The Algebra of Econometrics

D. S. G. POLLOCK

Queen Mary College
University of London

JOHN WILEY & SONS

Chichester · New York · Brisbane · Toronto

Library of Congress Cataloging in Publication Data:

Pollock, D. S. G.
The algebra of econometrics.
(Wiley series in probability and mathematical statistics)
1. Econometrics. I. Title.
HB139.P64 330'.01'82 78–27237
ISBN 0 471 99753 6

Printed and bound in Great Britain
at The Pitman Press, Bath

Probability and Mathematical Statistics (continued)

ROHATGI · An Introduction to Probability Theory and Mathematical Statistics
SCHEFFE · The Analysis of Variance
SEBER · Linear Regression Analysis
WILKS · Mathematical Statistics
WILLIAMS · Diffusions, Markov processes, and Martingales, Volume 1: Foundations
ZACKS · The Theory of Statistical Inference

Applied Probability and Statistics

BAILEY · The Elements of Stochastic Processes with Applications to the Natural Sciences
BAILEY · Mathematics, Statistics, and Systems for Health
BARNETT and LEWIS · Outliers in Statistical Data
BARTHOLOMEW and FORBES · Statistical Techniques for Manpower Planning
BARTHOLOMEW · Stochastic Models for Social Processes, *Second Edition*
BECK and ARNOLD · Parameter Estimation in Engineering and Science
BENNETT and FRANKLIN · Statistical Analysis in Chemistry and the Chemical Industry
BHAT · Elements of Applied Stochastic Processes
BLOOMFIELD · Fourier Analysis of Time Series: An Introduction
BOX · R. A. Fisher, The Life of a Scientist
BOX and DRAPER · Evolutionary Operation: A Statistical Method for Process Improvement
BOX, HUNTER, and HUNTER · Statistics for Experimenters: An Introduction to Design, Data Analysis, and Model Building
BROWN and HOLLANDER · Statistics: A Biomedical Introduction
BROWNLEE · Statistical Theory and Methodology in Science and Engineering, *Second Edition*
BURY · Statistical Models in Applied Science
CHAMBERS · Computational Methods for Data Analysis
CHATTERJEE and PRICE · Regression Analysis by Example
CHERNOFF and MOSES · Elementary Decision Theory
CHOW · Analysis and Control of Dynamic Economic Systems
CLELLAND, deCANI, BROWN, BURSK, and MURRAY · Basic Statistics with Business Applications, *Second Edition*
COCHRAN · Sampling Techniques, *Third Edition*
COCHRAN and COX · Experimental Designs, *Second Edition*
COX · Planning of Experiments
COX and MILLER · The Theory of Stochastic Processes. *Second Edition*
DANIEL · Biostatistics: A Foundation for Analysis in the Health Sciences, *Second Edition*
DANIEL · Application of Statistics to Industrial Experimentation
DANIEL and WOOD · Fitting Equations to Data
DAVID · Order Statistics
DEMING · Sample Design in Business Research
DODGE and ROMIG · Sampling Inspection Tables, *Second Edition*
DRAPER and SMITH · Applied Regression Analysis
DUNN · Basic Statistics: A Primer for the Biomedical Sciences, *Second Edition*
DUNN and CLARK · Applied Statistics: Analysis of Variance and Regression

continued on back

The Algebra of Econometrics

For A. M. B.

Contents

Preface

It is hoped that this book will serve as a text for graduate courses in econometrics and as a reference book for research workers in econometrics and statistics.

In writing the book, the aim has been to provide a unified treatment of the subject of theoretical econometrics by using certain general themes of the algebra of vector spaces. By emphasising the simple geometric notions that may be found at the basis of linear algebra, it should be possible to convey the underlying purpose of many of the econometric techniques in a direct and concise way. The detailed algebraic exposition of an econometric technique is often bound to be difficult and extensive, so that a prior understanding of its nature and its purpose is of great importance.

The book falls naturally into five parts. The first part, running from Chapter 1 to Chapter 4, is devoted to the development of the relevant algebra; and it contains a number of topics that have not hitherto been treated to any great extent in other texts of econometrics. These topics include the algebra of generalized inverses, projectors and tensor products. The topic of matrix differential calculus is also treated extensively with the use of tensor products and with one or two specially defined operators.

The second part contains detailed developments of the conventional estimators of the classical single-equation models of econometrics. It begins with Chapter 5, The Algebra of Econometrics, where an attempt is made to establish a broad framework wherein detailed developments may be placed. The general idea here is that virtually all the conventional estimators can be interpreted in terms of criteria for minimizing distances in vector spaces. This notion is applied both to the errors-in-variables model and to the various versions of the Gauss–Markov model. In Chapter 10, there is a treatment of the most general version of the Gauss–Markov model where no restriction is placed on either the rank of the data matrix or the rank of the variance–covariance matrix or dispersion matrix of the stochastic disturbances. The scope of the model is sufficient to accommodate both the classical Gauss–Markov model and the model with exact prior linear restrictions on the regression parameters. Admittedly, some people regard this level of generality as excessive; but others will, no doubt, agree that there is great aesthetic satisfaction in knowing that virtually every problem in Gauss–Markov estimation can be assimilated to a simple central model.

Part three of the book contains just two chapters: Chapter 11 on temporal stochastic processes and Chapter 12 on temporal regression models. The former includes a treatment of the autoregressive moving average model of the kind associated with the names of Box and Jenkins, whilst the latter includes material on regression models with serially correlated disturbances, regression models with lagged dependent variables and regression models with distributed lags amongst the explanatory variables. The notion of a general temporal regression model incorporating all these features is also posited and is used in an attempt to provide a taxonomy for temporal models.

The fourth part of the book deals mainly with the specifically econometric problem of estimating systems of simultaneous equations. Once more, the aim is to provide a unified treatment. To this end, the various estimating methods are presented both in the context of the errors-in-variables model and in the context of the Gauss–Markov model. The decision to devote a separate chapter to the two-stage and three-stage least-squares estimators was arrived at with some difficulty. For we would argue that these estimators can profitably be depicted as modified versions of the corresponding maximum-likelihood estimators. However, the derivations of the maximum-likelihood estimators are difficult; and, had these derivations preceded the two-stage and three-stage least-squares estimators, easy access to the latter might have been denied.

The fifth and final part of the book is the Appendix of Statistical Theory. There are numerous references within the text to the appendix which can be pursued as the occasions demand; yet the appendix is also designed to be read as a self-contained account.

The introductory chapter should also be mentioned here. Since books of this nature are often read back to front, I saw no great harm in placing the summary in the introduction. Yet there is a danger in this. For one of the purposes of an introduction is to propel the reader rapidly through the first stages of difficulty; and I fear that, in this case, readers who are new to econometric theory may find themselves overburdened. Their recourse should be to skim the surface of this chapter and to return to it at a later stage. Chapter 5, The Algebra of Econometrics, does offer an alternative point of entry to those who are already versed in some of the mathematical theory that is provided in the first part of the book.

I should like to acknowledge my indebtedness to three people. The first is Professor Gordon Fisher who taught a graduate course in econometrics at Southampton University which I attended during the academic year 1969–70. His is undoubtedly the seminal influence in this book; and some of his didactic methods are reflected in these pages. Next is my colleague Dick Allard. He was always prepared to listen to my tentative ideas and to comment on them. As a result, some errors of judgement and of analysis were averted much sooner than, otherwise, they would have been. Finally there is Sandra Place who typed the manuscript. Her prodigious speed and accuracy contributed greatly to the early publication of the book.

Stephen Pollock
November 1978
Queen Mary College

Introduction

Our intention in this introduction is to demonstrate that there is a remarkable unity in the classical methods of econometrics. We can only do this by invoking results that are derived in later chapters. Therefore the following account will be somewhat superficial, and it may oppress the reader with its many unsubstantiated statements. Nevertheless, we hope to provide a framework which will be sufficiently secure to bear the weight of later chapters and which will enable us to place related results in a meaningful juxtaposition.

We shall begin by considering some fundamental aspects of statistical inference.

STRUCTURE AND RANDOMNESS

The business of statistical inference is predicated upon the ancient notion that, underlying the apparent randomness and disorder of events that we observe in our universe, there is a set of regular and invariant structures. In attempting to identify its underlying structure, we may imagine that a statistical phenomenon is composed of a systematic or determinate component and a component that is essentially random or stochastic. The fundamental intellectual breakthrough that has accompanied the development of the modern science of statistical inference is the recognition that the random component has its own tenuous regularities that may be regarded as part of the underlying structure of the phenomenon.

In the sphere of social realities, statistical science has uncovered many regularities in the behaviour of large aggregates of apparently self-willed individuals. Examples spring readily to mind. Consider the expenditure on food and clothing of a group of individual households that might be observed over a given period. These expenditures vary widely, yet, when family income is taken into account, evident regularities emerge. Denoting the expenditure of the ith family by y_i and its income by x_i, we might postulate a statistical relationship of the form

(1) $$y_i = a + bx_i + \varepsilon_i$$

where a and b are parameters and ε_i is a random variable. In fitting the data to the model, we would find that the systematic component $\mu_i = a + bx_i$ would, in many cases, amount to a large proportion of y_i. The residual part of y_i would be attributed to the random variable ε_i. The precise details of the decomposition of each y_i would depend upon the values attributed to the parameters a and b. These values can be assigned only in view of the more or less specific assumptions that we make about the regularities inherent in the random variable ε_i. We might assume, for example, that the ε_i are distributed independently of each other with a common expected value of $E(\varepsilon_i) = 0$ and a common variance of $V(\varepsilon_i) = E(\varepsilon_i^2) = \sigma^2$. Then, as Chebyshev's inequality shows, there is an upper bound on the probability of large deviations of ε_i from zero; and it is appropriate to attribute to a and b the values that minimize the quantity $q = \sum_i (y_i - \hat{a} - \hat{b}x_i)^2$ which is the estimated sum of squares of the deviations. Alternatively, it might be more realistic to assume that the dispersion of the random component ε_i is related to the size of family income x_i. Then we might specify that $V(\varepsilon_i) = \sigma^2 x_i$; and the values of a and b would be found by minimizing $q = \sum_i x_i^{-1}(y_i - \hat{a} - \hat{b}x_i)^2$. The crucial assumptions concerning ε_i describe the stochastic structure of our model.

Doubtless, many would contend that the randomness in the variation of household expenditures is more apparent than real. For they would argue that the appearance of randomness is due to our failure to take into account a host of other factors contributing to this behaviour. They might suggest that, if every factor were taken into account, a perfect description of the behaviour could be derived. Fundamental though this objection might be, we can afford to ignore it; for it makes little difference to the practice of statistical inference whether the indeterminacy of the behaviour is the result of pure randomness or the result of our inability to comprehend more than a few of an infinite number of peculiar factors and circumstances affecting each household.

THE PARENT MODELS OF ECONOMETRICS

The theory of econometrics, which must be regarded as an integral part of multivariate statistical analysis, describes the methodology that is appropriate for making inferences about complex causal relationships that are beset by real or apparent randomness. The statistical models that are postulated in econometrics are often highly elaborate both in their systematic structures and in their stochastic structures. Nevertheless, most of the models that are peculiar to econometrics can be regarded as the hybrid offspring of two of the basic models of multivariate statistical analysis. These are the Gauss–Markov model and the so-called errors-in-variables model.

The Gauss–Markov model

The Gauss–Markov model postulates a linear system that transforms a set of k observable input variables in $\mathbf{x}_{t.}=[x_{t1},\ldots,x_{tk}]$ and an unobservable stochastic variable ε_t into a single output y_t. The relationship may be represented by

(2) $$y_t=\mathbf{x}_{t.}\boldsymbol{\beta}+\varepsilon_t,$$

where $\boldsymbol{\beta}'=[\beta_1,\ldots,\beta_k]$ contains the parameters of the systematic structure. A sequence of T realizations of the relationship may be compiled to give the equations

(3) $$\mathbf{y}=\mathbf{X}\boldsymbol{\beta}+\boldsymbol{\varepsilon},$$

where, for example, $\mathbf{y}'=[y_1,\ldots,y_T]$. The stochastic structure of the Gauss–Markov model is described by the assumptions

(4) $$E(\varepsilon_t)=0 \quad \text{for all } t, \text{ and}$$
$$E(\varepsilon_t\varepsilon_s)=\sigma_{ts} \quad \text{for all } t, s.$$

Using matrix notation, we write these as

(5) $$E(\boldsymbol{\varepsilon})=\mathbf{0}, \qquad D(\boldsymbol{\varepsilon})=E(\boldsymbol{\varepsilon}\boldsymbol{\varepsilon}')=[\sigma_{ts}]=\sigma^2\mathbf{Q}.$$

The positive-definite matrix $D(\boldsymbol{\varepsilon})=\sigma^2\mathbf{Q}$, which is called the dispersion matrix of $\boldsymbol{\varepsilon}$, contains all the variances and covariances of the elements of $\boldsymbol{\varepsilon}$. It describes an aspect of the statistical relationships existing amongst these elements, and it is usually assumed to be known except for the value of the scalar factor σ^2. (The classical assumptions, which effectively eliminate the statistical interdependencies from $\boldsymbol{\varepsilon}$, set $\mathbf{Q}=\mathbf{I}$.) It is often helpful to visualize the model in geometric terms. Thus we can regard the data vectors $[y_t, \mathbf{x}_{t.}]=[y_t, x_{t1},\ldots,x_{tk}]$; $t=1,\ldots,T$ as a scatter of points in a $(k+1)$-dimensional real space $\mathcal{R}^{k+1}$ in the vicinity of a regression hyperplane defined by the relationship $\mu_t=\mathbf{x}_{t.}\boldsymbol{\beta}$ where $\mu_t=y_t-\varepsilon_t$. Alternatively, we can visualize $\boldsymbol{\mu}=\mathbf{X}\boldsymbol{\beta}$, $\mathbf{y}$ and $\boldsymbol{\varepsilon}=\mathbf{y}-\mathbf{X}\boldsymbol{\beta}$ as vectors in a T-dimensional real space $\mathcal{R}^T$. In the main, we shall choose the latter interpretation.

In order to make inferences about the unknown structural parameters of the Gauss–Markov model, we must begin by decomposing $\mathbf{y}$ into two vectors $\hat{\mathbf{y}}$ and $\mathbf{e}$ representing, respectively, the estimate of the systematic component $\boldsymbol{\mu}=\mathbf{X}\boldsymbol{\beta}$ and the estimate of the stochastic component. Since we know that the systematic component $\boldsymbol{\mu}=\mathbf{X}\boldsymbol{\beta}$ is a linear combination of the columns of $\mathbf{X}$, we are bound to locate its estimate $\hat{\mathbf{y}}$ within the subspace $\mathcal{M}(\mathbf{X})$ consisting of all such linear combinations. Exactly how we locate this estimate depends upon the precise nature of our assumptions about the stochastic structure of the model. To simplify matters, let us begin with the assumptions of the classical model which has $D(\boldsymbol{\varepsilon})=\sigma^2\mathbf{I}$. Then the appropriate method is to locate $\hat{\mathbf{y}}$ at a minimum distance from $\mathbf{y}$ by dropping perpendicularly or orthogonally from $\mathbf{y}$ onto $\mathcal{M}(\mathbf{X})$. Then the vector $\hat{\mathbf{y}}$ represents the base of a right-angled triangle whose hypotenuse is $\mathbf{y}$ and whose third side is $\mathbf{e}$. In practice, we use the transformation $\mathbf{P}=\mathbf{X}(\mathbf{X}'\mathbf{X})^{-1}\mathbf{X}'$, known as the orthogonal projector of $\mathcal{R}^T$ on $\mathcal{M}(\mathbf{X})$, to find $\hat{\mathbf{y}}=\mathbf{Py}$. Then, by solving the equation $\mathbf{Py}=\mathbf{X}(\mathbf{X}'\mathbf{X})^{-1}\mathbf{X}'\mathbf{y}=\mathbf{X}\hat{\boldsymbol{\beta}}$, we get the estimate $\hat{\boldsymbol{\beta}}=(\mathbf{X}'\mathbf{X})^{-1}\mathbf{X}'\mathbf{y}$. As we shall see in Chapter 5, this expression for $\hat{\boldsymbol{\beta}}$ may be obtained directly from the criterion

(6) Minimize

$$\|\mathbf{y}-\hat{\mathbf{y}}\|^2=(\mathbf{y}-\mathbf{X}\hat{\boldsymbol{\beta}})'(\mathbf{y}-\mathbf{X}\hat{\boldsymbol{\beta}}) = \sum (y_t-\mathbf{x}_{t.}\hat{\boldsymbol{\beta}})^2$$

through the use of vector differential calculus. The expression on the LHS of the criterion function stands for the square of the distance between the vectors $\mathbf{y}$ and $\hat{\mathbf{y}}$ of the T-dimensional space. The term on the RHS is simply the sum of squares of the distances between the T data points $[y_t, \mathbf{x}_{t.}]=[y_t, x_{t1}, \ldots, x_{tk}]$ in the $(k+1)$-dimensional space and the corresponding points $[\hat{y}_t, \mathbf{x}_{t.}]=[\hat{y}_t, x_{t1}, \ldots, x_{tk}]$ within the estimated regression hyperplane; and this accounts for the common description of $\hat{\boldsymbol{\beta}}$ as the ordinary least-squares estimator.

We also require an estimate of the parameter σ^2 of the dispersion matrix $D(\boldsymbol{\varepsilon})=\sigma^2\mathbf{I}$. For this, we use the residual vector $\mathbf{e}'=[e_1, \ldots, e_T]$. Since e_t may be regarded as an estimate of the random variable ε_t, it seems reasonable to represent $\sigma^2=E(\varepsilon_t^2)$ by the average $\sum e_t^2/T=\mathbf{e}'\mathbf{e}/T$. Thus, with $\mathbf{e}=\mathbf{y}-\mathbf{Py}=[\mathbf{I}-\mathbf{X}(\mathbf{X}'\mathbf{X})^{-1}\mathbf{X}']\mathbf{y}$, we obtain the estimate

$$\hat{\sigma}^2=\mathbf{y}'[\mathbf{I}-\mathbf{X}(\mathbf{X}'\mathbf{X})^{-1}\mathbf{X}']\mathbf{y}/T=(\mathbf{y}-\mathbf{X}\hat{\boldsymbol{\beta}})'(\mathbf{y}-\mathbf{X}\hat{\boldsymbol{\beta}})/T. \tag{7}$$

In fact, this estimate is biased; and, for an unbiased estimate, we use $\tilde{\sigma}^2=\hat{\sigma}^2T/(T-k)$. However, the bias of $\hat{\sigma}^2$ vanishes as T tends to infinity.

Now let us briefly consider the problem of estimating the parameters of the more general model with a dispersion matrix of $D(\boldsymbol{\varepsilon})=\sigma^2\mathbf{Q}$. If we were to apply the method of ordinary least squares, we would fail to make proper use of the information about the stochastic structure. The resulting inferences might lack precision. The Gauss–Markov theorem proves that the efficient estimator is the one that satisfies the criterion

(8) Minimize

$$\|\mathbf{y}-\hat{\mathbf{y}}\|^2_{\mathbf{Q}^{-1}}=(\mathbf{y}-\mathbf{X}\hat{\boldsymbol{\beta}})'\mathbf{Q}^{-1}(\mathbf{y}-\mathbf{X}\hat{\boldsymbol{\beta}}).$$

The resulting estimator $\hat{\boldsymbol{\beta}}=(\mathbf{X}'\mathbf{Q}^{-1}\mathbf{X})^{-1}\mathbf{X}'\mathbf{Q}^{-1}\mathbf{y}$ is described alternatively as the minimum $\mathbf{Q}^{-1}$-distance estimator or as the generalized least-squares estimator. The transformation $\mathbf{P}=\mathbf{X}(\mathbf{X}'\mathbf{Q}^{-1}\mathbf{X})^{-1}\mathbf{X}'\mathbf{Q}^{-1}$ which gives us $\hat{\mathbf{y}}=\mathbf{Py}=\mathbf{X}\hat{\boldsymbol{\beta}}$ is called the $\mathbf{Q}^{-1}$-orthogonal projector on $\mathcal{M}(\mathbf{X})$. By generalizing our concepts of distance and angle, we are able to preserve the simple geometric interpretations that are associated with the ordinary least-squares estimator.

The errors-in-variables model

The errors-in-variables model postulates a linear relationship amongst the systematic components of a set of m random variables. Such a model arises whenever the observations on the variables of an exact linear relationship are beset by random errors. Let us denote the observation on the jth variable at time t by $y_{tj} = \mu_{tj} + \eta_{tj}$, where μ_{tj} represents the true value of the variable and η_{tj} represents the error in the observation. Then a vector of observations on the m variables is written as $\mathbf{y}_{t.} = \boldsymbol{\mu}_{t.} + \boldsymbol{\eta}_{t.} = [\mu_{t1} + \eta_{t1}, \ldots, \mu_{tm} + \eta_{tm}]$, and the exact relationship amongst the true variables is represented by

$$(9) \qquad (\mathbf{y}_{t.} - \boldsymbol{\eta}_{t.})\boldsymbol{\alpha} = 0,$$

where $\boldsymbol{\alpha}' = [\alpha_1, \ldots, \alpha_m]$. A set of T realizations of the relationship can be written as

$$(10) \qquad (\mathbf{Y} - \mathbf{H})\boldsymbol{\alpha} = \mathbf{0},$$

where $\mathbf{Y}' = [\mathbf{y}'_{1.}, \ldots, \mathbf{y}'_{T.}]$ and $\mathbf{H}' = [\boldsymbol{\eta}'_{1.}, \ldots, \boldsymbol{\eta}'_{T.}]$. According to the classical assumptions, the errors in the observations of the m variables are contemporaneously interdependent but are free of intertemporal dependencies. Thus, assuming that each error of observation has a zero expected value, we may describe the stochastic structure of the model by writing

$$(11) \qquad \begin{aligned} &E(\eta_{tj}) = 0 \quad \text{for all } t, j, \text{ and} \\ &E(\eta_{tj}\eta_{sk}) = \omega_{jk} \quad \text{if} \quad t = s \\ &\qquad\qquad\quad = 0 \quad \text{if} \quad t \neq s, \end{aligned}$$

where the subscripts j, k refer to variables and the subscripts t and s refer to the instants at which they are observed. Using matrix notation, we may write these assumptions more concisely as

$$(12) \qquad E(\boldsymbol{\eta}'_{t.}) = 0, \qquad D(\boldsymbol{\eta}'_{t.}) = \boldsymbol{\Omega} = [\omega_{jk}].$$

The problem that we wish to consider in relation to this model is one of estimating the parameter vector $\boldsymbol{\alpha}$ when $\boldsymbol{\Omega}$ is completely known or known up to a scalar factor. The method is to replace each observation $\mathbf{y}_{t.}$ by an estimate $\hat{\mathbf{y}}_{t.}$ of its systematic component $\boldsymbol{\mu}_{t.}$. then, provided that the matrix $\hat{\mathbf{Y}}' = [\hat{\mathbf{y}}'_{1.}, \ldots, \hat{\mathbf{y}}'_{T.}]$ has a rank of $m-1$, we can find an estimate of $\boldsymbol{\alpha}$ by solving the equation $\hat{\mathbf{Y}}\hat{\boldsymbol{\alpha}} = \mathbf{0}$ subject to some more or less arbitrary normalization on $\hat{\boldsymbol{\alpha}}$ such as $\hat{\boldsymbol{\alpha}}'\hat{\boldsymbol{\alpha}} = 1$. In geometric terms, the data vectors $\mathbf{y}_{t.}$; $t = 1, \ldots, T$ represent a scatter of points in the vicinity of a hyperplane defined by the relationship $\boldsymbol{\mu}_{t.}\boldsymbol{\alpha}=0$. Our problem is to locate the estimates $\hat{\mathbf{y}}_{t.}$; $t=1,\ldots,T$ of the systematic components within a single hyperplane so as to allow for the existence of an estimate $\hat{\boldsymbol{\alpha}}$ of the parameter vector which satisfies the equation $\hat{\mathbf{y}}_{t.}\hat{\boldsymbol{\alpha}}=0$ for all t. We can also envisage the problem as one of locating the column vectors $\hat{\mathbf{y}}_{.j}$; $j=1,\ldots,m$ within an $(m-1)$-dimensional subspace of $\mathcal{R}^T$; but this interpretation is less tractable.

The appropriate criterion for finding the vectors $\hat{\mathbf{y}}_{t.}$ is to minimize the sum of squares of the distances $\|\mathbf{y}_{t.}-\hat{\mathbf{y}}_{t.}\|_{\boldsymbol{\Omega}^{-1}}$. Thus we have the criterion

(13) Minimize

$$\sum \|\mathbf{y}_{t.}-\hat{\mathbf{y}}_{t.}\|^2_{\boldsymbol{\Omega}^{-1}}=\sum (\mathbf{y}_{t.}-\hat{\mathbf{y}}_{t.})\boldsymbol{\Omega}^{-1}(\mathbf{y}_{t.}-\hat{\mathbf{y}}_{t.})'$$

Subject to

$$\hat{\mathbf{y}}_{t.}\hat{\boldsymbol{\alpha}}=0 \quad \text{for all } t \text{ or, equivalently,} \quad \hat{\mathbf{Y}}\hat{\boldsymbol{\alpha}}=\mathbf{0}.$$

As we demonstrate in Chapter 5, this provides the estimating equation

$$(\mathbf{Y}'\mathbf{Y}-\lambda\boldsymbol{\Omega})\hat{\boldsymbol{\alpha}}=\mathbf{0}. \tag{14}$$

In order to solve this equation for $\hat{\boldsymbol{\alpha}}$, we attribute to λ the least value for which $(\mathbf{Y}'\mathbf{Y}-\lambda\boldsymbol{\Omega})$ has a rank of $m-1$.

The hybrid model

We shall now consider how these two basic models of multivariate statistical analysis may be combined to form a hybrid. Let us therefore imagine a linear relationship comprising both variables that are observed exactly and variables that are observed with errors. Let $\mathbf{x}_{t.}=[x_{t1},\ldots,x_{tk}]$ be a perfect observation on k variables, and let

$$\mathbf{y}_{t,}=[y_{t1},\ldots,y_{tm}]=[\mu_{t1}+\eta_{t1},\ldots,\mu_{tm}+\eta_{tm}]=\boldsymbol{\mu}_{t.}+\boldsymbol{\eta}_{t.}$$

be an observation on m variables beset by the error $\boldsymbol{\eta}_{t.}$. Then the relationship amongst the true variables is represented by

$$(\mathbf{y}_{t.}-\boldsymbol{\eta}_{t.})\boldsymbol{\gamma}+\mathbf{x}_{t.}\boldsymbol{\beta}=0, \tag{15}$$

and, by compiling T realizations, we obtain the equations

$$(\mathbf{Y}-\mathbf{H})\boldsymbol{\gamma}+\mathbf{X}\boldsymbol{\beta}=\mathbf{0}. \tag{16}$$

The assumptions concerning the vector of errors $\boldsymbol{\eta}_{t.}$ are borrowed from the pure errors-in-variables model so that, once more, we have $E(\boldsymbol{\eta}_{t.}')=\mathbf{0}$ and $D(\boldsymbol{\eta}_{t.}')=\boldsymbol{\Omega}$.

We may begin our investigation of the model by considering the relationship (15) from the point of view of the Gauss–Markov model. For this purpose, we may define the scalar random variable $\varepsilon_t=-\boldsymbol{\eta}_{t.}\boldsymbol{\gamma}$ which, in view of our assumptions about $\boldsymbol{\eta}_{t.}$, has $E(\varepsilon_t)=0$ and $V(\varepsilon_t)=\boldsymbol{\gamma}'\boldsymbol{\Omega}\boldsymbol{\gamma}=\sigma^2$ for all t.

Next, by extracting ε_t from the first term of the relationship in (15) and by rearranging the expression, we obtain

$$(17)\qquad -\mathbf{y}_{t.}\boldsymbol{\gamma} = \mathbf{x}_{t.}\boldsymbol{\beta} + \varepsilon_t.$$

A knowledge of the parameter $\boldsymbol{\gamma}$ would enable us to treat this relationship as an instance of the Gauss–Markov model. Accordingly, we would be able to estimate the unknown parameter $\boldsymbol{\beta}$ by

$$(18)\qquad \hat{\boldsymbol{\beta}} = -(\mathbf{X}'\mathbf{X})^{-1}\mathbf{X}'\mathbf{Y}\boldsymbol{\gamma}.$$

Thus the Gaussian aspect of the model is clearly apparent.

Let us now consider the relationship in (15) from the point of view of the errors-in-variables model. In reference to (13), it would appear that the appropriate way of estimating the parameters $\boldsymbol{\gamma}$ and $\boldsymbol{\beta}$ is to evaluate the criterion

(19) Minimize

$$\sum \|\mathbf{y}_{t.} - \hat{\mathbf{y}}_{t.}\|^2_{\Omega^{-1}} = \sum (\mathbf{y}_{t.} - \hat{\mathbf{y}}_{t.})\boldsymbol{\Omega}^{-1}(\mathbf{y}_{t.} - \hat{\mathbf{y}}_{t.})'$$

subject to

$$\hat{\mathbf{y}}_{t.}\hat{\boldsymbol{\gamma}} + \mathbf{x}_{t.}\hat{\boldsymbol{\beta}} = 0.$$

The criterion yields the estimating equations

$$(20)\qquad \begin{bmatrix} \mathbf{Y}'\mathbf{Y} - \lambda\boldsymbol{\Omega}, & \mathbf{Y}'\mathbf{X} \\ \mathbf{X}'\mathbf{Y}, & \mathbf{X}'\mathbf{X} \end{bmatrix} \begin{bmatrix} \hat{\boldsymbol{\gamma}} \\ \hat{\boldsymbol{\beta}} \end{bmatrix} = \begin{bmatrix} \mathbf{0} \\ \mathbf{0} \end{bmatrix}.$$

These provide a solution for $\hat{\boldsymbol{\beta}}$ in terms of $\hat{\boldsymbol{\gamma}}$ precisely in the form of (18). By substituting this solution into the first line of (20) and gathering the terms, we obtain

$$(21)\qquad \{\mathbf{Y}'[\mathbf{I} - \mathbf{X}(\mathbf{X}'\mathbf{X})^{-1}\mathbf{X}']\mathbf{Y} - \lambda\boldsymbol{\Omega}\}\hat{\boldsymbol{\gamma}} = \mathbf{0}.$$

Apart from the interpolation of $\mathbf{I} - \mathbf{P} = \mathbf{I} - \mathbf{X}(\mathbf{X}'\mathbf{X})^{-1}\mathbf{X}'$ into the term $\mathbf{Y}'\mathbf{Y}$ and the replacement of $\hat{\boldsymbol{\alpha}}$ by $\hat{\boldsymbol{\gamma}}$, this is the same as the expression in (14) which relates to the errors-in-variables model. The estimate $\hat{\boldsymbol{\gamma}}$ is found in the same manner as $\hat{\boldsymbol{\alpha}}$: by setting λ to the smallest value that induces linear dependence in the matrix $\{\mathbf{Y}'[\mathbf{I} - \mathbf{X}(\mathbf{X}'\mathbf{X})^{-1}\mathbf{X}']\mathbf{Y} - \lambda\boldsymbol{\Omega}\}$ and then solving the equation (21) subject to an appropriate normalization for $\hat{\boldsymbol{\gamma}}$. The estimate $\hat{\boldsymbol{\beta}}$ is then obtained by setting $\boldsymbol{\gamma} = \hat{\boldsymbol{\gamma}}$ in (18).

The considerable theoretical importance of this hybrid model from the point of view of econometric theory is due to the fact that the equation (15) is formally identical to any of the structural equations comprised within the linear simultaneous model of econometrics which we shall now describe.

THE LINEAR ECONOMETRIC MODEL

The linear model of econometrics is a system that describes a statistical relationship between k input variables and m output variables. Each of these output variables is presumed to be generated by a so-called structural relationship that comprises amongst its inputs not only some of the k primary inputs of the system but also some of the $m-1$ output variables that are generated by other structural relationships.

To take an example, let us consider an econometric model whose outputs include predictions of property values and of the activity of building contractors. Then, amongst the inputs to the structural equation generating the index of building activity, we would expect to find the index of property values which is generated elsewhere in the system.

The ith structural equation of the econometric model may be written in an unspecific manner as

$$(22) \qquad y_{ti} = \mathbf{y}_{t.}\mathbf{c}_{.i} + \mathbf{x}_{t.}\boldsymbol{\beta}_{.i} + \varepsilon_{ti}.$$

The parameter vector $\mathbf{c}_{.i}$ must have a zero element in at least the ith position in order to prevent the variable y_{ti} from entering on both sides of the equation. Usually, we presume that certain of the variables that are present in the system are absent from the ith equation, so that a number of the other elements of $\mathbf{c}_{.i}$ and $\boldsymbol{\beta}_{.i}$ are also zeros. By forming the parameter matrices $\mathbf{C} = [\mathbf{c}_{.1}, \ldots, \mathbf{c}_{.m}]$, $\mathbf{B} = [\boldsymbol{\beta}_{.1}, \ldots, \boldsymbol{\beta}_{.m}]$ and the stochastic vector $\varepsilon_{t.} = [\varepsilon_{t1}, \ldots, \varepsilon_{tm}]$, we may gather the m structural relationships into the equations

$$(23) \qquad \mathbf{y}_{t.} = \mathbf{y}_{t.}\mathbf{C} + \mathbf{x}_{t.}\mathbf{B} + \boldsymbol{\varepsilon}_{t.}.$$

Then, if we can assume that the elements of $\boldsymbol{\varepsilon}_{t.}$ are contemporaneously interdependent and that there are no dependencies between successive values of these elements, we may specify the stochastic structure of the model by

$$(24) \qquad E(\boldsymbol{\varepsilon}'_{t.}) = \mathbf{0}, \qquad D(\boldsymbol{\varepsilon}'_{t.}) = \boldsymbol{\Sigma}.$$

When we examine the equation (22), we see that randomness enters the structural relationships both via the additive disturbance term ε_{ti} and via the stochastic vector $\mathbf{y}_{t.}$. In estimating the parameters of the structural relationships, we endeavour to separate the systematic component from the various stochastic components. Therefore we rearrange the equation (23) so as to express the output vector $\mathbf{y}_{t.}$ as the sum of a random vector and a systematic vector which is a linear transformation of the vector of primary inputs $\mathbf{x}_{t.}$ alone. Thus, on defining new parameter matrices $-\boldsymbol{\Gamma} = \mathbf{I} - \mathbf{C}$ and $\boldsymbol{\Pi} = \mathbf{B}(\mathbf{I}-\mathbf{C})^{-1} = -\mathbf{B}\boldsymbol{\Gamma}^{-1}$ and a new stochastic vector $\boldsymbol{\eta}_{t.} = \boldsymbol{\varepsilon}_{t.}(\mathbf{I}-\mathbf{C})^{-1} = -\boldsymbol{\varepsilon}_{t.}\boldsymbol{\Gamma}^{-1}$, we obtain the equation

$$(25) \qquad \mathbf{y}_{t.} = \mathbf{x}_{t.}\mathbf{\Pi} + \boldsymbol{\eta}_{t.}$$

which is known as the reduced form of the econometric model. From the assumptions in (24), it follows that the reduced-form disturbances $\boldsymbol{\eta}_{t.}$ have

$$(26) \qquad E(\boldsymbol{\eta}'_{t.}) = E(\mathbf{\Gamma}^{-1\prime}\boldsymbol{\varepsilon}'_{t.}) = \mathbf{0},$$
$$D(\boldsymbol{\eta}'_{t.}) = \mathbf{\Gamma}^{-1\prime}D(\boldsymbol{\varepsilon}'_{t.})\mathbf{\Gamma}^{-1} = \mathbf{\Gamma}^{-1\prime}\mathbf{\Sigma}\mathbf{\Gamma}^{-1} = \mathbf{\Omega}.$$

We can now reconsider the ith structural equation in the light of the reduced-form relationship. By writing (22) in homogeneous form with $\mathbf{y}_{t.}\mathbf{c}_{.i} - y_{ti}$ expressed as $\mathbf{y}_{t.}\boldsymbol{\gamma}_{.i}$, where $\boldsymbol{\gamma}_{.i}$ is the ith column of $\mathbf{\Gamma}$, and by using the identity $\varepsilon_{ti} = -\boldsymbol{\eta}_{t.}\boldsymbol{\gamma}_{.i}$ which is comprised in the definition $\boldsymbol{\eta}_{t.} = -\boldsymbol{\varepsilon}_{t.}\mathbf{\Gamma}^{-1}$, we can express the structural relationship as

$$(27) \qquad (\mathbf{y}_{t.} - \boldsymbol{\eta}_{t.})\boldsymbol{\gamma}_{.i} + \mathbf{x}_{t.}\boldsymbol{\beta}_{.i} = 0.$$

Reference to (15) now shows that the ith structural equation of the econometric model takes the same form as the equation of the hybrid model. The only difference is in the fact that some of the elements of $\boldsymbol{\gamma}_{.i}$ and $\boldsymbol{\beta}_{.i}$ are known to be zeros. However, it is a straightforward matter to condense the equation (27) to eliminate these elements and their corresponding variables. Then, given the value of $D(\boldsymbol{\eta}'_{t.}) = \mathbf{\Omega}$, we may estimate the unknown parameters $\boldsymbol{\gamma}_{.i}$ and $\boldsymbol{\beta}_{.i}$ by exactly the methods that were outlined previously in connection with the hybrid model.

Consequences of interdependence

The fact that the relationship (27) is found within the context of a set of interdependent relationships has a number of important consequences which combine to give the econometric problem its own distinctive subtleties and difficulties.

In the first place, we need no longer presume that the dispersion matrix $\mathbf{\Omega}$ is known, for its elements are amongst the estimable parameters of the reduced form. Thus, for example, if we apply the Gauss–Markov method to the observations of the reduced-form relationship in (25), we can obtain an estimate of $\mathbf{\Omega}$ in the form of

$$(28) \qquad \hat{\mathbf{\Omega}} = \mathbf{Y}'[\mathbf{I} - \mathbf{X}(\mathbf{X}'\mathbf{X})^{-1}\mathbf{X}']\mathbf{Y}/T = (\mathbf{Y} - \mathbf{X}\hat{\mathbf{\Pi}})'(\mathbf{Y} - \mathbf{X}\hat{\mathbf{\Pi}})/T$$

which is an immediate generalization of (7). When we use $\hat{\mathbf{\Omega}}$ in our estimating equations in place of $\mathbf{\Omega}$, we obtain what is commonly known as the limited-information maximum-likelihood estimator.

A second consequence is that the possibility of identifying the parameters $\boldsymbol{\gamma}_{.i}$ and $\boldsymbol{\beta}_{.i}$ by finding meaningful estimates that are uniquely determined depends crucially on our having sufficient prior knowledge of the parameter values. Unless we have this, we cannot statistically distinguish the ith equation from a linear combination of the other equations. Typically, we have to make use of the knowledge that certain elements of $\boldsymbol{\gamma}_{.i}$ and $\boldsymbol{\beta}_{.i}$ are zeros, and of the fact that the element of $\boldsymbol{\gamma}_{.i}$ corresponding to y_{ti} has the value -1. In terms of such information, a necessary condition for identification is that there be at least $m-1$ zero elements in $\boldsymbol{\gamma}_{.i}$ and $\boldsymbol{\beta}_{.i}$ or, equivalently, that no more than $k+1$ of the system's variables be included in the ith equation. This is a specialized instance of a more general requirement that there should be at least $m-1$ independent linear restrictions on the elements of the vector $\boldsymbol{\theta}'_{.i}=[\boldsymbol{\gamma}'_{.i}, \boldsymbol{\beta}'_{.i}]$. If we count the restriction that $\gamma_{ii}=-1$, this number becomes m. If the restrictions, apart from the normalization rule, are homogeneous, then we may write them as $\mathbf{R}\boldsymbol{\theta}_{.i}=\mathbf{0}$. The appropriate criterion for finding estimates of $\boldsymbol{\gamma}_{.i}$ and $\boldsymbol{\beta}_{.i}$ is now

(29)
$$\text{Minimize} \quad \sum (\mathbf{y}_{t.}-\hat{\mathbf{y}}_{t.})\boldsymbol{\Omega}^{-1}(\mathbf{y}_{t.}-\hat{\mathbf{y}}_{t.})'$$
$$\text{Subject to} \quad \hat{\mathbf{y}}_{t.}\hat{\boldsymbol{\gamma}}_{.i}+\mathbf{x}_{t.}\hat{\boldsymbol{\beta}}_{.i}=0,$$
$$\text{and} \quad \mathbf{R}\begin{bmatrix}\hat{\boldsymbol{\gamma}}_{.i}\\ \hat{\boldsymbol{\beta}}_{.i}\end{bmatrix}=\mathbf{0},$$

where $\hat{\mathbf{y}}_{t.}$ represents an estimate of the systematic component $\mathbf{x}_{t.}\boldsymbol{\Pi}$ of $\mathbf{y}_{t.}$. When this criterion is evaluated, we obtain the estimating equations

(30)
$$\begin{bmatrix}\begin{bmatrix}\mathbf{Y}'\mathbf{Y}-\lambda\boldsymbol{\Omega}, & \mathbf{Y}'\mathbf{X}\\ \mathbf{X}'\mathbf{Y}, & \mathbf{X}'\mathbf{X}\end{bmatrix}, & \mathbf{R}'\\ \mathbf{R}, & \mathbf{0}\end{bmatrix}\begin{bmatrix}\begin{bmatrix}\hat{\boldsymbol{\gamma}}_{.i}\\ \hat{\boldsymbol{\beta}}_{.i}\end{bmatrix}\\ \boldsymbol{\mu}\end{bmatrix}=\begin{bmatrix}\mathbf{0}\\ \mathbf{0}\\ \mathbf{0}\end{bmatrix},$$

where $\boldsymbol{\mu}$ is the vector of Lagrangean multipliers associated with the restrictions $\mathbf{R}\hat{\boldsymbol{\theta}}_{.i}=\mathbf{0}$. In practice, we replace $\boldsymbol{\Omega}$ by $\hat{\boldsymbol{\Omega}}$ from (28).

A third consequence of the complex nature of the econometric model is the availability of a large number of viable alternative methods for estimating the structural equations. To illustrate the diversity of these methods, let us consider the method of two-stage least squares which, in all appearances, is quite different from the method of limited-information maximum likelihood. Let us re-examine the form of the ith structural equation given in (22). By substituting the reduced-form expression for $\mathbf{y}_{t.}$ given in (25) into the RHS, we obtain

(31)
$$y_{ti}=[\mathbf{x}_{t.}\boldsymbol{\Pi}, \mathbf{x}_{t.}]\begin{bmatrix}\mathbf{c}_{.i}\\ \boldsymbol{\beta}_{.i}\end{bmatrix}+(\varepsilon_{ti}+\boldsymbol{\eta}_{t.}\mathbf{c}_{.i}).$$

Thus we have a decomposition of y_{ti} into a systematic component $\mathbf{x}_{t.}\mathbf{\Pi c}_{.i}+\mathbf{x}_{t.}\boldsymbol{\beta}_{.i}$ and a random component $\varepsilon_{ti}+\boldsymbol{\eta}_{t.}\mathbf{c}_{.i}$. If $\mathbf{x}_{t.}\mathbf{\Pi}$ were an observable quantity, we could regard (31) as the equation of a Gauss–Markov model. Then, on condensing the equation to eliminate those elements of $\mathbf{c}_{.i}$ and $\boldsymbol{\beta}_{.i}$ that are known to be zeros, we could use the method of ordinary least squares to estimate the unknown structural parameters. In practice, we can replace the unknown reduced-form parameter $\mathbf{\Pi}$ by its ordinary least-squares estimate $\hat{\mathbf{\Pi}}=(\mathbf{X}'\mathbf{X})^{-1}\mathbf{X}'\mathbf{Y}$. Then, on applying ordinary least squares to the condensed version of the resulting equations

(32) $$y_{ti}=[\mathbf{x}_{t.}\hat{\mathbf{\Pi}},\mathbf{x}_{t.}]\begin{bmatrix}\mathbf{c}_{.i}\\ \boldsymbol{\beta}_{.i}\end{bmatrix}-\xi_{ti},$$

we can obtain the quasi Gauss–Markov estimates. We shall be able to show in Chapters 15 and 16 that, in spite of appearances, this method of two-stage least-squares estimation has a close affinity with the method of limited-information maximum likelihood.

Finally, let us consider what is perhaps the most significant consequence of the interdependent nature of the relationships comprised within the linear econometric model. This is the fact that, under any reasonable assumptions concerning the stochastic structure of the model, an efficient estimator must use all the information that is available on every aspect of the system.

To illustrate the problems of efficient system-wide estimation, we shall consider the full-information maximum-likelihood estimator. In order to specify the method, let us begin by considering the fact that, hitherto, we have approached the problem of estimating the structural parameters via the problem of finding an estimate of the systematic component $\mathbf{x}_{t.}\mathbf{\Pi}$ of the reduced-form relationship. We may recall that the reduced-form parameter matrix $\mathbf{\Pi}$ can be expressed as $\mathbf{\Pi}=-\mathbf{B}\mathbf{\Gamma}^{-1}$. Thus, using the notation $\mathbf{\Theta}'=[\mathbf{\Gamma}',\mathbf{B}']$, we can write $\mathbf{\Pi}=\mathbf{\Pi}(\mathbf{\Theta})$ to show that the value of $\mathbf{\Pi}$ is determined by the values of the structural parameters. We may assume that, in order to secure the statistical identifiability of the structural parameters, we have a set of linear restrictions of the form $\mathbf{R\Theta}^c=\mathbf{r}$ where $\mathbf{\Theta}^{c\prime}=[\boldsymbol{\gamma}'_{.1},\boldsymbol{\beta}'_{.1},\ldots,\boldsymbol{\gamma}'_{.m},\boldsymbol{\beta}'_{.m}]$ is a vector of the structural parameters. Any estimate of the reduced-form parameter $\mathbf{\Pi}$ that takes account of the system-wide information is bound to be constrained by these restrictions. Therefore, when we recall the criterion (29) for estimating the parameters of the ith structural equation, it seems appropriate to derive the estimate of $\mathbf{\Theta}'=[\mathbf{\Gamma}',\mathbf{B}']$ by evaluating the criterion

(33) Minimize

$$\sum(\mathbf{y}_{t.}-\hat{\mathbf{y}}_{t.})\mathbf{\Omega}^{-1}(\mathbf{y}_{t.}-\hat{\mathbf{y}}_{t.})'=\sum(\mathbf{y}_{t.}-\mathbf{x}_{t.}\hat{\mathbf{\Pi}})\mathbf{\Omega}^{-1}(\mathbf{y}_{t.}-\mathbf{x}_{t.}\hat{\mathbf{\Pi}})'$$

Subject to

$$\hat{\mathbf{y}}_{t.}\hat{\mathbf{\Gamma}}+\mathbf{x}_{t.}\hat{\mathbf{B}}=\mathbf{x}_{t.}\hat{\mathbf{\Pi}}\hat{\mathbf{\Gamma}}+\mathbf{x}_{t.}\hat{\mathbf{B}}=\mathbf{0} \quad \text{or, equivalently,}$$
$$\mathbf{\Pi}(\hat{\mathbf{\Theta}})\hat{\mathbf{\Gamma}}+\hat{\mathbf{B}}=\mathbf{0}$$

and

$$\mathbf{R}\hat{\mathbf{\Theta}}^c=\mathbf{r}.$$

In the process of evaluating this, we must also employ the identity $\hat{\mathbf{\Sigma}}=\hat{\mathbf{\Gamma}}'\mathbf{\Omega}\hat{\mathbf{\Gamma}}$ which reflects the assumptions made in (26). By dint of considerable labour involving, amongst other things, the use of the methods of matrix differential calculus provided in Chapter 4, we can obtain the estimating equations

$$\text{(34)} \qquad \begin{bmatrix} \hat{\mathbf{\Sigma}}\otimes\begin{bmatrix}\mathbf{Y}'\mathbf{Y}-T\mathbf{\Omega}, & \mathbf{Y}'\mathbf{X}\\ \mathbf{X}'\mathbf{Y}, & \mathbf{X}'\mathbf{X}\end{bmatrix}, & \mathbf{R}'\\ \mathbf{R}, & \mathbf{0}\end{bmatrix}\begin{bmatrix}\begin{bmatrix}\hat{\mathbf{\Gamma}}\\ \hat{\mathbf{B}}\end{bmatrix}^c\\ \boldsymbol{\mu}\end{bmatrix}=\begin{bmatrix}\mathbf{0}\\ \mathbf{0}\\ \mathbf{r}\end{bmatrix}$$

wherein

$$\hat{\mathbf{\Sigma}}\otimes\begin{bmatrix}\mathbf{Y}'\mathbf{Y}-T\mathbf{\Omega}, & \mathbf{Y}'\mathbf{X}\\ \mathbf{X}'\mathbf{Y}, & \mathbf{X}'\mathbf{X}\end{bmatrix}$$

is the $m(m+k)\times m(m+k)$ matrix whose ijth partition is the matrix

$$\hat{\sigma}_{ij}\begin{bmatrix}\mathbf{Y}'\mathbf{Y}-T\mathbf{\Omega}, & \mathbf{Y}'\mathbf{X}\\ \mathbf{X}'\mathbf{Y}, & \mathbf{X}'\mathbf{X}\end{bmatrix};$$

$\hat{\sigma}_{ij}$ being the ijth element of $\hat{\mathbf{\Sigma}}$. These estimating equations would require a knowledge of the reduced-form dispersion matrix $D(\boldsymbol{\eta}_{t.}')=\mathbf{\Omega}$. In the method of full-information maximum likelihood, this is replaced by its estimate

$$\text{(35)} \qquad \hat{\mathbf{\Omega}}=(\mathbf{Y}-\mathbf{X}\hat{\mathbf{\Pi}})'(\mathbf{Y}-\mathbf{X}\hat{\mathbf{\Pi}})/T$$

wherein $\hat{\mathbf{\Pi}}=-\hat{\mathbf{B}}\hat{\mathbf{\Gamma}}^{-1}$. The estimate of the dispersion matrix of the disturbances of the structural equations then becomes

$$\text{(36)} \qquad \hat{\mathbf{\Sigma}}=\hat{\mathbf{\Gamma}}'\hat{\mathbf{\Omega}}\hat{\mathbf{\Gamma}}.$$

The full-information maximum-likelihood estimates may be found by solving the equation derived from (34) by replacing $\mathbf{\Omega}$ by $\hat{\mathbf{\Omega}}$ together with the equations (35) and (36). For this, an iterative procedure is required.

The unity of econometric methods

The full-information maximum-likelihood estimating equations can be seen as a natural generalization of the equations in (30) which relate to the limited-information maximum-likelihood estimator. Despite their prodigious complexity, they preserve a strong family resemblance with the equations of the hybrid model given in (20). In fact, every estimating system that has been described in this chapter can be conceived, quite reasonably, as a specialization of the full-information maximum-likelihood system.

The remarkable unity of econometric methods is not wholly apparent in a synoptical comparison of their conventional algebraic expositions. This is partly on account of the tendency of a conventional exposition to emphasize the particularities of the method in question rather than to emphasize its affinities with other methods. Many such expositions, however, are redolent of the powerful seminal ideas which led to the devising of the method and, therefore, they have a strong intuitive content. It is the purpose of this book not only to render an account of the methods in the terms in which they were originally conceived, but also to draw the methods together into a framework which will enable us to make simple and direct comparisons. Thus, for example, we shall not only give a detailed exposition of the method of two-stage least squares in Chapter 15, proceeding along the lines that we have already indicated, but we shall also demonstrate that the method results from a straightforward modification to the method of limited-information maximum likelihood.

THE PREREQUISITES OF ECONOMETRIC THEORY

The method of full-information maximum likelihood is often regarded as the height of econometric theory. To reach this vantage point, it might seem appropriate to follow a straightforward and clear-cut path such as we have outlined. However, were we to do so, we would miss seeing much of the elaborate and often confusing scenery of theoretical econometrics. The purpose of this book is to make the journey in a slow and methodical way, often turning aside to explore avenues that are of general interest in multivariate statistical analysis. At the end, we shall conclude that, in fact, we have only reached a staging point from which one may embark in other directions with specialized aims. In order to be able to extend the journey beyond that point, we must carry a considerable burden of equipment. Among teachers of econometrics, there is a debate about the precise nature of the best equipment that can be carried. In this book, a very definite opinion is offered; and, while it is argued that what is presented in the first part of the book is in many respects lighter and more flexible than the conventional equipment, there is little tendency to underestimate the quantity that must be carried. Thus an impatient reader who wishes to travel lighter will still find the text accessible even if he does not study all of the first part. Nevertheless, he will run the risk that, if he wishes to explore things fully, he will be forced to return to the start.

The equipment that is offered in the first four chapters is the algebra of vector spaces. This is linear algebra presented in a way which does not pre-empt the choice of a specific co-ordinate framework and which is intended to accentuate its geometrical aspects.

The virtue of accentuating the geometric aspects of an econometric problem lies in the fact that we can often thereby gain a sense of concreteness such as is lacking in an entirely algebraic treatment. Thus, as we have already suggested in our introductory treatment of the Gauss–Markov model, we can base our intuitive understanding of the algebraic relationships of econometrics upon our ordinary understanding of 3-dimensional space. One might therefore expect to find in this book a large number of diagrams intended to assist his intuition. Their absence needs some explaining. An interesting comment on the propriety of using diagrams has been made by William Kruskal [**72,** p. 273]. He declares that he has been given to understand that

> . . . such aids to the mind are at best activities of child-like naivete, akin to rhythmic toe tapping by a string quartet player, and with analogous dangers of misrepresentation and social contempt. Nonetheless—he declares—, used quietly and with care not to substitute a highly special case for a proof, diagrams can be most useful, and it would be disingenuous to remain silent about their utility.

This statement, which evinces more than a hint of irony, seems to conform with the opinion that, whilst a reliance on geometric intuition is often the best means of discovering mathematical results, it is rarely an adequate way of communicating them. Because they cannot avoid incorporating much accidental detail which is likely to conflict with the reader's own visual interpretations, geometric diagrams are often difficult to understand unless accompanied by extensive verbal explanations. For these reasons, we leave the drawing of diagrams to the reader.

The other prerequisite of econometric theory is a wide knowledge of multivariate statistical theory. In econometrics, statistical theory and algebra go hand in hand. Therefore it makes no sense to talk of the algebraic approach and of the statistical approach as if they were alternatives. Nevertheless, within any exposition of econometric theory, one has a choice of how much space is to be devoted to either aspect of the problem.

Notwithstanding the title of this book, we shall not skimp the statistical aspects; and, indeed, the requisite statistical theory is expounded at some length in an appendix which represents the fifth part of the book. The title of the book alludes to the fact that the attempt to unify the material deals mainly with its algebraic aspect. Thus considerable attention is given to the algebraic nature of the criteria from which the econometric estimators are derived as well as to the comparative algebra of the estimating equations themselves. In particular, we attempt, wherever possible, to envisage the estimating criteria in terms of the minimization of distances in vector spaces.

Other unifying themes are available. For example, the majority of econometric estimators can be interpreted in terms of the criterion of maximizing the likelihood of the sample observations. Such was the approach of the members of the Cowles Commission who originally propounded the methods of full-information maximum likelihood and limited-information maximum likelihood. We shall also take this approach—not in the first instance, but as a means of providing the ultimate justification for estimators that have been derived from intuitively plausible algebraic criteria.

CHAPTER 1

Vector Spaces

DEFINITION OF A VECTOR SPACE

A set $\mathscr{G}$ is said to be closed under a binary operation if the application of that operation to any two elements of $\mathscr{G}$ results in a product which is also an element of $\mathscr{G}$.

The concept of a field provides a summary of the algebraic properties of the set of real numbers which is closed under the binary operations of addition and multiplication. However, the concept is not specific to the set of real numbers; and therefore, in the following definition, a broad interpretation must be given to an unspecified pair of binary operations which we shall persist in calling addition and multiplication.

(1.1) A field $\mathscr{F}$ is any set of elements which is closed under the binary operations of addition and multiplication such that, for any elements $x, y, z \in \mathscr{F}$, the following are true:

1. Multiplication is commutative, so that $xy = yx$.
2. Multiplication is associative, so that $x(yz) = (xy)z$.
3. There exists a unique element $1 \in \mathscr{F}$ such that $1x = x$.
4. For each $x \in \mathscr{F}$ there exists a unique element $x^{-1} \in \mathscr{F}$ such that $xx^{-1} = 1$.
5. Addition is commutative, so that $x + y = y + x$.
6. Addition is associative, so that

$$x + (y + z) = (x + y) + z.$$

7. There exists a unique element $0 \in \mathscr{F}$ such that $x + 0 = x$.
8. For each $x \in \mathscr{F}$ there exists a unique element $(-x) \in \mathscr{F}$ such that $x + (-x) = 0$.
9. Multiplication is distributive with respect to addition, so that $x(y + z) = xy + xz$.

The elements of a field are conveniently referred to as scalars. Examples of fields are the set of real numbers $\mathscr{R}$, the set of complex numbers $\mathscr{C}$ and the set of rational numbers $\mathscr{K}$. However, the set of integers $\mathscr{I}$ is not a field because condition 4 above is not satisfied.

For the definition of a vector space which follows, we assume that some field of scalars has been specified.

(1.2) A vector space $\mathscr{V}$ defined over a field $\mathscr{F}$ is a set of elements with the following properties:

$\mathscr{V}$ is closed under addition so that for any vectors $\mathbf{x}, \mathbf{y}, \mathbf{z} \in \mathscr{V}$

1. $\mathbf{x}+\mathbf{y}=\mathbf{y}+\mathbf{x}$,
2. $(\mathbf{x}+\mathbf{y})+\mathbf{z}=\mathbf{x}+(\mathbf{y}+\mathbf{z})$,
3. there exists a unique element $\mathbf{0} \in \mathscr{V}$ called the origin such that $\mathbf{0}+\mathbf{x}=\mathbf{x}$,
4. for every $\mathbf{x} \in \mathscr{V}$ there exists a unique element $(-\mathbf{x}) \in \mathscr{V}$ such that $\mathbf{x}+(-\mathbf{x})=\mathbf{0}$;

$\mathscr{V}$ is closed under the operation of scalar multiplication whereby any scalars $\lambda, \mu \in \mathscr{F}$, including 1, may be combined with vectors $\mathbf{x}, \mathbf{y} \in \mathscr{V}$ in such a way that

5. $\lambda(\mathbf{x}+\mathbf{y})=\lambda\mathbf{x}+\lambda\mathbf{y}$,
6. $(\lambda+\mu)\mathbf{x}=\lambda\mathbf{x}+\mu\mathbf{x}$,
7. $(\lambda\mu)\mathbf{x}=\lambda(\mu\mathbf{x})$,
8. $1\mathbf{x}=\mathbf{x}$.

We give three leading examples of vector spaces.

Example I. Let $\mathbf{x}'=[x_1, x_2, \ldots, x_n]$, $\mathbf{y}'=[y_1, y_2, \ldots, y_n]$; $x_i, y_i \in \mathscr{R}$ *represent ordered sets of n real numbers called n-tuples. Then the addition* $\mathbf{x}'+\mathbf{y}'$ *and the scalar multiplication* $\lambda\mathbf{x}'$; $\lambda \in \mathscr{R}$ *may be defined, respectively, by*

$$\mathbf{x}'+\mathbf{y}'=[x_1+y_1, x_2+y_2, \ldots, x_n+y_n]$$

and

$$\lambda\mathbf{x}'=[\lambda x_1, \lambda x_2, \ldots, \lambda x_n].$$

It can be confirmed that the set of all such n-tuples constitutes a vector space $\mathscr{R}^n$ *defined over the field of real numbers* $\mathscr{R}$.

Example II. Let $\mathbf{X}=[x_{ij}]$, $\mathbf{Y}=[y_{ij}]$, $\mathbf{Z}=[z_{ij}]$ *represent matrices of order* $m \times n$ *whose elements are scalars. Then, if we specify that* $\mathbf{X}+\mathbf{Y}=\mathbf{Z}$ *if and only if* $z_{ij}=x_{ij}+y_{ij}$ *for all i, j and that* $\lambda\mathbf{X}=\mathbf{Y}$ *if and only if* $\lambda x_{ij}=y_{ij}$ *for all i, j, we obtain a vector space over the specified field of scalars. In fact, the set of* $n \times n$ *matrices amounts to something more than a vector space if we also define operations of matrix multiplication in respect of which the set is certainly closed.*

Example III. Let n be a given integer and let $\mathscr{P}$ *be the set of all polynomials of degree n at most in some real variable x and with real coefficients. Then, if we take the usual definitions of the addition of polynomials and of their multiplication by a real number, we find that* $\mathscr{P}$ *is a vector space over the field of real numbers.*

LINEAR DEPENDENCE

We shall proceed to explore the relationships that subsist in a vector space. For this purpose we need various definitions.

(1.3) A vector $\mathbf{y} \in \mathscr{V}$ is said to be linearly dependent on a subset $\mathscr{X}$ if it can be written as a linear combination of some elements of $\mathscr{X}$.

Thus, if $\mathbf{y}$ is linearly dependent on $\mathscr{X}$, we will be able to find a finite set of vectors $\{\mathbf{x}_1, \mathbf{x}_2, \ldots, \mathbf{x}_r\} \subset \mathscr{X}$ such that $\mathbf{y} = \lambda_1\mathbf{x}_1 + \lambda_2\mathbf{x}_2 + \ldots + \lambda_r\mathbf{x}_r$ where $\lambda_i \in \mathscr{F}$ for all i.

(1.4) A subset $\mathscr{X}$ of a vector space $\mathscr{V}$ is said to be a linearly dependent set if at least one of its elements can be expressed as a linear combination of some of the others.

Equivalently, $\mathscr{X}$ is linearly dependent if there exists a finite subset $\{\mathbf{x}_1, \mathbf{x}_2, \ldots, \mathbf{x}_r\} \subset \mathscr{X}$ and a set of scalars $\{\lambda_1, \lambda_2, \ldots, \lambda_r\}$, not all zero, such that $\lambda_1\mathbf{x}_1 + \lambda_2\mathbf{x}_2 + \ldots + \lambda_r\mathbf{x}_r = \mathbf{0}$. These definitions imply that the set which contains the zero element alone is linearly dependent.

(1.5) A set is linearly independent if it is not linearly dependent.

Equivalently, a set $\mathscr{X}$ is linearly independent if it contains no subset $\{\mathbf{x}_1, \mathbf{x}_2, \ldots, \mathbf{x}_r\}$ for which $\sum \lambda_i\mathbf{x}_i = \mathbf{0}$ with $\lambda_i \neq 0$ for some i. A set containing a single non-zero vector is linearly independent.

(1.6) If the linearly dependent set $\{\mathbf{x}_1, \mathbf{x}_2, \ldots, \mathbf{x}_r\}$ contains a non-zero vector, then it contains a linearly independent subset in terms of which it is possible to express each $\mathbf{x}_i$; $i = 1, \ldots, r$.

Proof. Since $\{\mathbf{x}_1, \mathbf{x}_2, \ldots, \mathbf{x}_r\}$ is a linearly dependent set, there is a non-trivial relation $\sum \lambda_i\mathbf{x}_i = \mathbf{0}$. Let λ_s; $1 \leq s \leq r$ be a non-zero scalar in this expression. Then $\mathbf{x}_s = \sum_{i \neq s} (-\lambda_i/\lambda_s)\mathbf{x}_i$. Thus we may express the elements of the original set in terms of a reduced set $\{\mathbf{x}_1, \ldots, \mathbf{x}_{s-1}, \mathbf{x}_{s+1}, \ldots, \mathbf{x}_r\}$. By this process, we can always delete one vector from a linearly dependent set; and we may repeat the process until we arrive either at a plural linearly independent set or at a single non-zero vector which also constitutes a linearly independent set. All the vectors of the original set may then be expressed in terms of the vectors of the residual linearly independent set.

Bases

A set is said to span a vector space $\mathscr{V}$ if each of its elements belongs to $\mathscr{V}$ and if every vector in $\mathscr{V}$ can be expressed as a linear combination of these elements. A vector space is completely specified by any set that spans it. If the space $\mathscr{V}$ is spanned by a finite set, then this set may be reduced, according to (1.6), to a minimal set of linearly independent vectors also spanning $\mathscr{V}$. Such a set is said to constitute a basis. More precisely,

(1.7) A basis of a vector space $\mathscr{V}$ is a linearly independent set of vectors $[\mathbf{v}_1, \ldots, \mathbf{v}_n]$ such that any $\mathbf{x} \in \mathscr{V}$ may be expressed as $\mathbf{x} = \sum x_i \mathbf{v}_i$; $x_i \in \mathscr{F}$.

(1.8) The maximum number n of linearly independent vectors that may be contained in a vector space $\mathscr{V}$ is the dimension of that space, written as $\text{Dim}\,\mathscr{V} = n$.

A set containing a maximum number of linearly independent vectors must constitute a basis set, since any other vector in $\mathscr{V}$ can be written in terms of the elements of such a set. Conversely, every basis set contains the maximum number of linearly independent vectors; that is to say,

(1.9) The number of vectors in any basis of an n-dimensional space is n.

Proof. It is sufficient to prove that all bases of an n-space contain the same number of vectors; for this number must be equal to the maximum number n of linearly independent vectors. Thus consider any two bases of a vector space $\mathscr{V}$: $\mathscr{X} = [\mathbf{x}_1, \ldots, \mathbf{x}_r]$ and $\mathscr{Y} = [\mathbf{y}_1, \ldots, \mathbf{y}_s]$. Let $\mathscr{X}_1 = [\mathbf{y}_s, \mathbf{x}_1, \ldots, \mathbf{x}_r]$ be formed by adjoining the last element of $\mathscr{Y}$ to $\mathscr{X}$. This new set spans $\mathscr{V}$ since $[\mathbf{x}_1, \ldots, \mathbf{x}_r]$ does so, and it is also linearly dependent. We may reduce the set $\mathscr{X}_1$ by eliminating the first $\mathbf{x}_i$ which is linearly dependent upon its predecessors and $\mathbf{y}_s$. The reduced set still spans $\mathscr{V}$. We may proceed in this way—adjoining one vector and eliminating another—until the set $\mathscr{Y}$ is exhausted or all the $\mathbf{x}_i$ are eliminated. But, if $\mathscr{Y}$ is a linearly independent set, the $\mathbf{x}_i$ will not be exhausted before all the $\mathbf{y}_j$ are incorporated since, otherwise, the remaining $\mathbf{y}_j$ would have to be linear combinations of those already incorporated in the set which, by assumption, is not possible. Hence $r < s$ is not possible. By reversing the roles of $\mathscr{X}$ and $\mathscr{Y}$ in this argument, we may show that $s < r$ is not possible in view of our assumptions; so we must have $r = s$.

(1.10) If $[\mathbf{v}_1, \ldots, \mathbf{v}_n]$ is a basis of a vector space $\mathscr{V}$, then every $\mathbf{x} \in \mathscr{V}$ can be written uniquely in the form $\mathbf{x} = x_1\mathbf{v}_1 + \ldots + x_n\mathbf{v}_n$ with $x_i \in \mathscr{F}$.

Proof. To show that the set of scalars $[x_1, \ldots, x_n]$ is unique, consider another set $[y_1, \ldots, y_n]$. Then $\mathbf{x} = \sum x_i \mathbf{v}_i = \sum y_i \mathbf{v}_i$, whence $\mathbf{0} = \sum (x_i - y_i)\mathbf{v}_i$. But we must have $(x_i - y_i) = 0$ for all i since the vectors $[\mathbf{v}_1, \ldots, \mathbf{v}_n]$ are linearly independent; hence $x_i = y_i$ for all i.

We call the ordered set of scalars $[x_1, \ldots, x_n]$ the co-ordinates of the vector $\mathbf{x}$ relative to the basis $[\mathbf{v}_1, \ldots, \mathbf{v}_n]$. We shall establish the connection between the co-ordinates of a given vector relative to two different bases. To begin with,

(1.11) Let $[\mathbf{v}_1, \ldots, \mathbf{v}_n]$, $[\mathbf{u}_1, \ldots, \mathbf{u}_n]$ be two bases of a vector space $\mathscr{V}$, and let the scalars a_{ji}, b_{ij}; $i, j = 1, \ldots, n$ be defined by the equations

$$\mathbf{v}_i = \sum_j a_{ji}\mathbf{u}_j, \qquad \mathbf{u}_j = \sum_i b_{ij}\mathbf{v}_i. \quad \text{Then}$$

$$\mathbf{v}_i = \sum_j a_{ji} \sum_k b_{kj}\mathbf{v}_k = \sum_k \sum_j a_{ji}b_{kj}\mathbf{v}_k \quad \text{which}$$

implies that $\sum_j a_{ji}b_{kj} = \delta_{ik}$ where

$\delta_{ik} = 1$ if $k = i$ and $\delta_{ik} = 0$ if $k \neq i$.

Likewise $\sum_i b_{ij}a_{ki} = \delta_{jk}$.

If we use the notation $\mathbf{V} = [\mathbf{v}_1, \ldots, \mathbf{v}_n]$, $\mathbf{U} = [\mathbf{u}_1, \ldots, \mathbf{u}_n]$, $\mathbf{A} = [a_{ji}]$, $\mathbf{B} = [b_{ij}]$ and $\mathbf{I} = [\delta_{ij}]$, we can write $\mathbf{V} = \mathbf{UA}$, $\mathbf{U} = \mathbf{VB}$ for the equations defining a_{ji}, b_{ij}, and $\mathbf{BA} = \mathbf{I}$, $\mathbf{AB} = \mathbf{I}$ or $\mathbf{B} = \mathbf{A}^{-1}$ as a statement of the theorem. It follows from the theorem that

(1.12) If $\mathbf{p}' = [p_1, \ldots, p_n]$ and $\mathbf{q}' = [q_1, \ldots, q_n]$ are the co-ordinates of a vector $\mathbf{x} \in \mathscr{V}$ relative to the bases $[\mathbf{u}_1, \ldots, \mathbf{u}_n]$ and $[\mathbf{v}_1, \ldots, \mathbf{v}_n]$ respectively, then $q_i = \sum_j b_{ij}p_j$ and $p_j = \sum_i a_{ji}q_i$.

We can also express these relationships by writing $\mathbf{q} = \mathbf{Bp} = \mathbf{A}^{-1}\mathbf{p}$ and $\mathbf{p} = \mathbf{Aq}$.

VECTOR SUBSPACES

(1.13) A subspace $\mathscr{S}$ of a vector space $\mathscr{V}$ is any subset of $\mathscr{V}$ which constitutes a vector space in respect of the binary operations of addition and scalar multiplication that are defined for $\mathscr{V}$.

It follows from the properties of vector spaces that, if $\mathscr{S}$ is a vector space and if $\mathbf{x}, \mathbf{y} \in \mathscr{S}$, then $\lambda\mathbf{x} + \mu\mathbf{y} \in \mathscr{S}$ for any scalars $\lambda, \mu \in \mathscr{F}$. Conversely, if $\mathbf{x}, \mathbf{y} \in \mathscr{S}$ implies $\lambda\mathbf{x} + \mu\mathbf{y} \in \mathscr{S}$, then we may infer that $\mathbf{x} + \mathbf{y} \in \mathscr{S}$ (by setting $\lambda, \mu = 1$), that $\lambda\mathbf{x} \in \mathscr{S}$ (by setting $\mu = 0$) and that $\mu\mathbf{y} \in \mathscr{S}$ (by setting $\lambda = 0$); which shows that $\mathscr{S}$ is closed under vector addition and scalar multiplication. The remaining conditions of (1.2) are also satisfied for all $\mathbf{x}, \mathbf{y} \in \mathscr{S}$ since they are satisfied for all $\mathbf{x}, \mathbf{y} \in \mathscr{V}$ and we have $\mathscr{S} \subset \mathscr{V}$. In particular, $\mathscr{S}$ contains the origin $\mathbf{0}$. Hence $\mathcal{S}$ constitutes a vector space. Thus we may offer the following alternative definition which is equivalent to (1.13).

(1.14) A subspace of a vector space $\mathcal{V}$ is any set of vectors $\mathcal{S} \subset \mathcal{V}$ such that, if $\mathbf{x}, \mathbf{y} \in \mathcal{S}$, then $\lambda\mathbf{x}+\mu\mathbf{y} \in \mathcal{S}$ for any $\lambda, \mu \in \mathcal{F}$.

It follows from (1.14) that, if all possible linear combinations of an arbitrary set of vectors are taken together, the result is a linear subspace.

(1.15) The set of all linear combinations of an arbitrary finite set of vectors $\mathcal{G}$ is said to be the subspace spanned or generated by $\mathcal{G}$. Alternatively, it is described as the manifold of $\mathcal{G}$ denoted $\mathcal{M}(\mathcal{G})$.

(1.16) If $\mathcal{S} \subset \mathcal{V}$ is a subspace and $\text{Dim}\, \mathcal{S} = \text{Dim}\, \mathcal{V}$, then $\mathcal{S} = \mathcal{V}$.

Proof. If $\text{Dim}\, \mathcal{S} = \text{Dim}\, \mathcal{V}$, these spaces possess a common basis, and they must therefore be identical. We say then that $\mathcal{S}$ is an improper subspace of $\mathcal{V}$.

Sums and intersections of subspaces

(1.17) Let $\mathcal{U}$ and $\mathcal{W}$ be subspaces of a vector space $\mathcal{V}$. The sum of $\mathcal{U}$ and $\mathcal{W}$, written $\mathcal{U}+\mathcal{W}$, is the set of all elements of $\mathcal{V}$ which can be written as $\mathbf{u}+\mathbf{w}$ with $\mathbf{u} \in \mathcal{U}$ and $\mathbf{w} \in \mathcal{W}$. The intersection of $\mathcal{U}$ and $\mathcal{W}$, written $\mathcal{U} \cap \mathcal{W}$, is the set of all elements of $\mathcal{V}$ that are in both $\mathcal{U}$ and $\mathcal{W}$.

(1.18) If $\mathcal{U}, \mathcal{W} \subset \mathcal{V}$ are vector subspaces, then their sum $\mathcal{U}+\mathcal{W}$ and their intersection $\mathcal{U} \cap \mathcal{W}$ are also subspaces of $\mathcal{V}$.

Proof. Consider $\mathbf{u}_1, \mathbf{u}_2 \in \mathcal{U}$ and $\mathbf{w}_1, \mathbf{w}_2 \in \mathcal{W}$. If $\mathbf{p} = \mathbf{u}_1 + \mathbf{w}_1$, $\mathbf{q} = \mathbf{u}_2 + \mathbf{w}_2$, then $\mathbf{p}, \mathbf{q} \in (\mathcal{U}+\mathcal{W})$; and it follows that $\lambda\mathbf{p}+\mu\mathbf{q} = (\lambda\mathbf{u}_1+\mu\mathbf{u}_2)+(\lambda\mathbf{w}_1+\mu\mathbf{w}_2)$ is also in $\mathcal{U}+\mathcal{W}$ since $(\lambda\mathbf{u}_1+\mu\mathbf{u}_2) \in \mathcal{U}$ and $(\lambda\mathbf{w}_1+\mu\mathbf{w}_2) \in \mathcal{W}$ which, according to (1.14), proves that $\mathcal{U}+\mathcal{W}$ is a subspace.

Now consider $\mathbf{p}, \mathbf{q} \in (\mathcal{U} \cap \mathcal{W})$ which implies both $\mathbf{p}, \mathbf{q} \in \mathcal{U}$ and $\mathbf{p}, \mathbf{q} \in \mathcal{W}$. Then $\lambda\mathbf{p}, \mu\mathbf{q} \in \mathcal{U}$ and $\lambda\mathbf{p}, \mu\mathbf{q} \in \mathcal{W}$. This implies that $\lambda\mathbf{p}+\mu\mathbf{q} \in \mathcal{U}$ and $\lambda\mathbf{p}+\mu\mathbf{q} \in \mathcal{W}$, or $\lambda\mathbf{p}+\mu\mathbf{q} \in (\mathcal{U} \cap \mathcal{W})$; hence $\mathcal{U} \cap \mathcal{W}$ is a subspace.

(1.19) If $\mathcal{U}, \mathcal{W} \subset \mathcal{V}$ are vector subspaces, then $\text{Dim}(\mathcal{U}+\mathcal{W}) = \text{Dim}\, \mathcal{U} + \text{Dim}\, \mathcal{W} - \text{Dim}(\mathcal{U} \cap \mathcal{W})$.

Proof. Assume that $\text{Dim}\, \mathcal{U} = p$, $\text{Dim}\, \mathcal{W} = q$, $\text{Dim}(\mathcal{U} \cap \mathcal{W}) = r$, and let $[\mathbf{u}_1, \ldots, \mathbf{u}_p]$ and $[\mathbf{w}_1, \ldots, \mathbf{w}_q]$ be bases of $\mathcal{U}$ and $\mathcal{W}$ respectively. Each of these bases must contain a subset of elements which forms a basis of $\mathcal{U} \cap \mathcal{W}$. We may join the bases of $\mathcal{U}$ and $\mathcal{W}$ to form a set $[\mathbf{u}_1, \ldots, \mathbf{u}_p, \mathbf{w}_1, \ldots, \mathbf{w}_q]$ which spans $\mathcal{U}+\mathcal{W}$. To find a basis of $\mathcal{U}+\mathcal{W}$, we eliminate elements from this set; starting with the first vector which is linearly dependent on its predecessors and proceeding until we have a linearly independent set. At each stage the element which is eliminated must be some vector $\mathbf{w}_j \in (\mathcal{U} \cap \mathcal{W})$, since no vector $\mathbf{u}_i$ can be linearly dependent on its predecessors. By this process we succeed in eliminating the r elements of a basis of $\mathcal{U} \cap \mathcal{W}$ from the set $[\mathbf{w}_1, \ldots, \mathbf{w}_q]$. It follows that the number of elements remaining in the basis of $\mathcal{U} + \mathcal{W}$ is $\text{Dim}(\mathcal{U} + \mathcal{W}) = (p+q) - r = \text{Dim}\,\mathcal{U} + \text{Dim}\,\mathcal{W} - \text{Dim}(\mathcal{U} \cap \mathcal{W})$, which proves the theorem.

(1.20) If $\mathcal{U}$ and $\mathcal{W}$ have only the origin in common, so that $\mathcal{U} \cap \mathcal{W} = \mathbf{0}$, they are said to be virtually disjoint. In that case, their sum, written as $\mathcal{U} \oplus \mathcal{W}$, is called a direct sum.

Since $\mathcal{U} \cap \mathcal{W} = \mathbf{0}$ implies $\text{Dim}(\mathcal{U} \cap \mathcal{W}) = 0$, it follows from (1.19) that

(1.21) $\text{Dim}(\mathcal{U} \oplus \mathcal{W}) = \text{Dim}\,\mathcal{U} + \text{Dim}\,\mathcal{W}$.

(1.22) If $\mathcal{U}, \mathcal{W} \subset \mathcal{V}$ and $\mathcal{U} \oplus \mathcal{W} = \mathcal{V}$, we say that $\mathcal{U}$ and $\mathcal{W}$ are complementary subspaces.

Any vector $\mathbf{v} \in \mathcal{V} = \mathcal{U} \oplus \mathcal{W}$ may be uniquely decomposed with a component in $\mathcal{U}$ and a component in $\mathcal{W}$. Thus

(1.23) If $\mathbf{v} = \mathbf{u} + \mathbf{w}$ with $\mathbf{u} \in \mathcal{U}$, $\mathbf{w} \in \mathcal{W}$ and $\mathcal{U} \cap \mathcal{W} = \mathbf{0}$, then $\mathbf{u}$ and $\mathbf{w}$ are unique.

Proof. Imagine $\mathbf{v} = \mathbf{u} + \mathbf{w}$ and $\mathbf{v} = \mathbf{u}_* + \mathbf{w}_*$, with $\mathbf{u}, \mathbf{u}_* \in \mathcal{U}$ and $\mathbf{w}, \mathbf{w}_* \in \mathcal{W}$. Then $\mathbf{v} - \mathbf{v} = (\mathbf{u} - \mathbf{u}_*) + (\mathbf{w} - \mathbf{w}_*) = \mathbf{0}$. But, since $\mathcal{U} \cap \mathcal{W} = \mathbf{0}$, we cannot have $(\mathbf{u} - \mathbf{u}_*) = -(\mathbf{w} - \mathbf{w}_*) \neq \mathbf{0}$, so we must have $(\mathbf{u} - \mathbf{u}_*) = (\mathbf{w} - \mathbf{w}_*) = \mathbf{0}$; whence $\mathbf{u} = \mathbf{u}_*$, $\mathbf{w} = \mathbf{w}_*$.

AFFINE SUBSPACES

(1.24) An affine subspace of a vector space $\mathcal{V}$ is any set of vectors $\mathcal{A} \subset \mathcal{V}$ such that $(1-\lambda)\mathbf{x} + \lambda\mathbf{y} \in \mathcal{A}$ if $\mathbf{x}, \mathbf{y} \in \mathcal{A}$ and $\lambda \in \mathcal{F}$.

A vector space is clearly an affine subspace, but not all affine subspaces are vector spaces since, although it contains all linear combinations wherein the weights sum to unity, $\mathcal{A}$ does not necessarily contain every arbitrary linear combination of its own elements.

(1.25) An affine subspace which is not a vector space cannot contain the origin.

Proof. The affine subspace $\mathcal{A}$ cannot contain the zero vector since, if it did so, it would contain all linear combinations of its own elements contrary to the assumption. For, if $\mathbf{0} \in \mathcal{A}$, then, for any $\mathbf{x} \in \mathcal{A}$, $\lambda\mathbf{x} + (1-\lambda)\mathbf{0} = \lambda\mathbf{x} \in \mathcal{A}$; so that, for any $\mathbf{x}, \mathbf{y} \in \mathcal{A}$ and $\lambda, \mu \in \mathcal{F}$, we would have $\mu\mathbf{y}+(1-\mu)\lambda\mathbf{x}=\lambda\mathbf{y}+\rho\mathbf{x} \in \mathcal{A}$ where both λ and ρ are arbitrarily determined.

(1.26) If $\mathcal{U} \subset \mathcal{V}$ is a vector subspace of $\mathcal{V}$ and $\mathbf{a} \in \mathcal{V}$; $\mathbf{a} \notin \mathcal{U}$ is a fixed vector, then $\mathbf{a}+\mathcal{U}$ is an affine subspace which is not a vector space.

Proof. Let $\mathbf{x}, \mathbf{y}$ be arbitrary vectors of $\mathcal{U}$ so that $\mathbf{a}+\mathbf{x}$, $\mathbf{a}+\mathbf{y}$ are arbitrary vectors of $\mathbf{a}+\mathcal{U}$. Then $\lambda(\mathbf{a}+\mathbf{x})+(1-\lambda)(\mathbf{a}+\mathbf{y})=\mathbf{a}+[\lambda\mathbf{x}+(1-\lambda)\mathbf{y}] \in (\mathbf{a}+\mathcal{U})$; so that $\mathbf{a}+\mathcal{U}$ is an affine subspace. Moreover, if $\mathbf{a} \notin \mathcal{U}$, then $(-\mathbf{a}) \notin \mathcal{U}$ and therefore $\mathbf{a}+\mathcal{U}$ does not contain the origin and cannot be a vector space.

The converse of (1.26) is also true. Thus

(1.27) If $\mathcal{A}$ is an affine subspace, but not necessarily a vector space, then, for any $\mathbf{a} \in \mathcal{A}$, there exists a vector space $\mathcal{U}$ such that $\mathcal{A}=\mathbf{a}+\mathcal{U}$.

Proof. Let $\mathbf{a} \in \mathcal{A}$ be fixed and let $\mathbf{x}, \mathbf{y} \in \mathcal{A}$ be arbitrary. Then $\mathcal{A}$ is the set $\mathbf{a}+\mathcal{U}$ of all elements $\lambda\mathbf{x}+(1-\lambda)\mathbf{y}=\mathbf{a}+[\lambda(\mathbf{x}-\mathbf{a})+(1-\lambda)(\mathbf{y}-\mathbf{a})]$ where $\lambda \in \mathcal{F}$ is arbitrary. Furthermore, the set $\mathcal{U}$ of all elements $\lambda(\mathbf{x}-\mathbf{a})+(1-\lambda)(\mathbf{y}-\mathbf{a})$ constitutes an affine subspace. Setting $\lambda=0$ and $\mathbf{y}=\mathbf{a}$ shows that $\mathcal{U}$ contains the origin $\mathbf{0}$, so that, by (1.25), it must also be a vector space.

In view of (1.26) and (1.27) it is appropriate to refer to an affine subspace $\mathcal{A}=\mathbf{a}+\mathcal{U}$ which is not also a vector space as a translated vector space. The vector $\mathbf{a}$ is then termed the translation.

(1.28) A set of vectors $\{\mathbf{x}_1, \mathbf{x}_2, \ldots, \mathbf{x}_r\}$ is said to be affine dependent if there exists a set of scalars $\lambda_1, \lambda_2, \ldots, \lambda_r$, not all zero, such that $\lambda_1\mathbf{x}_1+\lambda_2\mathbf{x}_2 \ldots + \lambda_r\mathbf{x}_r=\mathbf{0}$ and $\lambda_1+\lambda_2+\ldots+\lambda_r=0$.

(1.29) A set of vectors is affine independent if it is not affine dependent.

The condition of affine dependence is stronger than the condition of linear dependence. Thus every affine dependent set is linearly dependent and every linearly independent set is affine independent; but the converse is not true.

It is useful to have the additional definition that

(1.30) A vector $\mathbf{y}$ is affine dependent on a set of vectors $\{\mathbf{x}_1, \ldots, \mathbf{x}_r\}$ if and only if $\mathbf{y}=\sum \lambda_i\mathbf{x}_i$ where $\sum \lambda_i=1$.

Clearly, (1.28) and (1.30) are equivalent definitions; for $\mathbf{y}$ is affine dependent on $\{\mathbf{x}_1, \ldots, \mathbf{x}_r\}$ if and only if the set $\{\mathbf{y}, \mathbf{x}_1, \ldots, \mathbf{x}_r\}$ is affine dependent.

The definitions of affine dependence and independence are intelligible in terms of 2-dimensional and 3-dimensional spaces. Thus three vectors are affine dependent if and only if they can be represented by three collinear points, and, likewise, four vectors are affine dependent if and only if they can be represented by four coplanar points.

(1.31) If $\{\mathbf{x}_1, \ldots, \mathbf{x}_r\}$ is linearly dependent such that $\lambda_1\mathbf{x}_1 + \ldots + \lambda_r\mathbf{x}_r = \mathbf{0}$, and if $\mathbf{x}_{r+1}$ is linearly dependent on this set such that $\mu_1\mathbf{x}_1 + \ldots + \mu_r\mathbf{x}_r + \mu_{r+1}\mathbf{x}_{r+1} = \mathbf{0}$, then $\{\mathbf{x}_1, \ldots, \mathbf{x}_r, \mathbf{x}_{r+1}\}$ is affine dependent.

Proof. Let $\sum^r \lambda_i = p$ and $\sum^{r+1} \mu_j = q$. Then $\sum^r (\lambda_i/p)\mathbf{x}_i - \sum^{r+1} (\mu_j/q)\mathbf{x}_j = \sum^{r+1} \eta_j\mathbf{x}_j = \mathbf{0}$, and $\sum \eta_j = \sum (\lambda_i/p) - \sum (\mu_j/q) = 1 - 1 = 0$, whence $\{\mathbf{x}_1, \ldots, \mathbf{x}_r, \mathbf{x}_{r+1}\}$ is affine dependent.

It follows from (1.31) that

(1.32) The number of affine independent vectors in an n-dimensional space cannot exceed $n+1$;

for every set of $n+2$ vectors in an n-dimensional space must contain a linearly dependent subset of $n+1$ vectors and a residual vector which is linearly dependent on this subset; which implies, according to (1.31), that the $n+2$ vectors must be affine dependent.

(1.33) If $\{\mathbf{x}_1, \ldots, \mathbf{x}_r\}$ is a linearly independent set, there exists a vector $\mathbf{x}_{r+1}$ such that $\{\mathbf{x}_1, \ldots, \mathbf{x}_r, \mathbf{x}_{r+1}\}$ is affine independent.

Proof. We may prove this by a single constructive example. Let us set $\mathbf{x}_{r+1} = \lambda_r\mathbf{x}_r$ where $\lambda_r \neq 1$. Then $\sum^{r+1} \lambda_j\mathbf{x}_j = \mathbf{0}$ only if $\lambda_j = 0$ for $j = 1, \ldots, r-1$ and $\lambda_{r+1} = -1$. Therefore, since $\sum^{r+1} \lambda_j \neq 0$, it follows that $\{\mathbf{x}_1, \ldots, \mathbf{x}_r, \mathbf{x}_{r+1}\}$ is affine independent.

It follows from (1.33) that the maximal set of affine independent vectors in any vector space must be a linearly dependent set; for otherwise, if it were linearly independent, we could find a more numerous set of affine independent vectors. Thus the maximum number of affine independent vectors in an n-dimensional space is at least $n+1$, since we can always find n linearly independent vectors in such a space. Taking this result together with (1.32), we deduce that

(1.34) The maximum number of affine independent vectors in an n-dimensional space is $n+1$.

However,

(1.35) The dimension of an affine subspace is defined as one less than the maximum number of affine independent vectors that can be contained therein.

The definition of the dimension of a vector space and the dimension of an affine space are clearly conformable since

(1.36) If $\mathcal{U}$ is a vector space of dimension r, it is also an affine space of dimension r.

Finally, let us consider the intersections of affine subspaces. It is clear that

(1.37) The intersection of two affine subspaces $\mathcal{A}, \mathcal{B}$ is also an affine subspace;

for, if $\mathbf{x}, \mathbf{y} \in \mathcal{A} \cap \mathcal{B}$, then $\mathbf{q} = \lambda\mathbf{x} + (1-\lambda)\mathbf{y} \in \mathcal{A}$ since $\mathbf{x}, \mathbf{y} \in \mathcal{A}$ and, likewise, $\mathbf{q} \in \mathcal{B}$ since $\mathbf{x}, \mathbf{y} \in \mathcal{B}$. Furthermore,

(1.38) Let $\mathcal{A}, \mathcal{B} \subset \mathcal{V}$ be intersecting affine subspaces within a vector space such that $\mathcal{A} \cap \mathcal{B} \neq \emptyset$. Then $\mathcal{A} = \boldsymbol{\mu} + \mathcal{P}$, $\mathcal{B} = \boldsymbol{\mu} + \mathcal{Q}$ and $\mathcal{A} \cap \mathcal{B} = \boldsymbol{\mu} + (\mathcal{P} \cap \mathcal{Q})$ where $\boldsymbol{\mu} \in (\mathcal{A} \cap \mathcal{B})$ is a vector and $\mathcal{P}, \mathcal{Q} \subset \mathcal{V}$ are vector subspaces.

Proof. The expressions $\mathcal{A} = \boldsymbol{\mu} + \mathcal{P}$, $\mathcal{B} = \boldsymbol{\mu} + \mathcal{Q}$ follow from (1.27), and then the expression $\mathcal{A} \cap \mathcal{B} = \boldsymbol{\mu} + (\mathcal{P} \cap \mathcal{Q})$ follows directly.

BIBLIOGRAPHY

Vector Spaces. Halmos [**49,** Chap. I], Shephard [**109,** Chap. I] Kreider et al. [**70,** Chap. 1]

Affine Subspaces. Shephard [**109,** pp. 33–35]

CHAPTER 2

Linear Transformations

THE DEFINITION OF A LINEAR TRANSFORMATION

If $\mathscr{V}$ and $\mathscr{W}$ are two sets, then a mapping from $\mathscr{V}$ to $\mathscr{W}$—which is also called a transformation or a function—is a rule which associates with each $\mathbf{x} \in \mathscr{V}$ a unique $\mathbf{y} \in \mathscr{W}$.

(2.1) Let $\mathscr{V}$ and $\mathscr{W}$ be two vector spaces defined over the same field $\mathscr{F}$; then a mapping $\mathbf{A}$ from $\mathscr{V}$ to $\mathscr{W}$ is defined to be a linear transformation if, for all $\mathbf{x}, \mathbf{y} \in \mathscr{V}$ and $\lambda \in \mathscr{F}$, it has the following properties:

1. $\mathbf{A}(\mathbf{x}+\mathbf{y}) = \mathbf{A}\mathbf{x}+\mathbf{A}\mathbf{y}$.
2. $\mathbf{A}(\lambda\mathbf{x}) = \lambda(\mathbf{A}\mathbf{x})$.

These conditions amount to a statement that vector addition and scalar multiplication are invariant with respect to the transformation $\mathbf{A}$; that is to say, it is immaterial whether these operations take place in $\mathscr{V}$ or $\mathscr{W}$. We may combine conditions 1 and 2 so as to define $\mathbf{A}$ to be a linear transformation from $\mathscr{V}$ to $\mathscr{W}$ if, for all $\mathbf{x}, \mathbf{y} \in \mathscr{V}$ and $\lambda, \mu \in \mathscr{F}$, we have

(2.2) $$\mathbf{A}(\lambda\mathbf{x}+\mu\mathbf{y}) = \lambda(\mathbf{A}\mathbf{x})+\mu(\mathbf{A}\mathbf{y}).$$

We shall denote the set of all linear transformations from $\mathscr{V}$ to $\mathscr{W}$ by $\mathscr{L}(\mathscr{V}, \mathscr{W})$.

(2.3) A linear transformation between the vector spaces $\mathscr{V}$ and $\mathscr{W}$, such that for every $\mathbf{x} \in \mathscr{V}$ there corresponds a unique $\mathbf{y} \in \mathscr{W}$ and for every $\mathbf{y} \in \mathscr{W}$ there corresponds a unique $\mathbf{x} \in \mathscr{V}$, is called a linear isomorphism.

Example. The relationship between the vectors in an n-dimensional vector space $\mathscr{V}$, defined over a field $\mathscr{F}$, and the n-tuple vectors in the vector space $\mathscr{F}^n$ is a linear isomorphism. To see this, let us recall that we have established in (1.10) *that, subject to the choice of a basis $[\mathbf{v}_1, \ldots, \mathbf{v}_n]$ for $\mathscr{V}$, there is a unique correspondence between the vectors $\mathbf{x} \in \mathscr{V}$ and the co-ordinates $[x_1, \ldots, x_n] \in \mathscr{F}^n$. To demonstrate that it is an isomorphism, we need only show that this relationship entails a linear transformation. Thus let $\mathbf{y} \in \mathscr{V}$ be another vector with co-ordinates, relative to the chosen basis, of $[y_1, \ldots, y_n]$. Then, for $\lambda, \mu \in \mathscr{F}$, we have $\lambda\mathbf{x} = \lambda \sum x_i\mathbf{v}_i$, $\mu\mathbf{y} = \mu \sum y_i\mathbf{v}_i$ and $\lambda\mathbf{x}+\mu\mathbf{y} = \sum (\lambda x_i + \mu y_i)\mathbf{v}_i$.*

The relationship between vectors in $\mathscr{V}$ and n-tuple vectors in $\mathscr{F}^n$ is expressed, in one direction, by writing,

$$\mathbf{Tx} = \mathbf{T}(\sum x_i \mathbf{v}_i) = [x_1, \ldots, x_n].$$

Therefore, since $\lambda\mathbf{Tx} = \lambda[x_1, \ldots, x_n]$, $\mu\mathbf{Ty} = \mu[x_1, \ldots, x_n]$ *and* $\mathbf{T}(\lambda\mathbf{x} + \mu\mathbf{y}) = [\lambda x_1 + \mu y_1, \ldots, \lambda x_n + \mu y_n]$, *we can write*

$$\mathbf{T}(\lambda\mathbf{x} + \mu\mathbf{y}) = \lambda\mathbf{Tx} + \mu\mathbf{Ty}$$

which establishes the linearity of the relationship and thereby demonstrates that it is a linear isomorphism.

If two spaces are related by an isomorphism, then they have an identical algebraic structure. This means that any true statement which applies to the elements of one space is necessarily true for the corresponding elements of the other space. It follows that any algebraic proposition that we can prove in terms of an abstract, co-ordinate free, space can be translated into the terminology of co-ordinate spaces. We shall prove many propositions in terms of abstract rather than co-ordinate spaces to assist an intuitive understanding, as well as to achieve an economy of expression. We shall also find that it is relatively easy to translate the proven propositions into co-ordinate terminology which we shall do whenever it is appropriate.

We now proceed to show, in various steps, that the transformation $\mathbf{y} = \mathbf{Ax}$ with $\mathbf{x} \in \mathscr{V}$, $\mathbf{y} \in \mathscr{W}$ and $\mathbf{A} \in \mathscr{L}(\mathscr{V}, \mathscr{W})$ has an equivalent representation in terms of an n-tuple vector $\mathbf{x} \in \mathscr{F}^n$, an m-tuple vector $\mathbf{y} \in \mathscr{F}^m$ and an $m \times n$ matrix $\mathbf{A} \in \mathscr{L}(\mathscr{F}^n, \mathscr{F}^m)$.

To begin with, we may state that

(2.4) Any transformation $\mathbf{A} \in \mathscr{L}(\mathscr{V}, \mathscr{W})$ can be completely characterized by the images under $\mathbf{A}$ of the some chosen basis of $\mathscr{V}$, say $[\mathbf{v}_1, \ldots, \mathbf{v}_n]$.

This is so because every $\mathbf{x} \in \mathscr{V}$ can be uniquely expressed as $\mathbf{x} = \sum \lambda_j \mathbf{v}_j$, and every transformed vector $\mathbf{y} = \mathbf{Ax}$ can be uniquely expressed as $\mathbf{y} = \sum \lambda_j \mathbf{Av}_j$.

Let us choose a basis $[\mathbf{w}_1, \ldots, \mathbf{w}_m]$ for $\mathscr{W}$. We may then express the characteristic image $\mathbf{Av}_j \in \mathscr{W}$ as $\mathbf{Av}_j = \sum_i a_{ij} \mathbf{w}_i$; $a_{ij} \in \mathscr{F}$, where $[a_{1j}, \ldots, a_{mj}]$ are, for each j, the unique co-ordinates of $\mathbf{Av}_j$ relative to the basis of $\mathscr{W}$. Since $j = 1, \ldots, n$, we obtain an $m \times n$ matrix $[a_{ij}]$ which, given the choice of bases, completely characterizes $\mathbf{A}$.

(2.5) Let $\mathbf{A} \in \mathscr{L}(\mathscr{V}, \mathscr{W})$ be characterized, relative to the bases $[\mathbf{v}_1, \ldots, \mathbf{v}_n]$, $[\mathbf{w}_1, \ldots, \mathbf{w}_m]$ of $\mathscr{V}$ and $\mathscr{W}$, by the matrix $[a_{ij}]$. Then the co-ordinates $[x_1, \ldots, x_n]$ of $\mathbf{x} \in \mathscr{V}$ and the co-ordinates $[y_1, \ldots, y_m]$ of $\mathbf{y} = \mathbf{Ax} \in \mathscr{W}$ are connected by the equations

$$y_i = \sum_{j=1}^{n} a_{ij} x_j, \qquad i = 1, \ldots, m,$$

or, in matrix notation,

$$\begin{bmatrix} y_1 \\ y_2 \\ \cdot \\ \cdot \\ \cdot \\ y_m \end{bmatrix} = \begin{bmatrix} a_{11}, & a_{12}, & \ldots, & a_{1n} \\ a_{21}, & a_{22}, & \ldots, & a_{2n} \\ \cdot & \cdot & & \cdot \\ \cdot & \cdot & & \cdot \\ \cdot & \cdot & & \cdot \\ a_{m1}, & a_{m2}, & \ldots, & a_{mn} \end{bmatrix} \begin{bmatrix} x_1 \\ x_2 \\ \cdot \\ \cdot \\ \cdot \\ x_n \end{bmatrix}$$

Proof. For any $\mathbf{x} \in \mathcal{V}$, we have

$$\mathbf{Ax} = \mathbf{A}\Big(\sum_j x_j \mathbf{v}_j\Big) = \sum_j x_j \mathbf{A v}_j = \sum_j x_j \sum_i a_{ij} \mathbf{w}_i = \sum_i \Big(\sum_j a_{ij} x_j\Big) \mathbf{w}_i.$$

But we also have $\mathbf{y} = \sum_i y_i \mathbf{w}_i$, whence we see, by equating the coefficients, that $y_i = \sum_j a_{ij} x_j$ for all i.

We shall now define a variety of vector spaces associated with any transformation $\mathbf{A} \in \mathcal{L}(\mathcal{V}, \mathcal{W})$.

Range spaces and null spaces

(2.6) The domain of a transformation $\mathbf{A} \in \mathcal{L}(\mathcal{V}, \mathcal{W})$ is the set of all elements $\mathbf{x} \in \mathcal{V}$ that are subject to the transformation. When $\mathbf{A}$ is defined over $\mathcal{V}$, $\mathcal{V}$ is the domain of $\mathbf{A}$. When $\mathbf{A}$ is defined over a subspace $\mathcal{U} \subset \mathcal{V}$ it is called the restriction of $\mathbf{A}$ to $\mathcal{U}$, written $\mathbf{A}_{\mathcal{U}}$.

(2.7) The range space of $\mathbf{A} \in \mathcal{L}(\mathcal{V}, \mathcal{W})$ is defined as the set $\{\mathbf{Ax}; \mathbf{x} \in \mathcal{V}\}$ and is denoted by $\mathcal{R}(\mathbf{A}) \subset \mathcal{W}$. The dimension of the range space is called the rank of the transformation, written $\mathrm{Dim}\, \mathcal{R}(\mathbf{A}) = \mathrm{Rank}(\mathbf{A})$.

(2.8) The null space of $\mathbf{A} \in \mathcal{L}(\mathcal{V}, \mathcal{W})$, also called the kernel, is defined as the set $\{\mathbf{x}; \mathbf{Ax} = \mathbf{0}\}$ and is denoted by $\mathcal{N}(\mathbf{A}) \subset \mathcal{V}$. The dimension of the null space is called the nullity of the transformation, written $\mathrm{Dim}\, \mathcal{N}(\mathbf{A}) = \mathrm{Null}(\mathbf{A})$.

We shall begin by showing that

(2.9) If $\mathbf{A} \in \mathcal{L}(\mathcal{V}, \mathcal{W})$ is a linear transformation from $\mathcal{V}$ to $\mathcal{W}$, then $\mathrm{Rank}(\mathbf{A}) + \mathrm{Null}(\mathbf{A}) = \mathrm{Dim}\, \mathcal{V}$

Proof. We choose a basis $[\mathbf{v}_1, \ldots, \mathbf{v}_g, \mathbf{v}_{g+1}, \ldots, \mathbf{v}_n]$ for $\mathcal{V}$, such that $[\mathbf{v}_1, \ldots, \mathbf{v}_g]$ is a basis for $\mathcal{N}(\mathbf{A}) \subset \mathcal{V}$. Then, for any $\mathbf{x} \in \mathcal{V}$,

$$\mathbf{A}\mathbf{x} = \mathbf{A}\Big(\sum_j x_j \mathbf{v}_j\Big) = \sum_{j=1}^{n} x_j \mathbf{A}\mathbf{v}_j = \sum_{j=g+1}^{n} x_j \mathbf{A}\mathbf{v}_j,$$

since, by definition, $\mathbf{A}\mathbf{v}_j = \mathbf{0}$ for $j = 1, \ldots, g$. Thus $[\mathbf{A}\mathbf{v}_{g+1}, \ldots, \mathbf{A}\mathbf{v}_n]$ spans $\mathcal{R}(\mathbf{A})$. It is also a basis of $\mathcal{R}(\mathbf{A})$; for, if this were not so, there would exist a set of scalars $\{\lambda_{g+1}, \ldots, \lambda_n\}$, not all zero, such that $\lambda_{g+1}\mathbf{A}\mathbf{v}_{g+1} + \ldots + \lambda_n \mathbf{A}\mathbf{v}_n = \mathbf{0}$. This implies $\mathbf{A}(\lambda_{g+1}\mathbf{v}_{g+1} + \ldots + \lambda_n \mathbf{v}_n) = \mathbf{0}$, which is impossible since the vectors $[\mathbf{v}_{g+1}, \ldots, \mathbf{v}_n]$ form no part of $\mathcal{N}(\mathbf{A})$. Thus $\text{Dim}\,\mathcal{R}(\mathbf{A}) = \text{Rank}(\mathbf{A}) = n - g$. Then, since $\text{Null}(\mathbf{A}) = g$ and $\text{Dim}\,\mathcal{V} = n$, we get $\text{Rank}(\mathbf{A}) + \text{Null}(\mathbf{A}) = \text{Dim}\,\mathcal{V}$.

(2.10) If $\text{Null}(\mathbf{A}) = 0$, which is to say $\text{Rank}(\mathbf{A}) = \text{Dim}\,\mathcal{V}$, then, equivalently, $\mathbf{A}$ is a one-to-one transformation from $\mathcal{V}$ to $\mathcal{R}(\mathbf{A})$.

Proof. If $\mathbf{A} \in \mathcal{L}(\mathcal{V}, \mathcal{W})$ is a one-to-one transformation, then $\mathbf{0} \in \mathcal{V}$ is the only element that maps into $\mathbf{0} \in \mathcal{R}(\mathbf{A}) \subset \mathcal{W}$, so $\text{Null}(\mathbf{A}) = 0$. Conversely, let $\text{Null}(\mathbf{A}) = 0$ and consider $\mathbf{x}, \mathbf{z} \in \mathcal{V}$ such that $\mathbf{y} = \mathbf{A}\mathbf{x} = \mathbf{A}\mathbf{z}$. Then $\mathbf{A}(\mathbf{x} - \mathbf{z}) = \mathbf{0}$. But, since $\text{Null}(\mathbf{A}) = 0$, $\mathbf{x} - \mathbf{z} = \mathbf{0}$ and $\mathbf{x} = \mathbf{z}$. Thus to every $\mathbf{y} \in \mathcal{R}(\mathbf{A})$ there corresponds a unique $\mathbf{x} \in \mathcal{V}$; and it is certainly true by the definition of a transformation that to every $\mathbf{x} \in \mathcal{V}$ there corresponds a unique $\mathbf{y} \in \mathcal{R}(\mathbf{A})$.

(2.11) If $\mathbf{A} \in \mathcal{L}(\mathcal{V}, \mathcal{W})$ has $\text{Rank}(\mathbf{A}) = \text{Dim}\,\mathcal{W}$, then it is a mapping onto $\mathcal{W}$.

For, if $\text{Rank}(\mathbf{A}) = \text{Dim}\,\mathcal{W}$, then $\mathcal{R}(\mathbf{A}) = \mathcal{W}$; and there is no element in $\mathcal{W}$ which does not correspond to some element in $\mathcal{V}$.

(2.12) If $\mathbf{A} \in \mathcal{L}(\mathcal{V}, \mathcal{W})$ has $\text{Null}(\mathbf{A}) = 0$ and $\text{Rank}(\mathbf{A}) = \text{Dim}\,\mathcal{W}$, then $\mathbf{A}$ is an isomorphism,

for in this case there exists no element in $\mathcal{W}$ which does not correspond to a unique element in $\mathcal{V}$, and conversely.

We are now in a position to state an important theorem which explains our ability to construct an isomorphic relationship between the abstract n-dimensional vector space $\mathcal{V}$ and the n-dimensional co-ordinate space $\mathcal{F}^n$. We can state quite simply that

(2.13) There exists an isomorphic relationship between two spaces $\mathcal{V}$ and $\mathcal{W}$ if and only if $\text{Dim}\,\mathcal{V} = \text{Dim}\,\mathcal{W}$.

Proof. Consider a transformation $\mathbf{A} \in \mathcal{L}(\mathcal{V}, \mathcal{W})$ with $\text{Null}(\mathbf{A}) = 0$. Then $\text{Rank}(\mathbf{A}) = \text{Dim}\,\mathcal{V}$. But if $\text{Dim}\,\mathcal{V} = \text{Dim}\,\mathcal{W}$, then $\text{Rank}(\mathbf{A}) = \text{Dim}\,\mathcal{W}$ and $\mathbf{A}$ is an isomorphism by (2.12). Conversely, if $\mathbf{A} \in \mathscr{L}(\mathscr{V}, \mathscr{W})$ is an isomorphism, then Null($\mathbf{A}$) = 0 and Rank($\mathbf{A}$) = Dim $\mathscr{W}$. Substituting these in the expression in (2.9) gives Dim $\mathscr{V}$ = Dim $\mathscr{W}$.

It is important to understand that the range space of a matrix transformation $\mathbf{A} \in \mathscr{L}(\mathscr{F}^n, \mathscr{F}^m)$ is precisely the linear manifold generated by the column vectors comprised in $\mathbf{A}$. For consider the $m \times n$ matrix $\mathbf{A} = [a_{ij}]$ written in columns as $[\mathbf{a}_{.1}, \ldots, \mathbf{a}_{.n}]$ with $\mathbf{a}_{.j} \in \mathscr{F}^m$ as well as an arbitrary vector $\mathbf{x} \in \mathscr{F}^n$ such that $\mathbf{x}' = [x_1, \ldots, x_n]$. Then $\mathbf{y} = \mathbf{A}\mathbf{x} = \mathbf{a}_{.1}x_1 + \ldots + \mathbf{a}_{.n}x_n$, and we can see that the set $\mathscr{R}(\mathbf{A}) = \{\mathbf{A}\mathbf{x}; \mathbf{x} \in \mathscr{F}^n\}$ is the set of all possible linear combinations of the vectors $\{\mathbf{a}_{.1}, \ldots, \mathbf{a}_{.n}\}$ which can also be written as $\mathscr{M}(\mathbf{A})$. Clearly, there is a redundancy of notation in having both $\mathscr{M}(\mathbf{A})$ and $\mathscr{R}(\mathbf{A})$; but we shall continue to use both on the grounds that they invoke different conceptualizations.

It follows immediately from what we understand about the range space of a matrix transformation that

(2.14) If $\mathbf{A} \in \mathscr{L}(\mathscr{F}^n, \mathscr{F}^m)$ is an $m \times n$ matrix with Null($\mathbf{A}$) = 0, then Rank($\mathbf{A}$) = Dim $\mathscr{R}(\mathbf{A}) = n$, and the columns of $\mathbf{A}$ constitute n linearly independent vectors. $\mathbf{A}$ is then said to have full column rank.

As a further definition;

(2.15) If $\mathbf{A} \in \mathscr{L}(\mathscr{F}^n, \mathscr{F}^m)$ is an $m \times n$ matrix with Rank($\mathbf{A}$) = Dim $\mathscr{F}^m$, so that $\mathbf{A}$ is a mapping onto $\mathscr{F}^m$, we say that $\mathbf{A}$ has full row rank.

Combining properties in (2.14) and (2.15), we have that

(2.16) If $\mathbf{A} \in \mathscr{L}(\mathscr{F}^n, \mathscr{F}^n)$ is an $n \times n$ matrix with Null($\mathbf{A}$) = 0 and Rank($\mathbf{A}$) = n, so that $\mathbf{A}$ is an isomorphism, then it is said to be non-singular.

THE ALGEBRA OF TRANSFORMATIONS

We have denoted linear transformations between the vector spaces $\mathscr{V}$ and $\mathscr{W}$ as elements of a set $\mathscr{L}(\mathscr{V}, \mathscr{W})$ of similar transformations but we have not, so far, examined the nature of this set, and we have not defined any operations with respect to its elements. We shall now proceed to do so.

(2.17) Let $\mathbf{A}, \mathbf{B} \in \mathscr{L}(\mathscr{V}, \mathscr{W})$ be any two transformations from $\mathscr{V}$ to $\mathscr{W}$. Then their sum, denoted $(\mathbf{A} + \mathbf{B})$, is a transformation from $\mathscr{V}$ to $\mathscr{W}$ such that, for any $\mathbf{x} \in \mathscr{V}$, $(\mathbf{A} + \mathbf{B})\mathbf{x} = \mathbf{A}\mathbf{x} + \mathbf{B}\mathbf{x}$.

We also postulate in respect of the set of transformations that

(2.18) There exists a zero transformation $\mathbf{0} \in \mathcal{L}(\mathcal{V}, \mathcal{W})$ such that $(\mathbf{A}+\mathbf{0})\mathbf{x}=\mathbf{Ax}$ for every $\mathbf{A} \in \mathcal{L}(\mathcal{V}, \mathcal{W})$; and there exists a $(-\mathbf{A}) \in \mathcal{L}(\mathcal{V}, \mathcal{W})$ such that $\mathbf{A}+(-\mathbf{A})=\mathbf{0}$.

We also define the scalar multiplication of transformations.

(2.19) If $\mathbf{A} \in \mathcal{L}(\mathcal{V}, \mathcal{W})$ and $\lambda \in \mathcal{F}$, then the scalar multiplication of $\mathbf{A}$ by λ, yielding $\lambda\mathbf{A} \in \mathcal{L}(\mathcal{V}, \mathcal{W})$, is such that, for any $\mathbf{x} \in \mathcal{V}$, $\lambda\mathbf{Ax}=\lambda(\mathbf{Ax})$.

In defining the addition and scalar multiplication of transformations, we have relied entirely upon the definition of these operations in $\mathcal{W}$. Thus the addition and scalar multiplication of transformations have all the properties that such operations have in vector spaces. This fact, allied with the postulates in (2.18), makes it very easy to prove that

(2.20) The set of all linear transformations from $\mathcal{V}$ to $\mathcal{W}$, denoted $\mathcal{L}(\mathcal{V}, \mathcal{W})$, constitutes a vector space.

The algebra of linear transformations is, of course, much more extensive than the algebra of vector spaces; and in fact (2.20) is of little interest until we attempt to represent matrices by co-ordinate vectors in Chapter 4. Returning to the addition of transformations, we have

(2.21) $\text{Rank}(\mathbf{A}+\mathbf{B}) \leqslant \text{Rank}(\mathbf{A})+\text{Rank}(\mathbf{B})$, and $\text{Rank}(\mathbf{A}+\mathbf{B})=\text{Rank}(\mathbf{A})+\text{Rank}(\mathbf{B})$ if and only if $\mathcal{R}(\mathbf{A}) \cap \mathcal{R}(\mathbf{B})=\mathbf{0}$.

Proof. We can write the set $\{(\mathbf{A}+\mathbf{B})\mathbf{x}; \mathbf{x} \in \mathcal{V}\}=(\mathbf{A}+\mathbf{B})\mathcal{V}$ as $\{\mathbf{Ax}+\mathbf{Bx}; \mathbf{x} \in \mathcal{V}\}=\mathbf{A}\mathcal{V}+\mathbf{B}\mathcal{V}$. Thus, in view of (1.19), we have $\text{Dim}(\mathbf{A}+\mathbf{B})\mathcal{V}=\text{Dim}(\mathbf{A}\mathcal{V}+\mathbf{B}\mathcal{V})=\text{Dim}\,\mathcal{R}(\mathbf{A})+\text{Dim}\,\mathcal{R}(\mathbf{B})-\text{Dim}(\mathcal{R}(\mathbf{A}) \cap \mathcal{R}(\mathbf{B}))$, from which the results follow.

The composition of linear transformations extends the algebra beyond that of a vector space.

(2.22) Let $\mathcal{U}$, $\mathcal{V}$, and $\mathcal{W}$ be vector spaces defined over the same field $\mathcal{F}$, and consider the transformations $\mathbf{B} \in \mathcal{L}(\mathcal{U}, \mathcal{V})$, $\mathbf{A} \in \mathcal{L}(\mathcal{V}, \mathcal{W})$. Then the composition of $\mathbf{A}$ and $\mathbf{B}$, denoted $\mathbf{AB} \in \mathcal{L}(\mathcal{U}, \mathcal{W})$, is a transformation from $\mathcal{U}$ to $\mathcal{W}$ such that, for any $\mathbf{x} \in \mathcal{U}$, $\mathbf{ABx}=\mathbf{A}(\mathbf{Bx})$.

(2.23) If $\mathbf{A} \in \mathcal{L}(\mathcal{V}, \mathcal{W})$ and $\mathbf{B} \in \mathcal{L}(\mathcal{U}, \mathcal{V})$ are two transformations for which the composition $\mathbf{AB} \in \mathcal{L}(\mathcal{U}, \mathcal{W})$ is defined, then $\text{Rank}(\mathbf{AB}) \leqslant \min\{\text{Rank}(\mathbf{A}), \text{Rank}(\mathbf{B})\}$.

Proof. Consider **AB** as the restriction of **A** to $\mathscr{R}(\mathbf{B})\subset\mathscr{V}$ to see that $\mathscr{R}(\mathbf{AB})=\mathbf{A}\mathscr{R}(\mathbf{B})$. Writing this restriction of **A** as $\mathbf{A}_{\mathscr{R}(\mathbf{B})}$, we have $\text{Rank}(\mathbf{AB})=\text{Rank}(\mathbf{A}_{\mathscr{R}(\mathbf{B})})=\text{Dim}\,\mathscr{R}(\mathbf{B})-\text{Null}(\mathbf{A}_{\mathscr{R}(\mathbf{B})})\leq\text{Dim}\,\mathscr{R}(\mathbf{B})=\text{Rank}(\mathbf{B})$. Also, $\text{Rank}(\mathbf{AB})=\text{Dim}\,\mathbf{A}\mathscr{R}(\mathbf{B})\leq\text{Dim}\,\mathbf{A}\mathscr{V}=\text{Rank}(\mathbf{A})$, since $\mathscr{R}(\mathbf{B})\subset\mathscr{V}$.

It is also apparent from the proof that

(2.24) If $\text{Null}(\mathbf{A})=0$, then $\text{Rank}(\mathbf{AB})=\text{Rank}(\mathbf{B})$,

and that

(2.25) If $\text{Rank}(\mathbf{B})=\text{Dim}\,\mathscr{V}$, so that **B** is a mapping onto $\mathscr{V}$, then $\text{Rank}(\mathbf{AB})=\text{Rank}(\mathbf{A})$.

In the case of (2.24) there is no loss of dimension in the mapping of $\mathscr{R}(\mathbf{B})$ into $\mathscr{W}$ by the one-to-one transformation **A**. In the case of (2.25) we have $\mathscr{R}(\mathbf{B})=\mathscr{V}$ so that **AB**, defined as the restriction of **A** to $\mathscr{R}(\mathbf{B})$, is equivalent to $\mathbf{A}\in\mathscr{L}(\mathscr{V},\mathscr{W})$.

We shall now begin to consider specific types of transformations.

PROJECTORS AND INVERSES

Projectors

Let us begin by defining the identity transformation.

(2.26) The identity transformation $\mathbf{I}\in\mathscr{L}(\mathscr{V},\mathscr{V})$ is such that $\mathbf{Ix}=\mathbf{x}$ for all $\mathbf{x}\in\mathscr{V}$.

A projector is a linear transformation on $\mathscr{V}=\mathscr{U}\oplus\mathscr{W}$ which acts as a zero transformation for all $\mathbf{w}\in\mathscr{W}$ and as an identity transformation for all $\mathbf{u}\in\mathscr{U}$. More precisely;

(2.27) Let $\mathbf{P}\in\mathscr{L}(\mathscr{V},\mathscr{V})$ be a transformation on $\mathscr{V}=\mathscr{U}\oplus\mathscr{W}$. Then **P** is a projector if, for every $\mathbf{x}=(\mathbf{u}+\mathbf{w})\in\mathscr{V}$, we have $\mathbf{Px}=\mathbf{P}(\mathbf{u}+\mathbf{w})=\mathbf{u}$ where $\mathbf{u}\in\mathscr{U}$ and $\mathbf{w}\in\mathscr{W}$.

Thus, if **P** is a projector, there is some decomposition $\mathscr{V}=\mathscr{U}\oplus\mathscr{W}$ such that $\mathbf{Pu}=\mathbf{u}$ for all $\mathbf{u}\in\mathscr{U}$ and $\mathbf{Pw}=\mathbf{0}$ for all $\mathbf{w}\in\mathscr{W}$; and it is clear that we may write $\mathscr{U}=\mathscr{R}(\mathbf{P})$ and $\mathscr{W}=\mathscr{N}(\mathbf{P})$. **P** is therefore called the projection of $\mathscr{V}$ on $\mathscr{U}$ along $\mathscr{W}$. This terminology alludes to a geometrical interpretation in a three-dimensional space $\mathscr{V}$ whereby $\mathbf{x}\in\mathscr{V}$ is first resolved into a component **u** in the plane $\mathscr{U}$ and a component **w** in the line $\mathscr{W}$ (not in $\mathscr{U}$), following which the component **w** is eliminated.

(2.28) **P** is a projector if and only if it is idempotent such that $\mathbf{P}^2=\mathbf{P}$.

Proof. If $\mathbf{P}$ is idempotent and if $\mathbf{u}=\mathbf{Px}$ for any $\mathbf{x}\in\mathscr{V}$, then $\mathbf{Pu}=\mathbf{PPx}=\mathbf{Px}=\mathbf{u}$, so that $\mathbf{Pu}=\mathbf{u}$ for all $\mathbf{u}\in\mathscr{U}=\mathscr{R}(\mathbf{P})$. Likewise, if $\mathbf{w}=(\mathbf{I}-\mathbf{P})\mathbf{x}$, then $\mathbf{Pw}=\mathbf{P}(\mathbf{I}-\mathbf{P})\mathbf{x}=(\mathbf{P}-\mathbf{P}^2)\mathbf{x}=\mathbf{0}$, so that $\mathbf{Pw}=\mathbf{0}$ for all $\mathbf{w}\in\mathscr{W}=\mathscr{R}(\mathbf{I}-\mathbf{P})$. Clearly we have $\mathscr{U}\cap\mathscr{W}=\mathbf{0}$. We also have $\mathscr{V}=\mathscr{U}+\mathscr{W}$ since any $\mathbf{x}\in\mathscr{V}$ can be written as $\mathbf{Px}+(\mathbf{I}-\mathbf{P})\mathbf{x}=\mathbf{u}+\mathbf{w}$ with $\mathbf{u}\in\mathscr{U}$ and $\mathbf{w}\in\mathscr{W}$ and, furthermore, $\mathbf{u}+\mathbf{w}\in\mathscr{V}$ for all $\mathbf{u}$ and $\mathbf{w}$. Therefore $\mathscr{V}=\mathscr{U}\oplus\mathscr{W}$ is a direct sum. Thus we see that, if it is idempotent, $\mathbf{P}$ satisfies the defining conditions of a projector. Conversely, if $\mathbf{P}$ is a projector, then $\mathbf{Px}=\mathbf{u}$ and $\mathbf{PPx}=\mathbf{Pu}=\mathbf{u}$, so that $\mathbf{Px}=\mathbf{PPx}$, and $\mathbf{P}$ is idempotent.

Another useful characterization of a projector is as follows:

(2.29) Let $\mathbf{P}\in\mathscr{L}(\mathscr{V},\mathscr{V})$ and $\mathbf{X}\in\mathscr{L}(\mathscr{U},\mathscr{V})$ be transformations. Then $\mathbf{P}$ is a projector on $\mathscr{R}(\mathbf{X})$ if and only if $\mathbf{PX}=\mathbf{X}$ and $\mathscr{R}(\mathbf{P})=\mathscr{R}(\mathbf{X})$.

Proof. Let $\mathbf{y}\in\mathscr{V}$ be any vector. Then, with $\mathscr{R}(\mathbf{P})=\mathscr{R}(\mathbf{X})$, we have $\mathbf{Py}=\mathbf{Xk}$ for some $\mathbf{k}$, whence $\mathbf{PX}=\mathbf{X}$ implies $\mathbf{PPy}=\mathbf{PXk}=\mathbf{Xk}=\mathbf{Py}$ so that $\mathbf{P}$ is an idempotent transformation and is, therefore, a projector on $\mathscr{R}(\mathbf{X})$. Conversely, if $\mathbf{P}$ is a projector on $\mathscr{R}(\mathbf{X})$, we must have $\mathscr{R}(\mathbf{P})=\mathscr{R}(\mathbf{X})$ and $\mathbf{PX}=\mathbf{X}$.

(2.30) If $\mathbf{P}\in\mathscr{L}(\mathscr{V},\mathscr{V})$ is a projector of $\mathscr{V}$ on $\mathscr{U}$ along $\mathscr{W}$, then $(\mathbf{I}-\mathbf{P})$ is the projector of $\mathscr{V}$ on $\mathscr{W}$ along $\mathscr{U}$.

For, clearly, $(\mathbf{I}-\mathbf{P})$ is idempotent if $\mathbf{P}$ is, since then $(\mathbf{I}-\mathbf{P})^2=(\mathbf{I}-2\mathbf{P}+\mathbf{P}^2)=(\mathbf{I}-\mathbf{P})$. Furthermore, we have $(\mathbf{I}-\mathbf{P})\mathbf{u}=\mathbf{0}$ for all $\mathbf{u}\in\mathscr{R}(\mathbf{P})=\mathscr{U}$ and $(\mathbf{I}-\mathbf{P})\mathbf{w}=\mathbf{w}$ for all $\mathbf{w}\in\mathscr{N}(\mathbf{P})=\mathscr{W}$, so that $\mathscr{N}(\mathbf{I}-\mathbf{P})=\mathscr{U}$ and $\mathscr{R}(\mathbf{I}-\mathbf{P})=\mathscr{W}$.

(2.31) Let $\mathbf{P}_1$ be a projector on $\mathscr{R}_1$ along $\mathscr{N}_1$ and let $\mathbf{P}_2$ be a projector on $\mathscr{R}_2$ along $\mathscr{N}_2$. If $\mathbf{P}_1\mathbf{P}_2=\mathbf{P}_2\mathbf{P}_1$, then $\mathbf{P}=\mathbf{P}_1\mathbf{P}_2$ is a projector on $\mathscr{R}=\mathscr{R}_1\cap\mathscr{R}_2$ along $\mathscr{N}=\mathscr{N}_1+\mathscr{N}_2$.

Proof. If $\mathbf{P}_1\mathbf{P}_2=\mathbf{P}_2\mathbf{P}_1$, then $\mathbf{P}^2=\mathbf{P}_1(\mathbf{P}_2\mathbf{P}_1)\mathbf{P}_2=\mathbf{P}_1(\mathbf{P}_1\mathbf{P}_2)\mathbf{P}_2=\mathbf{P}_1\mathbf{P}_2=\mathbf{P}$, so that $\mathbf{P}$ is idempotent, and hence it is a projector. Now if $\mathbf{x}\in(\mathscr{R}_1\cap\mathscr{R}_2)$, then $\mathbf{P}_1\mathbf{P}_2\mathbf{x}=\mathbf{P}_1\mathbf{x}=\mathbf{x}$, which implies $(\mathscr{R}_1\cap\mathscr{R}_2)\subset\mathscr{R}(\mathbf{P}_1\mathbf{P}_2)=\mathscr{R}$. Also, if $\mathbf{x}\in(\mathscr{N}_1+\mathscr{N}_2)$, then $\mathbf{P}_1\mathbf{P}_2\mathbf{x}=\mathbf{0}$, which implies that $(\mathscr{N}_1+\mathscr{N}_2)\subset\mathscr{N}(\mathbf{P}_1\mathbf{P}_2)=\mathscr{N}$. But, clearly, we also have $\mathscr{R}\subset(\mathscr{R}_1\cap\mathscr{R}_2)$ and $\mathscr{N}\subset(\mathscr{N}_1+\mathscr{N}_2)$; so $\mathscr{R}=(\mathscr{R}_1\cap\mathscr{R}_2)$ and $\mathscr{N}=(\mathscr{N}_1+\mathscr{N}_2)$.

It is easily understood that

(2.32) If $\mathbf{P}_1$ and $\mathbf{P}_2$ are projectors, then the conditions $\mathbf{P}_1\mathbf{P}_2=\mathbf{P}_2$ and $\mathbf{P}_2\mathbf{P}_1=\mathbf{P}_2$ are respectively equivalent to $\mathscr{R}(\mathbf{P}_2)\subset\mathscr{R}(\mathbf{P}_1)$ and $\mathscr{N}(\mathbf{P}_1)\subset\mathscr{N}(\mathbf{P}_2)$.

Combining the conditions of (2.32) we get

(2.33) If $\mathbf{P}_1$ and $\mathbf{P}_2$ are projectors, then $\mathbf{P}_1\mathbf{P}_2=\mathbf{P}_2\mathbf{P}_1=\mathbf{P}_2$ if and only if $\mathscr{R}(\mathbf{P}_2)\subset\mathscr{R}(\mathbf{P}_1)$ and $\mathscr{N}(\mathbf{P}_1)\subset\mathscr{N}(\mathbf{P}_2)$.

This result enables us to prove that

(2.34) If $\mathbf{P}_1$ is a projector on $\mathcal{R}_1$ along $\mathcal{N}_1$ and if $\mathbf{P}_2$ is a projector on $\mathcal{R}_2$ along $\mathcal{N}_2$, then $\mathbf{P}=\mathbf{P}_1-\mathbf{P}_2$ is a projector if and only if $\mathbf{P}_1\mathbf{P}_2=\mathbf{P}_2\mathbf{P}_1=\mathbf{P}_2$; in which case we can write $\mathbf{P}=\mathbf{P}_1-\mathbf{P}_2=\mathbf{P}_1(\mathbf{I}-\mathbf{P}_2)$. Furthermore, $\mathbf{P}$ is then a projector on $\mathcal{R}=\mathcal{R}_1\cap\mathcal{N}_2$ along $\mathcal{N}=\mathcal{N}_1+\mathcal{R}_2$.

Proof. If $\mathbf{P}_1\mathbf{P}_2=\mathbf{P}_2\mathbf{P}_1=\mathbf{P}_2$ then $\mathbf{P}^2=(\mathbf{P}_1-\mathbf{P}_2)^2=\mathbf{P}_1^2-\mathbf{P}_1\mathbf{P}_2-\mathbf{P}_2\mathbf{P}_1+\mathbf{P}_2^2=\mathbf{P}_1-\mathbf{P}_2$, so that $\mathbf{P}$ is idempotent and hence a projector. Conversely, if $\mathbf{P}$ is a projector, then $\mathbf{P}=\mathbf{P}^2$ implies $\mathbf{P}_1\mathbf{P}_2+\mathbf{P}_2\mathbf{P}_1=2\mathbf{P}_2$; that is, $\mathbf{P}_1\mathbf{P}_2\mathbf{x}+\mathbf{P}_2\mathbf{P}_1\mathbf{x}=2\mathbf{P}_2\mathbf{x}$ for all $\mathbf{x}\in\mathcal{V}$. Since we have $\mathbf{P}_1\mathbf{P}_2\mathbf{x}$, $\mathbf{P}_2\mathbf{P}_1\mathbf{x}\in(\mathcal{R}_1\cap\mathcal{R}_2)$ and $2\mathbf{P}_2\mathbf{x}\in\mathcal{R}_2$, this equality necessitates $\mathcal{R}_2\subset(\mathcal{R}_1\cap\mathcal{R}_2)$, which means $\mathcal{R}_2\subset\mathcal{R}_1$. Also, since $\mathcal{N}(\mathbf{P}_1\mathbf{P}_2)=\mathcal{N}(\mathbf{P}_2\mathbf{P}_1)=\mathcal{N}_1+\mathcal{N}_2$, we must have $\mathcal{N}_1+\mathcal{N}_2=\mathcal{N}_2$ or, equivalently, $\mathcal{N}_1\subset\mathcal{N}_2$ to ensure that we do not get a zero vector on the left at the same time as a non-zero vector on the right. According to (2.33) the conditions $\mathcal{R}_2\subset\mathcal{R}_1$, $\mathcal{N}_1\subset\mathcal{N}_2$ imply $\mathbf{P}_1\mathbf{P}_2=\mathbf{P}_2\mathbf{P}_1=\mathbf{P}_2$, so that the necessity of the latter condition is proved. It is then obvious that $\mathbf{P}_1-\mathbf{P}_2=\mathbf{P}_1(\mathbf{I}-\mathbf{P}_2)$. The other results follow immediately from (2.31) in view of the fact that $\mathcal{R}(\mathbf{I}-\mathbf{P}_2)=\mathcal{N}_2$.

Inverses

(2.35) Let $\mathbf{A}\in\mathcal{L}(\mathcal{V},\mathcal{W})$ and $\mathbf{B}\in\mathcal{L}(\mathcal{W},\mathcal{V})$ be linear transformations from $\mathcal{V}$ to $\mathcal{W}$ and from $\mathcal{W}$ to $\mathcal{V}$ respectively. We say that $\mathbf{B}=\mathbf{A}^L$ is a left inverse if

$$\mathbf{A}^L\mathbf{A}=\mathbf{I}\in\mathcal{L}(\mathcal{V},\mathcal{V}).$$

We say that $\mathbf{B}=\mathbf{A}^R$ is a right inverse if

$$\mathbf{A}\mathbf{A}^R=\mathbf{I}\in\mathcal{L}(\mathcal{W},\mathcal{W}).$$

If $\mathbf{B}$ is both a left inverse and a right inverse of $\mathbf{A}$, it is said to be a regular inverse of $\mathbf{A}$, denoted $\mathbf{B}=\mathbf{A}^{-1}$, and we have

$$\mathbf{A}^{-1}\mathbf{A}=\mathbf{I},\ \mathbf{A}\mathbf{A}^{-1}=\mathbf{I}.$$

We should notice that, if $\mathbf{A}^{-1}$ is a regular inverse of $\mathbf{A}$, then $\mathbf{A}$ is a regular inverse of $\mathbf{A}^{-1}$. Therefore we can say that the conditions for a regular inverse are reflexive. By contrast, the condition for a left inverse and the condition for a right inverse, taken separately, are not reflexive.

(2.36) The necessary and sufficient condition for the existence of a left inverse $\mathbf{A}^L$, such that $\mathbf{A}^L\mathbf{A}=\mathbf{I}$, is $\text{Null}(\mathbf{A})=0$.

Proof. If $\mathbf{A}^L$ exists, then, by (2.23), $\text{Rank}(\mathbf{A}^L\mathbf{A})=\text{Rank}(\mathbf{I})=\text{Dim}\,\mathcal{V}\leqslant\min\{\text{Rank}(\mathbf{A}),\text{Rank}(\mathbf{A}^L)\}$, whence $\text{Rank}(\mathbf{A})\geqslant\text{Dim}\,\mathcal{V}$. But, since $\mathcal{V}$ is the domain of $\mathbf{A}$, we must also have $\text{Rank}(\mathbf{A})\leqslant\text{Dim}\,\mathcal{V}$, so that $\text{Rank}(\mathbf{A})=\text{Dim}\,\mathcal{V}$ and, by (2.9), $\text{Null}(\mathbf{A})=0$. Conversely, the condition $\text{Null}(\mathbf{A})=0$ is sufficient for the existence of $\mathbf{A}^L$. For then $\mathbf{A}$ establishes a linear isomorphism between $\mathscr{V}$ and $\mathscr{R}(\mathbf{A}) \subset \mathscr{W}$, and therefore there must exist a transformation $\mathbf{A}^L$ from $\mathscr{W}$ to $\mathscr{V}$ whose restriction to $\mathscr{R}(\mathbf{A})$ finds the unique $\mathbf{x} \in \mathscr{V}$ corresponding to each $\mathbf{y} \in \mathscr{R}(\mathbf{A})$ as $\mathbf{x} = \mathbf{A}^L\mathbf{y} = \mathbf{A}^L\mathbf{A}\mathbf{x}$.

The argument here is readily extended to show that

(2.37) $$\text{Rank}(\mathbf{A}^L) = \text{Rank}(\mathbf{A}) = \text{Dim}\,\mathscr{V},$$

for $\mathbf{A}^L$ must be a mapping onto $\mathscr{V}$.

(2.38) The necessary and sufficient condition for the existence of a right inverse $\mathbf{A}^R$ such that $\mathbf{A}\mathbf{A}^R = \mathbf{I}$, where $\mathbf{A} \in \mathscr{L}(\mathscr{V}, \mathscr{W})$, is that $\text{Rank}(\mathbf{A}) = \text{Dim}\,\mathscr{W}$.

Proof. We may write $\mathbf{A}\mathbf{A}^R = \mathbf{I}$ as $\mathbf{B}^L\mathbf{B} = \mathbf{I}$ with $\mathbf{A} = \mathbf{B}^L$, $\mathbf{A}^R = \mathbf{B}$. The necessity of the condition $\text{Rank}(\mathbf{A}) = \text{Dim}\,\mathscr{W}$, which means that $\mathbf{A} = \mathbf{B}^L$ is a mapping onto $\mathscr{W}$, follows from (2.37) when the appropriate substitutions are made. For then we get $\text{Rank}(\mathbf{B}^L) = \text{Rank}(\mathbf{B}) = \text{Dim}\,\mathscr{W}$, which, using $\mathbf{B}^L = \mathbf{A}$ and $\mathbf{B} = \mathbf{A}^R$, gives $\text{Rank}(\mathbf{A}) = \text{Rank}(\mathbf{A}^R) = \text{Dim}\,\mathscr{W}$. The sufficiency of the condition can be established by an argument which is the image of that used in (2.36). That is to say, we argue for the existence of a $\mathbf{B} = \mathbf{A}^R$ given the existence of an 'onto', or surjective, mapping $\mathbf{B}^L = \mathbf{A}$.

Clearly, we can also state that

(2.39) $$\text{Null}(\mathbf{A}^R) = 0, \quad \text{and} \quad \text{Rank}(\mathbf{A}^R) = \text{Rank}(\mathbf{A}),$$

for this is entailed in the condition $\text{Rank}(\mathbf{A}) = \text{Rank}(\mathbf{A}^R) = \text{Dim}\,\mathscr{W}$ when $\mathscr{W}$ is the domain of $\mathbf{A}^R$.

It is clear that a species of duality exists for $\mathbf{A}^L$ and $\mathbf{A}^R$, so that propositions concerning one can be translated into the equivalent propositions for the other.

(2.40) $\mathbf{A} \in \mathscr{L}(\mathscr{V}, \mathscr{W})$ has a regular inverse $\mathbf{A}^{-1}$ such that $\mathbf{A}\mathbf{A}^{-1} = \mathbf{I}$, $\mathbf{A}^{-1}\mathbf{A} = \mathbf{I}$ if and only if $\mathbf{A}$ is an isomorphism between $\mathscr{V}$ and $\mathscr{W}$.

The regular inverse is both a left inverse and a right inverse. Thus, by (2.36), $\text{Null}(\mathbf{A}) = 0$ and, by (2.38), $\text{Rank}(\mathbf{A}) = \text{Dim}\,\mathscr{W}$, and so, by (2.12), $\mathbf{A}$ is, equivalently, an isomorphism or a non-singular transformation.

(2.41) If it exists, the regular inverse of a transformation is unique.

For, if $\mathbf{B}$ and $\mathbf{C}$ are both (regular) inverses of $\mathbf{A}$, then $\mathbf{B} = \mathbf{B}\mathbf{I} = \mathbf{B}(\mathbf{A}\mathbf{C}) = (\mathbf{B}\mathbf{A})\mathbf{C} = \mathbf{I}\mathbf{C} = \mathbf{C}$.

(2.42) If $\mathbf{AB}$, $\mathbf{A}$ and $\mathbf{B}$ are all non-singular, then $(\mathbf{AB})^{-1} = \mathbf{B}^{-1}\mathbf{A}^{-1}$.

For $\mathbf{AB}(\mathbf{AB})^{-1} = \mathbf{I} = \mathbf{A}\mathbf{A}^{-1} = \mathbf{A}(\mathbf{B}\mathbf{B}^{-1})\mathbf{A}^{-1} = \mathbf{AB}(\mathbf{B}^{-1}\mathbf{A}^{-1})$.

So far, we have defined inverses of one-to-one transformations (left inverses), of surjective transformations (right inverses), and of isomorphic transformations (regular inverses). It is possible to define, with varying degrees of specificity, classes of inverses which exist for all types of transformations.

(2.43) Consider $\mathbf{A} \in \mathcal{L}(\mathcal{V}, \mathcal{W})$ and $\mathbf{B} \in \mathcal{L}(\mathcal{W}, \mathcal{V})$. We say that $\mathbf{B}$ is a generalized inverse, or g-inverse, of $\mathbf{A}$, denoted $\mathbf{B} = \mathbf{A}^-$, if

$$\mathbf{A}\mathbf{A}^-\mathbf{A} = \mathbf{A}.$$

We say that $\mathbf{B}$ is a conjugate g-inverse of $\mathbf{A}$, denoted $\mathbf{B} = \mathbf{A}^\sim$, if

$$\mathbf{A}^\sim\mathbf{A}\mathbf{A}^\sim = \mathbf{A}^\sim.$$

If $\mathbf{B}$ is both a g-inverse and a conjugate g-inverse of $\mathbf{A}$, it is said to be a reflexive g-inverse, denoted $\mathbf{B} = \mathbf{A}^\simeq$, and we have

$$\mathbf{A}\mathbf{A}^\simeq\mathbf{A} = \mathbf{A}, \qquad \mathbf{A}^\simeq\mathbf{A}\mathbf{A}^\simeq = \mathbf{A}^\simeq.$$

We should notice that these conditions of (2.43) subsume the previously defined inverses; for $\mathbf{A}^L$, $\mathbf{A}^R$ and $\mathbf{A}^{-1}$ are all $\mathbf{A}^\simeq$, as can be seen by writing them in place of $\mathbf{A}^\simeq$ in its defining conditions. It is also helpful, in some respects, to consider $\mathbf{A}^-$, $\mathbf{A}^\sim$, and $\mathbf{A}^\simeq$ as generalizations of $\mathbf{A}^L$, $\mathbf{A}^R$, and $\mathbf{A}^{-1}$ respectively; although, of course, every inverse which we shall consider is a generalization of $\mathbf{A}^{-1}$ if it is not $\mathbf{A}^{-1}$ itself. For example, let us regard $\mathbf{A}^-$ as an extension of $\mathbf{A}^L$ to cases where $\text{Null}(\mathbf{A}) \neq 0$. In such cases it is not possible to recover a unique $\mathbf{x} \in \mathcal{V}$ from the value of the transform $\mathbf{y} = \mathbf{A}\mathbf{x}$, since there is no $\mathbf{A}^L$ such that $\mathbf{A}^L\mathbf{y} = \mathbf{A}^L\mathbf{A}\mathbf{x} = \mathbf{x}$. However, when $\text{Null}(\mathbf{A}) \neq 0$, we can at least find a $\mathbf{z} = \mathbf{A}^-\mathbf{y} = \mathbf{A}^-\mathbf{A}\mathbf{x}$, whose value is determined by the specific choice of $\mathbf{A}^-$, such that $\mathbf{A}\mathbf{z} = \mathbf{A}\mathbf{A}^-\mathbf{A}\mathbf{x} = \mathbf{A}\mathbf{x}$.

It is easy to construct an argument establishing the existence of a g-inverse in all cases. We shall therefore proceed to examine the properties of $\mathbf{A}^-$.

The following properties of $\mathbf{A}^-$ are easily deduced from (2.23)

(2.44)
1. $\text{Rank}(\mathbf{A}^-) \geqslant \text{Rank}(\mathbf{A})$.
2. $\text{Rank}(\mathbf{A}\mathbf{A}^-) = \text{Rank}(\mathbf{A}) = \text{Rank}(\mathbf{A}^-\mathbf{A})$.
3. $\text{Null}(\mathbf{A}\mathbf{A}^-) = \text{Null}(\mathbf{A}) = \text{Null}(\mathbf{A}^-\mathbf{A})$.

From the definition of $\mathbf{A}^-$ we readily deduce that

(2.45) $\mathbf{A}\mathbf{A}^-$ and $\mathbf{A}^-\mathbf{A}$ are idempotent transformations.

For with $\mathbf{A}\mathbf{A}^-\mathbf{A} = \mathbf{A}$ we have, if we postmultiply by $\mathbf{A}^-$, that $(\mathbf{A}\mathbf{A}^-)(\mathbf{A}\mathbf{A}^-) = \mathbf{A}\mathbf{A}^-$ and, if we premultiply by $\mathbf{A}^-$, that $(\mathbf{A}^-\mathbf{A})(\mathbf{A}^-\mathbf{A}) = \mathbf{A}^-\mathbf{A}$. It also follows from (2.28) that $\mathbf{A}\mathbf{A}^-$ and $\mathbf{A}^-\mathbf{A}$ are projectors.

The following are useful characterizations of the g-inverse:

(2.46) 1. If $\text{Rank}(\mathbf{BA}) = \text{Rank}(\mathbf{B})$, then $\mathbf{A}(\mathbf{BA})^-$ is $\mathbf{B}^-$.
2. If $\text{Rank}(\mathbf{BA}) = \text{Rank}(\mathbf{A})$, then $(\mathbf{BA})^-\mathbf{B}$ is $\mathbf{A}^-$.

Proof. 1. By (2.45), $\mathbf{BA}(\mathbf{BA})^-$ is a projector on $\mathcal{R}(\mathbf{BA}) \subset \mathcal{R}(\mathbf{B})$. But, if $\text{Rank}(\mathbf{BA}) = \text{Rank}(\mathbf{B})$, then $\mathcal{R}(\mathbf{BA}) = \mathcal{R}(\mathbf{B})$ and $\mathbf{BA}(\mathbf{BA})^-$ is also a projector on $\mathcal{R}(\mathbf{B})$. Therefore $\mathbf{BA}(\mathbf{BA})^-\mathbf{B} = \mathbf{B}$ and $\mathbf{A}(\mathbf{BA})^-$ is $\mathbf{B}^-$.

2. By definition, $\mathbf{BA}(\mathbf{BA})^-\mathbf{BA} = \mathbf{BA}$. But, if $\text{Rank}(\mathbf{BA}) = \text{Rank}(\mathbf{A})$, the restriction of $\mathbf{B}$ to $\mathcal{R}(\mathbf{A})$ becomes a one-to-one transformation, so that $\mathbf{A}(\mathbf{BA})^-\mathbf{BA} = \mathbf{A}$ and $(\mathbf{BA})^-\mathbf{B}$ is $\mathbf{A}^-$.

As a corollary of (2.46)2, we have that

(2.47) If $\text{Rank}(\mathbf{BA}) = \text{Rank}(\mathbf{A})$, then $\mathbf{A}(\mathbf{BA})^-\mathbf{B}$ is a projector on $\mathcal{R}(\mathbf{A})$.

Using (2.44) and (2.45) we can prove that

(2.48) If $\text{Null}(\mathbf{A}) = 0$, then $\mathbf{A}^-\mathbf{A} = \mathbf{I}$ and $\mathbf{A}^-$ is $\mathbf{A}^L$.

Proof. We already know that $\mathbf{A}^-\mathbf{A} \in \mathcal{L}(\mathcal{V}, \mathcal{V})$ is a projection of $\mathcal{V}$ into $\mathcal{V}$. If $\text{Null}(\mathbf{A}) = 0$, then $\text{Rank}(\mathbf{A}^-\mathbf{A}) = \text{Rank}(\mathbf{A}) = \text{Dim}\,\mathcal{V}$ and therefore $\mathcal{R}(\mathbf{A}^-\mathbf{A}) = \mathcal{V}$, which means that $\mathbf{A}^-\mathbf{A}$ is the projector of $\mathcal{V}$ on $\mathcal{V}$ such that $\mathbf{A}^-\mathbf{Ax} = \mathbf{x}$ for all $\mathbf{x} \in \mathcal{V}$. Thus $\mathbf{A}^-\mathbf{A} = \mathbf{I}$ and $\mathbf{A}^-$ is $\mathbf{A}^L$.

By a very similar deduction we can show that

(2.49) If $\mathbf{A} \in \mathcal{L}(\mathcal{V}, \mathcal{W})$ has $\text{Rank}(\mathbf{A}) = \text{Dim}\,\mathcal{W}$, then $\mathbf{AA}^- = \mathbf{I}$ and $\mathbf{A}^- = \mathbf{A}^R$.

It follows immediately, that

(2.50) If $\mathbf{A} \in \mathcal{L}(\mathcal{V}, \mathcal{W})$ has $\text{Null}(\mathbf{A}) = 0$ and $\text{Rank}(\mathbf{A}) = \text{Dim}\,\mathcal{W}$, then $\mathbf{A}^-$ is $\mathbf{A}^{-1}$, which is unique.

We shall not state the properties of the conjugate g-inverse $\mathbf{A}^{\sim}$, for we need only note that they are analogous to those of $\mathbf{A}^-$ by virtue of a duality that exists between these two. Nevertheless, in order to draw together the g-inverse and the conjugate g-inverse and to provide a basis for the subsequent definition of a Moore–Penrose inverse, we shall establish that

(2.51) The reflexive g-inverse of a transformation $\mathbf{A} \in \mathcal{L}(\mathcal{V}, \mathcal{W})$, defined as $\mathbf{A}^{\simeq} \in \mathcal{L}(\mathcal{W}, \mathcal{V})$ such that $\mathbf{AA}^{\simeq}\mathbf{A} = \mathbf{A}$ and $\mathbf{A}^{\simeq}\mathbf{AA}^{\simeq} = \mathbf{A}^{\simeq}$, exists for all $\mathbf{A}$.

Proof. To demonstrate the existence of the reflexive g-inverse $\mathbf{A}^{\simeq}$, consider the decomposition $\mathbf{A} = \mathbf{BC}$ where $\mathbf{C} \in \mathcal{L}(\mathcal{V}, \mathcal{Q})$ has $\text{Rank}(\mathbf{C}) = \text{Dim}\,\mathcal{Q}$, and $\mathbf{B} \in \mathcal{L}(\mathcal{Q}, \mathcal{W})$ has $\text{Null}(\mathbf{B}) = 0$. Then $\mathbf{C}^R$ and $\mathbf{B}^L$ exist, and we may specify

$\mathbf{A}^{\simeq}=\mathbf{C}^R\mathbf{B}^L$. We can then see that $\mathbf{A}\mathbf{A}^{\simeq}\mathbf{A}=\mathbf{B}\mathbf{C}(\mathbf{C}^R\mathbf{B}^L)\mathbf{B}\mathbf{C}=\mathbf{B}\mathbf{C}=\mathbf{A}$ and that $\mathbf{A}^{\simeq}\mathbf{A}\mathbf{A}^{\simeq}=\mathbf{C}^R\mathbf{B}^L(\mathbf{B}\mathbf{C})\mathbf{C}^R\mathbf{B}^L=\mathbf{C}^R\mathbf{B}^L=\mathbf{A}^{\simeq}$ which contains that $\mathbf{A}^{\simeq}=\mathbf{C}^R\mathbf{B}^L$ does indeed satisfy the conditions of a reflexive g-inverse.

(2.52) $\mathbf{A}^-$ is $\mathbf{A}^{\simeq}$ if and only if $\text{Rank}(\mathbf{A}^-)=\text{Rank}(\mathbf{A})$. Thus, for any reflexive g-inverse $\mathbf{A}^{\simeq}$, we must have $\text{Rank}(\mathbf{A}^{\simeq})=\text{Rank}(\mathbf{A})$.

Proof. Let $\mathbf{A}^-$ be $\mathbf{A}^{\simeq}$. Then by (2.44) the condition $\mathbf{A}\mathbf{A}^{\simeq}\mathbf{A}=\mathbf{A}$ implies $\text{Rank}(\mathbf{A}^{\simeq})\geqslant\text{Rank}(\mathbf{A})$. Likewise, the condition $\mathbf{A}^{\simeq}\mathbf{A}\mathbf{A}^{\simeq}=\mathbf{A}^{\simeq}$ implies $\text{Rank}(\mathbf{A})\geqslant\text{Rank}(\mathbf{A}^{\simeq})$. Together these give $\text{Rank}(\mathbf{A}^{\simeq})=\text{Rank}(\mathbf{A})$. Conversely, let $\text{Rank}(\mathbf{A}^-)=\text{Rank}(\mathbf{A})$. Then from (2.44) we get $\text{Rank}(\mathbf{A}^-\mathbf{A})=\text{Rank}(\mathbf{A})=\text{Rank}(\mathbf{A}^-)$. But $\mathbf{A}^-\mathbf{A}$ is an idempotent transformation and a projector onto $\mathcal{R}(\mathbf{A}^-\mathbf{A})\subset\mathcal{R}(\mathbf{A}^-)$, so that this implies $\mathcal{R}(\mathbf{A}^-\mathbf{A})=\mathcal{R}(\mathbf{A}^-)$, from which it follows that $\mathbf{A}^-\mathbf{A}\mathbf{A}^-=\mathbf{A}^-$, and $\mathbf{A}^-$ is $\mathbf{A}^{\simeq}$.

EQUATIONS

Consider the system $\mathbf{y}=\mathbf{A}\mathbf{x}$ where $\mathbf{A}\in\mathcal{L}(\mathcal{V},\mathcal{W})$ represents a linear transformation, $\mathbf{x}\in\mathcal{V}$ is an element subject to the transformation and $\mathbf{y}\in\mathcal{W}$ is its transform. If $\mathbf{y}\neq\mathbf{0}$, we call the system non-homogeneous. Otherwise, if $\mathbf{y}=\mathbf{0}$, we call it homogeneous.

The set $\{\mathbf{x};\mathbf{A}\mathbf{x}=\mathbf{0}\}$ is the solution set of the homogeneous system, and it is, of course, nothing but the null space of $\mathbf{A}$. If $\text{Null}(\mathbf{A})=0$, the solution space is of zero dimension and contains only the zero vector. We say then that $\mathbf{A}\mathbf{x}=\mathbf{0}$ has only a trivial solution. If $\text{Null}(\mathbf{A})=1$, the solution space is one-dimensional and it is conventional to say that the solution of $\mathbf{A}\mathbf{x}=\mathbf{0}$ is unique up to a scalar factor.

(2.53) The general solution of the homogeneous system $\mathbf{A}\mathbf{x}=\mathbf{0}$ is $\mathbf{x}=(\mathbf{I}-\mathbf{A}^-\mathbf{A})\mathbf{z}$, where $\mathbf{z}$ is arbitrary.

Proof. We must prove that $\mathcal{R}(\mathbf{I}-\mathbf{A}^-\mathbf{A})=\mathcal{N}(\mathbf{A})$. For a start, we certainly have $\mathcal{R}(\mathbf{I}-\mathbf{A}^-\mathbf{A})\subset\mathcal{N}(\mathbf{A})$, since, according to the definition of $\mathbf{A}^-$, $\mathbf{A}(\mathbf{I}-\mathbf{A}^-\mathbf{A})=\mathbf{0}$. We also have from (2.44) and (2.45) that $\mathbf{A}^-\mathbf{A}$ is a projector with $\text{Rank}(\mathbf{A}^-\mathbf{A})=\text{Rank}(\mathbf{A})$ and $\text{Null}(\mathbf{A}^-\mathbf{A})=\text{Null}(\mathbf{A})$. It follows that the projector $(\mathbf{I}-\mathbf{A}^-\mathbf{A})$ has $\text{Rank}(\mathbf{I}-\mathbf{A}^-\mathbf{A})=\text{Null}(\mathbf{A})$—and $\text{Null}(\mathbf{I}-\mathbf{A}^-\mathbf{A})=\text{Rank}(\mathbf{A})$—so that $\mathcal{R}(\mathbf{I}-\mathbf{A}^-\mathbf{A})=\mathcal{N}(\mathbf{A})$.

Now consider the non-homogeneous system $\mathbf{A}\mathbf{x}=\mathbf{y}$. The solution set $\{\mathbf{x};\mathbf{A}\mathbf{x}=\mathbf{y}\}$ will be empty unless $\mathbf{y}$ is in the range of $\mathbf{A}$. Whenever $\mathbf{y}\in\mathcal{R}(\mathbf{A})$, we say that the system is consistent. In fact

(2.54) The system $\mathbf{y}=\mathbf{A}\mathbf{x}$ is consistent if and only if $\mathbf{A}\mathbf{A}^-\mathbf{y}=\mathbf{y}$.

This is a straightforward consequence of the fact that $\mathbf{A}\mathbf{A}^-$ is a projector on $\mathcal{R}(\mathbf{A})$ whose restriction to that space is an identity transformation.

The solution set of $\mathbf{Ax}=\mathbf{y}$ may be characterized as the set which arises from adding any particular solution of $\mathbf{Ax}=\mathbf{y}$, say $\mathbf{a}$, to all the elements of the solution set of the associated homogeneous system $\mathbf{Az}=\mathbf{0}$. We may express this result by writing $\{\mathbf{x}; \mathbf{Ax}=\mathbf{y}\}=\mathbf{a}+\mathcal{U}$, where $\mathcal{U}=\{\mathbf{z}; \mathbf{Az}=\mathbf{0}\}$. To understand the result, consider subtracting $\mathbf{Aa}=\mathbf{y}$ from $\mathbf{Ax}=\mathbf{y}$ to give $\mathbf{A}(\mathbf{x}-\mathbf{a})=\mathbf{0}$. This shows that $\mathbf{z}=\mathbf{x}-\mathbf{a}$ satisfies the homogeneous equation. But $\mathbf{x}=\mathbf{a}+\mathbf{z}$, so the solution set or general solution of $\mathbf{Ax}=\mathbf{y}$ is the set $\{\mathbf{x}\}=\mathbf{a}+\mathcal{U}$. Also, it follows from (1.26) that, when $\mathbf{A}\in\mathcal{L}(\mathcal{V},\mathcal{W})$, the set of solutions of $\mathbf{Ax}=\mathbf{y}$ constitutes an affine subspace of $\mathcal{V}$ which is not a vector space.

(2.55) A consistent system $\mathbf{y}=\mathbf{Ax}$, $\mathbf{y}\in\mathcal{R}(\mathbf{A})$, has a unique solution $\mathbf{x}=\mathbf{A}^L\mathbf{y}$ if and only if $\text{Null}(\mathbf{A})=0$.

For if and only if $\text{Null}(\mathbf{A})=0$ does there exist a left inverse enabling us to write the solution uniquely as $\mathbf{x}=\mathbf{A}^L\mathbf{Ax}=\mathbf{A}^L\mathbf{y}$

(2.56) If $\mathbf{A}\in\mathcal{L}(\mathcal{V},\mathcal{W})$ has $\text{Null}(\mathbf{A})=0$ and $\text{Rank}(\mathbf{A})=\text{Dim}\,\mathcal{W}$, then the system $\mathbf{y}=\mathbf{Ax}$ is invariably consistent and has a unique solution $\mathbf{x}=\mathbf{A}^{-1}\mathbf{y}$.

For if $\text{Rank}(\mathbf{A})=\text{Dim}\,\mathcal{W}$, then $\mathcal{R}(\mathbf{A})=\mathcal{W}$, and $\mathbf{y}\in\mathcal{W}$ implies $\mathbf{y}\in\mathcal{R}(\mathbf{A})$ which ensures consistency. The conditions $\text{Null}(\mathbf{A})=0$, $\text{Rank}(\mathbf{A})=\text{Dim}\,\mathcal{W}$ are also necessary and sufficient for $\mathbf{A}^L$ to become $\mathbf{A}^{-1}$.

If $\text{Null}(\mathbf{A})\neq 0$, then $\mathbf{A}$ is not a one-to-one transformation and there are many $\mathbf{x}\in\mathcal{V}$ that might account for a given $\mathbf{y}\in\mathcal{R}(\mathbf{A})$. We may wish to find one such vector, for which purpose we may use any generalized inverse. To demonstrate this we shall prove that

(2.57) The necessary and sufficient condition for $\mathbf{x}=\mathbf{A}^-\mathbf{y}$ to be a solution of the consistent system $\mathbf{y}=\mathbf{Ax}$ is that $\mathbf{A}=\mathbf{AA}^-\mathbf{A}$.

Proof. If $\mathbf{A}\in\mathcal{L}(\mathcal{V},\mathcal{W})$ and $\mathbf{x}=\mathbf{A}^-\mathbf{y}$ is a solution to the consistent system $\mathbf{y}=\mathbf{Ax}$, then $\mathbf{y}=\mathbf{Ax}=\mathbf{AA}^-\mathbf{y}=\mathbf{AA}^-\mathbf{Ax}$. But, if this is true for all $\mathbf{x}\in\mathcal{V}$, we must have $\mathbf{A}=\mathbf{AA}^-\mathbf{A}$. Conversely, if $\mathbf{A}=\mathbf{AA}^-\mathbf{A}$ and $\mathbf{Ax}=\mathbf{y}$ is a consistent system, then $\mathbf{AA}^-\mathbf{Ax}=\mathbf{Ax}$ or $\mathbf{AA}^-\mathbf{y}=\mathbf{y}$. Hence $\mathbf{x}=\mathbf{A}^-\mathbf{y}$ is a solution to $\mathbf{Ax}=\mathbf{y}$.

For a particular choice of $\mathbf{A}^-$ in (2.57) we achieve a particular solution of $\mathbf{Ax}=\mathbf{y}$ in the form of $\mathbf{x}=\mathbf{A}^-\mathbf{y}$. The general solution of $\mathbf{Ax}=\mathbf{y}$ is the set which arises from adding any particular solution of $\mathbf{Ax}=\mathbf{y}$ to all solutions of $\mathbf{Ax}=\mathbf{0}$, which together constitute the general solution of $\mathbf{Ax}=\mathbf{0}$. Thus, from (2.53), we have that

(2.58) The general solution of the consistent system $\mathbf{Ax}=\mathbf{y}$ is $\mathbf{x}=\mathbf{A}^-\mathbf{y}+(\mathbf{I}-\mathbf{A}^-\mathbf{A})\mathbf{z}$ where $\mathbf{z}$ is arbitrary.

Even if the solution of $\mathbf{Ax}=\mathbf{y}$ is not unique, it may be that some function of the solution has a unique value. Thus

(2.59) If $\mathbf{K}\in\mathscr{L}(\mathscr{V},\mathscr{Q})$ and $\mathbf{A}\in\mathscr{L}(\mathscr{V},\mathscr{W})$, then $\mathbf{Kx}$ has a unique value for all solutions of $\mathbf{Ax}=\mathbf{y}$ if and only if $\mathbf{KA}^{-}\mathbf{A}=\mathbf{K}$.

This is understood by considering the form of the general solution in (2.58) and noting that the uniqueness of $\mathbf{Kx}$ is assured if and only if $\mathbf{K}(\mathbf{I}-\mathbf{A}^{-}\mathbf{A})\mathbf{z}=\mathbf{0}$ for all values of $\mathbf{z}$, which is equivalent to the condition that $\mathbf{K}=\mathbf{KA}^{-}\mathbf{A}$. By specifying $\mathbf{K}$ as the identity transformation $\mathbf{I}\in\mathscr{L}(\mathscr{V},\mathscr{V})$, we get the corollary that $\mathbf{x}=\mathbf{A}^{-}\mathbf{y}$ is a unique solution if and only if $\mathbf{I}=\mathbf{A}^{-}\mathbf{A}$; which is to say $\mathbf{A}^{-}$ is $\mathbf{A}^{L}$. This is precisely the result (2.55).

BIBLIOGRAPHY

Linear Transformations. Halmos [**49,** Chap. II], Kreider et al. [**70,** Chap. 2], Shephard [**109,** Chap. II], Shilov [**110,** Chap. 5].

Projectors. Afriat [**1**], Chipman and Rao [**19**], Rao and Mitra [**98,** Chap. 5].

Generalized Inverses. Kruskal [**72**], Pringle and Rayner [**92**], Rao [**94**], Rao and Mitra [**98**].

CHAPTER 3

Metric Spaces

Our formalization of a vector space, which we have abstracted from our ordinary understanding of three-dimensional space, has, so far, ignored those spatial relationships which are expressed in terms of distance and angle. We shall introduce such concepts in the present chapter by defining certain metric functions. However, to begin with, we must consider bilinear functionals in general.

METRIC RELATIONSHIPS

Bilinear functionals

(3.1) Let $\mathscr{V}, \mathscr{W}$ be two vector spaces defined over the same field of scalars $\mathscr{F}$. Then a bilinear functional ϕ is a scalar-valued function on $\mathscr{V}$ and $\mathscr{W}$ such that the following conditions hold for all $\mathbf{v} \in \mathscr{V}$, $\mathbf{w} \in \mathscr{W}$ and $\lambda, \mu \in \mathscr{F}$:

1. $\phi(\mathbf{v}, \mathbf{w}) \in \mathscr{F}$,
2. $\phi(\lambda \mathbf{v}_1 + \mu \mathbf{v}_2, \mathbf{w}) = \lambda\phi(\mathbf{v}_1, \mathbf{w}) + \mu\phi(\mathbf{v}_2, \mathbf{w})$,
3. $\phi(\mathbf{v}, \lambda \mathbf{w}_1 + \mu \mathbf{w}_2) = \lambda\phi(\mathbf{v}, \mathbf{w}_1) + \mu\phi(\mathbf{v}, \mathbf{w}_2)$.

We may indicate that ϕ is a member of the set of all bilinear functionals on $\mathscr{V}$ and $\mathscr{W}$ by writing $\phi \in \mathscr{L}(\mathscr{V} \times \mathscr{W}, \mathscr{F})$ where $\mathscr{V} \times \mathscr{W}$ denotes the Cartesian product of the spaces; that is to say, the set of all ordered pairs $(\mathbf{v}, \mathbf{w})$ with $\mathbf{v} \in \mathscr{V}$, $\mathbf{w} \in \mathscr{W}$.

We can readily find a matrix representation of a real-valued bilinear functional.

(3.2) Let $[\mathbf{v}_1, \ldots. \mathbf{v}_n], [\mathbf{w}_1, \ldots, \mathbf{w}_m]$ be bases of $\mathscr{V}, \mathscr{W}$ respectively, and let $\sum x_j \mathbf{v}_j = \mathbf{x} \in \mathscr{V}$ and $\sum y_i \mathbf{w}_i = \mathbf{y} \in \mathscr{W}$ be arbitrary vectors. Then, for any bilinear functional $\phi \in \mathscr{L}(\mathscr{V} \times \mathscr{W}, \mathscr{R})$, we may write $\phi(\mathbf{x}, \mathbf{y}) = \sum_i \sum_j y_i x_j q_{ij}$ where $q_{ij} = \phi(\mathbf{v}_j, \mathbf{w}_i)$ for all i, j. Thus, in matrix notation, we have

$$\phi(\mathbf{x}, \mathbf{y}) = [y_1, y_2, \ldots, y_m] \begin{bmatrix} q_{11}, q_{12}, \ldots, q_{1n} \\ q_{21}, q_{22}, \ldots, q_{2n} \\ \vdots \quad \vdots \quad \vdots \\ q_{m1}, q_{m2}, \ldots, q_{mn} \end{bmatrix} \begin{bmatrix} x_1 \\ x_2 \\ \vdots \\ x_n \end{bmatrix}$$

This follows from the defining conditions of a bilinear function whereby $\phi(\mathbf{x}, \mathbf{y}) = \phi(\sum x_j \mathbf{v}_j, \sum y_i \mathbf{w}_i) = \sum_i \sum_j y_i x_j \phi(\mathbf{v}_j, \mathbf{w}_i)$.

It is clear that any $m \times n$ matrix $\mathbf{Q} = [q_{ij}]$ with real-valued elements may be regarded as a member of the set of bilinear functions on $\mathcal{R}^n$ and $\mathcal{R}^m$, so that we may write $\mathbf{Q} \in \mathcal{L}(\mathcal{R}^n \times \mathcal{R}^m, \mathcal{R})$.

(3.3) The set of bilinear functionals $\mathcal{L}(\mathcal{V} \times \mathcal{W}, \mathcal{R})$, where Dim $\mathcal{V} = n$, Dim $\mathcal{W} = m$, constitutes a vector space of dimension mn when the operations of addition and scalar multiplication are appropriately defined.

The appropriate rules of addition and scalar multiplication may be given in terms of $\phi_1, \phi_2 \in \mathcal{L}(\mathcal{V} \times \mathcal{W}, \mathcal{R})$ and $\lambda, \mu \in \mathcal{R}$ by writing

(3.4) $$(\lambda\phi_1 + \mu\phi_2)(\mathbf{v}, \mathbf{w}) = \lambda\phi_1(\mathbf{v}, \mathbf{w}) + \mu\phi_2(\mathbf{v}, \mathbf{w}),$$

where, on the right, we use the established definitions of the two operations in respect of the field of scalars. When we recall that the set of all $m \times n$ matrices also constitutes a vector space of dimension mn, we can recognise that, in finding the matrix representation of a real-valued bilinear functional, we are exploiting a linear isomorphism existing between vector spaces of the same dimension. We can use this isomorphism to give a matrix representation of (3.4); for, if $\mathbf{y} \in \mathcal{R}^m$, $\mathbf{x} \in \mathcal{R}^n$ are vectors and $\mathbf{A}$ and $\mathbf{B}$ are $m \times n$ matrices associated with bilinear functionals on $\mathcal{R}^n \times \mathcal{R}^m$, we have

(3.5) $$\mathbf{y}'(\lambda\mathbf{A} + \mu\mathbf{B})\mathbf{x} = \lambda(\mathbf{y}'\mathbf{A}\mathbf{x}) + \mu(\mathbf{y}'\mathbf{B}\mathbf{x})$$

We shall now confine our attention to bilinear functions that are defined over a single space.

(3.6) A bilinear functional $\phi \in \mathcal{L}(\mathcal{V} \times \mathcal{V}, \mathcal{R})$ is called symmetric if $\phi(\mathbf{x}, \mathbf{y}) = \phi(\mathbf{y}, \mathbf{x})$ for every $\mathbf{x}, \mathbf{y} \in \mathcal{V}^n$. For any such symmetric bilinear functional, we call $\phi(\mathbf{x}, \mathbf{x})$ a quadratic form.

For co-ordinate vectors $\mathbf{x}, \mathbf{y} \in \mathcal{R}^n$, a symmetric bilinear functional has the form $\mathbf{y}'\mathbf{A}\mathbf{x} = \mathbf{x}'\mathbf{A}\mathbf{y}$, where the matrix $\mathbf{A} = [a_{ij}]$ has $a_{ij} = a_{ji}$ for all i, j, so that its transpose is $\mathbf{A}' = \mathbf{A}$. The quadratic form is simply $\mathbf{x}'\mathbf{A}\mathbf{x}$.

(3.7) A symmetric bilinear functional $\phi \in \mathcal{L}(\mathcal{V} \times \mathcal{V}, \mathcal{R})$ defined over a real vector space is said to be positive semidefinite if $\phi(\mathbf{x}, \mathbf{x}) \geq 0$ for all $\mathbf{x} \in \mathcal{V}$. If, additionally, $\phi(\mathbf{x}, \mathbf{x}) = 0$ implies $\mathbf{x} = \mathbf{0}$, it is said to be positive definite.

Inner products and metrics

(3.8) Any symmetric bilinear functional $\phi \in \mathcal{L}(\mathcal{V} \times \mathcal{V}, \mathcal{R})$ with a positive-definite quadratic form constitutes an inner product on the space $\mathscr{V}$. We denote the inner product of any $\mathbf{x}, \mathbf{y} \in \mathscr{V}$ by $\langle \mathbf{x}, \mathbf{y} \rangle^{\mathscr{V}}$ or simply $\langle \mathbf{x}, \mathbf{y} \rangle$; and we may observe that the following conditions are fulfilled:

1. $\langle \mathbf{x}, \mathbf{y} \rangle = \langle \mathbf{y}, \mathbf{x} \rangle$,
2. $\langle \lambda \mathbf{x} + \mu \mathbf{z}, \mathbf{y} \rangle = \lambda \langle \mathbf{x}, \mathbf{y} \rangle + \mu \langle \mathbf{z}, \mathbf{y} \rangle$,
3. $\langle \mathbf{x}, \mathbf{x} \rangle \geq 0$, and $\langle \mathbf{x}, \mathbf{x} \rangle = 0$ if and only if $\mathbf{x} = \mathbf{0}$,
4. $\langle \mathbf{0}, \mathbf{x} \rangle = 0$.

The last of these is true because $\langle \mathbf{0}, \mathbf{x} \rangle = \langle \mathbf{0} + \mathbf{0}, \mathbf{x} \rangle = \langle \mathbf{0}, \mathbf{x} \rangle + \langle \mathbf{0}, \mathbf{x} \rangle$ implies $\langle \mathbf{0}, \mathbf{x} \rangle = 0$. This argument also establishes that $\langle \mathbf{x}, \mathbf{x} \rangle = 0$ if $\mathbf{x} = \mathbf{0}$. The other conditions come from the definition of a positive-definite bilinear functional.

A real vector space with an inner product defined on it is called a Euclidean space, denoted $\mathscr{E}$. An inner product defined over a real co-ordinate space $\mathscr{R}^n$ is fully specified by the choice of a symmetric positive-definite matrix $\mathbf{Q}$ such that $\mathbf{x}'\mathbf{Q}\mathbf{x} > 0$ for all non-zero $\mathbf{x} \in \mathscr{R}^n$—for which $\mathbf{Q}$ must, clearly, be non-singular. For $\mathbf{x}, \mathbf{y} \in \mathscr{R}^n$, we shall denote the $\mathbf{Q}$-inner product by $\mathbf{x}'\mathbf{Q}\mathbf{y} = \langle \mathbf{x}, \mathbf{y} \rangle_{\mathbf{Q}}$ By specifying $\mathbf{Q} = \mathbf{I}$, we obtain $\langle \mathbf{x}, \mathbf{y} \rangle_{\mathbf{I}} = \mathbf{x}'\mathbf{y}$ which is the ordinary inner product of $\mathbf{x}, \mathbf{y} \in \mathscr{R}^n$.

(3.9) A translation-invariant metric defined on a vector space $\mathscr{V}$ is a real-valued function f mapping from $\mathscr{V} \times \mathscr{V}$ to $\mathscr{R}$ and obeying the following conditions for every $\mathbf{x}, \mathbf{y} \in \mathscr{V}$:

1. $f(\mathbf{x}, \mathbf{y}) \geq 0$; and $f(\mathbf{x}, \mathbf{y}) = 0$ if and only if $\mathbf{x} = \mathbf{y}$,
2. $f(\mathbf{x}, \mathbf{y}) = f(\mathbf{y}, \mathbf{x})$,
3. $f(\mathbf{x}, \mathbf{y}) + f(\mathbf{y}, \mathbf{z}) \geq f(\mathbf{x}, \mathbf{z})$,
4. $f(\mathbf{x} + \mathbf{z}, \mathbf{y} + \mathbf{z}) = f(\mathbf{x}, \mathbf{y})$.

In Euclidean space the function $\|\mathbf{x} - \mathbf{y}\| = \sqrt{\langle \mathbf{x} - \mathbf{y}, \mathbf{x} - \mathbf{y} \rangle}$ satisfies all the conditions of (3.9). We may therefore interpret this as the distance between the vectors $\mathbf{x}, \mathbf{y}$, or, equivalently, as the length of the vector $\mathbf{x} - \mathbf{y}$. The function $\|\mathbf{x}\| = \sqrt{\langle \mathbf{x}, \mathbf{x} \rangle}$ is called the length or norm of $\mathbf{x}$.

When the first condition of (3.9) is replaced by

(3.10) $f(\mathbf{x}, \mathbf{y}) \geq 0$; and $f(\mathbf{x}, \mathbf{y}) = 0$ if $\mathbf{x} = \mathbf{y}$.

it is no longer implied that the distance between two vectors is zero only when they coincide. A function which obeys (3.10) and the conditions (2–4) of (3.9) is called a degenerate metric, and the associated norm is called a semi-norm.

Metrics defined on $\mathscr{R}^n$ are specified in terms of positive-definite matrices. Thus the function $\|\mathbf{x} - \mathbf{y}\|_{\mathbf{Q}} = \sqrt{(\mathbf{x} - \mathbf{y})'\mathbf{Q}(\mathbf{x} - \mathbf{y})}$, for $\mathbf{x}, \mathbf{y} \in \mathscr{R}^n$, defines the distance between $\mathbf{x}$ and $\mathbf{y}$ in the $\mathbf{Q}$ metric, or, in other words, the $\mathbf{Q}$-distance of $\mathbf{x}$ and $\mathbf{y}$.

Before we introduce the further metric concept of the angle between two vectors, we will state, in convenient form, a well-known theorem.

(3.11) If $\mathbf{x}, \mathbf{y} \in \mathscr{E}$ are two vectors in a real inner-product space, then $\langle \mathbf{x}, \mathbf{y} \rangle^2 \leq \langle \mathbf{x}, \mathbf{x} \rangle \langle \mathbf{y}, \mathbf{y} \rangle$; and $\langle \mathbf{x}, \mathbf{y} \rangle^2 = \langle \mathbf{x}, \mathbf{x} \rangle \langle \mathbf{y}, \mathbf{y} \rangle$ for $\mathbf{x}, \mathbf{y} \neq \mathbf{0}$ if and only if $\lambda \mathbf{x} = \mathbf{y}$ for some scalar λ. This is the Cauchy–Schwarz inequality.

Proof. If $\langle \mathbf{x}, \mathbf{x} \rangle = 0$, then, by (3.8), $\mathbf{x} = \mathbf{0}$ and $\langle \mathbf{x}, \mathbf{y} \rangle = 0$, and both sides of the equality are zero which satisfies the theorem. Likewise, the theorem is satisfied if $\langle \mathbf{y}, \mathbf{y} \rangle = 0$. Therefore let $\langle \mathbf{x}, \mathbf{x} \rangle, \langle \mathbf{y}, \mathbf{y} \rangle > 0$, and consider $\langle \lambda \mathbf{x} - \mathbf{y}, \lambda \mathbf{x} - \mathbf{y} \rangle \geq 0$. Expanding this gives $\lambda^2 \langle \mathbf{x}, \mathbf{x} \rangle - 2\lambda \langle \mathbf{x}, \mathbf{y} \rangle + \langle \mathbf{y}, \mathbf{y} \rangle \geq 0$. On putting $\lambda = \langle \mathbf{x}, \mathbf{y} \rangle / \langle \mathbf{x}, \mathbf{x} \rangle$, we get $\langle \mathbf{x}, \mathbf{y} \rangle^2 / \langle \mathbf{x}, \mathbf{x} \rangle - 2\langle \mathbf{x}, \mathbf{y} \rangle^2 / \langle \mathbf{x}, \mathbf{x} \rangle + \langle \mathbf{y}, \mathbf{y} \rangle \geq 0$ which, after rearrangement, gives the desired inequality. For the second part, if $\langle \mathbf{x}, \mathbf{y} \rangle^2 = \langle \mathbf{x}, \mathbf{x} \rangle \langle \mathbf{y}, \mathbf{y} \rangle$, then it is evident from its expansion that $\langle \lambda \mathbf{x} - \mathbf{y}, \lambda \mathbf{x} - \mathbf{y} \rangle = 0$ when $\lambda = \langle \mathbf{x}, \mathbf{y} \rangle / \langle \mathbf{x}, \mathbf{x} \rangle$. This implies $\lambda \mathbf{x} - \mathbf{y} = \mathbf{0}$ and $\lambda \mathbf{x} = \mathbf{y}$. Conversely, if $\lambda \mathbf{x} = \mathbf{y}$, then $\lambda = \langle \mathbf{x}, \mathbf{y} \rangle / \langle \mathbf{x}, \mathbf{x} \rangle$ and $\langle \lambda \mathbf{x} - \mathbf{y}, \lambda \mathbf{x} - \mathbf{y} \rangle = 0$ are both identities. By expanding the latter and substituting for λ we may show that the Cauchy–Schwarz inequality becomes an equality.

(3.12) The angle θ between the non-zero vectors $\mathbf{x}, \mathbf{y} \in \mathscr{E}$ is defined by

$$\cos \theta = \frac{\langle \mathbf{x}, \mathbf{y} \rangle}{\sqrt{\langle \mathbf{x}, \mathbf{x} \rangle} \sqrt{\langle \mathbf{y}, \mathbf{y} \rangle}}.$$

The Cauchy–Schwarz inequality constrains this quantity to lie in the closed interval $[-1, 1]$, which conforms with our understanding of cosines. The interpretation of $\sqrt{\langle \mathbf{x}, \mathbf{x} \rangle} = \|\mathbf{x}\|$ as a length gives a further meaning to our definition of an angle; for, since $\|\mathbf{x}\|^2 + \|\mathbf{y}\|^2 - \|\mathbf{x} - \mathbf{y}\|^2 = 2\langle \mathbf{x}, \mathbf{y} \rangle$, we have

$$\cos \theta = \frac{\|\mathbf{x}\|^2 + \|\mathbf{y}\|^2 - \|\mathbf{x} - \mathbf{y}\|^2}{2\|\mathbf{x}\| \, \|\mathbf{y}\|}$$

or $\|\mathbf{x}\|^2 + \|\mathbf{y}\|^2 - \|\mathbf{x} - \mathbf{y}\|^2 = 2\|\mathbf{x}\| \, \|\mathbf{y}\| \cos \theta$ which may be construed as the law of cosines in respect of a triangle with sides of length $\|\mathbf{x}\|$, $\|\mathbf{y}\|$ and $\|\mathbf{x} - \mathbf{y}\|$.

Orthogonality

(3.13) Two vectors $\mathbf{x}, \mathbf{y}$ are said to be orthogonal if $\langle \mathbf{x}, \mathbf{y} \rangle = 0$. We may then write $\mathbf{x} \perp \mathbf{y}$.

A common synonym for orthogonal is 'perpendicular'. From (3.12) we see that if $\langle \mathbf{x}, \mathbf{y} \rangle = 0$, then $\cos \theta = 0$; whence θ, which is the angle between the vectors $\mathbf{x}$ and $\mathbf{y}$, has the value of a right angle. We should also note that

(3.14) The condition of orthogonality $\langle \mathbf{x}, \mathbf{y} \rangle = 0$ is equivalent to $\langle \mathbf{x} - \mathbf{y}, \mathbf{x} - \mathbf{y} \rangle = \langle \mathbf{x}, \mathbf{x} \rangle + \langle \mathbf{y}, \mathbf{y} \rangle$, or $\|\mathbf{x} - \mathbf{y}\|^2 = \|\mathbf{x}\|^2 + \|\mathbf{y}\|^2$. Thus two vectors are defined to be orthogonal if and only if the Pythagorean relationship holds.

It is clear that the relationship of orthogonality is specific to some chosen inner product. In terms of $\mathcal{R}^n$ we say that two vectors $\mathbf{x}, \mathbf{y}$ are $\mathbf{Q}$-orthogonal if $\langle \mathbf{x}, \mathbf{y}\rangle_{\mathbf{Q}} = \mathbf{x}'\mathbf{Q}\mathbf{y} = 0$. We may also write $\mathbf{x} \perp_{\mathbf{Q}} \mathbf{y}$ to denote the $\mathbf{Q}$-orthogonality of $\mathbf{x}$ and $\mathbf{y}$. If two vectors $\mathbf{x}, \mathbf{y} \in \mathcal{R}^n$ are such that $\langle \mathbf{x}, \mathbf{y}\rangle_{\mathbf{I}} = \mathbf{x}'\mathbf{y} = 0$, they are said to be orthogonal in the unitary metric, or simply orthogonal.

(3.15) A vector $\mathbf{y} \in \mathscr{E}$ is said to be orthogonal to a subspace $\mathscr{X} \subset \mathscr{E}$ if $\langle \mathbf{x}, \mathbf{y}\rangle = 0$ for all $\mathbf{x} \in \mathscr{X}$. We may then write $\mathbf{y} \perp \mathscr{X}$.

(3.16) Two subspaces $\mathscr{X}, \mathscr{Y} \subset \mathscr{E}$ are said to be orthogonal if, for every $\mathbf{x} \in \mathscr{X}$ and every $\mathbf{y} \in \mathscr{Y}$, we have $\langle \mathbf{x}, \mathbf{y}\rangle = 0$. We may then write $\mathscr{X} \perp \mathscr{Y}$.

(3.17) The orthogonal complement $\mathcal{O}(\mathscr{X})$ of a subspace $\mathscr{X} \subset \mathscr{E}$ is the set of all vectors $\mathbf{y} \in \mathscr{E}$ such that $\langle \mathbf{x}, \mathbf{y}\rangle = 0$ for all $\mathbf{x} \in \mathscr{X}$. We shall denote the orthogonal complement of $\mathcal{R}(\mathbf{A})$, the range space of a linear transformation, by $\mathcal{O}(\mathbf{A})$.

It is readily established that

(3.18)
1. $\mathcal{O}(\mathscr{X})$ is a subspace of $\mathscr{E}$,
2. The orthogonal complement of $\mathcal{O}(\mathscr{X})$ is $\mathscr{X}$ itself,
3. If $\mathscr{X}, \mathscr{Y} \subset \mathscr{E}$ are two subspaces, then

$$\mathcal{O}(\mathscr{X}+\mathscr{Y}) = \mathcal{O}(\mathscr{X}) \cap \mathcal{O}(\mathscr{Y}) \quad \text{and} \quad \mathcal{O}(\mathscr{X} \cap \mathscr{Y}) = \mathcal{O}(\mathscr{X}) + \mathcal{O}(\mathscr{Y}).$$

The second of these follows from the symmetrical nature of the relationship of orthogonality whereby $\mathcal{O}(\mathscr{X})$ and $\mathscr{X}$ are orthogonal complements of each other.

(3.19) A set of vectors $\{\mathbf{c}_1, \ldots, \mathbf{c}_r\}$ in $\mathscr{E}$ are orthonormal if $\langle \mathbf{c}_i, \mathbf{c}_j\rangle = 1$ when $i = j$ and $\langle \mathbf{c}_i, \mathbf{c}_j\rangle = 0$ when $i \neq j$. We may write $\langle \mathbf{c}_i, \mathbf{c}_j\rangle = \delta_{ij}$ where δ_{ij} is the Kronecker delta.

(3.20) The vectors of an orthonormal set are linearly independent.

Proof. Consider a set of scalars $\{\lambda_i; i = 1, \ldots, r\}$ such that $\sum \lambda_i \mathbf{c}_i = \mathbf{0}$. Then, since $\langle \mathbf{c}_i, \mathbf{c}_j\rangle = \delta_{ij}$, we have $0 = \langle \mathbf{0}, \mathbf{c}_j\rangle = \langle \sum \lambda_i \mathbf{c}_i, \mathbf{c}_j\rangle = \sum \lambda_i \langle \mathbf{c}_i, \mathbf{c}_j\rangle = \lambda_j$. Thus $\sum \lambda_i \mathbf{c}_i = \mathbf{0}$ implies $\lambda_i = 0$ for all i, and the vectors are therefore linearly independent.

We are particularly interested in sets of orthonormal vectors which also constitute bases.

Example. The natural basis in $\mathcal{R}^n$ is the set of n-tuple vectors $[\mathbf{e}_1, \ldots, \mathbf{e}_n] = \mathbf{I}$ comprised by the identity matrix. These constitute an orthonormal basis in respect of the ordinary inner product. The co-ordinates of a vector $\mathbf{y} \in \mathcal{R}^n$ relative to the natural basis are precisely the n elements of $\mathbf{y}$. Thus $\mathbf{y}$ is *specified by*

$$\begin{bmatrix} y_1 \\ y_2 \\ \cdot \\ \cdot \\ \cdot \\ y_n \end{bmatrix} = \begin{bmatrix} y_1 \\ 0 \\ \cdot \\ \cdot \\ \cdot \\ 0 \end{bmatrix} + \begin{bmatrix} 0 \\ y_2 \\ \cdot \\ \cdot \\ \cdot \\ 0 \end{bmatrix} + \dots + \begin{bmatrix} 0 \\ 0 \\ \cdot \\ \cdot \\ \cdot \\ y_n \end{bmatrix}$$

$$= y_1\mathbf{e}_1 + y_2\mathbf{e}_2 + \dots + y_n\mathbf{e}_n$$

$$= (\mathbf{y}'\mathbf{e}_1)\mathbf{e}_1 + (\mathbf{y}'\mathbf{e}_2)\mathbf{e}_2 + \dots + (\mathbf{y}'\mathbf{e}_n)\mathbf{e}_n.$$

A feature of this example is generalized in the following proposition:

(3.21) If $[\mathbf{c}_1, \dots, \mathbf{c}_n]$ is an orthonormal basis of $\mathscr{E}$ and $\mathbf{y}$ is any vector in $\mathscr{E}$, then $\mathbf{y} = \sum \langle \mathbf{y}, \mathbf{c}_i \rangle \mathbf{c}_i$; and $\langle \mathbf{y}, \mathbf{c}_j \rangle$ is the jth co-ordinate of $\mathbf{y}$ relative to this basis.

Proof. Let $[y_1, \dots, y_n]$ be the co-ordinates of $\mathbf{y}$. Then $\mathbf{y} = \sum y_i \mathbf{c}_i$, and $\langle \mathbf{y}, \mathbf{c}_j \rangle = \langle \sum y_i \mathbf{c}_i, \mathbf{c}_j \rangle = \sum y_i \langle \mathbf{c}_i, \mathbf{c}_j \rangle = \sum y_i \delta_{ij} = y_j$.

(3.22) If $\{\mathbf{c}_1, \dots, \mathbf{c}_r\}$ is an orthonormal set in $\mathscr{E}$ and $\mathbf{y} \in \mathscr{E}$ is any vector, then $\mathbf{q} = \mathbf{y} - \sum \langle \mathbf{y}, \mathbf{c}_i \rangle \mathbf{c}_i$ is orthogonal to each $\mathbf{c}_j$; $j = 1, \dots, r$.

Proof. For each $j = 1, \dots, r$, we have $\langle \mathbf{q}, \mathbf{c}_j \rangle = \langle \mathbf{y} - \sum \langle \mathbf{y}, \mathbf{c}_i \rangle \mathbf{c}_i, \mathbf{c}_j \rangle = \langle \mathbf{y}, \mathbf{c}_j \rangle - \sum \langle \mathbf{y}, \mathbf{c}_i \rangle \delta_{ij} = \langle \mathbf{y}, \mathbf{c}_j \rangle - \langle \mathbf{y}, \mathbf{c}_j \rangle = 0$.

It follows, as a simple corollary of this result, that

(3.23) If $\{\mathbf{c}_1, \dots, \mathbf{c}_r\}$ is an orthonormal set in $\mathscr{E}$, then any vector $\mathbf{y} \in \mathscr{E}$ may be written as $\mathbf{y} = \mathbf{p} + \mathbf{q}$ with $\langle \mathbf{p}, \mathbf{q} \rangle = \langle \sum \langle \mathbf{y}, \mathbf{c}_i \rangle \mathbf{c}_i, \mathbf{y} - \sum \langle \mathbf{y}, \mathbf{c}_i \rangle \mathbf{c}_i \rangle = 0$.

Thus, unless $\mathbf{y}$ is linearly dependent on the orthonormal set, such that $\mathbf{p} = \sum \langle \mathbf{y}, \mathbf{c}_i \rangle \mathbf{c}_i = \mathbf{y}$, or orthogonal to the set, such that $\mathbf{p} = \mathbf{0}$, we succeed in decomposing $\mathbf{y}$ into two orthogonal non-zero vectors. These results, (3.22) and (3.23), suggest a method by which we may find an orthonormal basis from an ordinary basis. For

(3.24) If $[\mathbf{x}_1, \dots, \mathbf{x}_n]$ is a basis of $\mathscr{E}$, we may find an orthonormal basis $[\mathbf{c}_1, \dots, \mathbf{c}_n]$ by the following process:

$$\mathbf{c}_1 = \mathbf{x}_1 / \|\mathbf{x}_1\|$$

$$\mathbf{c}_2 = (\mathbf{x}_2 - \langle \mathbf{x}_2, \mathbf{c}_1 \rangle \mathbf{c}_1) / \|\mathbf{x}_2 - \langle \mathbf{x}_2, \mathbf{c}_1 \rangle \mathbf{c}_1\|$$

$$\dots$$

$$\mathbf{c}_n = \left(\mathbf{x}_n - \sum_{i<n} \langle \mathbf{x}_n, \mathbf{c}_i \rangle \mathbf{c}_i\right) \Big/ \left\|\mathbf{x}_n - \sum_{i<n} \langle \mathbf{x}_n, \mathbf{c}_i \rangle \mathbf{c}_i\right\|.$$

This is the Gram–Schmidt orthogonalization procedure.

Since we can always find a basis for a vector space, this procedure provides a constructive proof of the fact that we can always find an orthonormal basis of a metric space. We use the proposition that there always exists an orthonormal basis to help prove that

(3.25) If $\mathscr{X} \subset \mathscr{E}$ is a vector subspace and $\mathscr{O}(\mathscr{X})$ is its orthogonal complement, then $\mathscr{X} \oplus \mathscr{O}(\mathscr{X}) = \mathscr{E}$.

Proof. Let $\mathbf{y} \in \mathscr{E}$ be any vector. Then, by (3.23), we may use an orthonormal basis of $\mathscr{X}$ to find $\mathbf{p} \in \mathscr{X}$, $\mathbf{q} \in \mathscr{O}(\mathscr{X})$ such that $\mathbf{y} = \mathbf{p} + \mathbf{q}$. Hence $\mathscr{E} = \mathscr{X} + \mathscr{O}(\mathscr{X})$. For this to be a direct sum, we must also have that $\mathscr{X} \cap \mathscr{O}(\mathscr{X}) = \mathbf{0}$. Thus consider $\mathbf{x} \in \mathscr{X} \cap \mathscr{O}(\mathscr{X})$. Then $\langle \mathbf{x}, \mathbf{x} \rangle = 0$, since we may assign the first term of this inner product to $\mathscr{X}$, and the second term to $\mathscr{O}(\mathscr{X})$. Hence $\mathbf{x} = \mathbf{0}$, $\mathscr{X} \cap \mathscr{O}(\mathscr{X}) = \mathbf{0}$ and $\mathscr{X} \oplus \mathscr{O}(\mathscr{X}) = \mathscr{E}$.

(3.26) Let $\mathscr{E} = \mathscr{X} \oplus \mathscr{O}(\mathscr{X})$ be the direct sum of orthogonal subspaces and let $\mathbf{y} = \mathbf{p} + \mathbf{q}$, with $\mathbf{p} \in \mathscr{X}$, $\mathbf{q} \in \mathscr{O}(\mathscr{X})$, be any vector in $\mathscr{E}$. Then the linear transformation defined by

$$\mathbf{P}\mathbf{y} = \mathbf{P}(\mathbf{p} + \mathbf{q}) = \mathbf{p}$$

is called the orthogonal projector of $\mathscr{E}$ on $\mathscr{X}$.

Example. Let $\mathbf{C} = [\mathbf{c}_1, \ldots, \mathbf{c}_r]$ *be an* $n \times r$ *matrix which constitutes an orthonormal basis of* $\mathscr{X} \subset \mathscr{R}^n$ *in respect of the ordinary inner product. Then* $\mathbf{CC}'$ *is the orthogonal projector of* $\mathscr{R}^n$ *on* $\mathscr{X}$, *and* $(\mathbf{I} - \mathbf{CC}')$ *is the orthogonal projector of* $\mathscr{R}^n$ *on* $\mathscr{O}(\mathscr{X})$. *To see this, consider* $\mathbf{y} \in \mathscr{R}^n$. *Then, in the manner of* (3.23),

$$\begin{aligned} \mathbf{y} &= \sum_{i=1}^{r} \mathbf{c}_i \mathbf{c}_i' \mathbf{y} + \left(\mathbf{y} - \sum_{i=1}^{r} \mathbf{c}_i \mathbf{c}_i' \mathbf{y} \right) \\ &= \mathbf{CC}'\mathbf{y} + (\mathbf{I} - \mathbf{CC}')\mathbf{y} \\ &= \mathbf{p} + \mathbf{q}. \end{aligned}$$

Moreover, since $\mathbf{C}'\mathbf{C} = \mathbf{I}$, *we have* $\mathbf{C}'(\mathbf{I} - \mathbf{CC}') = \mathbf{0}$, *whence* $\mathbf{p}'\mathbf{q} = \mathbf{y}'\mathbf{CC}'(\mathbf{I} - \mathbf{CC}')\mathbf{y} = \mathbf{0}$. *Thus* $\mathbf{p} \perp \mathbf{q}$, *with* $\mathbf{p} \in \mathscr{M}(\mathbf{C}) = \mathscr{X}$ *and* $\mathbf{q} \in \mathscr{N}(\mathbf{C}') = \mathscr{O}(\mathscr{X})$. *We may also note that the symmetric idempotent matrices* $\mathbf{CC}', \mathbf{I} - \mathbf{CC}'$ *are projectors by virtue of* (2.28), *and that* $\mathbf{C}'$ *is a reflexive g-inverse of* $\mathbf{C}$ *according to* (2.43).

TRANSFORMATIONS WITH METRIC PROPERTIES

Adjoint transformations

(3.27) If $\mathbf{A} \in \mathscr{L}(\mathscr{V}, \mathscr{W})$, then $\mathbf{A}^* \in \mathscr{L}(\mathscr{W}, \mathscr{V})$ is defined as the adjoint of $\mathbf{A}$ if $\langle \mathbf{x}, \mathbf{A}^*\mathbf{y} \rangle^{\mathscr{V}} = \langle \mathbf{A}\mathbf{x}, \mathbf{y} \rangle^{\mathscr{W}}$ for any $\mathbf{x} \in \mathscr{V}, \mathbf{y} \in \mathscr{W}$,

The matrix interpretation of an adjoint is readily accessible. For the simplest case,

(3.28) Let $[\mathbf{v}_1, \ldots, \mathbf{v}_n], [\mathbf{w}_1, \ldots, \mathbf{w}_m]$ be orthonormal bases of $\mathcal{V}$ and $\mathcal{W}$ in respect of certain inner products. Then, if $[a_{ij}]$ is the matrix representing $\mathbf{A}$ relative to these bases, the transposed matrix $[a_{ji}]$ represents the adjoint $\mathbf{A}^*$.

Proof. The elements of the matrix $[a_{ij}]$ are defined by $\mathbf{A}\mathbf{v}_k = \sum_i a_{ik}\mathbf{w}_i$; $k = 1, \ldots, j, \ldots, n$. Likewise, the elements of the matrix representing $\mathbf{A}^*$ are defined by $\mathbf{A}^*\mathbf{w}_l = \sum_j b_{jl}\mathbf{v}_j$; $l = 1, \ldots, i, \ldots, m$. Now

$$\langle \mathbf{A}\mathbf{v}_k, \mathbf{w}_l \rangle = \left\langle \sum_i a_{ik}\mathbf{w}_i, \mathbf{w}_l \right\rangle = \sum_i a_{ik}\delta_{il} = a_{lk}.$$

Likewise

$$\langle \mathbf{v}_k, \mathbf{A}^*\mathbf{w}_l \rangle = \left\langle \mathbf{v}_k, \sum_j b_{jl}\mathbf{v}_j \right\rangle = b_{kl}.$$

But, by the definition of the adjoint, these inner products have the same value, so that $a_{lk} = b_{kl}$. Hence, if $[a_{ij}]$ is the matrix of the original transformation, its transpose $[a_{ji}]$ is the matrix of the adjoint transformation.

Matters become more complicated when the bases of $\mathcal{V}$ and $\mathcal{W}$ are not orthonormal.

(3.29) Let $\mathbf{A}$ be an $m \times n$ matrix representing, in terms of the natural bases $\mathbf{I}_n, \mathbf{I}_m$, a transformation from $\mathcal{R}^n$ to $\mathcal{R}^m$. Let the inner products over $\mathcal{R}^n$ and $\mathcal{R}^m$ be defined respectively by $\langle \mathbf{x}_1, \mathbf{x}_2 \rangle_{\mathbf{N}} = \mathbf{x}_1'\mathbf{N}\mathbf{x}_2$ and $\langle \mathbf{y}_1, \mathbf{y}_2 \rangle_{\mathbf{Q}} = \mathbf{y}_1'\mathbf{Q}\mathbf{y}_2$. Then the $n \times m$ adjoint matrix $\mathbf{A}^*$ is defined by $\langle \mathbf{x}, \mathbf{A}^*\mathbf{y} \rangle_{\mathbf{N}} = \langle \mathbf{A}\mathbf{x}, \mathbf{y} \rangle_{\mathbf{Q}}$ or $\mathbf{x}'\mathbf{N}\mathbf{A}^*\mathbf{y} = \mathbf{x}'\mathbf{A}'\mathbf{Q}\mathbf{y}$; so that $\mathbf{A}^* = \mathbf{N}^{-1}\mathbf{A}'\mathbf{Q}$. If $\mathbf{N}$ and $\mathbf{Q}$ are, respectively, $\mathbf{I}_n$ and $\mathbf{I}_m$, then $\mathbf{A}^* = \mathbf{A}'$.

For transformations that are defined on a single space we have that

(3.30) If $\mathbf{x}, \mathbf{y} \in \mathcal{R}^m$, then the matrix $\mathbf{A}^*$ defined by $\langle \mathbf{x}, \mathbf{A}^*\mathbf{y} \rangle_{\mathbf{Q}} = \langle \mathbf{A}\mathbf{x}, \mathbf{y} \rangle_{\mathbf{Q}}$ or by $\mathbf{A}^* = \mathbf{Q}^{-1}\mathbf{A}'\mathbf{Q}$ is called the $\mathbf{Q}$-adjoint of $\mathbf{A}$. It follows that $\mathbf{Q}\mathbf{A}^* = \mathbf{A}'\mathbf{Q}$.

(3.31) Let $\mathbf{A}, \mathbf{B} \in \mathcal{L}(\mathcal{V}, \mathcal{W})$ and $\mathbf{C} \in \mathcal{L}(\mathcal{U}, \mathcal{V})$. Then

1. $(\mathbf{A}^*)^* = \mathbf{A}$,
2. $(\mathbf{A}\mathbf{C})^* = \mathbf{C}^*\mathbf{A}^*$,
3. $(\mathbf{A} + \mathbf{B})^* = \mathbf{A}^* + \mathbf{B}^*$,
4. $(\lambda\mathbf{A})^* = \lambda\mathbf{A}^*$.

These properties of the adjoint follow directly from the definition. It is also apparent that

(3.32) If $\mathbf{I}, \mathbf{0} \in \mathcal{L}(\mathcal{V}, \mathcal{V})$ are the identity and zero transformations, then

1. $\mathbf{I} = \mathbf{I}^*$,
2. $\mathbf{0} = \mathbf{0}^*$.

(3.33) If $\mathbf{A}$ is a non-singular, then $\mathbf{A}^{-1}$ exists and $(\mathbf{A}\mathbf{A}^{-1})^* = (\mathbf{A}^{-1})^*\mathbf{A}^* = \mathbf{I}$, and thus $(\mathbf{A}^{-1})^* = (\mathbf{A}^*)^{-1}$.

(3.34) If $\mathbf{A}^L$ is such that $\mathbf{A}^L\mathbf{A} = \mathbf{I}$, then $(\mathbf{A}^L\mathbf{A})^* = \mathbf{A}^*(\mathbf{A}^L)^* = \mathbf{I}$, and thus $(\mathbf{A}^L)^*$ is $(\mathbf{A}^*)^R$.

(3.35) If $\mathbf{A}^-$ is such that $\mathbf{A}\mathbf{A}^-\mathbf{A} = \mathbf{A}$, then $(\mathbf{A}\mathbf{A}^-\mathbf{A})^* = \mathbf{A}^*(\mathbf{A}^-)^*\mathbf{A}^* = \mathbf{A}^*$, and thus $(\mathbf{A}^-)^*$ is $(\mathbf{A}^*)^-$.

(3.36) Consider $\mathbf{A} \in \mathcal{L}(\mathcal{V}, \mathcal{W})$ and $\mathbf{A}^* \in \mathcal{L}(\mathcal{W}, \mathcal{V})$. Then

1. $\mathcal{N}(\mathbf{A}) = \mathcal{O}[\mathcal{R}(\mathbf{A}^*)] = \mathcal{O}(\mathbf{A}^*)$,
2. $\mathcal{R}(\mathbf{A}) = \mathcal{O}[\mathcal{N}(\mathbf{A}^*)]$.

Proof. For 1. we must show that $\mathcal{N}(\mathbf{A}) = \{\mathbf{x}; \mathbf{A}\mathbf{x} = \mathbf{0}\}$ is identical to the set $\mathcal{O}[\mathcal{R}(\mathbf{A}^*)] = \{\mathbf{x}; \langle \mathbf{x}, \mathbf{A}^*\mathbf{y}\rangle = 0, \mathbf{y} \in \mathcal{W}\}$. The latter is simply $\{\mathbf{x}; \langle \mathbf{A}\mathbf{x}, \mathbf{y}\rangle = 0, \mathbf{y} \in \mathcal{W}\}$. But $\langle \mathbf{A}\mathbf{x}, \mathbf{y}\rangle = 0$ for every $\mathbf{y} \in \mathcal{W}$ if and only if $\mathbf{A}\mathbf{x} = \mathbf{0}$. Thus $\mathcal{O}[\mathcal{R}(\mathbf{A}^*)]$ is the set of all $\mathbf{x} \in \mathcal{N}(\mathbf{A})$. To prove 2. we show that $\mathcal{O}[\mathcal{R}(\mathbf{A})] = \mathcal{N}(\mathbf{A}^*)$, whence $\mathcal{R}(\mathbf{A}) = \mathcal{O}[\mathcal{N}(\mathbf{A}^*)]$.

It is clear that, within the statements of (3.36), the positions of $\mathbf{A}$ and $\mathbf{A}^*$ are interchangeable. We use this fact in the proof of the following proposition.

(3.37) $\text{Rank}(\mathbf{A}^*) = \text{Rank}(\mathbf{A})$.

Proof. Since $\mathcal{R}(\mathbf{A}^*) = \mathcal{O}[\mathcal{N}(\mathbf{A})]$, we have $\text{Rank}(\mathbf{A}^*) = \text{Dim}\,\mathcal{V} - \text{Null}(\mathbf{A})$. We also have $\text{Rank}(\mathbf{A}) = \text{Dim}\,\mathcal{V} - \text{Null}(\mathbf{A})$ from (2.9), so that $\text{Rank}(\mathbf{A}) = \text{Rank}(\mathbf{A}^*)$.

If $\mathbf{X}^* = \mathbf{N}^{-1}\mathbf{X}'\mathbf{Q}$ is the adjoint of a matrix $\mathbf{X}$, then, according to this result, we have $\text{Rank}(\mathbf{X}) = \text{Rank}(\mathbf{N}^{-1}\mathbf{X}'\mathbf{Q}) = \text{Rank}(\mathbf{X}')$. The second equality follows since we are free to choose $\mathbf{N} = \mathbf{I}_n$, $\mathbf{Q} = \mathbf{I}_m$ in the definition of the adjoint when $\mathbf{X}$ is $m \times n$.

The result (3.37) also enables us to establish an outstanding duality between $\mathbf{A}$ and $\mathbf{A}^*$.

(3.38) $\mathbf{A}$ is a one-to-one transformation if and only if $\mathbf{A}^*$ is surjective and vice versa. Therefore, since $\mathbf{A}$ is one-to-one if and only if $\text{Null}(\mathbf{A}) = 0$, it follows that $\mathbf{A}$ is surjective if and only if $\text{Null}(\mathbf{A}^*) = 0$.

Proof. We are considering $\mathbf{A} \in \mathscr{L}(\mathscr{V}, \mathscr{W})$ and $\mathbf{A}^* \in \mathscr{L}(\mathscr{W}, \mathscr{V})$. If $\mathbf{A}$ is one-to-one, then $\text{Rank}(\mathbf{A}) = \text{Dim}\,\mathscr{V}$. If $\mathbf{A}^*$ is surjective, then $\text{Rank}(\mathbf{A}^*) = \text{Dim}\,\mathscr{V}$. But, by (3.37), $\text{Rank}(\mathbf{A}) = \text{Rank}(\mathbf{A}^*)$, so that these conditions on $\mathbf{A}$ and $\mathbf{A}^*$ are equivalent which means that $\mathbf{A}$ is one-to-one if and only if $\mathbf{A}^*$ is surjective. The positions of $\mathbf{A}$ and $\mathbf{A}^*$ in this argument are interchangeable, so it also follows that $\mathbf{A}$ is surjective if and only if $\mathbf{A}^*$ is one-to-one.

(3.39) 1. $\mathscr{R}(\mathbf{A}^*\mathbf{A}) = \mathscr{R}(\mathbf{A}^*)$.
2. $\mathscr{N}(\mathbf{A}^*\mathbf{A}) = \mathscr{N}(\mathbf{A})$.

Proof. With $\mathbf{A} \in \mathscr{L}(\mathscr{V}, \mathscr{W})$ and $\mathbf{A}^* \in \mathscr{L}(\mathscr{W}, \mathscr{V})$, we can write $\mathscr{R}(\mathbf{A}^*) = \mathbf{A}^*\mathscr{W}$. But, since $\mathscr{R}(\mathbf{A}) = \mathscr{O}[\mathscr{N}(\mathbf{A}^*)]$, we have $\mathscr{W} = \mathscr{N}(\mathbf{A}^*) \oplus \mathscr{R}(\mathbf{A})$. Hence $\mathscr{R}(\mathbf{A}^*) = \mathbf{A}^*\mathscr{N}(\mathbf{A}^*) \oplus \mathbf{A}^*\mathscr{R}(\mathbf{A}) = \mathbf{0} \oplus \mathscr{R}(\mathbf{A}^*\mathbf{A})$, which proves 1. To prove 2, we use $(\mathbf{A}^*\mathbf{A})^* = \mathbf{A}^*\mathbf{A}$ to give $\mathscr{N}(\mathbf{A}^*\mathbf{A}) = \mathscr{O}[\mathscr{R}(\mathbf{A}^*\mathbf{A})] = \mathscr{O}[\mathscr{R}(\mathbf{A}^*)] = \mathscr{N}(\mathbf{A})$.

An immediate implication of (3.39) is that $\text{Rank}(\mathbf{X}^*\mathbf{X}) = \text{Rank}(\mathbf{X}^*) = \text{Rank}(\mathbf{X})$. If $\mathbf{X}$ is a matrix with an adjoint $\mathbf{X}^* = \mathbf{N}^{-1}\mathbf{X}'\mathbf{Q}$, where $\mathbf{N}$ and $\mathbf{Q}$ are positive definite, then we have $\text{Rank}(\mathbf{N}^{-1}\mathbf{X}'\mathbf{Q}\mathbf{X}) = \text{Rank}(\mathbf{X}'\mathbf{Q}\mathbf{X}) = \text{Rank}(\mathbf{X}) = \text{Rank}(\mathbf{X}')$, where the first equality follows from (2.24) in consequence of the fact that $\text{Null}(\mathbf{N}^{-1}) = 0$.

Consideration of the adjoint leads us to define classes of transformations with specific metric properties.

(3.40) If $\mathbf{A} \in \mathscr{L}(\mathscr{V}, \mathscr{V})$ is a non-singular transformation such that $\mathbf{A}^* = \mathbf{A}^{-1}$, it is called an isometry; and it has the property that $\langle \mathbf{Ax}, \mathbf{Ay} \rangle = \langle \mathbf{x}, \mathbf{A}^*\mathbf{Ay} \rangle = \langle \mathbf{x}, \mathbf{y} \rangle$ for all $\mathbf{x}, \mathbf{y}$.

The name isometry derives from the fact that any vector which is subject to this transformation preserves its length, as is evident in the definition. It also follows, in reference to (3.12), that the angle between two vectors is unchanged by an isometric transformation. In $\mathscr{R}^n$ we represent an isometry, with respect to the ordinary inner product, by some $n \times n$ matrix $\mathbf{C}$ such that $\mathbf{x}'\mathbf{C}'\mathbf{C}\mathbf{y} = \mathbf{x}'\mathbf{y}$ for all $\mathbf{x}, \mathbf{y} \in \mathscr{R}^n$. Therefore $\mathbf{C}'\mathbf{C} = \mathbf{I}$; and $\mathbf{C}\mathbf{C}'\mathbf{C} = \mathbf{C}$, so $\mathbf{C}\mathbf{C}' = \mathbf{I}$. A matrix, such as $\mathbf{C}$, which constitutes an orthonormal basis of $\mathscr{R}^n$ is called an orthogonal matrix.

(3.41) If $\mathbf{A} \in \mathscr{L}(\mathscr{V}, \mathscr{V})$ and $\mathbf{A} = \mathbf{A}^*$, then $\langle \mathbf{x}, \mathbf{Ay} \rangle = \langle \mathbf{Ax}, \mathbf{y} \rangle$, and $\mathbf{A}$ is called a self-adjoint transformation.

An obvious example of a self-adjoint transformation is the product $\mathbf{T}^*\mathbf{T} \in \mathscr{L}(\mathscr{V}, \mathscr{V})$ where $\mathbf{T} \in \mathscr{L}(\mathscr{V}, \mathscr{W})$ is arbitrary.

A simple matrix interpretation of a self-adjoint transformation is indicated by (3.28) which states that, for a given orthonormal basis of $\mathscr{V}$, the matrix corresponding to $\mathbf{A}^*$ is the transpose of the matrix corresponding to $\mathbf{A}$. Thus, when $\mathbf{A} = \mathbf{A}^*$, the matrix and its transpose are equal, which must imply that it is symmetric.

Consider also the case of the matrix transformation $\mathbf{A} \in \mathscr{L}(\mathscr{R}^m, \mathscr{R}^m)$. Then, when the inner product is defined in terms of a positive-definite symmetric matrix $\mathbf{Q}$, $\mathbf{A}$ will be defined as self adjoint if, for any $\mathbf{x}, \mathbf{y} \in \mathscr{R}^m$, $\langle \mathbf{Ax}, \mathbf{y} \rangle_{\mathbf{Q}} = \langle \mathbf{x}, \mathbf{Ay} \rangle_{\mathbf{Q}}$. Thus

(3.42) The matrix $\mathbf{A}$ represents a self-adjoint transformation in respect of the $\mathbf{Q}$-inner product if $\mathbf{A}'\mathbf{Q} = \mathbf{QA}$, or, equivalently, $(\mathbf{QA})' = \mathbf{QA}$; in which case we say that $\mathbf{A}$ is $\mathbf{Q}$-symmetric.

(3.43) $\mathbf{A} \in \mathscr{L}(\mathscr{V}, \mathscr{V})$ is a self-adjoint transformation if and only if $\mathscr{R}(\mathbf{A}) = \mathscr{O}[\mathscr{N}(\mathbf{A})]$.

This follows directly from (3.36) when $\mathbf{A}^* = \mathbf{A}$.

Orthogonal projectors

If we combine the proposition (3.43) that the range space and null space of self-adjoint transformations are orthogonal complements with the proposition (2.28) that projectors are synonymous with idempotent transformations, we get the result that

(3.44) $\mathbf{P}$ is an orthogonal projector if and only if it is self adjoint and idempotent such that $\mathbf{P} = \mathbf{P}^* = \mathbf{P}^2$. Equivalently, $\mathbf{P}$ is an orthogonal projector if and only if $\mathbf{P}^*(\mathbf{I} - \mathbf{P}) = \mathbf{0}$.

To establish the equivalence of these conditions is straightforward. Thus $\mathbf{P}^*(\mathbf{I} - \mathbf{P}) = \mathbf{0}$ is equivalent to the expression $\mathbf{P}^* = \mathbf{P}^*\mathbf{P}$ and to the adjoint thereof which is $\mathbf{P} = \mathbf{P}^*\mathbf{P}$. Therefore $\mathbf{P} = \mathbf{P}^* = \mathbf{P}^*\mathbf{P} = \mathbf{P}^2$ is equivalent to the first condition.

When we translate (3.44) into the terms of co-ordinate spaces we have the result that

(3.45) $\mathbf{P} \in \mathscr{L}(\mathscr{R}^m, \mathscr{R}^m)$ is a $\mathbf{Q}$-orthogonal projector if and only if it is idempotent, such that $\mathbf{P} = \mathbf{P}^2$, and $\mathbf{Q}$-symmetric, such that $(\mathbf{QP})' = \mathbf{QP}$.

The conditions $\mathbf{P}^2 = \mathbf{P}$ and $\mathbf{P}'\mathbf{Q} = \mathbf{QP}$ are jointly equivalent to the condition $\mathbf{P}'\mathbf{QP} = \mathbf{QP}^2 = \mathbf{QP} = \mathbf{P}'\mathbf{Q}$ or simply $\mathbf{P}'\mathbf{Q} = \mathbf{P}'\mathbf{QP} = \mathbf{QP}$. Alternatively, we may write the condition $\mathbf{P}'\mathbf{Q} = \mathbf{QP}$ as $\mathbf{Q}^{-1}\mathbf{P}' = \mathbf{PQ}^{-1}$, whence, with $\mathbf{P}^2 = \mathbf{P}$, we get $\mathbf{PQ}^{-1}\mathbf{P}' = \mathbf{P}^2\mathbf{Q}^{-1} = \mathbf{PQ}^{-1} = \mathbf{Q}^{-1}\mathbf{P}'$ or simply $\mathbf{PQ}^{-1} = \mathbf{PQ}^{-1}\mathbf{P}' = \mathbf{Q}^{-1}\mathbf{P}'$. In summary we state that

(3.46) $\mathbf{P} \in \mathscr{L}(\mathscr{R}^m, \mathscr{R}^m)$ is a $\mathbf{Q}$-orthogonal projector if and only if $\mathbf{P}'\mathbf{Q} = \mathbf{P}'\mathbf{QP} = \mathbf{QP}$ or, equivalently, $\mathbf{PQ}^{-1} = \mathbf{PQ}^{-1}\mathbf{P}' = \mathbf{Q}^{-1}\mathbf{P}'$.

We have already constructed an orthogonal projector of $\mathscr{V}$ onto $\mathscr{X}$ from a basis of $\mathscr{X}$. We shall now find a more general form for this projector. Our problem is to find a transformation $\mathbf{P} \in \mathscr{L}(\mathscr{V}, \mathscr{V})$ such that, for every $\mathbf{y} \in \mathscr{V}$,

$\mathbf{Py}=\mathbf{p}\in\mathscr{X}$ and $\mathbf{y}-\mathbf{p}=\mathbf{q}\in\mathscr{O}(\mathscr{X})$. Let $\mathbf{X}\in\mathscr{L}(\mathscr{U},\mathscr{V})$ be any transformation with $\mathscr{R}(\mathbf{X})=\mathscr{X}$. Then $\mathbf{p}\in\mathscr{R}(\mathbf{X})$, and so $\mathbf{p}=\mathbf{Xb}$ for some $\mathbf{b}$. We can therefore give the condition $(\mathbf{y}-\mathbf{p})\in\mathscr{O}(\mathscr{X})$ in the form $(\mathbf{y}-\mathbf{Xb})\perp\mathscr{R}(\mathbf{X})$, or as $0=\langle\mathbf{y}-\mathbf{Xb},\mathbf{Xz}\rangle=\langle\mathbf{X}^*\mathbf{y}-\mathbf{X}^*\mathbf{Xb},\mathbf{z}\rangle$ for all $\mathbf{z}\in\mathscr{U}$. This implies that $\mathbf{X}^*\mathbf{y}-\mathbf{X}^*\mathbf{Xb}=\mathbf{0}$. Solving for $\mathbf{b}$ gives $\mathbf{b}=(\mathbf{X}^*\mathbf{X})^-\mathbf{X}^*\mathbf{y}$, whence $\mathbf{p}=\mathbf{Xb}=\mathbf{X}(\mathbf{X}^*\mathbf{X})^-\mathbf{X}^*\mathbf{y}$; and we conclude that

(3.47) The orthogonal projector of $\mathscr{V}$ on $\mathscr{X}$ is given by $\mathbf{P}=\mathbf{X}(\mathbf{X}^*\mathbf{X})^-\mathbf{X}^*$ where $\mathbf{X}$ is any transformation with $\mathscr{R}(\mathbf{X})=\mathscr{X}$.

The idempotency of $\mathbf{P}$, which is implicit in the fact that $\mathbf{P}$ is a projector, may be established directly from (2.47) by using the fact that $\text{Rank}(\mathbf{X}^*\mathbf{X})=\text{Rank}(\mathbf{X})$.

(3.48) The $\mathbf{Q}$-orthogonal projector of $\mathscr{R}^m$ on a p-dimensional subspace $\mathscr{X}\subset\mathscr{R}^m$ is given by $\mathbf{P}=\mathbf{X}(\mathbf{X}'\mathbf{QX})^-\mathbf{X}'\mathbf{Q}$ where $\mathbf{X}$ is any $m\times p$ matrix with $\mathscr{M}(\mathbf{X})=\mathscr{X}$.

Proof. First, we note that, if $\mathbf{N}$ is non-singular, then $\mathbf{B}^-\mathbf{N}$ is $(\mathbf{N}^{-1}\mathbf{B})^-$, for we have $\mathbf{N}^{-1}\mathbf{B}(\mathbf{B}^-\mathbf{N})\mathbf{N}^{-1}\mathbf{B}=\mathbf{N}^{-1}(\mathbf{BB}^-\mathbf{B})=\mathbf{N}^{-1}\mathbf{B}$. Taking $\mathbf{X}^*=\mathbf{N}^{-1}\mathbf{X}'\mathbf{Q}$ as the adjoint of $\mathbf{X}$, we may now write the formula of (3.47) as $\mathbf{X}(\mathbf{X}^*\mathbf{X})^-\mathbf{X}^*=\mathbf{X}(\mathbf{N}^{-1}\mathbf{X}'\mathbf{QX})^-\mathbf{N}^{-1}\mathbf{X}'\mathbf{Q}=\mathbf{X}(\mathbf{X}'\mathbf{QX})^-\mathbf{NN}^{-1}\mathbf{X}'\mathbf{Q}=\mathbf{X}(\mathbf{X}'\mathbf{QX})^-\mathbf{X}'\mathbf{Q}$. This matrix is certainly $\mathbf{Q}$-symmetric and idempotent, and therefore it conforms with the conditions of (3.45).

We shall now establish that, for a given metric or inner product, the orthogonal projector is identical to the minimum-distance projector. That is to say,

(3.49) $\mathbf{P}\in\mathscr{L}(\mathscr{V},\mathscr{V})$ is an orthogonal projector, such that $\mathbf{P}^*=\mathbf{P}=\mathbf{P}^2$, if and only if $\|\mathbf{y}-\mathbf{Py}\|\leqslant\|\mathbf{y}-\mathbf{z}\|$ for all $\mathbf{y}\in\mathscr{V}$ and all $\mathbf{z}\in\mathscr{R}(\mathbf{P})$.

Proof. By Pythagoras' Theorem, as expressed in (3.14), we have $\|\mathbf{y}-\mathbf{z}\|^2=\|(\mathbf{y}-\mathbf{Py})-(\mathbf{z}-\mathbf{Py})\|^2=\|\mathbf{y}-\mathbf{Py}\|^2+\|\mathbf{z}-\mathbf{Py}\|^2$ or, equivalently, $\|\mathbf{y}-\mathbf{z}\|\geqslant\|\mathbf{y}-\mathbf{Py}\|$, if and only if $(\mathbf{z}-\mathbf{Py})\perp(\mathbf{y}-\mathbf{Py})$. But $\mathbf{z}=\mathbf{Pq}$ for some $\mathbf{q}\in\mathscr{V}$, so that the latter condition may be written as $\mathbf{P}(\mathbf{q}-\mathbf{y})\perp(\mathbf{I}-\mathbf{P})\mathbf{y}$. If this condition holds for all $\mathbf{y},\mathbf{q}\in\mathscr{V}$, it must be equivalent to $\mathbf{P}^*(\mathbf{I}-\mathbf{P})=\mathbf{0}$ or $\mathbf{P}^*=\mathbf{P}=\mathbf{P}^2$.

Thus the orthogonal projector $\mathbf{P}$ is the minimum-distance projector of $\mathbf{y}\in\mathscr{V}$ on $\mathscr{R}(\mathbf{P})$.

Alternative forms of projectors

Let us recall that

(3.50) If $\mathscr{V}=\mathscr{U}\oplus\mathscr{W}$, then $\mathbf{P}\in\mathscr{L}(\mathscr{V},\mathscr{V})$ is defined as a projector on $\mathscr{R}(\mathbf{P})=\mathscr{U}$ along $\mathscr{N}(\mathbf{P})=\mathscr{W}$ if, for every $\mathbf{y}=\mathbf{u}+\mathbf{w}$ where $\mathbf{u}\in\mathscr{U}$ and $\mathbf{w}\in\mathscr{W}$, we have $\mathbf{Py}=\mathbf{u}$.

If $\mathcal{U}$ and $\mathcal{W}$ are fully specified, then it is straightforward to construct the projector. Let $\mathcal{R}(\mathbf{A})=\mathcal{U}$ and $\mathcal{R}(\mathbf{B})=\mathcal{W}$. Then the projector is specified by the condition $\mathbf{P}(\mathbf{Aa}+\mathbf{Bb})=\mathbf{Aa}$ for every $\mathbf{a}, \mathbf{b}\in\mathcal{V}$ or, equivalently, by the conditions $\mathbf{PA}=\mathbf{A}, \mathbf{PB}=\mathbf{0}$. Consider the decomposition $\mathbf{P}=\mathbf{RQ}$. The condition $\mathbf{PB}=\mathbf{RQB}=\mathbf{0}$ is satisfied if $\mathbf{Q}$ is chosen so that $\mathcal{R}(\mathbf{B})=\mathcal{N}(\mathbf{Q})$. The condition $\mathbf{PA}=\mathbf{RQA}=\mathbf{A}$ is satisfied by choosing $\mathbf{R}=\mathbf{A}(\mathbf{QA})^-$ where $\text{Rank}(\mathbf{QA})=\text{Rank}(\mathbf{A})$; for then $\mathbf{QPA}=\mathbf{QRQA}=\mathbf{QA}(\mathbf{QA})^-\mathbf{QA}=\mathbf{QA}$, which implies $\mathbf{PA}=\mathbf{A}(\mathbf{QA})^-\mathbf{QA}=\mathbf{A}$. In summary,

(3.51) If $\mathcal{R}(\mathbf{A})\oplus\mathcal{R}(\mathbf{B})=\mathcal{V}$, then the projector on $\mathcal{R}(\mathbf{A})$ along $\mathcal{R}(\mathbf{B})$ is given by $\mathbf{P}=\mathbf{A}(\mathbf{QA})^-\mathbf{Q}$ where $\mathbf{Q}$ is such that $\mathcal{N}(\mathbf{Q})=\mathcal{R}(\mathbf{B})$ and $\text{Rank}(\mathbf{QA})=\text{Rank}(\mathbf{A})$.

In fact, this is largely a repetition of the result in (2.47).

The formula for the projector in (3.51) naturally subsumes previous formulae. For example, if $\mathcal{R}(\mathbf{A})$ and $\mathcal{R}(\mathbf{B})$ are orthogonal complements in $\mathcal{V}$, then, by (3.36), $\mathcal{R}(\mathbf{B})=\mathcal{O}(\mathbf{A})=\mathcal{N}(\mathbf{A}^*)$, and we can choose $\mathbf{Q}=\mathbf{A}^*$ to obtain $\mathbf{P}=\mathbf{A}(\mathbf{A}^*\mathbf{A})^-\mathbf{A}^*$ which is the formula for the orthogonal projector given in (3.47).

The formula of (3.51) also enables us to establish a useful result that relates alternative forms of the same projector. Thus,

(3.52) If $\mathbf{V}_1$ and $\mathbf{V}_2$ are (self-adjoint) positive-definite transformations, then $\mathbf{P}=\mathbf{A}(\mathbf{A}^*\mathbf{V}_1\mathbf{A})^-\mathbf{A}^*\mathbf{V}_1=\mathbf{A}(\mathbf{A}^*\mathbf{V}_2\mathbf{A})^-\mathbf{A}^*\mathbf{V}_2$ if and only if $\mathcal{R}(\mathbf{V}_1\mathbf{A})=\mathcal{R}(\mathbf{V}_2\mathbf{A})$.

Proof. If $\mathbf{P}\in\mathcal{L}(\mathcal{V},\mathcal{V})$ is a projector on $\mathcal{R}(\mathbf{A})$, then it is uniquely specified by its null space $\mathcal{R}(\mathbf{B})$. Thus $\mathbf{P}=\mathbf{A}(\mathbf{A}^*\mathbf{V}_i\mathbf{A})^-\mathbf{A}^*\mathbf{V}_i$; $i=1,2$, is unique if and only if $\mathcal{R}(\mathbf{B})=\mathcal{N}(\mathbf{A}^*\mathbf{V}_1)=\mathcal{N}(\mathbf{A}^*\mathbf{V}_2)$. The equivalent condition in terms of the orthogonal complement of the null space is $\mathcal{R}(\mathbf{V}_1\mathbf{A})=\mathcal{R}(\mathbf{V}_2\mathbf{A})$.

Another useful specialization of the general formula (3.51) is as follows:

(3.53) If the transformations $\mathbf{A}$, $\mathbf{B}$ have $\mathcal{R}(\mathbf{A})\oplus\mathcal{R}(\mathbf{B})=\mathcal{V}$, then the projector of $\mathcal{V}$ on $\mathcal{R}(\mathbf{A})$ along $\mathcal{R}(\mathbf{B})$ is given by $\mathbf{P}=\mathbf{A}[\mathbf{A}^*(\mathbf{I}-\mathbf{P}_\mathbf{B})\mathbf{A}]^-\mathbf{A}^*(\mathbf{I}-\mathbf{P}_\mathbf{B})$ where $\mathbf{I}-\mathbf{P}_\mathbf{B}=\mathbf{I}-\mathbf{B}(\mathbf{B}^*\mathbf{B})^-\mathbf{B}^*$ is an orthogonal projection of $\mathcal{V}$ on $\mathcal{O}(\mathbf{B})$.

This form of $\mathbf{P}=\mathbf{A}(\mathbf{QA})^-\mathbf{Q}$ has $\mathbf{Q}=\mathbf{A}^*(\mathbf{I}-\mathbf{P}_\mathbf{B})$. To show that the condition $\mathcal{R}(\mathbf{B})=\mathcal{N}(\mathbf{Q})$ of (3.51) is satisfied, we write

$$\begin{aligned}\mathcal{N}(\mathbf{Q})&=\mathcal{N}(\mathbf{I}-\mathbf{P}_\mathbf{B})+[\mathcal{N}(\mathbf{A}^*)\cap\mathcal{R}(\mathbf{I}-\mathbf{P}_\mathbf{B})]\\&=\mathcal{R}(\mathbf{B})+[\mathcal{O}(\mathbf{A})\cap\mathcal{O}(\mathbf{B})]=\mathcal{R}(\mathbf{B})+\mathcal{O}[\mathcal{R}(\mathbf{A})\oplus\mathcal{R}(\mathbf{B})]=\mathcal{R}(\mathbf{B})\end{aligned}$$

where we use (3.18) for the third equality, and $\mathcal{O}(\mathcal{V})=\mathbf{0}$ for the fourth.

(3.54) If $\mathcal{R}(\mathbf{A}), \mathcal{R}(\mathbf{B})\subset\mathcal{V}$, then the projector on $\mathcal{R}(\mathbf{A})\cap\mathcal{O}(\mathbf{B})$ along $\mathcal{R}(\mathbf{B})+\mathcal{O}(\mathbf{A})$ is given by

$$\mathbf{P}=(\mathbf{I}-\mathbf{P}_\mathbf{B})\mathbf{A}[\mathbf{A}^*(\mathbf{I}-\mathbf{P}_\mathbf{B})\mathbf{A}]^-\mathbf{A}^*(\mathbf{I}-\mathbf{P}_\mathbf{B}).$$

Proof. Since $(\mathbf{I}-\mathbf{P_B})$ is an orthogonal projector, we have $(\mathbf{I}-\mathbf{P_B})=(\mathbf{I}-\mathbf{P_B})^*(\mathbf{I}-\mathbf{P_B})$. Therefore, by defining $\mathbf{X}=(\mathbf{I}-\mathbf{P_B})\mathbf{A}$, we can write the projector of (3.54) as $\mathbf{P}=\mathbf{X}(\mathbf{X}^*\mathbf{X})^-\mathbf{X}^*$, which shows that it is an orthogonal projector on $\mathcal{R}[(\mathbf{I}-\mathbf{P_B})\mathbf{A}]=\mathcal{R}(\mathbf{A})\cap\mathcal{O}(\mathbf{B})$. Using (3.18), we find that the orthogonal complement of this space is $\mathcal{R}(\mathbf{B})+\mathcal{O}(\mathbf{A})$. The latter also constitutes the null space of $\mathbf{P}$.

(3.55) If $\mathcal{R}(\mathbf{B})\subset\mathcal{R}(\mathbf{A})\subset\mathcal{V}$, then the projector on $\mathcal{R}(\mathbf{A})\cap\mathcal{O}(\mathbf{B})$ along $\mathcal{R}(\mathbf{B})+\mathcal{O}(\mathbf{A})$ is given by

$$(\mathbf{I}-\mathbf{P_B})\mathbf{A}[\mathbf{A}^*(\mathbf{I}-\mathbf{P_B})\mathbf{A}]^-\mathbf{A}^*(\mathbf{I}-\mathbf{P_B})=\mathbf{P_A}-\mathbf{P_B},$$

where $\mathbf{P_A}=\mathbf{A}(\mathbf{A}^*\mathbf{A})^-\mathbf{A}^*$, and $\mathbf{P_B}=\mathbf{B}(\mathbf{B}^*\mathbf{B})^-\mathbf{B}^*$ are orthogonal projectors on $\mathcal{R}(\mathbf{A})$ and $\mathcal{R}(\mathbf{B})$ respectively.

Proof. Our ability to represent the projector by $\mathbf{P_A}-\mathbf{P_B}$ follows directly from (2.34) in consequence of the fact that $\mathbf{P_A}\mathbf{P_B}=\mathbf{P_B}\mathbf{P_A}=\mathbf{P_B}$. The alternative representation is established in (3.54) above.

Example. Let $\mathbf{X}=[\mathbf{X}_1,\mathbf{X}_2]$ *be a partitioned matrix with* Null$(\mathbf{X})=0$ *so that* $\mathcal{M}(\mathbf{X})=\mathcal{M}(\mathbf{X}_1)\oplus\mathcal{M}(\mathbf{X}_2)$, *and let* $\mathbf{P}=\mathbf{X}(\mathbf{X}'\mathbf{X})^-\mathbf{X}'$ *and* $\mathbf{P}_2=\mathbf{X}_2(\mathbf{X}_2'\mathbf{X}_2)^-\mathbf{X}_2'$. *Then, according to* (3.53), *the projector of* $\mathcal{M}(\mathbf{X})$ *on* $\mathcal{M}(\mathbf{X}_1)$ *along* $\mathcal{M}(\mathbf{X}_2)$ *is* $\mathbf{P}_{1/2}=\mathbf{X}_1[\mathbf{X}_1'(\mathbf{I}-\mathbf{P}_2)\mathbf{X}_1]^-\mathbf{X}_1'(\mathbf{I}-\mathbf{P}_2)$. *According to* (3.54), *the orthogonal projector on* $\mathcal{M}(\mathbf{X}_1)\cap\mathcal{O}(\mathbf{X}_2)$ *is* $\mathbf{P}_*=(\mathbf{I}-\mathbf{P}_2)\mathbf{X}_1[\mathbf{X}_1'(\mathbf{I}-\mathbf{P}_2)\mathbf{X}_1]^-\mathbf{X}_1'(\mathbf{I}-\mathbf{P}_2)$, *whereas, according to* (3.55), *the orthogonal projector on* $\mathcal{M}(\mathbf{X})\cap\mathcal{O}(\mathbf{X}_2)$ *is* $(\mathbf{I}-\mathbf{P}_2)\mathbf{X}[\mathbf{X}'(\mathbf{I}-\mathbf{P}_2)\mathbf{X}]^-\mathbf{X}'(\mathbf{I}-\mathbf{P}_2)=\mathbf{P}-\mathbf{P}_2$. *But* $\mathcal{M}(\mathbf{X})\cap\mathcal{O}(\mathbf{X}_2)=\mathcal{M}(\mathbf{X}_1)\cap\mathcal{O}(\mathbf{X}_2)$, *so* $\mathbf{P}_*=\mathbf{P}-\mathbf{P}_2$. *Also, it is clear that* $(\mathbf{I}-\mathbf{P}_2)\mathbf{P}_{1/2}=\mathbf{P}_*=\mathbf{P}-\mathbf{P}_2$.

Inverses with metric properties

(3.56) Let $\mathbf{x}=\mathbf{A}^-\mathbf{y}$ be a solution to the consistent system $\mathbf{y}=\mathbf{A}\mathbf{x}$. Then $\mathbf{x}$ has a minimum norm $\|\mathbf{x}\|$ if and only if $\mathbf{A}\mathbf{A}^-\mathbf{A}$ and $(\mathbf{A}^-\mathbf{A})^*=(\mathbf{A}^-\mathbf{A})$; in which case $\mathbf{A}^-$ is called a minimum-norm g-inverse denoted $\mathbf{A}_m^-$.

Proof. The general solution of $\mathbf{y}=\mathbf{A}\mathbf{x}$ is $\mathbf{x}=\mathbf{A}^-\mathbf{y}+(\mathbf{I}-\mathbf{A})\mathbf{z}$ where $\mathbf{A}^-$ is some g-inverse of $\mathbf{A}$ such that $\mathbf{A}=\mathbf{A}\mathbf{A}^-\mathbf{A}$ and $\mathbf{z}$ is arbitrary. If $\|\mathbf{A}^-\mathbf{y}\|$ is minimized, we must have $\|\mathbf{A}^-\mathbf{y}\|\leqslant\|\mathbf{A}^-\mathbf{A}\mathbf{x}+(\mathbf{I}-\mathbf{A}^-\mathbf{A})\mathbf{z}\|$ for all $\mathbf{x},\mathbf{z}$. But this is equivalent to the condition $\mathbf{A}^-\mathbf{A}\mathbf{x}\perp(\mathbf{I}-\mathbf{A}^-\mathbf{A})\mathbf{z}$ for all $\mathbf{x},\mathbf{z}$ or $(\mathbf{A}^-\mathbf{A})^*(\mathbf{I}-\mathbf{A}^-\mathbf{A})=\mathbf{0}$ or $(\mathbf{A}^-\mathbf{A})^*=\mathbf{A}^-\mathbf{A}$.

(3.57) Let $\mathbf{A}\in\mathcal{L}(\mathcal{V},\mathcal{W})$, and consider $\mathbf{x}\in\mathcal{V}$, $\mathbf{y}\in\mathcal{W}$; $\mathbf{y}\notin\mathcal{R}(\mathbf{A})$ such that the system $\mathbf{y}=\mathbf{A}\mathbf{x}$ is inconsistent. Then the distance $\|\mathbf{y}-\mathbf{A}\mathbf{A}^-\mathbf{y}\|=\|\mathbf{y}-\mathbf{A}\hat{\mathbf{x}}\|$ is minimized if $\mathbf{A}^-$ is such that $\mathbf{A}\mathbf{A}^-\mathbf{A}=\mathbf{A}$ and $(\mathbf{A}\mathbf{A}^-)^*=\mathbf{A}\mathbf{A}^-$; in which case we call $\hat{\mathbf{x}}=\mathbf{A}^-\mathbf{y}$ a minimum-distance (approximative) solution, and we call $\mathbf{A}^-$ a minimum-distance g-inverse, denoted $\mathbf{A}_l^-$.

Proof. By (3.49), we have $\|\mathbf{y}-\mathbf{A}\mathbf{A}_l^-\mathbf{y}\| \leq \|\mathbf{y}-\mathbf{A}\mathbf{A}^-\mathbf{y}\|$ for every other $\mathbf{A}^-$ if and only if $(\mathbf{A}\mathbf{A}_l^-)^* = \mathbf{A}\mathbf{A}_l^-$ and $(\mathbf{A}\mathbf{A}_l^-)(\mathbf{A}\mathbf{A}_l^-) = \mathbf{A}\mathbf{A}_l^-$. The latter condition is satisfied if $\mathbf{A}\mathbf{A}_l^-\mathbf{A} = \mathbf{A}$. Thus the defining conditions of a minimum-distance g-inverse are established.

A simple duality that is of considerable importance in the theory of linear statistical models exists between the minimum-norm and minimum-distance g-inverses. It is as follows:

(3.58) $\quad (\mathbf{A}_m^-)^* = (\mathbf{A}^*)_l^-$ or, equivalently, $(\mathbf{A}^*)_m^- = (\mathbf{A}_l^-)^*$.

Proof. The conditions $\mathbf{A}\mathbf{A}_m^-\mathbf{A} = \mathbf{A}$, $(\mathbf{A}_m^-\mathbf{A})^* = \mathbf{A}_m^-\mathbf{A}$ which define $\mathbf{A}_m^-$ may be given in an adjoint form as $\mathbf{A}^*(\mathbf{A}_m^-)^*\mathbf{A}^* = \mathbf{A}^*$, $\mathbf{A}^*(\mathbf{A}_m^-)^* = [\mathbf{A}_m^-)^*]^*$; which shows that $(\mathbf{A}_m^-)^*$ satisfies the defining conditions for $(\mathbf{A}^*)_l^-$. Hence $(\mathbf{A}_m^-)^* = (\mathbf{A}^*)_l^-$. Interchanging $\mathbf{A}$ and $\mathbf{A}^*$ gives the equivalent result that $[(\mathbf{A}^*)_m^-]^* = \mathbf{A}_l^-$ or $(\mathbf{A}^*)_m^- = (\mathbf{A}_l^-)^*$.

Example. The minimum $\mathbf{Q}$*-norm g-inverse of* $\mathbf{X}'$ *is* $(\mathbf{X}')_{m\mathbf{Q}}^- = \mathbf{Q}^{-1}\mathbf{X}(\mathbf{X}'\mathbf{Q}^{-1}\mathbf{X})^-$. *The fact that this is a g-inverse of* $\mathbf{X}'$ *follows from* (2.46) *when we use* $\text{Rank}(\mathbf{X}'\mathbf{Q}^{-1}\mathbf{X}) = \text{Rank}(\mathbf{X}')$. *To demonstrate that* $\mathbf{R} = (\mathbf{X}')_{m\mathbf{Q}}^-\mathbf{X}'$ *is* $\mathbf{Q}$*-symmetric we write* $\mathbf{R}^* = \mathbf{Q}^{-1}\mathbf{R}'\mathbf{Q} = \mathbf{Q}^{-1}[\mathbf{X}(\mathbf{X}'\mathbf{Q}^{-1}\mathbf{X})^-\mathbf{X}'\mathbf{Q}^{-1}]\mathbf{Q} = \mathbf{Q}^{-1}\mathbf{X}(\mathbf{X}'\mathbf{Q}^{-1}\mathbf{X})^-\mathbf{X}' = \mathbf{R}$, *whence* $\mathbf{Q}\mathbf{R} = \mathbf{R}'\mathbf{Q} = (\mathbf{Q}\mathbf{R})'$.

The minimum $\mathbf{Q}^{-1}$*-distance g-inverse of* $\mathbf{X}$ *is* $\mathbf{X}_{l\mathbf{Q}^{-1}}^- = (\mathbf{X}'\mathbf{Q}^{-1}\mathbf{X})^-\mathbf{X}'\mathbf{Q}^{-1}$. *The fact that this is a g-inverse of* $\mathbf{X}$ *follows from* (2.46) *when we use* $\text{Rank}(\mathbf{X}'\mathbf{Q}^{-1}\mathbf{X}) = \text{Rank}(\mathbf{X})$. *To demonstrate the* $\mathbf{Q}^{-1}$*-symmetry of* $\mathbf{P} = \mathbf{X}\mathbf{X}_{l\mathbf{Q}^{-1}}^-$ *we write* $\mathbf{P}^* = \mathbf{Q}\mathbf{P}'\mathbf{Q}^{-1} = \mathbf{Q}[\mathbf{Q}^{-1}\mathbf{X}(\mathbf{X}'\mathbf{Q}^{-1}\mathbf{X})^-\mathbf{X}']\mathbf{Q}^{-1} = \mathbf{X}(\mathbf{X}'\mathbf{Q}^{-1}\mathbf{X})^-\mathbf{X}'\mathbf{Q}^{-1} = \mathbf{P}$, *whence* $\mathbf{Q}^{-1}\mathbf{P} = \mathbf{P}'\mathbf{Q}^{-1} = (\mathbf{Q}^{-1}\mathbf{P})$.

It is clear from the example that $[(\mathbf{X}')_{m\mathbf{Q}}^-]' = \mathbf{X}_{l\mathbf{Q}^{-1}}^-$.

The Moore–Penrose inverse

(3.59) The Moore–Penrose inverse of a transformation $\mathbf{A} \in \mathscr{L}(\mathscr{V}, \mathscr{W})$ is a transformation $\mathbf{A}^+ \in \mathscr{L}(\mathscr{W}, \mathscr{V})$ such that

1. $\mathbf{A}\mathbf{A}^+\mathbf{A} = \mathbf{A}$,
2. $\mathbf{A}^+\mathbf{A}\mathbf{A}^+ = \mathbf{A}^+$,
3. $(\mathbf{A}\mathbf{A}^+)^* = \mathbf{A}\mathbf{A}^+$,
4. $(\mathbf{A}^+\mathbf{A})^* = \mathbf{A}^+\mathbf{A}$.

Taken together, the conditions 1. and 2. specify that $\mathbf{A}^+$ is a reflexive g-inverse $\mathbf{A}^{\approx}$. The conditions 3. and 4. specify that $\mathbf{A}\mathbf{A}^+$ and $\mathbf{A}^+\mathbf{A}$ are self adjoint in terms of the given inner products of $\mathscr{W}$ and $\mathscr{V}$ respectively.

Since these two products are also idempotent it follows by (3.44) that they are orthogonal projectors. In fact,

(3.60) 1. $\mathbf{A}\mathbf{A}^+$ is the orthogonal projector on $\mathscr{R}(\mathbf{A})$,
2. $\mathbf{A}^+\mathbf{A}$ is the orthogonal projector on $\mathscr{R}(\mathbf{A}^*)$.

The first of these is obvious. To establish the second we note that, by (2.44), $\mathcal{N}(\mathbf{A}^+\mathbf{A})=\mathcal{N}(\mathbf{A})$. Then, since $\mathbf{A}^+\mathbf{A}$ is an orthogonal projector, we have $\mathcal{R}(\mathbf{A}^+\mathbf{A})=\mathcal{O}[\mathcal{N}(\mathbf{A}^+\mathbf{A})]=\mathcal{O}[\mathcal{N}(\mathbf{A})]=\mathcal{R}(\mathbf{A}^*)$, the last equality of which is from (3.36).

(3.61) For any transformation $\mathbf{A}$ there is a unique $\mathbf{A}^+$.

Proof. To establish the existence of $\mathbf{A}^+$, consider decomposing $\mathbf{A}\in\mathcal{L}(\mathcal{V},\mathcal{W})$ as $\mathbf{A}=\mathbf{BC}$ where $\mathbf{C}\in\mathcal{L}(\mathcal{V},\mathcal{Q})$ has $\text{Rank}(\mathbf{C})=\text{Dim}\,\mathcal{Q}$ and $\mathbf{B}\in\mathcal{L}(\mathcal{Q},\mathcal{W})$ has $\text{Null}(\mathbf{B})=0$. We may then construct $\mathbf{C}^R=\mathbf{C}^*(\mathbf{CC}^*)^{-1}$, and $\mathbf{B}^L=(\mathbf{B}^*\mathbf{B})^{-1}\mathbf{B}^*$. Using these, we specify $\mathbf{A}^+=\mathbf{C}^R\mathbf{B}^L=\mathbf{C}^*(\mathbf{CC}^*)^{-1}(\mathbf{B}^*\mathbf{B})^{-1}\mathbf{B}^*$; and it can be confirmed that this obeys the conditions of (3.59).

To show that $\mathbf{A}^+$ is unique, suppose that $\mathbf{G}$ also satisfies the conditions of (3.59). Then, since, by (3.60), both $\mathbf{A}^+\mathbf{A}$ and $\mathbf{GA}$ constitute the unique orthogonal projector on $\mathcal{R}(\mathbf{A}^*)$ along $\mathcal{N}(\mathbf{A})$, we must have $\mathbf{A}^+\mathbf{A}=\mathbf{GA}$. Thus $\mathbf{A}^+\mathbf{AG}=\mathbf{GAG}=\mathbf{G}$. We also argue from (3.60) that $\mathbf{AA}^+=\mathbf{AG}$. Thus $\mathbf{A}^+\mathbf{AG}=\mathbf{A}^+\mathbf{AA}^+=\mathbf{A}^+$. Therefore $\mathbf{G}=\mathbf{A}^+\mathbf{AG}=\mathbf{A}^+$, which proves that $\mathbf{A}^+$ is unique.

We may notice in connection with the proof of the existence of $\mathbf{A}^+$ that, if $\text{Null}(\mathbf{A})=0$, the appropriate decomposition is $\mathbf{A}=\mathbf{AI}$, whence $\mathbf{A}^+=(\mathbf{A}^*\mathbf{A})^{-1}\mathbf{A}^*$, and $\mathbf{AA}^+=\mathbf{A}(\mathbf{A}^*\mathbf{A})^{-1}\mathbf{A}^*$ has the form of the orthogonal projector given in (3.47). Conversely, if $\text{Rank}(\mathbf{A})=\text{Dim}\,\mathcal{W}$, the appropriate decomposition is $\mathbf{A}=\mathbf{IA}$, whence $\mathbf{A}^+=\mathbf{A}^*(\mathbf{AA}^*)^{-1}$. If $\mathbf{A}$ is non-singular, either of these expressions may be reduced to give $\mathbf{A}^+=\mathbf{A}^{-1}$.

Example. Let $\mathbf{R}$ *be a matrix of full row rank, so that* $\text{Null}(\mathbf{R}')=0$, *and let* $\mathbf{Q}$ *be a positive-definite matrix of the appropriate order. Then* $\mathbf{R}^+=\mathbf{Q}^{-1}\mathbf{R}'(\mathbf{RQ}^{-1}\mathbf{R}')^{-1}$ *is a Moore–Penrose inverse such that* $\mathbf{RR}^+=\mathbf{I}$ *is symmetric in terms of the ordinary inner product, and* $\mathbf{R}^+\mathbf{R}=\mathbf{Q}^{-1}\mathbf{R}'(\mathbf{RQ}^{-1}\mathbf{R}')^{-1}\mathbf{R}$ *is* $\mathbf{Q}$*-symmetric. Also,* $[\mathbf{I}-\mathbf{Q}^{-1}\mathbf{R}'(\mathbf{RQ}^{-1}\mathbf{R}')^{-1}\mathbf{R}]$ *is the* $\mathbf{Q}$*-orthogonal projector on* $\mathcal{N}(\mathbf{R})$ *along* $\mathcal{M}(\mathbf{R}^*)=\mathcal{M}(\mathbf{Q}^{-1}\mathbf{R}')$.

CHARACTERISTIC ROOTS

(3.62) If $\mathbf{A}\in\mathcal{L}(\mathcal{V},\mathcal{V})$, then a subspace $\mathcal{U}\subset\mathcal{V}$ such that $\mathbf{Ax}\in\mathcal{U}$ for every $\mathbf{x}\in\mathcal{U}$ is called an invariant subspace of $\mathbf{A}$.

(3.63) If $\mathbf{A}\in\mathcal{L}(\mathcal{V},\mathcal{V})$ and $\mathbf{Ax}=\lambda\mathbf{x}$ where $\mathbf{x}$ is non-zero and λ is a scalar, we say that $\mathbf{x}$ is a characteristic vector of $\mathbf{A}$ corresponding to a characteristic root λ.

(3.64) The set $\{\mathbf{x};\mathbf{Ax}=\lambda_i\mathbf{x}\}$ is called the characteristic subspace of $\mathbf{A}$ corresponding to the root λ_i. The characteristic subspace constitutes a vector space whose dimension m_i is termed the geometric multiplicity of the root λ_i.

We shall be concerned in detail only with the characteristic roots and vectors of self-adjoint transformations, of which we are able to give a simple and definitive account. It may be demonstrated, in fact, that the roots of a self-adjoint transformation are always real regardless of whether the transformation is defined on real or complex spaces. Therefore it does not detract from the account if we deal only with real spaces defined over $\mathcal{R}$.

Working with real spaces, we shall proceed to show that, for a self-adjoint transformation $\mathbf{A}=\mathbf{A}^*$, there always exist a characteristic root and vector. We base the proof of existence upon the fact that there exists a maximal unit vector $\mathbf{x}_0 \in \mathcal{V}; \|\mathbf{x}_0\|=1$ defined by the condition that $\|\mathbf{Ax}_0\| \geqslant \|\mathbf{Az}\|$ for every $\mathbf{z} \in \mathcal{V}; \|\mathbf{z}\|=1$, or by the equivalent condition that $\|\mathbf{Ax}_0\| \geqslant \|\mathbf{A}(\mathbf{x}/\|\mathbf{x}\|)\|$ for every $\mathbf{x} \in \mathcal{V}$. To begin, we prove that

(3.65) If $\mathbf{A}=\mathbf{A}^*$ is self adjoint and if $\mathbf{x}_0 \in \mathcal{V}$ is such that $\|\mathbf{x}_0\|=1$ and $\|\mathbf{Ax}_0\| \geqslant \|\mathbf{A}(\mathbf{x}/\|\mathbf{x}\|)\|$ for all $\mathbf{x} \in \mathcal{V}$, then $\mathbf{A}^2\mathbf{x}_0 = \lambda \mathbf{x}_0$ with $\lambda = \|\mathbf{Ax}_0\|^2$, so that $\mathbf{x}_0$ is a characteristic vector of $\mathbf{A}^2$.

Proof. We have, by definition, $\langle \mathbf{Ax}_0, \mathbf{Ax}_0\rangle = \langle \mathbf{A}^2\mathbf{x}_0, \mathbf{x}_0\rangle$ and $\surd\langle \mathbf{x}_0, \mathbf{x}_0\rangle = \|\mathbf{x}_0\| = 1$. Therefore we may use the Cauchy–Schwarz inequality to write $\|\mathbf{Ax}_0\|^2 = \langle \mathbf{Ax}_0, \mathbf{Ax}_0\rangle = \langle \mathbf{A}^2\mathbf{x}_0, \mathbf{x}_0\rangle \leqslant \surd\langle \mathbf{A}^2\mathbf{x}_0, \mathbf{A}^2\mathbf{x}_0\rangle \surd\langle \mathbf{x}_0, \mathbf{x}_0\rangle = \|\mathbf{A}^2\mathbf{x}_0\|$, or simply $\|\mathbf{Ax}_0\|^2 \leqslant \|\mathbf{A}^2\mathbf{x}_0\|$. Now, the condition $\|\mathbf{A}(\mathbf{x}/\|\mathbf{x}\|)\| \leqslant \|\mathbf{Ax}_0\|$ implies $\|\mathbf{Ax}\| \leqslant \|\mathbf{Ax}_0\|\,\|\mathbf{x}\|$, so, for the maximal vector $\mathbf{x}_0$, we also have $\|\mathbf{A}^2\mathbf{x}_0\| = \|\mathbf{A}(\mathbf{Ax}_0)\| \leqslant \|\mathbf{Ax}_0\|\,\|\mathbf{Ax}_0\|$ or simply $\|\mathbf{A}^2\mathbf{x}_0\| \leqslant \|\mathbf{Ax}_0\|^2$. Thus $\|\mathbf{Ax}_0\|^2 = \|\mathbf{A}^2\mathbf{x}_0\|$, and the Cauchy–Schwarz inequality reduces to an equality which indicates that $\mathbf{A}^2\mathbf{x}_0$ and $\mathbf{x}_0$ are collinear such that $\mathbf{A}^2\mathbf{x}_0 = \lambda\mathbf{x}_0$. It follows that $\|\mathbf{Ax}_0\|^2 = \|\mathbf{A}^2\mathbf{x}_0\| = \|\lambda\mathbf{x}_0\| = \lambda$.

Having shown that $\mathbf{A}^2$ has a characteristic root and vector if $\mathbf{A}=\mathbf{A}^*$, we can proceed to prove that

(3.66) Any self-adjoint transformation $\mathbf{A}=\mathbf{A}^*$ has a characteristic vector which is associated with a characteristic root $\mu = \mp\|\mathbf{Ax}_0\|$ where $\mathbf{x}_0$ is the maximal vector of $\mathbf{A}$.

Proof. Defining $\mu^2=\lambda$, we have, from (3.65), $\mathbf{A}^2\mathbf{x}_0 - \mu^2\mathbf{x}_0 = (\mathbf{A}-\mu\mathbf{I})(\mathbf{A}+\mu\mathbf{I})\mathbf{x}_0 = \mathbf{0}$. If $\mathbf{z} = (\mathbf{A}+\mu\mathbf{I})\mathbf{x}_0 \neq \mathbf{0}$, then $(\mathbf{A}-\mu\mathbf{I})\mathbf{z} = \mathbf{0}$, and $\mathbf{z}$ is a characteristic vector corresponding to $\mu = \|\mathbf{Ax}_0\|$. Alternatively, if $(\mathbf{A}+\mu\mathbf{I})\mathbf{x}_0 = \mathbf{0}$, then $\mathbf{x}_0$ is a characteristic vector of $\mathbf{A}$ corresponding to $\mu = -\|\mathbf{Ax}_0\|$.

This fundamental result (3.66) implies that

(3.67) Every invariant subspace of a self-adjoint transformation has at least one characteristic root and vector.

For, if $\mathcal{U} \subset \mathcal{V}$ is an invariant subspace of a self-adjoint transformation $\mathbf{A} \in \mathcal{L}(\mathcal{V}, \mathcal{V})$, then the theorem (3.66) also applies to the restriction of $\mathbf{A}$ to $\mathcal{U}$, written $\mathbf{A}_{\mathcal{U}} \in \mathcal{L}(\mathcal{U}, \mathcal{U})$.

(3.68) If $\mathbf{A} = \mathbf{A}^*$ is a self-adjoint transformation, then the characteristic subspaces corresponding to two distinct roots are orthogonal.

Proof. Consider λ_i, λ_j and $\mathbf{x}_i, \mathbf{x}_j$ such that $\mathbf{A}\mathbf{x}_i = \lambda_i \mathbf{x}_i$ and $\mathbf{A}\mathbf{x}_j = \lambda_j \mathbf{x}_j$. Then, since $\mathbf{A} = \mathbf{A}^*$, we have $\langle \mathbf{x}_i, \mathbf{A}\mathbf{x}_j \rangle = \langle \mathbf{A}\mathbf{x}_i, \mathbf{x}_j \rangle$ or $\lambda_j \langle \mathbf{x}_i, \mathbf{x}_j \rangle = \lambda_i \langle \mathbf{x}_i, \mathbf{x}_j \rangle$. But $\lambda_i \neq \lambda_j$, so the equality implies $\langle \mathbf{x}_i, \mathbf{x}_j \rangle = 0$.

(3.69) Let $\mathbf{A} \in \mathscr{L}(\mathscr{V}, \mathscr{V})$ be a self-adjoint transformation. If $\lambda_1, \ldots, \lambda_r$ are the distinct characteristic roots of $\mathbf{A}$ and if $\mathscr{Q}_1, \ldots, \mathscr{Q}_r$ are their corresponding characteristic subspaces, then $\mathscr{V} = \mathscr{Q}_1 \oplus \ldots \oplus \mathscr{Q}_r$ is an orthogonal decomposition.

Proof. We have shown that, if $\mathbf{A}$ is $\mathscr{Q}$ self adjoint, the characteristic subspaces corresponding to distinct roots are orthogonal. It remains to show that $\mathscr{Q}_1 + \ldots + \mathscr{Q}_r = \mathscr{Q} = \mathscr{V}$. Assume that $\mathscr{Q} \neq \mathscr{V}$ so that it has an orthogonal complement $\mathscr{Q}^*$ such that $\mathscr{Q}^* \oplus \mathscr{Q} = \mathscr{V}$ and $\mathscr{Q}^* \perp \mathscr{Q}$. Then, for every $\mathbf{x} \in \mathscr{Q}_i$, $\mathbf{y} \in \mathscr{Q}^*$, we have $\langle \mathbf{x}, \mathbf{y} \rangle = 0$ and $\langle \mathbf{x}, \mathbf{A}\mathbf{y} \rangle = \langle \mathbf{A}\mathbf{x}, \mathbf{y} \rangle = \lambda_i \langle \mathbf{x}, \mathbf{y} \rangle = 0$; so that $\mathbf{A}\mathbf{y} \in \mathscr{Q}^*$ if $\mathbf{y} \in \mathscr{Q}^*$. Thus $\mathscr{Q}^*$ is an invariant subspace of $\mathbf{A}$; and it follows from (3.67) that there is some characteristic vector $\mathbf{z} \in \mathscr{Q}^*$ such that $\mathbf{A}\mathbf{z} = \lambda \mathbf{z}$. But then, by definition, $\mathbf{z} \in \mathscr{Q}$; and it follows that $\mathbf{z} \in (\mathscr{Q}^* \cap \mathscr{Q}) = \mathbf{0}$. Thus $\mathscr{Q}^*$, which has no non-zero characteristic vectors, is a space of zero dimension, and the theorem is proved.

It follows directly from this result that

(3.70) If $\mathbf{A} = \mathbf{A}^*$ is a self-adjoint transformation on $\mathscr{V}$, then $\mathscr{V}$ has an orthonormal basis $[\mathbf{c}_1, \ldots, \mathbf{c}_n]$ where each $\mathbf{c}_i$ is a characteristic vector of $\mathbf{A}$.

For such a basis is formed by the collection of the orthonormal bases of the characteristic subspaces $\mathscr{Q}_i$ of $\mathbf{A}$.

(3.71) If a self-adjoint transformation $\mathbf{A} = \mathbf{A}^*$ has r non-zero characteristic roots, including multiplicities, then $\text{Rank}(\mathbf{A}) = r$.

Proof. We may order the basis $[\mathbf{c}_1, \ldots, \mathbf{c}_r, \mathbf{c}_{r+1}, \ldots, \mathbf{c}_n]$ of $\mathscr{V} = \mathscr{R}(\mathbf{A}) \oplus \mathscr{N}(\mathbf{A})$, comprising the characteristic vectors of $\mathbf{A}$, so that $[\mathbf{c}_1, \ldots, \mathbf{c}_r]$ is the basis of $\mathscr{R}(\mathbf{A})$ and $[\mathbf{c}_{r+1}, \ldots, \mathbf{c}_n]$ is the basis of $\mathscr{N}(\mathbf{A})$. Then $\mathbf{A}\mathbf{c}_i = \lambda_i \mathbf{c} \neq \mathbf{0}$ for $i = 1, \ldots, r$ implies $\lambda_i \neq 0$, and $\mathbf{A}\mathbf{c}_i = \lambda_i \mathbf{c}_i = 0$ for $i = r+1, \ldots, n$ implies $\lambda_i = 0$; whence $r = \text{Dim}\, \mathscr{R}(\mathbf{A}) = \text{Rank}(\mathbf{A})$ is the number of non-zero roots.

(3.72) If $\mathbf{A} = \mathbf{A}^*$ is a self-adjoint transformation, then (i) $\langle \mathbf{A}\mathbf{x}, \mathbf{x} \rangle \geqslant 0$ for every $\mathbf{x} \in \mathscr{V}$ if and only if the characteristic roots of $\mathbf{A}$ are non-negative—in which case $\mathbf{A}$ is said to be positive semidefinite—, and (ii) $\langle \mathbf{A}\mathbf{x}, \mathbf{x} \rangle > 0$ for every non-zero $\mathbf{x}$ if and only if the roots of $\mathbf{A}$ are strictly positive—in which case $\mathbf{A}$ is said to be positive definite.

Proof. Let $[\mathbf{c}_1, \ldots, \mathbf{c}_n]$ be a set of characteristic vectors of $\mathbf{A}$ constituting an orthonormal basis of $\mathcal{V}$. Then any $\mathbf{x} \in \mathcal{V}$ may be expressed as $\mathbf{x} = \sum \mu_i \mathbf{c}_i$. Furthermore, since $\mathbf{A}\mathbf{c}_i = \lambda_i \mathbf{c}_i$, we also have $\mathbf{A}\mathbf{x} = \mathbf{A}(\sum \mu_i \mathbf{c}_i) = \sum \mu_i \lambda_i \mathbf{c}_i$. Thus $\langle \mathbf{A}\mathbf{x}, \mathbf{x} \rangle = \sum_i \sum_j \mu_i \mu_j \lambda_i \langle \mathbf{c}_i, \mathbf{c}_j \rangle = \sum \mu_i^2 \lambda_i$. For this to be non-negative we must have $\lambda_i \geqslant 0$ for all i; which proves (i). For it to be strictly positive we must have $\lambda_i > 0$ for all i; which proves (ii).

A leading example of a positive-semidefinite transformation is the product $\mathbf{T}^*\mathbf{T}$; for it follows from the definition of an inner product that $\langle \mathbf{T}^*\mathbf{T}\mathbf{x}, \mathbf{x} \rangle = \langle \mathbf{T}\mathbf{x}, \mathbf{T}\mathbf{x} \rangle \geqslant 0$. Furthermore, if $\text{Null}(\mathbf{T}) = 0$, then $\mathbf{T}\mathbf{x} \neq \mathbf{0}$ for any non-zero $\mathbf{x}$, whence $\langle \mathbf{T}^*\mathbf{T}\mathbf{x}, \mathbf{x} \rangle > 0$, and $\mathbf{T}^*\mathbf{T}$ is positive definite.

(3.73) If $\mathbf{P} = \mathbf{P}^2$ is an idempotent transformation, then its roots are either zero or unity.

Proof. If λ and $\mathbf{x}$ are respectively a characteristic root and an associated characteristic vector of $\mathbf{P}$, then $\mathbf{P}\mathbf{x} = \lambda \mathbf{x}$, and, by the idempotency of $\mathbf{P}$, $\mathbf{P}\mathbf{x} = \mathbf{P}\mathbf{P}\mathbf{x} = \lambda \mathbf{P}\mathbf{x} = \lambda^2 \mathbf{x}$. Thus λ and λ^2 are the same characteristic root, which can only be the case if $\lambda = 0, 1$.

(3.74) Let $\lambda_1, \ldots, \lambda_r$ be the set of distinct characteristic roots of a self-adjoint transformation $\mathbf{A} = \mathbf{A}^*$, and let the scalars $m_1, \ldots, m_r$ be their geometric multiplicities. Then we may define the trace of $\mathbf{A}$ by

$$\text{Trace}(\mathbf{A}) = \sum_{i=1}^{r} m_i \lambda_i,$$

and the determinant of $\mathbf{A}$ by

$$\text{Det}(\mathbf{A}) = \prod_{i=1}^{r} \lambda_i^{m_i}.$$

The determinant of $\mathbf{A}$ is also denoted by $|\mathbf{A}|$.

We shall develop the theory of determinants and traces at a later stage on the basis of alternative definitions which are specific to matrices but which do not require that these matrices be symmetric.

Diagonalization of symmetric matrices

(3.75) Let $\mathbf{C}$ be an orthonormal matrix comprising the characteristic vectors of a symmetric matrix $\mathbf{A}$. Then $\mathbf{\Lambda} = \mathbf{C}'\mathbf{A}\mathbf{C}$ is a diagonal matrix containing the characteristic roots of $\mathbf{A}$.

Proof. Since $\mathbf{C} = [\mathbf{c}_1, \ldots, \mathbf{c}_n]$ and $\mathbf{A}\mathbf{c}_i = \lambda_i \mathbf{c}_i$ for $i = 1, \ldots, n$, we have $\mathbf{A}\mathbf{C} = \mathbf{C}\mathbf{\Lambda}$. Then, since $\mathbf{C}'\mathbf{C} = \mathbf{C}\mathbf{C}' = \mathbf{I}$, we get $\mathbf{C}'\mathbf{A}\mathbf{C} = \mathbf{C}'\mathbf{C}\mathbf{\Lambda} = \mathbf{\Lambda}$ and $\mathbf{A} = \mathbf{A}\mathbf{C}\mathbf{C}' = \mathbf{C}\mathbf{\Lambda}\mathbf{C}'$. Thus $\mathbf{C}$ is effective in diagonalizing $\mathbf{A}$.

(3.76) If $\mathbf{Q}$ is a symmetric (positive-semidefinite) matrix with non-negative characteristic roots, there exists a transformation $\mathbf{T}$ such that

$$\mathbf{TQT}' = \mathbf{J} = \begin{bmatrix} \mathbf{I}_r, & \mathbf{0} \\ \mathbf{0}, & \mathbf{0} \end{bmatrix},$$

where r is the number of non-zero roots of $\mathbf{Q}$.

To obtain the matrix $\mathbf{J}$ we order the sequence of the characteristic vectors of $\mathbf{Q}$ in the matrix $\mathbf{C}$ in such a way that r non-zero roots $\lambda_1, \ldots, \lambda_r$ appear as the first r diagonal elements of $\mathbf{\Lambda} = \mathbf{C}'\mathbf{QC}$. Then, if $\mathbf{D}$ is a diagonal matrix whose ith element is $d_i = 1/\sqrt{\lambda_i}$ if $i \leq r$, and $d_i = 0$ if $i > r$, we have $\mathbf{J} = \mathbf{D}'\mathbf{\Lambda D} = \mathbf{D}'\mathbf{C}'\mathbf{QCD} = \mathbf{TQT}'$, where $\mathbf{T} = \mathbf{D}'\mathbf{C}'$.

(3.77) If $\mathbf{Q}$ is a positive-definite matrix, then there exists a non-singular transformation $\mathbf{T}$ such that $\mathbf{TQT}' = \mathbf{I}$. It follows that $\mathbf{Q} = \mathbf{T}^{-1}\mathbf{T}^{-1\prime}$ and that $\mathbf{Q}^{-1} = \mathbf{T}'\mathbf{T}$.

This result, which is a specialization of (3.76), depends upon the fact that the roots of a positive-definite matrix are all positive. We can also deduce that

(3.78) If $\mathbf{Q}$ is positive definite then $\mathbf{x}'\mathbf{Q}^{-1}\mathbf{x} = \mathbf{x}'\mathbf{T}'\mathbf{Tx} = (\mathbf{Tx})'\mathbf{Tx} > 0$ for any non-zero $\mathbf{x}$, whence $\mathbf{Q}^{-1}$ is also positive definite.

For another specialization of (3.75) and (3.76), we use the fact that the characteristic roots of an idempotent matrix are zeros and units to deduce that

(3.79) If $\mathbf{P} = \mathbf{P}' = \mathbf{P}^2$ is an $n \times n$ symmetric idempotent matrix of rank r, then there is some choice of orthonormal matrix $\mathbf{C} = [\mathbf{C}_r, \mathbf{C}_{n-r}]$ such that

$$\mathbf{C}'\mathbf{PC} = \begin{bmatrix} \mathbf{I}_r, & \mathbf{0} \\ \mathbf{0}, & \mathbf{0} \end{bmatrix},$$

and

$$\mathbf{P} = \mathbf{CC}'\mathbf{PCC}' = \mathbf{C}\begin{bmatrix} \mathbf{I}_r, & \mathbf{0} \\ \mathbf{0}, & \mathbf{0} \end{bmatrix}\mathbf{C}' = \mathbf{C}_r\mathbf{C}_r'.$$

Example. Consider the symmetric idempotent matrix $\mathbf{P} = \mathbf{X}(\mathbf{X}'\mathbf{X})^{-1}\mathbf{X}'$, *and define* $\mathbf{T}$ *such that* $\mathbf{T}(\mathbf{X}'\mathbf{X})\mathbf{T}' = \mathbf{I}$, *and* $\mathbf{T}'\mathbf{T} = (\mathbf{X}'\mathbf{X})^{-1}$. *Then* $\mathbf{P} = \mathbf{XT}'\mathbf{TX}' = \mathbf{C}_*\mathbf{C}_*'$. *Thus* $\mathbf{C}_* = \mathbf{XT}'$ *is such that* $\mathbf{C}_*'\mathbf{C}_* = \mathbf{T}(\mathbf{X}'\mathbf{X})\mathbf{T}' = \mathbf{I}$; *and we can see that we have derived precisely the form of the orthogonal projector which was given in the example following (3.26).*

BIBLIOGRAPHY

Metric Spaces. Halmos [**49,** Chap. III], Kreider et al. [**70,** Chap. 7], Shephard [**109,** Chap. V], Shilov [**110,** Chap. 7]

Projectors and Inverses with Metric Properties. Kruskal [**72**], Rao [**97**], Rao and Mitra [**98,** Chap. 3]

Characteristic Roots and Vectors. Shilov [**110,** Chap. 9]

CHAPTER 4

Extensions of Matrix Algebra

In this chapter, we shall develop some aspects of matrix algebra. We shall adopt a more concrete approach than hitherto. Thus, instead of developing the theory, in the first instance, in terms of abstract spaces, we shall adopt a co-ordinate specific approach throughout.

MATRIX DETERMINANTS

To facilitate the development of the theory of matrix determinants, we shall first give a few definitions and results concerning permutations.

(4.1) A permutation α defined on the set of integers $\mathscr{I}_n = [1, \ldots, n]$ is a one-to-one mapping of $\mathscr{I}_n$ onto itself. Thus, for every $i \in \mathscr{I}_n$, there is a unique $\alpha(i) = j \in \mathscr{I}_n$ and, for every $i \in \mathscr{I}_n$, there is a unique $l \in \mathscr{I}_n$ such that $\alpha(l) = i$.

It is well known that there are exactly $n!$ permutations defined on $\mathscr{I}_n$. Furthermore, every permutation can be expressed as the product of transpositions which are permutations that interchange only two numbers. Thus, if we denote the permutation which interchanges the ith and jth elements of $\mathscr{I}_n$, and affects no others, by (i, j), it is possible to write factorizations of α of the form $\alpha = (i, j)(k, l) \ldots (p, q)$.

Example. The permutation of the first six integers defined by $[\alpha(1), \alpha(2), \alpha(3), \alpha(4), \alpha(5), \alpha(6)] = [1, 4, 3, 2, 6, 5]$ *may be expressed as the product* $(5, 6)(3, 4)(2, 3)(3, 4)$ *comprising four transpositions. This is evident in the following tabulation which shows the results of applying each transposition successively to the integers*:

$$1, 2, \overbrace{3, 4}, 5, 6$$

$$1, \overbrace{2, 4}, 3, 5, 6$$

$$1, 4, \overbrace{2, 3}, 5, 6$$

$$1, 4, 3, 2, \overbrace{5, 6}$$

$$1, 4, 3, 2, 6, 5$$

The permutation can also be factorized as $\alpha = (2, 4)(5, 6)$.

The factorization of a permutation is clearly not unique; however

(4.2) A given permutation α has either an odd number or an even number of transpositions in every factorization. If α decomposes to an odd number of transpositions, then its sign is $\text{sgn}(\alpha)=-1$. If α decomposes to an even number of transpositions, then its sign is $\text{sgn}(\alpha)=1$.

We can determine the sign of a permutation α by inspecting the mapping under α of the integers $[1, \ldots, n]$. Thus

(4.3) For the permutation $[\alpha(1), \alpha(2), \ldots, \alpha(n)]$, let p be the number of pairs of elements $[\alpha(i), \alpha(j)]$; $i<j$ such that $\alpha(i)>\alpha(j)$. Then $\text{sgn}(\alpha)=(-1)^p$.

This is made clear by the fact that p is precisely the minimum number of transpositions of adjacent elements required to generate the permutation. We call p the number of inversions of α.

Associated with any square $n\times n$ matrix $\mathbf{A}$ is a real scalar-valued function of its elements called the determinant, written Det($\mathbf{A}$) or $|\mathbf{A}|$. We may define the determinant recursively.

(4.4) Let $|\mathbf{A}|$ be the determinant of an $n\times n$ matrix $\mathbf{A}=[a_{ij}]$ and let $|\mathbf{A}_{ij}|$ be the determinant of the submatrix of $\mathbf{A}$ formed by deleting the ith row and the jth column. Then, given the rule that the determinant of a minimal submatrix a_{ij} is $|a_{ij}|=a_{ij}$, we may define $|\mathbf{A}|$ by the expansion $|\mathbf{A}|=\sum_i a_{ij}(-1)^{i+j}\,|\mathbf{A}_{ij}|=\sum_i a_{ij}c_{ij}$, where the choice of $j=1,\ldots,n$ is arbitrary. The scalar $c_{ij}=(-1)^{i+j}\,|\mathbf{A}_{ij}|$ is called the cofactor of a_{ij} comprising the minor $|\mathbf{A}_{ij}|$.

Thus the determinant of $\mathbf{A}$ is found by successive expansions of determinants of matrices of decreasing order, terminating with the determinants of matrices of single elements.

The definition (4.4) allows for any choice of $j=1,\ldots,n$. However, if we adopt the convention of always choosing the lowest value for j, and if we use (4.3), we find that the ultimate expansion of $|\mathbf{A}|$ is

(4.5) $$|\mathbf{A}|=\sum_{\alpha} \text{sgn}(\alpha)a_{\alpha(1),1}a_{\alpha(2),2}\cdots a_{\alpha(n),n},$$

which is a sum of $n!$ terms, each corresponding to a different permutation. We can also describe a typical term of this expansion as the product of n elements selected from successive columns of the matrix in such a way that no two elements come from the same row of the matrix. It is clear from this characterization of the determinant that

(4.6) If $\mathbf{A}$ is a diagonal matrix, then $|\mathbf{A}| = a_{11}a_{22} \ldots a_{nn} = \prod_i a_{ii}$. That is, the determinant of $\mathbf{A}$ is the product of the diagonal elements.

The next proposition also follows immediately from (4.5).

(4.7) Consider the $n \times n$ matrix $\mathbf{A}$ and the matrix $\mathbf{A}(\lambda \mathbf{a}_{.k})$ which differs from $\mathbf{A}$ only in its kth column $\lambda \mathbf{a}_{.k}$ which is λ times the kth column of $\mathbf{A}$. Then $|\lambda \mathbf{A}| = \lambda^n |\mathbf{A}|$, whereas $|\mathbf{A}(\lambda \mathbf{a}_{.k})| = \lambda |\mathbf{A}|$.

Using the properties of permutations we can prove that

(4.8) $|\mathbf{A}'| = |\mathbf{A}|$.

Proof. Define $\mathbf{B} = \mathbf{A}'$. Then, since $b_{ij} = a_{ji}$, we have

$$\begin{aligned} |\mathbf{B}| &= \sum \operatorname{sgn}(\alpha) b_{\alpha(1),1} b_{\alpha(2),2} \ldots b_{\alpha(n),n} \\ &= \sum \operatorname{sgn}(\alpha) a_{1,\alpha(1)} a_{2,\alpha(2)} \ldots a_{n,\alpha(n)}. \end{aligned}$$

Now consider a permutation ϕ. Clearly, since $\{\phi(1), \ldots, \phi(n)\}$ is the set of integers, and since $\alpha\phi$ is also a permutation, the products

$$a_{1,\alpha(1)} a_{2,\alpha(2)} \ldots a_{n,\alpha(n)} \quad \text{and}$$

$$a_{\phi(1),\alpha\phi(1)} a_{\phi(2),\alpha\phi(2)} \ldots a_{\phi(n),\alpha\phi(n)}$$

differ only in respect of the order of their factors; so that, while retaining $\operatorname{sgn}(\alpha)$, we may use either of these in the expansion of $|\mathbf{B}|$. Furthermore, if we choose $\phi = \alpha^{-1}$ and make use of the fact that $\operatorname{sgn}(\alpha) = \operatorname{sgn}(\alpha^{-1}) = \operatorname{sgn}(\phi)$, we can write

$$|\mathbf{B}| = \sum \operatorname{sgn}(\phi) a_{\phi(1),1} a_{\phi(2),2} \ldots a_{\phi(n),n}.$$

But, apart from a change of notation, this is precisely the expansion of $|\mathbf{A}|$, so that $|\mathbf{B}| = |\mathbf{A}'| = |\mathbf{A}|$.

Since $\mathbf{A}' = [a_{ji}]$, we can write $|\mathbf{A}| = |\mathbf{A}'| = \sum_i a_{ji} c_{ji} = \sum_j a_{ij} c_{ij}$, where the last equality involves nothing but a change of notation. Thus the result (4.8) enables us to see that a determinant may be expanded in terms of the column index j as well as the row index i as it was in the definition (4.4).

(4.9) Interchanging any two columns, or rows, of the matrix $\mathbf{A}$ alters the sign of its determinant.

Proof. Interchanging two of the columns of $\mathbf{A}$ is equivalent to multiplying each permutation in the expansion of $|\mathbf{A}|$ in (4.5) by an appropriate transposition. Therefore, since the number of transpositions in each permutation increases by one, the sign of each permutation is changed, and hence the sign of the determinant is changed. Since $|\mathbf{A}|=|\mathbf{A}'|$, we can transpose the matrix and apply the same argument to its rows.

It follows immediately from (4.9) that

(4.10) If a matrix has two identical columns or rows, then its determinant is zero;

for, in this case, interchanging the columns, or the rows, must change the sign of the determinant and yet leave its value unaltered, which can only happen if the determinant is zero.

(4.11) Let $\mathbf{A}(\lambda\mathbf{b}_{.k}+\mu\mathbf{c}_{.k})=[\mathbf{a}_{.1},\ldots,\lambda\mathbf{b}_{.k}+\mu\mathbf{c}_{.k},\ldots,\mathbf{a}_{.n}]$, $\mathbf{A}(\mathbf{b}_{.k})=[\mathbf{a}_{.1},\ldots,\mathbf{b}_{.k},\ldots,\mathbf{a}_{.n}]$ and $\mathbf{A}(\mathbf{c}_{.k})=[\mathbf{a}_{.1},\ldots,\mathbf{c}_{.k},\ldots\mathbf{a}_{.n}]$ be matrices which differ only in respect of the kth column. Then $|\mathbf{A}(\lambda\mathbf{b}_{.k}+\mu\mathbf{c}_{.k})|=\lambda\,|\mathbf{A}(\mathbf{b}_{.k})|+\mu\,|\mathbf{A}(\mathbf{c}_{.k})|$.

Proof

$$\begin{aligned}
&|\mathbf{A}(\lambda\mathbf{b}_{.k}+\mu\mathbf{c}_{.k})|\\
&\qquad=\sum \operatorname{sgn}(\alpha)a_{\alpha(1),1}\ldots[\lambda b_{\alpha(k),k}+\mu c_{\alpha(k),k}]\ldots a_{\alpha(n),n}\\
&\qquad=\sum \operatorname{sgn}(\alpha)a_{\alpha(1),1}\ldots\lambda b_{\alpha(k),k}\ldots a_{\alpha(n),n}\\
&\qquad\quad+\sum \operatorname{sgn}(\alpha)a_{\alpha(1),1}\ldots\mu c_{\alpha(k),k}\ldots a_{\alpha(n),n}\\
&\qquad=\lambda\,|\mathbf{A}(\mathbf{b}_{.k})|+\mu\,|\mathbf{A}(\mathbf{c}_{.k})|.
\end{aligned}$$

The generalization of (4.11) to any number of matrices is immediate. Thus

(4.12) $$|\mathbf{A}(\lambda\mathbf{b}_{.k}+\cdots+\omega\mathbf{z}_{.k})|=\lambda|\mathbf{A}(\mathbf{b}_{.k})|+\cdots+\omega\,|\mathbf{A}(\mathbf{z}_{.k})|.$$

Our results enable us to prove that

(4.13) Adding multiples of any column of a matrix to another column does not change the value of the determinant.

Proof. We may add λ times the jth column of $\mathbf{A}$ to its kth column to give $\mathbf{A}(\mathbf{a}_{.k}+\lambda\mathbf{a}_{.j})$. Then, by (4.11), we get $|\mathbf{A}(\mathbf{a}_{.k}+\lambda\mathbf{a}_{.j})|=|\mathbf{A}(\mathbf{a}_{.k})|+\lambda\,|\mathbf{A}(\mathbf{a}_{.j})|=|\mathbf{A}|$. The last equality follows since $\mathbf{A}(\mathbf{a}_{.k})=\mathbf{A}$, and $|\mathbf{A}(\mathbf{a}_{.j})|=0$, by (4.10), because $\mathbf{A}(\mathbf{a}_{.j})$ is a matrix whose kth column is identical to its jth column.

(4.14) If $\mathbf{A}$ is a matrix whose columns are linearly dependent, then $|\mathbf{A}|=0$.

Proof. Let the kth column of $\mathbf{A}$ be $\mathbf{a}_{.k}=\sum_{j\neq k}\lambda_j\mathbf{a}_{.j}$. Then, by (4.12), $|\mathbf{A}|=\sum_{j\neq k}\lambda_j\,|\mathbf{A}(\mathbf{a}_{.j})|$. But, since $j\neq k$, every matrix $\mathbf{A}(\mathbf{a}_{.j})$ has identical columns in the jth and kth positions, whence $|\mathbf{A}(\mathbf{a}_{.j})|=0$ for all j, by (4.10), and therefore $|\mathbf{A}|=0$.

(4.15) Let $c_{ik}=(-1)^{i+k}\,|\mathbf{A}_{ik}|$ be the cofactor of a_{ik}. Then $\sum_i a_{ij}c_{ik}=0$. We express this result by saying that an expansion in terms of alien cofactors is identically zero.

Proof. The expansion $\sum_i a_{ij}c_{ik}$ is the expression we would obtain for the determinant of a matrix whose jth and kth columns are identical. But this determinant is necessarily zero by (4.10).

The result (4.15) may be stated equally in terms of an expansion by the column index. Thus we also have $\sum_j a_{ij}c_{kj}=0$ if $i\neq k$.

(4.16) If $\mathbf{A}$, $\mathbf{B}$ are $n\times n$ matrices, then $|\mathbf{AB}|=|\mathbf{A}|\,|\mathbf{B}|$.

Proof. The kth column of $\mathbf{C}=\mathbf{AB}$ is $\mathbf{c}_{.k}=\sum_j b_{jk}\mathbf{a}_{.j}$. Thus the determinant $|\mathbf{AB}|$ is

$$|\mathbf{C}|=\left|\left[\sum b_{j1}\mathbf{a}_{.j},\ldots,\sum b_{jn}\mathbf{a}_{.j}\right]\right|.$$

Expanding this according to (4.12) gives a sum of $n!$ determinants

$$\sum_{\alpha}|[b_{\alpha(1),1}\mathbf{a}_{.\alpha(1)},\ldots,b_{\alpha(n),n}\mathbf{a}_{.\alpha(n)}]|$$

$$=\sum_{\alpha}b_{\alpha(1),1}\ldots b_{\alpha(n),n}\,|[\mathbf{a}_{.\alpha(1)},\ldots,\mathbf{a}_{.\alpha(n)}]|$$

$$=\sum_{\alpha}\operatorname{sgn}(\alpha)b_{\alpha(1),1}\ldots b_{\alpha(n),n}\,|\mathbf{A}|,$$

where the last equality uses $|[\mathbf{a}_{,\alpha(1)},\ldots,\mathbf{a}_{,\alpha(n)}]|=\operatorname{sgn}(\alpha)\,|[\mathbf{a}_{.1},\ldots,\mathbf{a}_{.n}]|=\operatorname{sgn}(\alpha)\,|\mathbf{A}|$. The result of the expansion is recognizably the product $|\mathbf{B}|\,|\mathbf{A}|$.

(4.17) $|\mathbf{A}|\neq 0$ is the necessary and sufficient condition for the existence of the inverse $\mathbf{A}^{-1}=|\mathbf{A}|^{-1}\operatorname{adj}(\mathbf{A})$, where $\operatorname{adj}(\mathbf{A})=[c_{ji}]$ is the transposed matrix of the cofactors of $\mathbf{A}$.

Proof. If $\mathbf{A}^{-1}$ exists, then $|\mathbf{A}|\,|\mathbf{A}^{-1}|=|\mathbf{AA}^{-1}|=|\mathbf{I}|=1$, which shows that $|\mathbf{A}|\neq 0$. Conversely, let $|\mathbf{A}|\neq 0$ and consider the matrix $\mathbf{B}=[b_{ij}]$ where $b_{ij}=|\mathbf{A}|^{-1}c_{ji}$ with c_{ji} as the cofactor of a_{ji}. Then, according to the result (4.15) on expansions by alien cofactors, the ijth element of $\mathbf{AB}$ is $\sum a_{ik}b_{kj}=|\mathbf{A}|^{-1}\sum a_{ik}c_{jk}=\delta_{ij}$, where $\delta_{ij}=1$ if $i=j$ and $\delta_{ij}=0$ if $i\neq j$. Thus $\mathbf{AB}=\mathbf{I}$, and $\mathbf{A}^{-1}=\mathbf{B}$ exists.

We are now in a position to demonstrate that our present definition of a matrix determinant is conformable with the definition of the determinant of a self-adjoint transformation given in (3.74). Thus

(4.18) If $\mathbf{A}$ is a symmetric matrix with characteristic roots $\lambda_1,\ldots,\lambda_r$ of multiplicities $m_1,\ldots,m_r$, then $|\mathbf{A}|=\prod\lambda_i^{m_i}$.

Proof. Let $\boldsymbol{\Lambda}$ be a diagonal matrix containing the roots of $\mathbf{A}$. Then, by (3.75), $\boldsymbol{\Lambda}=\mathbf{C}'\mathbf{AC}$ where $\mathbf{C}$ is an orthonormal matrix comprising the characteristic vectors of $\mathbf{A}$. Therefore $\prod\lambda_i^{m_i}=|\boldsymbol{\Lambda}|=|\mathbf{C}'\mathbf{AC}|=|\mathbf{C}'|\,|\mathbf{C}|\,|\mathbf{A}|=|\mathbf{C}'\mathbf{C}|\,|\mathbf{A}|=|\mathbf{A}|$, since $\mathbf{C}'\mathbf{C}=\mathbf{I}$, and $|\mathbf{I}|=1$.

MATRIX TRACES

(4.19) The trace of a square $n \times n$ matrix is the sum of its diagonal elements, written $\text{Trace}(\mathbf{A}) = \sum a_{ii}$.

A few results which follow readily from the definition may be listed together.

(4.20)
1. $\text{Trace}(\mathbf{A}+\mathbf{B}) = \text{Trace}(\mathbf{A}) + \text{Trace}(\mathbf{B})$.
2. $\text{Trace}(\mathbf{A}') = \text{Trace}(\mathbf{A})$.
3. $\text{Trace}(\lambda\mathbf{A}) = \lambda\,\text{Trace}(\mathbf{A})$.
4. $\text{Trace}(\mathbf{AB}) = \text{Trace}(\mathbf{BA})$.

The last of these results may be extended to give $\text{Trace}(\mathbf{ABC}) = \text{Trace}(\mathbf{BCA}) = \text{Trace}(\mathbf{CAB}) = \sum_i \sum_k \sum_j a_{ik} b_{kj} c_{ji}$. More generally, we might say that the trace of a matrix product is invariant with respect to the cyclical permutation of its factors.

A result which is similar to one given for determinants in (4.18) and which also shows that the definition of a matrix trace is conformable with the definition of the trace of a self-adjoint transformation, given in (3.74), is as follows:

(4.21) If $\mathbf{A}$ is a symmetric matrix with characteristic roots $\lambda_1, \ldots, \lambda_r$ of multiplicities $m_1, \ldots, m_r$, then $\text{Trace}(\mathbf{A}) = \sum m_i \lambda_i$.

Proof. Let $\mathbf{\Lambda} = \mathbf{C}'\mathbf{AC}$ be the diagonal matrix containing the roots of $\mathbf{A}$, given in (3.75). Then $\sum m_i\lambda_i = \text{Trace}(\mathbf{\Lambda}) = \text{Trace}(\mathbf{C}'\mathbf{AC}) = \text{Trace}(\mathbf{CC}'\mathbf{A}) = \text{Trace}(\mathbf{A})$, since $\mathbf{C}'\mathbf{C} = \mathbf{I}$.

Another useful result is that

(4.22) If $\mathbf{A}$ is a symmetric idempotent matrix such that $\mathbf{A} = \mathbf{A}^2 = \mathbf{A}'$, then $\text{Rank}(\mathbf{A}) = \text{Trace}(\mathbf{A})$.

This follows from the fact that the $r = \text{Rank}(\mathbf{A})$ non-zero roots of the matrix are all units, whence their sum is $\text{Trace}(\mathbf{A}) = r = \text{Rank}(\mathbf{A})$.

TENSOR PRODUCTS

Consider a matrix equation in $\mathbf{X}$ and $\mathbf{Y}$ of the form

(4.23) $$\mathbf{Y} = \mathbf{AXB}'$$

where

$$\mathbf{Y}=[y_{kl}] \text{ is an } r\times s \text{ matrix,}$$
$$\mathbf{X}=[x_{ij}] \text{ is an } m\times n \text{ matrix,}$$
$$\mathbf{A}=[a_{ki}] \text{ is an } r\times m \text{ matrix, and}$$
$$\mathbf{B}=[b_{lj}] \text{ is an } s\times n \text{ matrix.}$$

If λ_1, λ_2 are scalars and $\mathbf{X}_1$, $\mathbf{X}_2$ are both $m\times n$ matrices, we can write $\mathbf{A}(\lambda_1\mathbf{X}_1+\lambda_2\mathbf{X}_2)\mathbf{B}'=\lambda_1\mathbf{A}\mathbf{X}_1\mathbf{B}'+\lambda_2\mathbf{A}\mathbf{X}_2\mathbf{B}'$. This shows that the equation (4.23) constitutes a linear transformation from $\mathbf{X}$ to $\mathbf{Y}$; so that the set of transformations of this form must be isomorphic to a set of ordinary matrix transformations from one co-ordinate vector space to another. Thus, when we write $y_{kl}=\sum_i\sum_j b_{lj}a_{ki}x_{ij}$, we can regard y_{kl} and x_{ij} as elements of $rs\times 1$ and $mn\times 1$ vectors respectively, and the product $b_{lj}a_{ki}$ as an element of an $rs\times mn$ matrix. The position of $b_{lj}a_{ki}$ within this matrix is determined by the ordering of the elements y_{kl}, x_{ij} within their respective vectors. When we adopt a lexicographic ordering using the column subscripts of these elements as their leading indices, we derive the expression

(4.24)
$$\begin{bmatrix} \mathbf{y}_{.1} \\ \mathbf{y}_{.2} \\ \cdot \\ \cdot \\ \cdot \\ \mathbf{y}_{.s} \end{bmatrix} = \begin{bmatrix} b_{11}\mathbf{A}, b_{12}\mathbf{A}, \dots, b_{1n}\mathbf{A} \\ b_{21}\mathbf{A}, b_{22}\mathbf{A}, \dots, b_{2n}\mathbf{A} \\ \cdot \quad \cdot \quad\quad \cdot \\ \cdot \quad \cdot \quad\quad \cdot \\ \cdot \quad \cdot \quad\quad \cdot \\ b_{s1}\mathbf{A}, b_{s2}\mathbf{A}, \dots, b_{sn}\mathbf{A} \end{bmatrix} \begin{bmatrix} \mathbf{x}_{.1} \\ \mathbf{x}_{.2} \\ \cdot \\ \cdot \\ \cdot \\ \mathbf{x}_{.n} \end{bmatrix},$$

where $\mathbf{y}_{.l}$, $\mathbf{x}_{.j}$ are the lth and jth columns of $\mathbf{Y}$ and $\mathbf{X}$ respectively. The expression is written in summary notation as

(4.25)
$$\mathbf{Y}^c=(\mathbf{B}\otimes\mathbf{A})\mathbf{X}^c.$$

Thus, by writing $\mathbf{Y}=\mathbf{AXB}'$, we obtain the identity

(4.26)
$$(\mathbf{AXB}')^c=(\mathbf{B}\otimes\mathbf{A})\mathbf{X}^c.$$

Although the method by which the equations (4.24) and (4.25) are derived from (4.23) is self evident, there is a considerable amount of algebraic detail which may be developed in respect of these and similar expressions. The relevant algebra is known as the algebra of tensor products. We may begin its development with an abstract definition.

(4.27) A tensor product, mapping from $\mathcal{V}\times\mathcal{W}$ onto $\mathcal{T}$, where $\mathcal{V}$, $\mathcal{W}$, $\mathcal{T}$ are spaces defined over the same field, is a vector-valued bilinear function, written $(\mathbf{v}\otimes\mathbf{w})\in\mathcal{T}$ for $\mathbf{v}\in\mathcal{V}$, $\mathbf{w}\in\mathcal{W}$, which has the following properties:

1. $\mathbf{v}\otimes(\lambda\mathbf{w}_1+\mu\mathbf{w}_2)=\lambda(\mathbf{v}\otimes\mathbf{w}_1)+\mu(\mathbf{v}\otimes\mathbf{w}_2)$,
2. $(\lambda\mathbf{v}_1+\mu\mathbf{v}_2)\otimes\mathbf{w}=\lambda(\mathbf{v}_1\otimes\mathbf{w})+\mu(\mathbf{v}_2\otimes\mathbf{w})$,
3. $\mathbf{v}\otimes\mathbf{w}=\mathbf{0}$ only if $\mathbf{v}=\mathbf{0}$, $\mathbf{w}=\mathbf{0}$, or both.

The conditions 1 and 2 of this definition imply that $\mathbf{0}\otimes\mathbf{w}=\mathbf{v}\otimes\mathbf{0}=\mathbf{0}\otimes\mathbf{0}$ which is the converse of 3. Thus, for example, by the first condition, we get $\mathbf{v}\otimes\mathbf{w}=\mathbf{v}\otimes(\mathbf{w}+\mathbf{0})=(\mathbf{v}\otimes\mathbf{w})+(\mathbf{v}\otimes\mathbf{0})$, which implies that $\mathbf{v}\otimes\mathbf{0}=\mathbf{0}\otimes\mathbf{0}$, which is the zero element in $\mathcal{T}$. The definition also implies that

(4.28) The tensor space $\mathcal{T}=\mathcal{V}\otimes\mathcal{W}$ is the set of all sums $\sum_i\sum_j\lambda_{ij}(\mathbf{v}_j\otimes\mathbf{w}_i)$ which have a finite number of non-zero coefficients.

This is the result of defining $\mathcal{T}$ as a vector space which must necessarily contain every arbitrary linear combination of its own elements. We should note that not every element of $\mathcal{V}\otimes\mathcal{W}$ of the form $\sum\sum\lambda_{ij}(\mathbf{v}_j\otimes\mathbf{w}_i)$ can be expressed as $\mathbf{v}\otimes\mathbf{w}=(\sum_j\mu_j\mathbf{v}_j\otimes\sum_i\eta_i\mathbf{w}_i)$; for this is only possible if $\lambda_{ij}=\mu_j\eta_i$ for all i, j.

(4.29) If $[\mathbf{v}_1,\ldots,\mathbf{v}_n]$ and $[\mathbf{w}_1,\ldots,\mathbf{w}_m]$ are bases of $\mathcal{V}$ and $\mathcal{W}$ respectively, then the products $\mathbf{v}_j\otimes\mathbf{w}_i$, $j=1,\ldots,n$; $i=1,\ldots,m$ form a basis of $\mathcal{T}=\mathcal{V}\otimes\mathcal{W}$.

Proof. Every vector of $\mathcal{T}$ may be written in the form $\sum_i\sum_j\lambda_{ij}(\mathbf{v}_j\otimes\mathbf{w}_i)$, which shows that the set of tensor products spans the space. The set is also linearly independent. For, if $(\mathbf{0}\otimes\mathbf{0})=\sum_i\sum_j\lambda_{ij}(\mathbf{v}_j\otimes\mathbf{w}_i)=(\sum_j\mu_j\mathbf{v}_j\otimes\sum_i\eta_i\mathbf{w}_i)$, we must have $\mu_j=0$ for all j, or $\eta_i=0$ for all i, and hence $\lambda_{ij}=\mu_j\eta_i=0$ for all i, j.

It follows immediately from (4.29) that

(4.30) $\mathrm{Dim}(\mathcal{V}\otimes\mathcal{W})=\mathrm{Dim}\,\mathcal{V}\times\mathrm{Dim}\,\mathcal{W}$.

If $\mathbf{x}\in\mathcal{R}^n$, $\mathbf{y}\in\mathcal{R}^m$ are co-ordinate vectors such that $\mathbf{x}'=[x_1,\ldots,x_n]$, $\mathbf{y}'=[y_1,\ldots,y_m]$, then any formal array of the products $y_iq_{ij}x_j$, with $q_{ij}\neq 0$ for all i, j, constitutes a tensor product of $\mathbf{x}$ and $\mathbf{y}$. Our practical concern, however, will be the tensor product of $\mathbf{x}$ and $\mathbf{y}$ defined by $(\mathbf{x}\otimes\mathbf{y})=[y_ix_j]^c=(\mathbf{y}\mathbf{x}')^c$, which is formed by the lexicographic ordering of the elements y_ix_j and which constitutes a vector in $\mathcal{R}^n\otimes\mathcal{R}^m=\mathcal{R}^{nm}$. Under this definition, the vectorization $\mathbf{X}^c$ of any $m\times n$ matrix $\mathbf{X}$ is an element of the tensor space $\mathcal{R}^n\otimes\mathcal{R}^m$.

Transformations of tensor products

(4.31) If $\mathbf{A}\in\mathcal{L}(\mathcal{W},\mathcal{Q})$, $\mathbf{B}\in\mathcal{L}(\mathcal{V},\mathcal{P})$ are linear transformations, then the Kronecker product of $\mathbf{B}$ and $\mathbf{A}$, written $\mathbf{B}\otimes\mathbf{A}$, is a linear transformation from $(\mathcal{V}\otimes\mathcal{W})$ to $(\mathcal{P}\otimes\mathcal{Q})$ such that $(\mathbf{B}\otimes\mathbf{A})(\mathbf{v}\otimes\mathbf{w})=(\mathbf{B}\mathbf{v}\otimes\mathbf{A}\mathbf{w})$ for $\mathbf{v}\in\mathcal{V}$, $\mathbf{w}\in\mathcal{W}$.

The following relationships are easily established from the definition of $\mathbf{B}\otimes\mathbf{A}$.

(4.32)
1. $(\mathbf{B}\otimes\mathbf{A})(\mathbf{D}\otimes\mathbf{C})=\mathbf{BD}\otimes\mathbf{AC}$.
2. $\mathbf{B}\otimes(\mathbf{D}+\mathbf{C})=(\mathbf{B}\otimes\mathbf{D})+(\mathbf{B}\otimes\mathbf{C})$.
3. $(\mathbf{B}+\mathbf{D})\otimes\mathbf{C}=(\mathbf{B}\otimes\mathbf{C})+(\mathbf{D}\otimes\mathbf{C})$.
4. $\alpha\mathbf{B}\otimes\beta\mathbf{A}=\alpha\beta(\mathbf{B}\otimes\mathbf{A})$.
5. $\mathbf{0}\otimes\mathbf{A}=\mathbf{A}\otimes\mathbf{0}=\mathbf{0}\otimes\mathbf{0}$.
6. $\mathbf{B}\otimes\mathbf{A}=(\mathbf{B}\otimes\mathbf{I})(\mathbf{I}\otimes\mathbf{A})=(\mathbf{I}\otimes\mathbf{A})(\mathbf{B}\otimes\mathbf{I})$.
7. $(\mathbf{B}\otimes\mathbf{A})^{-1}=\mathbf{B}^{-1}\otimes\mathbf{A}^{-1}$.

It follows immediately from (4.30) that

$$\text{Rank}(\mathbf{B}\otimes\mathbf{A})=\text{Rank}(\mathbf{B})\text{Rank}(\mathbf{A}). \tag{4.33}$$

The transformation $(\mathbf{B}\otimes\mathbf{A})\in\mathcal{L}(\mathcal{V}\otimes\mathcal{W},\mathcal{P}\otimes\mathcal{Q})$ can be represented in terms of a matrix of order $\text{Dim}(\mathcal{P}\otimes\mathcal{Q})\times\text{Dim}(\mathcal{V}\otimes\mathcal{W})$ once bases are chosen. We may specify the bases $[\mathbf{v}_j\otimes\mathbf{w}_i;\ i=1,\ldots,m;\ j=1,\ldots,n]$ and $[\mathbf{p}_l\otimes\mathbf{q}_k;\ k=1,\ldots,r;\ l=1,\ldots,s]$ for $\mathcal{V}\otimes\mathcal{W}$ and $\mathcal{P}\otimes\mathcal{Q}$ respectively. The ijth column of the matrix will, by definition, contain the co-ordinates, relative to the basis of $\mathcal{P}\otimes\mathcal{Q}$, of the image of the ijth basis vector of $\mathcal{V}\otimes\mathcal{W}$ under the mappings of $\mathbf{B}\otimes\mathbf{A}$. The elements of this column are therefore the scalars $b_{lj}a_{ki}$ that are given by the relationship $(\mathbf{B}\otimes\mathbf{A})(\mathbf{v}_j\otimes\mathbf{w}_i)=\sum_l b_{lj}\mathbf{p}_l\otimes\sum_k a_{ki}\mathbf{q}_k=\sum_k\sum_l b_{lj}a_{ki}(\mathbf{p}_l\otimes\mathbf{q}_k)$. It remains to determine the ordering of the matrix columns and to determine the ordering of the elements within these columns which is also the ordering of the matrix rows. These orderings will depend upon the choice of ordering for the bases of $\mathcal{V}\otimes\mathcal{W}$ and $\mathcal{P}\otimes\mathcal{Q}$. In fact, we conventionally adopt a lexicographic ordering with the indices j and l as the leading classifiers of the two bases respectively. The basis of $\mathcal{V}\otimes\mathcal{W}$ is therefore written in the order

$$(\mathbf{v}_1\otimes\mathbf{w}_1),(\mathbf{v}_1\otimes\mathbf{w}_2),\ldots,(\mathbf{v}_1\otimes\mathbf{w}_m),(\mathbf{v}_2\otimes\mathbf{w}_1),$$
$$\ldots,(\mathbf{v}_2\otimes\mathbf{w}_m),\ldots,(\mathbf{v}_n\otimes\mathbf{w}_1),\ldots,(\mathbf{v}_n\otimes\mathbf{w}_m),$$

whilst the basis of $\mathcal{P}\otimes\mathcal{Q}$ is written, likewise, in the order

$$(\mathbf{p}_1\otimes\mathbf{q}_1),(\mathbf{p}_1\otimes\mathbf{q}_2),\ldots,(\mathbf{p}_1\otimes\mathbf{q}_r),(\mathbf{p}_2\otimes\mathbf{q}_1),$$
$$\ldots,(\mathbf{p}_2\otimes\mathbf{q}_r),\ldots,(\mathbf{p}_s\otimes\mathbf{q}_1),\ldots,(\mathbf{p}_s\otimes\mathbf{q}_r).$$

Thus, in each column of the matrix, the indices i, j are fixed whilst the indices k, l are varied. The lexicographic ordering of the basis of $\mathcal{P}\otimes\mathcal{Q}$ implies that the index k varies between elements of the column and that the index l varies in intervals of r elements. The ordering of the basis of $\mathcal{V}\otimes\mathcal{W}$

gives, likewise, the ordering of the columns of the matrix. Thus we derive a matrix array of a form that is given in (4.24).

It is possible to establish, with reference to the matrix form of $(\mathbf{B}\otimes\mathbf{A})$ given in (4.24), that

(4.34) If $\mathbf{A}$ and $\mathbf{B}$ are matrices of orders $m\times m$ and $n\times n$ respectively, then $|\mathbf{B}\otimes\mathbf{A}|=|\mathbf{B}|^n\,|\mathbf{A}|^m$.

For this purpose we consider the expansion $|\mathbf{B}\otimes\mathbf{A}|=\sum_\alpha\sum_\beta \operatorname{sgn}(\alpha)\operatorname{sgn}(\beta)$ $[\prod_i\prod_j b_{\beta(j),j}a_{\alpha(i),i}]$ which derives from (4.5).

A more specific result is that

(4.35) If $\mathbf{A}$ and $\mathbf{B}$ are symmetric matrices with roots, including multiplicities, of $\lambda_1,\ldots,\lambda_m$ and $\mu_1,\ldots,\mu_n$ respectively, then $|\mathbf{B}\otimes\mathbf{A}|=\prod_i\prod_j\mu_j\lambda_i=(\prod_j\mu_j)^n(\prod_i\lambda_i)^m=|\mathbf{B}|^n\,|\mathbf{A}|^m$.

Proof. Let $\mathbf{w}_1,\ldots,\mathbf{w}_m$ and $\mathbf{v}_1,\ldots,\mathbf{v}_n$ be the characteristic vectors corresponding to the roots of $\mathbf{A}$ and $\mathbf{B}$ respectively. Then, since $\mathbf{A}\mathbf{w}_i=\lambda_i\mathbf{w}_i$, $\mathbf{B}\mathbf{v}_j=\mu_j\mathbf{v}_j$, we have $(\mathbf{B}\otimes\mathbf{A})(\mathbf{v}_j\otimes\mathbf{w}_i)=\mu_j\lambda_i(\mathbf{v}_j\otimes\mathbf{w}_i)$ for all i,j; whence the roots of $\mathbf{B}\otimes\mathbf{A}$ are $u_j\lambda_i$; $i=1,\ldots,m$; $j=1,\ldots,n$. It follows from (4.18) that the determinant of the symmetric matrix $\mathbf{B}\otimes\mathbf{A}$ is $\prod_i\prod_j\mu_j\lambda_i$.

We can also readily deduce from the form of the matrix that

(4.36) $\operatorname{Trace}(\mathbf{B}\otimes\mathbf{A})=\operatorname{Trace}(\mathbf{B})\operatorname{Trace}(\mathbf{A})$.

Inner products

We may define an inner product on the tensor space $\mathcal{T}=\mathcal{V}\otimes\mathcal{W}$ in precisely the way that we define an inner product on an ordinary vector space. Thus, for example, if $\mathcal{T}=\mathcal{R}^n\otimes\mathcal{R}^m$ is a co-ordinate space and $\mathbf{Y}^c,\mathbf{X}^c\in\mathcal{T}$ are two vectors, we may form the ordinary inner product $\langle\mathbf{Y}^c,\mathbf{X}^c\rangle_{\mathbf{I}\otimes\mathbf{I}}=\mathbf{Y}^{c\prime}\mathbf{X}^c=\sum_i\sum_j y_{ij}x_{ij}=\operatorname{Trace}(\mathbf{Y}'\mathbf{X})$. More generally, if $\mathbf{Q}$ is a positive-definite matrix of order $mn\times mn$, we may form the inner product $\langle\mathbf{Y}^c,\mathbf{X}^c\rangle_{\mathbf{Q}}=\mathbf{Y}^{c\prime}\mathbf{Q}\mathbf{X}^c$. Our primary concern, however, is not with the broadly defined class of inner products but with the specialized class of natural inner products.

(4.37) A natural inner product on $\mathcal{T}=\mathcal{V}\otimes\mathcal{W}$ has the form $\langle\mathbf{v}_1\otimes\mathbf{w}_1,\mathbf{v}_2\otimes\mathbf{w}_2\rangle=\langle\mathbf{v}_1,\mathbf{v}_2\rangle^{\mathcal{V}}\cdot\langle\mathbf{w}_1,\mathbf{w}_2\rangle^{\mathcal{W}}$.

We will show that

(4.38) If $\mathbf{A}$, $\mathbf{B}$ are positive-definite matrices of orders $m\times m$ and $n\times n$ respectively and if $\mathbf{Y}^c$, $\mathbf{X}^c$ are vectors in $\mathcal{T}=\mathcal{R}^n\otimes\mathcal{R}^m$, then $\langle\mathbf{Y}^c,\mathbf{X}^c\rangle_{\mathbf{B}\otimes\mathbf{A}}=\mathbf{Y}^{c\prime}(\mathbf{B}\otimes\mathbf{A})\mathbf{X}^c=\operatorname{Trace}(\mathbf{Y}'\mathbf{A}\mathbf{X}\mathbf{B}')$ is a natural inner product on $\mathcal{T}$.

Proof. We use the identity $(\mathbf{AXB}')^c = (\mathbf{B}\otimes\mathbf{A})\mathbf{X}^c$ of (4.26) to obtain $\mathbf{Y}^{c\prime}(\mathbf{B}\otimes\mathbf{A})\mathbf{X}^c = \mathbf{Y}^{c\prime}(\mathbf{AXB}')^c = \text{Trace}(\mathbf{Y}'\mathbf{AXB}')$. Now let $\mathbf{Y}^c = (\mathbf{v}_1\otimes\mathbf{w}_1) = (\mathbf{w}_1\mathbf{v}_1')^c$ and $\mathbf{X}^c = (\mathbf{v}_2\otimes\mathbf{w}_2) = (\mathbf{w}_2\mathbf{v}_2')^c$. Then $\mathbf{Y}^{c\prime}(\mathbf{B}\otimes\mathbf{A})\mathbf{X}^c = \text{Trace}(\mathbf{v}_1\mathbf{w}_1'\mathbf{A}\mathbf{w}_2\mathbf{v}_2'\mathbf{B}') = (\mathbf{w}_1'\mathbf{A}\mathbf{w}_2)(\mathbf{v}_1'\mathbf{B}\mathbf{v}_2)$. This enables us to write $\langle\mathbf{Y}^c, \mathbf{X}^c\rangle_{\mathbf{B}\otimes\mathbf{A}} = \langle\mathbf{v}_1\otimes\mathbf{w}_1, \mathbf{v}_2\otimes\mathbf{w}_2\rangle_{\mathbf{B}\otimes\mathbf{A}} = \langle\mathbf{v}_1, \mathbf{v}_2\rangle_{\mathbf{B}}\langle\mathbf{w}_1, \mathbf{w}_2\rangle_{\mathbf{A}}$, which shows that we have a natural inner product.

(4.39) For any natural inner product on $\mathcal{T} = \mathcal{V}\otimes\mathcal{W}$, the adjoint of $(\mathbf{B}\otimes\mathbf{A})$ is $(\mathbf{B}\otimes\mathbf{A})^* = \mathbf{B}^*\otimes\mathbf{A}^*$.

Proof. For a natural inner product we have $\langle\mathbf{v}_1\otimes\mathbf{w}_1, (\mathbf{B}\otimes\mathbf{A})(\mathbf{v}_2\otimes\mathbf{w}_2)\rangle = \langle\mathbf{v}_1, \mathbf{B}\mathbf{v}_2\rangle\langle\mathbf{w}_1, \mathbf{A}\mathbf{w}_2\rangle = \langle\mathbf{B}^*\mathbf{v}_1, \mathbf{v}_2\rangle\langle\mathbf{A}^*\mathbf{w}_1, \mathbf{w}_2\rangle = \langle(\mathbf{B}^*\otimes\mathbf{A}^*)(\mathbf{v}_1\otimes\mathbf{w}_1), \mathbf{v}_2\otimes\mathbf{w}_2\rangle$, whence $(\mathbf{B}\otimes\mathbf{A})^* = \mathbf{B}^*\otimes\mathbf{A}^*$.

When we interpret this result (4.39) in terms of the ordinary inner product on $\mathcal{T} = \mathcal{R}^n\otimes\mathcal{R}^m$ we obtain the result that

(4.40) $(\mathbf{B}\otimes\mathbf{A})' = \mathbf{B}'\otimes\mathbf{A}'$.

The tensor commutator

In order to facilitate the subsequent development of the theory of matrix differential calculus, we shall now define the tensor commutator and investigate its properties.

(4.41) The tensor commutator is a transformation Ⓣ defined on $\mathcal{T} = \mathcal{V}\otimes\mathcal{W}$ such that, for any vector of $\mathcal{T}$ of the form $\mathbf{v}\otimes\mathbf{w}$, we have Ⓣ $(\mathbf{v}\otimes\mathbf{w}) = \mathbf{w}\otimes\mathbf{v}$.

Clearly, both $\mathbf{v}\otimes\mathbf{w}$ and $\mathbf{w}\otimes\mathbf{v}$ are elements of $\mathcal{T} = \mathcal{V}\otimes\mathcal{W} = \mathcal{W}\otimes\mathcal{V}$. Thus

(4.42) If Ⓣ is the tensor commutator on $\mathcal{V}\otimes\mathcal{W}$ such that Ⓣ $(\mathbf{v}\otimes\mathbf{w}) = \mathbf{w}\otimes\mathbf{v}$, we may define an inverse commutator by Ⓣ$^{-1}$ $(\mathbf{w}\otimes\mathbf{v}) =$ Ⓣ$^{-1}$ Ⓣ $(\mathbf{v}\otimes\mathbf{w}) = \mathbf{v}\otimes\mathbf{w}$.

However,

(4.43) If $\mathcal{T} = \mathcal{V}\otimes\mathcal{V}$, then Ⓣ$^{-1}$Ⓣ$(\mathbf{v}_1\otimes\mathbf{v}_2) =$ Ⓣ$^2(\mathbf{v}_1\otimes\mathbf{v}_2)$, so that Ⓣ$^2 = \mathbf{I}\otimes\mathbf{I}$ and Ⓣ = Ⓣ$^{-1}$.

In practice, we are only concerned with tensor commutators defined on co-ordinate spaces. Thus

(4.44) If $\mathcal{T} = \mathcal{R}^n\otimes\mathcal{R}^m$ and $\mathbf{v}\in\mathcal{R}^n$, $\mathbf{w}\in\mathcal{R}^m$ are any two vectors, then Ⓣ$(\mathbf{v}\otimes\mathbf{w}) =$ Ⓣ$(\mathbf{w}\mathbf{v}')^c = (\mathbf{v}\mathbf{w}')^c$. More generally, if $\mathbf{X}^c\in\mathcal{T}$, then Ⓣ$\mathbf{X}^c = \mathbf{X}'^c$.

(4.45) The tensor commutator on $\mathcal{T} = \mathcal{R}^n\otimes\mathcal{R}^m$ is an orthonormal matrix transformation in respect of the ordinary inner product, so that Ⓣ$^{-1} =$ Ⓣ$'$.

Proof. For the ordinary inner product on $\mathcal{T}=\mathcal{R}^n\otimes\mathcal{R}^m$, we have $\langle \mathbf{V}_1\otimes\mathbf{w}_1,\ \mathbf{v}_2\otimes\mathbf{w}_2\rangle_{\mathbf{I}\otimes\mathbf{I}}=(\mathbf{w}_1\mathbf{v}_1')^{c\prime}(\mathbf{w}_2\mathbf{v}_2')^c=\text{Trace}(\mathbf{v}_1\mathbf{w}_1'\mathbf{w}_2\mathbf{v}_2')\mathbf{w}_1'\mathbf{w}_2\mathbf{v}_1'\mathbf{v}_2$ and $\langle \textcircled{T}(\mathbf{v}_1\otimes\mathbf{w}_1),\ \textcircled{T}(\mathbf{v}_2\otimes\mathbf{w}_2)\rangle_{\mathbf{I}\otimes\mathbf{I}}=(\mathbf{v}_1\mathbf{w}_1')^{c\prime}(\mathbf{v}_2\mathbf{w}_2')^c=\text{Trace}(\mathbf{w}_1\mathbf{v}_1'\mathbf{v}_2\mathbf{w}_2')=\mathbf{v}_1'\mathbf{v}_2\mathbf{w}_1'\mathbf{w}_2$. Hence $\langle \mathbf{v}_1\otimes\mathbf{w}_1,\ \mathbf{v}_2\otimes\mathbf{w}_2\rangle_{\mathbf{I}\otimes\mathbf{I}}=\langle \textcircled{T}(\mathbf{v}_1\otimes\mathbf{w}_1),\ \textcircled{T}(\mathbf{v}_2\otimes\mathbf{w}_2)\rangle_{\mathbf{I}\otimes\mathbf{I}}$. But if we use the fact that the adjoint of $\textcircled{T}$ in respect of the ordinary inner product is $\textcircled{T}'$, we can augment this identity to get $\langle \mathbf{v}_1\otimes\mathbf{w}_1,\ \textcircled{T}^{-1}\textcircled{T}(\mathbf{v}_2\otimes\mathbf{w}_2)\rangle=\langle \mathbf{w}_1,\ \mathbf{v}_2\otimes\mathbf{w}_2\rangle=\langle \textcircled{T}(\mathbf{v}_1\otimes\mathbf{w}_1),\ \textcircled{T}(\mathbf{v}_2\otimes\mathbf{w}_2)\rangle=\langle \mathbf{v}_1\otimes\mathbf{w}_1,\ \textcircled{T}'\textcircled{T}(\mathbf{v}_2\otimes\mathbf{w}_2)\rangle$. This shows that $\textcircled{T}^{-1}\textcircled{T}=\textcircled{T}'\textcircled{T}$, whence $\textcircled{T}^{-1}=\textcircled{T}'$.

Example. Let $\mathcal{T}=\mathcal{R}^2\otimes\mathcal{R}^2$. Then

$$\textcircled{T}=\begin{bmatrix}1, & 0, & 0, & 0\\ 0, & 0, & 1, & 0\\ 0, & 1, & 0, & 0\\ 0, & 0, & 0, & 1\end{bmatrix}$$

is a tensor commutator defined on $\mathcal{T}$. Thus, if $[y_1x_1,\ y_2x_1,\ y_1x_2,\ y_2x_2]'=(\mathbf{x}\otimes\mathbf{y})\in\mathcal{T}$, we have $\textcircled{T}(\mathbf{x}\otimes\mathbf{y})=(\mathbf{y}\otimes\mathbf{x})=[y_1x_1,\ y_1x_2,\ y_2x_1,\ y_2x_2]'$. Observe that, in accordance with (4.43), *we have $\textcircled{T}^2=\mathbf{I}_2\otimes\mathbf{I}_2=\mathbf{I}_4$.*

In using the tensor commutator, it is appropriate to define the row vector $\mathbf{X}^r=[\mathbf{x}_1,\mathbf{x}_2,\ldots,\mathbf{x}_{m.}]$ which is formed from the rows of the $m\times n$ matrix $\mathbf{X}$ in a manner which is analogous to the formation of $\mathbf{X}^c$ from the columns of $\mathbf{X}$. It is easy to confirm that $\mathbf{X}^r=\mathbf{X}'^{c\prime}$. We use $\mathbf{X}^r$ in the following list of the properties of $\textcircled{T}$:

(4.46) If $\mathbf{X}^r=[\mathbf{x}_{1.},\mathbf{x}_{2.},\ldots,\mathbf{x}_{m.}]=\mathbf{X}'^{c\prime}$, then

1. $\textcircled{T}\mathbf{X}^c=\mathbf{X}'^c=\mathbf{X}^{r\prime}$,
2. $\textcircled{T}'\mathbf{X}'^c=\mathbf{X}^c=\mathbf{X}'^{r\prime}$,
3. $\mathbf{X}^r\textcircled{T}=\mathbf{X}'^r$,
4. $\mathbf{X}'^r\textcircled{T}'=\mathbf{X}^r$.

The results 1. and 2. repeat the definitions of $\textcircled{T}$ and $\textcircled{T}'=\textcircled{T}^{-1}$. The results 3. and 4. are simply transpositions of the results 2. and 1. respectively.

The next two results are also easily accessible.

(4.47) If $\mathbf{Y}=\mathbf{AXB}'$, so that $\mathbf{Y}^c=(\mathbf{B}\otimes\mathbf{A})\mathbf{X}^c$, then $\textcircled{T}\mathbf{Y}^c=\mathbf{Y}'^c=(\mathbf{A}\otimes\mathbf{B})\mathbf{X}'^c$.

(4.48) If $\mathbf{Y}=\mathbf{AXB}'$, then $\mathbf{Y}^r=\mathbf{X}^r(\mathbf{A}'\otimes\mathbf{B}')$ and $\mathbf{Y}^r\textcircled{T}=\mathbf{Y}'^r=\mathbf{X}'^r(\mathbf{B}'\otimes\mathbf{A}')$.

The first of these may be verified by considering $\textcircled{T}(\mathbf{B}\otimes\mathbf{A})(\mathbf{v}\otimes\mathbf{w})=\textcircled{T}(\mathbf{Bv}\otimes\mathbf{Aw})=(\mathbf{Aw}\otimes\mathbf{Bv})=(\mathbf{A}\otimes\mathbf{B})(\mathbf{w}\otimes\mathbf{v})$. The second may be obtained by transposing the first. Thus $\mathbf{Y}^r=\mathbf{Y}'^{c\prime}=\mathbf{X}'^{c\prime}(\mathbf{A}'\otimes\mathbf{B}')=\mathbf{X}^r(\mathbf{A}'\otimes\mathbf{B}')$, and $\mathbf{Y}'^r=\mathbf{Y}^{c\prime}=\mathbf{X}^{c\prime}(\mathbf{B}'\otimes\mathbf{A}')=\mathbf{X}'^r(\mathbf{B}'\otimes\mathbf{A}')$.

MATRIX DIFFERENTIAL CALCULUS

One of the more onerous tasks of multivariate statistical analysis is that of finding the first-order and second-order partial derivatives of complicated likelihood functions involving vectors or matrices as their arguments. To lighten our burden, it is appropriate to compile some of the results that we shall need later.

We shall consider both derivatives of vector functions of vectors and derivatives of matrix functions of matrices. The case of vector functions of vectors subsumes scalar functions of vectors and vector functions of scalars. Likewise, the case of matrix functions of matrices subsumes scalar and vector functions of matrices as well as matrix functions of scalars or vectors.

The derivative of a vector function of a vector is easily defined. Consider $\mathbf{y}=\mathbf{y}(\mathbf{x})$ where $\mathbf{y}'=[y_1, \ldots, y_m]$ and $\mathbf{x}'=[x_1, \ldots, x_n]$. The derivative $\partial\mathbf{y}/\partial\mathbf{x}$ is simply an $m\times n$ array of the elements $\partial y_i/\partial x_j$. Thus it is a matrix function of $\mathbf{x}$ which assumes specific values in the set $\mathscr{L}(\mathscr{R}^n, \mathscr{R}^m)$ of linear transformations mapping from the space $\mathscr{R}^n$ containing $\mathbf{x}$ to the space $\mathscr{R}^m$ containing $\mathbf{y}$.

The problem of defining the derivative of a matrix function is more complicated. Consider the function $\mathbf{Y}=\mathbf{Y}(\mathbf{X})$ where $\mathbf{Y}=[y_{kl}]$ is an $r\times s$ matrix and $\mathbf{X}=[x_{ij}]$ is an $m\times n$ matrix. On differentiating the elements of $\mathbf{Y}$ with respect to the elements of $\mathbf{X}$, we obtain a set of $rsmn$ derivatives of the form $\partial y_{kl}/\partial x_{ij}$. Since each of these derivatives has four subscripts, there is no immediately obvious way of containing them within a formal array. We shall examine two different approaches to the problem.

The classical approach of Dwyer and MacPhail avoids the difficulties inherent in a fully fledged theory of matrix differential calculus by confining attention to the component derivatives $\partial y_{kl}/\partial\mathbf{X}$ and $\partial\mathbf{Y}/\partial x_{ij}$. The former is defined as an $n\times m$ matrix of the same order as $\mathbf{X}'$ whose jith element is $\partial y_{kl}/\partial x_{ij}$. The latter is defined as an $r\times s$ matrix whose klth element is $\partial y_{kl}/\partial x_{ij}$. Dwyer and MacPhail have established in **[33]** and **[34]** the general theory which links these two component forms.

The alternative approach is to treat the problem of matrix differentiation within the framework of vector differentiation. The function $\mathbf{Y}=\mathbf{Y}(\mathbf{X})$ may be written in vector form as $\mathbf{Y}^c=\mathbf{Y}^c(\mathbf{X}^c)$, and on this basis we may define the derivative of $\mathbf{Y}$ with respect to $\mathbf{X}$ to be the $rs\times mn$ matrix $\partial\mathbf{Y}^c/\partial\mathbf{X}^c$ comprising all the elements $\partial y_{kl}/\partial x_{ij}$ in a two-dimensional lexicographic ordering. For a given value of $\mathbf{X}$, this derivative constitutes an element in the set $\mathscr{L}(\mathscr{R}^n\otimes\mathscr{R}^m, \mathscr{R}^s\otimes\mathscr{R}^r)$ of linear transformations mapping from the tensor product space $\mathscr{R}^n\otimes\mathscr{R}^m$ containing $\mathbf{X}^c$ to the space $\mathscr{R}^s\otimes\mathscr{R}^r$ containing $\mathbf{Y}^c$.

Although we can usefully treat the problem of matrix differentiation within a vector framework, we have to contend with additional complications that are peculiar to matrices. The presence of these complications reflects the fact that the algebra of matrices is far more extensive than the algebra of vectors: it comprises not only the operations of addition and scalar multiplication which are common to vectors, but it comprises also the operation of matrix multiplication which has no counterpart amongst vectors. Thus, for example, we find ourselves articulating a product rule for matrix differentiation which has no counterpart amongst the rules of vector differentiation.

Vector differentiation

Let us now provide some precise definitions.

(4.49) If $\mathbf{x}$ is an $n \times 1$ vector and $\mathbf{y} = \mathbf{y}(\mathbf{x})$ is an $m \times 1$ vector whose elements are functions of $\mathbf{x}$, then the derivative of $\mathbf{y}$ with respect to $\mathbf{x}$ is the $m \times n$ matrix

$$\frac{\partial \mathbf{y}}{\partial \mathbf{x}} = \left[\frac{\partial y_i}{\partial x_j}\right].$$

This definition is at variance with a common convention which arrays the partial derivatives in an $n \times m$ matrix. As a leading example of (4.49) we have the result that

(4.50) If $\mathbf{y} = \mathbf{A}\mathbf{x}$, then $\partial \mathbf{y}/\partial \mathbf{x} = \mathbf{A}$.

We may specialize the definition in (4.49) to the case of a scalar function of a vector and to the case of a vector function of a scalar. Thus

(4.51) If $y = y(\mathbf{x})$ is a scalar function of the $n \times 1$ vector $\mathbf{x}$, then the derivative of y with respect to $\mathbf{x}$ is the row vector

$$\frac{\partial y}{\partial \mathbf{x}} = \left[\frac{\partial y}{\partial x_1}, \ldots, \frac{\partial y}{\partial x_n}\right].$$

whereas

(4.52) If $\mathbf{y} = \mathbf{y}(x)$ is an $m \times 1$ vector function of the scalar x, then the derivative of $\mathbf{y}$ with respect to x is the column vector

$$\frac{\partial \mathbf{y}}{\partial x} = \left[\frac{\partial y_1}{\partial x}, \ldots, \frac{\partial y_m}{\partial x}\right]'.$$

The only formal rule of vector differentiation which we shall use hereafter is the chain rule which states that

(4.53) If $\mathbf{u} = \mathbf{u}(\mathbf{y})$ is a vector function of $\mathbf{y}$ and if $\mathbf{y} = \mathbf{y}(\mathbf{x})$ is a function of the vector $\mathbf{x}$, so that $\mathbf{u} = \mathbf{u}[\mathbf{y}(\mathbf{x})]$, then

$$\frac{\partial \mathbf{u}}{\partial \mathbf{x}} = \frac{\partial \mathbf{u}}{\partial \mathbf{y}} \frac{\partial \mathbf{y}}{\partial \mathbf{x}}.$$

A derivative which we shall frequently encounter is that of a quadratic form.

(4.54) If $y = \mathbf{x}'\mathbf{A}\mathbf{x}$, then $\partial y/\partial \mathbf{x} = \mathbf{x}'(\mathbf{A}+\mathbf{A}')$; and, if $\mathbf{A} = \mathbf{A}'$, then $\partial y/\partial \mathbf{x} = 2\mathbf{x}'\mathbf{A}$.

This result is understood by noting that the qth element of the row vector $\partial y/\partial \mathbf{x}$ is

$$\frac{\partial}{\partial x_q}\left(\sum_i \sum_j a_{ij} x_i x_j\right) = \sum_i a_{iq} x_i + \sum_j a_{qj} x_j.$$

In most cases it would be more convenient to define the derivative to be the column vector $(\mathbf{A}+\mathbf{A}')\mathbf{x}$, and this is the conventional practice. However, we choose to sacrifice such convenience for the sake of conforming with the definition in (4.49) which provides such straightforward results as (4.50).

Classical matrix derivatives

(4.55) If $\mathbf{Y} = \mathbf{Y}(x)$ is an $r \times s$ matrix whose elements are functions of the scalar x, then the classical derivative of $\mathbf{Y}$ with respect to x is the $r \times s$ matrix

$$\frac{\partial \mathbf{Y}}{\partial x} = \left[\frac{\partial y_{kl}}{\partial x}\right].$$

On the other hand,

(4.56) If $y = y(\mathbf{X})$ is a scalar function of an $m \times n$ matrix $\mathbf{X}$, then the classical derivative of y with respect to $\mathbf{X}$ is the $n \times m$ matrix

$$\frac{\partial y}{\partial \mathbf{X}} = \left[\frac{\partial y}{\partial x_{ij}}\right]'$$

which has the same order as $\mathbf{X}'$.

Examples of the derivative $\partial y/\partial \mathbf{X}$ are common in multivariate statistical analysis where probability distributions are represented by scalar functions of vectors or matrices. We may cite the derivatives

(4.57) $$\frac{\partial \mathrm{Trace}(\mathbf{X})}{\partial \mathbf{X}} = \left[\frac{\partial}{\partial x_{ij}} \sum_i x_{ii}\right]' = [\delta_{ij}]' = \mathbf{I}$$

and

(4.58) $$\frac{\partial\, \mathrm{Det}(\mathbf{X})}{\partial \mathbf{X}} = \mathrm{Det}(\mathbf{X})\mathbf{X}^{-1}.$$

To derive the latter, we write

$$\partial\,\mathrm{Det}(\mathbf{X})/\partial\mathbf{X} = \left[\frac{\partial}{\partial x_{ij}} \sum_i x_{ij}c_{ij}\right]' = [c_{ij}]'$$

where c_{ij} is the cofactor of x_{ij} in the expansion of Det(**X**) given in (4.4). Then, by using $\mathbf{X}^{-1} = \mathrm{Det}^{-1}(\mathbf{X})[c_{ij}]'$ from (4.17), we get the result.

Now let us consider the matrix function $\mathbf{Y} = \mathbf{Y}(\mathbf{X})$. For this function we may define rs classical derivatives $\partial y_{kl}/\partial\mathbf{X}$ of orders $n \times m$ and mn classical derivatives $\partial\mathbf{Y}/\partial x_{ij}$ of orders $r \times s$. Dwyer and MacPhail have remarked that it is often easier to evaluate $\partial\mathbf{Y}/\partial x_{ij}$ than to evaluate its counterpart $\partial y_{kl}/\partial\mathbf{X}$. Thus, for example,

(4.59) If $\mathbf{Y} = \mathbf{UVW}$ is a matrix product wherein **U**, **V** and **W** are matrix functions of **X**, then

$$\frac{\partial\mathbf{Y}}{\partial x_{ij}} = \frac{\partial\mathbf{U}}{\partial x_{ij}}\mathbf{VW} + \mathbf{U}\frac{\partial\mathbf{V}}{\partial x_{ij}}\mathbf{W} + \mathbf{UV}\frac{\partial\mathbf{W}}{\partial x_{ij}},$$

whereas

$$\frac{\partial y_{kl}}{\partial\mathbf{X}} = \sum_p\sum_q \frac{\partial u_{kp}}{\partial\mathbf{X}} v_{pq}w_{ql} + \sum_p\sum_q u_{kp}\frac{\partial v_{pq}}{\partial\mathbf{X}} w_{ql} + \sum_p\sum_q u_{kp}v_{pq}\frac{\partial w_{ql}}{\partial\mathbf{X}}.$$

Since in multivariate statistical analysis we require the derivative $\partial y_{kl}/\partial\mathbf{X}$ more commonly, it is unfortunate that it is less accessible than its counterpart $\partial\mathbf{Y}/\partial x_{ij}$. To overcome this difficulty Dwyer and MacPhail have proposed that, instead of finding $\partial y_{kl}/\partial\mathbf{X}$ directly, one should obtain it from $\partial\mathbf{Y}/\partial x_{ij}$ via certain rules of conversion. We shall establish these rules after we have investigated the derivative $\partial\mathbf{Y}^c/\partial\mathbf{X}^c$.

Matrix differentiation in a vector framework

(4.60) Let the function $\mathbf{Y} = \mathbf{Y}(\mathbf{X})$ be written as $\mathbf{Y}^c = \mathbf{Y}^c(\mathbf{X}^c)$ where $\mathbf{X}^{c\prime} = [\mathbf{x}'_{.1}, \ldots, \mathbf{x}'_{.n}]$ and $\mathbf{Y}^{c\prime} = [\mathbf{y}'_{.1}, \ldots, \mathbf{y}'_{.s}]$. Then the derivative of $\mathbf{Y}^c$ with respect to $\mathbf{X}^c$ is the $rs \times mn$ matrix

$$\frac{\partial\mathbf{Y}^c}{\partial\mathbf{X}^c} = \begin{bmatrix} \partial\mathbf{y}_{.1}/\partial\mathbf{x}_{.1}, & \partial\mathbf{y}_{.1}/\partial\mathbf{x}_{.2}, \ldots, & \partial\mathbf{y}_{.1}/\partial\mathbf{x}_{.n} \\ \partial\mathbf{y}_{.2}/\partial\mathbf{x}_{.1}, & \partial\mathbf{y}_{.2}/\partial\mathbf{x}_{.2}, \ldots, & \partial\mathbf{y}_{.2}/\partial\mathbf{x}_{.n} \\ \cdot & \cdot & \cdot \\ \cdot & \cdot & \cdot \\ \cdot & \cdot & \cdot \\ \partial\mathbf{y}_{.s}/\partial\mathbf{x}_{.1}, & \partial\mathbf{y}_{.s}/\partial\mathbf{x}_{.2}, \ldots. & \partial\mathbf{y}_{.s}/\partial\mathbf{x}_{.n} \end{bmatrix}$$

This is a matrix array of the elements $\partial y_{kl}/\partial x_{ij}$ which has the same structure as the matrix Kronecker product $\mathbf{B}\otimes\mathbf{A}$ defined in (4.24). It also has the same order and structure as the tensor product $(\mathbf{X}^c\otimes\mathbf{Y}^c) = \mathbf{Y}^c\mathbf{X}^{c\prime}$. From the display in (4.60) it is easy to see that

(4.61) The ijth column of $\partial\mathbf{Y}^c/\partial\mathbf{X}^c$ is $\partial\mathbf{Y}^c/\partial x_{ij} = (\partial\mathbf{Y}/\partial x_{ij})^c$

and that

(4.62) The klth row of $\partial\mathbf{Y}^c/\partial\mathbf{X}^c$ is $\partial y_{kl}/\partial\mathbf{X}^c = (\partial y_{kl}/\partial\mathbf{X})^r = (\partial y_{kl}/\partial\mathbf{X})'^{c\prime}$.

Two fundamental consequences of our definition are that

$$(4.63)\qquad \frac{\partial\mathbf{Y}^c}{\partial\mathbf{Y}^c} = \mathbf{I}_r \otimes \mathbf{I}_s = \mathbf{I}_{rs},$$

and that

$$(4.64)\qquad \frac{\partial\mathbf{X}'^c}{\partial\mathbf{X}^c} = Ⓣ.$$

The latter follows immediately from the definition of the tensor commutator given in (4.44) whereby $\mathbf{X}'^c = Ⓣ\mathbf{X}^c$. Other leading consequences are that

(4.65) If $\mathbf{Y} = \mathbf{AXB}'$, so that $\mathbf{Y}^c = (\mathbf{B}\otimes\mathbf{A})\mathbf{X}^c$, then

$$\frac{\partial\mathbf{Y}^c}{\partial\mathbf{X}^c} = (\mathbf{B}\otimes\mathbf{A}),$$

(4.66) If $\mathbf{Y} = \mathbf{CX'D}'$, so that $\mathbf{Y}^c = (\mathbf{D}\otimes\mathbf{C})\mathbf{X}'^c$, then

$$\frac{\partial\mathbf{Y}^c}{\partial\mathbf{X}^c} = (\mathbf{D}\otimes\mathbf{C})Ⓣ.$$

The latter is derived by applying the chain rule of (4.53) to the function $\mathbf{Y}^c = \mathbf{Y}^c(\mathbf{X}'^c)$ to obtain $\partial\mathbf{Y}^c/\partial\mathbf{X}^c = (\partial\mathbf{Y}^c/\partial\mathbf{X}'^c)(\partial\mathbf{X}'^c/\partial\mathbf{X}^c) = (\partial\mathbf{Y}^c/\partial\mathbf{X}'^c)Ⓣ$.

Apart from the chain rule, the basic rule which we shall exploit most extensively is the following product rule:

(4.67) If $\mathbf{Y} = \mathbf{UVW}$ is a matrix product wherein $\mathbf{U} = \mathbf{U}(\mathbf{X})$, $\mathbf{V} = \mathbf{V}(\mathbf{X})$ and $\mathbf{W} = \mathbf{W}(\mathbf{X})$ are functions of $\mathbf{X}$, then

$$\frac{\partial\mathbf{Y}^c}{\partial\mathbf{X}^c} = ([\mathbf{VW}]'\otimes\mathbf{I})\frac{\partial\mathbf{U}^c}{\partial\mathbf{X}^c} + (\mathbf{W}'\otimes\mathbf{U})\frac{\partial\mathbf{V}^c}{\partial\mathbf{X}^c} + (\mathbf{I}\otimes\mathbf{UV})\frac{\partial\mathbf{W}^c}{\partial\mathbf{X}^c}.$$

This rule depends upon the fact that we can write the equation $\mathbf{Y}^c = (\mathbf{UVW})^c$ in any of the alternative forms provided by the identity $\mathbf{Y}^c = ([\mathbf{VW}]'\otimes\mathbf{I})\mathbf{U}^c = (\mathbf{W}'\otimes\mathbf{U})\mathbf{V}^c = (\mathbf{I}\otimes\mathbf{UV})\mathbf{W}^c$. The rule is readily established by writing $\partial\mathbf{Y}/\partial x_{ij}$ of (4.59) in vector form to give

$$\left(\frac{\partial\mathbf{Y}}{\partial x_{ij}}\right)^c = ([\mathbf{VW}]'\otimes\mathbf{I})\left(\frac{\partial\mathbf{U}}{\partial x_{ij}}\right)^c + (\mathbf{W}'\otimes\mathbf{U})\left(\frac{\partial\mathbf{V}}{\partial x_{ij}}\right)^c + (\mathbf{I}\otimes\mathbf{UV})\left(\frac{\partial\mathbf{W}}{\partial x_{ij}}\right)^c,$$

and then recognizing, with the help of (4.61) that this is simply the ijth column of $\partial\mathbf{Y}^c/\partial\mathbf{X}^c$.

Relationships between classical matrix derivatives

Having investigated the derivative $\partial\mathbf{Y}^c/\partial\mathbf{X}^c$, we are in a position to examine the relationships existing between the component derivatives $\partial y_{kl}/\partial\mathbf{X}$ and $\partial\mathbf{Y}/\partial x_{ij}$.

Let us begin by finding the classical components of a derivative of the form $\partial\mathbf{Y}^c/\partial\mathbf{X}^c=\mathbf{B}\otimes\mathbf{A}$ wherein $\mathbf{B}$ and $\mathbf{A}$ may themselves be functions of $\mathbf{X}$. Consider first an $m\times n$ matrix $\mathbf{J}_{ij}$ with a unit in the ijth position and zeros elsewhere. By postmultiplying $\mathbf{B}\otimes\mathbf{A}$ by the vector $\mathbf{J}^c_{ij}$, we can extract the ijth column. Thus it follows from (4.61) that $(\mathbf{B}\otimes\mathbf{A})\mathbf{J}^c_{ij}=\partial\mathbf{Y}^c/\partial x_{ij}=(\partial\mathbf{Y}/\partial x_{ij})^c$; and, on restoring this equation to matrix notation, we get

(4.68) $$\frac{\partial\mathbf{Y}}{\partial x_{ij}}=\mathbf{A}\mathbf{J}_{ij}\mathbf{B}'.$$

Now consider an $r\times s$ matrix $\mathbf{K}_{kl}$ with a unit in the klth position and zeros elsewhere. By premultiplying $\mathbf{B}\otimes\mathbf{A}$ by the row vector $\mathbf{K}^{c\prime}_{kl}=\mathbf{K}'^{r}_{kl}$, we can extract the klth row. Thus $\mathbf{K}'^{r}_{kl}(\mathbf{B}\otimes\mathbf{A})=\partial y_{kl}/\partial\mathbf{X}^c=(\partial y_{kl}/\partial\mathbf{X})^r$ and, using (4.48) to restore the equation to matrix notation, we find that

(4.69) $$\partial y_{kl}/\partial\mathbf{X}=\mathbf{B}'\mathbf{K}'_{kl}\mathbf{A}.$$

The results under (4.68) and (4.69) indicate that

(4.70) The derivative $\partial\mathbf{Y}^c/\partial\mathbf{X}^c=\mathbf{B}\otimes\mathbf{A}$ may be decomposed into the components $\partial\mathbf{Y}/\partial x_{ij}=\mathbf{A}\mathbf{J}_{ij}\mathbf{B}'$ where $i=1,\ldots,m$ and $j=1,\ldots,n$; or, alternatively, it may be decomposed into the components $\partial y_{kl}/\partial\mathbf{X}=\mathbf{B}'\mathbf{K}'_{kl}\mathbf{A}$ where $k=1,\ldots,r$ and $l=1,\ldots,s$.

We shall now find the classical components of a derivative of the form $\partial\mathbf{Y}^c/\partial\mathbf{X}^c=(\mathbf{D}\otimes\mathbf{C})\textcircled{T}$. On postmultiplying the derivative by $\mathbf{J}^c_{ij}$, we get $\partial\mathbf{Y}^c/\partial x_{ij}=(\mathbf{D}\otimes\mathbf{C})\textcircled{T}\mathbf{J}^c_{ij}=(\mathbf{D}\otimes\mathbf{C})\mathbf{J}'^{c}_{ij}$. Hence

(4.71) $$\frac{\partial\mathbf{Y}}{\partial x_{ij}}=\mathbf{C}\mathbf{J}'_{ij}\mathbf{D}'.$$

On premultiplying the derivative by $\mathbf{K}^{c\prime}_{kl}=\mathbf{K}'^{r}_{kl}$ and using the second part of (4.48), we get $(\partial y_{kl}/\partial\mathbf{X})^r=\mathbf{K}'^{r}_{kl}(\mathbf{D}\otimes\mathbf{C})\textcircled{T}=\mathbf{K}^{r}_{kl}(\mathbf{C}\otimes\mathbf{D})$. Using (4.48) again, we find that

(4.72) $$\frac{\partial y_{kl}}{\partial\mathbf{X}}=\mathbf{C}'\mathbf{K}_{kl}\mathbf{D}.$$

The results under (4.71) and (4.72) indicate that

(4.73) The derivative $\partial\mathbf{Y}^c/\partial\mathbf{X}^c = (\mathbf{D}\otimes\mathbf{C})Ⓣ$ may be decomposed into the components $\partial\mathbf{Y}/\partial x_{ij} = \mathbf{C}\mathbf{J}'_{ij}\mathbf{D}'$ where $i = 1, \ldots, m$ and $j = 1, \ldots, n$; or, alternatively, it may be decomposed into the components $\partial y_{kl}/\partial\mathbf{X} = \mathbf{C}'\mathbf{K}_{kl}\mathbf{D}$ where $k = 1, \ldots, r$ and $l = 1, \ldots, s$.

It is important to understand that (4.70) and (4.73) are simply statements about relationships that exist between various matrix formats. Thus, if the expression $\partial\mathbf{Y}^c/\partial\mathbf{X}^c$ contains terms in the forms of $\mathbf{B}\otimes\mathbf{A}$ and $(\mathbf{D}\otimes\mathbf{C})Ⓣ$, then $\partial\mathbf{Y}/\partial x_{ij}$ will contain corresponding terms in the forms of $\mathbf{A}\mathbf{J}_{ij}\mathbf{B}'$ and $\mathbf{C}\mathbf{J}'_{ij}\mathbf{D}'$, while likewise, $\partial y_{kl}/\partial\mathbf{X}$ will contain terms in the forms of $\mathbf{B}'\mathbf{K}'_{kl}\mathbf{A}$ and $\mathbf{C}'\mathbf{K}_{kl}\mathbf{D}$. It is upon these relationships that Dwyer and MacPhail have based their classical treatment of matrix differential calculus.

Some leading matrix derivatives

In this section we shall list some of the matrix derivatives that are commonly used in various forms in multivariate statistical analysis.

(4.74)

1. $$\frac{\partial\mathbf{X}^{-1c}}{\partial\mathbf{X}^c} = -(\mathbf{X}^{-1\prime}\otimes\mathbf{X}^{-1}),$$

2. $$\frac{\partial\mathbf{X}^{-1}}{\partial x_{ij}} = -\mathbf{X}^{-1}\mathbf{J}_{ij}\mathbf{X}^{-1}.$$

3. $$\frac{\partial(\mathbf{X}^{-1})_{kl}}{\partial\mathbf{X}} = -\mathbf{X}^{-1}\mathbf{K}'_{kl}\mathbf{X}^{-1}.$$

To establish the first of these, we differentiate $(\mathbf{X}\mathbf{X}^{-1})^c = \mathbf{I}^c$ according to the product rule (4.67) to give $\partial(\mathbf{X}\mathbf{X}^{-1})^c/\partial\mathbf{X}^c = (\mathbf{X}^{-1\prime}\otimes\mathbf{I}) + (\mathbf{I}\otimes\mathbf{X})\partial\mathbf{X}^{-1c}/\partial\mathbf{X}^c = \partial\mathbf{I}^c/\partial\mathbf{X}^c = \mathbf{0}$. After rearranging, we have $\partial\mathbf{X}^{-1c}/\partial\mathbf{X}^c = -(\mathbf{I}\otimes\mathbf{X})^{-1}(\mathbf{X}^{-1\prime}\otimes\mathbf{I}) = -(\mathbf{X}^{-1\prime}\otimes\mathbf{X}^{-1})$. We can then use (4.70) to establish 2. and 3.

(4.75)

1. $$\frac{\partial(\mathbf{X}'\mathbf{A}\mathbf{X})^c}{\partial\mathbf{X}^c} = ([\mathbf{A}\mathbf{X}]'\otimes\mathbf{I})Ⓣ + (\mathbf{I}\otimes\mathbf{X}'\mathbf{A}),$$

2. $$\frac{\partial\mathbf{X}'\mathbf{A}\mathbf{X}}{\partial x_{ij}} = \mathbf{J}'_{ij}\mathbf{A}\mathbf{X} + \mathbf{X}'\mathbf{A}\mathbf{J}_{ij},$$

3. $$\frac{\partial(\mathbf{X}'\mathbf{A}\mathbf{X})_{kl}}{\partial\mathbf{X}} = \mathbf{K}_{kl}(\mathbf{A}\mathbf{X})' + \mathbf{K}'_{kl}\mathbf{X}'\mathbf{A}.$$

We use $(\mathbf{X}'\mathbf{A}\mathbf{X})^c = ([\mathbf{A}\mathbf{X}]'\otimes\mathbf{I})\mathbf{X}'^c = (\mathbf{I}\otimes\mathbf{X}'\mathbf{A})\mathbf{X}^c$ to give $\partial(\mathbf{X}'\mathbf{A}\mathbf{X})^c/\partial\mathbf{X}^c = ([\mathbf{A}\mathbf{X}]'\otimes\mathbf{I})\partial\mathbf{X}'^c/\partial\mathbf{X} + (\mathbf{I}\otimes\mathbf{X}'\mathbf{A})\partial\mathbf{X}^c/\partial\mathbf{X}^c$, from which we get the first result. The other results follow immediately as implications of (4.70) and (4.73). As a specialization of (4.75), we have the result, familiar from (4.54), that

(4.76) $$\frac{\partial \mathbf{x}'\mathbf{A}\mathbf{x}}{\partial \mathbf{x}} = \mathbf{x}'(\mathbf{A}'+\mathbf{A}) \quad \text{and, if} \quad \mathbf{A}=\mathbf{A}', \quad \text{then} \quad \frac{\partial \mathbf{x}'\mathbf{A}\mathbf{x}}{\partial \mathbf{x}} = 2\mathbf{x}'\mathbf{A}.$$

This follows from (4.75) 3 when, in view of the fact that $y=\mathbf{x}'\mathbf{A}\mathbf{x}$ is a scalar, we put $\mathbf{K}_{kl}=\mathbf{K}'_{kl}=1$.

(4.77)

1. $$\frac{\partial(\mathbf{X}\mathbf{A}\mathbf{X}')^{\mathrm{c}}}{\partial \mathbf{X}^{\mathrm{c}}} = (\mathbf{X}\mathbf{A}'\otimes\mathbf{I})+(\mathbf{I}\otimes\mathbf{X}\mathbf{A})Ⓣ,$$

2. $$\frac{\partial \mathbf{X}\mathbf{A}\mathbf{X}'}{\partial x_{ij}} = \mathbf{J}_{ij}\mathbf{A}\mathbf{X}'+\mathbf{X}\mathbf{A}\mathbf{J}'_{ij},$$

3. $$\frac{\partial(\mathbf{X}\mathbf{A}\mathbf{X}')_{kl}}{\partial \mathbf{X}} = \mathbf{A}\mathbf{X}'\mathbf{K}'_{kl}+(\mathbf{X}\mathbf{A})'\mathbf{K}_{kl}.$$

These are established in the same way as the results of (4.76).

The chain rule in (4.53) is applicable to the differentiation of a scalar function of a matrix function. Thus

(4.78) If $u=u(\mathbf{Y})$ is a scalar function of $\mathbf{Y}$ and $\mathbf{Y}=\mathbf{Y}(\mathbf{X})$ is a matrix function of a matrix $\mathbf{X}$, so that $u=u[\mathbf{Y}(\mathbf{X})]$, then

$$\frac{\partial u}{\partial \mathbf{X}^{\mathrm{c}}} = \frac{\partial u}{\partial \mathbf{Y}^{\mathrm{c}}}\frac{\partial \mathbf{Y}^{\mathrm{c}}}{\partial \mathbf{X}^{\mathrm{c}}}$$

where $\partial u/\partial \mathbf{X}^{\mathrm{c}}$ and $\partial u/\partial \mathbf{Y}^{\mathrm{c}}$ are row vectors of the appropriate orders.

As examples, we have

(4.79) $$\frac{\partial\,|\mathbf{Y}|}{\mathbf{X}^{\mathrm{c}}} = \frac{\partial\,|\mathbf{Y}|}{\mathbf{Y}^{\mathrm{c}}}\frac{\partial \mathbf{Y}^{\mathrm{c}}}{\mathbf{X}^{\mathrm{c}}} = |\mathbf{Y}|\,\mathbf{Y}^{-1\mathrm{r}}\frac{\partial \mathbf{Y}^{\mathrm{c}}}{\partial \mathbf{X}^{\mathrm{c}}},$$

which derives from (4.58), and

(4.80) $$\frac{\partial \log|\mathbf{Y}|}{\partial \mathbf{X}^{\mathrm{c}}} = \mathbf{Y}^{-1\mathrm{r}}\frac{\partial \mathbf{Y}^{\mathrm{c}}}{\partial \mathbf{X}^{\mathrm{c}}}.$$

A further example which gathers together a variety of results is the derivative of $\log|\mathbf{X}'\mathbf{A}\mathbf{X}|$ where $\mathbf{A}=\mathbf{A}'$ is symmetric. From (4.80) we have $\partial \log|\mathbf{X}'\mathbf{A}\mathbf{X}|/\partial \mathbf{X}^{\mathrm{c}} = (\mathbf{X}'\mathbf{A}\mathbf{X})^{-1\mathrm{r}}\,\partial(\mathbf{X}'\mathbf{A}\mathbf{X})^{\mathrm{c}}/\partial \mathbf{X}^{\mathrm{c}} = \mathbf{Q}$ let us say. Using (4.75), we get $\mathbf{Q}=(\mathbf{X}'\mathbf{A}\mathbf{X})^{-1\mathrm{r}}\{([\mathbf{A}\mathbf{X}]'\otimes\mathbf{I})Ⓣ+(\mathbf{I}\otimes\mathbf{X}'\mathbf{A})\}$. Then, since by (4.48) $\mathbf{X}^{\mathrm{r}}(\mathbf{A}'\otimes\mathbf{B}')=(\mathbf{A}\mathbf{X}\mathbf{B}')^{\mathrm{r}}$, we get $\mathbf{Q}=[\mathbf{A}\mathbf{X}(\mathbf{X}'\mathbf{A}\mathbf{X})^{-1}]^{\mathrm{r}}Ⓣ+[(\mathbf{X}'\mathbf{A}\mathbf{X})^{-1}\mathbf{X}'\mathbf{A}]^{\mathrm{r}}$, whence, using $\mathbf{X}^{\mathrm{r}}Ⓣ=\mathbf{X}'^{\mathrm{r}}$ from (4.46), we get

(4.81)

1. $$\frac{\partial \log|\mathbf{X}'\mathbf{A}\mathbf{X}|}{\partial \mathbf{X}^{\mathrm{c}}} = 2[(\mathbf{X}'\mathbf{A}\mathbf{X})^{-1}\mathbf{X}'\mathbf{A}]^{\mathrm{r}},$$

2. $$\frac{\partial \log|\mathbf{X}'\mathbf{A}\mathbf{X}|}{\partial \mathbf{X}} = 2(\mathbf{X}'\mathbf{A}\mathbf{X})^{-1}\mathbf{X}'\mathbf{A}.$$

The trace operator provides further examples of scalar functions of matrices. Thus

(4.82)
$$1.\ \frac{\partial\,\mathrm{Trace}(\mathbf{X}'\mathbf{A}\mathbf{X}\mathbf{B}')}{\partial \mathbf{X}^{c}} = \mathbf{X}^{c\prime}(\mathbf{B}\otimes\mathbf{A}) + \mathbf{X}^{c\prime}(\mathbf{B}'\otimes\mathbf{A}'),$$
$$2.\ \frac{\partial\,\mathrm{Trace}(\mathbf{X}'\mathbf{A}\mathbf{X}\mathbf{B}')}{\partial \mathbf{X}} = \mathbf{B}'\mathbf{X}'\mathbf{A} + \mathbf{B}\mathbf{X}'\mathbf{A}'.$$

To demonstrate the first of these, we write $\mathrm{Trace}(\mathbf{X}'\mathbf{A}\mathbf{X}\mathbf{B}') = \mathbf{X}^{c\prime}(\mathbf{B}\otimes\mathbf{A})\mathbf{X}^{c}$ to which we can apply (4.76). The second is found by writing $\mathbf{X}^{c\prime} = \mathbf{X}^{\prime r}$ and applying (4.48). Another useful result is

(4.83)
$$\frac{\partial\,\mathrm{Trace}(\mathbf{A}'\mathbf{A}\mathbf{X})}{\partial \mathbf{X}^{c}} = (\mathbf{A}'\mathbf{A})^{r}.$$

BIBLIOGRAPHY

Matrix Determinants. Kreider et al. [**70,** Appendix III], Lang [**73,** Chap. VI], Shilov [**110,** Chap. 1]

Tensor Products. Halmos [**49,** pp. 38–41], Shephard [**109,** Chap. IV]

Kronecker Products. Halmos [**49,** pp. 95–98]

Matrix Differential Calculus. Dwyer [**33**], Dwyer and MacPhail [**34**], MacRae [**77**], Neudecker [**88**]

CHAPTER 5

The Algebra of Econometrics

We shall now consider some of the algebraic methods for inferring the parametric structure of an empirical relationship involving a number of variables. At this stage we shall provide only weak justification for the proposed techniques. For, in order to demonstrate the optimality of any method of inference, we must make detailed assumptions about the statistical nature of the relationship; and we shall reserve such detail for later chapters.

INCONSISTENT SYSTEMS OF OBSERVATIONS

Let us, for example, consider a system which transforms a vector-valued input into a scalar-valued output. We may write such a transformation, in the tth instance, as

(5.1) $$y_t = \mathbf{x}_{t.}\boldsymbol{\beta}$$

where.

y_t is the scalar-valued output,

$\mathbf{x}_{t.} = [x_{t1}, \ldots, x_{tk}]$ is a row vector of inputs, and

$\boldsymbol{\beta}$ is a $k \times 1$ vector of parameters.

A set of T observations on the system may be represented in the equations

(5.2) $$\mathbf{y} = \mathbf{X}\boldsymbol{\beta},$$

where

$\mathbf{y}$ is a vector of T values of the output, and $\mathbf{X} = [x_{ij}] = [\mathbf{x}_{.1}, \ldots, \mathbf{x}_{.k}]$ is a $T \times k$ matrix comprising vectors of T values of each of the k inputs.

If $\mathbf{y} \in \mathcal{M}(\mathbf{X})$, then the equations (5.2) would be consistent, and, provided $\text{Rank}(\mathbf{X}) = k$, it would be a simple matter to find the unique value of $\boldsymbol{\beta}$. However, when dealing with an empirical relationship, it is common to find that the actual observations of the variables cannot be comprised in a consistent set of equations. The reasons for this may be any of the following:

1. The transformation represented by (5.1) may be inherently variable so that $\boldsymbol{\beta}$ will assume different values on different occasions. Thus it might be

appropriate to specify $y_t = \mathbf{x}_{t.}\boldsymbol{\beta}_t$ where $\boldsymbol{\beta}_t = (\boldsymbol{\beta} + \boldsymbol{\theta}_t)$ contains a random component.

2. The system may be subject to more inputs than are recorded in the vector $\mathbf{x}_{t.}$ of (5.1). In that case, the equation provides an incomplete description of the processes at work; and we might represent the overall contribution of the unrecorded inputs to the value of y_t by an element ε_t so as to write $y_t = \mathbf{x}_{t.}\boldsymbol{\beta} + \varepsilon_t$. It is presumed that the unrecorded inputs are of secondary importance. If they are also very numerous and are liable to cancel each other out, we may be justified in regarding ε_t as a random variable of zero mean.

3. Our observations of the system's variables may be afflicted by errors. Thus, in place of the true values y_t and $\mathbf{x}_{t.}$, we might record $q_t = (y_t + \zeta_t)$ and $\mathbf{z}_{t.} = (\mathbf{x}_{t.} + \boldsymbol{\eta}_{t.})$ where ζ_t and $\boldsymbol{\eta}_{t.}$ are random errors.

In each of these cases, we would want to find, as a surrogate of the unknown $\boldsymbol{\beta}$, a vector $\hat{\mathbf{b}}$ which is roughly descriptive of the relationship between the observations. We shall see that it is possible to decompose the procedure for finding such a $\hat{\mathbf{b}}$ into two stages. In the first, we reform the observations so that the equations comprising them become algebraically consistent. In the second, we find a solution to the reformed system by the normal methods of solving linear equations. The particular method that we adopt, in the first stage, for resolving the inconsistency will be chosen largely in view of our beliefs about the predominant causes of that inconsistency.

GAUSSIAN REGRESSION

Gaussian regression in the $\mathbf{Q}^{-1}$-metric

If either of the systems $y_t = \mathbf{x}_{t.}\boldsymbol{\beta} + \varepsilon_t$ and $y_t = \mathbf{x}_{t.}(\boldsymbol{\beta} + \boldsymbol{\theta}_t)$ underlie our observations $\mathbf{y}$, $\mathbf{X}$, we can safely presume that $\mathbf{y} \notin \mathcal{M}(\mathbf{x})$ and that there is no solution to the equations $\mathbf{y} = \mathbf{X}\boldsymbol{\beta}$. We might be satisfied, however, with finding an approximate solution $\hat{\mathbf{b}}$ according to the criterion of minimizing the distance, somehow defined, between $\mathbf{y}$ and $\hat{\mathbf{y}} = \mathbf{X}\hat{\mathbf{b}}$. Let us define this distance as $\|\mathbf{y} - \hat{\mathbf{y}}\|_{\mathbf{Q}^{-1}} = \sqrt{(\mathbf{y} - \hat{\mathbf{y}})'\mathbf{Q}^{-1}(\mathbf{y} - \hat{\mathbf{y}})}$ where $\mathbf{Q}$ is some positive-definite matrix. Then $\hat{\mathbf{b}}$ may be found by minimizing

$$(5.3) \qquad (\mathbf{y} - \mathbf{X}\mathbf{b})'\mathbf{Q}^{-1}(\mathbf{y} - \mathbf{X}\mathbf{b}) = \mathbf{y}'\mathbf{Q}^{-1}\mathbf{y} - 2\mathbf{y}'\mathbf{Q}^{-1}\mathbf{X}\mathbf{b} + \mathbf{b}'\mathbf{X}'\mathbf{Q}^{-1}\mathbf{X}\mathbf{b},$$

where we have used the fact that the scalar values $\mathbf{b}'\mathbf{X}'\mathbf{Q}^{-1}\mathbf{y}$ and $\mathbf{y}'\mathbf{Q}^{-1}\mathbf{X}\mathbf{b}$ are equal. Differentiating this expression with respect to $\mathbf{b}$ and setting the result to zero gives, after trivial simplification,

$$(5.4) \qquad \mathbf{X}'\mathbf{Q}^{-1}\mathbf{y} - \mathbf{X}'\mathbf{Q}^{-1}\mathbf{X}\hat{\mathbf{b}} = \mathbf{0},$$

which are described as the normal equations of Gaussian regression in the $\mathbf{Q}^{-1}$-metric.

The vector

$$(5.5)\qquad \mathbf{X}\hat{\mathbf{b}} = \mathbf{X}(\mathbf{X}'\mathbf{Q}^{-1}\mathbf{X})^{-}\mathbf{X}'\mathbf{Q}^{-1}\mathbf{y}$$

is uniquely determined by these equations. For, according to the result in (2.59), $\mathbf{X}\hat{\mathbf{b}}$ has a unique value for all $\hat{\mathbf{b}} = (\mathbf{X}'\mathbf{Q}^{-1}\mathbf{X})^{-}\mathbf{X}'\mathbf{Q}^{-1}\mathbf{y}$ if and only if $\mathbf{X}(\mathbf{X}'\mathbf{Q}^{-1}\mathbf{X})^{-}\mathbf{X}'\mathbf{Q}^{-1}\mathbf{X} = \mathbf{X}$; and this condition is clearly fulfilled since $\mathbf{P} = \mathbf{X}(\mathbf{X}'\mathbf{Q}^{-1}\mathbf{X})^{-}\mathbf{X}'\mathbf{Q}^{-1}$ is, according to (3.48), the $\mathbf{Q}^{-1}$-orthogonal projector of $\mathscr{R}^T$ on $\mathscr{M}(\mathbf{X})$. Also, it is clear from the result in (3.49) concerning the minimum-distance properties of orthogonal projections that we have indeed succeeded in minimizing the distance $\|\mathbf{y} - \hat{\mathbf{y}}\|_{\mathbf{Q}^{-1}}$ between $\mathbf{y}$ and $\hat{\mathbf{y}} = \mathbf{X}\hat{\mathbf{b}}$.

If $\text{Null}(\mathbf{X}) = 0$, then, of course, $(\mathbf{X}'\mathbf{Q}^{-1}\mathbf{X})^{-1}$ exists, and we can obtain directly from (5.4) the unique solution

$$(5.6)\qquad \hat{\mathbf{b}} = (\mathbf{X}'\mathbf{Q}^{-1}\mathbf{X})^{-1}\mathbf{X}'\mathbf{Q}^{-1}\mathbf{y}.$$

The method of projection is the way in which we resolve the inconsistency of the equations $\mathbf{y} = \mathbf{X}\boldsymbol{\beta}$. It may be regarded as the first step of a procedure whose second step is to find $\hat{\mathbf{b}}$ from the consistent system $\hat{\mathbf{y}} = \mathbf{X}\hat{\mathbf{b}}$. It is notable that, in Gaussian regression, the whole burden of the adjustments to the data $[\mathbf{y}, \mathbf{X}]$ that are necessary to achieve consistency is placed on the vector $\mathbf{y}$ of the observations on the dependent variable.

If we wish to envisage the method of finding $\hat{\mathbf{b}}$ as a one-step procedure, it is appropriate to write (5.6) as $\hat{\mathbf{b}} = \mathbf{X}^L\mathbf{y}$ where $\mathbf{X}^L = (\mathbf{X}'\mathbf{Q}^{-1}\mathbf{X})^{-1}\mathbf{X}'\mathbf{Q}^{-1}$ is a left inverse of $\mathbf{X}$.

An obvious specialization of Gaussian regression is to choose $\mathbf{Q} = \mathbf{I}$ to obtain, from (5.5) and (5.6) respectively, the equations

$$(5.7)\qquad \mathbf{X}\hat{\mathbf{b}} = \mathbf{X}(\mathbf{X}'\mathbf{X})^{-}\mathbf{X}'\mathbf{y},$$

$$(5.8)\qquad \hat{\mathbf{b}} = (\mathbf{X}'\mathbf{X})^{-1}\mathbf{X}'\mathbf{y}.$$

The equation (5.8), which depends upon the assumption $\text{Null}(\mathbf{X}) = 0$, gives the ordinary least-squares regression estimate of $\boldsymbol{\beta}$.

It is possible to convert a regression in the $\mathbf{Q}^{-1}$-metric to an ordinary least-squares regression if we first transform the data in an appropriate manner. For this purpose we use a non-singular matrix $\mathbf{T}$ such that $\mathbf{T}'\mathbf{T} = \mathbf{Q}^{-1}$, and we define $\mathbf{Z} = \mathbf{T}\mathbf{X}$, $\mathbf{q} = \mathbf{T}\mathbf{y}$. Then, if we apply the ordinary least-squares procedure to $\mathbf{Z}$ and $\mathbf{q}$, we find, assuming $\text{Null}(\mathbf{X}) = 0$, that

$$(5.9)\qquad (\mathbf{Z}'\mathbf{Z})^{-1}\mathbf{Z}'\mathbf{q} = (\mathbf{X}'\mathbf{T}'\mathbf{T}\mathbf{X})^{-1}\mathbf{X}'\mathbf{T}'\mathbf{T}\mathbf{y} = (\mathbf{X}'\mathbf{Q}^{-1}\mathbf{X})^{-1}\mathbf{X}'\mathbf{Q}^{-1}\mathbf{y}.$$

This demonstrates the equivalence of the ordinary least-squares regression of the transformed variables and the regression of the original variables in the $\mathbf{Q}^{-1}$-metric.

Equivalent metrics

The regression in the $\mathbf{Q}^{-1}$-metric is completely specified by the manifold $\mathcal{M}(\mathbf{X})$ and its $\mathbf{Q}^{-1}$-orthogonal complement. The latter may be orthogonal to $\mathcal{M}(\mathbf{X})$ in terms of an alternative metric. In that case, we can say that the $\mathbf{Q}^{-1}$-metric and the alternative metric, which clearly serve to define the same projection on $\mathcal{M}(\mathbf{X})$, are equivalent regression metrics. We may express this more formally:

(5.10) Let $\mathbf{P}_1$ and $\mathbf{P}_2$ be the minimum-distance projectors on $\mathcal{M}(\mathbf{X})$ in the $\mathbf{Q}_1^{-1}$-metric, and the $\mathbf{Q}_2^{-1}$-metric respectively. Then, for any vector $\mathbf{y} \in \mathscr{E}$, we have $\mathbf{P}_1\mathbf{y} = \mathbf{P}_2\mathbf{y} = \mathbf{X}\hat{\mathbf{b}}$ and $(\mathbf{I}-\mathbf{P}_1)\mathbf{y} = (\mathbf{I}-\mathbf{P}_2)\mathbf{y}$ if and only if $\mathbf{Q}_1^{-1}\mathcal{M}(\mathbf{X}) = \mathbf{Q}_2^{-1}\mathcal{M}(\mathbf{X})$.

Proof. Imagine that $\mathbf{P}_1$ and $\mathbf{P}_2$ are defined over the Euclidean space $\mathscr{E}$. Then the decomposition $\mathbf{y} = (\mathbf{I}-\mathbf{P}_i)\mathbf{y} + \mathbf{P}_i\mathbf{y}$; $i = 1, 2$ is unique if and only if the direct sum $\mathscr{E} = (\mathbf{I}-\mathbf{P}_i)\mathscr{E} \oplus \mathbf{P}_i\mathscr{E}$ is unique. This requirement is equivalent to the condition that $(\mathbf{I}-\mathbf{P}_i)\mathscr{E}$ has a unique orthogonal complement in the unitary metric and, since $\mathbf{y}'(\mathbf{I}-\mathbf{P}_i)'\mathbf{Q}_i^{-1}\mathbf{P}_i\mathbf{y} = 0$ for all $\mathbf{y} \in \mathscr{E}$, the latter must be of the form $\mathbf{Q}_i^{-1}\mathbf{P}_i\mathscr{E}$. On writing $\mathbf{P}_i\mathscr{E} = \mathcal{M}(\mathbf{X})$; $i = 1, 2$, we may express this necessary and sufficient condition as $\mathbf{Q}_1^{-1}\mathcal{M}(\mathbf{X}) = \mathbf{Q}_2^{-1}\mathcal{M}(\mathbf{X})$.

In fact, (5.10) simply restates the result (3.52) in a more specialised form.

Interpretive aspects of Gaussian regression

Our tendency has been to visualize Gaussian regressions in terms of the T-dimensional space containing the column vectors of the data matrix $[\mathbf{y}, \mathbf{X}]$. In these terms, we are projecting $\mathbf{y} \in \mathscr{R}^T$ onto the k-dimensional subspace $\mathcal{M}(\mathbf{X}) \subset \mathscr{R}^T$ in order to find $\mathbf{P}\mathbf{y} = \hat{\mathbf{y}} = \mathbf{X}\hat{\mathbf{b}}$.

An alternative interpretation of the geometric aspects of the regressions arises if we choose to represent the rows of the data matrix $[\mathbf{y}, \mathbf{X}]$ as a set of T vectors, or points, in the $(k+1)$-dimensional space spanned by the axes $\{[y, 0, \ldots, 0], [0, x_1, \ldots, 0], \ldots, [0, 0, \ldots, x_k]\}$. A relationship between $k+1$ variables is represented by a k-dimensional hyperplane within this space. Thus, if they were wholly consistent with the fixed relationship postulated in (5.1), the set of observations in $[\mathbf{y}, \mathbf{X}]$ would correspond to a set of coplanar points. In practice the observations must be adjusted in order to achieve such consistency.

The method of Gaussian regression is to make the observations coplanar by adjusting them in respect of only one of their co-ordinates; that is to say, a vector $[y_t, x_{t1}, \ldots, x_{tk}]$ is replaced by $[\hat{y}_t, x_{t1}, \ldots, x_{tk}]$, where $\hat{y}_t = x_{t1}\hat{b}_1 + x_{t2}\hat{b}_2 + \ldots + x_{tk}\hat{b}_k$ for some $[\hat{b}_1, \hat{b}_2, \ldots, \hat{b}_k] = \hat{\mathbf{b}}'$. In general, the parameter vector $\hat{\mathbf{b}}$ is determined so as to minimize a weighted sum of squares and cross-products of the adjustments $(y_t - \hat{y}_t)$. Thus a criterion is adopted which has the form of

(5.11) Minimize

$$\sum_t \sum_s q^{ts}(y_t - \hat{y}_t)(y_s - \hat{y}_s),$$

where the scalars q^{ts} are elements of a positive-definite matrix $\mathbf{Q}^{-1}$. We may rewrite (5.11) as

(5.12) Minimize

$$(\mathbf{y}-\hat{\mathbf{y}})'\mathbf{Q}^{-1}(\mathbf{y}-\hat{\mathbf{y}}) = \|\mathbf{y}-\hat{\mathbf{y}}\|^2_{\mathbf{Q}^{-1}},$$

which is precisely the criterion that gave rise to the normal equations (5.4).

Synthetic estimation

Let us now imagine that we have some prior estimate of $\boldsymbol{\beta}$, denoted $\hat{\mathbf{b}}$, which is considered to be a useful approximation to the true value, and let us assume that we also have some *a priori* information about $\boldsymbol{\beta}$ that can be represented in the restrictions

(5.13) $\mathbf{R}\boldsymbol{\beta} = \mathbf{r}$,

where

$\mathbf{R}$ is a $j \times k$ matrix with $j < k$ and $\text{Null}(\mathbf{R}') = 0$.

The condition $\text{Null}(\mathbf{R}') = 0$, giving $\mathbf{R}$ full row rank, ensures that the restrictions of (5.13) are both mutually independent and consistent; and the condition $j < k$ implies that there are insufficient restrictions to determine the k elements of $\boldsymbol{\beta}$ uniquely. Since the prior estimate $\hat{\mathbf{b}}$ does not incorporate the information of the restrictions, it is presumed that it fails to satisfy the equation (5.13). Our problem is therefore to find a new estimate $\overset{*}{\mathbf{b}}$ which compounds the information in the original estimate $\hat{\mathbf{b}}$ with the information of the restrictions.

The effect of (5.13) is to specify that the true value of $\boldsymbol{\beta}$ lies in the affine subspace $\mathscr{A} = \{\mathbf{b}; \mathbf{Rb} = \mathbf{r}\}$ within the total parameter space. Therefore an appropriate way of determining the new estimate $\overset{*}{\mathbf{b}}$ is to locate it in $\mathscr{A}$ at a minimum distance from $\hat{\mathbf{b}}$, according to the criterion

(5.14) Minimize

$$\|\hat{\mathbf{b}} - \overset{*}{\mathbf{b}}\|_{\mathbf{Q}} = \sqrt{(\hat{\mathbf{b}} - \overset{*}{\mathbf{b}})'\mathbf{Q}(\hat{\mathbf{b}} - \overset{*}{\mathbf{b}})}$$

Subject to

$$\mathbf{R}\overset{*}{\mathbf{b}} = \mathbf{r}.$$

In fact, it is sufficient to minimize $(\hat{\mathbf{b}}-\overset{*}{\mathbf{b}})'\mathbf{Q}(\hat{\mathbf{b}}-\overset{*}{\mathbf{b}})$, so that the appropriate Lagrangean expression is

(5.15) $$\begin{aligned} L &= (\hat{\mathbf{b}}-\mathbf{b})'\mathbf{Q}(\hat{\mathbf{b}}-\mathbf{b})+2\boldsymbol{\lambda}'(\mathbf{Rb}-\mathbf{r}) \\ &= \hat{\mathbf{b}}'\mathbf{Q}\hat{\mathbf{b}}-2\hat{\mathbf{b}}'\mathbf{Qb}+\mathbf{b}'\mathbf{Qb}+2\boldsymbol{\lambda}'(\mathbf{Rb}-\mathbf{r}), \end{aligned}$$

wherein $\boldsymbol{\lambda}$ is a $j\times 1$ vector of Lagrangean multipliers. Differentiating this with respect to $\mathbf{b}$ and setting the results to zero gives, after trivial simplification, $\mathbf{Q}\overset{*}{\mathbf{b}}-\mathbf{Q}\hat{\mathbf{b}}+\mathbf{R}'\boldsymbol{\lambda}=\mathbf{0}$, whence

(5.16) $$\overset{*}{\mathbf{b}}=\hat{\mathbf{b}}-\mathbf{Q}^{-1}\mathbf{R}'\boldsymbol{\lambda}.$$

Substituting this expression of $\overset{*}{\mathbf{b}}$ into the restrictions $\mathbf{Rb}-\mathbf{r}=\mathbf{0}$, obtained from (5.15) by differentiating L with respect to $\boldsymbol{\lambda}$, and setting the result to zero, gives $\mathbf{0}=\mathbf{R}\hat{\mathbf{b}}-\mathbf{RQ}^{-1}\mathbf{R}'\boldsymbol{\lambda}-\mathbf{r}$, from which

$$\boldsymbol{\lambda}=(\mathbf{RQ}^{-1}\mathbf{R}')^{-1}(\mathbf{R}\hat{\mathbf{b}}-\mathbf{r}).$$

Substituting the latter into the expression of (5.16) gives

(5.17) $$\overset{*}{\mathbf{b}}=\hat{\mathbf{b}}-\mathbf{Q}^{-1}\mathbf{R}'(\mathbf{RQ}^{-1}\mathbf{R}')^{-1}(\mathbf{R}\hat{\mathbf{b}}-\mathbf{r}).$$

It is instructive to consider the case where $\mathbf{R}\boldsymbol{\beta}=\mathbf{r}=\mathbf{0}$. The expression for $\overset{*}{\mathbf{b}}$ then becomes

(5.18) $$\overset{*}{\mathbf{b}}=[\mathbf{I}-\mathbf{Q}^{-1}\mathbf{R}'(\mathbf{RQ}^{-1}\mathbf{R}')^{-1}\mathbf{R}]\hat{\mathbf{b}};$$

where $\mathbf{P}=[\mathbf{I}-\mathbf{Q}^{-1}\mathbf{R}'(\mathbf{RQ}^{-1}\mathbf{R}')^{-1}\mathbf{R}]$, which is idempotent and $\mathbf{Q}$-symmetric, is the $\mathbf{Q}$-orthogonal projector on $\mathcal{N}(\mathbf{R})=\mathcal{O}(\mathbf{R}')$, given in the example following (3.61). Thus $\overset{*}{\mathbf{b}}$ is obtained from $\hat{\mathbf{b}}$ by projecting the latter onto the vector subspace $\{\mathbf{b};\mathbf{Rb}=\mathbf{0}\}$.

MULTILATERAL REGRESSION

The equation (5.1) defines a relationship between a dependent variable y_t, described as the output, and a set of independent variables $x_{t1},\ldots,x_{tk}$, described as inputs. However, in postulating a relationship between p variables we need not distinguish a dependent variable; and in place of (5.1) we might wish to consider a homogeneous equation of the form

(5.19) $$\mathbf{x}_{t.}\boldsymbol{\alpha}=0,$$

where

$\mathbf{x}_{t.}=[x_{t1},\ldots,x_{tp}]$ is a row vector of related variables and $\boldsymbol{\alpha}$ is a vector of parameters determined up to a scalar factor.

This relationship (5.19) defines a $(p-1)$-dimensional hyperplane $\{\mathbf{x}'_{t.}\} = \mathcal{N}(\boldsymbol{\alpha}') = \mathcal{O}(\boldsymbol{\alpha})$ within the p-dimensional space spanned by the axes $\{[x_1, \ldots, 0]', \ldots, [0, \ldots, x_p]'\}$.

It is possible that, in attempting to observe $\mathbf{x}_{t.}$, we should record a vector $\mathbf{z}_{t.} = \mathbf{x}_{t.} + \boldsymbol{\eta}_{t.}$ where $\boldsymbol{\eta}_{t.}$ is a vector of random errors. These errors of observation are liable to obscure the relationship, so that, if

> $\mathbf{Z}' = [\mathbf{z}'_{1.}, \ldots, \mathbf{z}'_{T.}]$ is a $p \times T$ matrix comprising $T > p$ observations on each of the p variables,

we might find that Rank$(\mathbf{Z}) = p$, and that the system $\mathbf{Z}\boldsymbol{\alpha} = \mathbf{0}$ has only a trivial solution $\boldsymbol{\alpha} = \mathbf{0}$. Our recourse in that case is to replace the set of observations $\mathbf{z}_{t.}; t = 1, \ldots, T$ that span the p-dimensional space by a set of close approximations $\hat{\mathbf{z}}_{t.}$; $t = 1, \ldots, T$ that lie within a $(p-1)$-dimensional hyperplane. The reformed system $\hat{\mathbf{Z}}\mathbf{a} = \mathbf{0}$, comprising the new values, will have a non-zero solution $\hat{\mathbf{a}}$ which will, hopefully, approximate to the true value of $\boldsymbol{\alpha}$.

Orthogonal regression

We may find the vector $\hat{\mathbf{a}}$ by determining the values $\hat{\mathbf{z}}_{t.}$; $t = 1, \ldots, T$ in such a way as to minimize the sum of squares of the distances $\|\mathbf{z}_{t.} - \hat{\mathbf{z}}_{t.}\|_{\mathbf{I}}$. Thus, adopting the arbitrary normalization $\mathbf{a}'\mathbf{a} = 1$, our criterion becomes

(5.20) Minimize

$$\sum_{t=1}^{T} (\mathbf{z}_{t.} - \hat{\mathbf{z}}_{t.})(\mathbf{z}_{t.} - \hat{\mathbf{z}}_{t.})'$$

Subject to

$$\hat{\mathbf{z}}_{t.}\mathbf{a} = 0, \quad \text{for all } t; \qquad \text{and} \quad \mathbf{a}'\mathbf{a} = 1.$$

To investigate this criterion, we may consider the problem of finding a single value $\hat{\mathbf{z}}_{t.}$ at a minimum distance from $\mathbf{z}_{t.}$, such as to obey the relationship $\hat{\mathbf{z}}_{t.}\mathbf{a} = 0$ for a fixed value of $\mathbf{a}$. The problem gives rise to the Lagrangean expression

$$L = (\mathbf{z}_{t.} - \hat{\mathbf{z}}_{t.})(\mathbf{z}_{t.} - \hat{\mathbf{z}}_{t.})' + 2\mu(\hat{\mathbf{z}}_{t.}\mathbf{a}) + 2\lambda(\mathbf{a}'\mathbf{a} - 1). \tag{5.21}$$

Differentiating with respect to $\hat{\mathbf{z}}'_{t.}$, μ, and λ and setting the results to zero gives the conditions

$$(\mathbf{z}_{t.} - \hat{\mathbf{z}}_{t.})' = \mu\mathbf{a}, \tag{5.22}$$

$$\hat{\mathbf{z}}_{t.}\mathbf{a} = 0, \tag{5.23}$$

$$\mathbf{a}'\mathbf{a} = 1. \tag{5.24}$$

To find the solution for μ, we premultiply the equation of (5.22) by $\mathbf{a}'$ to give $\mathbf{a}'(\mathbf{z}_{t.} - \hat{\mathbf{z}}_{t.})' = \mu\mathbf{a}'\mathbf{a}$. Then, by applying (5.23) and (5.24) to the LHS and

RHS respectively, we get

$$(5.25) \qquad \mu = \mathbf{a}'\mathbf{z}'_{t.}.$$

By substituting the latter into (5.22) and by rearranging the result, we obtain

$$(5.26) \qquad \hat{\mathbf{z}}'_{t.} = (\mathbf{I} - \mathbf{aa}')\mathbf{z}'_{t.}.$$

The symmetric idempotent matrix $(\mathbf{I} - \mathbf{aa}')$ is the orthogonal projector on $\mathcal{N}(\mathbf{a}') = \mathcal{O}(\mathbf{a})$. Thus $\hat{\mathbf{z}}'_{t.}$ is obtained by a minimum-distance projection of $\mathbf{z}'_{t.}$ onto a $(p-1)$-dimensional hyperplane.

It also follows from (5.26), by way of (5.24), that

$$(5.27) \qquad (\mathbf{z}_{t.} - \hat{\mathbf{z}}_{t.})(\mathbf{z}_{t.} - \hat{\mathbf{z}}_{t.})' = (\mathbf{z}_{t.}\mathbf{a})^2.$$

This gives an expression for the squared distance $\|\mathbf{z}_{t.} - \hat{\mathbf{z}}_{t.}\|^2_{\mathbf{I}}$ which we may use to rewrite the criterion (5.20) in the form

(5.28) Minimize

$$\sum_{t=1}^{T} (\mathbf{z}_{t.}\mathbf{a})^2 = \mathbf{a}'\mathbf{Z}'\mathbf{Z}\mathbf{a}$$

Subject to

$$\mathbf{a}'\mathbf{a} = 1.$$

To determine the value of $\hat{\mathbf{a}}$ according to (5.28) we form the Lagrangean

$$(5.29) \qquad L = \mathbf{a}'\mathbf{Z}'\mathbf{Z}\mathbf{a} - \lambda(\mathbf{a}'\mathbf{a} - 1).$$

Differentiating with respect to $\mathbf{a}$ and setting the result to zero gives the condition

$$(5.30) \qquad (\mathbf{Z}'\mathbf{Z} - \lambda\mathbf{I})\mathbf{a} = \mathbf{0}.$$

A vector $\mathbf{a}$ satisfying this expression is a characteristic vector of $\mathbf{Z}'\mathbf{Z}$. Premultiplying by $\mathbf{a}'$ gives $\mathbf{a}'\mathbf{Z}'\mathbf{Z}\mathbf{a} = \lambda\mathbf{a}'\mathbf{a} = \lambda$; and it is apparent from this that the sum of squares in the criterion (5.28) is minimized by choosing $\hat{\mathbf{a}}$ as the vector corresponding to the smallest root of $\mathbf{Z}'\mathbf{Z}$. We then have the solution to the problem of orthogonal regression.

Interpretive aspects of orthogonal regression

A fundamental contrast between orthogonal regression and Gaussian regression concerns the nature of the adjustments that are made to the data in order to obtain a system of equations that allows us to find the parameter estimate as a simple algebraic solution. In Gaussian regression, the tth observation $[y_t, \mathbf{x}_{t.}] = [y_t, x_{t1}, \ldots, x_{tk}]$ is adjusted only in respect of its leading co-ordinate to give $[\hat{y}_t, \mathbf{x}_{t.}] = [\hat{y}_t, x_{t1}, \ldots, x_{tk}]$. In orthogonal regression, every co-ordinate of the observation $\mathbf{z}_{t.} = [\mathbf{z}_{t1}, \ldots, \mathbf{z}_{tp}]$ is adjusted to give $\hat{\mathbf{z}}_{t.} = [\hat{z}_{t1}, \ldots, \hat{z}_{tp}]$. Thus, in Gaussian regression, the data points are projected onto a k-dimensional hyperplane in a direction that is parallel to the y-axis; whereas, in orthogonal regression, the data points are projected orthogonally onto a $(p-1)$-dimensional hyperplane in a manner that is represented by (5.26). The fact that every co-ordinate of the data is thereby adjusted leads us to describe orthogonal regression as a multilateral regression.

We prefer to visualize Gaussian regressions in terms of the T-dimensional space containing the columns of the data matrix $[\mathbf{y}, \mathbf{X}]$; for this enables us to describe the column vector $\hat{\mathbf{y}}$, where $\hat{\mathbf{y}}' = [\hat{y}_1, \ldots, \hat{y}_T]$, as a projection of $\mathbf{y}$ on $\mathcal{M}(\mathbf{X})$. When orthogonal regression is visualized in these terms, it becomes a matter of finding a $(p-1)$-dimensional subspace of $\mathcal{R}^T$ containing the minimum-distance approximations $\hat{\mathbf{z}}_{.j}$; $j = 1, \ldots, p$ of the column vectors $\mathbf{z}_{.j}$; $j = 1, \ldots, p$ comprised in the data matrix $\mathbf{Z}$.

In fact, by minimizing the sum of squares of the distances $\|\mathbf{z}_{t.} - \hat{\mathbf{z}}_{t.}\|_{\mathbf{I}_p}$ according to the criterion (5.20), we also succeed in minimizing the sum of squares of the distances $\|\mathbf{z}_{.j} - \hat{\mathbf{z}}_{.j}\|_{\mathbf{I}_T}$. The equivalence of the two minimands is demonstrated in the following identities:

$$\begin{aligned}(5.31)\qquad \sum_t (\mathbf{z}_{t.} - \hat{\mathbf{z}}_{t.})(\mathbf{z}_{t.} - \hat{\mathbf{z}}_{t.})' &= \sum_t \left[\sum_j (z_{tj} - \hat{z}_{tj})^2\right] \\ &= \operatorname{Trace}[(\mathbf{Z} - \hat{\mathbf{Z}})(\mathbf{Z} - \hat{\mathbf{Z}})'] = \operatorname{Trace}[(\mathbf{Z} - \hat{\mathbf{Z}})'(\mathbf{Z} - \hat{\mathbf{Z}})] \\ &= \sum_j \left[\sum_t (z_{tj} - \hat{z}_{tj})^2\right] = \sum_j (\mathbf{z}_{.j} - \hat{\mathbf{z}}_{.j})'(\mathbf{z}_{.j} - \hat{\mathbf{z}}_{.j}).\end{aligned}$$

Thus, as an alternative to (5.20), we may give the following criterion for orthogonal regression:

(5.32) Minimize

$$\sum_j (\mathbf{z}_{.j} - \hat{\mathbf{z}}_{.j})'(\mathbf{z}_{.j} - \hat{\mathbf{z}}_{.j})$$

Subject to

$\mathbf{B}'\hat{\mathbf{z}}_{.j} = 0$ for all j, where $\mathbf{B}'$ is a freely determined $\{T - (p-1)\} \times T$ matrix such that $\mathbf{B}'\mathbf{B} = \mathbf{I}$.

This criterion may be investigated in the same way as (5.20) was, by considering the problem of finding a single value $\hat{\mathbf{z}}_{.j}$ at a minimum distance from $\mathbf{z}_{.j}$ and obeying the relationship $\mathbf{B}'\hat{\mathbf{z}}_{.j}$ for a fixed matrix $\mathbf{B}'$. Thus we find that

$$(5.33)\qquad \hat{\mathbf{z}}_{.j} = (\mathbf{I} - \mathbf{B}\mathbf{B}')\mathbf{z}_{.j},$$

where $(\mathbf{I}-\mathbf{BB}')$ is the orthogonal projector on $\mathcal{O}(\mathbf{B})=\mathcal{N}(\mathbf{B}')$, and that

$$(5.34)\qquad (\mathbf{z}_{.j}-\hat{\mathbf{z}}_{.j})'(\mathbf{z}_{.j}-\hat{\mathbf{z}}_{.j})=\mathbf{z}'_{.j}\mathbf{BB}'\mathbf{z}_{.j}.$$

Substituting the latter into the minimand of (5.32) and using $\sum_j \mathbf{z}'_{.j}\mathbf{BB}'\mathbf{z}_{.j}=\text{Trace}(\mathbf{Z}'\mathbf{BB}'\mathbf{Z})=\text{Trace}(\mathbf{B}'\mathbf{ZZ}'\mathbf{B})=\sum \mathbf{b}'_{.l}\mathbf{ZZ}'\mathbf{b}_{.l}$ enables us to rewrite the criterion as

(5.35) Minimize

$$\sum_j \mathbf{z}'_{.j}\mathbf{BB}'\mathbf{z}_{.j}=\sum_l \mathbf{b}'_{.l}\mathbf{ZZ}'\mathbf{b}_{.l}$$

Subject to

$\mathbf{B}'\mathbf{B}=\mathbf{I}$, or, equivalently, $\mathbf{b}'_{.l}\mathbf{b}_{.s}=\delta_{ls}$.

The appropriate Lagrangean for this problem is

$$(5.36)\qquad L=\sum_l \mathbf{b}'_{.l}\mathbf{ZZ}'\mathbf{b}_{.l}-\sum_l\sum_s \lambda_{ls}(\mathbf{b}'_{.l}\mathbf{b}_{.s}),$$

where $\lambda_{ls}=\lambda_{sl}$. Differentiating with respect to $\mathbf{b}_{.l}$ and setting the result to zero yields

$$(5.37)\qquad (\mathbf{ZZ}'-\lambda_{ll}\mathbf{I})\mathbf{b}_{.l}-\sum_{s\neq l}\lambda_{sl}\mathbf{b}_{.s}=\mathbf{0}$$

for each $l=1,\ldots,T-(p-1)$. These equations are satisfied by the characteristic vectors of $\mathbf{ZZ}'$ which are mutually orthogonal such that $\mathbf{b}'_{.l}\mathbf{b}_{.s}=\delta_{ls}$. Furthermore, the criterion function $\sum_l \mathbf{b}'_{.l}\mathbf{ZZ}'\mathbf{b}_{.l}$ is minimized by choosing the vectors $\mathbf{b}_{.l}$ to correspond to the $T-(p-1)$ smallest roots of $\mathbf{ZZ}'$. In fact, since $\text{Rank}(\mathbf{ZZ}')=\text{Rank}(\mathbf{Z})=p$, the first $T-p$ roots of $\mathbf{ZZ}'$ are all zeros and the corresponding vectors form an orthogonal basis of $\mathcal{N}(\mathbf{ZZ}')=\mathcal{N}(\mathbf{Z}')=\mathcal{O}(\mathbf{Z})$.

It is, perhaps, instructive to consider the fact that, when $p=T$, the problem of orthogonal regression has an identical representation in the column space $\mathcal{R}^T$ and in the row space $\mathcal{R}^p$. Clearly, the same is not true of the problem of Gaussian regression.

Principal components

Another interesting characterization of orthogonal regression is obtained when we consider the principal components of the data matrix $\mathbf{Z}$.

(5.38) The first principal component of a matrix $\mathbf{Z}$ is a vector $\mathbf{b}_1=\mathbf{Z}\mathbf{a}_1$ such that $\|\mathbf{b}_1\|_\mathbf{I}=\sqrt{\mathbf{a}'\mathbf{Z}'\mathbf{Z}\mathbf{a}}$ is maximized for all $\mathbf{a}$ subject to $\|\mathbf{a}\|_\mathbf{I}=\mathbf{a}'\mathbf{a}=1$.

To find $\mathbf{b}_1$ we form the Lagrangean

$$L = \mathbf{a}'\mathbf{Z}'\mathbf{Z}\mathbf{a} - \lambda(\mathbf{a}'\mathbf{a} - 1), \tag{5.39}$$

which is precisely the expression (5.29). Differentiating with respect to **a** and setting the result to zero gives the condition

$$(\mathbf{Z}'\mathbf{Z} - \lambda\mathbf{I})\mathbf{a} = \mathbf{0}. \tag{5.40}$$

Then, with $\mathbf{a}'\mathbf{a} = 1$, the value which maximizes $\|\mathbf{b}\|_{\mathbf{I}} = \sqrt{\mathbf{a}'\mathbf{Z}'\mathbf{Z}\mathbf{a}} = \sqrt{\lambda}$ is the vector $\mathbf{a}_1$ corresponding to the largest characteristic root λ_1 of $\mathbf{Z}'\mathbf{Z}$. In general

(5.41) The jth principal component of $\mathbf{Z}$ is the vector $\mathbf{b}_j = \mathbf{Z}\mathbf{a}_j$ such that $\|\mathbf{b}_j\|$ is maximized subject to $\|\mathbf{a}_j\| = 1$ and $\mathbf{b}_i'\mathbf{b}_j = 0$ for all $i < j$, where $\mathbf{b}_i$ is the ith principal component.

The vector $\mathbf{a}_j$ satisfying this definition is simply the normalized characteristic vector corresponding to the jth largest root λ_j of $\mathbf{Z}'\mathbf{Z}$. The orthogonality condition $\mathbf{b}_i'\mathbf{b}_j$ is satisfied by virtue of the fact that characteristic vectors $\mathbf{a}_i$, $\mathbf{a}_j$ are orthogonal on account of the symmetry of the matrix $\mathbf{Z}'\mathbf{Z}$. For, with $\mathbf{a}_i'\mathbf{a}_j = 0$, we have $\mathbf{b}_i'\mathbf{b}_j = \mathbf{a}_i'\mathbf{Z}'\mathbf{Z}\mathbf{a}_j = \lambda_j\mathbf{a}_i'\mathbf{a}_j = 0$. It follows that

(5.42) For any $T \times p$ matrix $\mathbf{Z}$ with Rank$(\mathbf{Z}) = p$, we can find a $p \times p$ orthogonal matrix $[\mathbf{a}_1, \ldots, \mathbf{a}_p] = \mathbf{A}$ which generates a $T \times p$ matrix of principal components $[\mathbf{b}_1, \ldots, \mathbf{b}_p] = \mathbf{Z}\mathbf{A}$.

Moreover, since $\mathbf{a}_i'\mathbf{Z}'\mathbf{Z}\mathbf{a}_i = \mathbf{b}_i'\mathbf{b}_i = \lambda_i$ and $\mathbf{a}_i'\mathbf{Z}'\mathbf{Z}\mathbf{a}_j = \mathbf{b}_i'\mathbf{b}_j = 0$, it also follows that

$$\mathbf{A}'\mathbf{Z}'\mathbf{Z}\mathbf{A} = \mathbf{B}'\mathbf{B} = \boldsymbol{\Lambda}, \tag{5.43}$$

where

$\boldsymbol{\Lambda}$ is a $p \times p$ diagonal matrix containing the characteristic roots of $\mathbf{Z}'\mathbf{Z}$ in descending order of magnitude.

We should also note that, if Rank$(\mathbf{Z}) =$ Rank$(\mathbf{Z}'\mathbf{Z}) = q < p$, then the values of the last $p - q$ latent roots will be identically zero. Thus, for $\mathbf{a}_i$; $i = q+1, \ldots, p$, we will have $\mathbf{Z}'\mathbf{Z}\mathbf{a}_i = \mathbf{0}$ and $\mathbf{Z}\mathbf{a}_i = \mathbf{0}$, and there will be no corresponding principal components of $\mathbf{Z}$.

Given the principal components of $\mathbf{Z}$, we can easily find those of the transposed matrix $\mathbf{Z}'$. The relationship between the two sets of principal components is established by means of the following result.

(5.44) If **a** is a characteristic vector of $\mathbf{Z}'\mathbf{Z}$ corresponding to the root λ, then $(\mathbf{Z}'\mathbf{Z} - \lambda\mathbf{I})\mathbf{a} = \mathbf{0}$ and $\mathbf{Z}(\mathbf{Z}'\mathbf{Z} - \lambda\mathbf{I})\mathbf{a} = (\mathbf{Z}\mathbf{Z}' - \lambda\mathbf{I})\mathbf{Z}\mathbf{a} = (\mathbf{Z}\mathbf{Z}' - \lambda\mathbf{I})\mathbf{b}$, whence $\mathbf{b} = \mathbf{Z}\mathbf{a}$ is a characteristic vector of $\mathbf{Z}\mathbf{Z}'$ corresponding to λ. Conversely, if **b** is a characteristic vector of $\mathbf{Z}\mathbf{Z}'$ corresponding to a root λ, then

$(\mathbf{ZZ}' - \lambda\mathbf{I})\mathbf{b} = \mathbf{0}$ and $\mathbf{Z}'(\mathbf{ZZ}' - \lambda\mathbf{I})\mathbf{b} = (\mathbf{Z}'\mathbf{Z} - \lambda\mathbf{I})\mathbf{Z}'\mathbf{b} = (\mathbf{Z}'\mathbf{Z} - \lambda\mathbf{I})\mathbf{a}$, whence $\mathbf{a} = \mathbf{Z}'\mathbf{b}$ is a characteristic vector of $\mathbf{Z}'\mathbf{Z}$ corresponding to λ.

This result implies that $\mathbf{Z}'\mathbf{Z}$ and $\mathbf{ZZ}'$ have the same non-zero characteristic roots. It also establishes the fact that the principal components $\mathbf{b}_j$; $j = 1, \ldots, p$ of $\mathbf{Z}$ are characteristic vectors of $\mathbf{ZZ}'$ corresponding to the roots λ_j; $j = 1, \ldots, p$. Let us define p normalized characteristic vectors of $\mathbf{ZZ}'$ by $\mathbf{b}_j^* = \mathbf{b}_j/\|\mathbf{b}_j\| = \mathbf{b}_j/\sqrt{\lambda_j}$. Then it follows, by definition, that

(5.45) The jth principal component of $\mathbf{Z}'$ is $\overset{*}{\mathbf{a}}_j = \mathbf{Z}'\overset{*}{\mathbf{b}}_j = \mathbf{Z}'\mathbf{b}_j/\sqrt{\lambda_j}$ where $\mathbf{b}_j$ is the jth principal component of $\mathbf{Z}$ and $\lambda_j = \mathbf{b}_j'\mathbf{b}_j$ is the jth largest root of $\mathbf{Z}'\mathbf{Z}$ and $\mathbf{ZZ}'$.

The problem of orthogonal regression can be described either in terms of finding the normalized characteristic vectors $\mathbf{a}_1, \ldots, \mathbf{a}_p$ of $\mathbf{Z}'\mathbf{Z}$ or in terms of finding the principal components $\overset{*}{\mathbf{a}}_1, \ldots, \overset{*}{\mathbf{a}}_p$ of $\mathbf{Z}'$. Thus the vector $\mathbf{a}_p = \overset{*}{\mathbf{a}}_p/\|\overset{*}{\mathbf{a}}_p\|$ is the estimate of the parameter $\boldsymbol{\alpha}$ of (5.19), whilst $\mathbf{a}_1, \ldots, \mathbf{a}_{p-1}$ and $\overset{*}{\mathbf{a}}_1, \ldots, \overset{*}{\mathbf{a}}_{p-1}$ span the $(p-1)$-dimensional hyperplane in $\mathcal{R}^p$ containing the adjusted data points $\hat{\mathbf{z}}_{t.}'$; $t = 1, \ldots, T$. In view of (5.37), we can equally well describe the problem of orthogonal regression in terms of finding the normalized characteristic vectors $\overset{*}{\mathbf{b}}_1, \ldots, \overset{*}{\mathbf{b}}_T$ of $\mathbf{ZZ}'$ which are related, in an obvious way, to the principal components $\mathbf{b}_1, \ldots, \mathbf{b}_p$ of $\mathbf{Z}$. Thus the matrix $\mathbf{B}$ defined in (5.32) is formed as $[\overset{*}{\mathbf{b}}_p, \ldots, \overset{*}{\mathbf{b}}_T]$, whilst $\overset{*}{\mathbf{b}}_1, \ldots, \overset{*}{\mathbf{b}}_{p-1}$ and $\mathbf{b}_1, \ldots, \mathbf{b}_{p-1}$ span the $(p-1)$-dimensional subspace of $\mathcal{R}^T$ containing the adjusted vectors $\hat{\mathbf{z}}_{.j}$; $j = 1, \ldots, p$.

Orthogonal regression in the $\boldsymbol{\Omega}^{-1}$-metric

Orthogonal regression has been considered so far only in terms of the unitary metric. When we replace the latter by the $\boldsymbol{\Omega}^{-1}$-metric we obtain, as a generalization of (5.20), the criterion

(5.46) Minimize

$$\sum_{t=1}^{T} (\mathbf{z}_{t.} - \hat{\mathbf{z}}_{t.})\boldsymbol{\Omega}^{-1}(\mathbf{z}_{t.} - \hat{\mathbf{z}}_{t.})'$$

Subject to

$$\hat{\mathbf{z}}_{t.}\boldsymbol{\Omega}^{-1}\mathbf{a} = \hat{\mathbf{z}}_{t.}\mathbf{c} = 0 \text{ for all } t \text{ and}$$

$$\mathbf{a}'\boldsymbol{\Omega}^{-1}\mathbf{a} = \mathbf{c}'\boldsymbol{\Omega}\mathbf{c} = 1,$$

where we define $\mathbf{c} = \boldsymbol{\Omega}^{-1}\mathbf{a}$. In order to establish an alternative form of the criterion, not in terms of $\hat{\mathbf{z}}_{t.}$, we consider the Lagrangean expression

(5.47) $$L = (\mathbf{z}_{t.} - \hat{\mathbf{z}}_{t.})\mathbf{\Omega}^{-1}(\mathbf{z}_{t.} - \hat{\mathbf{z}}_{t.})' + 2\mu(\hat{\mathbf{z}}_{t.}\mathbf{c}) + 2\lambda(\mathbf{c}'\mathbf{\Omega}\mathbf{c} - 1),$$

which relates to the problem of finding a single value $\hat{\mathbf{z}}_{t.}$ subject to $\hat{\mathbf{z}}_{t.}\mathbf{c} = 0$ for a fixed value of $\mathbf{c}$. The conditions for minimizing the expression are

(5.48) $$\begin{aligned} &\mathbf{\Omega}^{-1}(\mathbf{z}_{t.} - \hat{\mathbf{z}}_{t.})' = \mu\mathbf{c}, \\ &\hat{\mathbf{z}}_{t.}\mathbf{c} = 0, \\ &\mathbf{c}'\mathbf{\Omega}\mathbf{c} = 1. \end{aligned}$$

From these we find that

(5.49) $$\hat{\mathbf{z}}'_{t.} = (\mathbf{I} - \mathbf{\Omega}\mathbf{c}\mathbf{c}')\mathbf{z}'_{t.} = (\mathbf{I} - \mathbf{a}\mathbf{a}'\mathbf{\Omega}^{-1})\mathbf{z}'_{t.},$$

and that

(5.50) $$(\mathbf{z}_{t.} - \hat{\mathbf{z}}_{t.})\mathbf{\Omega}^{-1}(\mathbf{z}_{t.})' = (\mathbf{z}_{t.}\mathbf{c})^2 = (\mathbf{z}_{t.}\mathbf{\Omega}^{-1}\mathbf{a})^2$$

Therefore the restated criterion is

(5.51) Minimize

$$\mathbf{c}'\mathbf{Z}'\mathbf{Z}\mathbf{c} = \mathbf{a}'\mathbf{\Omega}^{-1}\mathbf{Z}'\mathbf{Z}\mathbf{\Omega}^{-1}\mathbf{a},$$

Subject to

$$\mathbf{c}'\mathbf{\Omega}\mathbf{c} = \mathbf{a}'\mathbf{\Omega}^{-1}\mathbf{a} = 1.$$

The appropriate Lagrangean expression for this problem is

(5.52) $$L = \mathbf{c}'\mathbf{Z}'\mathbf{Z}\mathbf{c} - \lambda(\mathbf{c}'\mathbf{\Omega}\mathbf{c} - 1).$$

Differentiating with respect to $\mathbf{c}$ and setting the result to zero gives

(5.53) $$(\mathbf{Z}'\mathbf{Z} - \lambda\mathbf{\Omega})\mathbf{c} = \mathbf{0},$$

which is equivalent to

(5.54) $$(\mathbf{\Omega}^{-1}\mathbf{Z}'\mathbf{Z} - \lambda\mathbf{I})\mathbf{c} = \mathbf{0}.$$

We can obtain a solution $\hat{\mathbf{c}}$ which minimizes the criterion function $\mathbf{c}'\mathbf{Z}'\mathbf{Z}\mathbf{c}$ by choosing a characteristic vector of $\mathbf{\Omega}^{-1}\mathbf{Z}'\mathbf{Z}$ corresponding to the smallest root and having a finite norm. In fact, the criterion (5.46) specifies the normalization $\hat{\mathbf{c}}'\mathbf{\Omega}\hat{\mathbf{c}} = 1$ for $\hat{\mathbf{c}}$, since this enables the equation (5.53) to be deduced most readily. Nevertheless, we are free to discard this particular normalization when we come to solve (5.53).

It is possible to convert an orthogonal regression in the $\mathbf{\Omega}^{-1}$-metric to an orthogonal regression in the unitary metric by applying an appropriate transformation to each of the T observations of the variables. For this purpose, we define a transformation of the data matrix of the form

(5.55) $$\mathbf{X} = \mathbf{Z}\mathbf{P},$$

where

$$\mathbf{P}'\mathbf{\Omega}\mathbf{P}=\mathbf{I}, \qquad \mathbf{P}\mathbf{P}'=\mathbf{\Omega}^{-1}.$$

Since $\mathbf{P}$ is non-singular, we can express the vector $\mathbf{c}$ as the transform of some vector $\mathbf{d}$, so that $\mathbf{c}=\mathbf{Pd}$. Thus, premultiplying (5.53) by $\mathbf{P}'$ gives

(5.56) $$(\mathbf{P}'\mathbf{Z}'\mathbf{Z}\mathbf{P}-\lambda\mathbf{P}'\mathbf{\Omega}\mathbf{P})\mathbf{d}=(\mathbf{X}'\mathbf{X}-\lambda\mathbf{I})\mathbf{d}=\mathbf{0}$$

which defines an orthogonal regression of the transformed variables in the unitary metric.

Ordinary least squares as a limiting case of orthogonal regression

It is particularly interesting to realize that the normal equations of the ordinary least-squares estimator are subsumed by the equation (5.53) so long as we allow $\mathbf{\Omega}$ to be singular. To demonstrate this, we replace $\mathbf{\Omega}$ in (5.53) by the matrix

(5.57) $$\mathbf{J}_{11}=\begin{bmatrix}1, & \mathbf{0}\\ \mathbf{0}, & \mathbf{0}\end{bmatrix},$$

which has a unit as its leading element and zeros elsewhere. We also replace the normalization $\mathbf{c}'\mathbf{\Omega}\mathbf{c}=1$ by $\mathbf{c}'\mathbf{J}_{11}\mathbf{c}=1$, with the effect that the leading element of $\mathbf{c}$ is now ±1, enabling us to write $\mathbf{c}'=[1,-\mathbf{b}']$. The data matrix is written conformably as $\mathbf{Z}=[\mathbf{y},\mathbf{X}]$. By substituting these particulars into (5.53), we obtain

(5.58) $$\left(\begin{bmatrix}\mathbf{y}'\mathbf{y}, & \mathbf{y}'\mathbf{X}\\ \mathbf{X}'\mathbf{y}, & \mathbf{X}'\mathbf{X}\end{bmatrix}-\lambda\begin{bmatrix}1, & \mathbf{0}\\ \mathbf{0}, & \mathbf{0}\end{bmatrix}\right)\begin{bmatrix}1\\ -\mathbf{b}\end{bmatrix}=\begin{bmatrix}0\\ \mathbf{0}\end{bmatrix},$$

from which

(5.59) $$\hat{\mathbf{b}}=(\mathbf{X}'\mathbf{X})^{-1}\mathbf{X}'\mathbf{y},$$

and

(5.60) $$\lambda=\mathbf{y}'\mathbf{y}-\mathbf{y}'\mathbf{X}(\mathbf{X}'\mathbf{X})^{-1}\mathbf{X}'\mathbf{y}.$$

The first of these (5.59) is identical to (5.8) which defines the ordinary least-squares estimator. By exploiting the symmetry and idempotency of the projector $\mathbf{P}=\mathbf{X}(\mathbf{X}'\mathbf{X})^{-1}\mathbf{X}'$ we can write the second equation (5.60) as $\lambda=\mathbf{y}'(\mathbf{I}-\mathbf{P})\mathbf{y}=\mathbf{y}'(\mathbf{I}-\mathbf{P})'(\mathbf{I}-\mathbf{P})\mathbf{y}=(\mathbf{y}-\mathbf{X}\hat{\mathbf{b}})'(\mathbf{y}-\mathbf{X}\hat{\mathbf{b}})$. Using the notation $\hat{\mathbf{y}}=\mathbf{X}\hat{\mathbf{b}}$, this becomes $\lambda=\|\mathbf{y}-\hat{\mathbf{y}}\|^2_{\mathbf{I}}$. Thus λ is seen to represent the value of the minimand in ordinary least-squares regression.

REGRESSIONS IN TENSOR SPACES

We have been able to represent the problems of Gaussian regression both in the space $\mathcal{R}^T$ comprising the column vectors of the data matrix $\mathbf{Z}=[\mathbf{y},\mathbf{X}]$

and in the space $\mathcal{R}^p$ comprising the row vectors. Nevertheless, it is more natural to visualize Gaussian regression in terms of $\mathcal{R}^T$, since it is in respect of this space that the $\mathbf{Q}^{-1}$-metric is defined; and, conversely, it is more natural to visualize orthogonal regression in terms of $\mathcal{R}^p$, upon which the $\mathbf{\Omega}^{-1}$-metric is defined. However, we can avoid having to particularize a regression problem in terms of either $\mathcal{R}^p$ or $\mathcal{R}^T$ by choosing to represent it in the tensor product space $\mathcal{T} = \mathcal{R}^p \otimes \mathcal{R}^T$. Thus, for example, the criterion function of orthogonal regression in the $\mathbf{\Omega}^{-1}$-metric is a natural inner product on $\mathcal{T}$ according to the definition (4.38). This is demonstrated when, with reference to (5.46), we write the criterion function as

$$\begin{aligned}\sum (\mathbf{z}_{t.} - \hat{\mathbf{z}}_{t.})\mathbf{\Omega}^{-1}(\mathbf{z}_{t.} - \hat{\mathbf{z}}_{t.})' &= \text{Trace}[(\mathbf{Z} - \hat{\mathbf{Z}})\mathbf{\Omega}^{-1}(\mathbf{Z} - \hat{\mathbf{Z}})'] \\ &= \text{Trace}[(\mathbf{Z} - \hat{\mathbf{Z}})'\mathbf{I}(\mathbf{Z} - \hat{\mathbf{Z}})\mathbf{\Omega}^{-1}] \\ &= (\mathbf{Z} - \hat{\mathbf{Z}})^{c\prime}(\mathbf{\Omega}^{-1} \otimes \mathbf{I})(\mathbf{Z} - \hat{\mathbf{Z}})^c,\end{aligned}$$

where it is understood that $(\mathbf{Z} - \hat{\mathbf{Z}})^c = \mathbf{Z}^c - \hat{\mathbf{Z}}^c$. Thus the criterion (5.46) may be rewritten in the form

(5.61) Minimize

$$(\mathbf{Z} - \hat{\mathbf{Z}})^{c\prime}(\mathbf{\Omega}^{-1} \otimes \mathbf{I})(\mathbf{Z} - \hat{\mathbf{Z}})^c$$

Subject to

$$(\mathbf{a}' \otimes \mathbf{I})(\mathbf{\Omega}^{-1} \otimes \mathbf{I})\mathbf{Z}^c = (\mathbf{c}' \otimes \mathbf{I})\mathbf{Z}^c = \mathbf{0}^c,$$

where we have omitted to specify any normalization for $\mathbf{c}$ or $\mathbf{a}$.

In order to depict the criterion of Gaussian regression in the $\mathbf{Q}^{-1}$-metric in the same terms as (5.61), we may rewrite (5.12) as

(5.62) Minimize

$$[\mathbf{y} - \hat{\mathbf{y}}, \mathbf{0}]^{c\prime}(\mathbf{I} \otimes \mathbf{Q}^{-1})[\mathbf{y} - \hat{\mathbf{y}}, \mathbf{0}]^c,$$

where $[\mathbf{y} - \hat{\mathbf{y}}, \mathbf{0}] = [\mathbf{y}, \mathbf{X}] - [\hat{\mathbf{y}}, \mathbf{X}] = \mathbf{Z} - \hat{\mathbf{Z}}$ and $\hat{\mathbf{y}} \in \mathcal{M}(\mathbf{X})$. This clearly indicates that the data is adjusted only in respect of the vector $\mathbf{y}$.

We can also regard the criterion of Gaussian regression as a limiting case of a criterion of a multilateral regression. For this purpose, we may consider a multilateral criterion whereby adjustments to all but the vector $\mathbf{y}$ are inhibited by being associated with indefinitely large weights. Let us therefore define a non-singular diagonal matrix $\overset{*}{\mathbf{J}}_{11}$ of order $p \times p$, having a unit as its leading element and values of $1/n$ elsewhere on the diagonal. We may note that the limit of $\overset{*}{\mathbf{J}}_{11}$, as n tends to infinity, is the singular matrix $\mathbf{J}_{11}$ defined in (5.57); and we may also note that the inverse matrix $\overset{*}{\mathbf{J}}{}_{11}^{-1}$ differs from $\overset{*}{\mathbf{J}}_{11}$ only by having values of n in place of $1/n$. Using $\overset{*}{\mathbf{J}}{}_{11}^{-1}$, we may form the criterion

(5.63) Minimize

$$(\mathbf{Z}-\hat{\mathbf{Z}})^{c\prime}(\overset{*}{\mathbf{J}}{}_{11}^{-1}\otimes\mathbf{Q}^{-1})(\mathbf{Z}-\hat{\mathbf{Z}})^{c}$$

Subject to

$$(\mathbf{c}'\otimes\mathbf{I})\hat{\mathbf{Z}}^{c}=\mathbf{0}^{c}, \quad \text{where} \quad \mathbf{c}'=[-1,\mathbf{b}'].$$

Then it is easy to see that, as n tends to infinity, the multilateral regression resulting from (5.63) tends towards Gaussian regression in the $\mathbf{Q}^{-1}$-metric; for, as their associated weights—of value n—increase indefinitely, the adjustments $\mathbf{x}_{.j}-\hat{\mathbf{x}}_{.j}$, within $\mathbf{Z}-\hat{\mathbf{Z}}=[\mathbf{y}-\hat{\mathbf{y}},\mathbf{X}-\hat{\mathbf{X}}]$, must become negligible in any metric in order to ensure that the criterion function retains a finite value. If, in particular, we specify $\mathbf{Q}=\mathbf{I}$, we obtain, from (5.63), a multilateral regression whose limit, as n tends to infinity, is represented by the equations of ordinary least squares in the form of (5.58).

Not every practical problem of econometric estimation can be associated with a criterion function that has the form of a natural inner product on a tensor product space $\mathcal{T}$. Some problems give rise to criteria that can only be expressed in terms of non-decomposable inner products on $\mathcal{T}$. Nevertheless, many of the classical econometric procedures do involve relatively simple natural inner products.

BIBLIOGRAPHY

Equivalent Regression Metrics. Kruskal [**71**]

Interpretive Aspects of Gaussian Regression. Barnard [**11**], Durbin and Kendall [**32**], Scheffé [**106,** pp. 10–13]

Principal Components. Anderson [**8,** Chap. 11], Morrison [**86,** Chap. 7]

CHAPTER 6

The Gauss–Markov Model

We shall now consider in detail the problems of inference that are associated with a stochastic model of the form

$$y_t = \mathbf{x}_{t.}\boldsymbol{\beta} + \varepsilon_t, \tag{6.1}$$

which relates an observable scalar-valued output y_t to a set of observable inputs $\mathbf{x}_{t.} = [x_{t1}, \ldots, x_{tk}]$ and an unobservable stochastic component ε_t. A set of T realizations of the relationship is written as

$$\mathbf{y} = \mathbf{X}\boldsymbol{\beta} + \boldsymbol{\varepsilon}, \tag{6.2}$$

where $\mathbf{y}, \mathbf{X}$ comprise the observations. Within this framework, we begin by making the sole assumptions that the stochastic vector $\boldsymbol{\varepsilon}$ has

$$E(\boldsymbol{\varepsilon}) = \mathbf{0}, \qquad D(\boldsymbol{\varepsilon}) = E(\boldsymbol{\varepsilon}\boldsymbol{\varepsilon}') = \sigma^2\mathbf{Q}, \tag{6.3}$$

where $\mathbf{Q}$ is a known positive-definite matrix and σ^2 is an unknown scalar. That is to say, we assume that $\boldsymbol{\varepsilon}$ is a non-degenerate random vector with a zero mean and a dispersion matrix that is known up to a scalar factor. If the input variables are regarded as non-stochastic, we can depict the output vector $\mathbf{y}$ as a random vector with

$$E(\mathbf{y}) = \mathbf{X}\boldsymbol{\beta}, \qquad D(\mathbf{y}) = E\{[\mathbf{y} - E(\mathbf{y})][\mathbf{y} - E(\mathbf{y})]'\} = \sigma^2\mathbf{Q}. \tag{6.4}$$

Thus it becomes appropriate to denote the distribution of this vector by $\mathbf{y} \sim (\mathbf{X}\boldsymbol{\beta}, \sigma^2\mathbf{Q})$. However, we shall also denote the model by $(\mathbf{y}, \mathbf{X}\boldsymbol{\beta}, \sigma^2\mathbf{Q})$.

MINIMUM VARIANCE LINEAR UNBIASED ESTIMATION

Estimating parametric functions of $\boldsymbol{\beta}$

In order to obtain an unbiased estimator of the mean vector $\boldsymbol{\mu} = \mathbf{X}\boldsymbol{\beta}$, we use the method of Gaussian regression which is to project $\mathbf{y}$ on $\mathcal{M}(\mathbf{X})$ to obtain $\hat{\mathbf{y}} = \mathbf{P}\mathbf{y} = \mathbf{X}\hat{\boldsymbol{\beta}}$. Then we have $E(\hat{\mathbf{y}}) = E(\mathbf{P}\mathbf{y}) = \mathbf{P}E(\mathbf{y}) = \mathbf{P}\mathbf{X}\boldsymbol{\beta} = \mathbf{X}\boldsymbol{\beta}$, since $\mathbf{P}\mathbf{X} = \mathbf{X}$.

We are also interested in estimating scalar functions of the parameter vector $\boldsymbol{\beta}$, including single elements of the vector.

(6.5) A linear parametric function $\mathbf{p}'\boldsymbol{\beta}$ is said to be estimable if there exists a vector $\mathbf{q}$ such that $E(\mathbf{q}'\mathbf{y}) = \mathbf{p}'\boldsymbol{\beta}$.

In fact, the set of estimable parametric functions of $\boldsymbol{\beta}$ may be limited by the nature of $\mathbf{X}$ in such a way that not all elements of $\boldsymbol{\beta}$ are estimable.

(6.6) A parametric function $\mathbf{p}'\boldsymbol{\beta}$ is estimable if and only if there exists a vector $\mathbf{q}$ such that $\mathbf{p}'=\mathbf{q}'\mathbf{X}$; that is to say, if and only if $\mathbf{p}'$ may be expressed as a linear combination of the rows of $\mathbf{X}$.

Proof. If $\mathbf{p}'\boldsymbol{\beta}$ is estimable there exists, by definition, a vector $\mathbf{q}$ such that, for all $\boldsymbol{\beta}$, $E(\mathbf{q}'\mathbf{y})=\mathbf{q}'E(\mathbf{y})=\mathbf{q}'\mathbf{X}\boldsymbol{\beta}=\mathbf{p}'\boldsymbol{\beta}$, whence $\mathbf{p}'=\mathbf{q}'\mathbf{X}$. Conversely, if $\mathbf{p}'=\mathbf{q}'\mathbf{X}$, then $\mathbf{p}'\boldsymbol{\beta}=\mathbf{q}'\mathbf{X}\boldsymbol{\beta}=\mathbf{q}'E(\mathbf{y})=E(\mathbf{q}'\mathbf{y})$, and $\mathbf{p}'\boldsymbol{\beta}$ is an estimable parametric function for all $\boldsymbol{\beta}$.

Clearly, if $\text{Null}(\mathbf{X})=0$, then the rows of $\mathbf{X}$ span the space of all $\mathbf{p}'$; and every parametric function of $\boldsymbol{\beta}$, including each element of $\boldsymbol{\beta}$, is therefore estimable.

Given the specification $(\mathbf{y}, \mathbf{X}\boldsymbol{\beta}, \sigma^2\mathbf{Q})$, we can find the minimum variance unbiased linear estimator of every estimable parametric function from the minimum $\mathbf{Q}^{-1}$-distance projection of $\mathbf{y}$ on $\mathcal{M}(\mathbf{X})$. The latter is said to be the minimum variance linear unbiased estimator of $\mathbf{X}\boldsymbol{\beta}$. These results are established by the Gauss–Markov theorem which is as follows:

(6.7) Let $\mathbf{y}\sim(\mathbf{X}\boldsymbol{\beta}, \sigma^2\mathbf{Q})$ and let $\mathbf{P}$ be the $\mathbf{Q}^{-1}$-orthogonal projector on $\mathcal{M}(\mathbf{X})$. Then, if $\mathbf{q}$ is any vector such that $\mathbf{q}'\mathbf{X}=\mathbf{p}'$ or, equivalently, $E(\mathbf{q}'\mathbf{y})=\mathbf{p}'\boldsymbol{\beta}$, we have $E(\mathbf{q}'\mathbf{P}\mathbf{y})=\mathbf{p}'\boldsymbol{\beta}$ and $V(\mathbf{q}'\mathbf{P}\mathbf{y})\leq V(\mathbf{q}'\mathbf{y})$. Furthermore, if $\mathbf{F}$ is any other matrix such that $E(\mathbf{q}'\mathbf{F}\mathbf{y})=\mathbf{p}'\boldsymbol{\beta}$, then $V(\mathbf{q}'\mathbf{P}\mathbf{y})\leq V(\mathbf{q}'\mathbf{F}\mathbf{y})$.

Proof. The condition $E(\mathbf{q}'\mathbf{P}\mathbf{y})=\mathbf{q}'\mathbf{P}E(\mathbf{y})=\mathbf{q}'\mathbf{P}\mathbf{X}\boldsymbol{\beta}=\mathbf{q}'\mathbf{X}\boldsymbol{\beta}=\mathbf{p}'\boldsymbol{\beta}$, which asserts that $\mathbf{q}'\mathbf{P}\mathbf{y}$ is an unbiased estimator of $\mathbf{q}'\mathbf{X}\boldsymbol{\beta}=\mathbf{p}'\boldsymbol{\beta}$, is fulfilled for all $\boldsymbol{\beta}$ if and only if $\mathbf{P}\mathbf{X}=\mathbf{X}$. The latter condition is satisfied since $\mathbf{P}$ is a projector on $\mathcal{M}(\mathbf{X})$. Now let us recall that $\mathbf{P}$ is idempotent such that $\mathbf{P}^2=\mathbf{P}$ and $\mathbf{Q}^{-1}$-symmetric such that $(\mathbf{Q}^{-1}\mathbf{P})'=\mathbf{P}'\mathbf{Q}^{-1}=\mathbf{Q}^{-1}\mathbf{P}$. These conditions on $\mathbf{P}$ are jointly equivalent to $\mathbf{P}\mathbf{Q}=\mathbf{Q}\mathbf{P}'=\mathbf{P}\mathbf{Q}\mathbf{P}'$. The latter may be used to confirm the identity $\mathbf{Q}=\mathbf{P}\mathbf{Q}\mathbf{P}'+(\mathbf{I}-\mathbf{P})\mathbf{Q}(\mathbf{I}-\mathbf{P})'$. Thus we have $V(\mathbf{q}'\mathbf{y})=\mathbf{q}'D(\mathbf{y})\mathbf{q}=\sigma^2\mathbf{q}'\mathbf{Q}\mathbf{q}=\sigma^2\mathbf{q}'\mathbf{P}\mathbf{Q}\mathbf{P}'\mathbf{q}+\sigma^2\mathbf{q}'(\mathbf{I}-\mathbf{P})\mathbf{Q}(\mathbf{I}-\mathbf{P})'\mathbf{q}\geq\sigma^2\mathbf{q}'\mathbf{P}\mathbf{Q}\mathbf{P}'\mathbf{q}=V(\mathbf{q}'\mathbf{P}\mathbf{y})$, or simply $V(\mathbf{q}'\mathbf{y})\geq V(\mathbf{q}'\mathbf{P}\mathbf{y})$. Now consider any other estimator $\mathbf{q}'\mathbf{F}\mathbf{y}$ such that $E(\mathbf{q}'\mathbf{F}\mathbf{y})=\mathbf{q}'\mathbf{X}\boldsymbol{\beta}=\mathbf{p}'\boldsymbol{\beta}$ or, equivalently, $\mathbf{F}\mathbf{X}=\mathbf{X}$. Then, since $\mathcal{M}(\mathbf{P})=\mathcal{M}(\mathbf{X})$, we have $\mathbf{F}\mathbf{P}=\mathbf{P}$, and, on replacing $\mathbf{q}'$ in the inequality by $\mathbf{q}'\mathbf{F}$, we get $V(\mathbf{q}'\mathbf{F}\mathbf{P}\mathbf{y})=V(\mathbf{q}'\mathbf{P}\mathbf{y})\leq V(\mathbf{q}'\mathbf{F}\mathbf{y})$.

The estimator $\mathbf{p}'\hat{\boldsymbol{\beta}}=\mathbf{q}'\mathbf{X}\hat{\boldsymbol{\beta}}=\mathbf{q}'\mathbf{P}\mathbf{y}$, specified in the Gauss–Markov theorem, is commonly known as the best linear unbiased estimator, or BLUE, of $\mathbf{p}'\boldsymbol{\beta}$.

An explicit form of the estimator is given by

$$\mathbf{q'Py} = \mathbf{q'X(X'Q^{-1}X)^{-}X'Q^{-1}y} \tag{6.8}$$
$$= \mathbf{p'(X'Q^{-1}X)^{-}X'Q^{-1}y}$$
$$= \mathbf{p'X^{-}_{lQ^{-1}}y},$$

where $\mathbf{X}^{-}_{l\mathbf{Q}^{-1}}$ is the minimum $\mathbf{Q}^{-1}$-distance g-inverse given in the example following (3.58). Using the functional form $\mathbf{P} = \mathbf{X(X'Q^{-1}X)^{-}X'Q^{-1}}$ and the condition $\mathbf{PQP'} = \mathbf{PQ}$, we may also find a convenient expression for the variance of $\mathbf{p'\hat{\boldsymbol{\beta}}}$. Thus we have $V(\mathbf{p'\hat{\boldsymbol{\beta}}}) = V(\mathbf{q'Py}) = \sigma^2\mathbf{q'PQP'q} = \sigma^2\mathbf{q'PQq} = \sigma^2\mathbf{q'X(X'Q^{-1}X)^{-}X'Q^{-1}Qq} = \sigma^2\mathbf{p'(X'Q^{-1}X)^{-}p}$, or simply

$$V(\mathbf{p'\hat{\boldsymbol{\beta}}}) = \sigma^2\mathbf{p'(X'Q^{-1}X)^{-}p} \tag{6.9}$$

The Gauss–Markov theorem is the traditional means of establishing the equivalence of the minimum-distance and the minimum variance estimators within the class of linear unbiased estimators of $\mathbf{X}\boldsymbol{\beta}$. The theorem demonstrates the minimum variance property of the estimator that is derived from the minimum-distance criterion. We might, equally, take the estimator that is derived from the minimum variance criterion and proceed to demonstrate the minimum-distance property. Therefore let us consider the criterion

(6.10) Minimize

$$V(\mathbf{q'y}) = \sigma^2\mathbf{q'Qq} = \sigma^2\,\|\mathbf{q}\|^2_{\mathbf{Q}}$$

Subject to

$$E(\mathbf{q'y}) = \mathbf{p'}\boldsymbol{\beta} \quad \text{or, equivalently,} \quad \mathbf{X'q} = \mathbf{p}.$$

All that is at issue here is the problem of finding the minimum $\mathbf{Q}$-norm solution of the equation $\mathbf{X'q} = \mathbf{p}$. Thus the criterion specifies $\mathbf{q} = (\mathbf{X'})^{-}_{m\mathbf{Q}}\mathbf{p}$; and, using the form $(\mathbf{X'})^{-}_{m\mathbf{Q}} = \mathbf{Q^{-1}X(X'Q^{-1}X)^{-}}$ given in the example following (3.58), we obtain

$$\mathbf{q'y} = \mathbf{p'}[(\mathbf{X'})^{-}_{m\mathbf{Q}}]'\mathbf{y} \tag{6.11}$$
$$= \mathbf{p'(X'Q^{-1}X)^{-}X'Q^{-1}y},$$

which we recognize as the minimum-distance estimator. In comparing (6.8) and (6.11) we may also recall the identity $[(\mathbf{X'})^{-}_{m\mathbf{Q}}]' = \mathbf{X}^{-}_{l\mathbf{Q}^{-1}}$.

In order to derive the estimator more directly from the criterion (6.10), we may form the Lagrangean expression

$$L = \mathbf{q'Qq} - 2\boldsymbol{\lambda}'(\mathbf{X'q} - \mathbf{p}). \tag{6.12}$$

Differentiating this with respect to $\mathbf{q}$ and setting the results to zero gives, after eliminating the factor, the condition $\mathbf{q'Q} - \boldsymbol{\lambda}'\mathbf{X'} = \mathbf{0}$, whence

$$\mathbf{q'} = \boldsymbol{\lambda}'\mathbf{X'Q^{-1}}. \tag{6.13}$$

Postmultiplying by $\mathbf{X}$ and using $\mathbf{q}'\mathbf{X}=\mathbf{p}'$ gives $\mathbf{q}'\mathbf{X}=\mathbf{p}'=\boldsymbol{\lambda}'\mathbf{X}'\mathbf{Q}^{-1}\mathbf{X}$, whence

$$\boldsymbol{\lambda}'=\mathbf{q}'\mathbf{X}(\mathbf{X}'\mathbf{Q}^{-1}\mathbf{X})^{-}=\mathbf{p}'(\mathbf{X}'\mathbf{Q}^{-1}\mathbf{X})^{-}. \tag{6.14}$$

Thus, on postmultiplying (6.13) by $\mathbf{y}$ and substituting for $\boldsymbol{\lambda}'$, we get

$$\begin{aligned}\mathbf{q}'\mathbf{y}&=\mathbf{q}'\mathbf{X}(\mathbf{X}'\mathbf{Q}^{-1}\mathbf{X})^{-}\mathbf{X}'\mathbf{Q}^{-1}\mathbf{y}\\&=\mathbf{p}'(\mathbf{X}'\mathbf{Q}^{-1}\mathbf{X})^{-}\mathbf{X}'\mathbf{Q}^{-1}\mathbf{y}.\end{aligned}$$

Estimating σ^2

To form an unbiased estimator of σ^2, we use the information contained in the residual vector $\mathbf{y}-\mathbf{X}\hat{\boldsymbol{\beta}}=(\mathbf{I}-\mathbf{P})\mathbf{y}=(\mathbf{I}-\mathbf{P})(\mathbf{X}\boldsymbol{\beta}+\boldsymbol{\varepsilon})=(\mathbf{I}-\mathbf{P})\boldsymbol{\varepsilon}$. By the assumptions of (6.3), we have $\boldsymbol{\varepsilon}\sim(\mathbf{0},\sigma^2\mathbf{Q})$. Thus, if we define $\mathbf{T}$ such that $\mathbf{T}'\mathbf{T}=\mathbf{Q}^{-1}$ and $\mathbf{T}\mathbf{Q}\mathbf{T}'=\mathbf{I}$, we obtain the result that

$$\mathbf{T}\mathbf{P}\boldsymbol{\varepsilon}+\mathbf{T}(\mathbf{I}-\mathbf{P})\boldsymbol{\varepsilon}=\mathbf{T}\boldsymbol{\varepsilon}\sim(\mathbf{0},\sigma^2\mathbf{I}_T), \tag{6.15}$$

where $\mathbf{T}\mathbf{P}\boldsymbol{\varepsilon}$ and $\mathbf{T}(\mathbf{I}-\mathbf{P})\boldsymbol{\varepsilon}$ are vectors that reside in complementary spaces which are orthogonal in terms of the ordinary inner product. It is now possible to find an orthonormal matrix $\mathbf{C}$, such that $\mathbf{C}'\mathbf{C}=\mathbf{I}$, which represents a rotation that translates these vectors into subspaces spanned by the first $h=\text{Rank}(\mathbf{P})$, and the remaining $T-h$ vectors of the natural basis of $\mathscr{R}^T$. Thus we may obtain

$$\mathbf{C}\mathbf{T}\mathbf{P}\boldsymbol{\varepsilon}+\mathbf{C}\mathbf{T}(\mathbf{I}-\mathbf{P})\boldsymbol{\varepsilon}=\mathbf{C}\mathbf{T}\boldsymbol{\varepsilon}=\boldsymbol{\eta}\sim(\mathbf{0},\sigma^2\mathbf{I}_T), \tag{6.16}$$

where

$$\mathbf{C}\mathbf{T}\mathbf{P}\boldsymbol{\varepsilon}=\begin{bmatrix}\boldsymbol{\eta}_1\\\mathbf{0}\end{bmatrix}\sim\left(\begin{bmatrix}\mathbf{0}\\\mathbf{0}\end{bmatrix},\ \sigma^2\begin{bmatrix}\mathbf{I}_h, & \mathbf{0}\\\mathbf{0}, & \mathbf{0}\end{bmatrix}\right), \tag{6.17}$$

and

$$\mathbf{C}\mathbf{T}(\mathbf{I}-\mathbf{P})\boldsymbol{\varepsilon}=\begin{bmatrix}\mathbf{0}\\\boldsymbol{\eta}_2\end{bmatrix}\sim\left(\begin{bmatrix}\mathbf{0}\\\mathbf{0}\end{bmatrix},\ \sigma^2\begin{bmatrix}\mathbf{0}, & \mathbf{0}\\\mathbf{0}, & \mathbf{I}_{T-h}\end{bmatrix}\right). \tag{6.18}$$

From (6.18) it follows that $E(\boldsymbol{\eta}_2'\boldsymbol{\eta}_2)=E(\sum_{j=h+1}^{T}\eta_j^2)=(T-h)\sigma^2$. But $\boldsymbol{\eta}_2'\boldsymbol{\eta}_2=\boldsymbol{\varepsilon}'(\mathbf{I}-\mathbf{P})'\mathbf{T}'\mathbf{C}'\mathbf{C}\mathbf{T}(\mathbf{I}-\mathbf{P})\boldsymbol{\varepsilon}=(\mathbf{y}-\mathbf{P}\mathbf{y})'\mathbf{Q}^{-1}(\mathbf{y}-\mathbf{P}\mathbf{y})$, so $E[(\mathbf{y}-\mathbf{P}\mathbf{y})'\mathbf{Q}^{-1}(\mathbf{y}-\mathbf{P}\mathbf{y})]=\sigma^2(T-h)$; and we may define an unbiased estimator of σ^2 by

$$\hat{\sigma}^2=\frac{(\mathbf{y}-\mathbf{P}\mathbf{y})'\mathbf{Q}^{-1}(\mathbf{y}-\mathbf{P}\mathbf{y})}{T-h}. \tag{6.19}$$

The coefficient of determination

We may wish to have a summary measure of the extent to which an estimated regression model accounts for the observed vector $\mathbf{y}$. An appropriate measure, which is invariant with respect to the units in which the data in $[\mathbf{y}, \mathbf{X}]$ are measured, is the correlation coefficient of $\mathbf{y}$ and $\hat{\mathbf{y}} = \mathbf{X}\hat{\boldsymbol{\beta}}$. This is defined simply as the cosine of the angle θ between these vectors. On the assumption that $\mathbf{y} \sim (\mathbf{X}\boldsymbol{\beta}, \sigma^2\mathbf{Q})$ it seems appropriate to measure this angle in the $\mathbf{Q}^{-1}$-metric. Thus from (3.12) we obtain

$$\rho_{\mathbf{Q}^{-1}} = \cos\theta = \frac{\langle \mathbf{y}, \hat{\mathbf{y}} \rangle_{\mathbf{Q}^{-1}}}{\sqrt{\langle \hat{\mathbf{y}}, \hat{\mathbf{y}} \rangle_{\mathbf{Q}^{-1}}} \sqrt{\langle \mathbf{y}, \mathbf{y} \rangle_{\mathbf{Q}^{-1}}}}.$$

This gives $\rho_{\mathbf{Q}^{-1}} = \mathbf{y}'\mathbf{Q}^{-1}\mathbf{P}\mathbf{y}/\sqrt{\mathbf{y}'\mathbf{P}'\mathbf{Q}^{-1}\mathbf{P}\mathbf{y}}\,\sqrt{\mathbf{y}'\mathbf{Q}^{-1}\mathbf{y}}$. Using $\mathbf{Q}^{-1}\mathbf{P} = \mathbf{P}'\mathbf{Q}^{-1}\mathbf{P}$, we can express the numerator as $\mathbf{y}'\mathbf{P}'\mathbf{Q}^{-1}\mathbf{P}\mathbf{y}$; and this enables us to write

$$\rho_{\mathbf{Q}^{-1}} = \frac{\sqrt{\mathbf{y}'\mathbf{P}'\mathbf{Q}^{-1}\mathbf{P}\mathbf{y}}}{\sqrt{\mathbf{y}'\mathbf{Q}^{-1}\mathbf{y}}} = \frac{\|\hat{\mathbf{y}}\|_{\mathbf{Q}^{-1}}}{\|\mathbf{y}\|_{\mathbf{Q}^{-1}}}. \tag{6.20}$$

The properties of cosines are such that $-1 \leq \rho_{\mathbf{Q}^{-1}} = \cos\theta \leq 1$, which gives $0 \leq \rho^2_{\mathbf{Q}^{-1}} \leq 1$. The measure $\rho^2_{\mathbf{Q}^{-1}}$ is known as the coefficient of determination in the $\mathbf{Q}^{-1}$-metric. In practice the coefficient of determination is commonly defined in terms of the unitary metric and denoted by $R^2 = \hat{\mathbf{y}}'\hat{\mathbf{y}}/\mathbf{y}'\mathbf{y}$. It is then described as the ratio of the regression sum of squares and the total sum of squares. It is important to understand that $R^2 = 1$ whenever $\text{Null}(\mathbf{X}') = 0$. This results from the fact that, when $\mathbf{X}$ is $T \times k$ and $\text{Null}(\mathbf{X}') = 0$, we have $\mathcal{M}(\mathbf{X}) = \mathcal{R}^T$. For then $\mathbf{P} \in \mathcal{L}(\mathcal{R}^T, \mathcal{R}^T)$, which is the projector on $\mathcal{M}(\mathbf{X})$, becomes the identity transformation on $\mathcal{R}^T$, and we get $\mathbf{P}\mathbf{y} = \hat{\mathbf{y}} = \mathbf{y}$.

STATISTICAL INFERENCE IN THE NORMAL REGRESSION MODEL

The assumption of normality

In the absence of a specification of the functional form of the statistical distribution of $\mathbf{y}$ in the model $(\mathbf{y}, \mathbf{X}\boldsymbol{\beta}, \sigma^2\mathbf{Q})$, we are unable to construct confidence intervals for estimates of $\mathbf{X}\boldsymbol{\beta}$ or to test hypotheses in respect of estimable functions of $\boldsymbol{\beta}$. It is reasonable to assume that $\mathbf{y}$ is normally distributed. This is expressed by writing $\mathbf{y} \sim N_T(\mathbf{X}\boldsymbol{\beta}, \sigma^2\mathbf{Q})$. The functional form of the distribution of $\mathbf{y}$ is given as

$$N_T(\mathbf{y}; \mathbf{X}\boldsymbol{\beta}, \sigma^2\mathbf{Q}) = (2\pi)^{-T/2}\,|\sigma^2\mathbf{Q}|^{-1/2} \times \exp\left\{-\frac{1}{2\sigma^2}(\mathbf{y} - \mathbf{X}\boldsymbol{\beta})'\mathbf{Q}^{-1}(\mathbf{y} - \mathbf{X}\boldsymbol{\beta})\right\}. \tag{6.21}$$

As a probability distribution, $N(\mathbf{y}; \mathbf{X}\boldsymbol{\beta}, \sigma^2\mathbf{Q})$ is a function of the distance $\|\mathbf{y} - \mathbf{X}\boldsymbol{\beta}\|_{\mathbf{Q}^{-1}}$. When it is considered, alternatively, as a function of the parameters $\boldsymbol{\beta}, \sigma^2$ with fixed data values, $N(\mathbf{y}; \mathbf{X}\boldsymbol{\beta}, \sigma^2\mathbf{Q})$ becomes a likelihood function and is then denoted by $L(\boldsymbol{\beta}, \sigma^2)$.

For a given value of σ^2 the likelihood function is maximized by minimizing the quadratic $(\mathbf{y}-\mathbf{X\beta})'\mathbf{Q}^{-1}(\mathbf{y}-\mathbf{X\beta})$ in respect of $\boldsymbol{\beta}$. Thus Gaussian regression in the $\mathbf{Q}^{-1}$-metric provides the maximum-likelihood estimator of $\boldsymbol{\beta}$. In order to derive the maximum-likelihood estimator of σ^2, we maximize $L(\boldsymbol{\beta}, \sigma^2)$ in respect of σ^2. The value that maximizes $L(\boldsymbol{\beta}, \sigma^2)$ also maximizes the log-likelihood function $L^*(\boldsymbol{\beta}, \sigma^2) = \log L(\boldsymbol{\beta}, \sigma^2)$. The latter is written explicitly as

$$L^*(\boldsymbol{\beta}, \sigma^2 \mid \mathbf{y}, \mathbf{X}) = -\frac{T}{2}\log(2\pi) - \tfrac{1}{2}\log|\mathbf{Q}| - T\log\sigma - \frac{1}{2\sigma^2}(\mathbf{y}-\mathbf{X\beta})'\mathbf{Q}^{-1}(\mathbf{y}-\mathbf{X\beta}), \tag{6.22}$$

which is derived from (6.21) by using the identities $\log|\sigma^2\mathbf{Q}|^{-1/2} = \log(\sigma^{2T}|\mathbf{Q}|)^{-1/2} = -\tfrac{1}{2}\log|\mathbf{Q}| - T\log\sigma$. Differentiating (6.22) with respect to σ and setting the result to zero for a maximum gives

$$-\frac{T}{\sigma} + \frac{1}{\sigma^3}(\mathbf{y}-\mathbf{X\beta})'\mathbf{Q}^{-1}(\mathbf{y}-\mathbf{X\beta}) = 0.$$

By replacing $\mathbf{X\beta}$ in this expression by the maximum-likelihood estimator $\mathbf{X}\tilde{\boldsymbol{\beta}} = \mathbf{Py}$ and solving for σ^2, we get

$$\tilde{\sigma}^2 = \frac{(\mathbf{y}-\mathbf{Py})'\mathbf{Q}^{-1}(\mathbf{y}-\mathbf{Py})}{T} = \hat{\sigma}^2(T-h)/T, \tag{6.23}$$

where $\hat{\sigma}^2$ is the estimator of σ^2 defined in (6.19). Since $\hat{\sigma}^2$ is an unbiased estimator, it is clear that $\tilde{\sigma}^2$ is biased. However, as the sample size T increases, the factor $(T-h)/T$ tends to unity, and so $\tilde{\sigma}^2$ tends to $\hat{\sigma}^2$.

Hypothesis testing under the assumption of normality

The assumption that $\mathbf{y}$ is normally distributed enables us to derive the sampling distributions of the statistics that are used to test the validity of hypotheses relating to the unknown parameters of the regression model. Fortunately, many of the tests may be subsumed under a relatively simple general model of which we shall consider three examples.

In the first example, we consider an hypothesis that postulates, in the context of the model $\mathbf{y} \sim N(\mathbf{X\beta}, \sigma^2\mathbf{Q})$, that $\mathbf{X\beta}$ has the specific value $\boldsymbol{\mu}_0 = \mathbf{X\beta}_0$. Unless $\text{Null}(\mathbf{X}) = 0$, it is unnecessary to assume that $\boldsymbol{\beta}_0$ is uniquely identified by this hypothesis. Ignoring the hypothesis, we would estimate the mean vector $\boldsymbol{\mu} = \mathbf{X\beta}$ under the general assumptions of the model by $\hat{\mathbf{y}} = \mathbf{Py} = \mathbf{X}\hat{\boldsymbol{\beta}}$, where $\mathbf{P}$ is the minimum $\mathbf{Q}^{-1}$-distance projector on $\mathcal{M}(\mathbf{X})$. This estimator freely expresses the properties of the data. The validity of the hypothesis will therefore be reflected, in the light of the sample data, by the proximity of $\boldsymbol{\mu}_0$ and $\hat{\mathbf{y}}$. A measure of proximity is provided by the square of the distance between the two vectors in terms of the $(\sigma^2\mathbf{Q})^{-1}$-metric. This is $\sigma^{-2}\|\hat{\mathbf{y}}-\boldsymbol{\mu}_0\|^2_{\mathbf{Q}^{-1}}=\sigma^{-2}(\hat{\mathbf{y}}-\boldsymbol{\mu}_0)'\mathbf{Q}^{-1}(\hat{\mathbf{y}}-\boldsymbol{\mu}_0)=\sigma^{-2}(\mathbf{y}-\boldsymbol{\mu}_0)'\mathbf{P}'\mathbf{Q}^{-1}\mathbf{P}(\mathbf{y}-\boldsymbol{\mu}_0)$.

The hypothesis that the mean vector is $\boldsymbol{\mu}_0$ implies that $(\mathbf{y}-\boldsymbol{\mu}_0)\sim N(\mathbf{0},\sigma^2\mathbf{Q})$. Therefore it follows directly from (17.46), in view of the fact that $\mathbf{P}$ is a $\mathbf{Q}^{-1}$-symmetric idempotent matrix, that $\sigma^{-2}(\mathbf{y}-\boldsymbol{\mu}_0)'\mathbf{P}'\mathbf{Q}^{-1}\mathbf{P}(\mathbf{y}-\boldsymbol{\mu}_0)\sim\chi^2(h)$, where $h=\text{Rank}(\mathbf{P})=\text{Rank}(\mathbf{X})$. Thus

(6.24) On the hypothesis that $\mathbf{y}\sim N_T(\boldsymbol{\mu}_0,\sigma^2\mathbf{Q})$; $\boldsymbol{\mu}_0\in\mathcal{M}(\mathbf{X})$, we have $\sigma^{-2}(\hat{\mathbf{y}}-\boldsymbol{\mu}_0)'\mathbf{Q}^{-1}(\hat{\mathbf{y}}-\boldsymbol{\mu}_0)\sim\chi^2(h)$, where $\hat{\mathbf{y}}=\mathbf{P}\mathbf{y}$ is the minimum $\mathbf{Q}^{-1}$-distance projector on $\mathcal{M}(\mathbf{X})$ and $h=\text{Rank}(\mathbf{P})=\text{Rank}(\mathbf{X})$.

To test the hypothesis, we define a critical region for the statistic $\sigma^{-2}(\hat{\mathbf{y}}-\boldsymbol{\mu}_0)'\mathbf{Q}^{-1}(\hat{\mathbf{y}}-\boldsymbol{\mu}_0)$ by referring to the table of the distribution of the $\chi^2(h)$ variate. The critical values of the statistic, leading to the rejection of the hypothesis, will be those in the upper tail of the distribution which are significantly greater than the expected value $E[\chi^2(h)]=h$.

The result (6.24), on the distribution of the statistic $\sigma^{-2}(\hat{\mathbf{y}}-\boldsymbol{\mu}_0)'\mathbf{Q}^{-1}(\hat{\mathbf{y}}-\boldsymbol{\mu}_0)$ when $\mathbf{y}\sim N_T(\boldsymbol{\mu}_0,\sigma^2\mathbf{Q})$, can also be deduced by way of (6.17) when we introduce the assumption that the random vector $\boldsymbol{\varepsilon}=(\mathbf{y}-\boldsymbol{\mu}_0)$ has a normal distribution. Thus, in the notation of (6.17), we have $\sigma^{-2}(\hat{\mathbf{y}}-\boldsymbol{\mu}_0)'\mathbf{Q}^{-1}(\hat{\mathbf{y}}-\boldsymbol{\mu}_0)=\sigma^{-2}\boldsymbol{\varepsilon}'\mathbf{P}'\mathbf{Q}^{-1}\mathbf{P}\boldsymbol{\varepsilon}=\sigma^{-2}\boldsymbol{\varepsilon}'\mathbf{P}'\mathbf{T}'\mathbf{C}'\mathbf{C}\mathbf{T}\mathbf{P}\boldsymbol{\varepsilon}=\sigma^{-2}\boldsymbol{\eta}_1'\boldsymbol{\eta}_1$, where $\boldsymbol{\eta}_1\sim N_h(\mathbf{0},\sigma^2\mathbf{I})$. It is clear from this that $\sigma^{-2}(\hat{\mathbf{y}}-\boldsymbol{\mu}_0)'\mathbf{Q}^{-1}(\hat{\mathbf{y}}-\boldsymbol{\mu}_0)=\sigma^{-2}\boldsymbol{\eta}_1'\boldsymbol{\eta}_1\sim\chi^2(h)$.

If σ^2 is unknown, which is likely to be the case, it may be replaced in (6.24) by an unbiased estimator which avoids using the *a priori* information that is under test. This is provided by $\hat{\sigma}^2=(\mathbf{y}-\hat{\mathbf{y}})'\mathbf{Q}^{-1}(\mathbf{y}-\hat{\mathbf{y}})/(T-h)=\|\mathbf{y}-\hat{\mathbf{y}}\|^2_{\mathbf{Q}^{-1}}/(T-h)$ from (6.19). Thus, ignoring the factor $(T-h)$, we derive the measure

$$\lambda=\frac{\|\hat{\mathbf{y}}-\boldsymbol{\mu}_0\|^2_{\mathbf{Q}^{-1}}}{\|\mathbf{y}-\hat{\mathbf{y}}\|^2_{\mathbf{Q}^{-1}}}=\frac{(\hat{\mathbf{y}}-\boldsymbol{\mu}_0)'\mathbf{Q}^{-1}(\hat{\mathbf{y}}-\boldsymbol{\mu}_0)}{(\mathbf{y}-\hat{\mathbf{y}})'\mathbf{Q}^{-1}(\mathbf{y}-\hat{\mathbf{y}})}. \tag{6.25}$$

The sampling distribution of $\lambda(T-h)/h$ under the assumptions of the hypothesis is readily accessible. For, given that $\mathbf{P}(\mathbf{y}-\boldsymbol{\mu}_0)+(\mathbf{I}-\mathbf{P})(\mathbf{y}-\boldsymbol{\mu}_0)=\mathbf{y}-\boldsymbol{\mu}_0$ is a $\mathbf{Q}^{-1}$-orthogonal decomposition of $(\mathbf{y}-\boldsymbol{\mu}_0)\sim N(\mathbf{0},\sigma^2\mathbf{Q})$, it follows from (17.46) that $\sigma^{-2}(\mathbf{y}-\boldsymbol{\mu}_0)'\mathbf{P}'\mathbf{Q}^{-1}\mathbf{P}(\mathbf{y}-\boldsymbol{\mu}_0)=\sigma^{-2}(\hat{\mathbf{y}}-\boldsymbol{\mu}_0)'\mathbf{Q}^{-1}(\hat{\mathbf{y}}-\boldsymbol{\mu}_0)\sim\chi^2(h)$ and $\sigma^{-2}(\mathbf{y}-\boldsymbol{\mu}_0)'(\mathbf{I}-\mathbf{P})'\mathbf{Q}^{-1}(\mathbf{I}-\mathbf{P})(\mathbf{y}-\boldsymbol{\mu}_0)=\sigma^{-2}(\mathbf{y}-\hat{\mathbf{y}})'\mathbf{Q}^{-1}(\mathbf{y}-\hat{\mathbf{y}})\sim\chi^2(T-h)$ constitute mutually independent chi-square variates. Thus

(6.26) On the hypothesis that $\mathbf{y}\sim N_T(\boldsymbol{\mu}_0,\sigma^2\mathbf{Q})$; $\boldsymbol{\mu}_0\in\mathcal{M}(\mathbf{X})$, we have

$$\left\{\frac{(\hat{\mathbf{y}}-\boldsymbol{\mu}_0)'\mathbf{Q}^{-1}(\hat{\mathbf{y}}-\boldsymbol{\mu}_0)}{h}\bigg/\frac{(\mathbf{y}-\hat{\mathbf{y}})'\mathbf{Q}^{-1}(\mathbf{y}-\hat{\mathbf{y}})}{T-h}\right\}\sim F(h,T-h),$$

where $\hat{\mathbf{y}}=\mathbf{P}\mathbf{y}$ is the minimum $\mathbf{Q}^{-1}$-distance projection of $\mathbf{y}$ on $\mathcal{M}(\mathbf{X})$, and $h=\text{Rank}(\mathbf{P})=\text{Rank}(\mathbf{X})$.

Thus the statistic $\lambda(T-h)/h$ is seen to have an F distribution of h and $T-h$ degrees of freedom on the assumptions of the hypothesis. To test this hypothesis, we construct a critical region for the statistic containing values that are significantly larger than $E[F(h, T-h)] \simeq 1$; and we reject the hypothesis if the statistic falls in this region.

For our second example, we consider an hypothesis which maintains, within the context of the model $\mathbf{y} \sim N(\mathbf{X\beta}, \sigma^2\mathbf{Q})$, that $\boldsymbol{\mu} = \mathbf{X\beta}$ lies in some subspace $\mathcal{M}(\mathbf{Z}) \subset \mathcal{M}(\mathbf{X})$. Under the general assumptions of the model, we would estimate $\boldsymbol{\mu}$ by $\hat{\mathbf{y}} = \mathbf{P_X y}$, where $\mathbf{P_X}$ is the minimum $\mathbf{Q}^{-1}$-distance projector on $\mathcal{M}(\mathbf{X})$. Under the specific assumptions of the hypothesis, we would estimate the mean vector $\boldsymbol{\mu}$ by $\overset{*}{\mathbf{y}} = \mathbf{P_Z y}$, where $\mathbf{P_Z}$ is the minimum $\mathbf{Q}^{-1}$-distance projector on $\mathcal{M}(\mathbf{Z})$. The estimate $\hat{\mathbf{y}}$ freely reflects the properties of the data. Thus, by measuring the proximity of $\overset{*}{\mathbf{y}}$ and $\hat{\mathbf{y}}$, we are able to gauge the extent to which the additional *a priori* information of the hypothesis, which has been incorporated in $\overset{*}{\mathbf{y}}$, is in conformity with the data. We can thereby assess the validity of the hypothesis. The appropriate measure of proximity is

$$\begin{aligned}\sigma^{-2}\|\hat{\mathbf{y}} - \overset{*}{\mathbf{y}}\|^2_{\mathbf{Q}^{-1}} &= \sigma^{-2}(\hat{\mathbf{y}} - \overset{*}{\mathbf{y}})'\mathbf{Q}^{-1}(\hat{\mathbf{y}} - \overset{*}{\mathbf{y}})\\ &= \sigma^{-2}\mathbf{y}'(\mathbf{P_X} - \mathbf{P_Z})'\mathbf{Q}^{-1}(\mathbf{P_X} - \mathbf{P_Z})\mathbf{y}.\end{aligned}$$

On replacing σ^2 by $\hat{\sigma}^2$ and omitting the factor $T-h$, we obtain

$$\text{(6.27)} \qquad \lambda = \frac{\|\hat{\mathbf{y}} - \overset{*}{\mathbf{y}}\|^2_{\mathbf{Q}^{-1}}}{\|\mathbf{y} - \hat{\mathbf{y}}\|^2_{\mathbf{Q}^{-1}}} = \frac{(\hat{\mathbf{y}} - \overset{*}{\mathbf{y}})'\mathbf{Q}^{-1}(\hat{\mathbf{y}} - \overset{*}{\mathbf{y}})}{(\mathbf{y} - \hat{\mathbf{y}})'\mathbf{Q}^{-1}(\mathbf{y} - \hat{\mathbf{y}})}.$$

To derive a sampling distribution of a multiple of λ on the assumption that $\boldsymbol{\mu} \in \mathcal{M}(\mathbf{Z})$ and $(\mathbf{y} - \boldsymbol{\mu}) \sim N_T(\mathbf{0}, \sigma^2\mathbf{Q})$, we consider the identity

$$\begin{aligned}\mathbf{I} &= (\mathbf{I} - \mathbf{P_Z}) + \mathbf{P_Z} = \mathbf{P_X}(\mathbf{I} - \mathbf{P_Z}) + (\mathbf{I} - \mathbf{P_X})(\mathbf{I} - \mathbf{P_Z}) + \mathbf{P_Z}\\ &= (\mathbf{P_X} - \mathbf{P_Z}) + (\mathbf{I} - \mathbf{P_X}) + \mathbf{P_Z},\end{aligned}$$

which depends on the fact that $\mathbf{P_X P_Z} = \mathbf{P_Z}$ since $\mathcal{M}(\mathbf{Z}) \subset \mathcal{M}(\mathbf{X})$. The identity $\mathbf{I} = (\mathbf{P_X} - \mathbf{P_Z}) + (\mathbf{I} - \mathbf{P_X}) + \mathbf{P_Z}$ comprises a sum of mutually $\mathbf{Q}^{-1}$-orthogonal matrices. Thus, when $\text{Rank}(\mathbf{P_Z}) = z$, it follows from (17.46) that

(6.28)

1. $(\mathbf{y} - \boldsymbol{\mu})'\mathbf{Q}^{-1}(\mathbf{y} - \boldsymbol{\mu}) \sim \chi^2(T)\sigma^2$,
2. $(\mathbf{y} - \boldsymbol{\mu})'(\mathbf{P_X} - \mathbf{P_Z})'\mathbf{Q}^{-1}(\mathbf{P_X} - \mathbf{P_Z})(\mathbf{y} - \boldsymbol{\mu})$ $= (\hat{\mathbf{y}} - \overset{*}{\mathbf{y}})'\mathbf{Q}^{-1}(\hat{\mathbf{y}} - \overset{*}{\mathbf{y}}) \sim \chi^2(h-z)\sigma^2$,
3. $(\mathbf{y} - \boldsymbol{\mu})'(\mathbf{I} - \mathbf{P_X})'\mathbf{Q}^{-1}(\mathbf{I} - \mathbf{P_X})(\mathbf{y} - \boldsymbol{\mu})$ $= (\mathbf{y} - \hat{\mathbf{y}})'\mathbf{Q}^{-1}(\mathbf{y} - \hat{\mathbf{y}}) \sim \chi^2(T-h)\sigma^2$,
4. $(\mathbf{y} - \boldsymbol{\mu})'\mathbf{P_Z}'\mathbf{Q}^{-1}\mathbf{P_Z}(\mathbf{y} - \boldsymbol{\mu}) = (\overset{*}{\mathbf{y}} - \boldsymbol{\mu})'\mathbf{Q}^{-1}(\overset{*}{\mathbf{y}} - \boldsymbol{\mu}) \sim \chi^2(z)\sigma^2$,

where the expressions under 2, 3 and 4 are for mutually independent variates. Therefore

(6.29) On the hypothesis that $\mathbf{y} \sim N_T(\boldsymbol{\mu}, \sigma^2\mathbf{Q})$; $\boldsymbol{\mu} \in \mathcal{M}(\mathbf{Z}) \subset \mathcal{M}(\mathbf{X})$, we have

$$\left\{\frac{(\hat{\mathbf{y}}-\overset{*}{\mathbf{y}})'\mathbf{Q}^{-1}(\hat{\mathbf{y}}-\overset{*}{\mathbf{y}})}{h-z} \Big/ \frac{(\mathbf{y}-\hat{\mathbf{y}})'\mathbf{Q}^{-1}(\mathbf{y}-\hat{\mathbf{y}})}{T-h}\right\} \sim F(h-z, T-h),$$

where $\hat{\mathbf{y}} = \mathbf{P_X y}$ and $\overset{*}{\mathbf{y}} = \mathbf{P_Z y}$ are the minimum $\mathbf{Q}^{-1}$-distance projectors of $\mathbf{y}$ on $\mathcal{M}(\mathbf{X})$ and $\mathcal{M}(\mathbf{Z})$ respectively and $h = \text{Rank}(\mathbf{P_X}) = \text{Rank}(\mathbf{X})$, $z = \text{Rank}(\mathbf{P_Z}) = \text{Rank}(\mathbf{Z})$.

Thus $\lambda\{(T-h)/(h-z)\}$, which is seen to have an F distribution of $h-z$ and $T-h$ degrees of freedom on the assumptions of the hypothesis, is the appropriate test statistic.

For the third example, we may consider testing an hypothesis in respect of several estimable parametric functions of $\boldsymbol{\beta}$. Let this hypothesis specify that $\mathbf{y} \sim N(\mathbf{X}\boldsymbol{\beta}, \sigma^2\mathbf{Q})$ subject to $\mathbf{R}\boldsymbol{\beta} = \mathbf{r}$; and let $\mathbf{R} = \mathbf{HX}$ to ensure that every element of $\mathbf{R}\boldsymbol{\beta}$ is estimable. To test the hypothesis, we estimate $\boldsymbol{\mu} = \mathbf{X}\boldsymbol{\beta}$ by $\hat{\mathbf{y}} = \mathbf{Py} = \mathbf{X}\hat{\mathbf{b}}$ where $\mathbf{P}$ is the minimum $\mathbf{Q}^{-1}$-distance projector on $\mathcal{M}(\mathbf{X})$. Then, under the hypothesis, we have $\mathbf{R}\hat{\boldsymbol{\beta}} = \mathbf{HX}\hat{\boldsymbol{\beta}} = \mathbf{HPy} \sim N(\mathbf{R}\boldsymbol{\beta} = \mathbf{r}, \sigma^2\mathbf{HPQP'H'})$. Using $\mathbf{PQP'} = \mathbf{PQ}$ and $\mathbf{PQ} = \mathbf{X}(\mathbf{X'Q}^{-1}\mathbf{X})^-\mathbf{X'}$, we may re-express this as $\mathbf{R}\hat{\boldsymbol{\beta}} \sim N(\mathbf{r}, \sigma^2\mathbf{R}(\mathbf{X'Q}^{-1}\mathbf{X})^-\mathbf{R'})$ or $(\mathbf{R}\hat{\boldsymbol{\beta}} - \mathbf{r}) \sim N(\mathbf{0}, \sigma^2\mathbf{R}(\mathbf{X'Q}^{-1}\mathbf{X})^-\mathbf{R'})$. It then follows directly from (17.41) that $\sigma^{-2}(\mathbf{R}\hat{\boldsymbol{\beta}} - \mathbf{r})'[\mathbf{R}(\mathbf{X'Q}^{-1}\mathbf{X})^-\mathbf{R'}]^-(\mathbf{R}\hat{\boldsymbol{\beta}} - \mathbf{r}) \sim \chi^2(q)$, where $q = \text{Rank}[\mathbf{R}(\mathbf{X'Q}^{-1}\mathbf{X})^-\mathbf{R'}]$. As in previous examples, we are liable to replace σ^2 in this expression by $\hat{\sigma}^2 = (\mathbf{y} - \mathbf{Py})'\mathbf{Q}^{-1}(\mathbf{y} - \mathbf{Py})/(T-h) = (\mathbf{y} - \mathbf{X}\hat{\boldsymbol{\beta}})'\mathbf{Q}^{-1}(\mathbf{y} - \mathbf{X}\hat{\boldsymbol{\beta}})/(T-h)$ which is distributed as $\sigma^2/(T-h)$ times a $\chi^2(T-h)$ variate. Since $\hat{\sigma}^2$ is statistically independent of $\hat{\mathbf{y}} = \mathbf{Py}$, it must also be statistically independent of $(\mathbf{R}\hat{\boldsymbol{\beta}} - \mathbf{r}) = (\mathbf{H}\hat{\mathbf{y}} - \mathbf{r})$. Thus we deduce that

(6.30) On the hypothesis that $\mathbf{y} \sim N(\mathbf{X}\boldsymbol{\beta} \mid \mathbf{R}\boldsymbol{\beta} = \mathbf{r}, \sigma^2\mathbf{Q})$, we have

$$\left\{\frac{(\mathbf{R}\hat{\boldsymbol{\beta}} - \mathbf{r})'[\mathbf{R}(\mathbf{X'Q}^{-1}\mathbf{X})^-\mathbf{R'}]^-(\mathbf{R}\hat{\boldsymbol{\beta}} - \mathbf{r})}{q} \Big/ \frac{(\mathbf{y} - \mathbf{X}\hat{\boldsymbol{\beta}})'\mathbf{Q}^{-1}(\mathbf{y} - \mathbf{X}\hat{\boldsymbol{\beta}})}{T-h}\right\}$$
$$\sim F(q, T-h),$$

where $q = \text{Rank}[\mathbf{R}(\mathbf{X'Q}^{-1}\mathbf{X})^-\mathbf{R'}]$, and $h = \text{Rank}(\mathbf{X})$.

We may simplify the expression for the test statistic in (6.30) by ensuring that $\mathbf{R}$ has full row rank such that $\text{Null}(\mathbf{R'}) = 0$; for then $\mathbf{R}(\mathbf{X'Q}^{-1}\mathbf{X})^-\mathbf{R'}$ is non-singular, and $[\mathbf{R}(\mathbf{X'Q}^{-1}\mathbf{X})^-\mathbf{R'}]^-$ becomes a regular inverse. To demonstrate this, we use $\mathcal{M}(\mathbf{X'Q}^{-1}\mathbf{X}) = \mathcal{M}(\mathbf{X'})$ to write $\mathbf{R'} = \mathbf{X'H'} = \mathbf{X'Q}^{-1}\mathbf{XS'}$ for some $\mathbf{S}'$. Then the condition $\text{Null}(\mathbf{R}')=0$ implies that $\text{Null}(\mathbf{H}')=\text{Null}(\mathbf{Q}^{-1}\mathbf{X}\mathbf{S}')=\text{Null}(\mathbf{X}\mathbf{S}')=0$, and it follows immediately that

$$\mathbf{R}(\mathbf{X}'\mathbf{Q}^{-1}\mathbf{X})^{-}\mathbf{R}'=\mathbf{S}\mathbf{X}'\mathbf{Q}^{-1}\mathbf{X}(\mathbf{X}'\mathbf{Q}^{-1}\mathbf{X})^{-}\mathbf{X}'\mathbf{Q}^{-1}\mathbf{X}\mathbf{S}'=\mathbf{S}\mathbf{X}'\mathbf{Q}^{-1}\mathbf{X}\mathbf{S}'$$

is non-singular. It is also clear that, under these circumstances, the system $\mathbf{R}\boldsymbol{\beta}=\mathbf{r}$ constitutes a set of $q=\text{Rank}(\mathbf{R})$ independent restrictions on $\boldsymbol{\beta}$, each of which is capable of being tested by virtue of the assumption that $\mathbf{R}=\mathbf{H}\mathbf{X}$.

The arguments by which we have constructed this test differ from those in the two previous examples where we have used measures of the proximity of the two estimates of the mean vector $\boldsymbol{\mu}$ which are formed, respectively, under the general assumptions of the model $\mathbf{y}\sim N(\mathbf{X}\boldsymbol{\beta}, \sigma^2\mathbf{Q})$ and the specific assumptions of the hypothesis to be tested. Nevertheless, it is possible to show that the present test is based on a measure of proximity of the form $\sigma^{-2}\|\hat{\mathbf{y}}-\overset{*}{\mathbf{y}}\|^2_{\mathbf{Q}^{-1}}$ where $\hat{\mathbf{y}}=\mathbf{P}\mathbf{y}=\mathbf{X}\hat{\boldsymbol{\beta}}$ and $\overset{*}{\mathbf{y}}$ is the minimum $\mathbf{Q}^{-1}$-distance estimate of $\boldsymbol{\mu}=\mathbf{X}\boldsymbol{\beta}$ subject to the restrictions $\mathbf{R}\boldsymbol{\beta}=\mathbf{r}$. In fact, we shall demonstrate this in Chapter 10 where we shall specify the dispersion matrix as $D(\boldsymbol{\varepsilon})=\sigma^2\mathbf{Q}=\sigma^2\mathbf{I}$.

THE LIKELIHOOD-RATIO PRINCIPLE

The convenient statistical properties of the F-test are not sufficient in themselves to justify its use; for it is possible that a test which is more powerful, albeit less tractable, is available. One argument which justifies the F-test consists of showing that it is a likelihood-ratio test. We shall demonstrate this argument for our second example where the general assumptions of the model imply that $\boldsymbol{\mu}\in\mathcal{M}(\mathbf{X})$ and the hypothesis asserts, more specifically, that $\boldsymbol{\mu}\in\mathcal{M}(\mathbf{Z})\subset\mathcal{M}(\mathbf{X})$. The likelihood-ratio test involves a comparison of the values of the likelihood function associated with the alternative maximum-likelihood estimates that are formed under the general assumptions of the model and under the specific assumptions of the hypothesis. The value of the likelihood function under the general assumptions represents a global maximum over $\mathcal{M}(\mathbf{X})$, whereas its value under the assumptions of the hypothesis represents, by contrast, a restricted maximum over $\mathcal{M}(\mathbf{Z})$. The principle of the test is that we should reject the hypothesis if the value of the local maximum is significantly less than the value of the global maximum. For the comparison of the two maxima, we form the ratio

$$\phi=\frac{\max[\boldsymbol{\mu}\in\mathcal{M}(\mathbf{Z})]L(\boldsymbol{\mu},\sigma^2)}{\max[\boldsymbol{\mu}\in\mathcal{M}(\mathbf{X})]L(\boldsymbol{\mu},\sigma^2)}=\frac{L_{\mathbf{Z}}}{L_{\mathbf{X}}}. \tag{6.31}$$

Since the maximum of the likelihood function over $\mathcal{M}(\mathbf{Z})$ cannot exceed the maximum over $\mathcal{M}(\mathbf{X})$, we have $0\leqslant\phi\leqslant1$. Values of ϕ close to 1 are favourable to the hypothesis, whereas values close to 0 are critical. We can see, by reference to (6.21), that, given σ^2,

$$L_{\mathbf{Z}} = (2\pi)^{-T/2}\,|\sigma^2\mathbf{Q}|^{-1/2} \times \exp\left\{-\frac{1}{2\sigma^2}(\mathbf{y}-\mathbf{P_Z y})'\mathbf{Q}^{-1}(\mathbf{y}-\mathbf{P_Z y})\right\} \tag{6.32}$$

is the maximum of the likelihood function over $\mathcal{M}(\mathbf{Z})$, and that

$$L_{\mathbf{X}} = (2\pi)^{-T/2}\,|\sigma^2\mathbf{Q}|^{-1/2} \times \exp\left\{-\frac{1}{2\sigma^2}(\mathbf{y}-\mathbf{P_X y})'\mathbf{Q}^{-1}(\mathbf{y}-\mathbf{P_X y})\right\} \tag{6.33}$$

is the maximum over $\mathcal{M}(\mathbf{X})$. Morever, since

$$(\mathbf{y}-\mathbf{P_Z y})'\mathbf{Q}^{-1}(\mathbf{y}-\mathbf{P_Z y}) = (\mathbf{y}-\mathbf{P_X y})'\mathbf{Q}^{-1}(\mathbf{y}-\mathbf{P_X y}) + (\mathbf{P_X y}-\mathbf{P_Z y})'\mathbf{Q}^{-1}(\mathbf{P_X y}-\mathbf{P_Z y}), \tag{6.34}$$

we have

$$\frac{L_{\mathbf{Z}}}{L_{\mathbf{X}}} = \exp\left\{-\frac{1}{2\sigma^2}(\mathbf{P_X y}-\mathbf{P_Z y})'\mathbf{Q}^{-1}(\mathbf{P_X y}-\mathbf{P_Z y})\right\}. \tag{6.35}$$

Thus, when σ^2 is known, the test statistic of the likelihood-ratio test is a simple function of the measure of proximity of $\hat{\mathbf{y}} = \mathbf{P_X y}$ and $\overset{*}{\mathbf{y}} = \mathbf{P_Z y}$. If both $\boldsymbol{\mu}$ and σ^2 are unknown, we must find $L_{\mathbf{Z}}$, $L_{\mathbf{X}}$ by maximizing the likelihood function over the appropriate spaces with respect to both these parameters. The form of the maximum-likelihood estimator of σ^2 is given in (6.23). Thus, under the hypothesis, the estimator is $\tilde{\sigma}^2_{\mathbf{Z}} = (\mathbf{y}-\mathbf{P_Z y})'\mathbf{Q}^{-1}(\mathbf{y}-\mathbf{P_Z y})/T$. Inserting this in (6.32) gives

$$L_{\mathbf{Z}} = (2\pi)^{-T/2}\left|\frac{(\mathbf{y}-\mathbf{P_Z y})'\mathbf{Q}^{-1}(\mathbf{y}-\mathbf{P_Z y})\mathbf{Q}}{T}\right|^{-1/2}\exp\left\{-\frac{T}{2}\right\}. \tag{6.36}$$

Likewise, we derive

$$L_{\mathbf{X}} = (2\pi)^{-T/2}\left|\frac{(\mathbf{y}-\mathbf{P_X y})'\mathbf{Q}^{-1}(\mathbf{y}-\mathbf{P_X y})\mathbf{Q}}{T}\right|^{-1/2}\exp\left\{-\frac{T}{2}\right\}. \tag{6.37}$$

Thus the likelihood ratio becomes

$$\frac{L_{\mathbf{Z}}}{L_{\mathbf{X}}} = \left[\frac{(\mathbf{y}-\mathbf{P_Z y})'\mathbf{Q}^{-1}(\mathbf{y}-\mathbf{P_Z y})}{(\mathbf{y}-\mathbf{P_X y})'\mathbf{Q}^{-1}(\mathbf{y}-\mathbf{P_X y})}\right]^{-T/2}, \tag{6.38}$$

which, in view of (6.34), can also be expressed as

$$\begin{aligned}\frac{L_{\mathbf{Z}}}{L_{\mathbf{X}}} &= \left[1+\frac{(\mathbf{P_X y}-\mathbf{P_Z y})'\mathbf{Q}^{-1}(\mathbf{P_X y}-\mathbf{P_Z y})}{(\mathbf{y}-\mathbf{P_X y})'\mathbf{Q}^{-1}(\mathbf{y}-\mathbf{P_X y})}\right]^{-T/2} \\ &= (1+\lambda)^{-T/2},\end{aligned} \tag{6.39}$$

where λ is the quantity defined in (6.27). The fact that the F-test and the likelihood-ratio test are both based on the random variable λ signifies that they are equivalent.

BIBLIOGRAPHY

The Gauss–Markov Model. Anderson [**8,** Chap. 8], Malinvaud [**82,** Chap. 5], Scheffé [**106,** Chap. 1, 2], Seber [**108**].

The Likelihood-ratio Principle. Kendall and Stuart [**62,** Chap. 24], Scheffé [**106,** pp. 32–51], Wilks [**122,** Chap. 13].

CHAPTER 7

The Classical Linear Model

We have dealt broadly in Chapter 6 with the Gauss–Markov model $(\mathbf{y}, \mathbf{X\beta}, \sigma^2\mathbf{Q})$ and with the corresponding method of estimation which we have called Gaussian regression in the $\mathbf{Q}^{-1}$-metric. We shall now develop some practical details of the more specialized classical linear model $(\mathbf{y}, \mathbf{X\beta} \mid \text{Null}(\mathbf{X}) = 0, \sigma^2\mathbf{I})$ for which the appropriate method of estimation is ordinary least-squares regression. In putting aside the generality of the previous chapter, there are fewer disadvantages than might be imagined. For, in the first place, we may easily regain such generality if it is required, and, in the second place, we may often, in practice, reduce a problem of Gaussian regression in the $\mathbf{Q}^{-1}$-metric to a problem of ordinary least squares by applying a prior transformation to the data. This method of transforming the data is depicted in (5.9).

ORDINARY LEAST-SQUARES ESTIMATION

The classical linear model comprises the equations

$$\mathbf{y} = \mathbf{X\beta} + \boldsymbol{\varepsilon} \tag{7.1}$$

where $\mathbf{y}$ and $\mathbf{X}$ contain T observations on a scalar output y_t and a k-element vector input $\mathbf{x}_{t.} = [x_{t1}, \ldots, x_{tk}]$ respectively, and $\boldsymbol{\varepsilon}$ is a vector of T values of the unobserved random variable ε_t. It is assumed that $\mathbf{X}$ is a non-stochastic matrix of full column rank so that

$$\text{Null}(\mathbf{X}) = 0 \quad \text{or, equivalently,} \quad \text{Rank}(\mathbf{X}) = k. \tag{7.2}$$

It is also assumed that $\boldsymbol{\varepsilon}$ has

$$E(\boldsymbol{\varepsilon}) = \mathbf{0}, \qquad D(\boldsymbol{\varepsilon}) = E(\boldsymbol{\varepsilon}\boldsymbol{\varepsilon}') = \sigma^2\mathbf{I}. \tag{7.3}$$

This implies that successive values of ε_t are uncorrelated. Using the identity $\mathbf{y} - \mathbf{X\beta} = \boldsymbol{\varepsilon}$, we deduce from (7.3) that

$$E(\mathbf{y}) = \mathbf{X\beta}, \qquad D(\mathbf{y}) = E\{[\mathbf{y} - E(\mathbf{y})][\mathbf{y} - E(\mathbf{y})]'\} = \sigma^2\mathbf{I}. \tag{7.4}$$

It is often appropriate to have T units in the leading column of $\mathbf{X}$ in place of T observations on a genuine variable x_{t1}. The coefficient associated with these units is called the intercept term. In order to distinguish the intercept term from the remaining coefficients, we may write the equations $\mathbf{y}=\mathbf{X\beta}+\boldsymbol{\varepsilon}$ as

$$\mathbf{y}=[\mathbf{i},\mathbf{Z}]\begin{bmatrix}\beta_1\\ \boldsymbol{\beta}_\mathbf{Z}\end{bmatrix}+\boldsymbol{\varepsilon} \tag{7.5}$$

where $\mathbf{i}'=[1,\ldots,1]=\mathbf{x}'_{.1}$ and $\mathbf{Z}=[\mathbf{x}_{.2},\ldots,\mathbf{x}_{.k}]$.

The ordinary least-squares estimator of $\boldsymbol{\beta}$ is

$$\hat{\boldsymbol{\beta}}=(\mathbf{X}'\mathbf{X})^{-1}\mathbf{X}'\mathbf{y}. \tag{7.6}$$

This is an unbiased estimator, since its expectation is $E(\hat{\boldsymbol{\beta}})=(\mathbf{X}'\mathbf{X})^{-1}\mathbf{X}'E(\mathbf{y})=(\mathbf{X}'\mathbf{X})^{-1}\mathbf{X}'\mathbf{X\beta}=\boldsymbol{\beta}$. Its dispersion matrix is $D(\hat{\boldsymbol{\beta}})=(\mathbf{X}'\mathbf{X})^{-1}\mathbf{X}'D(\mathbf{y})\mathbf{X}(\mathbf{X}'\mathbf{X})^{-1}=\sigma^2(\mathbf{X}'\mathbf{X})^{-1}$. Thus

$$E(\hat{\boldsymbol{\beta}})=\boldsymbol{\beta},\qquad D(\hat{\boldsymbol{\beta}})=\sigma^2(\mathbf{X}'\mathbf{X})^{-1}. \tag{7.7}$$

A proof that $\hat{\boldsymbol{\beta}}$ is a minimum variance linear unbiased estimator of $\boldsymbol{\beta}$ is obtained by specializing the Gauss–Markov theorem of (6.7) to the case of the classical linear model. For an alternative proof, let us consider $\boldsymbol{\beta}^*=\mathbf{Ay}$ to be any other linear unbiased estimator of $\boldsymbol{\beta}$. Then the condition that $E(\mathbf{Ay})=\mathbf{A}E(\mathbf{y})=\mathbf{AX\beta}=\boldsymbol{\beta}$ for all $\boldsymbol{\beta}$ implies that $\mathbf{AX}=\mathbf{I}$. Writing $\mathbf{A}$ as $\mathbf{A}=(\mathbf{X}'\mathbf{X})^{-1}\mathbf{X}'+\mathbf{B}$ gives $\mathbf{AX}=\mathbf{I}+\mathbf{BX}=\mathbf{I}$; whence $\mathbf{BX}=\mathbf{0}$. Using this condition, we find that the dispersion matrix of $\boldsymbol{\beta}^*=\mathbf{Ay}$ is $D(\boldsymbol{\beta}^*)=\mathbf{A}D(\mathbf{y})\mathbf{A}'=\sigma^2\mathbf{AA}'=\sigma^2(\mathbf{X}'\mathbf{X})^{-1}+\sigma^2\mathbf{BB}'=D(\hat{\boldsymbol{\beta}})+\sigma^2\mathbf{BB}'$, where $\mathbf{BB}'$ is a positive-semidefinite matrix. Thus, for any $k\times 1$ vector $\mathbf{p}$, we have $V(\mathbf{p}'\boldsymbol{\beta}^*)=\mathbf{p}'D(\hat{\boldsymbol{\beta}})\mathbf{p}+\sigma^2\mathbf{p}'\mathbf{BB}'\mathbf{p}\geqslant\mathbf{p}'D(\hat{\boldsymbol{\beta}})\mathbf{p}=V(\mathbf{p}'\hat{\boldsymbol{\beta}})$, or simply $V(\mathbf{p}'\boldsymbol{\beta}^*)\geqslant V(\mathbf{p}'\hat{\boldsymbol{\beta}})$, which proves the theorem.

To provide an unbiased estimator of σ^2, we use

$$\hat{\sigma}^2=\frac{\mathbf{y}'(\mathbf{I}-\mathbf{P})\mathbf{y}}{T-k}=\frac{(\mathbf{y}-\mathbf{X}\hat{\boldsymbol{\beta}})'(\mathbf{y}-\mathbf{X}\hat{\boldsymbol{\beta}})}{T-k}, \tag{7.8}$$

wherein $\mathbf{P}=\mathbf{X}(\mathbf{X}'\mathbf{X})^{-1}\mathbf{X}'$ and $\mathbf{Py}=\mathbf{X}\hat{\boldsymbol{\beta}}$.

To demonstrate the unbiasedness of $\hat{\sigma}^2$, we must evaluate the expectation of $\mathbf{y}'(\mathbf{I}-\mathbf{P})\mathbf{y}$. We may do so via the identity

$$\begin{aligned}E[\mathbf{y}'(\mathbf{I}-\mathbf{P})\mathbf{y}]&=E[(\mathbf{y}-\mathbf{X\beta})'(\mathbf{I}-\mathbf{P})(\mathbf{y}-\mathbf{X\beta})]\\&=E(\boldsymbol{\varepsilon}'\boldsymbol{\varepsilon})-E(\boldsymbol{\varepsilon}'\mathbf{P}\boldsymbol{\varepsilon})\end{aligned} \tag{7.9}$$

which follows from the condition $(\mathbf{I}-\mathbf{P})\mathbf{X}=\mathbf{0}$ and the identity $\mathbf{y}-\mathbf{X\beta}=\boldsymbol{\varepsilon}$. Since $\boldsymbol{\varepsilon}\sim(\mathbf{0},\sigma^2\mathbf{I}_T)$, the first term of the final expression is $E(\boldsymbol{\varepsilon}'\boldsymbol{\varepsilon})=\sigma^2T$. To evaluate the second term $E(\boldsymbol{\varepsilon}'\mathbf{P}\boldsymbol{\varepsilon})$, we may use the fact that the trace of a scalar has the value of the scalar itself. Thus $E(\boldsymbol{\varepsilon}'\mathbf{P}\boldsymbol{\varepsilon})=E[\text{Trace}(\boldsymbol{\varepsilon}'\mathbf{P}\boldsymbol{\varepsilon})]=E[\text{Trace}(\boldsymbol{\varepsilon}\boldsymbol{\varepsilon}'\mathbf{P})]=\text{Trace}[E(\boldsymbol{\varepsilon}\boldsymbol{\varepsilon}')\mathbf{P}]=\sigma^2\,\text{Trace}(\mathbf{P})$. But $\mathbf{P}$ is a symmetric idempotent matrix with $\text{Rank}(\mathbf{P})=\text{Rank}(\mathbf{X})=k$, so, by (4.22), $\text{Trace}(\mathbf{P})=k$.

Therefore $E(\boldsymbol{\varepsilon}'\mathbf{P}\boldsymbol{\varepsilon}) = \sigma^2 \,\text{Trace}(\mathbf{P}) = \sigma^2 k$. Substituting the two results in (7.9) gives

$$E[\mathbf{y}'(\mathbf{I}-\mathbf{P})\mathbf{y}] = E[(\mathbf{y}-\mathbf{X}\hat{\boldsymbol{\beta}})'(\mathbf{y}-\mathbf{X}\hat{\boldsymbol{\beta}})] = \sigma^2(T-k), \tag{7.10}$$

from which $E(\hat{\sigma}^2) = E[(\mathbf{y}-\mathbf{X}\hat{\boldsymbol{\beta}})'(\mathbf{y}-\mathbf{X}\hat{\boldsymbol{\beta}})/(T-k)] = \sigma^2$ follows immediately, and the unbiasedness of the estimator is demonstrated.

THE PARTITIONED MODEL

The partitioned inverse and various projectors

In order to find explicit expressions for the estimators of subvectors of $\boldsymbol{\beta}$ in the model $(\mathbf{y}, \mathbf{X}\boldsymbol{\beta}, \sigma^2\mathbf{I})$, we must consider the formula of a partitioned inverse of $\mathbf{X}'\mathbf{X}$. If $\mathbf{X}$ is partitioned as $\mathbf{X} = [\mathbf{X}_1, \mathbf{X}_2]$, then

$$\begin{aligned}(\mathbf{X}'\mathbf{X})^{-1} &= \begin{bmatrix}\mathbf{X}_1'\mathbf{X}_1, & \mathbf{X}_1'\mathbf{X}_2\\ \mathbf{X}_2'\mathbf{X}_1, & \mathbf{X}_2'\mathbf{X}_2\end{bmatrix}^{-1}\\ &= \begin{bmatrix}[\mathbf{X}_1'(\mathbf{I}-\mathbf{P}_2)\mathbf{X}_1]^{-1}, & -[\mathbf{X}_1'(\mathbf{I}-\mathbf{P}_2)\mathbf{X}_1]^{-1}\mathbf{X}_1'\mathbf{X}_2(\mathbf{X}_2'\mathbf{X}_2)^{-1}\\ -[\mathbf{X}_2'(\mathbf{I}-\mathbf{P}_1)\mathbf{X}_2]^{-1}\mathbf{X}_2'\mathbf{X}_1(\mathbf{X}_1'\mathbf{X}_1)^{-1}, & [\mathbf{X}_2'(\mathbf{I}-\mathbf{P}_1)\mathbf{X}_2]^{-1}\end{bmatrix}\end{aligned} \tag{7.11}$$

where

$$\begin{aligned}\mathbf{P}_1 &= \mathbf{X}_1(\mathbf{X}_1'\mathbf{X}_1)^{-1}\mathbf{X}_1',\\ \mathbf{P}_2 &= \mathbf{X}_2(\mathbf{X}_2'\mathbf{X}_2)^{-1}\mathbf{X}_2',\end{aligned} \tag{7.12}$$

are orthogonal projectors on $\mathcal{M}(\mathbf{X}_1)$ and $\mathcal{M}(\mathbf{X}_2)$ respectively. The result in (7.11) is easily verified by multiplying the matrix on the RHS by the partitioned form of $\mathbf{X}'\mathbf{X}$ to give a partitioned form of the identity matrix.

It is also helpful to define

$$\begin{aligned}\mathbf{P}_{1/2} &= \mathbf{X}_1[\mathbf{X}_1'(\mathbf{I}-\mathbf{P}_2)\mathbf{X}_1]^{-1}\mathbf{X}_1'(\mathbf{I}-\mathbf{P}_2),\\ \mathbf{P}_{2/1} &= \mathbf{X}_2[\mathbf{X}_2'(\mathbf{I}-\mathbf{P}_1)\mathbf{X}_2]^{-1}\mathbf{X}_2'(\mathbf{I}-\mathbf{P}_1).\end{aligned} \tag{7.13}$$

Using the partitioned inverse defined in (7.11), we can readily establish that

$$\mathbf{X}(\mathbf{X}'\mathbf{X})^{-1}\mathbf{X}' = \mathbf{P} = \mathbf{P}_{1/2} + \mathbf{P}_{2/1}.$$

It can be verified directly that $\mathbf{P}_{1/2}^2 = \mathbf{P}_{1/2}$ and that $\mathbf{P}_{1/2}\mathbf{X}_1 = \mathbf{X}_1$ and $\mathbf{P}_{1/2}\mathbf{X}_2 = \mathbf{0}$. Thus we see that the restriction of $\mathbf{P}_{1/2}$ to $\mathcal{M}(\mathbf{X}) = \mathcal{M}(\mathbf{X}_1) \oplus \mathcal{M}(\mathbf{X}_2)$ is a projector on $\mathcal{M}(\mathbf{X}_1)$ along $\mathcal{M}(\mathbf{X}_2)$. When $\mathbf{P}_{1/2}$ is defined over $\mathcal{R}^T$, it becomes the projector on $\mathcal{M}(\mathbf{X}_1)$ along $\mathcal{M}(\mathbf{X}_2) \oplus \mathcal{O}(\mathbf{X})$. Similar deductions may be made for $\mathbf{P}_{2/1}$.

It will be helpful to record some of the relationships existing amongst these various projectors. To begin with, it is clear from our characterizations of $\mathbf{P}_{1/2}$ and $\mathbf{P}_{2/1}$ that

(7.14) $$\text{(i) } \mathbf{P}_{1/2}\mathbf{P}_1=\mathbf{P}_1, \qquad \text{(ii) } \mathbf{P}_{1/2}\mathbf{P}_2=\mathbf{0},$$
$$\text{(iii) } \mathbf{P}_{2/1}\mathbf{P}_1=\mathbf{0}, \qquad \text{(iv) } \mathbf{P}_{2/1}\mathbf{P}_2=\mathbf{P}_2.$$

These relationships may be confirmed directly. It is also easy to confirm that

(7.15) $$\mathbf{P}_1\mathbf{P}_{1/2}=\mathbf{P}_{1/2} \quad \text{and, likewise,} \quad \mathbf{P}_2\mathbf{P}_{2/1}=\mathbf{P}_{2/1}.$$

Next, by referring to (i) and (iii) of (7.14), we can see that $\mathbf{P}\mathbf{P}_1=(\mathbf{P}_{1/2}+\mathbf{P}_{2/1})\mathbf{P}_1=\mathbf{P}_1$ or simply $\mathbf{P}\mathbf{P}_1=\mathbf{P}_1$. From the symmetry of $\mathbf{P}$ and $\mathbf{P}_1$ it follows that $\mathbf{P}_1=\mathbf{P}_1\mathbf{P}$. Thus we have

(7.16) $$\mathbf{P}_1=\mathbf{P}_1\mathbf{P}=\mathbf{P}\mathbf{P}_1 \quad \text{and, likewise,} \quad \mathbf{P}_2=\mathbf{P}_2\mathbf{P}=\mathbf{P}\mathbf{P}_2.$$

By substituting $\mathbf{P}=\mathbf{P}_{1/2}+\mathbf{P}_{2/1}$ in the first of these and using the first result under (7.15), we find that $\mathbf{P}_1=\mathbf{P}_1(\mathbf{P}_{1/2}+\mathbf{P}_{2/1})=\mathbf{P}_{1/2}+\mathbf{P}_1\mathbf{P}_{2/1}$. Thus we deduce the important results that

(7.17) $$\mathbf{P}_{1/2}=\mathbf{P}_1-\mathbf{P}_1\mathbf{P}_{2/1} \quad \text{and, likewise,} \quad \mathbf{P}_{2/1}=\mathbf{P}_2-\mathbf{P}_2\mathbf{P}_{1/2}.$$

We can use the second of these expressions to show that $\mathbf{P}_{1/2}-\mathbf{P}_2\mathbf{P}_{1/2}=\mathbf{P}_{1/2}+\mathbf{P}_{2/1}-\mathbf{P}_2$ or simply

(7.18) $$(\mathbf{I}-\mathbf{P}_2)\mathbf{P}_{1/2}=\mathbf{P}-\mathbf{P}_2.$$

However, it also follows from (7.16) that

(7.19) $$(\mathbf{I}-\mathbf{P}_2)\mathbf{P}(\mathbf{I}-\mathbf{P}_2)=\mathbf{P}-\mathbf{P}_2.$$

Therefore, on gathering the last two results, we find that

(7.20) $$(\mathbf{I}-\mathbf{P}_2)\mathbf{P}_{1/2}=(\mathbf{I}-\mathbf{P}_2)\mathbf{P}(\mathbf{I}-\mathbf{P}_2)=\mathbf{P}-\mathbf{P}_2.$$

This is an important result which we shall use frequently. On representing it more explicitly, we find that

(7.21) $$\begin{aligned}(\mathbf{I}-\mathbf{P}_2)\mathbf{X}_1[\mathbf{X}_1'(\mathbf{I}-\mathbf{P}_2)\mathbf{X}_1]^{-1}\mathbf{X}_1'(\mathbf{I}-\mathbf{P}_2) \\ =(\mathbf{I}-\mathbf{P}_2)\mathbf{X}(\mathbf{X}'\mathbf{X})^{-1}\mathbf{X}'(\mathbf{I}-\mathbf{P}_2) \\ =\mathbf{X}(\mathbf{X}'\mathbf{X})^{-1}\mathbf{X}'-\mathbf{X}_2(\mathbf{X}_2'\mathbf{X}_2)^{-1}\mathbf{X}_2'.\end{aligned}$$

In fact, one of these identities has already been established in the example following (3.55).

Estimates of subvectors of $\boldsymbol{\beta}$

Let us consider writing the equations $\mathbf{y}=\mathbf{X}\boldsymbol{\beta}+\boldsymbol{\varepsilon}$ as

(7.22) $$\mathbf{y}=[\mathbf{X}_1, \mathbf{X}_2]\begin{bmatrix}\boldsymbol{\beta}_1\\ \boldsymbol{\beta}_2\end{bmatrix}+\boldsymbol{\varepsilon},$$

where $\mathbf{X}_1$ is $T\times k_1$ and $\mathbf{X}_2$ is $T\times k_2$, with $k_1+k_2=k$. The estimator $\mathbf{Py}=\mathbf{X}\hat{\boldsymbol{\beta}}$ may be written conformably as $\mathbf{Py}=\mathbf{P}_{1/2}\mathbf{y}+\mathbf{P}_{2/1}\mathbf{y}=\mathbf{X}_1\hat{\boldsymbol{\beta}}_1+\mathbf{X}_2\hat{\boldsymbol{\beta}}_2$. Since $\text{Null}(\mathbf{X})=0$, the estimates $\hat{\boldsymbol{\beta}}_1$, $\hat{\boldsymbol{\beta}}_2$ are uniquely determined. Therefore, using the expressions for $\mathbf{P}_{1/2}$, $\mathbf{P}_{2/1}$ in (7.13), we can solve the equations $\mathbf{P}_{1/2}\mathbf{y}=\mathbf{X}_1\hat{\boldsymbol{\beta}}_1$, $\mathbf{P}_{2/1}\mathbf{y}=\mathbf{X}_2\hat{\boldsymbol{\beta}}_2$ to obtain

$$\text{(7.23)}\qquad \begin{aligned}\hat{\boldsymbol{\beta}}_1&=[\mathbf{X}_1'(\mathbf{I}-\mathbf{P}_2)\mathbf{X}_1]^{-1}\mathbf{X}_1'(\mathbf{I}-\mathbf{P}_2)\mathbf{y},\\ \hat{\boldsymbol{\beta}}_2&=[\mathbf{X}_2'(\mathbf{I}-\mathbf{P}_1)\mathbf{X}_2]^{-1}\mathbf{X}_2'(\mathbf{I}-\mathbf{P}_1)\mathbf{y}.\end{aligned}$$

These expressions for $\hat{\boldsymbol{\beta}}_1$, $\hat{\boldsymbol{\beta}}_2$ may also be derived directly from the equations

$$\text{(7.24)}\qquad \begin{bmatrix}\hat{\boldsymbol{\beta}}_1\\ \hat{\boldsymbol{\beta}}_2\end{bmatrix}=\begin{bmatrix}\mathbf{X}_1'\mathbf{X}_1, & \mathbf{X}_1'\mathbf{X}_2\\ \mathbf{X}_2'\mathbf{X}_1, & \mathbf{X}_2'\mathbf{X}_2\end{bmatrix}^{-1}\begin{bmatrix}\mathbf{X}_1'\mathbf{y}\\ \mathbf{X}_2'\mathbf{y}\end{bmatrix}$$

by using the form of the partitioned inverse of $\mathbf{X}'\mathbf{X}$ given in (7.11).

Alternative expressions for $\mathbf{X}_1\hat{\boldsymbol{\beta}}_1$ and $\mathbf{X}_2\hat{\boldsymbol{\beta}}_2$ and for $\hat{\boldsymbol{\beta}}_1$ and $\hat{\boldsymbol{\beta}}_2$ may be derived by using the identities $\mathbf{P}_{1/2}=\mathbf{P}_1-\mathbf{P}_1\mathbf{P}_{2/1}$ and $\mathbf{P}_{2/1}=\mathbf{P}_2-\mathbf{P}_2\mathbf{P}_{1/2}$ from (7.17). Substituting these in $\mathbf{X}_1\hat{\boldsymbol{\beta}}_1=\mathbf{P}_{1/2}\mathbf{y}$, and $\mathbf{X}_2\hat{\boldsymbol{\beta}}_2=\mathbf{P}_{2/1}\mathbf{y}$ and solving for $\hat{\boldsymbol{\beta}}_1$, $\hat{\boldsymbol{\beta}}_2$ gives

$$\text{(7.25)}\qquad \begin{aligned}\hat{\boldsymbol{\beta}}_1&=(\mathbf{X}_1'\mathbf{X}_1)^{-1}\mathbf{X}_1'\mathbf{y}\\ &\quad-(\mathbf{X}_1'\mathbf{X}_1)^{-1}\mathbf{X}_1'\mathbf{X}_2[\mathbf{X}_2'(\mathbf{I}-\mathbf{P}_1)\mathbf{X}_2]^{-1}\mathbf{X}_2'(\mathbf{I}-\mathbf{P}_1)\mathbf{y}\\ \hat{\boldsymbol{\beta}}_2&=(\mathbf{X}_2'\mathbf{X}_2)^{-1}\mathbf{X}_2'\mathbf{y}\\ &\quad-(\mathbf{X}_2'\mathbf{X}_2)^{-1}\mathbf{X}_2'\mathbf{X}_1[\mathbf{X}_1'(\mathbf{I}-\mathbf{P}_2)\mathbf{X}_1]^{-1}\mathbf{X}_1'(\mathbf{I}-\mathbf{P}_2)\mathbf{y}\\ &=(\mathbf{X}_2'\mathbf{X}_2)^{-1}\mathbf{X}_2'(\mathbf{y}-\mathbf{X}_1\hat{\boldsymbol{\beta}}_1).\end{aligned}$$

To find the dispersion matrix $D(\hat{\boldsymbol{\beta}}_1)$, we use the expression for $\hat{\boldsymbol{\beta}}_1$ in (7.23) to give $D(\hat{\boldsymbol{\beta}}_1)=[\mathbf{X}_1'(\mathbf{I}-\mathbf{P}_2)\mathbf{X}_1]^{-1}\mathbf{X}_1'(\mathbf{I}-\mathbf{P}_2)D(\mathbf{y})(\mathbf{I}-\mathbf{P}_2)\mathbf{X}_1[\mathbf{X}_1'(\mathbf{I}-\mathbf{P}_2)\mathbf{X}_1]^{-1}=\sigma^2[\mathbf{X}_1'(\mathbf{I}-\mathbf{P}_2)\mathbf{X}_1]^{-1}$. Thus

$$\text{(7.26)}\qquad \begin{aligned}D(\hat{\boldsymbol{\beta}}_1)&=\sigma^2[\mathbf{X}_1'(\mathbf{I}-\mathbf{P}_2)\mathbf{X}_1]^{-1}\quad\text{and, likewise,}\\ D(\hat{\boldsymbol{\beta}}_2)&=\sigma^2[\mathbf{X}_2'(\mathbf{I}-\mathbf{P}_1)\mathbf{X}_2]^{-1}.\end{aligned}$$

Reference to (7.11) shows that $D(\hat{\boldsymbol{\beta}}_1)$ is simply the leading submatrix of $D(\hat{\boldsymbol{\beta}})=\sigma^2(\mathbf{X}'\mathbf{X})^{-1}$.

An alternative derivation of the estimator $\hat{\boldsymbol{\beta}}_1$

To provide an alternative derivation of the estimator $\hat{\boldsymbol{\beta}}_1$, let us consider a $T\times(T-k_2)$ orthonormal matrix with vectors that constitute a basis of $\mathcal{O}(\mathbf{X}_2)$. With this matrix, we may form $\mathbf{C}'\mathbf{C}=\mathbf{I}_{T-k_2}$ and $\mathbf{CC}'=(\mathbf{I}-\mathbf{P}_2)$. If we premultiply the equations $\mathbf{y}=\mathbf{X}\boldsymbol{\beta}+\boldsymbol{\varepsilon}$ by $\mathbf{C}'$, we get

$$\text{(7.27)}\qquad \mathbf{C}'\mathbf{y}=\mathbf{C}'[\mathbf{X}_1,\mathbf{X}_2]\begin{bmatrix}\boldsymbol{\beta}_1\\ \boldsymbol{\beta}_2\end{bmatrix}+\mathbf{C}'\boldsymbol{\varepsilon}=\mathbf{C}'\mathbf{X}_1\boldsymbol{\beta}_1+\mathbf{C}'\boldsymbol{\varepsilon}$$

where

$$E(\mathbf{C}'\boldsymbol{\varepsilon})=\mathbf{0}, \qquad D(\mathbf{C}'\boldsymbol{\varepsilon})=\mathbf{C}'D(\boldsymbol{\varepsilon})\mathbf{C}=\sigma^2\mathbf{I}_{T-k_2}. \tag{7.28}$$

Thus, by transforming the equations of the model $(\mathbf{y}, \mathbf{X}\boldsymbol{\beta}, \sigma^2\mathbf{I})$, we obtain a pseudo-model $(\mathbf{C}'\mathbf{y}, \mathbf{C}'\mathbf{X}_1\boldsymbol{\beta}_1, \sigma^2\mathbf{I})$ which also conforms to the assumptions of the classical linear model. Therefore we can apply ordinary least-squares regression to find the minimum variance linear unbiased estimator of $\boldsymbol{\beta}_1$ in the form of

$$\hat{\boldsymbol{\beta}}_1=(\mathbf{X}_1'\mathbf{C}\mathbf{C}'\mathbf{X}_1)^{-1}\mathbf{X}_1'\mathbf{C}\mathbf{C}'\mathbf{y}=[\mathbf{X}_1'(\mathbf{I}-\mathbf{P}_2)\mathbf{X}_1]^{-1}\mathbf{X}_1'(\mathbf{I}-\mathbf{P}_2)\mathbf{y}. \tag{7.29}$$

We may perceive that this is precisely the expression in (7.23).

We might also consider finding an estimate of σ^2 from this regression. By analogy with the formula $\hat{\sigma}^2=\mathbf{y}'[\mathbf{I}-\mathbf{X}(\mathbf{X}'\mathbf{X})^{-1}\mathbf{X}']\mathbf{y}/(T-k)$ of (7.8), we obtain an unbiased estimator

$$\begin{aligned}\hat{\sigma}^2&=\frac{\mathbf{y}'\mathbf{C}[\mathbf{I}-\mathbf{C}'\mathbf{X}_1(\mathbf{X}_1'\mathbf{C}\mathbf{C}'\mathbf{X}_1)^{-1}\mathbf{X}_1'\mathbf{C}]\mathbf{C}'\mathbf{y}}{(T-k_2)-k_1}\\&=\frac{\mathbf{y}'\{(\mathbf{I}-\mathbf{P}_2)-(\mathbf{I}-\mathbf{P}_2)\mathbf{X}_1[\mathbf{X}_1'(\mathbf{I}-\mathbf{P}_2)\mathbf{X}_1]^{-1}\mathbf{X}_1'(\mathbf{I}-\mathbf{P}_2)\}\mathbf{y}}{T-k}.\end{aligned} \tag{7.30}$$

Using the identity $(\mathbf{I}-\mathbf{P}_2)\mathbf{X}_1[\mathbf{X}_1'(\mathbf{I}-\mathbf{P}_2)\mathbf{X}_1]^{-1}\mathbf{X}_1'(\mathbf{I}-\mathbf{P}_2)=\mathbf{P}-\mathbf{P}_2$ taken from (7.20) and (7.21), we find that this reduces to $\hat{\sigma}^2=\mathbf{y}'(\mathbf{I}-\mathbf{P})\mathbf{y}/(T-k)$ which is precisely the expression in (7.8). Thus, by applying the ordinary least-squares method to the pseudo-model $(\mathbf{C}'\mathbf{y}, \mathbf{C}'\mathbf{X}_1\boldsymbol{\beta}_1, \sigma^2\mathbf{I})$, we obtain the same estimates of $\boldsymbol{\beta}_1$ and σ^2 as we would obtain by applying the method to the model $(\mathbf{y}, \mathbf{X}_1\boldsymbol{\beta}_1+\mathbf{X}_2\boldsymbol{\beta}_2, \sigma^2\mathbf{I})$.

A biased estimator of $\boldsymbol{\beta}_1$

One might consider estimating $\mathbf{X}_1\boldsymbol{\beta}_1$ by $\mathbf{X}_1\tilde{\boldsymbol{\beta}}_1=\mathbf{P}_1\mathbf{y}$ instead of by $\mathbf{X}_1\hat{\boldsymbol{\beta}}_1=\mathbf{P}_{1/2}\mathbf{y}$. To investigate the consequences of so doing, let us write the expression for $\hat{\boldsymbol{\beta}}_1$ in (7.25) as $\hat{\boldsymbol{\beta}}_1=(\mathbf{X}_1'\mathbf{X}_1)^{-1}\mathbf{X}_1'\mathbf{y}-(\mathbf{X}_1'\mathbf{X}_1)^{-1}\mathbf{X}_1'\mathbf{X}_2\hat{\boldsymbol{\beta}}_2$. Then

$$\tilde{\boldsymbol{\beta}}_1=(\mathbf{X}_1'\mathbf{X}_1)^{-1}\mathbf{X}_1'\mathbf{y}=\hat{\boldsymbol{\beta}}_1+(\mathbf{X}_1'\mathbf{X}_1)^{-1}\mathbf{X}_1'\mathbf{X}_2\hat{\boldsymbol{\beta}}_2. \tag{7.31}$$

From this it follows that $\tilde{\boldsymbol{\beta}}_1\neq\hat{\boldsymbol{\beta}}_1$ unless $\mathbf{X}_1'\mathbf{X}_2=\mathbf{0}$ or $\hat{\boldsymbol{\beta}}_2=\mathbf{0}$. Moreover, taking expectations, we find that

$$E(\tilde{\boldsymbol{\beta}}_1)=\boldsymbol{\beta}_1+(\mathbf{X}_1'\mathbf{X}_1)^{-1}\mathbf{X}_1'\mathbf{X}_2\boldsymbol{\beta}_2, \tag{7.32}$$

so that $\tilde{\boldsymbol{\beta}}_1$ is a biased estimator of $\boldsymbol{\beta}_1$ unless $\mathbf{X}_1'\mathbf{X}_2=\mathbf{0}$ or $\boldsymbol{\beta}_2=\mathbf{0}$.

Regression with an intercept

We may use the expressions for $\hat{\boldsymbol{\beta}}_1, \hat{\boldsymbol{\beta}}_2$ in (7.25) in order to find estimators of the parameters β_1, $\boldsymbol{\beta}_{\mathbf{Z}}$ of the regression model $(\mathbf{y}, \mathbf{i}\beta_1+\mathbf{Z}\boldsymbol{\beta}_{\mathbf{Z}}, \sigma^2\mathbf{I})$. For this purpose we assimilate the equations $\mathbf{y}=\mathbf{i}\beta_1+\mathbf{Z}\boldsymbol{\beta}_\mathbf{Z}+\boldsymbol{\varepsilon}$ to the equations $\mathbf{y}=\mathbf{X}_1\boldsymbol{\beta}_1+\mathbf{X}_2\boldsymbol{\beta}_2+\boldsymbol{\varepsilon}$ by setting $\mathbf{X}_1=\mathbf{i}$, $\mathbf{X}_2=[\mathbf{x}_{.2},\ldots,\mathbf{x}_{.k}]=\mathbf{Z}$, $\boldsymbol{\beta}_1=\beta_1$ and $\boldsymbol{\beta}_2'=\boldsymbol{\beta}_\mathbf{Z}'=[\beta_2,\ldots,\beta_k]$.

To assist us in finding the formulae for the estimators, let us consider the projector

$$(7.33)\qquad \mathbf{P}_1=\mathbf{P}_\mathbf{i}=\mathbf{i}(\mathbf{i}'\mathbf{i})^{-1}\mathbf{i}'=\mathbf{i}\mathbf{i}'/T.$$

Applying this to the vector $\mathbf{y}$, we get

$$(7.34)\qquad \mathbf{P}_\mathbf{i}\mathbf{y}=\mathbf{i}(\mathbf{i}'\mathbf{y}/T)=\mathbf{i}(\textstyle\sum y_t/T)=\mathbf{i}\bar{y}=\bar{\mathbf{y}}.$$

Applying it likewise to the matrix $\mathbf{Z}$, we get

$$(7.35)\qquad \begin{aligned}\mathbf{P}_\mathbf{i}\mathbf{Z}&=\mathbf{i}[\textstyle\sum x_{t2},\ldots,\sum x_{tk}]/T=\mathbf{i}[\bar{x}_2,\ldots,\bar{x}_k]\\&=[\bar{\mathbf{x}}_{.2},\ldots,\bar{\mathbf{x}}_{.k}]=\bar{\mathbf{Z}}.\end{aligned}$$

On substituting $\mathbf{Z}=\mathbf{X}_2$ and $\mathbf{i}=\mathbf{X}_1$ in the formula for $\hat{\boldsymbol{\beta}}_2=\hat{\boldsymbol{\beta}}_\mathbf{Z}$ in (7.23), and using the identity $(\mathbf{I}-\mathbf{P}_\mathbf{i})=(\mathbf{I}-\mathbf{P}_\mathbf{i})'(\mathbf{I}-\mathbf{P}_\mathbf{i})$ and the notation $\mathbf{P}_\mathbf{i}\mathbf{y}=\bar{\mathbf{y}}$, $\mathbf{P}_\mathbf{i}\mathbf{Z}=\bar{\mathbf{Z}}$, we obtain

$$(7.36)\qquad \begin{aligned}\hat{\boldsymbol{\beta}}_\mathbf{Z}&=[\mathbf{Z}'(\mathbf{I}-\mathbf{P}_\mathbf{i})\mathbf{Z}]^{-1}\mathbf{Z}'(\mathbf{I}-\mathbf{P}_\mathbf{i})\mathbf{y}\\&=[(\mathbf{Z}-\bar{\mathbf{Z}})'(\mathbf{Z}-\bar{\mathbf{Z}})]^{-1}(\mathbf{Z}-\bar{\mathbf{Z}})'(\mathbf{y}-\bar{\mathbf{y}}).\end{aligned}$$

Thus the coefficients $\beta_2,\ldots,\beta_k$ may be estimated by applying ordinary least-squares regression to data which has been adjusted by subtracting from each observation its respective sample mean.

To find an estimate of the intercept term $\beta_1=\boldsymbol{\beta}_1$, we substitute $\mathbf{i}=\mathbf{X}_1$ and $\mathbf{Z}=\mathbf{X}_2$ in the formula for $\hat{\boldsymbol{\beta}}_1$ in (7.25) to get

$$(7.37)\qquad \begin{aligned}\hat{\beta}_1&=(\mathbf{i}'\mathbf{i})^{-1}\mathbf{i}'\mathbf{y}-(\mathbf{i}'\mathbf{i})^{-1}\mathbf{i}'\mathbf{Z}[\mathbf{Z}'(\mathbf{I}-\mathbf{P}_\mathbf{i})\mathbf{Z}]^{-1}\mathbf{Z}'(\mathbf{I}-\mathbf{P}_\mathbf{i})\mathbf{y}\\&=\mathbf{i}'\mathbf{y}/T-\mathbf{i}'\mathbf{Z}\hat{\boldsymbol{\beta}}_\mathbf{Z}/T\\&=\bar{y}-\sum_{j=2}^{k}\hat{\beta}_j\bar{x}_j.\end{aligned}$$

COEFFICIENTS OF DETERMINATION

To provide a summary measure of the extent to which the ordinary least-squares regression accounts for the observed vector $\mathbf{y}$, we may use the ordinary coefficient of determination. This is defined by

$$(7.38)\qquad R^2(\mathbf{y},\mathbf{X})=\frac{\mathbf{y}'\mathbf{P}\mathbf{y}}{\mathbf{y}'\mathbf{y}}=\frac{\hat{\boldsymbol{\beta}}'\mathbf{X}'\mathbf{X}\hat{\boldsymbol{\beta}}}{\mathbf{y}'\mathbf{y}}.$$

If $\mathbf{y}\in\mathcal{M}(\mathbf{X})$, then $\mathbf{X}\hat{\boldsymbol{\beta}}=\mathbf{P}\mathbf{y}=\mathbf{y}$; and it follows that $R^2=1$. The value of $\mathbf{y}$ is then completely accounted for by the regression. If $\mathbf{y}$ is distributed continuously in $\mathcal{R}^T$, then the event $\mathbf{y}\in\mathcal{M}(\mathbf{X})$ has a probability measure of zero unless $\mathcal{M}(\mathbf{X})=\mathcal{R}^T$, in which case the event is a certainty. The condition $\mathcal{M}(\mathbf{X})=\mathcal{R}^T$ is equivalent to the condition $\text{Null}(\mathbf{X}')=0$ which means that $\mathbf{X}$ has full row rank which, in turn, implies that the number of rows in $\mathbf{X}$ cannot exceed the number of columns. For the parameter vector $\boldsymbol{\beta}$ to be estimable, the condition $\text{Null}(\mathbf{X})=0$ must also be fulfilled. Thus $\mathbf{X}$ must have full column rank and the number of columns must not exceed the number of rows. It follows that we can expect the regression to yield both a coefficient of determination of unity and a uniquely determined estimate $\hat{\boldsymbol{\beta}}$ if and only if $\mathbf{X}$ is a non-singular square matrix comprising equal numbers of variables and observations.

If $\mathbf{y}\perp\mathcal{M}(\mathbf{X})$ or, equivalently, $\mathbf{y}\in\mathcal{N}(\mathbf{P})$, then $\mathbf{Py}=\mathbf{0}$; and it follows that $R^2=0$. The regression then fails to account for any part of $\mathbf{y}$. However, on the assumption that $\mathbf{y}$ is distributed continuously in $\mathcal{R}^T$, the event $\mathbf{y}\perp\mathcal{M}(\mathbf{X})$ has a probability measure of zero, and thus we would never expect to find $R^2=0$ in practice.

The inequality $0\leqslant R^2\leqslant 1$ also follows from the properties of cosines once we recognize, on the basis of (3.12), that

$$\rho=\frac{\langle\mathbf{y},\mathbf{Py}\rangle}{\sqrt{\langle\mathbf{y},\mathbf{y}\rangle}\sqrt{\langle\mathbf{Py},\mathbf{Py}\rangle}}=\frac{\mathbf{y}'\mathbf{Py}}{\sqrt{\mathbf{y}'\mathbf{y}}\sqrt{\mathbf{y}'\mathbf{Py}}}=\sqrt{R^2} \tag{7.39}$$

is the cosine of the angle between the vectors $\mathbf{y}$ and $\hat{\mathbf{y}}=\mathbf{Py}$.

We may also wish to measure the peculiar contribution of the variables in $\mathbf{X}_1$ to the explanation of $\mathbf{y}$ when $\mathbf{y}$ is regressed on $\mathbf{X}=[\mathbf{X}_1,\mathbf{X}_2]$. To do so, we must remove from $\mathbf{y}$ the component that is attributable to $\mathbf{X}_2$ by subtracting $\mathbf{P}_2\mathbf{y}$ to give $(\mathbf{I}-\mathbf{P}_2)\mathbf{y}$. We must also find the components that are peculiar to $\mathbf{X}_1$ by subtracting $\mathbf{P}_2\mathbf{X}_1$ to give $(\mathbf{I}-\mathbf{P}_2)\mathbf{X}_1$. We can then obtain a measure of the contribution by finding the ordinary coefficient of determination $R^2[(\mathbf{I}-\mathbf{P}_2)\mathbf{y},(\mathbf{I}-\mathbf{P}_2)\mathbf{X}_1]$ of the regression of $(\mathbf{I}-\mathbf{P}_2)\mathbf{y}$ on $(\mathbf{I}-\mathbf{P}_2)\mathbf{X}_1$. In the context of the regression of $\mathbf{y}$ on $\mathbf{X}$, this is called the partial coefficient of determination of $\mathbf{y}$ and $\mathbf{X}_1$ given $\mathbf{X}_2$ and is denoted by $R^2(\mathbf{y},\mathbf{X}_1\,|\,\mathbf{X}_2)$. Using the symmetry and idempotency of $\mathbf{I}-\mathbf{P}_2$ and the identities of (7.20) and (7.21), we find that

$$\begin{aligned} R^2(\mathbf{y},\mathbf{X}_1\,|\,\mathbf{X}_2)&=\frac{\mathbf{y}'(\mathbf{I}-\mathbf{P}_2)\mathbf{X}_1[\mathbf{X}_1'(\mathbf{I}-\mathbf{P}_2)\mathbf{X}_1]^{-1}\mathbf{X}_1'(\mathbf{I}-\mathbf{P}_2)\mathbf{y}}{\mathbf{y}'(\mathbf{I}-\mathbf{P}_2)'(\mathbf{I}-\mathbf{P}_2)\mathbf{y}}\\ &=\frac{\mathbf{y}'(\mathbf{I}-\mathbf{P}_2)'\mathbf{P}(\mathbf{I}-\mathbf{P}_2)\mathbf{y}}{\mathbf{y}'(\mathbf{I}-\mathbf{P}_2)'(\mathbf{I}-\mathbf{P}_2)\mathbf{y}}=\frac{\mathbf{y}'(\mathbf{P}-\mathbf{P}_2)\mathbf{y}}{\mathbf{y}'(\mathbf{I}-\mathbf{P}_2)\mathbf{y}}\mathbf{y}. \end{aligned} \tag{7.40}$$

From the second equality it is also apparent that $R^2(\mathbf{y},\mathbf{X}_1\,|\,\mathbf{X}_2)=R^2[(\mathbf{I}-\mathbf{P}_2)\mathbf{y},\mathbf{X}]$.

A further interpretation of the partial coefficient of determination arises when we consider the regression of $\mathbf{C}'\mathbf{y}$ on $\mathbf{C}'\mathbf{X}_1$ in the context of the pseudo-model $(\mathbf{C}'\mathbf{y},\mathbf{C}'\mathbf{X}_1\boldsymbol{\beta}_1,\sigma^2\mathbf{I})$. Using $\mathbf{CC}'=(\mathbf{I}-\mathbf{P}_2)$, it is readily confirmed that $R^2(\mathbf{y},\mathbf{X}_1\,|\,\mathbf{X}_2)=R^2(\mathbf{C}'\mathbf{y},\mathbf{C}'\mathbf{X}_1)$.

In the case of the model $(\mathbf{y}, \mathbf{i}\beta_1+\mathbf{Z}\boldsymbol{\beta}_Z, \sigma^2\mathbf{I})$, which we also write as $(\mathbf{y}, \mathbf{X}\boldsymbol{\beta}, \sigma^2\mathbf{I})$ where $\mathbf{X}=[\mathbf{i}, \mathbf{Z}]$ and $\boldsymbol{\beta}'=[\beta_1, \boldsymbol{\beta}_2']$, it is conventional to measure the explanatory power of the regression in terms of the partial coefficient of determination $R^2(\mathbf{y}, \mathbf{Z}\,|\,\mathbf{i})$. This practice is justified by the argument that the explanatory power of the vector $\mathbf{i}$ is gratuitous. Using the notations $\mathbf{P}_i\mathbf{y}=\bar{\mathbf{y}}$ and $\mathbf{P}_i\mathbf{Z}=\bar{\mathbf{Z}}$ of (7.34) and (7.35) respectively, we find from (7.40) that

$$(7.41) \qquad R^2(\mathbf{y}, \mathbf{Z}\,|\,\mathbf{i})=\frac{(\mathbf{y}-\bar{\mathbf{y}})'(\mathbf{Z}-\bar{\mathbf{Z}})[(\mathbf{Z}-\bar{\mathbf{Z}})'(\mathbf{Z}-\bar{\mathbf{Z}})]^{-1}(\mathbf{Z}-\bar{\mathbf{Z}})'(\mathbf{y}-\bar{\mathbf{y}})}{(\mathbf{y}-\bar{\mathbf{y}})'(\mathbf{y}-\bar{\mathbf{y}})}$$

$$=\frac{\mathbf{y}'\mathbf{P}\mathbf{y}-\mathbf{y}'\mathbf{P}_i\mathbf{y}}{\mathbf{y}'(\mathbf{I}-\mathbf{P}_i)\mathbf{y}}=\frac{\hat{\boldsymbol{\beta}}'\mathbf{X}'\mathbf{X}\hat{\boldsymbol{\beta}}-\bar{\mathbf{y}}'\bar{\mathbf{y}}}{\mathbf{y}'\mathbf{y}-\bar{\mathbf{y}}'\bar{\mathbf{y}}}.$$

The first equality shows that $R^2(\mathbf{y}, \mathbf{Z}\,|\,\mathbf{i})$ is the ordinary coefficient of determination of the regression (7.36) wherein the variables are the deviations of the observations about their sample means. The final term, which suggests a straightforward way of computing the coefficient, has an interesting comparison with $R^2(\mathbf{y}, \mathbf{X})=\hat{\boldsymbol{\beta}}'\mathbf{X}'\mathbf{X}\hat{\boldsymbol{\beta}}/\mathbf{y}'\mathbf{y}$ defined in (7.38).

THE ASSUMPTION OF NORMALITY

In order to test hypotheses relating to the parameter vector $\boldsymbol{\beta}$, or to construct confidence intervals, we must make further statistical assumptions about the model $(\mathbf{y}, \mathbf{X}\boldsymbol{\beta}, \sigma^2\mathbf{I})$. It is conventional to assume that the vector of disturbances $\boldsymbol{\varepsilon}=(\mathbf{y}-\mathbf{X}\boldsymbol{\beta})$ is distributed normally so that

$$(7.42) \qquad \mathbf{y}\sim N(\mathbf{X}\boldsymbol{\beta}, \sigma^2\mathbf{I}).$$

This assumption is supported by the central limit theorem if we assume that the elements of $\boldsymbol{\varepsilon}$ are sums of a large number of independent random variables with small finite variances.

The distributions of the vectors $\hat{\boldsymbol{\beta}}$ and $\mathbf{y}-\mathbf{X}\hat{\boldsymbol{\beta}}$

A linear function of a normally distributed vector is itself normally distributed. Thus it follows that, if $\mathbf{y}\sim N(\mathbf{X}\boldsymbol{\beta}, \sigma^2\mathbf{I})$, then

$$(7.43) \qquad \hat{\boldsymbol{\beta}}\sim N_k(\boldsymbol{\beta}, \sigma^2(\mathbf{X}'\mathbf{X})^{-1}).$$

The marginal distributions of $\hat{\boldsymbol{\beta}}_1$, $\hat{\boldsymbol{\beta}}_2$ within $\hat{\boldsymbol{\beta}}'=[\hat{\boldsymbol{\beta}}_1', \hat{\boldsymbol{\beta}}_2']$ are given by

$$(7.44) \qquad \hat{\boldsymbol{\beta}}_1\sim N_{k_1}(\boldsymbol{\beta}_1, \sigma^2[\mathbf{X}_1'(\mathbf{I}-\mathbf{P}_2)\mathbf{X}_1]^{-1}),$$

$$\hat{\boldsymbol{\beta}}_2\sim N_{k_2}(\boldsymbol{\beta}_2, \sigma^2[\mathbf{X}_2'(\mathbf{I}-\mathbf{P}_1)\mathbf{X}_2]^{-1}).$$

The marginal distribution of the jth element of $\hat{\boldsymbol{\beta}}$ is given by

$$(7.45) \qquad \hat{\beta}_j\sim N(\beta_j, \sigma^2\omega_{jj}),$$

where ω_{jj} is the jth diagonal element of $(\mathbf{X}'\mathbf{X})^{-1}$.

On applying the result (17.38) of the Appendix of Statistical Theory to (7.43), we find that

$$\sigma^{-2}(\hat{\boldsymbol\beta}-\boldsymbol\beta)'\mathbf{X}'\mathbf{X}(\hat{\boldsymbol\beta}-\boldsymbol\beta)\sim\chi^2(k). \tag{7.46}$$

Similarly, it follows from (7.44) that

$$\begin{aligned}\sigma^{-2}(\hat{\boldsymbol\beta}_1-\boldsymbol\beta_1)'\mathbf{X}_1'(\mathbf{I}-\mathbf{P}_2)\mathbf{X}_1(\hat{\boldsymbol\beta}_1-\boldsymbol\beta_1)&\sim\chi^2(k_1),\\ \sigma^{-2}(\hat{\boldsymbol\beta}_2-\boldsymbol\beta_2)'\mathbf{X}_2'(\mathbf{I}-\mathbf{P}_1)\mathbf{X}_2(\hat{\boldsymbol\beta}_2-\boldsymbol\beta_2)&\sim\chi^2(k_2).\end{aligned} \tag{7.47}$$

The distribution of the residual vector $\mathbf{y}-\mathbf{X}\hat{\boldsymbol\beta}=(\mathbf{I}-\mathbf{P})\mathbf{y}$ is degenerate, since $\mathbf{I}-\mathbf{P}$ is a singular transformation. To find the distribution of the corresponding quadratic form $(\mathbf{y}-\mathbf{X}\hat{\boldsymbol\beta})'(\mathbf{y}-\mathbf{X}\hat{\boldsymbol\beta})=\mathbf{y}'(\mathbf{I}-\mathbf{P})\mathbf{y}$, we consider a $T\times(T-k)$ orthonormal matrix $\mathbf{C}$ whose columns constitute a basis of $\mathcal{O}(\mathbf{X})$ such that $\mathbf{C}'\mathbf{X}=\mathbf{0}$. With this matrix we may form $\mathbf{C}'\mathbf{C}=\mathbf{I}_{T-k}$ and $\mathbf{C}\mathbf{C}'=\mathbf{I}-\mathbf{P}$. Thus, on premultiplying $\mathbf{y}\sim N_T(\mathbf{X}\boldsymbol\beta,\sigma^2\mathbf{I})$ by $\mathbf{C}'$, we get $\mathbf{C}'\mathbf{y}\sim N_{T-k}(\mathbf{0},\sigma^2\mathbf{I})$. It follows that $\sigma^{-2}\mathbf{y}'\mathbf{C}\mathbf{C}'\mathbf{y}\sim\chi^2(T-k)$ or, equivalently,

$$\sigma^{-2}\mathbf{y}'(\mathbf{I}-\mathbf{P})\mathbf{y}=\sigma^{-2}(\mathbf{y}-\mathbf{X}\hat{\boldsymbol\beta})'(\mathbf{y}-\mathbf{X}\hat{\boldsymbol\beta})\sim\chi^2(T-k). \tag{7.48}$$

The covariance structure of $\mathbf{X}\hat{\boldsymbol\beta}=\mathbf{P}\mathbf{y}$ and $\mathbf{y}-\mathbf{X}\hat{\boldsymbol\beta}=(\mathbf{I}-\mathbf{P})\mathbf{y}$ is given by

$$\begin{aligned}C(\mathbf{X}\hat{\boldsymbol\beta},\mathbf{y}-\mathbf{X}\hat{\boldsymbol\beta})&=C(\mathbf{P}\mathbf{y},(\mathbf{I}-\mathbf{P})\mathbf{y})\\ &=\mathbf{P}D(\mathbf{y})(\mathbf{I}-\mathbf{P})'=\sigma^2\mathbf{P}(\mathbf{I}-\mathbf{P})=\mathbf{0}.\end{aligned} \tag{7.49}$$

If two normally distributed random vectors have a zero covariance matrix, then, according to (17.26), the vectors are statistically independent. Thus (7.49) implies that $\mathbf{X}\hat{\boldsymbol\beta}$ and $\mathbf{y}-\mathbf{X}\hat{\boldsymbol\beta}$ are statistically independent, and it follows that

$$\begin{aligned}&\sigma^{-2}(\hat{\boldsymbol\beta}-\boldsymbol\beta)'\mathbf{X}'\mathbf{X}(\hat{\boldsymbol\beta}-\boldsymbol\beta)\sim\chi^2(k)\quad\text{and}\\ &\sigma^{-2}(\mathbf{y}-\mathbf{X}\hat{\boldsymbol\beta})'(\mathbf{y}-\mathbf{X}\hat{\boldsymbol\beta})\sim\chi^2(T-k)\end{aligned} \tag{7.50}$$

are mutually independent chi-square variates.

From this we may deduce that

$$\left\{\frac{(\hat{\boldsymbol\beta}-\boldsymbol\beta)'\mathbf{X}'\mathbf{X}(\hat{\boldsymbol\beta}-\boldsymbol\beta)}{k}\Big/\frac{(\mathbf{y}-\mathbf{X}\hat{\boldsymbol\beta})'(\mathbf{y}-\mathbf{X}\hat{\boldsymbol\beta})}{T-k}\right\}=\frac{(\hat{\boldsymbol\beta}-\boldsymbol\beta)'\mathbf{X}'\mathbf{X}(\hat{\boldsymbol\beta}-\boldsymbol\beta)}{\hat\sigma^2k}\sim F(k,T-k) \tag{7.51}$$

is an F variate with k and $T-k$ degrees of freedom.

Taking the subvector $\hat{\boldsymbol\beta}_2$, we can also deduce that

$$\frac{(\hat{\boldsymbol\beta}_2-\boldsymbol\beta_2)'\mathbf{X}_2'(\mathbf{I}-\mathbf{P}_1)\mathbf{X}_2(\hat{\boldsymbol\beta}_2-\boldsymbol\beta_2)}{\hat\sigma^2k_2}\sim F(k_2,T-k). \tag{7.52}$$

Finally, for the jth element of $\hat{\boldsymbol{\beta}}$ we have

(7.53) $$(\hat{\beta}_j - \beta_j)^2/\hat{\sigma}^2\omega_{jj} \sim F(1, T-k) \quad \text{or, equivalently,}$$
$$(\hat{\beta}_j - \beta_j)/\sqrt{\hat{\sigma}^2\omega_{jj}} \sim t(T-k),$$

where ω_{jj} is the jth diagonal element of $(\mathbf{X}'\mathbf{X})^{-1}$ and $t(T-k)$ denotes the t distribution of $T-k$ degrees of freedom.

Confidence intervals for the elements of β

Let F_α be a number such that the probability of the event $F(k, T-k) > F_\alpha$ is α. Then it follows from (7.51) that the probability of the event $(\hat{\boldsymbol{\beta}} - \boldsymbol{\beta})'\mathbf{X}'\mathbf{X}(\hat{\boldsymbol{\beta}} - \boldsymbol{\beta}) \leq F_\alpha \hat{\sigma}^2 k$ is $1-\alpha$. Therefore

(7.54) The set $\{\mathbf{b}; (\hat{\boldsymbol{\beta}} - \mathbf{b})'\mathbf{X}'\mathbf{X}(\hat{\boldsymbol{\beta}} - \mathbf{b}) \leq F_\alpha \hat{\sigma}^2 k\}$ is a confidence region with a probability of $1-\alpha$ of containing the true value of $\boldsymbol{\beta}$.

This confidence region has the form of an ellipsoid centred on $\hat{\boldsymbol{\beta}}$. An analogous confidence interval may be constructed for $\hat{\boldsymbol{\beta}}_1$ using the result in (7.47).

Finally, consider the scalar estimate $\hat{\beta}_j$, and let t_α be a number such that the probability of the event $-t_\alpha < t(T-k) < +t_\alpha$ is $1-\alpha$. Then

(7.55) The set $\{\hat{\beta}_j - t_\alpha\sqrt{\hat{\sigma}^2\omega_{jj}} < b < \hat{\beta}_j + t_\alpha\sqrt{\hat{\sigma}^2\omega_{jj}}\}$ is a confidence interval with a probability of $1-\alpha$ of containing the true value of β_j.

HYPOTHESIS TESTING UNDER THE ASSUMPTION OF NORMALITY

We shall now develop procedures for testing some of the hypotheses that are commonly maintained in the context of the model $(\mathbf{y}, \mathbf{X}\boldsymbol{\beta}, \sigma^2\mathbf{I})$. Each of these procedures is based on an F-statistic, and each may be justified in terms of the likelihood-ratio principle.

In Chapter 6 we derived the test statistics for the various hypotheses relating to the model $(\mathbf{y}, \mathbf{X}\boldsymbol{\beta}, \sigma^2\mathbf{Q})$ from the quadratic products of the components of the appropriate $\mathbf{Q}^{-1}$-orthogonal decomposition of the random vector $(\mathbf{y} - \mathbf{X}\boldsymbol{\beta}) \sim N(\mathbf{0}, \sigma^2\mathbf{Q})$. We found the distributions of these products by invoking Cochran's theorem. In the present context, we shall derive our test statistics in a manner which is less general, by relying on the results concerning the distributions of the vectors $\hat{\boldsymbol{\beta}}$ and $\mathbf{y} - \mathbf{X}\hat{\boldsymbol{\beta}}$ which have been given in the previous section.

Testing hypotheses on the complete vector $\boldsymbol{\beta}$

Under some circumstances, we might be able to assert an hypothesis specifying every element of $\boldsymbol{\beta}$. Let us denote the vector of hypothesized values by $\boldsymbol{\beta}_*$. Then reference to (7.51) shows that

(7.56) On the hypothesis $\mathbf{y} \sim N(\mathbf{X}\boldsymbol{\beta}_*, \sigma^2\mathbf{I})$, we have

$$(\hat{\boldsymbol{\beta}} - \boldsymbol{\beta}_*)'\mathbf{X}'\mathbf{X}(\hat{\boldsymbol{\beta}} - \boldsymbol{\beta}_*)/\hat{\sigma}^2 k \sim F(k, T-k);$$

and this provides the appropriate statistic for testing the hypothesis.

An example is the hypothesis which maintains that $\boldsymbol{\beta} = \boldsymbol{\beta}_* = \mathbf{0}$ or, equivalently, that $\mathbf{y} \sim N(\mathbf{0}, \sigma^2\mathbf{I})$. However, this is unlikely to be a reasonable hypothesis, for, even when we believe that the variables of the matrix $\mathbf{Z}$ within $\mathbf{X} = [\mathbf{i}, \mathbf{Z}]$ have no explanatory power, we do not normally expect $\mathbf{y}$ to be distributed with zero mean. We are more likely to maintain an hypothesis of the form $\mathbf{y} \sim N(\beta_1\mathbf{i}, \sigma^2\mathbf{I})$ which specifies that $\mathbf{y}$ is a vector of independent random variables sampled from the normal distribution $N(\beta_1, \sigma^2)$. We shall develop a test for this in the following section.

Hypotheses on a subvector of $\boldsymbol{\beta}$

We might wish to test an hypothesis relating to a subvector of the elements of $\boldsymbol{\beta}$ without presuming anything about the remaining elements. We might, for example, presume that $\boldsymbol{\beta}_2 = \boldsymbol{\beta}_{2*}$ in the vector $\boldsymbol{\beta}' = [\boldsymbol{\beta}_1', \boldsymbol{\beta}_2']$. Reference to (7.52) helps us to establish that

(7.57) On the hypothesis that $\boldsymbol{\beta}_2 = \boldsymbol{\beta}_{2*}$ in the model $\mathbf{y} \sim N(\mathbf{X}_1\boldsymbol{\beta}_1 + \mathbf{X}_2\boldsymbol{\beta}_2, \sigma^2\mathbf{I})$, we have

$$\frac{(\hat{\boldsymbol{\beta}}_2 - \boldsymbol{\beta}_{2*})'\mathbf{X}_2'(\mathbf{I} - \mathbf{P}_1)\mathbf{X}_2(\hat{\boldsymbol{\beta}}_2 - \boldsymbol{\beta}_{2*})}{\hat{\sigma}^2 k_2} \sim F(k_2, T-k);$$

and this provides the appropriate test statistic.

To construct a test of an hypothesis relating to the single element β_j, we may refer to the result in (7.53).

An important hypothesis which falls in the present category is one which asserts that, amongst the variables in $\mathbf{X} = [\mathbf{X}_1, \mathbf{X}_2]$, the variables in $\mathbf{X}_2$ are irrelevant for the explanation of the values in $\mathbf{y}$. This leads to the specification that $\boldsymbol{\beta}_2 = \boldsymbol{\beta}_{2*} = \mathbf{0}$, so that the numerator of the statistic of (7.57) becomes

(7.58) $$\hat{\boldsymbol{\beta}}_2'\mathbf{X}_2'(\mathbf{I} - \mathbf{P}_1)\mathbf{X}_2\hat{\boldsymbol{\beta}}_2 = \mathbf{y}'(\mathbf{P} - \mathbf{P}_1)\mathbf{y},$$

where the second expression comes from using the formula for $\hat{\boldsymbol{\beta}}_2$ in (7.23) and an identity in the form of that of (7.21). On writing the expression as $(\mathbf{P}\mathbf{y} - \mathbf{P}_1\mathbf{y})'(\mathbf{P}\mathbf{y} - \mathbf{P}_1\mathbf{y}) = (\mathbf{X}\hat{\boldsymbol{\beta}} - \mathbf{X}_1\tilde{\boldsymbol{\beta}}_1)'(\mathbf{X}\hat{\boldsymbol{\beta}} - \mathbf{X}_1\tilde{\boldsymbol{\beta}}_1) = \|\mathbf{X}\hat{\boldsymbol{\beta}} - \mathbf{X}_1\tilde{\boldsymbol{\beta}}_1\|^2$, we can see that the test statistic comprises a measure of the proximity of the ordinary least-squares estimates of the mean vectors of the models $(\mathbf{y}, \mathbf{X}_1\boldsymbol{\beta}_1 + \mathbf{X}_2\boldsymbol{\beta}_2, \sigma^2\mathbf{I})$ and $(\mathbf{y}, \mathbf{X}_1\boldsymbol{\beta}_1, \sigma^2\mathbf{I})$. A specialized example of the hypothesis presently under consideration is the one that asserts that the variables of the matrix $\mathbf{Z}$ within $\mathbf{X} = [\mathbf{i}, \mathbf{Z}]$ have no explanatory power. Using the form $\mathbf{y}'(\mathbf{P} - \mathbf{P}_i)\mathbf{y} = \boldsymbol{\beta}'\mathbf{X}'\mathbf{X}\boldsymbol{\beta} - \bar{\mathbf{y}}'\bar{\mathbf{y}}$ in the numerator of the test statistic, we find that

(7.59) The appropriate statistic for testing the hypothesis $\mathbf{y} \sim N(\beta_1\mathbf{i}, \sigma^2\mathbf{I})$ in the context of the model $\mathbf{y} \sim N(\beta_1\mathbf{i} + \mathbf{Z}\boldsymbol{\beta}_Z, \sigma^2\mathbf{I})$ is

$$(\hat{\boldsymbol{\beta}}'\mathbf{X}'\mathbf{X}\hat{\boldsymbol{\beta}} - \bar{\mathbf{y}}'\bar{\mathbf{y}})/\hat{\sigma}^2(k-1) \sim F(k-1, T-k).$$

This statistic has a close affinity to the partial coefficient of determination $R^2(\mathbf{y}, \mathbf{Z} \mid \mathbf{i})$ defined in (7.41). It gives a better indication of the explanatory power of the regression, since it enables us to make precise probabilistic statements about the likelihood that the variables in $\mathbf{Z}$ are devoid of genuine explanatory power.

THE ASYMPTOTIC PROPERTIES OF THE ORDINARY LEAST-SQUARES ESTIMATORS

We shall now consider how the sampling properties of the ordinary least-squares estimates evolve as the number of observations increases indefinitely. These properties depend largely upon the nature of the matrix $\mathbf{X}$ comprising the T observations on the k input variables. We have assumed that $\mathbf{X}$ is non-stochastic. In fact, this assumption is rather more appropriate to the experimental sciences, where the values of the variables can be fixed according to a design, than it is to econometrics. Nevertheless, to regard $\mathbf{X}$ as non-stochastic for heuristic purposes is a fiction which does little to prejudice the wider validity of our results.

We have also assumed that $\mathbf{X}$ has full column rank, from which it follows that $\mathbf{X}'\mathbf{X}$ is positive definite. We shall now assume, in addition, that the elements of the matrix have the same order as T so that $\mathbf{X}'\mathbf{X}/T$ converges to a positive-definite matrix $\mathbf{W}$ as $T \to \infty$. For heuristic purposes, it is sometimes helpful to add further detail to this assumption. Thus we may imagine a perpetual cycle of observations in which the typical row vector $\mathbf{x}_{t.}$ recurs after $s \geqslant k$ periods. If we denote the first s rows by $\mathbf{X}_*$, and if we record our observations in batches of s at a time, then the data matrix can be written as $\mathbf{X} = [\mathbf{X}_*', \mathbf{X}_*', \ldots, \mathbf{X}_*']'$.

The consistency of the least-squares estimators

To show that $\hat{\boldsymbol{\beta}}$ is a consistent estimator, it is sufficient to show that it is unbiased and that its dispersion matrix tends to zero as $T \to \infty$. Since the unbiasedness is already established, we may establish the consistency simply by confirming that

$$\text{(7.60)} \qquad \lim(T\to\infty)D(\hat{\boldsymbol{\beta}})=\lim\left[\frac{\sigma^2}{T}\left(\frac{\mathbf{X}'\mathbf{X}}{T}\right)^{-1}\right]=0\mathbf{W}^{-1}=\mathbf{0}.$$

To establish that the estimator $\hat{\sigma}^2=\mathbf{y}'(\mathbf{I}-\mathbf{P})\mathbf{y}/(T-k)$ is consistent, we shall write it as

$$\text{(7.61)} \qquad \hat{\sigma}^2=\frac{\boldsymbol{\varepsilon}'\boldsymbol{\varepsilon}}{T-k}-\frac{(\boldsymbol{\varepsilon}'\mathbf{X}/\sqrt{T})(\mathbf{X}'\mathbf{X}/T)^{-1}(\mathbf{X}'\boldsymbol{\varepsilon}/\sqrt{T})}{T-k}.$$

Then, given that $\boldsymbol{\varepsilon}'=[\varepsilon_1,\ldots,\varepsilon_T]$ is a vector of independent and identically distributed variates with $E(\varepsilon_t^2)=\sigma^2$ for all t, it follows from Khintchine's theorem in (17.64) that $\text{plim}(\boldsymbol{\varepsilon}'\boldsymbol{\varepsilon}/T)=\text{plim}(\sum_{t=1}^{T}\varepsilon_t^2/T)=\sigma^2$. Hence $\text{plim}[\boldsymbol{\varepsilon}'\boldsymbol{\varepsilon}/(T-k)]=\sigma^2$. Therefore the consistency of the estimator may be demonstrated by showing that the second term on the RHS tends to zero in probability as $T\to\infty$.

Consider the numerator of the second term. This is a quadratic function of the random vector $\boldsymbol{\eta}_T=\mathbf{X}'\boldsymbol{\varepsilon}/\sqrt{T}$. Since $\boldsymbol{\varepsilon}\sim(\mathbf{0},\sigma^2\mathbf{I})$, we have $\boldsymbol{\eta}_T\sim(\mathbf{0},\sigma^2\mathbf{X}'\mathbf{X}/T)$; and from the fact that $\mathbf{X}'\mathbf{X}/T\to\mathbf{W}$ as $T\to\infty$, it follows that $\boldsymbol{\eta}_T$ tends in distribution to $\boldsymbol{\eta}\sim(\mathbf{0},\sigma^2\mathbf{W})$. Also $(\mathbf{X}'\mathbf{X}/T)^{-1}$ tends to $\mathbf{W}^{-1}$. Therefore the quadratic function tends in distribution to a random variable with a finite mean and variance. It follows that the term as a whole tends to a probability limit of zero as $T\to\infty$; and this proves our proposition.

The asymptotic normality of $\hat{\boldsymbol{\beta}}$

So far, we have relied upon an assumption that the vector of disturbances $\boldsymbol{\varepsilon}$ is normally distributed to justify our assumption that $\hat{\boldsymbol{\beta}}$ is normal. We shall now show that, when the sample is large, $\hat{\boldsymbol{\beta}}$ has a distribution that is approximately normal no matter how $\boldsymbol{\varepsilon}$ is distributed. The basic result is that

(7.62) If $\lim(\mathbf{X}'\mathbf{X}/T)=\mathbf{W}$, and if $\boldsymbol{\varepsilon}$ has $E(\boldsymbol{\varepsilon})=\mathbf{0}$ and $D(\boldsymbol{\varepsilon})=\sigma^2\mathbf{I}$, then the random vector $\mathbf{X}'\boldsymbol{\varepsilon}/\sqrt{T}$ tends in distribution to $\boldsymbol{\eta}\sim N(\mathbf{0},\sigma^2\mathbf{W})$.

The method of proving this depends upon the assumptions that we make about the matrix $\mathbf{X}$. Let us adopt the heuristic assumption that $\mathbf{X}=[\mathbf{X}_*',\mathbf{X}_*',\ldots,\mathbf{X}_*']'$ is composed of n repetitions of the $s\times k$ matrix $\mathbf{X}_*$. Then

$$\frac{\mathbf{X}'\boldsymbol{\varepsilon}}{\sqrt{T}}=\frac{1}{\sqrt{n}}\sum_{i=1}^{n}\frac{\mathbf{X}_*'\boldsymbol{\varepsilon}_i}{\sqrt{s}}=\frac{1}{\sqrt{n}}\sum_{i=1}^{n}\boldsymbol{\eta}_i$$

where $\boldsymbol{\varepsilon}_i\sim(\mathbf{0},\sigma^2\mathbf{I}_s)$ and $\mathbf{X}_*'\boldsymbol{\varepsilon}_i/\sqrt{s}=\boldsymbol{\eta}_i\sim(\mathbf{0},\sigma^2\mathbf{W})$. Thus the conditions of the basic central limit theorem in (17.67) are precisely fulfilled and the result in

(7.62) follows immediately. Given that $\mathbf{X}'\boldsymbol{\varepsilon}/\sqrt{T}$ has the limiting distribution $N(\mathbf{0}, \sigma^2\mathbf{W})$, and given that $\lim(\mathbf{X}'\mathbf{X}/T)^{-1} = \mathbf{W}^{-1}$, it is straightforward to deduce that

(7.63) The vector $\sqrt{T}(\hat{\boldsymbol{\beta}} - \boldsymbol{\beta}) = (\mathbf{X}'\mathbf{X}/T)^{-1}(\mathbf{X}'\boldsymbol{\varepsilon}/\sqrt{T})$ has a limiting distribution of $N(\mathbf{0}, \sigma^2\mathbf{W}^{-1})$.

If we wish to avoid the heuristic assumption regarding the nature of **X**, then we must prove (7.63) by a more sophisticated method such as the one in the Appendix of Statistical Theory preceding (17.68).

BIBLIOGRAPHY

The Classical Linear Model. Goldberger [**41,** Chap. 4], Kendall and Stuart [**62,** Chap. 19].

Coefficients of Determination: Partial and Multiple Correlation. Anderson [**8,** Chap. 4], Kendall and Stuart [**62,** Chap. 27], Theil [**115,** Chap. 4].

CHAPTER 8

Models with Errors in Variables

In econometrics, we commonly assume that the variables comprised in our functional relationships are observed without error. Often such an assumption is too optimistic. Therefore we ought to investigate the effect that errors in observations are likely to have upon the performance of our usual estimators; and we ought also to suggest alternative methods of estimation to take account of these errors.

In order to take account of the errors, we need quite detailed information relating either to the distribution of the errors or to the distribution of the true values underlying the observations. Since such information is hard to come by, our ability to cope in practice with the problem of errors in observations is limited. Nevertheless, the problem provides a useful context in which to study a variety of methods of estimation that have wider application. Thus, in later chapters, we shall discover in quite unrelated contexts several models that are formally identical to a model with errors in observations, and to which the methods are equally applicable.

One example is the model of a single structural relationship within a simultaneous econometric system. Another example is provided by the autoregressive form of a model with a geometrically weighted distributed lag which will be investigated in Chapter 12. We shall describe the common problem that is posed by such models as the errors-in-variables problem.

ESTIMATION WHEN THE ERROR DISPERSION MATRIX IS KNOWN

Let us assume that the underlying structure of the system that we wish to investigate is described by the classical regression equation

$$(8.1) \qquad y_t = \mathbf{x}_{t.}\boldsymbol{\beta} + \varepsilon_t$$

which explains the output variable y_t in terms of k input variables in $\mathbf{x}_{t.}$. A set of T realizations of this relationship would give rise to the equations

$$(8.2) \qquad \mathbf{y} = \mathbf{X}\boldsymbol{\beta} + \boldsymbol{\varepsilon}$$

where $\boldsymbol{\varepsilon}$ is a vector of independently and identically distributed random variables such that

$$(8.3) \qquad E(\boldsymbol{\varepsilon}) = \mathbf{0}, \qquad D(\boldsymbol{\varepsilon}) = \sigma_\varepsilon^2 \mathbf{I}.$$

However, let us imagine that, instead of observing the true values y_t, $\mathbf{x}_{t.}$, we observe $q_t = y_t + \zeta_t$ and $\mathbf{z}_{t.} = \mathbf{x}_{t.} + \boldsymbol{\eta}_{t.}$ and that we form the data $\mathbf{q} = \mathbf{y} + \boldsymbol{\zeta}$ and $\mathbf{Z} = \mathbf{X} + \mathbf{H}$. Then, in place of (8.1), we have to contend with the relationship

$$(8.4) \qquad (q_t - \zeta_t) = (\mathbf{z}_{t.} - \boldsymbol{\eta}_{t.})\boldsymbol{\beta} + \varepsilon_t$$

which gives rise over T periods to the system

$$(8.5) \qquad (\mathbf{q} - \boldsymbol{\zeta}) = (\mathbf{Z} - \mathbf{H})\boldsymbol{\beta} + \boldsymbol{\varepsilon}.$$

We shall assume that the errors of observation ζ_t and $\boldsymbol{\eta}_{t.}$ have zero expected values and that they are distributed independently of the true values of the variables and of the structural disturbances ε_t. If we also assume that they are distributed independently of time, then we may specify that for all t

$$(8.6) \qquad \begin{aligned} &E(\zeta_t) = 0, & &V(\zeta_t) = \sigma_\zeta^2, \\ &E(\boldsymbol{\eta}_{t.}) = \mathbf{0}, & &D(\boldsymbol{\eta}'_{t.}) = \boldsymbol{\Omega}_{\eta\eta}, \\ &C(\boldsymbol{\eta}_{t.}, \zeta_t) = \boldsymbol{\omega}_{\eta\zeta}. \end{aligned}$$

It is natural to assume that the probability limits of various sample moments are equal to the values of the population or theoretical moments. If we take the further assumptions that $\text{plim}(\mathbf{X}'\mathbf{X}/T) = \mathbf{M}$ and $\text{plim}(\mathbf{X}'\boldsymbol{\varepsilon}/T) = \mathbf{0}$ from the classical regression model, then we can deduce that

$$(8.7) \qquad \begin{aligned} \text{plim}\left(\frac{\mathbf{Z}'\mathbf{Z}}{T}\right) &= \mathbf{M} + \boldsymbol{\Omega}_{\eta\eta}, \\ \text{plim}\left(\frac{\mathbf{Z}'\mathbf{q}}{T}\right) &= \mathbf{M}\boldsymbol{\beta} + \boldsymbol{\omega}_{\eta\zeta}. \end{aligned}$$

Let us now examine the effect that the errors of observation have upon our usual estimates. We know that, given exact observations, we could use the method of ordinary least squares to obtain an efficient and consistent estimator of the parameter $\boldsymbol{\beta}$ in (8.1) in the form of $\hat{\boldsymbol{\beta}} = (\mathbf{X}'\mathbf{X})^{-1}\mathbf{X}'\mathbf{y}$. On applying the same method to the erroneous data, we obtain the estimator

$$(8.8) \qquad \overset{*}{\boldsymbol{\beta}} = (\mathbf{Z}'\mathbf{Z})^{-1}\mathbf{Z}'\mathbf{q}.$$

Using (8.7), we deduce that the probability limit of $\overset{*}{\boldsymbol{\beta}}$ is

$$(8.9) \qquad \begin{aligned} \text{plim}(\overset{*}{\boldsymbol{\beta}}) &= \text{plim}\left(\frac{\mathbf{Z}'\mathbf{Z}}{T}\right)^{-1} \text{plim}\left(\frac{\mathbf{Z}'\mathbf{q}}{T}\right) \\ &= (\mathbf{M} + \boldsymbol{\Omega}_{\eta\eta})^{-1}(\mathbf{M}\boldsymbol{\beta} + \boldsymbol{\omega}_{\eta\zeta}) \end{aligned}$$

which cannot be equal in general to the true parameter value $\boldsymbol{\beta}$. Hence $\overset{*}{\boldsymbol{\beta}}$ is an inconsistent estimator.

However, a knowledge of the error dispersion matrices is sufficient to enable us to find a consistent estimator of $\boldsymbol{\beta}$. In fact, from the conditions in (8.7) it follows that the estimator

$$\text{(8.10)} \qquad \tilde{\boldsymbol{\beta}} = (\mathbf{Z}'\mathbf{Z} - T\boldsymbol{\Omega}_{\eta\eta})^{-1}(\mathbf{Z}'\mathbf{q} - T\boldsymbol{\omega}_{\eta\zeta})$$

has the same probability limit as $\hat{\boldsymbol{\beta}} = (\mathbf{X}'\mathbf{X})^{-1}\mathbf{X}'\mathbf{y}$.

At first glance, the estimator $\tilde{\boldsymbol{\beta}}$ appears to be nothing but a modified version of the ordinary least-squares estimator derived in an *ad hoc* fashion. We might prefer an estimator that could be derived by evaluating an appropriate estimating criterion. To establish such a criterion, let us consider representing the systematic structure of the relationship in (8.1) by the equation

$$\text{(8.11)} \qquad [\mu_t, \mathbf{x}_{t.}]\begin{bmatrix} -1 \\ \boldsymbol{\beta} \end{bmatrix} = 0.$$

Then, in view of the identities

$$\text{(8.12)} \qquad \begin{aligned} \mu_t &= y_t - \varepsilon_t = q_t - \{\zeta_t + \varepsilon_t\}, \\ \mathbf{x}_{t.} &= \mathbf{z}_{t.} - \boldsymbol{\eta}_{t.}, \end{aligned}$$

we get

$$\text{(8.13)} \qquad [q_t - \{\zeta_t + \varepsilon_t\}, \mathbf{z}_{t.} - \boldsymbol{\eta}_{t.}]\begin{bmatrix} -1 \\ \boldsymbol{\beta} \end{bmatrix} = 0,$$

which expresses the relationship in terms of the observations q_t, $\mathbf{z}_{t.}$ and the errors $\{\zeta_t + \varepsilon_t\}$, $\boldsymbol{\eta}_{t.}$.

These errors have zero expectations and a dispersion matrix

$$\text{(8.14)} \qquad D\begin{bmatrix} \zeta_t + \varepsilon_t \\ \boldsymbol{\eta}_{t.} \end{bmatrix} = \begin{bmatrix} \sigma_\zeta^2 + \sigma_\varepsilon^2, & \boldsymbol{\omega}'_{\eta\zeta} \\ \boldsymbol{\omega}_{\eta\zeta}, & \boldsymbol{\Omega}_{\eta\eta} \end{bmatrix} = \boldsymbol{\Omega}$$

whose elements we shall assume to be known *a priori*. Within this framework, the problem of estimating $\boldsymbol{\beta}$ may be described as one of finding estimates of the T values of $[\mu_t, \mathbf{x}_{t.}]$ that will simultaneously satisfy the equation (8.11). It is appropriate, in view of the statistical specification of the model, to locate these estimated values in such a way as to minimize the sum of squares of the $\boldsymbol{\Omega}^{-1}$-distances from the corresponding observations $[q_t, \mathbf{z}_{t.}]$. Thus our criterion is to minimize the function

$$\text{(8.15)} \qquad \sum_{t=1}^{T} ([\mu_t, \mathbf{x}_{t.}] - [q_t, \mathbf{z}_{t.}])\boldsymbol{\Omega}^{-1}\left(\begin{bmatrix} \mu_t \\ \mathbf{x}'_{t.} \end{bmatrix} - \begin{bmatrix} q_t \\ \mathbf{z}'_{t.} \end{bmatrix}\right).$$

As we have demonstrated in Chapter 5, this yields the estimating equations

$$\left(\begin{bmatrix}\mathbf{q}'\mathbf{q}, & \mathbf{q}'\mathbf{Z}\\ \mathbf{Z}'\mathbf{q}, & \mathbf{Z}'\mathbf{Z}\end{bmatrix}-\lambda\begin{bmatrix}\sigma_\zeta^2+\sigma_\varepsilon^2, & \boldsymbol{\omega}'_{\eta\zeta}\\ \boldsymbol{\omega}_{\eta\zeta}, & \boldsymbol{\Omega}_{\eta\eta}\end{bmatrix}\right)\begin{bmatrix}-1\\ \boldsymbol{\beta}\end{bmatrix}=\begin{bmatrix}0\\ \mathbf{0}\end{bmatrix}. \tag{8.16}$$

To solve these in accordance with the criterion, we must attribute to λ the smallest value that renders the system algebraically consistent. We can then find the value of $\boldsymbol{\beta}$ by solving the second line of the system to give

$$\hat{\boldsymbol{\beta}}=(\mathbf{Z}'\mathbf{Z}-\lambda\boldsymbol{\Omega}_{\eta\eta})^{-1}(\mathbf{Z}'\mathbf{q}-\lambda\boldsymbol{\omega}_{\eta\zeta}). \tag{8.17}$$

This estimator differs from the estimator specified in (8.10) only in having λ in place of T. Indeed, the latter estimator may be derived from the equations in (8.16) by setting $\lambda = T$ and allowing $\phi=\sigma_\zeta^2+\sigma_\varepsilon^2$ to be determined by the solution of the system. With these substitutions, we find that

$$\begin{aligned}T\phi&=\mathbf{q}'\mathbf{q}-(\mathbf{q}'\mathbf{Z}-T\boldsymbol{\omega}'_{\eta\zeta})(\mathbf{Z}'\mathbf{Z}-T\boldsymbol{\Omega}_{\eta\eta})^{-1}(\mathbf{Z}'\mathbf{q}-T\boldsymbol{\omega}_{\eta\zeta})\\ &=\mathbf{q}'\mathbf{q}-\tilde{\boldsymbol{\beta}}'(\mathbf{Z}'\mathbf{Z}-T\boldsymbol{\Omega}_{\eta\eta})\tilde{\boldsymbol{\beta}}.\end{aligned} \tag{8.18}$$

This expression, which is analogous to the residual sum of squares of an ordinary least-squares regression, provides an estimate of $\phi=(\sigma_\zeta^2+\sigma_\varepsilon^2)$.

A procedure for determining the characteristic root and vector

Although we are rarely capable of implementing the method of estimation that we have just described, we shall encounter analogous methods in later chapters that are wholly practical. It is therefore appropriate for us to discuss a method for finding the value λ in the equation (8.16). To simplify the notation, let us consider a model where the systematic structure is given by the equation

$$\mathbf{x}_{t.}\boldsymbol{\alpha}=0 \tag{8.19}$$

and where the tth observation

$$\mathbf{q}_{t.}=\mathbf{x}_{t.}+\boldsymbol{\eta}_{t.} \tag{8.20}$$

contains an error $\boldsymbol{\eta}_{t.}$ with $E(\boldsymbol{\eta}_{t.})=\mathbf{0}$ and $D(\boldsymbol{\eta}'_{t.})=\boldsymbol{\Omega}$. By the method of orthogonal regression in the $\boldsymbol{\Omega}^{-1}$-metric we obtain the estimating equation

$$(\mathbf{Z}'\mathbf{Z}-\lambda\boldsymbol{\Omega})\boldsymbol{\alpha}=\mathbf{0} \tag{8.21}$$

or, equivalently,

$$(\boldsymbol{\Omega}^{-1}\mathbf{Z}'\mathbf{Z}-\lambda\mathbf{I})\boldsymbol{\alpha}=\mathbf{0}. \tag{8.22}$$

To find the latent root λ_p of $\boldsymbol{\Omega}^{-1}\mathbf{Z}'\mathbf{Z}$ with the smallest absolute value, we find the largest latent root $\gamma_1=1/\lambda_p$ of the inverse matrix $\mathbf{A}=(\boldsymbol{\Omega}^{-1}\mathbf{Z}'\mathbf{Z})^{-1}$.

For this purpose we form a sequence

$$\begin{aligned}(8.23)\qquad & \mathbf{x}_0 \\ & \mathbf{x}_1 = \mathbf{A}\mathbf{x}_0 \\ & \mathbf{x}_2 = \mathbf{A}\mathbf{x}_1 = \mathbf{A}^2\mathbf{x}_0 \\ & \cdots\cdots \\ & \mathbf{x}_n = \mathbf{A}\mathbf{x}_{n-1} = \mathbf{A}^n\mathbf{x}_0\end{aligned}$$

beginning with an arbitrary vector $\mathbf{x}_0$. The ratio of corresponding elements of $\mathbf{x}_n$ and $\mathbf{x}_{n-1}$ will tend to γ_1 as n tends to infinity.

To demonstrate this, consider writing $\mathbf{x}_0$ as a linear combination of the characteristic vectors $\mathbf{v}_1, \ldots, \mathbf{v}_p$ of $\mathbf{A}$ corresponding to the roots $\gamma_1, \ldots, \gamma_p$ ordered in terms of their declining absolute values. Since a characteristic vector is determined only up to a scalar factor, there is no loss of generality if we put

$$(8.24)\qquad \mathbf{x}_0 = \mathbf{v}_1 + \mathbf{v}_2 + \ldots + \mathbf{v}_p.$$

On multiplying $\mathbf{x}_0$ by $\mathbf{A}$ we get

$$\begin{aligned}(8.25)\qquad \mathbf{x}_1 &= \mathbf{A}\mathbf{v}_1 + \mathbf{A}\mathbf{v}_2 + \ldots + \mathbf{A}\mathbf{v}_p \\ &= \gamma_1\mathbf{v}_1 + \gamma_2\mathbf{v}_2 + \ldots + \gamma_p\mathbf{v}_p.\end{aligned}$$

and, after repeated multiplications, we arrive at

$$\begin{aligned}(8.26)\qquad \mathbf{x}_n &= \mathbf{A}^n\mathbf{v}_1 + \mathbf{A}^n\mathbf{v}_2 + \ldots + \mathbf{A}^n\mathbf{v}_p \\ &= \gamma_1^n\mathbf{v}_1 + \gamma_2^n\mathbf{v}_2 + \ldots + \gamma_p^n\mathbf{v}_p \\ &= \gamma_1^n\left[\mathbf{v}_1 + \left(\frac{\gamma_2}{\gamma_1}\right)^n\mathbf{v}_2 + \ldots + \left(\frac{\gamma_p}{\gamma_1}\right)^n\mathbf{v}_p\right].\end{aligned}$$

Since γ_1 is the root with the largest absolute value, it follows that, as n tends to infinity, all but the first of the terms in the brackets of the final expression in (8.26) tend to zero. Thus, if x_n, x_{n-1} and ν_1 are corresponding elements within $\mathbf{x}_n$, $\mathbf{x}_{n-1}$ and $\mathbf{v}_1$ respectively, we have

$$(8.27)\qquad \lim(n \to \infty)\frac{x_n}{x_{n-1}} = \frac{\gamma_1^n v_1}{\gamma_1^{n-1} v_1} = \gamma_1.$$

The consistency of the estimator

We now wish to demonstrate the consistency of the estimate of the parameter $\boldsymbol{\alpha}$ which is derived from the equations

$$(8.28)\qquad (\mathbf{Z}'\mathbf{Z} - \lambda\boldsymbol{\Omega})\boldsymbol{\alpha} = \mathbf{0}$$

or, equivalently, from the equations

$$(8.29)\qquad T\left(\mathbf{\Omega}^{-1}\frac{\mathbf{Z'Z}}{T}-\phi\mathbf{I}\right)\boldsymbol{\alpha}=\mathbf{0}$$

where $\phi=\lambda/T$.

We should begin by recognizing that, if the true value of the parameter is provided by a normalized solution of the equations $\mathbf{X}\boldsymbol{\alpha}=\mathbf{0}$, where $\mathbf{X}$ is a matrix of $T\geqslant p$ values or the unobservable vector $\mathbf{x}_{t.}=[\mathbf{x}_{t1},\ldots,\mathbf{x}_{tp}]$, then it is also provided by the solution of the equation $\mathbf{\Omega}^{-1}\mathbf{M}\boldsymbol{\alpha}=\mathbf{0}$ where $\mathbf{M}=\operatorname{plim}(\mathbf{X'X}/T)$. Therefore, to demonstrate the consistency of the estimate provided by (8.28), we need only show that

$$(8.30)\qquad \operatorname{plim}\left(\mathbf{\Omega}^{-1}\frac{\mathbf{Z'Z}}{T}-\phi\mathbf{I}\right)=\mathbf{\Omega}^{-1}\mathbf{M}.$$

To establish this equality, we begin by deducing from the assumption that $\operatorname{plim}(\mathbf{Z'Z}/T)=\mathbf{M}+\mathbf{\Omega}$ the result that

$$(8.31)\qquad \operatorname{plim}\left(\mathbf{\Omega}^{-1}\frac{\mathbf{Z'Z}}{T}\right)=\mathbf{\Omega}^{-1}(\mathbf{M}+\mathbf{\Omega})$$
$$=\mathbf{\Omega}^{-1}\mathbf{M}+\mathbf{I}.$$

Next we assert that, since the roots of a matrix are continuous functions of its elements, the probability limit of ϕ, the smallest root of $\mathbf{\Omega}^{-1}\mathbf{Z'Z}/T$, must be the smallest root of $\operatorname{plim}(\mathbf{\Omega}^{-1}\mathbf{Z'Z}/T)=\mathbf{\Omega}^{-1}\mathbf{M}+\mathbf{I}$. The smallest root of $\mathbf{\Omega}^{-1}\mathbf{M}$ is clearly zero on account of the fact that there exists a vector $\boldsymbol{\alpha}$ such that $\mathbf{\Omega}^{-1}\mathbf{M}\boldsymbol{\alpha}=\mathbf{0}$. It follows that the smallest root of $\mathbf{\Omega}^{-1}\mathbf{M}+\mathbf{I}$ is unity; and hence we have

$$(8.32)\qquad \operatorname{plim}(\phi)=1.$$

By substituting the results under (8.31) and (8.32) into the expression $\operatorname{plim}(\mathbf{\Omega}^{-1}\mathbf{Z'Z}/T-\phi\mathbf{I})=\operatorname{plim}(\mathbf{\Omega}^{-1}\mathbf{Z'Z}/T)-\operatorname{plim}(\phi)\mathbf{I}$, we establish the equality in (8.30); and this, as we have already shown, is sufficient to prove the consistency of the estimator.

MODELS CONTAINING EXACT OBSERVATIONS

In some cases of our model, not all the variables are associated with errors. For example, amongst the explanatory variables there may be one which records the occasional presence of a causal factor that has a unique and invariant effect. This variable, which might assume the value of unity in the presence of the factor and zero in its absence, is unlikely to be associated with any error.

Let us represent such a model by the equation

$$(8.33)\qquad (\mathbf{y}_{t.}-\boldsymbol{\eta}_{t.})\boldsymbol{\gamma}+\mathbf{x}_{t.}\boldsymbol{\beta}=0$$

wherein $\mathbf{x}_{t.}$ is a vector of exact observations and

$$(8.34)\qquad \mathbf{y}_{t.}=\mathbf{z}_{t.}+\boldsymbol{\eta}_{t.}$$

is a vector of observations comprising the error $\boldsymbol{\eta}_{t.}$. We shall assume that

$$(8.35)\qquad E(\boldsymbol{\eta}_{t.})=\mathbf{0}, \qquad D(\boldsymbol{\eta}'_{t.})=\boldsymbol{\Omega}$$

for all t.

To estimate the parameters of the model, we adopt the criterion of minimizing the function.

$$(8.36)\qquad \sum_{t=1}^{T}\boldsymbol{\eta}_{t.}\boldsymbol{\Omega}^{-1}\boldsymbol{\eta}'_{t.}=\sum_{t=1}^{T}(\mathbf{y}_{t.}-\mathbf{z}_{t.})\boldsymbol{\Omega}^{-1}(\mathbf{y}_{t.}-\mathbf{z}_{t.})'$$

subject to the condition that $\mathbf{z}_{t.}\boldsymbol{\gamma}+\mathbf{x}_{t.}\boldsymbol{\beta}=0$ and an appropriate normalization of the parameter vector which we shall take to be $\boldsymbol{\gamma}'\boldsymbol{\Omega}\boldsymbol{\gamma}=1$.

To express the criterion in terms of the observations, we must differentiate the Lagrangean expression

$$(8.37)\qquad L=(\mathbf{y}_{t.}-\mathbf{z}_{t.})\boldsymbol{\Omega}^{-1}(\mathbf{y}_{t.}-\mathbf{z}_{t.})'+2\lambda(\mathbf{z}_{t.}\boldsymbol{\gamma}+\mathbf{x}_{t.}\boldsymbol{\beta})+2\mu(\boldsymbol{\gamma}'\boldsymbol{\Omega}\boldsymbol{\gamma}-1)$$

in respect of $\mathbf{z}'_{t.}$, λ, and μ. By setting the results to zero we obtain the conditions

$$(8.38)\qquad (\mathbf{y}_{t.}-\mathbf{z}_{t.})\boldsymbol{\Omega}^{-1}=\lambda\boldsymbol{\gamma}',$$

$$(8.39)\qquad \mathbf{z}_{t.}\boldsymbol{\gamma}+\mathbf{x}_{t.}\boldsymbol{\beta}=0,$$

$$(8.40)\qquad \boldsymbol{\gamma}'\boldsymbol{\Omega}\boldsymbol{\gamma}=1.$$

On postmultiplying both sides of (8.38) by $\boldsymbol{\Omega}\boldsymbol{\gamma}$ and using (8.40), we get

$$(8.41)\qquad \begin{aligned}(\mathbf{y}_{t.}-\mathbf{z}_{t.})\boldsymbol{\gamma}&=\lambda\boldsymbol{\gamma}'\boldsymbol{\Omega}\boldsymbol{\gamma}\\&=\lambda.\end{aligned}$$

But, according to (8.39), $-\mathbf{z}_{t.}\boldsymbol{\gamma}=\mathbf{x}_{t.}\boldsymbol{\beta}$, so we have

$$(8.42)\qquad \lambda=\mathbf{y}_{t.}\boldsymbol{\gamma}+\mathbf{x}_{t.}\boldsymbol{\beta}.$$

We can use the latter to show that

$$(8.43)\qquad \begin{aligned}(\mathbf{y}_{t.}-\mathbf{z}_{t.})\boldsymbol{\Omega}^{-1}(\mathbf{y}_{t.}-\mathbf{z}_{t.})'&=\lambda^2\boldsymbol{\gamma}'\boldsymbol{\Omega}\boldsymbol{\gamma}\\&=\lambda^2\\&=(\mathbf{y}_{t.}\boldsymbol{\gamma}+\mathbf{x}_{t.}\boldsymbol{\beta})^2\end{aligned}$$

It follows that our criterion function in (8.36) can be replaced by

$$\sum_{t=1}^{T} (\mathbf{y}_{t.}\boldsymbol{\gamma}+\mathbf{x}_{t.}\boldsymbol{\beta})^2 = (\mathbf{Y}\boldsymbol{\gamma}+\mathbf{X}\boldsymbol{\beta})'(\mathbf{Y}\boldsymbol{\gamma}+\mathbf{X}\boldsymbol{\beta}) \tag{8.44}$$

where $\mathbf{Y}$ and $\mathbf{X}$ are matrices comprising the observations $\mathbf{y}_{t.}$ and $\mathbf{x}_{t.}$ respectively.

To find the estimates of the unknown parameters, we form the Lagrangean expression

$$L = (\mathbf{Y}\boldsymbol{\gamma}+\mathbf{X}\boldsymbol{\beta})'(\mathbf{Y}\boldsymbol{\gamma}+\mathbf{X}\boldsymbol{\beta}) - \lambda(\boldsymbol{\gamma}'\boldsymbol{\Omega}\boldsymbol{\gamma}-1). \tag{8.45}$$

On differentiating with respect to $\boldsymbol{\gamma}$ and $\boldsymbol{\beta}$ and setting the results to zero, we obtain the equations

$$\left(\begin{bmatrix}\mathbf{Y}'\mathbf{Y}, & \mathbf{Y}'\mathbf{X}\\ \mathbf{X}'\mathbf{Y}, & \mathbf{X}'\mathbf{X}\end{bmatrix} - \lambda\begin{bmatrix}\boldsymbol{\Omega}, & \mathbf{0}\\ \mathbf{0}, & \mathbf{0}\end{bmatrix}\right)\begin{bmatrix}\boldsymbol{\gamma}\\ \boldsymbol{\beta}\end{bmatrix} = \begin{bmatrix}\mathbf{0}\\ \mathbf{0}\end{bmatrix}. \tag{8.46}$$

Premultiplying these by $[\boldsymbol{\gamma}', \boldsymbol{\beta}']$ shows that the value of our minimand is

$$\begin{aligned}(\mathbf{Y}\boldsymbol{\gamma}+\mathbf{X}\boldsymbol{\beta})'(\mathbf{Y}\boldsymbol{\gamma}+\mathbf{X}\boldsymbol{\beta}) &= \lambda\boldsymbol{\gamma}'\boldsymbol{\Omega}\boldsymbol{\gamma}\\ &= \lambda.\end{aligned} \tag{8.47}$$

Thus, to find estimates that fulfil the criterion, we must solve the equations in (8.46) subject to the condition that λ assumes the smallest value that renders the system algebraically consistent.

In practice, we decompose the system in (8.46) in order to solve it recursively. The second line of the system gives

$$-\boldsymbol{\beta} = (\mathbf{X}'\mathbf{X})^{-1}\mathbf{X}'\mathbf{Y}\boldsymbol{\gamma}. \tag{8.48}$$

On substituting this in the first line, we find that

$$[\mathbf{Y}'\mathbf{Y} - \mathbf{Y}'\mathbf{X}(\mathbf{X}'\mathbf{X})^{-1}\mathbf{X}'\mathbf{Y} - \lambda\boldsymbol{\Omega}]\boldsymbol{\gamma} = \mathbf{0}. \tag{8.49}$$

This means that λ may be found as the smallest characteristic root of the matrix

$$\boldsymbol{\Omega}^{-1}\mathbf{Y}'(\mathbf{I}-\mathbf{P})\mathbf{Y} \tag{8.50}$$

where $\mathbf{P} = \mathbf{X}(\mathbf{X}'\mathbf{X})^{-1}\mathbf{X}'$. Once the estimate $\hat{\boldsymbol{\gamma}}$ is determined from the solution of equation (8.49), we can find $\hat{\boldsymbol{\beta}}$ directly from equation (8.48).

It may be instructive to regard the expression in (8.48) as the equation of an ordinary least-squares regression. From this point of view, we see that the vector $\mathbf{X}\hat{\boldsymbol{\beta}}$ is determined by the orthogonal projection of the vector $\mathbf{Y}\hat{\boldsymbol{\gamma}}$ onto the manifold $\mathcal{M}(\mathbf{X})$. In fact, we can visualize the classical regression model $(\mathbf{y}, \mathbf{X}\boldsymbol{\beta}, \sigma^2\mathbf{I})$, to which the method of ordinary least squares is properly applicable, as a limiting case of the present model which arises when only a single variable y_t is subject to error.

Amongst the models that can be usefully assimilated to the present system is one which is described by the equation

$$(8.51) \qquad (\mathbf{y}_{t.} - \boldsymbol{\eta}_{t.})\boldsymbol{\gamma} = \beta$$

where β is a constant term. If we associate with this term a dummy variable $x_t = -1$ that has the same value in all periods, then equation (8.51) can be seen as a straightforward specialization of equation (8.33). The estimating equations for $\boldsymbol{\gamma}$, $-\beta$ are derived from those in (8.46) by replacing the matrix $\mathbf{X}$ by a vector $\mathbf{i}$ containing T units to obtain

$$(8.52) \qquad \left(\begin{bmatrix} \mathbf{Y}'\mathbf{Y}, & \mathbf{Y}'\mathbf{i} \\ \mathbf{i}'\mathbf{Y}, & \mathbf{i}'\mathbf{i} \end{bmatrix} - \lambda \begin{bmatrix} \boldsymbol{\Omega}, & \mathbf{0} \\ \mathbf{0}, & \mathbf{0} \end{bmatrix}\right)\begin{bmatrix} \boldsymbol{\gamma} \\ -\beta \end{bmatrix} = \begin{bmatrix} \mathbf{0} \\ \mathbf{0} \end{bmatrix}.$$

The second line of the equation gives

$$(8.53) \qquad \beta = (\mathbf{i}'\mathbf{i})^{-1}\mathbf{i}'\mathbf{Y}\boldsymbol{\gamma},$$

and, on substituting this in the first line, we find that

$$(8.54) \qquad \{\mathbf{Y}'[\mathbf{I} - \mathbf{i}(\mathbf{i}'\mathbf{i})^{-1}\mathbf{i}']\mathbf{Y} - \lambda\boldsymbol{\Omega}\}\boldsymbol{\gamma} = \mathbf{0}$$

which can also be written as

$$(8.55) \qquad [(\mathbf{Y} - \bar{\mathbf{Y}})'(\mathbf{Y} - \bar{\mathbf{Y}}) - \lambda\boldsymbol{\Omega}]\boldsymbol{\gamma} = \mathbf{0}$$

where $\bar{\mathbf{Y}} = \mathbf{i}(\mathbf{i}'\mathbf{i})^{-1}\mathbf{i}'\mathbf{Y}$ is a matrix wherein every element of the jth column is

$$\bar{y}_j = \sum_{t=1}^{T} y_{tj}/T$$

INSTRUMENTAL VARIABLES

An essential part of the specification of the classical linear model is the assumption that there is no correlation between the disturbances ε_t and the input variables $\mathbf{x}_{t.}$ in the equation $y_t = \mathbf{x}_{t.}\boldsymbol{\beta} + \varepsilon_t$. This assumption, which may be expressed as $E(\mathbf{x}'_{t.}\varepsilon_t) = \mathbf{0}$, implies that when we premultiply the regression equation by $\mathbf{x}'_{t.}$ and take expectations we get

$$(8.56) \qquad \begin{aligned} E(\mathbf{x}'_{t.}y_t) &= E(\mathbf{x}'_{t.}\mathbf{x}_{t.})\boldsymbol{\beta} + E(\mathbf{x}'_{t.}\varepsilon_t) \\ &= E(\mathbf{x}'_{t.}\mathbf{x}_{t.})\boldsymbol{\beta}. \end{aligned}$$

In the method of ordinary least squares, we replace the theoretical moments $E(\mathbf{x}'_{t.}y_t)$ and $E(\mathbf{x}'_{t.}\mathbf{x}_{t.})$ in equation (8.56) by the corresponding sample moments $\mathbf{X}'\mathbf{y}/T$ and $\mathbf{X}'\mathbf{X}/T$ to obtain the normal equations

$$(8.57) \qquad \frac{\mathbf{X}'\mathbf{y}}{T} = \frac{\mathbf{X}'\mathbf{X}}{T}\boldsymbol{\beta}.$$

By solving these equations, we obtain the estimator $\hat{\boldsymbol{\beta}}=(\mathbf{X}'\mathbf{X})^{-1}\mathbf{X}'\mathbf{y}$ which is bound to be statistically consistent if the sample moments tend in probability to the theoretical moment as the sample size increases.

Let us now consider replacing $\mathbf{x}_{t.}$ by a vector $\mathbf{w}_{t.}$ containing variables that are closely related to those in $\mathbf{x}_{t.}$ and are equal to them in number. If there is no correlation between the variables in $\mathbf{w}_{t.}$ and the disturbance term ε_t, then $E(\mathbf{w}'_{t.}\varepsilon_t)=\mathbf{0}$; and, on premultiplying the regression equation by $\mathbf{w}_{t.}$ and taking expectations, we get

$$(8.58)\qquad \begin{aligned} E(\mathbf{w}'_{t.}y_t)&=E(\mathbf{w}'_{t.}\mathbf{x}_{t.})\boldsymbol{\beta}+E(\mathbf{w}'_{t.}\varepsilon_t)\\ &=E(\mathbf{w}'_{t.}\mathbf{x}_{t.})\boldsymbol{\beta}. \end{aligned}$$

As in the ordinary least-squares procedure, we can replace the theoretical moments of this equation by the corresponding sample moments $\mathbf{W}'\mathbf{y}/T$ and $\mathbf{W}'\mathbf{X}/T$. This gives the equation

$$(8.59)\qquad \frac{\mathbf{W}'\mathbf{y}}{T}=\frac{\mathbf{W}'\mathbf{X}}{T}\boldsymbol{\beta}$$

from which we may derive the estimator

$$(8.60)\qquad \overset{*}{\boldsymbol{\beta}}=(\mathbf{W}'\mathbf{X})^{-1}\mathbf{W}'\mathbf{y}.$$

Once more, if the sample moments tend in probability to the theoretical moments, we are bound to obtain a consistent estimator. This is readily confirmed by writing

$$(8.61)\qquad \begin{aligned} \overset{*}{\boldsymbol{\beta}}&=(\mathbf{W}'\mathbf{X})^{-1}\mathbf{W}'(\mathbf{X}\boldsymbol{\beta}+\boldsymbol{\varepsilon})\\ &=\boldsymbol{\beta}+\left(\frac{\mathbf{W}'\mathbf{X}}{T}\right)^{-1}\frac{\mathbf{W}'\boldsymbol{\varepsilon}}{T} \end{aligned}$$

and finding that

$$(8.62)\qquad \begin{aligned} \operatorname{plim}(\overset{*}{\boldsymbol{\beta}})&=\boldsymbol{\beta}+\operatorname{plim}\left(\frac{\mathbf{W}'\mathbf{X}}{T}\right)^{-1}\operatorname{plim}\left(\frac{\mathbf{W}'\boldsymbol{\varepsilon}}{T}\right)\\ &=\boldsymbol{\beta}+\operatorname{plim}\left(\frac{\mathbf{W}'\mathbf{X}}{T}\right)^{-1}\mathbf{0}\\ &=\boldsymbol{\beta}. \end{aligned}$$

The variables comprised in the vector $\mathbf{w}_{t.}$ are called instruments and the estimator given in (8.60) is an instrumental variables estimator of $\boldsymbol{\beta}$. In general, an instrument may be described as a variable which is independent of or uncorrelated with the disturbances of the regression equation yet correlated with the input variables of the equation. In fact, the efficiency of the instrumental variables estimator depends directly upon the degree of correlation between the instruments and the input variables.

The properties of the instrumental variables estimator can be deduced in the same way as the properties of the ordinary least-squares estimator. Thus, under our present assumptions, the sample moments of $\boldsymbol{\beta}^*$ conditional upon $\mathbf{X}$ and $\mathbf{W}$ are

$$(8.63) \qquad E(\overset{*}{\boldsymbol{\beta}}) = \boldsymbol{\beta}, \qquad D(\overset{*}{\boldsymbol{\beta}}) = \sigma^2(\mathbf{W}'\mathbf{X})^{-1}\mathbf{W}'\mathbf{W}(\mathbf{X}'\mathbf{W})^{-1}.$$

Moreover, under the usual assumptions concerning the disturbance term, it can be shown that the limiting distribution of the vector $\sqrt{T}(\overset{*}{\boldsymbol{\beta}} - \boldsymbol{\beta})$ is a normal distribution.

The relevance of the instrumental variables procedure to the problem of errors in variables lies in the fact that it is sometimes possible to find a set of instruments $\mathbf{w}_{t.}$ that are statistically independent of both the structural disturbance ε_t and the errors $\boldsymbol{\eta}_{t.}$, ζ_t of the model represented by equation (8.4). Such instruments should enable us to obtain a consistent estimator of the regression parameter $\boldsymbol{\beta}$. By merging the various stochastic terms, the equation (8.4) can be written as

$$(8.64) \qquad q_t = \mathbf{z}_{t.}\boldsymbol{\beta} + \xi_t$$

where $\xi_t = \varepsilon_t + \zeta_t - \boldsymbol{\eta}_{t.}\boldsymbol{\beta}$. Our estimate based on the instruments in $\mathbf{w}_{t.}$ is

$$(8.65) \qquad \overset{*}{\boldsymbol{\beta}} = (\mathbf{W}'\mathbf{Z})^{-1}\mathbf{W}'\mathbf{q}.$$

Having a sufficient set of instruments amounts to having a partial knowledge of the distribution of the true values y_t, $\mathbf{x}_{t.}$ underlying the observations q_t, $\mathbf{z}_{t.}$. In some circumstances the instruments also enable us to estimate the error dispersion matrix. Consider the case where the unobserved explanatory variables in $\mathbf{x}_{t.}$ are exact linear combinations of the instruments in $\mathbf{w}_{t.}$. Then $\mathbf{x}_{t.} = \mathbf{w}_{t.}\boldsymbol{\Pi}$ for some matrix $\boldsymbol{\Pi}$; and $\mathbf{z}_{t.} = \mathbf{w}_{t.}\boldsymbol{\Pi} + \boldsymbol{\eta}_{t.}$. By regressing $\mathbf{z}_{t.}$ on $\mathbf{w}_{t.}$, we can find an estimate $\hat{\boldsymbol{\Pi}} = (\mathbf{W}'\mathbf{W})^{-1}\mathbf{W}'\mathbf{Z}$. An estimate of the dispersion matrix $\boldsymbol{\Omega} = D(\boldsymbol{\eta}'_{t.})$ is provided by $\hat{\boldsymbol{\Omega}} = (\mathbf{Z} - \mathbf{W}\hat{\boldsymbol{\Pi}})'(\mathbf{Z} - \mathbf{W}\hat{\boldsymbol{\Pi}})/T$.

BIBLIOGRAPHY

Models with Errors in Variables. Madansky [**78**], Malinvaud [**82,** Chap. 10]
Instrumental Variables. Sargan [**102**]

CHAPTER 9

The Gauss–Markov Model with a Singular Dispersion Matrix

Hitherto, we have imposed upon the Gauss–Markov model $(\mathbf{y}, \mathbf{X\beta}, \sigma^2\mathbf{Q})$ the assumption that $\text{Null}(\mathbf{Q}) = 0$. That is to say, for the stochastic equation $\mathbf{y} = \mathbf{X\beta} + \boldsymbol{\varepsilon}$, we have assumed that $\boldsymbol{\varepsilon} \sim (\mathbf{0}, \sigma^2\mathbf{Q})$ is a non-degenerate random vector. We shall relax this assumption and embark upon a search for the specification of the minimum variance linear unbiased estimator of $\mathbf{X\beta}$ in the most general case of the model where no rank condition is imposed on either $\mathbf{X}$ or $\mathbf{Q}$. The scope of this general case is sufficient to accommodate the model $(\mathbf{q}, \mathbf{Z\beta} \mid \mathbf{R\beta} = \mathbf{r}, \sigma^2\mathbf{I})$, where the exact *a priori* restrictions $\mathbf{R\beta} = \mathbf{r}$ are imposed on the stochastic system $\mathbf{q} = \mathbf{Z\beta} + \boldsymbol{\eta}$. To show this, we combine the stochastic equations and the restrictions to form a system

$$\text{(9.1)} \qquad \mathbf{y} = \begin{bmatrix} \mathbf{q} \\ \mathbf{r} \end{bmatrix} = \begin{bmatrix} \mathbf{Z} \\ \mathbf{R} \end{bmatrix} \boldsymbol{\beta} + \begin{bmatrix} \boldsymbol{\eta} \\ \mathbf{0} \end{bmatrix} = \mathbf{X\beta} + \boldsymbol{\varepsilon},$$

which has a singular dispersion matrix of the form

$$\text{(9.2)} \qquad D(\boldsymbol{\varepsilon}) = E(\boldsymbol{\varepsilon\varepsilon}') = \sigma^2\mathbf{Q} = \sigma^2 \begin{bmatrix} \mathbf{I}, & \mathbf{0} \\ \mathbf{0}, & \mathbf{0} \end{bmatrix}.$$

Conversely, the model $(\mathbf{y}, \mathbf{X\beta}, \sigma^2\mathbf{Q})$ with a singular dispersion matrix $\sigma^2\mathbf{Q}$ may be transformed to the particular form of the model $(\mathbf{q}, \mathbf{Z\beta} \mid \mathbf{R\beta} = \mathbf{r}, \sigma^2\mathbf{I})$ by premultiplying the equation $\mathbf{y} = \mathbf{X\beta} + \boldsymbol{\varepsilon}$ by a matrix $\mathbf{T}$ such that

$$\text{(9.3)} \qquad \mathbf{TQT}' = \begin{bmatrix} \mathbf{I}, & \mathbf{0} \\ \mathbf{0}, & \mathbf{0} \end{bmatrix},$$

and by defining $[\mathbf{q}', \mathbf{r}'] = \mathbf{y}'\mathbf{T}'$, $[\mathbf{Z}', \mathbf{R}'] = \mathbf{X}'\mathbf{T}'$ and $[\boldsymbol{\eta}', \mathbf{0}'] = \boldsymbol{\varepsilon}'\mathbf{T}'$.

In the present chapter, we shall concentrate on the general model $(\mathbf{y}, \mathbf{X\beta}, \sigma^2\mathbf{Q})$. In a later chapter, we shall develop the algebra of the restricted model $(\mathbf{q}, \mathbf{Z\beta} \mid \mathbf{R\beta} = \mathbf{r}, \sigma^2\mathbf{I})$ under a variety of specialized assumptions and with the aid of the results pertaining to the general model. It should be mentioned, however, that a number of authors, including Goldman and Zelen in their seminal article [**44**] and Theil in his textbook [**115**], have chosen to treat the general model by assimilating it to various versions of the restricted model.

THE SINGULAR DISPERSION MATRIX

If the symmetric matrix $\mathbf{Q}$ is singular, then there exists a non-zero matrix $\mathbf{R}$, with $\mathcal{N}(\mathbf{R})=\mathcal{M}(\mathbf{Q})$, such that $\mathbf{RQ}=\mathbf{0}$ and $\mathbf{QR}'=\mathbf{0}$. It follows that

(9.4) If $\boldsymbol{\varepsilon}\sim(\mathbf{0},\sigma^2\mathbf{Q})$ and $\mathbf{RQ}=\mathbf{0}$, then $E(\mathbf{R}\boldsymbol{\varepsilon})=\mathbf{0}$ and $D(\mathbf{R}\boldsymbol{\varepsilon})=E(\mathbf{R}\boldsymbol{\varepsilon}\boldsymbol{\varepsilon}'\mathbf{R}')=\sigma^2\mathbf{RQR}'=\mathbf{0}$, which implies that $\mathbf{R}\boldsymbol{\varepsilon}=\mathbf{0}$ with probability 1.

Conversely,

(9.5) If $\mathbf{R}\boldsymbol{\varepsilon}=\mathbf{0}$ for all $\boldsymbol{\varepsilon}\sim(\mathbf{0},\sigma^2\mathbf{Q})$, then $E(\mathbf{R}\boldsymbol{\varepsilon}\boldsymbol{\varepsilon}'\mathbf{R}')=\sigma^2\mathbf{RQR}'=\mathbf{0}$, which implies that $\mathbf{RQ}=\mathbf{0}$.

The conditions $\mathbf{R}\boldsymbol{\varepsilon}=\mathbf{0}$, $\mathbf{RQ}=\mathbf{0}$ are therefore equivalent; and, from the fact that $\mathcal{N}(\mathbf{R})=\mathcal{M}(\mathbf{Q})$, it follows that $\boldsymbol{\varepsilon}\in\mathcal{M}(\mathbf{Q})$ or, equivalently, that $\boldsymbol{\varepsilon}=\mathbf{Q}\boldsymbol{\lambda}=\mathbf{LL}'\boldsymbol{\lambda}=\mathbf{L}\boldsymbol{\eta}$ where $\boldsymbol{\lambda}$ and $\mathbf{L}'\boldsymbol{\lambda}=\boldsymbol{\eta}\sim(\mathbf{0},\sigma^2\mathbf{I})$ are stochastic vectors. Thus

(9.6) If $\mathbf{y}\sim(\mathbf{X}\boldsymbol{\beta},\sigma^2\mathbf{Q})$ and $\mathbf{RQ}=\mathbf{0}$, then $\boldsymbol{\varepsilon}=(\mathbf{y}-\mathbf{X}\boldsymbol{\beta})=\mathbf{Q}\boldsymbol{\lambda}$ and $\mathbf{R}\boldsymbol{\varepsilon}=\mathbf{R}(\mathbf{y}-\mathbf{X}\boldsymbol{\beta})=\mathbf{RQ}\boldsymbol{\lambda}=\mathbf{0}$. Equivalently, $\mathbf{y}=\mathbf{X}\boldsymbol{\beta}+\mathbf{Q}\boldsymbol{\lambda}$ and $\mathbf{Ry}=\mathbf{RX}\boldsymbol{\beta}$.

We see from this that the linear subspace $\mathcal{M}(\mathbf{Q})$ contains all possible values of $\boldsymbol{\varepsilon}$. Hence the affine subspace $\mathscr{A}=\boldsymbol{\mu}+\mathcal{M}(\mathbf{Q})$, where $\boldsymbol{\mu}=\mathbf{X}\boldsymbol{\beta}$, contains all possible values of $\mathbf{y}$. The set $\mathscr{A}$ is clearly the general solution of the restrictions $\mathbf{Ry}=\mathbf{R}\boldsymbol{\mu}$; for $\boldsymbol{\mu}$ is a particular solution and $\mathcal{M}(\mathbf{Q})$ is the general solution of the associated homogeneous equations $\mathbf{Rz}=\mathbf{0}$. We also have the condition $\boldsymbol{\mu}=\mathbf{X}\boldsymbol{\beta}\in\mathcal{M}(\mathbf{X})$; and, therefore, the set of all possible values of the mean vector $\boldsymbol{\mu}$ is further confined to the intersection $\mathscr{B}=\mathscr{A}\cap\mathcal{M}(\mathbf{X})$. According to (1.38), we can write this intersection as $\mathscr{B}=\boldsymbol{\mu}+\mathcal{M}(\mathbf{Q})\cap\mathcal{M}(\mathbf{X})$; where it is understood that any fixed vector in $\mathscr{B}$ may stand in place of $\boldsymbol{\mu}$.

To find an unbiased estimator of the mean vector $\boldsymbol{\mu}=\mathbf{X}\boldsymbol{\beta}$, we would normally use the method of Gaussian regression which consists of projecting $\mathbf{y}$ on $\mathcal{M}(\mathbf{X})$ to obtain $\mathbf{Py}=\mathbf{X}\hat{\boldsymbol{\beta}}$. In the present case, we know that $\boldsymbol{\mu}$ actually lies in an affine subspace $\mathscr{B}$ within $\mathcal{M}(\mathbf{X})$; and, if it is to be efficient, our estimate must also be an element of this set. We can be certain of obtaining an estimate within $\mathscr{B}$ if and only if $\mathbf{P}$ is a transformation whose restriction to $\mathcal{M}(\mathbf{Q})$ is a projector on $\mathcal{M}(\mathbf{Q})\cap\mathcal{M}(\mathbf{X})$. To demonstrate this result, let us write $\mathbf{y}=\boldsymbol{\mu}+\boldsymbol{\varepsilon}$ where $\boldsymbol{\mu}\in\mathscr{B}$ and $\boldsymbol{\varepsilon}\in\mathcal{M}(\mathbf{Q})$. Then, from the condition that $\mathbf{P}\boldsymbol{\mu}=\mathbf{PX}\boldsymbol{\beta}=\mathbf{X}\boldsymbol{\beta}=\boldsymbol{\mu}$, we obtain $\mathbf{Py}=\boldsymbol{\mu}+\mathbf{P}\boldsymbol{\varepsilon}$. Hence $\mathbf{X}\hat{\boldsymbol{\beta}}=\mathbf{Py}\in\mathscr{B}$ if and only if $\mathbf{P}\boldsymbol{\varepsilon}\in\mathcal{M}(\mathbf{Q})\cap\mathcal{M}(\mathbf{X})$; and for this it is necessary and sufficient that $\mathbf{P}$ be a projector of $\mathcal{M}(\mathbf{Q})$ on $\mathcal{M}(\mathbf{Q})\cap\mathcal{M}(\mathbf{X})$.

A special case of the model $(\mathbf{y},\mathbf{X}\boldsymbol{\beta},\sigma^2\mathbf{Q}\,|\,\mathbf{RQ}=\mathbf{0})$ arises when $\mathcal{M}(\mathbf{X})\subset\mathcal{M}(\mathbf{Q})$. With $\mathbf{RQ}=\mathbf{0}$, this condition implies $\mathbf{RX}=\mathbf{0}$ and $\mathbf{Ry}=\mathbf{RX}\boldsymbol{\beta}=\mathbf{0}$. Thus the set $\mathscr{A}$ of all possible values of $\mathbf{y}$ becomes the linear subspace $\mathcal{N}(\mathbf{R})=\mathcal{M}(\mathbf{Q})$, and the set $\mathscr{B}$ of all possible values of $\boldsymbol{\mu}=\mathbf{X}\boldsymbol{\beta}$ becomes the linear subspace $\mathcal{M}(\mathbf{Q}) \cap \mathcal{M}(\mathbf{X}) = \mathcal{M}(\mathbf{X})$. Therefore the fact that $\mathbf{Q}$ is singular no longer provides us with any extra restrictions to impose on our estimate of the mean vector. However, the condition $\mathbf{Ry} = \mathbf{0}$ does provide a natural means of testing whether there is any inconsistency between the observed vector $\mathbf{y}$ and the statistical specification of the model.

We shall proceed to derive the necessary specification of the minimum variance linear unbiased estimator of $\mathbf{X\beta}$ in the most general case of the model, and we shall then demonstrate that this estimator does indeed find a value within $\mathcal{B}$.

THE MINIMUM VARIANCE LINEAR UNBIASED ESTIMATOR OF $\mathbf{X\beta}$

We say that $\mathbf{Py} = \mathbf{X}\hat{\boldsymbol{\beta}}$ is the minimum variance linear unbiased estimator of $\mathbf{X\beta}$ in the model $(\mathbf{y}, \mathbf{X\beta}, \sigma^2\mathbf{Q})$ if $\mathbf{q}'\mathbf{X}\hat{\boldsymbol{\beta}} = \mathbf{p}'\hat{\boldsymbol{\beta}}$ is the minimum variance linear unbiased estimator of $\mathbf{q}'\mathbf{X\beta} = \mathbf{p}'\boldsymbol{\beta}$ for every $\mathbf{q}$. The requisite specification of this estimator is given by the following version of the Gauss–Markov Theorem.

(9.7) Let $\mathbf{y} \sim (\mathbf{X\beta}, \sigma^2\mathbf{Q})$, and let $\mathbf{Py}$ and $\mathbf{Fy}$ be unbiased estimators of $\mathbf{X\beta}$. Then the condition $E(\mathbf{q}'\mathbf{Py}) = E(\mathbf{q}'\mathrm{Fy}) = \mathbf{q}'\mathbf{X\beta}$ is equivalent to $\mathbf{PX} = \mathbf{FX} = \mathbf{X}$. Furthermore, if $\mathcal{M}(\mathbf{P}) = \mathcal{M}(\mathbf{X})$ we have $V(\mathbf{q}'\mathbf{Py}) \leqslant V(\mathbf{q}'\mathbf{Fy})$ for all $\mathbf{q}$ if and only if $\mathbf{PQ}(\mathbf{I} - \mathbf{P})' = \mathbf{0}$ or, equivalently, $\mathbf{PQ} = \mathbf{PQP}' = \mathbf{QP}'$.

Proof. We have $E(\mathbf{q}'\mathbf{Py}) = \mathbf{q}'\mathbf{P}E(\mathbf{y}) = \mathbf{q}'\mathbf{PX\beta} = \mathbf{q}'\mathbf{X\beta}$ for all $\boldsymbol{\beta}$ if and only if $\mathbf{PX} = \mathbf{X}$. Likewise, $E(\mathbf{q}'\mathbf{Fy}) = \mathbf{q}'\mathbf{X\beta}$ if and only if $\mathbf{FX} = \mathbf{X}$. Now let $\mathbf{F} = \mathbf{I}$ so that the condition $V(\mathbf{q}'\mathrm{Fy}) \geqslant V(\mathbf{q}'\mathbf{Py})$ becomes $V(\mathbf{q}'\mathbf{y}) \geqslant V(\mathbf{q}'\mathbf{Py})$. Then $V(\mathbf{q}'\mathbf{y}) = V[\mathbf{q}'\mathbf{Py} + \mathbf{q}'(\mathbf{I} - \mathbf{P})\mathbf{y}] = V(\mathbf{q}'\mathbf{Py}) + V[\mathbf{q}'(\mathbf{I} - \mathbf{P})\mathbf{y}] + 2C[\mathbf{q}'\mathbf{Py}, \mathbf{q}'(\mathbf{I} - \mathbf{P})\mathbf{y}] \geqslant V(\mathbf{q}'\mathbf{Py})$ for all $\mathbf{q}$ if and only if $C[\mathbf{q}'\mathbf{Py}, \mathbf{q}'(\mathbf{I} - \mathbf{P})\mathbf{y}] = \sigma^2\mathbf{q}'\mathbf{PQ}(\mathbf{I} - \mathbf{P})'\mathbf{q} = \mathbf{0}$ which is equivalent to the condition $\mathbf{PQ}(\mathbf{I} - \mathbf{P})' = \mathbf{0}$ or to $\mathbf{PQ} = \mathbf{PQP}' = \mathbf{QP}'$, using the symmetry of $\mathbf{PQP}'$. Replacing $\mathbf{q}'$ by $\mathbf{q}'\mathbf{F}$ in this inequality gives $V(\mathbf{q}'\mathbf{Fy}) \geqslant V(\mathbf{q}'\mathbf{FPy})$. But $\mathbf{FX} = \mathbf{X}$ and $\mathcal{M}(\mathbf{P}) = \mathcal{M}(\mathbf{X})$ imply $\mathbf{FP} = \mathbf{P}$, so that the latter is equivalent to the inequality $V(\mathbf{q}'\mathbf{Fy}) \geqslant V(\mathbf{q}'\mathbf{Py})$. This proves the theorem.

As an immediate corollary, we have that

(9.8) If $\mathrm{Null}(\mathbf{Q}) = 0$ such that $\mathbf{Q}^{-1}$ exists, then $\mathbf{P} = \mathbf{P}^2$ and $\mathbf{P}$ is necessarily idempotent.

This follows since $\mathbf{PQ} = \mathbf{PQP}' = \mathbf{QP}'$ implies that $\mathbf{PQ} = \mathbf{P}(\mathbf{QP}') = \mathbf{P}(\mathbf{PQ}) = \mathbf{P}^2\mathbf{Q}$, whence $\mathbf{P} = \mathbf{P}^2$ is implied if $\mathbf{Q}^{-1}$ exists.

We shall now demonstrate that the minimum variance linear unbiased estimator $\mathbf{Py} = \mathbf{X}\hat{\boldsymbol{\beta}}$ obeys the restriction $\mathbf{Ry} = \mathbf{RX}\hat{\boldsymbol{\beta}} = \mathbf{RX}\boldsymbol{\beta}$. That is to say,

(9.9) Let $\mathbf{y} \sim (\mathbf{X}\boldsymbol{\beta}, \sigma^2\mathbf{Q})$ with $\mathbf{RQ} = \mathbf{0}$, and let $\hat{\mathbf{y}} = \mathbf{X}\hat{\boldsymbol{\beta}} = \mathbf{Py}$ be the minimum variance linear unbiased estimator of $\mathbf{X}\boldsymbol{\beta}$. Then, since $\mathbf{PQ} = \mathbf{PQP}' = \mathbf{QP}'$ and $\mathbf{PX} = \mathbf{X}$, we have $\mathbf{Ry} = \mathbf{RX}\hat{\boldsymbol{\beta}} = \mathbf{RX}\boldsymbol{\beta}$.

Proof. From (9.6) we have $\mathbf{Ry} = \mathbf{R}(\mathbf{X}\boldsymbol{\beta} + \mathbf{Q}\boldsymbol{\lambda}) = \mathbf{RX}\boldsymbol{\beta} + \mathbf{RQ}\boldsymbol{\lambda} = \mathbf{RX}\boldsymbol{\beta}$, since $\mathbf{RQ} = \mathbf{0}$. Now, $\mathbf{RX}\hat{\boldsymbol{\beta}} = \mathbf{RPy} = \mathbf{RP}(\mathbf{X}\boldsymbol{\beta} + \mathbf{Q}\boldsymbol{\lambda}) = \mathbf{RPX}\boldsymbol{\beta} + \mathbf{RPQ}\boldsymbol{\lambda}$. But $\mathbf{PX} = \mathbf{X}$ and $\mathbf{PQ} = \mathbf{QP}'$, so that $\mathbf{RX}\hat{\boldsymbol{\beta}} = \mathbf{RX}\boldsymbol{\beta} + \mathbf{RQP}'\boldsymbol{\lambda} = \mathbf{RX}\boldsymbol{\beta}$, since $\mathbf{RQ} = \mathbf{0}$. Thus $\mathbf{Ry} = \mathbf{RX}\hat{\boldsymbol{\beta}} = \mathbf{RX}\boldsymbol{\beta}$.

This result shows that the estimate $\mathbf{Py} = \mathbf{X}\hat{\boldsymbol{\beta}}$ is indeed an element of the set $\mathcal{B} = \boldsymbol{\mu} + \mathcal{M}(\mathbf{X}) \cap \mathcal{M}(\mathbf{Q})$ defined by the restrictions $\mathbf{Ry} = \mathbf{RX}\boldsymbol{\beta}$. Also, in the light of the result in (2.29), it is clear that the conditions $\mathcal{M}(\mathbf{P}) = \mathcal{M}(\mathbf{X})$, $\mathbf{PX} = \mathbf{X}$ and $\mathbf{PQ} = \mathbf{QP}'$ imply that the restriction of $\mathbf{P}$ to $\mathcal{M}(\mathbf{Q})$ is a projector on $\mathcal{M}(\mathbf{Q}) \cap \mathcal{M}(\mathbf{X})$; and, as we have already shown, this property of $\mathbf{P}$ is both necessary and sufficient for obtaining an estimate of $\mathbf{X}\boldsymbol{\beta}$ within the set $\mathcal{B}$.

When it comes to finding a specific functional form for the projector, we can rely upon a simple generalization of the formula of the minimum $\mathbf{Q}^{-1}$-distance projector on $\mathcal{M}(\mathbf{X})$ given in (6.8). We shall deal first with the special case where $\mathcal{M}(\mathbf{X}) \subset \mathcal{M}(\mathbf{Q})$ and then with the general case.

When $\mathcal{M}(\mathbf{X}) \subset \mathcal{M}(\mathbf{Q})$ in the model $(\mathbf{y}, \mathbf{X}\boldsymbol{\beta}, \sigma^2\mathbf{Q})$, the matrix $\mathbf{P}$ in the minimum variance unbiased estimate $\mathbf{X}\hat{\boldsymbol{\beta}} = \mathbf{Py}$ may be specified as $\mathbf{P} = \mathbf{X}(\mathbf{X}'\mathbf{Q}^{-}\mathbf{X})^{-}\mathbf{X}'\mathbf{Q}$. We prove this in two steps. First,

(9.10) If $\mathcal{M}(\mathbf{X}) \subset \mathcal{M}(\mathbf{Q})$, then $\mathbf{P} = \mathbf{X}(\mathbf{X}'\mathbf{Q}^{-}\mathbf{X})^{-}\mathbf{X}'\mathbf{Q}^{-}$ satisfies the conditions $\mathbf{PX} = \mathbf{X}$ and $\mathcal{M}(\mathbf{P}) = \mathcal{M}(\mathbf{X})$.

Proof. We may show that $\mathbf{PX} = \mathbf{X}$ and $\mathcal{M}(\mathbf{P}) = \mathcal{M}(\mathbf{X})$ by demonstrating that $\mathbf{P} = \mathbf{X}(\mathbf{X}'\mathbf{Q}^{-}\mathbf{X})^{-}\mathbf{X}'\mathbf{Q}^{-}$ is a projector on $\mathcal{M}(\mathbf{X})$. For this it is sufficient, according to (2.47), to show that $\text{Rank}(\mathbf{X}'\mathbf{Q}^{-}\mathbf{X}) = \text{Rank}(\mathbf{X})$. Therefore we observe that $\mathcal{M}(\mathbf{X}) \subset \mathcal{M}(\mathbf{Q})$ implies that $\mathbf{X} = \mathbf{QS}$ for some $\mathbf{S}$. This enables us to write $\mathbf{X}'\mathbf{Q}^{-}\mathbf{X} = \mathbf{S}'\mathbf{QQ}^{-}\mathbf{QS} = \mathbf{S}'\mathbf{QS}$. Thus $\text{Rank}(\mathbf{X}'\mathbf{Q}^{-}\mathbf{X}) = \text{Rank}(\mathbf{S}'\mathbf{QS}) = \text{Rank}(\mathbf{QS}) = \text{Rank}(\mathbf{X})$, where the second equality follows from the fact that $\mathbf{Q}$ is positive semidefinite.

Next we prove that

(9.11) If $\mathcal{M}(\mathbf{X}) \subset \mathcal{M}(\mathbf{Q})$, then $\mathbf{P} = \mathbf{X}(\mathbf{X}'\mathbf{Q}^{-}\mathbf{X})^{-}\mathbf{X}'\mathbf{Q}^{-}$ satisfies the condition $\mathbf{PQ}(\mathbf{I} - \mathbf{P})' = \mathbf{0}$.

Proof. To prove that $\mathbf{X}(\mathbf{X}'\mathbf{Q}^{-}\mathbf{X})^{-}\mathbf{X}'\mathbf{Q}^{-}\mathbf{Q}(\mathbf{I} - \mathbf{P})' = \mathbf{0}$, it is sufficient to show that $\mathbf{X}'\mathbf{Q}^{-}\mathbf{Q}(\mathbf{I} - \mathbf{P})' = \mathbf{0}$. Thus, using $\mathbf{X} = \mathbf{QS}$, we have $\mathbf{X}'\mathbf{Q}^{-}\mathbf{Q}(\mathbf{I} - \mathbf{P})' = \mathbf{S}'\mathbf{QQ}^{-}\mathbf{Q}(\mathbf{I} - \mathbf{P})' = \mathbf{S}'\mathbf{Q}(\mathbf{I} - \mathbf{P})' = \mathbf{X}'(\mathbf{I} - \mathbf{P})' = \mathbf{0}$, where the last equality follows from the condition $\mathbf{PX} = \mathbf{X}$ which is already established.

We may also find a convenient expression for the variance of the function $\mathbf{q'Py}=\mathbf{q'X\hat{\beta}}=\mathbf{p'\hat{\beta}}$, which is the minimum variance linear unbiased estimator of $\mathbf{p'\beta}$. Thus, using $V(\mathbf{q'Py})=\sigma^2\mathbf{q'PQP'q}=\sigma^2\mathbf{q'PQq}$ and $\mathbf{P}=\mathbf{X}(\mathbf{X'Q^-X})^-\mathbf{X'Q^-}$, we get $V(\mathbf{p'\hat{\beta}})=\sigma^2\mathbf{q'X}(\mathbf{X'Q^-X})^-\mathbf{Q^-Qq}=\sigma^2\mathbf{q'X}(\mathbf{X'Q^-X})^-\mathbf{X'q}=\sigma^2\mathbf{p'}(\mathbf{X'Q^-X})^-\mathbf{p}$, where the second equality depends upon the fact that $\mathbf{X'Q^-Q}=\mathbf{S'QQ^-Q}=\mathbf{S'Q}=\mathbf{X'}$.

To summarize our results, we may state that

(9.12) If $\mathcal{M}(\mathbf{X})\subset\mathcal{M}(\mathbf{Q})$ in the model $(\mathbf{y},\mathbf{X\beta},\sigma^2\mathbf{Q})$, then the minimum variance linear unbiased estimator of $\mathbf{X\beta}$ is given by $\mathbf{X\hat{\beta}}=\mathbf{Py}=\mathbf{X}(\mathbf{X'Q^-X})^-\mathbf{X'Q^-y}$ with $D(\mathbf{X\hat{\beta}})=\sigma^2\mathbf{X}(\mathbf{X'Q^-X})^-\mathbf{X'}$.

In the general case of the model $(\mathbf{y},\mathbf{X\beta},\sigma^2\mathbf{Q})$, the matrix $\mathbf{P}$ in the minimum variance unbiased estimator $\mathbf{X\hat{\beta}}=\mathbf{Py}$ may be specified as $\mathbf{P}=\mathbf{X}[\mathbf{X'}(\mathbf{Q}+\mathbf{M})^-\mathbf{X}]^-\mathbf{X'}(\mathbf{Q}+\mathbf{M})^-$, where $\mathbf{M}$ is any positive-semidefinite matrix such that $\mathcal{M}(\mathbf{Q}+\mathbf{M})=\mathcal{M}(\mathbf{X},\mathbf{Q})$ and $\mathcal{M}(\mathbf{M})\subset\mathcal{M}(\mathbf{X})$. To help us establish this result, we first prove the following Lemma.

(9.13) If $\mathbf{Q},\mathbf{M}$ are positive semidefinite, then $(\mathbf{Q}+\mathbf{M})$ is positive semidefinite and $\mathcal{M}(\mathbf{Q}+\mathbf{M})=\mathcal{M}(\mathbf{Q})+\mathcal{M}(\mathbf{M})=\mathcal{M}(\mathbf{Q},\mathbf{M})$.

Proof. A matrix $\mathbf{A}$ is positive semidefinite if and only if there exists a matrix $\mathbf{B}$ such that $\mathbf{A}=\mathbf{BB'}$. Let $\mathbf{Q}=\mathbf{LL'}$ and $\mathbf{M}=\mathbf{JJ'}$, and define $\mathbf{Z}=[\mathbf{L},\mathbf{J}]$. Then $\mathbf{ZZ'}=(\mathbf{LL'}+\mathbf{JJ'})=(\mathbf{Q}+\mathbf{M})$ is positive semidefinite. Furthermore, since $\mathcal{M}(\mathbf{L})=\mathcal{M}(\mathbf{Q})$, $\mathcal{M}(\mathbf{J})=\mathcal{M}(\mathbf{M})$ and $\mathcal{M}(\mathbf{L},\mathbf{J})=\mathcal{M}(\mathbf{Z})=\mathcal{M}(\mathbf{ZZ'})$, it follows that $\mathcal{M}(\mathbf{Q},\mathbf{M})=\mathcal{M}(\mathbf{L},\mathbf{J})=\mathcal{M}(\mathbf{Z})=\mathcal{M}(\mathbf{Q}+\mathbf{M})$.

We may now prove that

(9.14) If $(\mathbf{Q}+\mathbf{M})$ is positive semidefinite with $\mathcal{M}(\mathbf{Q}+\mathbf{M})=\mathcal{M}(\mathbf{Q},\mathbf{X})$, then $\mathbf{P}=\mathbf{X}[\mathbf{X'}(\mathbf{Q}+\mathbf{M})^-\mathbf{X}]^-\mathbf{X'}(\mathbf{Q}+\mathbf{M})^-$ satisfies the conditions $\mathbf{PX}=\mathbf{X}$ and $\mathcal{M}(\mathbf{P})=\mathcal{M}(\mathbf{X})$.

Proof. It is sufficient to show that $\mathbf{P}$ is a projector on $\mathcal{M}(\mathbf{X})$ by virtue of the condition $\text{Rank}[\mathbf{X'}(\mathbf{Q}+\mathbf{M})^-\mathbf{X}]=\text{Rank}(\mathbf{X})$. To show that this is satisfied, we observe that $\mathbf{X}=(\mathbf{Q}+\mathbf{M})\mathbf{S}$ for some $\mathbf{S}$. It follows that $\mathbf{X'}(\mathbf{Q}+\mathbf{M})^-\mathbf{X}=\mathbf{S'}(\mathbf{Q}+\mathbf{M})(\mathbf{Q}+\mathbf{M})^-(\mathbf{Q}+\mathbf{M})\mathbf{S}=\mathbf{S'}(\mathbf{Q}+\mathbf{M})\mathbf{S}$. Therefore $\text{Rank}[\mathbf{X'}(\mathbf{Q}+\mathbf{M})^-\mathbf{X}]=\text{Rank}[\mathbf{S'}(\mathbf{Q}+\mathbf{M})\mathbf{S}]=\text{Rank}[(\mathbf{Q}+\mathbf{M})\mathbf{S}]=\text{Rank}(\mathbf{X})$, which proves the proposition.

Next we prove that

(9.15) If $\mathcal{M}(\mathbf{Q}+\mathbf{M})=\mathcal{M}(\mathbf{Q},\mathbf{X})$ and $\mathcal{M}(\mathbf{M})\subset\mathcal{M}(\mathbf{X})$, where $\mathbf{Q}$ and $\mathbf{M}$ are symmetric and positive semidefinite, then $\mathbf{P}=\mathbf{X}[\mathbf{X'}(\mathbf{Q}+\mathbf{M})^-\mathbf{X}]^-\mathbf{X'}(\mathbf{Q}+\mathbf{M})^-$ satisfies the condition $\mathbf{PQ}(\mathbf{I}-\mathbf{P})'=\mathbf{0}$.

Proof. It is sufficient to show that $\mathbf{X}'(\mathbf{Q}+\mathbf{M})^-\mathbf{Q}(\mathbf{I}-\mathbf{P})'=\mathbf{0}$. We observe that $\mathbf{PX}=\mathbf{X}$ from (9.14) implies $\mathbf{X}'(\mathbf{I}-\mathbf{P})'=\mathbf{0}$, whence $\mathcal{M}(\mathbf{M})\subset\mathcal{M}(\mathbf{X})$ with $\mathbf{M}=\mathbf{M}'$ implies $\mathbf{M}(\mathbf{I}-\mathbf{P})'=\mathbf{0}$ and $\mathbf{Q}(\mathbf{I}-\mathbf{P})'=(\mathbf{Q}+\mathbf{M})(\mathbf{I}-\mathbf{P})'$. Therefore, using $\mathcal{M}(\mathbf{Q}+\mathbf{M})=\mathcal{M}(\mathbf{Q},\mathbf{X})$ to write $\mathbf{X}=(\mathbf{Q}+\mathbf{M})\mathbf{S}$ for some $\mathbf{S}$, we obtain $\mathbf{X}'(\mathbf{Q}+\mathbf{M})^-\mathbf{Q}(\mathbf{I}-\mathbf{P})'=\mathbf{S}'(\mathbf{Q}+\mathbf{M})(\mathbf{Q}+\mathbf{M})^-(\mathbf{Q}+\mathbf{M})(\mathbf{I}-\mathbf{P})'=\mathbf{S}'(\mathbf{Q}+\mathbf{M})(\mathbf{I}-\mathbf{P})'=\mathbf{X}'(\mathbf{I}-\mathbf{P})'=\mathbf{0}$, and the theorem is proved.

By collecting the results (9.14), (9.15) and relating them to (9.7) we may establish that

(9.16) The minimum variance linear unbiased estimator of $\mathbf{X}\boldsymbol{\beta}$ in the model $(\mathbf{y},\mathbf{X}\boldsymbol{\beta},\sigma^2\mathbf{Q})$, where $\mathbf{Q}$ may be singular, is given by $\mathbf{X}\hat{\boldsymbol{\beta}}=\mathbf{Py}=\mathbf{X}[\mathbf{X}'(\mathbf{Q}+\mathbf{M})^-\mathbf{X}]^-\mathbf{X}'(\mathbf{Q}+\mathbf{M})^-\mathbf{y}$ where $\mathcal{M}(\mathbf{Q}+\mathbf{M})=\mathcal{M}(\mathbf{Q},\mathbf{X})$, $\mathcal{M}(\mathbf{M})\subset\mathcal{M}(\mathbf{X})$ and $\mathbf{M}$ is symmetric positive semidefinite.

In the absence of the condition $\mathcal{M}(\mathbf{X})\subset\mathcal{M}(\mathbf{Q})$, we are unable to find a simple form for $D(\mathbf{X}\hat{\boldsymbol{\beta}})$ such as is given in (9.12).

An obvious choice of $(\mathbf{Q}+\mathbf{M})$ in (9.16) is $(\mathbf{Q}+\mathbf{XX}')$. However, $(\mathbf{Q}+\mathbf{XX}')^-$ is not generally a g-inverse of $\mathbf{Q}$. To ensure that $(\mathbf{Q}+\mathbf{M})^-$ is $\mathbf{Q}^-$, the columns of $\mathbf{M}$ must be chosen so as to be linearly independent of the columns of $\mathbf{Q}$. We establish this result by proving that

(9.17) If $\mathbf{Q}$ and $\mathbf{M}$ are positive semidefinite, so that $\mathcal{M}(\mathbf{Q}+\mathbf{M})=\mathcal{M}(\mathbf{Q})+\mathcal{M}(\mathbf{M})$, then $(\mathbf{Q}+\mathbf{M})^-$ is $\mathbf{Q}^-$ if and only if $\mathcal{M}(\mathbf{Q})\cap\mathcal{M}(\mathbf{M})=\mathbf{0}$.

Proof. First we recall that the condition $\mathcal{M}(\mathbf{Q})\cap\mathcal{M}(\mathbf{M})=\mathbf{0}$ is necessary and sufficient for the existence of a projector $\mathbf{P}$ on $\mathcal{M}(\mathbf{Q})$ along $\mathcal{M}(\mathbf{M})$ such that $\mathbf{PQ}=\mathbf{Q}$ and $\mathbf{PM}=\mathbf{0}$.

Let $\mathcal{M}(\mathbf{Q})\cap\mathcal{M}(\mathbf{M})=\mathbf{0}$ so that there exists a $\mathbf{P}$ such that $\mathbf{PQ}=\mathbf{Q}$ and $\mathbf{PM}=\mathbf{0}$. Then $\mathbf{P}(\mathbf{Q}+\mathbf{M})(\mathbf{Q}+\mathbf{M})^-(\mathbf{Q}+\mathbf{M})\mathbf{P}'=\mathbf{Q}(\mathbf{Q}+\mathbf{M})^-\mathbf{Q}$. But, also, $\mathbf{P}(\mathbf{Q}+\mathbf{M})(\mathbf{Q}+\mathbf{M})^-(\mathbf{Q}+\mathbf{M})\mathbf{P}'=\mathbf{P}(\mathbf{Q}+\mathbf{M})\mathbf{P}'=\mathbf{Q}$. Thus $\mathbf{Q}(\mathbf{Q}+\mathbf{M})^-\mathbf{Q}=\mathbf{Q}$, which shows that $(\mathbf{Q}+\mathbf{M})^-$ is $\mathbf{Q}^-$. By replacing $\mathbf{P}$ in this argument by $(\mathbf{I}-\mathbf{P})$ such that $(\mathbf{I}-\mathbf{P})\mathbf{Q}=\mathbf{0}$ and $(\mathbf{I}-\mathbf{P})\mathbf{M}=\mathbf{M}$, we can also show that $(\mathbf{Q}+\mathbf{M})^-$ is $\mathbf{M}^-$.

For the converse, we assume that $(\mathbf{Q}+\mathbf{M})^-$ is $\mathbf{Q}^-$ so that $\mathbf{Q}(\mathbf{Q}+\mathbf{M})^-\mathbf{Q}=\mathbf{Q}$. Then $\mathbf{Q}(\mathbf{Q}+\mathbf{M})^-(\mathbf{Q}+\mathbf{M})=\mathbf{Q}+\mathbf{Q}(\mathbf{Q}+\mathbf{M})^-\mathbf{M}$. But, since $\mathbf{Q}=(\mathbf{Q}+\mathbf{M})\mathbf{S}$ for some $\mathbf{S}$, we also have $\mathbf{Q}(\mathbf{Q}+\mathbf{M})^-(\mathbf{Q}+\mathbf{M})=\mathbf{S}'(\mathbf{Q}+\mathbf{M})(\mathbf{Q}+\mathbf{M})^-(\mathbf{Q}+\mathbf{M})=\mathbf{S}(\mathbf{Q}+\mathbf{M})=\mathbf{Q}$. Thus $\mathbf{Q}+\mathbf{Q}(\mathbf{Q}+\mathbf{M})^-\mathbf{M}=\mathbf{Q}$ which implies $\mathbf{Q}(\mathbf{Q}+\mathbf{M})^-\mathbf{M}=\mathbf{0}$. Therefore, since both $\mathbf{Q}(\mathbf{Q}+\mathbf{M})^-\mathbf{Q}=\mathbf{Q}$ and $\mathbf{Q}(\mathbf{Q}+\mathbf{M})^-\mathbf{M}=\mathbf{0}$, we must have $\mathcal{M}(\mathbf{Q})\cap\mathcal{M}(\mathbf{M})=\mathbf{0}$.

An alternative derivation of the estimator of $\mathbf{p}'\boldsymbol{\beta}$

The minimum variance linear unbiased estimator of the estimable parametric function $\mathbf{p}'\boldsymbol{\beta}$ of $\boldsymbol{\beta}$ in the model $(\mathbf{y},\mathbf{X}\boldsymbol{\beta},\sigma^2\mathbf{Q})$ may also be obtained directly from the criterion

(9.18) Minimize

$$V(\mathbf{q}'\mathbf{y})=\sigma^2\mathbf{q}'\mathbf{Q}\mathbf{q}=\sigma^2\|\mathbf{q}\|^2_{\mathbf{Q}}$$

Subject to

$$E(\mathbf{q}'\mathbf{y})=\mathbf{p}'\boldsymbol{\beta} \quad \text{or, equivalently,} \quad \mathbf{X}'\mathbf{q}=\mathbf{p}.$$

The appropriate Lagrangean expression for evaluating this is $L=\mathbf{q}'\mathbf{Q}\mathbf{q}-2\boldsymbol{\lambda}'(\mathbf{X}'\mathbf{q}-\mathbf{p})$. The conditions for minimizing L are

(9.19)
$$\mathbf{Q}\mathbf{q}=\mathbf{X}\boldsymbol{\lambda}, \qquad \mathbf{X}'\mathbf{q}=\mathbf{p}.$$

Adding $\mathbf{M}\mathbf{q}=\mathbf{X}\mathbf{k}$ to both sides of the first of these gives $(\mathbf{Q}+\mathbf{M})\mathbf{q}=\mathbf{X}(\boldsymbol{\lambda}+\mathbf{k})$. If $\mathbf{M}$ is chosen such that $\mathcal{M}(\mathbf{X})\subset\mathcal{M}(\mathbf{Q}+\mathbf{M})$, then this equation may be solved without any restriction on the choice of $(\mathbf{Q}+\mathbf{M})^-$ to give $\mathbf{q}=(\mathbf{Q}+\mathbf{M})^-\mathbf{X}(\boldsymbol{\lambda}+\mathbf{k})$; whence, from the second equation, $\mathbf{p}=\mathbf{X}'\mathbf{q}=\mathbf{X}'(\mathbf{Q}+\mathbf{M})^-\mathbf{X}(\boldsymbol{\lambda}+\mathbf{k})$. Then, a solution for $(\boldsymbol{\lambda}+\mathbf{k})$ is $(\boldsymbol{\lambda}+\mathbf{k})=[\mathbf{X}'(\mathbf{Q}+\mathbf{M})^-\mathbf{X}]^-\mathbf{p}$. Thus $(\mathbf{Q}+\mathbf{M})\mathbf{q}=\mathbf{X}(\boldsymbol{\lambda}+\mathbf{k})=\mathbf{X}[\mathbf{X}'(\mathbf{Q}+\mathbf{M})^-\mathbf{X}]^-\mathbf{p}$, and $\mathbf{q}=(\mathbf{Q}+\mathbf{M})^-\mathbf{X}[\mathbf{X}'(\mathbf{Q}+\mathbf{M})^-\mathbf{X}]^-\mathbf{p}$; whence

$$\mathbf{q}'\mathbf{y}=\mathbf{p}'[\mathbf{X}'(\mathbf{Q}+\mathbf{M})^-\mathbf{X}]^-\mathbf{X}'(\mathbf{Q}+\mathbf{M})^-\mathbf{y}$$

is the solution to the problem.

ESTIMATING σ^2

We shall demonstrate in two different ways that

(9.20) If $\mathbf{y}\sim(\mathbf{X}\boldsymbol{\beta},\sigma^2\mathbf{Q})$, and if $\mathbf{X}\hat{\boldsymbol{\beta}}=\mathbf{P}\mathbf{y}$ is the minimum variance linear unbiased estimator of $\mathbf{X}\boldsymbol{\beta}$, then $E[(\mathbf{y}-\mathbf{X}\hat{\boldsymbol{\beta}})'\mathbf{Q}^-(\mathbf{y}-\mathbf{X}\hat{\boldsymbol{\beta}})]=\sigma^2(q-s)$, where $q=\text{Rank}(\mathbf{Q})$, $s=\text{Rank}(\mathbf{P}\mathbf{Q})=\text{Dim}\,\mathcal{M}(\mathbf{X})\cap\mathcal{M}(\mathbf{Q})$ and $\mathbf{Q}^-$ is any choice of g-inverse of $\mathbf{Q}$.

Once this proposition is established, it follows immediately that

(9.21)
$$\hat{\sigma}^2=\frac{(\mathbf{y}-\mathbf{P}\mathbf{y})'\mathbf{Q}^-(\mathbf{y}-\mathbf{P}\mathbf{y})}{q-s}$$

provides an unbiased estimator of σ^2.

The invariance of $E[(\mathbf{y}-\mathbf{X}\hat{\boldsymbol{\beta}})'\mathbf{Q}^-(\mathbf{y}-\mathbf{X}\hat{\boldsymbol{\beta}})]$ with respect to the choice of $\mathbf{Q}^-$ is explained by the following result:

(9.22) If $\mathbf{j}\in\mathcal{M}(\mathbf{Q})$, then $\mathbf{j}=\mathbf{Q}\mathbf{k}$ for some $\mathbf{k}$, whence $\mathbf{j}'\mathbf{Q}^-\mathbf{j}=\mathbf{k}'\mathbf{Q}\mathbf{Q}^-\mathbf{Q}\mathbf{k}=\mathbf{k}'\mathbf{Q}\mathbf{k}$ is invariant with respect to the choice of $\mathbf{Q}^-$.

The fact that $\mathbf{X}\hat{\boldsymbol{\beta}}$ satisfies the restrictions $\mathbf{R}(\mathbf{y}-\mathbf{X}\hat{\boldsymbol{\beta}})=\mathbf{0}$, where $\mathcal{N}(\mathbf{R})=\mathcal{M}(\mathbf{Q})$, implies that $(\mathbf{y}-\mathbf{X}\hat{\boldsymbol{\beta}})=\mathbf{Qk}$ for some $\mathbf{k}$. Therefore (9.22) implies that $(\mathbf{y}-\mathbf{X}\hat{\boldsymbol{\beta}})'\mathbf{Q}^-(\mathbf{y}-\mathbf{X}\hat{\boldsymbol{\beta}})$ is invariant with respect to the choice of $\mathbf{Q}^-$; and the same is clearly true for $E[(\mathbf{y}-\mathbf{X}\hat{\boldsymbol{\beta}})'\mathbf{Q}^-(\mathbf{y}-\mathbf{X}\hat{\boldsymbol{\beta}})]$.

The proof that $E[(\mathbf{y}-\mathbf{X}\hat{\boldsymbol{\beta}})'\mathbf{Q}^-(\mathbf{y}-\mathbf{X}\hat{\boldsymbol{\beta}})]=\sigma^2(q-s)$ is facilitated by choosing $\mathbf{Q}^-$ as the Moore–Penrose g-inverse of $\mathbf{Q}$ in respect of the ordinary inner product.

(9.23) The Moore–Penrose g-inverse of $\mathbf{Q}$ in respect of the ordinary inner product is given by $\mathbf{Q}^+=\mathbf{T}'\mathbf{T}$, where $\mathbf{T}$ is such that $\mathbf{TQT}'=\mathbf{J}$ is a diagonal matrix whose sole non-zero elements are $q=\text{Rank}(\mathbf{Q})$ units on the principal diagonal.

To demonstrate this, let us consider an orthonormal matrix $\mathbf{C}$ such that $\mathbf{CC}'=\mathbf{C}'\mathbf{C}=\mathbf{I}$, the columns of which constitute the characteristic vectors of $\mathbf{Q}$. Then, if the columns are appropriately ordered, we can form

$$(9.24)\qquad \mathbf{C}'\mathbf{QC}=\begin{bmatrix}\boldsymbol{\Lambda}, & \mathbf{0}\\ \mathbf{0}, & \mathbf{0}\end{bmatrix},$$

where $\boldsymbol{\Lambda}$ is a $q\times q$ diagonal matrix containing the q non-zero characteristic roots of $\mathbf{Q}$, denoted $\lambda_1,\ldots,\lambda_q$, which are all positive since $\mathbf{Q}$ is positive semidefinite. Since $\mathbf{CC}'=\mathbf{I}$, we can also write

$$(9.25)\qquad \mathbf{Q}=\mathbf{CC}'\mathbf{QCC}'=\mathbf{C}\begin{bmatrix}\boldsymbol{\Lambda}, & \mathbf{0}\\ \mathbf{0}, & \mathbf{0}\end{bmatrix}\mathbf{C}',$$

which is described as the canonical form of $\mathbf{Q}$. Let us now define a diagonal matrix $\mathbf{D}$ whose ith element is $d_i=1/\sqrt{\lambda_i}$ if $i\leqslant q$, and $d_i=0$ if $i>q$. Then

$$(9.26)\qquad \mathbf{D}'\mathbf{D}=\mathbf{DD}'=\begin{bmatrix}\boldsymbol{\Lambda}^{-1}, & \mathbf{0}\\ \mathbf{0}, & \mathbf{0}\end{bmatrix},$$

and, defining $\mathbf{T}=\mathbf{D}'\mathbf{C}'$, we have

$$(9.27)\qquad \mathbf{TQT}'=\mathbf{D}'\mathbf{C}'\mathbf{QCD}=\begin{bmatrix}\mathbf{I}_q, & \mathbf{0}\\ \mathbf{0}, & \mathbf{0}\end{bmatrix}=\mathbf{J}.$$

Thus $\mathbf{T}=\mathbf{D}'\mathbf{C}'$ is the matrix defined in the proposition (9.23). The proposition is verified by showing that

$$(9.28)\qquad \mathbf{Q}^+=\mathbf{T}'\mathbf{T}=\mathbf{CDD}'\mathbf{C}'=\mathbf{C}\begin{bmatrix}\boldsymbol{\Lambda}^{-1}, & \mathbf{0}\\ \mathbf{0}, & \mathbf{0}\end{bmatrix}\mathbf{C}'$$

obeys the defining conditions of $\mathbf{Q}^+$ which are $\mathbf{QQ}^+\mathbf{Q}=\mathbf{Q}, \mathbf{Q}^+\mathbf{QQ}^+=\mathbf{Q}^+$, $(\mathbf{QQ}^+)'=\mathbf{QQ}^+$ and $(\mathbf{Q}^+\mathbf{Q})'=\mathbf{Q}^+\mathbf{Q}$. This is readily accomplished by using the canonical form of $\mathbf{Q}$ from the RHS of (9.25) and the partitioned matrix on the RHS of (9.28) above. Thus, for example,

$$\mathbf{QQ}^{+}\mathbf{Q}=\mathbf{C}\begin{bmatrix}\mathbf{\Lambda}, & \mathbf{0}\\ \mathbf{0}, & \mathbf{0}\end{bmatrix}\mathbf{C}'\mathbf{C}\begin{bmatrix}\mathbf{\Lambda}^{-1}, & \mathbf{0}\\ \mathbf{0}, & \mathbf{0}\end{bmatrix}\mathbf{C}'\mathbf{C}\begin{bmatrix}\mathbf{\Lambda}, & \mathbf{0}\\ \mathbf{0}, & \mathbf{0}\end{bmatrix}\mathbf{C} \tag{9.29}$$

$$=\mathbf{C}\begin{bmatrix}\mathbf{\Lambda}, & \mathbf{0}\\ \mathbf{0}, & \mathbf{0}\end{bmatrix}\mathbf{C}'=\mathbf{Q}.$$

To prove (9.20), let us consider that, if $(\mathbf{y}-\mathbf{X\beta})=\boldsymbol{\varepsilon}\sim(\mathbf{0},\sigma^2\mathbf{Q})$, then

$$\mathbf{TP}\boldsymbol{\varepsilon}+\mathbf{T}(\mathbf{I}-\mathbf{P})\boldsymbol{\varepsilon}=\mathbf{T}\boldsymbol{\varepsilon}\sim\left(\begin{bmatrix}\mathbf{0}\\ \mathbf{0}\end{bmatrix},\ \sigma^2\begin{bmatrix}\mathbf{I}_q, & \mathbf{0}\\ \mathbf{0}, & \mathbf{0}\end{bmatrix}\right). \tag{9.30}$$

Moreover, since $\boldsymbol{\varepsilon}=\mathbf{Q}\boldsymbol{\lambda}$ by (9.6), we also have $(\mathbf{TP}\boldsymbol{\varepsilon})'\mathbf{T}(\mathbf{I}-\mathbf{P})\boldsymbol{\varepsilon}=\boldsymbol{\lambda}'\mathbf{QP}'\mathbf{Q}^{+}(\mathbf{I}-\mathbf{P})\mathbf{Q}\boldsymbol{\lambda}=\boldsymbol{\lambda}'\mathbf{PQQ}^{+}\mathbf{Q}(\mathbf{I}-\mathbf{P})'\boldsymbol{\lambda}=\boldsymbol{\lambda}'\mathbf{PQ}(\mathbf{I}-\mathbf{P}')\boldsymbol{\lambda}=0$, wherein the conditions $\mathbf{PQ}=\mathbf{QP}'$ and $\mathbf{PQ}(\mathbf{I}-\mathbf{P}')=\mathbf{0}$ of (9.7) account for the second and the final equalities respectively. Thus the effect of $\mathbf{T}$ is to transform the space $\mathcal{M}(\mathbf{PQ})=\mathcal{M}(\mathbf{X})\cap\mathcal{M}(\mathbf{Q})$ containing $\mathbf{P}\boldsymbol{\varepsilon}$ and the space $\mathcal{M}[(\mathbf{I}-\mathbf{P})\mathbf{Q}]$ containing $(\mathbf{I}-\mathbf{P})\boldsymbol{\varepsilon}$ into orthogonal complements within the space spanned by the leading q vectors of the natural basis. It is now possible to find an orthonormal matrix $\mathbf{S}$, such that $\mathbf{SS}'=\mathbf{S}'\mathbf{S}=\mathbf{I}$, which translates these orthogonal complements into those spanned by the first $s=\text{Rank}(\mathbf{PQ})$ and the succeeding $(q-s)=\text{Rank}[(\mathbf{I}-\mathbf{P})\mathbf{Q}]$ vectors of the natural basis. Thus we may obtain

$$\mathbf{STP}\boldsymbol{\varepsilon}+\mathbf{ST}(\mathbf{I}-\mathbf{P})\boldsymbol{\varepsilon}=\mathbf{ST}\boldsymbol{\varepsilon}=\boldsymbol{\eta}\sim\left(\begin{bmatrix}\mathbf{0}\\ \mathbf{0}\end{bmatrix},\ \sigma^2\begin{bmatrix}\mathbf{I}_q, & \mathbf{0}\\ \mathbf{0}, & \mathbf{0}\end{bmatrix}\right) \tag{9.31}$$

with

$$\mathbf{STP}\boldsymbol{\varepsilon}=\begin{bmatrix}\boldsymbol{\eta}_1\\ \mathbf{0}\end{bmatrix}\sim\left(\begin{bmatrix}\mathbf{0}\\ \mathbf{0}\end{bmatrix},\ \sigma^2\begin{bmatrix}\mathbf{I}_s, & \mathbf{0}\\ \mathbf{0}, & \mathbf{0}\end{bmatrix}\right), \tag{9.32}$$

and

$$\mathbf{ST}(\mathbf{I}-\mathbf{P})\boldsymbol{\varepsilon}=\begin{bmatrix}\mathbf{0}\\ \boldsymbol{\eta}_2\\ \mathbf{0}\end{bmatrix}\sim\left(\begin{bmatrix}\mathbf{0}\\ \mathbf{0}\\ \mathbf{0}\end{bmatrix},\ \sigma^2\begin{bmatrix}\mathbf{0}, & \mathbf{0}, & \mathbf{0}\\ \mathbf{0}, & \mathbf{I}_{q-s} & \mathbf{0}\\ \mathbf{0}, & \mathbf{0}, & \mathbf{0}\end{bmatrix}\right). \tag{9.33}$$

It follows that $E(\boldsymbol{\eta}_2'\boldsymbol{\eta}_2)=\sigma^2(q-s)$. But $\boldsymbol{\eta}_2'\boldsymbol{\eta}_2=\boldsymbol{\varepsilon}'(\mathbf{I}-\mathbf{P})'\mathbf{T}'\mathbf{S}'\mathbf{ST}(\mathbf{I}-\mathbf{P})\boldsymbol{\varepsilon}=\boldsymbol{\varepsilon}'(\mathbf{I}-\mathbf{P})'\mathbf{Q}^{+}(\mathbf{I}-\mathbf{P})\boldsymbol{\varepsilon}=(\mathbf{y}-\mathbf{X}\hat{\boldsymbol{\beta}})'\mathbf{Q}^{-}(\mathbf{y}-\mathbf{X}\hat{\boldsymbol{\beta}})$, so that $E[(\mathbf{y}-\mathbf{X}\hat{\boldsymbol{\beta}})'\mathbf{Q}^{-}(\mathbf{y}-\mathbf{X}\hat{\boldsymbol{\beta}})]=\sigma^2(q-s)$, and (9.20) is proved.

The alternative proof of (9.20) depends upon the following result:

(9.34) Let $\mathbf{P}_i\mathbf{Q}=\mathbf{P}_i\mathbf{QP}_i'=\mathbf{QP}_i'$ where $\mathbf{Q}=\mathbf{LL}'$ with $\text{Null}(\mathbf{L})=0$. Then, if $\mathbf{A}_i=\mathbf{L}'\mathbf{P}_i'\mathbf{Q}^{-}\mathbf{P}_i\mathbf{L}$, we have

(i) $\mathbf{A}_i=\mathbf{A}_i^2$,

(ii) $\mathbf{A}_i=\mathbf{A}_i'$,

(iii) $\text{Rank}(\mathbf{A}_i)=\text{Rank}(\mathbf{P}_i\mathbf{Q})$.

Proof. To begin, we use $\mathbf{P}_i\mathbf{Q} = \mathbf{P}_i\mathbf{Q}\mathbf{P}_i' = \mathbf{Q}\mathbf{P}_i'$ to establish that $\mathbf{Q}(\mathbf{P}_i'\mathbf{Q}^-\mathbf{P}_i)\mathbf{Q}(\mathbf{P}_i'\mathbf{Q}^-\mathbf{P}_i)\mathbf{Q} = (\mathbf{Q}\mathbf{P}_i')\mathbf{Q}^-(\mathbf{P}_i\mathbf{Q}\mathbf{P}_i')\mathbf{Q}^-\mathbf{P}_i\mathbf{Q} = \mathbf{P}_i(\mathbf{Q}\mathbf{Q}^-\mathbf{Q})\mathbf{P}_i'\mathbf{Q}^-\mathbf{P}_i\mathbf{Q} = (\mathbf{P}_i\mathbf{Q}\mathbf{P}_i')\mathbf{Q}^-\mathbf{P}_i\mathbf{Q} = \mathbf{Q}(\mathbf{P}_i'\mathbf{Q}^-\mathbf{P}_i)\mathbf{Q}$.

To prove (i) we note that $\mathcal{M}(\mathbf{L}) = \mathcal{M}(\mathbf{L}\mathbf{L}') = \mathcal{M}(\mathbf{Q})$ implies that $\mathbf{L} = \mathbf{Q}\mathbf{K}$ for some $\mathbf{K}$. Thus $\mathbf{A}_i^2 = (\mathbf{L}'\mathbf{P}_i'\mathbf{Q}^-\mathbf{P}_i\mathbf{L})^2 = \mathbf{K}'\mathbf{Q}(\mathbf{P}_i'\mathbf{Q}^-\mathbf{P}_i)\mathbf{Q}(\mathbf{P}_i'\mathbf{Q}^-\mathbf{P}_i)\mathbf{Q}\mathbf{K} = \mathbf{K}'\mathbf{Q}(\mathbf{P}_i'\mathbf{Q}^-\mathbf{P}_i)\mathbf{Q}\mathbf{K} = \mathbf{L}'\mathbf{P}_i'\mathbf{Q}^-\mathbf{P}_i\mathbf{L} = \mathbf{A}_i$.

To prove (ii) we write $\mathbf{A}_i = \mathbf{L}'\mathbf{P}_i'\mathbf{Q}^-\mathbf{P}_i\mathbf{L} = \mathbf{K}'(\mathbf{Q}\mathbf{P}_i')\mathbf{Q}^-(\mathbf{P}_i\mathbf{Q})\mathbf{K} = \mathbf{K}'\mathbf{P}_i(\mathbf{Q}\mathbf{Q}^-\mathbf{Q})\mathbf{P}_i'\mathbf{K} = \mathbf{K}'\mathbf{P}_i\mathbf{Q}\mathbf{P}_i'\mathbf{K}$, from which the symmetry of $\mathbf{A}_i$ is obvious.

To prove (iii) we use $\mathbf{Q}\mathbf{P}_i'\mathbf{Q}^-\mathbf{P}_i\mathbf{Q} = \mathbf{P}_i\mathbf{Q}\mathbf{Q}^-\mathbf{Q}\mathbf{P}_i' = \mathbf{P}_i\mathbf{Q}\mathbf{P}_i' = \mathbf{P}_i\mathbf{Q}$. Thus, with $\text{Null}(\mathbf{L}) = 0$, we have $\text{Rank}(\mathbf{A}_i) = \text{Rank}(\mathbf{L}'\mathbf{P}_i'\mathbf{Q}^-\mathbf{P}_i\mathbf{L}) = \text{Rank}(\mathbf{Q}\mathbf{P}_i'\mathbf{Q}^-\mathbf{P}_i\mathbf{Q}) = \text{Rank}(\mathbf{P}_i\mathbf{Q})$.

For the proof of (9.20) itself, we first note that if $\mathbf{Q} = \mathbf{L}\mathbf{L}'$ and $\mathbf{y} \sim (\mathbf{X}\boldsymbol{\beta}, \sigma^2\mathbf{Q})$ or, equivalently, $(\mathbf{y} - \mathbf{X}\boldsymbol{\beta}) \sim (\mathbf{0}, \sigma^2\mathbf{Q})$, then $(\mathbf{y} - \mathbf{X}\boldsymbol{\beta}) = \boldsymbol{\varepsilon} = \mathbf{L}\boldsymbol{\eta}$ for some $\boldsymbol{\eta} \sim (\mathbf{0}, \sigma^2\mathbf{I})$. Therefore it follows that $(\mathbf{y} - \mathbf{X}\hat{\boldsymbol{\beta}})'\mathbf{Q}^-(\mathbf{y} - \mathbf{X}\hat{\boldsymbol{\beta}}) = \boldsymbol{\varepsilon}'(\mathbf{I} - \mathbf{P})'\mathbf{Q}^-(\mathbf{I} - \mathbf{P})\boldsymbol{\varepsilon} = \boldsymbol{\eta}'\mathbf{L}'(\mathbf{I} - \mathbf{P})'\mathbf{Q}^-(\mathbf{I} - \mathbf{P})\mathbf{L}\boldsymbol{\eta} = \boldsymbol{\eta}'\mathbf{A}\boldsymbol{\eta}$, where $\mathbf{A}$ obeys the conditions (i), (ii), (iii) of (9.34). Thus $\mathbf{A}$ is a symmetric idempotent matrix with $\text{Trace}(\mathbf{A}) = \text{Rank}(\mathbf{A}) = \text{Rank}[(\mathbf{I} - \mathbf{P})\mathbf{Q}] = q - s$. On taking the expectation, we find that $E[\boldsymbol{\varepsilon}'(\mathbf{I} - \mathbf{P})'\mathbf{Q}^-(\mathbf{I} - \mathbf{P})\boldsymbol{\varepsilon}] = E(\boldsymbol{\eta}'\mathbf{A}\boldsymbol{\eta}) = E[\text{Trace}(\boldsymbol{\eta}'\mathbf{A}\boldsymbol{\eta})] = E[\text{Trace}(\boldsymbol{\eta}\boldsymbol{\eta}'\mathbf{A})] = \text{Trace}[E(\boldsymbol{\eta}\boldsymbol{\eta}')\mathbf{A}] = \sigma^2\text{Trace}(\mathbf{A}) = \sigma^2\text{Rank}[(\mathbf{I} - \mathbf{P})\mathbf{Q}] = \sigma^2(q - s)$. Thus $E[\boldsymbol{\varepsilon}'(\mathbf{I} - \mathbf{P})'\mathbf{Q}^-(\mathbf{I} - \mathbf{P})\boldsymbol{\varepsilon}] = E[(\mathbf{y} - \mathbf{X}\hat{\boldsymbol{\beta}})'\mathbf{Q}^-(\mathbf{y} - \mathbf{X}\hat{\boldsymbol{\beta}})] = \sigma^2(q - s)$ which proves (9.20).

To provide a further interpretation of the estimator $\hat{\sigma}^2 = (\mathbf{y} - \mathbf{X}\hat{\boldsymbol{\beta}})'\mathbf{Q}^-(\mathbf{y} - \mathbf{X}\hat{\boldsymbol{\beta}})/(q - s)$, we may consider the fact that the function $\|\mathbf{j}\|_{\mathbf{Q}^-} = \sqrt{\mathbf{j}'\mathbf{Q}^-\mathbf{j}}$ defines a unique norm for any $\mathbf{j} \in \mathcal{M}(\mathbf{Q})$. Thus $(\mathbf{y} - \mathbf{X}\hat{\boldsymbol{\beta}})'\mathbf{Q}^-(\mathbf{y} - \mathbf{X}\hat{\boldsymbol{\beta}})$ may be interpreted as the squared length of the vector of regression residuals. The estimate $\hat{\sigma}^2$ is formed by dividing this squared length by a number of degrees of freedom equal to the dimension of the subspace $\mathcal{M}[(\mathbf{I} - \mathbf{P})\mathbf{Q}] \subset \mathcal{M}(\mathbf{Q})$ in which the vector is confined.

An alternative expression for the degrees of freedom associated with the residual vector is provided by the following equality:

$$(9.35) \qquad \text{Rank}(\mathbf{Q}) - \text{Rank}(\mathbf{P}\mathbf{Q}) = \text{Rank}(\mathbf{Q}, \mathbf{X}) - \text{Rank}(\mathbf{X}).$$

To establish this, we write $\text{Rank}(\mathbf{Q}) - \text{Rank}(\mathbf{P}\mathbf{Q}) = \text{Dim}\,\mathcal{M}(\mathbf{Q}) - \text{Dim}\,\mathcal{M}(\mathbf{Q}) \cap \mathcal{M}(\mathbf{X})$, and we use (1.19) to write

$$\begin{aligned}
\text{Rank}(\mathbf{Q}, \mathbf{X}) - \text{Rank}(\mathbf{X}) &= \{\text{Dim}\,\mathcal{M}(\mathbf{Q}) + \mathcal{M}(\mathbf{X})\} - \text{Dim}\,\mathcal{M}(\mathbf{X}) \\
&= \{\text{Dim}\,\mathcal{M}(\mathbf{Q}) + \text{Dim}\,\mathcal{M}(\mathbf{X}) - \text{Dim}\,\mathcal{M}(\mathbf{Q}) \cap \mathcal{M}(\mathbf{X})\} - \text{Dim}\,\mathcal{M}(\mathbf{X}) \\
&= \text{Dim}\,\mathcal{M}(\mathbf{Q}) - \text{Dim}\,\mathcal{M}(\mathbf{Q}) \cap \mathcal{M}(\mathbf{X}),
\end{aligned}$$

and the equality in (9.35) follows.

THE ASSUMPTION OF NORMALITY

The additional assumption that $\mathbf{y}$ has a normal distribution is required to enable us to find confidence intervals for the estimable parametric functions of $\boldsymbol{\beta}$ and to test hypotheses. The theory in Chapter 6 on hypothesis testing is, in fact, easily generalized to accommodate the case where $\mathbf{y} \sim N(\mathbf{X}\boldsymbol{\beta}, \sigma^2\mathbf{Q})$ has a singular dispersion matrix $\mathbf{Q}$.

The following theorem, which is a generalization of Cochran's theorem (17.45), provides the basis from which to derive the distributions of the various statistics that are used in testing linear hypotheses in respect of the model $(\mathbf{y}, \mathbf{X}\boldsymbol{\beta}, \sigma^2\mathbf{Q})$

(9.36) Let $\mathbf{PQ} = \sum_{i=1}^{k} \mathbf{P}_i\mathbf{Q}$ be a sum of k matrices such that $\mathbf{P}_i\mathbf{Q} = \mathbf{P}_i\mathbf{QP}_i' = \mathbf{QP}_i'$ for all i and $\mathbf{P}_i\mathbf{QP}_j' = \mathbf{0}$ if $i \neq j$, and let $\text{Rank}(\mathbf{P}_i\mathbf{Q}) = r_i$. Then, if $(\mathbf{y} - \mathbf{X}\boldsymbol{\beta}) = \boldsymbol{\varepsilon} \sim N(\mathbf{0}, \sigma^2\mathbf{Q})$, it follows that $\sigma^{-2}\boldsymbol{\varepsilon}'\mathbf{P}_i'\mathbf{Q}^-\mathbf{P}_i\boldsymbol{\varepsilon} \sim \chi^2(r_i); i = 1, \ldots, k$ are independent chi-square variates; whence $\sigma^{-2}\sum_i \boldsymbol{\varepsilon}'\mathbf{P}_i'\mathbf{Q}^-\mathbf{P}_i\boldsymbol{\varepsilon} = \sigma^{-2}\boldsymbol{\varepsilon}'\mathbf{P}'\mathbf{Q}^-\mathbf{P}\boldsymbol{\varepsilon} \sim \chi^2(r)$ where $r = \text{Rank}(\mathbf{PQ}) = \sum r_i = \sum \text{Rank}(\mathbf{P}_i\mathbf{Q})$.

This theorem is stated and proved in the Appendix of Statistical Theory under (17.48). However, we shall also prove it here using (9.34). For this purpose, we must invoke the result that

(9.37) If $\zeta_i \sim \chi^2(r_i)$; $i = 1, \ldots, k$ are independent chi-square variates of r_i degrees of freedom, then $\sum_i \zeta_i = \zeta \sim \chi^2(r)$ is a chi-square variate of $r = \sum_i r_i$ degrees of freedom.

To prove the theorem (9.36) it is then sufficient to prove (i) that $\sigma^{-2}\boldsymbol{\varepsilon}'\mathbf{P}_i'\mathbf{Q}^-\mathbf{P}_i\boldsymbol{\varepsilon}$ and $\sigma^{-2}\boldsymbol{\varepsilon}'\mathbf{P}_j'\mathbf{Q}^-\mathbf{P}_j\boldsymbol{\varepsilon}$ are independent chi-square variates of $r_i = \text{Rank}(\mathbf{P}_i\mathbf{Q})$ and $r_j = \text{Rank}(\mathbf{P}_j\mathbf{Q})$ degrees of freedom respectively, (ii) that $\sigma^{-2}\boldsymbol{\varepsilon}'\mathbf{P}'\mathbf{Q}^-\mathbf{P}\boldsymbol{\varepsilon}$ is a chi-square variate of $r = \text{Rank}(\mathbf{PQ})$ degrees of freedom, and (iii) that $\boldsymbol{\varepsilon}'\mathbf{P}'\mathbf{Q}^-\mathbf{P}\boldsymbol{\varepsilon} = \sum_i \boldsymbol{\varepsilon}'\mathbf{P}_i'\mathbf{Q}^-\mathbf{P}_i\boldsymbol{\varepsilon}$.

To prove (i), we express $\boldsymbol{\varepsilon} \sim N(\mathbf{0}, \sigma^2\mathbf{Q})$ as $\boldsymbol{\varepsilon} = \mathbf{Q}\boldsymbol{\lambda} = \mathbf{LL}'\boldsymbol{\lambda} = \mathbf{L}\boldsymbol{\eta}$, where $\boldsymbol{\eta} \sim N(\mathbf{0}, \sigma^2\mathbf{I})$; and we use (9.34) to write $\sigma^{-2}\boldsymbol{\varepsilon}'\mathbf{P}_i'\mathbf{Q}^-\mathbf{P}_i\boldsymbol{\varepsilon} = \sigma^{-2}\boldsymbol{\eta}'\mathbf{L}'\mathbf{P}_i'\mathbf{Q}^-\mathbf{P}_i\mathbf{L}\boldsymbol{\eta} = \sigma^{-2}\boldsymbol{\eta}'\mathbf{A}_i\boldsymbol{\eta}$, where $\mathbf{A}_i = \mathbf{A}_i^2 = \mathbf{A}_i'$ and $\text{Rank}(\mathbf{A}_i) = \text{Rank}(\mathbf{P}_i\mathbf{Q}) = r_i$. It then follows immediately from (17.39) that $\sigma^{-2}\boldsymbol{\eta}'\mathbf{A}_i\boldsymbol{\eta} \sim \chi^2(r_i)$. Next, to see that $\sigma^{-2}\boldsymbol{\varepsilon}'\mathbf{P}_i'\mathbf{Q}^-\mathbf{P}_i\boldsymbol{\varepsilon}$ and $\sigma^{-2}\boldsymbol{\varepsilon}'\mathbf{P}_j'\mathbf{Q}^-\mathbf{P}_j\boldsymbol{\varepsilon}$ are independent variates, it is sufficient to recognize that $\mathbf{P}_i\boldsymbol{\varepsilon}$ and $\mathbf{P}_j\boldsymbol{\varepsilon}$ are independent by virtue of being normally distributed with a covariance structure of $C(\mathbf{P}_i\boldsymbol{\varepsilon}, \mathbf{P}_j\boldsymbol{\varepsilon}) = E(\mathbf{P}_i\boldsymbol{\varepsilon\varepsilon}'\mathbf{P}_j') = \mathbf{P}_i\mathbf{QP}_j' = \mathbf{0}$.

The proof of (ii) follows along the same lines as the first part of the proof of (i) once it is established that $\mathbf{PQ} = \mathbf{PQP}' = \mathbf{QP}'$. First, $\mathbf{PQ} = \sum \mathbf{P}_i\mathbf{Q} = \mathbf{QP}'$ follows from the fact that $\mathbf{P}_i\mathbf{Q} = \mathbf{QP}_i'$ for all i. Next, using $\mathbf{P}_i\mathbf{QP}_j' = \mathbf{0}$, we find that $\mathbf{PQP}' = \sum_i \sum_j \mathbf{P}_i\mathbf{QP}_j' = \sum \mathbf{P}_i\mathbf{QP}_i' = \sum \mathbf{P}_i\mathbf{Q} = \mathbf{PQ}$.

To prove (iii), we use $\boldsymbol{\varepsilon} = \mathbf{Q}\boldsymbol{\lambda}$ and $\boldsymbol{\varepsilon}'\mathbf{P}_i'\mathbf{Q}^-\mathbf{P}_i\boldsymbol{\varepsilon} = \boldsymbol{\lambda}'(\mathbf{QP}_i')\mathbf{Q}^-(\mathbf{P}_i\mathbf{Q})\boldsymbol{\lambda} =$

$\boldsymbol{\lambda}'\mathbf{P}_i(\mathbf{QQ}^-\mathbf{Q})\mathbf{P}_i'\boldsymbol{\lambda}=\boldsymbol{\lambda}'\mathbf{P}_i\mathbf{QP}_i'\boldsymbol{\lambda}$. Then $\boldsymbol{\varepsilon}'\mathbf{P}'\mathbf{Q}^-\mathbf{P}\boldsymbol{\varepsilon}=\boldsymbol{\lambda}'(\mathbf{QP}')\mathbf{Q}^-(\mathbf{PQ})\boldsymbol{\lambda}=\boldsymbol{\lambda}'\mathbf{P}(\mathbf{QQ}^-\mathbf{Q})\mathbf{P}'\boldsymbol{\lambda}=\boldsymbol{\lambda}'\mathbf{PQP}'\boldsymbol{\lambda}=\sum\boldsymbol{\lambda}'\mathbf{P}_i\mathbf{QP}_i'\boldsymbol{\lambda}=\sum\boldsymbol{\varepsilon}'\mathbf{P}_i'\mathbf{Q}^-\mathbf{P}_i\boldsymbol{\varepsilon}$.

The test of an hypothesis

We may illustrate the application of the theorem (9.36) by considering a test of an hypothesis which maintains, in the context of the model $\mathbf{y}\sim N(\mathbf{X}\boldsymbol{\beta},\sigma^2\mathbf{Q})$, that $\boldsymbol{\mu}=\mathbf{X}\boldsymbol{\beta}\in\mathcal{M}(\mathbf{Z})\subset\mathcal{M}(\mathbf{X})$. Under the general assumptions of the model, we would estimate the mean vector $\boldsymbol{\mu}=\mathbf{X}\boldsymbol{\beta}$ by $\hat{\mathbf{y}}=\mathbf{P_X y}$, where $\mathbf{P_X}$ is such that $\mathcal{M}(\mathbf{P_X})=\mathcal{M}(\mathbf{X})$, $\mathbf{P_X X}=\mathbf{X}$ and $\mathbf{P_X Q}(\mathbf{I}-\mathbf{P_X})'=\mathbf{0}$. Under the specific assumptions of the hypothesis, we would estimate the mean vector by $\overset{*}{\mathbf{y}}=\mathbf{P_Z y}$, where $\mathbf{P_Z}$ is such that $\mathcal{M}(\mathbf{P_Z})=\mathcal{M}(\mathbf{Z})$, $\mathbf{P_Z Z}=\mathbf{Z}$ and$\mathbf{P_Z Q}(\mathbf{I}-\mathbf{P_Z})'=\mathbf{0}$. Then the function $\sigma^{-2}\|\hat{\mathbf{y}}-\overset{*}{\mathbf{y}}\|^2_{\mathbf{Q}^-}=\sigma^{-2}(\hat{\mathbf{y}}-\overset{*}{\mathbf{y}})'\mathbf{Q}^-(\hat{\mathbf{y}}-\overset{*}{\mathbf{y}})$, which is a measure of the proximity of $\hat{\mathbf{y}}$ and $\overset{*}{\mathbf{y}}$, would give us an indication of the extent to which the extra assumptions of the hypothesis conform to the evidence of the data as reflected in $\hat{\mathbf{y}}$. On replacing the unknown σ^2 by $\hat{\sigma}^2=(\mathbf{y}-\mathbf{P_X y})'\mathbf{Q}^-(\mathbf{y}-\mathbf{P_X y})/(q-s)$ and ignoring the factor $(q-s)=\text{Rank}[(\mathbf{I}-\mathbf{P_X})\mathbf{Q}]$, we obtain

(9.38) $$\rho=\frac{\|\hat{\mathbf{y}}-\overset{*}{\mathbf{y}}\|^2_{\mathbf{Q}^-}}{\|\mathbf{y}-\hat{\mathbf{y}}\|^2_{\mathbf{Q}^-}}=\frac{(\hat{\mathbf{y}}-\overset{*}{\mathbf{y}})'\mathbf{Q}^-(\hat{\mathbf{y}}-\overset{*}{\mathbf{y}})}{(\mathbf{y}-\hat{\mathbf{y}})'\mathbf{Q}^-(\mathbf{y}-\hat{\mathbf{y}})}.$$

We can now show how the theorem (9.36) enables us to find distribution of a scalar multiple of ρ on the assumptions of the hypothesis. Therefore, let us first confirm that the identity

$$\mathbf{Q}=(\mathbf{P_X}-\mathbf{P_Z})\mathbf{Q}+(\mathbf{I}-\mathbf{P_X})\mathbf{Q}+\mathbf{P_Z Q}$$

conforms to the conditions of the theorem. For this we use the identity $\mathbf{P_X QP_Z'}=\mathbf{P_X P_Z Q}=\mathbf{P_Z Q}$ to confirm that $(\mathbf{P_X}-\mathbf{P_Z})\mathbf{Q}(\mathbf{I}-\mathbf{P_X})'=\mathbf{0}$, $(\mathbf{P_X}-\mathbf{P_Z})\mathbf{QP_Z'}=\mathbf{0}$ and $(\mathbf{I}-\mathbf{P_X})\mathbf{QP_Z'}=\mathbf{0}$. Then, from the hypothesis that $(\mathbf{y}-\boldsymbol{\mu})=\boldsymbol{\varepsilon}\sim N(\mathbf{0},\sigma^2\mathbf{Q})$; $\boldsymbol{\mu}\in\mathcal{M}(\mathbf{Z})$, it follows that

(9.39)
1. $\sigma^{-2}(\mathbf{y}-\boldsymbol{\mu})'\mathbf{Q}^-(\mathbf{y}-\boldsymbol{\mu})\sim\chi^2(q)$,
2. $\sigma^{-2}(\mathbf{y}-\boldsymbol{\mu})'(\mathbf{P_X}-\mathbf{P_Z})'\mathbf{Q}^-(\mathbf{P_X}-\mathbf{P_Z})(\text{Y}-\boldsymbol{\mu})$
$=\sigma^{-2}(\hat{\mathbf{y}}-\overset{*}{\mathbf{y}})'\mathbf{Q}^-(\hat{\mathbf{y}}-\overset{*}{\mathbf{y}})\sim\chi^2(s-z)$,
3. $\sigma^{-2}(\mathbf{y}-\boldsymbol{\mu})'(\mathbf{I}-\mathbf{P_X})'\mathbf{Q}^-(\mathbf{I}-\mathbf{P_X})(\mathbf{y}-\boldsymbol{\mu})$
$=\sigma^{-2}(\mathbf{y}-\hat{\mathbf{y}})'\mathbf{Q}^-(\mathbf{y}-\hat{\mathbf{y}})\sim\chi^2(q-s)$,
4. $\sigma^{-2}(\mathbf{y}-\boldsymbol{\mu})'\mathbf{P_Z'}\mathbf{Q}^-\mathbf{P_Z}(\mathbf{y}-\boldsymbol{\mu})=\sigma^{-2}(\overset{*}{\mathbf{y}}-\boldsymbol{\mu})'\mathbf{Q}^-(\overset{*}{\mathbf{y}}-\boldsymbol{\mu})\sim\chi^2(z)$,

where $q=\text{Rank}(\mathbf{Q})$, $s=\text{Rank}(\mathbf{P_X Q})$ and $z=\text{Rank}(\mathbf{P_Z Q})$. From the fact that the chi-square variates under 2. and 3. are statistically independent, we can deduce that

(9.40) On the hypothesis $\mathbf{y}\sim N(\boldsymbol{\mu},\sigma^2\mathbf{Q})$; $\boldsymbol{\mu}\in\mathcal{M}(\mathbf{Z})\subset\mathcal{M}(\mathbf{X})$, we have

$$\left\{\frac{(\hat{\mathbf{y}}-\overset{*}{\mathbf{y}})'\mathbf{Q}^-(\hat{\mathbf{y}}-\overset{*}{\mathbf{y}})}{s-z}\Big/\frac{(\mathbf{y}-\hat{\mathbf{y}})'\mathbf{Q}^-(\mathbf{y}-\hat{\mathbf{y}})}{q-s}\right\}\sim F(s-z,q-s),$$

where $\hat{\mathbf{y}} = \mathbf{P_X y}$, $\overset{*}{\mathbf{y}} = \mathbf{P_Z y}$, and where $q = \text{Rank}(\mathbf{Q})$, $s = \text{Rank}(\mathbf{P_X Q})$ and $z = \text{Rank}(\mathbf{P_Z Q})$.

Thus we see that the test statistic $\rho[(q-s)/(s-z)]$ has an F-distribution of $s-z$ and $q-s$ degrees of freedom under the assumptions of the hypothesis.

BIBLIOGRAPHY

The Gauss–Markov Model with a Singular Dispersion Matrix. Goldman and Zelen [**44**], Mitra [**85**], Rao [**95**], [**96**], [**97**], Schönfeld [**107**], Theil [**115**, Chap. 6 §7–9], Zyskind and Martin [**129**].

CHAPTER 10

The Gauss–Markov Model with Linear Restrictions on Parameters

In this chapter, we shall consider the regression model $(\mathbf{g}, \mathbf{Z}\boldsymbol{\beta} \mid \mathbf{R}\boldsymbol{\beta} = \mathbf{r}, \sigma^2\mathbf{V})$ where the parameter vector $\boldsymbol{\beta}$ of the stochastic system $\mathbf{g} = \mathbf{Z}\boldsymbol{\beta} + \boldsymbol{\eta}$ is known to conform to the restrictions $\mathbf{R}\boldsymbol{\beta} = \mathbf{r}$. The effect of these restrictions is to confine $\boldsymbol{\beta}$ to an affine subspace $\mathcal{A} = \{\boldsymbol{\beta} = \mathbf{R}^- \mathbf{r} + (\mathbf{I} - \mathbf{R}^- \mathbf{R})\mathbf{q};\ \mathbf{q} \text{ is arbitrary}\}$ contained within the total parameter space. The set $\mathcal{A}$ may also be expressed as $\mathcal{A} = \boldsymbol{\beta} + \mathcal{N}(\mathbf{R})$, where $\boldsymbol{\beta}$ stands for a particular solution of $\mathbf{R}\boldsymbol{\beta} = \mathbf{r}$ and $\mathcal{N}(\mathbf{R})$ is the general solution of the associated homogeneous equations $\mathbf{R}\mathbf{q} = \mathbf{0}$.

The mapping of $\mathcal{A}$ under $\mathbf{Z}$ is the set $\mathcal{B} = \{\mathbf{Z}\boldsymbol{\beta}; \mathbf{R}\boldsymbol{\beta} = \mathbf{r}\}$ comprising all possible values of the mean vector $\boldsymbol{\mu} = \mathbf{Z}\boldsymbol{\beta}$ for which $\boldsymbol{\beta}$ obeys the restrictions $\mathbf{R}\boldsymbol{\beta} = \mathbf{r}$. The set $\mathcal{B}$ constitutes an affine subspace of $\mathcal{M}(\mathbf{Z})$ according to the definition (1.24); for if $\mathbf{Z}\boldsymbol{\beta}_1, \mathbf{Z}\boldsymbol{\beta}_2 \in \mathcal{B}$ by virtue of the condition $\boldsymbol{\beta}_1, \boldsymbol{\beta}_2 \in \mathcal{A}$, then $\lambda\mathbf{Z}\boldsymbol{\beta}_1 + (1-\lambda)\mathbf{Z}\boldsymbol{\beta}_2 = \mathbf{Z}[\lambda\boldsymbol{\beta}_1 + (1-\lambda)\boldsymbol{\beta}_2] \in \mathcal{B}$ by virtue of the condition $\lambda\boldsymbol{\beta}_1 + (1-\lambda)\boldsymbol{\beta}_2 \in \mathcal{A}$. In general, we cannot expect $\mathcal{B} = \mathbf{Z}\mathcal{A}$ to be a vector space unless $\mathcal{A}$ is a vector space. For $\mathcal{A}$ to be a vector space it is necessary and sufficient that $\mathbf{0} \in \mathcal{A}$ or, equivalently, $\mathbf{r} = \mathbf{0}$.

When $\mathcal{B} \subset \mathcal{M}(\mathbf{Z})$ is not a vector space, we cannot find a linear transformation that will map every value of the unrestricted vector $\mathbf{g}$ into $\mathcal{B}$. Thus, although we can use the ordinary method of Gaussian regression to find an unbiased estimator of $\boldsymbol{\mu} = \mathbf{Z}\boldsymbol{\beta}$ in the form of $\hat{\mathbf{g}} = \mathbf{P}_z\mathbf{g}$ where $\mathbf{P}_z$ is a projector on $\mathcal{M}(\mathbf{Z})$, we cannot use such a method to find an estimator $\overset{*}{\mathbf{g}} \in \mathcal{B}$ conforming to the *a priori* restrictions of $\boldsymbol{\beta}$.

One approach to the problem of obtaining estimates of $\boldsymbol{\mu} = \mathbf{Z}\boldsymbol{\beta}$ obeying the restrictions $\mathbf{R}\boldsymbol{\beta} = \mathbf{r}$ is to assimilate the model $(\mathbf{g}, \mathbf{Z}\boldsymbol{\beta} \mid \mathbf{R}\boldsymbol{\beta} = \mathbf{r}, \sigma^2\mathbf{V})$ to the general model $(\mathbf{y}, \mathbf{X}\boldsymbol{\beta}, \sigma^2\mathbf{Q} \mid \mathbf{N}\mathbf{Q} = \mathbf{0})$ containing a singular dispersion matrix. To do this, we combine the stochastic equations $\mathbf{g} = \mathbf{Z}\boldsymbol{\beta} + \boldsymbol{\eta}$ with the restrictions $\mathbf{R}\boldsymbol{\beta} = \mathbf{r}$ to form

$$\mathbf{y} = \begin{bmatrix} \mathbf{g} \\ \mathbf{r} \end{bmatrix} = \begin{bmatrix} \mathbf{Z} \\ \mathbf{R} \end{bmatrix}\boldsymbol{\beta} + \begin{bmatrix} \boldsymbol{\eta} \\ \mathbf{0} \end{bmatrix} = \mathbf{X}\boldsymbol{\beta} + \boldsymbol{\varepsilon}.$$

Then, by defining $\mathbf{N} = [\mathbf{0}, \mathbf{I}]$ such that $\mathbf{N}\mathbf{y} = \mathbf{r} = \mathbf{R}\boldsymbol{\beta} = \mathbf{N}\mathbf{X}\boldsymbol{\beta}$, we can write the restrictions as $\mathbf{N}\mathbf{y} = \mathbf{N}\mathbf{X}\boldsymbol{\beta}$. Reference to (9.5) shows that $\mathbf{N}(\mathbf{y} - \mathbf{X}\boldsymbol{\beta}) = \mathbf{N}\boldsymbol{\varepsilon} = \mathbf{0}$ is equivalent to $\mathbf{N}\mathbf{Q} = \mathbf{0}$ when $\sigma^2\mathbf{Q} = E(\boldsymbol{\varepsilon}\boldsymbol{\varepsilon}') = D(\boldsymbol{\varepsilon})$. Thus we obtain the model $(\mathbf{y}, \mathbf{X}\boldsymbol{\beta}, \sigma^2\mathbf{Q} \mid \mathbf{N}\mathbf{Q} = \mathbf{0})$.

To find an unbiased estimate of $\mathbf{X}\boldsymbol{\beta}$ subject to the restrictions $\mathbf{Ny}=\mathbf{NX}\boldsymbol{\beta}$ or $\mathbf{NQ}=\mathbf{0}$, we use the estimator specified in (9.16). That is to say, we estimate $\mathbf{X}\boldsymbol{\beta}$ by $\overset{*}{\mathbf{y}}=\mathbf{P}_x\mathbf{y}=\mathbf{X}\overset{*}{\boldsymbol{\beta}}$ where $\mathbf{P}_x$ is a projector on $\mathcal{M}(\mathbf{X})$ whose restriction to $\mathcal{M}(\mathbf{Q})$ is a projector on $\mathcal{M}(\mathbf{Q})\cap\mathcal{M}(\mathbf{X})$. The estimate $\overset{*}{\mathbf{y}}=\mathbf{X}\overset{*}{\boldsymbol{\beta}}$ incorporates the desired estimate $\overset{*}{\mathbf{g}}=\mathbf{Z}\overset{*}{\boldsymbol{\beta}}$. Moreover, the set of all estimable parametric functions of the form $\mathbf{q}'\mathbf{X}\boldsymbol{\beta}=\mathbf{p}'\boldsymbol{\beta}$ relating to the model $(\mathbf{y}, \mathbf{X}\boldsymbol{\beta}, \sigma^2\mathbf{Q} \mid \mathbf{NQ}=\mathbf{0})$ is identical to the set of all estimable parametric functions of the form $(\mathbf{k}'\mathbf{Z}+\boldsymbol{\lambda}'\mathbf{R})\boldsymbol{\beta}=\mathbf{p}'\boldsymbol{\beta}$ relating to the model $(\mathbf{g}, \mathbf{Z}\boldsymbol{\beta} \mid \mathbf{R}\boldsymbol{\beta}=\mathbf{r}, \sigma^2\mathbf{V})$; and it follows that the problem of obtaining restricted estimates of the estimable parametric functions of $\boldsymbol{\beta}$ is completely solved.

We shall, nevertheless, develop an equivalent theory of restricted Gaussian regression along alternative lines. A reason for doing so is that the very generality of the model $(\mathbf{y}, \mathbf{X}\boldsymbol{\beta}, \sigma^2\mathbf{Q} \mid \mathbf{NQ}=\mathbf{0})$ serves to conceal the interesting particularities of the model $(\mathbf{g}, \mathbf{Z}\boldsymbol{\beta} \mid \mathbf{R}\boldsymbol{\beta}=\mathbf{r}, \sigma^2\mathbf{V})$. Moreover, within the context of the general model, it is more difficult to exploit, in a manner which simplifies the estimation procedures, some of the assumptions that we are liable to make about the data $[\mathbf{g}, \mathbf{Z}]$.

ALTERNATIVE ESTIMATORS OF $\boldsymbol{\beta}$ IN THE RESTRICTED MODEL

We shall consider the model

(10.1) $$\mathbf{g}=\mathbf{Z}\boldsymbol{\beta}+\boldsymbol{\eta}$$

where $\mathbf{g}$ and $\mathbf{Z}$ comprise T observations on a scalar output and a k-element vector input respectively and $\boldsymbol{\eta}$ is a vector of T unobserved random variables with

(10.2) $$E(\boldsymbol{\eta})=\mathbf{0}, \qquad D(\boldsymbol{\eta})=E(\boldsymbol{\eta}\boldsymbol{\eta}')=\sigma^2\mathbf{I}.$$

The somewhat specific assumption that $D(\boldsymbol{\eta})=\sigma^2\mathbf{I}$, which is made largely in order to simplify the subsequent algebra, may be easily generalized to $D(\boldsymbol{\eta})=\sigma^2\mathbf{V}$ where $\mathbf{V}$ is positive definite. We shall also suppose that we have *a priori* information, relating to the parameter vector $\boldsymbol{\beta}$ of the form

(10.3) $$\mathbf{R}\boldsymbol{\beta}=\mathbf{r},$$

where $\mathbf{R}$ is a $j\times k$ matrix such that

(10.4) $$\mathbf{r}\in\mathcal{M}(\mathbf{R}) \quad \text{and} \quad \text{Null}(\mathbf{R}')=\mathbf{0}.$$

These conditions together imply that the j equations of $\mathbf{R}\boldsymbol{\beta}=\mathbf{r}$ are consistent and that none of them is redundant. By combining (10.1) and (10.3), we obtain

$$\begin{bmatrix}\mathbf{g}\\ \mathbf{r}\end{bmatrix}=\begin{bmatrix}\mathbf{Z}\\ \mathbf{R}\end{bmatrix}\boldsymbol{\beta}+\begin{bmatrix}\boldsymbol{\eta}\\ \mathbf{0}\end{bmatrix}. \tag{10.5}$$

Our concern is to estimate functions of the parameter $\boldsymbol{\beta}$ including, if possible, the elements of $\boldsymbol{\beta}$ itself.

(10.6) A scalar parametric function $\mathbf{p}'\boldsymbol{\beta}$ of $\boldsymbol{\beta}$ is said to be estimable if and only if there exist vectors $\mathbf{k}$, $\boldsymbol{\lambda}$ such that $E(\mathbf{k}'\mathbf{g}+\boldsymbol{\lambda}'\mathbf{r})=\mathbf{p}'\boldsymbol{\beta}$.

Given this definition, we may prove that

(10.7) A parametric function $\mathbf{p}'\boldsymbol{\beta}$ is estimable if and only if $\mathbf{p}'=\mathbf{k}'\mathbf{Z}+\boldsymbol{\lambda}'\mathbf{R}=\mathbf{q}'\mathbf{X}$ for some $\mathbf{q}'=[\mathbf{k}',\boldsymbol{\lambda}']$; that is, if and only if $\mathbf{p}$ lies in the manifold $\mathcal{M}(\mathbf{Z}',\mathbf{R}')=\mathcal{M}(\mathbf{X}')$.

Proof. If $\mathbf{p}'\boldsymbol{\beta}$ is estimable, there exist, by definition, vectors $\mathbf{k}$, $\boldsymbol{\lambda}$ such that $E(\mathbf{k}'\mathbf{g}+\boldsymbol{\lambda}'\mathbf{r})=E[\mathbf{k}'(\mathbf{Z}\boldsymbol{\beta}+\boldsymbol{\eta})+\boldsymbol{\lambda}'\mathbf{R}\boldsymbol{\beta}]=(\mathbf{k}'\mathbf{Z}+\boldsymbol{\lambda}'\mathbf{R})\boldsymbol{\beta}=\mathbf{p}'\boldsymbol{\beta}$ for every $\boldsymbol{\beta}$. Hence $\mathbf{p}'=\mathbf{k}'\mathbf{Z}+\boldsymbol{\lambda}'\mathbf{R}=\mathbf{q}'\mathbf{X}$. Conversely, if $\mathbf{p}'=\mathbf{k}'\mathbf{Z}+\boldsymbol{\lambda}'\mathbf{R}=\mathbf{q}'\mathbf{X}$, then $\mathbf{p}'\boldsymbol{\beta}=\mathbf{k}'\mathbf{Z}\boldsymbol{\beta}+\boldsymbol{\lambda}'\mathbf{R}\boldsymbol{\beta}=E(\mathbf{k}'\mathbf{g}+\boldsymbol{\lambda}'\mathbf{r})$, and $\mathbf{p}'\boldsymbol{\beta}$ is an estimable function for all $\boldsymbol{\beta}$.

It follows that

$$\mathbf{p}'=[\mathbf{k}',\boldsymbol{\lambda}']\begin{bmatrix}\mathbf{Z}\\ \mathbf{R}\end{bmatrix}=\mathbf{q}'\mathbf{X} \tag{10.8}$$

for every $\mathbf{p}$ if and only if $\text{Null}(\mathbf{X})=\text{Null}([\mathbf{Z}',\mathbf{R}']')=0$, which is interpreted to mean that the rows of $\mathbf{Z}$ and $\mathbf{R}$ jointly span the space of all $\mathbf{p}'$. In such a case, every linear parametric function of $\boldsymbol{\beta}$ is estimable, including each element of $\boldsymbol{\beta}$ itself; and it follows that

(10.9) In the model $(\mathbf{g},\mathbf{Z}\boldsymbol{\beta}\,|\,\mathbf{R}\boldsymbol{\beta}=\mathbf{r},\sigma^2\mathbf{V})$ the vector $\boldsymbol{\beta}$ is uniquely estimable if and only if $\text{Null}\left[\begin{smallmatrix}\mathbf{Z}\\ \mathbf{R}\end{smallmatrix}\right]=\mathbf{0}$.

To find an efficient estimate of $\boldsymbol{\beta}$ in the model $(\mathbf{g},\mathbf{Z}\boldsymbol{\beta}\,|\,\mathbf{R}\boldsymbol{\beta}=\mathbf{r},\sigma^2\mathbf{I})$, we may adopt either of two methods.

In the first method we find the general solution to the consistent equations $\mathbf{R}\boldsymbol{\beta}=\mathbf{r}$ in the form

$$\boldsymbol{\beta}=\mathbf{R}^-\mathbf{r}+(\mathbf{I}-\mathbf{R}^-\mathbf{R})\mathbf{q}, \tag{10.10}$$

where $\mathbf{q}$ is arbitrary. We then use the information that is provided by the system (10.1) to impose statistical restrictions on $\boldsymbol{\beta}$. Thus, substituting (10.10) in (10.1), we get

$$\mathbf{g}-\mathbf{Z}\mathbf{R}^-\mathbf{r}=\mathbf{Z}(\mathbf{I}-\mathbf{R}^-\mathbf{R})\mathbf{q}+\boldsymbol{\eta}. \tag{10.11}$$

Then, defining $\mathbf{j} = \mathbf{g} - \mathbf{Z}\mathbf{R}^{-}\mathbf{r}$ and $\mathbf{W} = \mathbf{Z}(\mathbf{I} - \mathbf{R}^{-}\mathbf{R})$, we may write

$$\mathbf{j} = \mathbf{W}\mathbf{q} + \boldsymbol{\eta} \tag{10.12}$$

so as to obtain the pseudo-model $(\mathbf{j}, \mathbf{W}\mathbf{q}, \sigma^2\mathbf{I})$ which has the same statistical properties as the original model $(\mathbf{g}, \mathbf{Z}\boldsymbol{\beta}, \sigma^2\mathbf{I})$ but contains a reduced number of parameters. Assuming that Null($\mathbf{W}$) = 0, we may apply ordinary least squares to (10.12) to find a unique estimate $\hat{\mathbf{q}}$. Then, on substituting $\hat{\mathbf{q}}$ for $\mathbf{q}$ in (10.10), we get a unique estimate of $\boldsymbol{\beta}$ in the form of

$$\overset{*}{\boldsymbol{\beta}} = \mathbf{R}^{-}\mathbf{r} + (\mathbf{I} - \mathbf{R}^{-}\mathbf{R})\hat{\mathbf{q}}. \tag{10.13}$$

The second method is to evaluate the criterion

(10.14) Minimize

$$\|\mathbf{g} - \mathbf{Z}\boldsymbol{\beta}\|_{\mathbf{I}} = \sqrt{(\mathbf{g} - \mathbf{Z}\boldsymbol{\beta})'(\mathbf{g} - \mathbf{Z}\boldsymbol{\beta})}$$

Subject to

$$\mathbf{R}\boldsymbol{\beta} = \mathbf{r}.$$

For this we must minimize the Lagrangean $L = (\mathbf{g} - \mathbf{Z}\boldsymbol{\beta})'(\mathbf{g} - \mathbf{Z}\boldsymbol{\beta}) + 2\boldsymbol{\lambda}'(\mathbf{R}\boldsymbol{\beta} - \mathbf{r}) = \mathbf{g}'\mathbf{g} - 2\mathbf{g}'\mathbf{Z}\boldsymbol{\beta} + \boldsymbol{\beta}'\mathbf{Z}'\mathbf{Z}\boldsymbol{\beta} + 2\boldsymbol{\lambda}'(\mathbf{R}\boldsymbol{\beta} - \mathbf{r})$. By differentiating with respect to $\boldsymbol{\beta}$ and $\boldsymbol{\lambda}$ and setting the results to zero, we obtain the conditions

$$\begin{aligned} -\mathbf{Z}'\mathbf{g} + \mathbf{Z}'\mathbf{Z}\overset{*}{\boldsymbol{\beta}} + \mathbf{R}'\boldsymbol{\lambda} &= \mathbf{0}, \\ \mathbf{R}\overset{*}{\boldsymbol{\beta}} - \mathbf{r} &= \mathbf{0}, \end{aligned} \tag{10.15}$$

from which we may form the system

$$\begin{bmatrix} \mathbf{Z}'\mathbf{Z}, & \mathbf{R}' \\ \mathbf{R}, & \mathbf{0} \end{bmatrix} \begin{bmatrix} \overset{*}{\boldsymbol{\beta}} \\ \boldsymbol{\lambda} \end{bmatrix} = \begin{bmatrix} \mathbf{Z}'\mathbf{g} \\ \mathbf{r} \end{bmatrix}. \tag{10.16}$$

This may be solved for $\overset{*}{\boldsymbol{\beta}}$ which will acquire a unique value if and only if the partitioned matrix is non-singular.

We shall proceed to develop the second of these two methods under a variety of more detailed assumptions.

THE ASSUMPTION THAT Null($\mathbf{Z}$) = 0

If Null($\mathbf{Z}$) = 0, then, from the first equation of (10.15), we may find

$$\overset{*}{\boldsymbol{\beta}} = (\mathbf{Z}'\mathbf{Z})^{-1}\mathbf{Z}'\mathbf{g} - (\mathbf{Z}'\mathbf{Z})^{-1}\mathbf{R}'\boldsymbol{\lambda} = \hat{\boldsymbol{\beta}} - (\mathbf{Z}'\mathbf{Z})^{-1}\mathbf{R}'\boldsymbol{\lambda}, \tag{10.17}$$

where $\hat{\boldsymbol{\beta}} = (\mathbf{Z}'\mathbf{Z})^{-1}\mathbf{Z}'\mathbf{g}$ is the ordinary least-squares estimator of $\boldsymbol{\beta}$. Premultiplying (10.17) by $\mathbf{R}$ and using $\mathbf{R}\overset{*}{\boldsymbol{\beta}} = \mathbf{r}$ from the second equation of (10.15) gives $\mathbf{r} = \mathbf{R}\overset{*}{\boldsymbol{\beta}} = \mathbf{R}\hat{\boldsymbol{\beta}} - \mathbf{R}(\mathbf{Z}'\mathbf{Z})^{-1}\mathbf{R}'\boldsymbol{\lambda}$. Then, since Null($\mathbf{R}'$) = 0 implies

$\text{Null}[\mathbf{R}(\mathbf{Z}'\mathbf{Z})^{-1}\mathbf{R}'] = 0$, we can obtain $\boldsymbol{\lambda} = [\mathbf{R}(\mathbf{Z}'\mathbf{Z})^{-1}\mathbf{R}']^{-1}(\mathbf{R}\hat{\boldsymbol{\beta}} - \mathbf{r})$ uniquely. On substituting for $\boldsymbol{\lambda}$ in (10.17), we get

$$\text{(10.18)} \qquad \overset{*}{\boldsymbol{\beta}} = \hat{\boldsymbol{\beta}} - (\mathbf{Z}'\mathbf{Z})^{-1}\mathbf{R}'[\mathbf{R}(\mathbf{Z}'\mathbf{Z})^{-1}\mathbf{R}']^{-1}(\mathbf{R}\hat{\boldsymbol{\beta}} - \mathbf{r}).$$

We can see from (10.18) that the restricted estimator $\boldsymbol{\beta}$ differs from the unrestricted estimator $\hat{\boldsymbol{\beta}}$ by a linear function of the amount $\mathbf{R}\hat{\boldsymbol{\beta}} - \mathbf{r}$ by which $\hat{\boldsymbol{\beta}}$ fails to obey the restrictions. To further examine the relationship between $\overset{*}{\boldsymbol{\beta}}$ and $\hat{\boldsymbol{\beta}}$, let us take $\boldsymbol{\beta}$ from both sides of (10.18). Then, using $\mathbf{r} = \mathbf{R}\boldsymbol{\beta}$, we find that

$$\text{(10.19)} \qquad \begin{aligned} \overset{*}{\boldsymbol{\beta}} - \boldsymbol{\beta} &= \{\mathbf{I} - (\mathbf{Z}'\mathbf{Z})^{-1}\mathbf{R}'[\mathbf{R}(\mathbf{Z}'\mathbf{Z})^{-1}\mathbf{R}']^{-1}\mathbf{R}\}(\hat{\boldsymbol{\beta}} - \boldsymbol{\beta}) \\ &= \mathbf{P_N}(\hat{\boldsymbol{\beta}} - \boldsymbol{\beta}), \end{aligned}$$

where

(10.20) $\mathbf{P_N} = \mathbf{I} - (\mathbf{Z}'\mathbf{Z})^{-1}\mathbf{R}'[\mathbf{R}(\mathbf{Z}'\mathbf{Z})^{-1}\mathbf{R}']^{-1}\mathbf{R}$ is the $\mathbf{Z}'\mathbf{Z}$-symmetric idempotent projector on $\mathcal{N}(\mathbf{R})$ along $\mathcal{M}(\mathbf{R}^*) = \mathcal{M}[(\mathbf{Z}'\mathbf{Z})^{-1}\mathbf{R}']$, such that $\mathbf{P_N} = \mathbf{P_N^2}$, $\mathbf{Z}'\mathbf{Z}\mathbf{P_N} = \mathbf{P_N'}\mathbf{Z}'\mathbf{Z}\mathbf{P_N} = \mathbf{P_N'}\mathbf{Z}'\mathbf{Z}$ and $\mathbf{P_N}(\mathbf{Z}'\mathbf{Z})^{-1} = \mathbf{P_N}(\mathbf{Z}'\mathbf{Z})^{-1}\mathbf{P_N'} = (\mathbf{Z}'\mathbf{Z})^{-1}\mathbf{P_N'}$.

Thus $\overset{*}{\boldsymbol{\beta}} - \boldsymbol{\beta}$, which obeys the restriction $\mathbf{R}(\overset{*}{\boldsymbol{\beta}} - \boldsymbol{\beta}) = \mathbf{0}$, is obtained from $\hat{\boldsymbol{\beta}} - \boldsymbol{\beta}$ by projecting the latter on $\mathcal{N}(\mathbf{R})$ in such a way as to minimize the distance $\|(\hat{\boldsymbol{\beta}} - \boldsymbol{\beta}) - (\overset{*}{\boldsymbol{\beta}} - \boldsymbol{\beta})\|_{\mathbf{Z}'\mathbf{Z}} = \|\hat{\boldsymbol{\beta}} - \overset{*}{\boldsymbol{\beta}}\|_{\mathbf{Z}'\mathbf{Z}}$. The resulting $\mathbf{Z}'\mathbf{Z}$-orthogonal decomposition of $\hat{\boldsymbol{\beta}} - \boldsymbol{\beta}$ can be written as

$$\text{(10.21)} \qquad \begin{aligned} (\hat{\boldsymbol{\beta}} - \boldsymbol{\beta}) &= \mathbf{P_N}(\hat{\boldsymbol{\beta}} - \boldsymbol{\beta}) + (\mathbf{I} - \mathbf{P_N})(\hat{\boldsymbol{\beta}} - \boldsymbol{\beta}) \\ &= (\overset{*}{\boldsymbol{\beta}} - \boldsymbol{\beta}) + (\hat{\boldsymbol{\beta}} - \overset{*}{\boldsymbol{\beta}}). \end{aligned}$$

The procedure for finding the restricted least-squares estimate $\overset{*}{\boldsymbol{\beta}}$ consists, therefore, of (i) finding the ordinary least-squares estimate $\hat{\boldsymbol{\beta}}$ and then (ii) locating $\overset{*}{\boldsymbol{\beta}} \in \mathcal{A} = \{\boldsymbol{\beta}; \mathbf{R}\boldsymbol{\beta} = \mathbf{r}\}$ at a minimum $\mathbf{Z}'\mathbf{Z}$-distance from $\hat{\boldsymbol{\beta}} \notin \mathcal{A}$. By recognizing that the assumption $\mathbf{g} \sim (\mathbf{Z}\boldsymbol{\beta}, \sigma^2\mathbf{I})$ implies the condition $(\hat{\boldsymbol{\beta}} - \boldsymbol{\beta}) \sim (\mathbf{0}, \sigma^2(\mathbf{Z}'\mathbf{Z})^{-1})$, we can understand the appropriateness of using the $\mathbf{Z}'\mathbf{Z}$-metric in the second stage (ii) of the procedure.

Our present interpretation of the restricted estimator $\boldsymbol{\beta}$ is reaffirmed when we realize that we may also derive the expression for $\overset{*}{\boldsymbol{\beta}}$ in (10.18) by using the method of Lagrangean multipliers to evaluate the criterion

(10.22) Minimize

$$\|\hat{\boldsymbol{\beta}} - \overset{*}{\boldsymbol{\beta}}\|_{\mathbf{Z}'\mathbf{Z}} = \sqrt{(\hat{\boldsymbol{\beta}} - \overset{*}{\boldsymbol{\beta}})'\mathbf{Z}'\mathbf{Z}(\hat{\boldsymbol{\beta}} - \overset{*}{\boldsymbol{\beta}})} = \|\mathbf{Z}\hat{\boldsymbol{\beta}} - \mathbf{Z}\overset{*}{\boldsymbol{\beta}}\|_{\mathbf{I}}$$

Subject to

$$\mathbf{R}\overset{*}{\boldsymbol{\beta}} = \mathbf{r}.$$

The algebra of this derivation is provided in the section in Chapter 5 following (5.14) when we specify $\mathbf{Q}=\mathbf{Z}'\mathbf{Z}$.

An alternative interpretation of the estimator $\overset{*}{\boldsymbol{\beta}}$ can be obtained by resolving the procedure for finding $\mathbf{Z}\overset{*}{\boldsymbol{\beta}}\in\mathscr{B}=\{\mathbf{Z}\boldsymbol{\beta};\mathbf{R}\boldsymbol{\beta}=\mathbf{r}\}$ into two stages. The first stage (i) consists of finding $\mathbf{Z}\hat{\boldsymbol{\beta}}\in\mathcal{M}(\mathbf{Z})$ by minimizing $\|\mathbf{g}-\mathbf{Z}\hat{\boldsymbol{\beta}}\|_{\mathbf{I}}$. The second stage (ii) consists of finding $\mathbf{Z}\overset{*}{\boldsymbol{\beta}}\in\mathscr{B}\subset\mathcal{M}(\mathbf{Z})$ by minimizing $\|\mathbf{Z}\hat{\boldsymbol{\beta}}-\mathbf{Z}\overset{*}{\boldsymbol{\beta}}\|_{\mathbf{I}}$. Since $(\mathbf{g}-\mathbf{Z}\hat{\boldsymbol{\beta}})=(\mathbf{I}-\mathbf{P}_{\mathbf{Z}})\mathbf{g}\perp_{\mathbf{I}}\mathcal{M}(\mathbf{Z})$, and $(\overset{*}{\boldsymbol{\beta}}-\boldsymbol{\beta})\perp_{\mathbf{Z}'\mathbf{Z}}(\hat{\boldsymbol{\beta}}-\overset{*}{\boldsymbol{\beta}})$ or, equivalently, $(\mathbf{Z}\overset{*}{\boldsymbol{\beta}}-\mathbf{Z}\boldsymbol{\beta})\perp_{\mathbf{I}}(\mathbf{Z}\hat{\boldsymbol{\beta}}-\mathbf{Z}\overset{*}{\boldsymbol{\beta}})$, it follows that

$$(10.23)\qquad (\mathbf{g}-\mathbf{Z}\boldsymbol{\beta})=(\mathbf{g}-\mathbf{Z}\hat{\boldsymbol{\beta}})+(\mathbf{Z}\hat{\boldsymbol{\beta}}-\mathbf{Z}\overset{*}{\boldsymbol{\beta}})+(\mathbf{Z}\overset{*}{\boldsymbol{\beta}}-\mathbf{Z}\boldsymbol{\beta})$$

is an orthogonal decomposition of $(\mathbf{g}-\mathbf{Z}\boldsymbol{\beta})=\boldsymbol{\eta}\sim(\mathbf{0},\sigma^2\mathbf{I})$ in respect of the ordinary inner product.

To derive the dispersion matrix of the restricted estimator $\overset{*}{\boldsymbol{\beta}}$, we use $D(\overset{*}{\boldsymbol{\beta}})=E[(\overset{*}{\boldsymbol{\beta}}-\boldsymbol{\beta})(\overset{*}{\boldsymbol{\beta}}-\boldsymbol{\beta})']=E[\mathbf{P}_{\mathbf{N}}(\hat{\boldsymbol{\beta}}-\boldsymbol{\beta})(\hat{\boldsymbol{\beta}}-\boldsymbol{\beta})'\mathbf{P}_{\mathbf{N}}']=\mathbf{P}_{\mathbf{N}}E[(\hat{\boldsymbol{\beta}}-\boldsymbol{\beta})(\hat{\boldsymbol{\beta}}-\boldsymbol{\beta})']\mathbf{P}_{\mathbf{N}}'$ $=\mathbf{P}_{\mathbf{N}}D(\hat{\boldsymbol{\beta}})\mathbf{P}_{\mathbf{N}}'$. Then, since $D(\hat{\boldsymbol{\beta}})=\sigma^2(\mathbf{Z}'\mathbf{Z})^{-1}$, we obtain $D(\overset{*}{\boldsymbol{\beta}})=$ $\sigma^2\mathbf{P}_{\mathbf{N}}(\mathbf{Z}'\mathbf{Z})^{-1}\mathbf{P}_{\mathbf{N}}'=\sigma^2\mathbf{P}_{\mathbf{N}}(\mathbf{Z}'\mathbf{Z})^{-1}$. Thus

(10.24) If $\overset{*}{\boldsymbol{\beta}}$ is the restricted least-squares estimator of $\boldsymbol{\beta}$ in the model $(\mathbf{g},\mathbf{Z}\boldsymbol{\beta}\,|\,\mathbf{R}\boldsymbol{\beta}=\mathbf{r},\sigma^2\mathbf{I})$ such that $\|\mathbf{g}-\mathbf{Z}\overset{*}{\boldsymbol{\beta}}\|_{\mathbf{I}}$ is minimized, then $D(\overset{*}{\boldsymbol{\beta}})=\sigma^2\{(\mathbf{Z}'\mathbf{Z})^{-1}-(\mathbf{Z}'\mathbf{Z})^{-1}\mathbf{R}'[\mathbf{R}(\mathbf{Z}'\mathbf{Z})^{-1}\mathbf{R}']^{-1}\mathbf{R}(\mathbf{Z}'\mathbf{Z})^{-1}\}$.

We may write $D(\overset{*}{\boldsymbol{\beta}})=\sigma^2(\mathbf{Z}'\mathbf{Z})^{-1}-\mathbf{Q}=D(\hat{\boldsymbol{\beta}})-\mathbf{Q}$ where $\mathbf{Q}$ is a positive-definite matrix. Thus, for any $\mathbf{p}$, we have $V(\mathbf{p}'\overset{*}{\boldsymbol{\beta}})=\mathbf{p}'D(\overset{*}{\boldsymbol{\beta}})\mathbf{p}\leqslant\mathbf{p}'D(\hat{\boldsymbol{\beta}})\mathbf{p}=$ $V(\mathbf{p}'\hat{\boldsymbol{\beta}})$. This shows that the variance of a restricted estimate of a parametric function $\mathbf{p}'\boldsymbol{\beta}$ cannot exceed the variance of an unrestricted estimate.

Estimating σ^2

We may use the residual vector $(\mathbf{g}-\mathbf{Z}\overset{*}{\boldsymbol{\beta}})$ from the restricted regression in order to find an efficient estimate of σ^2. It follows from (10.23), by consolidating the first two terms on the RHS, that $(\mathbf{g}-\mathbf{Z}\boldsymbol{\beta})=$ $(\mathbf{g}-\mathbf{Z}\overset{*}{\boldsymbol{\beta}})+(\mathbf{Z}\overset{*}{\boldsymbol{\beta}}-\mathbf{Z}\boldsymbol{\beta})$ is an orthogonal decomposition in terms of the ordinary inner product. Therefore $(\mathbf{g}-\mathbf{Z}\boldsymbol{\beta})'(\mathbf{g}-\mathbf{Z}\boldsymbol{\beta})=(\mathbf{g}-\mathbf{Z}\overset{*}{\boldsymbol{\beta}})'(\mathbf{g}-\mathbf{Z}\overset{*}{\boldsymbol{\beta}})+$ $(\mathbf{Z}\overset{*}{\boldsymbol{\beta}}-\mathbf{Z}\boldsymbol{\beta})'(\mathbf{Z}\overset{*}{\boldsymbol{\beta}}-\mathbf{Z}\boldsymbol{\beta})$. On taking expectations and rearranging, we get

$$(10.25)\qquad \begin{aligned}&E[(\mathbf{g}-\mathbf{Z}\overset{*}{\boldsymbol{\beta}})'(\mathbf{g}-\mathbf{Z}\overset{*}{\boldsymbol{\beta}})]\\&=E[(\mathbf{g}-\mathbf{Z}\boldsymbol{\beta})'(\mathbf{g}-\mathbf{Z}\boldsymbol{\beta})]-E[(\mathbf{Z}\overset{*}{\boldsymbol{\beta}}-\mathbf{Z}\boldsymbol{\beta})'(\mathbf{Z}\overset{*}{\boldsymbol{\beta}}-\mathbf{Z}\boldsymbol{\beta})].\end{aligned}$$

To evaluate $E[(\mathbf{g}-\mathbf{Z}\overset{*}{\boldsymbol{\beta}})'(\mathbf{g}-\mathbf{Z}\overset{*}{\boldsymbol{\beta}})]$, we must evaluate the terms on the RHS of (10.25). First, from the assumption that $(\mathbf{g}-\mathbf{Z}\boldsymbol{\beta})=\boldsymbol{\eta}\sim(\mathbf{0},\sigma^2\mathbf{I})$, we immediately deduce that $E[(\mathbf{g}-\mathbf{Z}\boldsymbol{\beta})'(\mathbf{g}-\mathbf{Z}\boldsymbol{\beta})]=\sigma^2 T$. Next, to find $E[(\mathbf{Z}\overset{*}{\boldsymbol{\beta}}-\mathbf{Z}\boldsymbol{\beta})'(\mathbf{Z}\overset{*}{\boldsymbol{\beta}}-\mathbf{Z}\boldsymbol{\beta})]$, we take the identity $\mathbf{Z}(\overset{*}{\boldsymbol{\beta}}-\boldsymbol{\beta})=\mathbf{Z}\mathbf{P}_\mathbf{N}(\hat{\boldsymbol{\beta}}-\boldsymbol{\beta})=\mathbf{Z}\mathbf{P}_\mathbf{N}[(\mathbf{Z}'\mathbf{Z})^{-1}\mathbf{Z}'(\mathbf{Z}\boldsymbol{\beta}+\boldsymbol{\eta})-\boldsymbol{\beta}]=\mathbf{Z}\mathbf{P}_\mathbf{N}(\mathbf{Z}'\mathbf{Z})^{-1}\mathbf{Z}'\boldsymbol{\eta}$. Then, from the properties of $\mathbf{P}_\mathbf{N}$ given in (10.20), we get $(\mathbf{Z}\overset{*}{\boldsymbol{\beta}}-\mathbf{Z}\boldsymbol{\beta})'(\mathbf{Z}\overset{*}{\boldsymbol{\beta}}-\mathbf{Z}\boldsymbol{\beta})=\boldsymbol{\eta}'\mathbf{Z}(\mathbf{Z}'\mathbf{Z})^{-1}\mathbf{P}_\mathbf{N}'\mathbf{Z}'\mathbf{Z}\mathbf{P}_\mathbf{N}(\mathbf{Z}'\mathbf{Z})^{-1}\mathbf{Z}'\boldsymbol{\eta}=\boldsymbol{\eta}'\mathbf{Z}\mathbf{P}_\mathbf{N}(\mathbf{Z}'\mathbf{Z})^{-1}\mathbf{Z}'\boldsymbol{\eta}$. To find the expectation of this, we use the fact that the trace of a scalar is the value of the scalar itself, and we thereby obtain

$$\begin{aligned}E[(\mathbf{Z}\overset{*}{\boldsymbol{\beta}}-\mathbf{Z}\boldsymbol{\beta})'(\mathbf{Z}\overset{*}{\boldsymbol{\beta}}-\mathbf{Z}\boldsymbol{\beta})]&=E\{\text{Trace}[\boldsymbol{\eta}'\mathbf{Z}\mathbf{P}_\mathbf{N}(\mathbf{Z}'\mathbf{Z})^{-1}\mathbf{Z}'\boldsymbol{\eta}]\}\\&=\text{Trace}[E(\boldsymbol{\eta}\boldsymbol{\eta}')\mathbf{Z}\mathbf{P}_\mathbf{N}(\mathbf{Z}'\mathbf{Z})^{-1}\mathbf{Z}']=\sigma^2\,\text{Trace}[\mathbf{Z}\mathbf{P}_\mathbf{N}(\mathbf{Z}'\mathbf{Z})^{-1}\mathbf{Z}']\\&=\sigma^2\,\text{Trace}(\mathbf{P}_\mathbf{N}).\end{aligned}$$

But

$$\begin{aligned}&\text{Trace}(\mathbf{P}_\mathbf{N})=\text{Trace}(\mathbf{I}_k)-\text{Trace}\{(\mathbf{Z}'\mathbf{Z})^{-1}\mathbf{R}'[\mathbf{R}(\mathbf{Z}'\mathbf{Z})^{-1}\mathbf{R}']^{-1}\mathbf{R}\}\\&\text{Trace}(\mathbf{I}_k)-\text{Trace}\{\mathbf{R}(\mathbf{Z}'\mathbf{Z})^{-1}\mathbf{R}'[\mathbf{R}(\mathbf{Z}'\mathbf{Z})^{-1}\mathbf{R}']^{-1}\}=k-j.\end{aligned}$$

Therefore $E[(\mathbf{Z}\overset{*}{\boldsymbol{\beta}}-\mathbf{Z}\boldsymbol{\beta})'(\mathbf{Z}\overset{*}{\boldsymbol{\beta}}-\mathbf{Z}\boldsymbol{\beta})]=\sigma^2(k-j)$. Substituting these two results in (10.25) above, we find that $E[(\mathbf{g}-\mathbf{Z}\overset{*}{\boldsymbol{\beta}})'(\mathbf{g}-\mathbf{Z}\overset{*}{\boldsymbol{\beta}})]=\sigma^2(T+j-k)$. It follows that

$$\overset{*}{\sigma}{}^2=\frac{(\mathbf{g}-\mathbf{Z}\overset{*}{\boldsymbol{\beta}})'(\mathbf{g}-\mathbf{Z}\overset{*}{\boldsymbol{\beta}})}{T+j-k} \tag{10.26}$$

provides an unbiased estimator of σ^2. It can also be shown that the variance of $\overset{*}{\sigma}{}^2$ does not exceed the variance of the estimator $\hat{\sigma}^2=(\mathbf{g}-\mathbf{Z}\hat{\boldsymbol{\beta}})'(\mathbf{g}-\mathbf{Z}\hat{\boldsymbol{\beta}})/(T-k)$ which is based upon the residual vector from the ordinary least-squares regression. The number $k-j$ is both the dimension of the affine subspace $\mathscr{A}=\{\boldsymbol{\beta};\mathbf{R}\boldsymbol{\beta}=\mathbf{r}\}$ and the dimension of the affine subspace $\mathscr{B}=\mathbf{Z}\mathscr{A}=\{\mathbf{Z}\boldsymbol{\beta};\mathbf{R}\boldsymbol{\beta}=\mathbf{r}\}$ when $\text{Null}(\mathbf{Z})=0$. The vector $\overset{*}{\mathbf{g}}=\mathbf{Z}\overset{*}{\boldsymbol{\beta}}$ is contained in $\mathscr{B}$. Thus $T-(k-j)=T+j-k$ in the denominator of (10.26) is clearly the number of degrees of freedom of the vector $(\mathbf{g}-\overset{*}{\mathbf{g}})=(\mathbf{g}-\mathbf{Z}\overset{*}{\boldsymbol{\beta}})$. We might also recall that $T+j$ is the total number of rows in the matrix $\mathbf{X}$ comprising the matrix $\mathbf{Z}$ of T rows, and the matrix $\mathbf{R}$ of j rows.

Testing linear restrictions

We may test the validity of the restrictions $\mathbf{R}\boldsymbol{\beta}=\mathbf{r}$ in the model $\mathbf{g}\sim N(\mathbf{Z}\boldsymbol{\beta},\sigma^2\mathbf{I})$ by using the ordinary least-squares estimate $\hat{\boldsymbol{\beta}}$ and without computing the restricted estimate $\overset{*}{\boldsymbol{\beta}}$. The distribution of the ordinary least-squares estimator is given by $\hat{\boldsymbol{\beta}} \sim N(\boldsymbol{\beta}, \sigma^2(\mathbf{Z}'\mathbf{Z})^{-1})$. Thus, under the hypothesis that $\mathbf{R}\boldsymbol{\beta} = \mathbf{r}$, it follows that $\mathbf{R}\hat{\boldsymbol{\beta}} \sim N(\mathbf{R}\boldsymbol{\beta} = \mathbf{r}, \sigma^2\mathbf{R}(\mathbf{Z}'\mathbf{Z})^{-1}\mathbf{R}')$, whence $(\mathbf{R}\hat{\boldsymbol{\beta}} - \mathbf{r}) \sim N(\mathbf{0}, \sigma^2\mathbf{R}(\mathbf{Z}'\mathbf{Z})^{-1}\mathbf{R}')$. Therefore

$$(10.27) \qquad \sigma^{-2}(\mathbf{R}\hat{\boldsymbol{\beta}} - \mathbf{r})'[\mathbf{R}(\mathbf{Z}'\mathbf{Z})^{-1}\mathbf{R}']^{-1}(\mathbf{R}\hat{\boldsymbol{\beta}} - \mathbf{r}) \sim \chi^2(j),$$

where $j = \text{Rank}[\mathbf{R}(\mathbf{Z}'\mathbf{Z})^{-1}\mathbf{R}'] = \text{Rank}(\mathbf{R})$. If σ^2 is unknown, we may replace it in (10.27) by the estimator $\hat{\sigma}^2 = \mathbf{g}'(\mathbf{I} - \mathbf{P_Z})\mathbf{g}/(T-k) = (\mathbf{g} - \mathbf{Z}\hat{\boldsymbol{\beta}})'(\mathbf{g} - \mathbf{Z}\hat{\boldsymbol{\beta}})/(T-k) \sim [\sigma^2/(T-k)]\chi^2(T-k)$. Since $\hat{\sigma}^2$ is statistically independent of $\mathbf{Z}\hat{\boldsymbol{\beta}} = \mathbf{P_Z g}$, it must also be independent of $(\mathbf{R}\hat{\boldsymbol{\beta}} - \mathbf{r})$. Thus we deduce that

(10.28) Under the hypothesis that $\mathbf{g} \sim N(\mathbf{Z}\boldsymbol{\beta} \mid \mathbf{R}\boldsymbol{\beta} = \mathbf{r}, \sigma^2\mathbf{I})$, we have

$$\left\{\frac{(\mathbf{R}\hat{\boldsymbol{\beta}} - \mathbf{r})'[\mathbf{R}(\mathbf{Z}'\mathbf{Z})^{-1}\mathbf{R}']^{-1}(\mathbf{R}\hat{\boldsymbol{\beta}} - \mathbf{r})}{j} \Big/ \frac{(\mathbf{y} - \mathbf{Z}\hat{\boldsymbol{\beta}})'(\mathbf{y} - \mathbf{Z}\hat{\boldsymbol{\beta}})}{T-k}\right\}$$
$$\sim F(j, T-k)$$

where $\hat{\boldsymbol{\beta}}$ is the ordinary least-squares estimator of $\boldsymbol{\beta}$, $\mathbf{R}$ is $j \times k$ with $\text{Rank}(\mathbf{R}) = j$ and $\mathbf{Z}$ is $T \times k$ with $\text{Rank}(\mathbf{Z}) = k$.

This statistic provides the means for testing the restrictions $\mathbf{R}\boldsymbol{\beta} = \mathbf{r}$.

It is interesting to note that, with the use of (10.18), the expression in (10.27) may be rewritten as $\sigma^{-2}(\mathbf{R}\hat{\boldsymbol{\beta}} - \mathbf{r})'[\mathbf{R}(\mathbf{Z}'\mathbf{Z})^{-1}\mathbf{R}']^{-1}(\mathbf{R}\hat{\boldsymbol{\beta}} - \mathbf{r}) = \sigma^{-2}(\mathbf{Z}\hat{\boldsymbol{\beta}} - \mathbf{Z}\overset{*}{\boldsymbol{\beta}})'(\mathbf{Z}\hat{\boldsymbol{\beta}} - \mathbf{Z}\overset{*}{\boldsymbol{\beta}}) = \sigma^{-2}\|\mathbf{Z}\hat{\boldsymbol{\beta}} - \mathbf{Z}\overset{*}{\boldsymbol{\beta}}\|_{\mathbf{I}}$. Thus we can interpret (10.27), and (10.28) likewise, as a measure of the proximity of the constrained and unconstrained estimators of $\boldsymbol{\mu} = \mathbf{Z}\boldsymbol{\beta}$.

Let us denote the assumption that $\mathbf{g} \sim N(\mathbf{Z}\boldsymbol{\beta}, \sigma^2\mathbf{I})$ by G, and let us consider a situation where, in addition to the primary hypothesis $H_1 : \mathbf{R}_1\boldsymbol{\beta} = \mathbf{r}_1$, we have a secondary hypothesis $H_2 : \mathbf{R}_2\boldsymbol{\beta} = \mathbf{r}_2$. We shall presume that, although the two hypotheses are independent in the sense that the equations

$$(10.29) \qquad \mathbf{R}\boldsymbol{\beta} = \begin{bmatrix} \mathbf{R}_1 \\ \mathbf{R}_2 \end{bmatrix} \boldsymbol{\beta} = \begin{bmatrix} \mathbf{r}_1 \\ \mathbf{r}_2 \end{bmatrix} = \mathbf{r}$$

are mutually independent, the validity of the secondary hypothesis is conditional upon the validity of the primary hypothesis. Denoting the likelihood function of the model $(\mathbf{g}, \mathbf{Z}\boldsymbol{\beta} \mid \mathbf{R}\boldsymbol{\beta} = \mathbf{r}, \sigma^2\mathbf{I})$ by $L(H_1 \cap H_2 \mid G)$, we may write

$$(10.30) \qquad L(H_1 \cap H_2 \mid G) = L(H_1 \cap H_2 \mid H_1 \cap G)L(H_1 \mid G).$$

This decomposition suggests the following sequence of tests:

(i) The test of $\mathbf{R}_1\boldsymbol{\beta} = \mathbf{r}_1$ given that $\mathbf{g} \sim N(\mathbf{Z}\boldsymbol{\beta}, \sigma^2\mathbf{I})$; that is to say, the test of H_1 given G,

(ii) The test of $\mathbf{R}_2\boldsymbol{\beta} = \mathbf{r}_2$ given that $\mathbf{g} \sim N(\mathbf{Z}\boldsymbol{\beta} \mid \mathbf{R}_1\boldsymbol{\beta} = \mathbf{r}_1, \sigma^2\mathbf{I})$; that it to say, the test of H_2 given H_1 and G,

(iii) The test of $\mathbf{R\beta}=\mathbf{r}$ given that $\mathbf{g}\sim N(\mathbf{Z\beta}, \sigma^2\mathbf{I})$; that is to say, the test of H_1 and H_2 given G.

For the first test, we may use an F statistic in the form of the statistic of (10.28), albeit with $\mathbf{R}_1$ in place of $\mathbf{R}$. We will accept the hypothesis H_1 if the value of the statistic is below the level of significance; and this is equivalent to accepting the hypothesis if the value of the likelihood ratio $L(H_1 \mid G)= L(H_1 \cap G)/L(G)$ is not significantly less than unity.

If the hypothesis H_1 is accepted in the first test, then we may proceed to the second test. For this we require to estimate the parameter $\boldsymbol{\beta}$ subject to the restrictions $\mathbf{R}_1\boldsymbol{\beta}=\mathbf{r}_1$. Denoting the restricted estimator by $\overset{*}{\boldsymbol{\beta}}$ and its dispersion by $D(\overset{*}{\boldsymbol{\beta}})$, we deduce that

(10.31) Under the hypothesis that $\mathbf{R}_2\boldsymbol{\beta}=\mathbf{r}_2$ in the model $\mathbf{g}\sim N(\mathbf{Z\beta} \mid \mathbf{R}_1\boldsymbol{\beta}=\mathbf{r}_1, \sigma^2\mathbf{I})$, we have

$$\left\{\frac{(\mathbf{R}_2\overset{*}{\boldsymbol{\beta}}-\mathbf{r}_2)'[\mathbf{R}_2D(\overset{*}{\boldsymbol{\beta}})\mathbf{R}_2']^{-1}(\mathbf{R}_2\overset{*}{\boldsymbol{\beta}}-\mathbf{r})}{q}\bigg/\frac{(\mathbf{g}-\mathbf{Z}\overset{*}{\boldsymbol{\beta}})'(\mathbf{g}-\mathbf{Z}\overset{*}{\boldsymbol{\beta}})}{T+j-k}\right\}$$
$$\sim F(q, T+j-k),$$

where $\overset{*}{\boldsymbol{\beta}}$ is the minimum-distance estimator of $\boldsymbol{\beta}$ subject to $\mathbf{R}_1\boldsymbol{\beta}=\mathbf{r}_1$, $\mathbf{R}_1$ is $j\times k$ with $\text{Rank}(\mathbf{R}_1)=j$, $\mathbf{R}_2$ is $q\times k$ with $\text{Rank}(\mathbf{R}_2)=q$ and $\mathbf{Z}$ is $T\times k$ with $\text{Rank}(\mathbf{Z})=k$.

We will accept the hypothesis H_2 if the value of the F statistic in (10.31) is below the significance level. The value of the likelihood ratio $L(H_1\cap H_2 \mid H_1\cap G)=L(H_1\cap H_2\cap G)/L(H_1\cap G)$ will, in that case, be close to unity.

To check the results of our two tests, we might perform the third test. For this, we would use the F statistic of (10.28) wherein the matrix $\mathbf{R}$ would have the form specified in (10.29). In this test we are facing the possibility that the joint hypothesis of H_1 and H_2 given G will be rejected in spite of the acceptance of H_1 and H_2 in the first and second tests respectively. This will not happen, however, if both of the likelihood-ratio statistics on the RHS of (10.30) have values sufficiently close to unity to ensure that their product, in its turn, is not significantly different from unity.

THE ASSUMPTION THAT $\text{Null}(\mathbf{X})=0$; $\mathbf{X}'=[\mathbf{Z}', \mathbf{R}']$

For the unique estimability of $\boldsymbol{\beta}$ in the model $(\mathbf{g}, \mathbf{Z\beta}, \sigma^2\mathbf{I})$, the condition $\text{Null}(\mathbf{Z})=0$ is necessary and sufficient. However, for the model $(\mathbf{g}, \mathbf{Z\beta} \mid \mathbf{R\beta}=\mathbf{r}, \sigma^2\mathbf{I})$, comprising the *a priori* information $\mathbf{R\beta}=\mathbf{r}$, the necessary and sufficient condition for the unique estimability of $\boldsymbol{\beta}$ is, according to (10.19), $\text{Null}([\mathbf{Z}', \mathbf{R}']')=0$. This condition is also necessary and sufficient for the non-singularity of the partitioned matrix in equation (10.16) which must be solved in order to obtain the restricted estimate $\overset{*}{\boldsymbol{\beta}}$. That is to say,

(10.32) $$\begin{bmatrix} \mathbf{Z}'\mathbf{Z}, & \mathbf{R}' \\ \mathbf{R}, & \mathbf{0} \end{bmatrix} \text{ is non-singular if and only if}$$

$$\text{Null}(\mathbf{R}')=0 \quad \text{and} \quad \text{Null}\begin{bmatrix} \mathbf{Z} \\ \mathbf{R} \end{bmatrix}=0.$$

Proof. Since $\mathcal{N}(\mathbf{Z}'\mathbf{Z})=\mathcal{N}(\mathbf{Z})$, it is easy to see that, if the matrix is non-singular, then $\text{Null}\left[\begin{smallmatrix}\mathbf{Z}\\ \mathbf{R}\end{smallmatrix}\right]=0$ and $\text{Null}(\mathbf{R}')=0$.

For the converse, let $\text{Null}\left[\begin{smallmatrix}\mathbf{Z}\\ \mathbf{R}\end{smallmatrix}\right]=0$ and $\text{Null}(\mathbf{R}')=0$, and let $\mathbf{a}$ and $\mathbf{b}$ be such that

$$\text{(i)}\ \mathbf{Z}'\mathbf{Z}\mathbf{a}+\mathbf{R}'\mathbf{b}=\mathbf{0},$$
$$\text{(ii)}\ \mathbf{R}\mathbf{a}=\mathbf{0}.$$

Premultiplying (i) by $\mathbf{a}'$ gives $\mathbf{a}'\mathbf{Z}'\mathbf{Z}\mathbf{a}-\mathbf{a}'\mathbf{R}'\mathbf{b}=\mathbf{0}$, which implies $\mathbf{a}'\mathbf{Z}'\mathbf{Z}\mathbf{a}=\mathbf{0}$ and $\mathbf{Z}\mathbf{a}=\mathbf{0}$, since $\mathbf{a}'\mathbf{R}'\mathbf{b}=\mathbf{0}$ by (ii). Next, with $\mathbf{Z}'\mathbf{Z}\mathbf{a}=\mathbf{0}$ in (i), we have $\mathbf{R}'\mathbf{b}=\mathbf{0}$. Thus $\left[\begin{smallmatrix}\mathbf{Z}\\ \mathbf{R}\end{smallmatrix}\right]\mathbf{a}=\mathbf{0}$ and $\mathbf{R}'\mathbf{b}=\mathbf{0}$, and hence $\mathbf{a}, \mathbf{b}=\mathbf{0}$. It follows that the square matrix $\left[\begin{smallmatrix}\mathbf{Z}'\mathbf{Z}, & \mathbf{R}'\\ \mathbf{R} & \mathbf{0}\end{smallmatrix}\right]$ must be non-singular, since the only vector in its null space is the zero vector $\mathbf{0}=[\mathbf{a}', \mathbf{b}']'$.

On taking this result to the equation (10.16), we see that, when $\text{Null}([\mathbf{Z}', \mathbf{R}']')=0$, we can obtain a unique estimate of $\boldsymbol{\beta}$ from

$$\begin{bmatrix} \overset{*}{\boldsymbol{\beta}} \\ \boldsymbol{\lambda} \end{bmatrix}=\begin{bmatrix} \mathbf{Z}'\mathbf{Z}, & \mathbf{R}' \\ \mathbf{R}, & \mathbf{0} \end{bmatrix}^{-1}\begin{bmatrix} \mathbf{Z}'\mathbf{g} \\ \mathbf{r} \end{bmatrix}=\begin{bmatrix} \mathbf{C}_1, & \mathbf{C}_2 \\ \mathbf{C}_2', & \mathbf{C}_3 \end{bmatrix}\begin{bmatrix} \mathbf{Z}'\mathbf{g} \\ \mathbf{r} \end{bmatrix}$$

in the form of

(10.33) $$\overset{*}{\boldsymbol{\beta}}=\mathbf{C}_1\mathbf{Z}'\mathbf{g}+\mathbf{C}_2\mathbf{r}.$$

To find explicit forms for the submatrices $\mathbf{C}_1$, $\mathbf{C}_2$, and $\mathbf{C}_3$, let us consider the identity

$$\begin{bmatrix} \mathbf{Z}'\mathbf{Z}, & \mathbf{R}' \\ \mathbf{R}, & \mathbf{0} \end{bmatrix}\begin{bmatrix} \mathbf{C}_1, & \mathbf{C}_2 \\ \mathbf{C}_2', & \mathbf{C}_3 \end{bmatrix}=\begin{bmatrix} \mathbf{I}, & \mathbf{0} \\ \mathbf{0}, & \mathbf{I} \end{bmatrix}.$$

This gives us

(10.34) $$\text{(i)}\ \mathbf{Z}'\mathbf{Z}\mathbf{C}_1+\mathbf{R}'\mathbf{C}_2'=\mathbf{I}, \qquad \text{(ii)}\ \mathbf{Z}'\mathbf{Z}\mathbf{C}_2+\mathbf{R}'\mathbf{C}_3=\mathbf{0},$$
$$\text{(iii)}\ \mathbf{R}\mathbf{C}_1=\mathbf{0}, \qquad \text{(iv)}\ \mathbf{R}\mathbf{C}_2=\mathbf{I}.$$

Adding $\mathbf{R}'\mathbf{R}\mathbf{C}_1=\mathbf{0}$ to both sides of (i), we get $(\mathbf{R}'\mathbf{R}+\mathbf{Z}'\mathbf{Z})\mathbf{C}_1+\mathbf{R}'\mathbf{C}_2'=\mathbf{I}$, whence

(10.35) $$\mathbf{C}_1=(\mathbf{R}'\mathbf{R}+\mathbf{Z}'\mathbf{Z})^{-1}-(\mathbf{R}'\mathbf{R}+\mathbf{Z}'\mathbf{Z})^{-1}\mathbf{R}'\mathbf{C}_2'.$$

Premultiplying this by $\mathbf{R}$ and using (iii), we get $\mathbf{RC}_1 = \mathbf{0} = \mathbf{R}(\mathbf{R'R}+\mathbf{Z'Z})^{-1} - \mathbf{R}(\mathbf{R'R}+\mathbf{Z'Z})^{-1}\mathbf{R'C}_2'$, from which

$$\text{(10.36)} \qquad \mathbf{C}_2 = (\mathbf{R'R}+\mathbf{Z'Z})^{-1}\mathbf{R'}[\mathbf{R}(\mathbf{R'R}+\mathbf{Z'Z})^{-1}\mathbf{R'}]^{-1}.$$

By substituting this in (10.35), we find

$$\text{(10.37)} \qquad \mathbf{C}_1 = \{\mathbf{I} - (\mathbf{R'R}+\mathbf{Z'Z})^{-1}\mathbf{R'}[\mathbf{R}(\mathbf{R'R}+\mathbf{Z'Z})^{-1}\mathbf{R'}]^{-1}\mathbf{R}\} \times (\mathbf{R'R}+\mathbf{Z'Z})^{-1}.$$

To find $\mathbf{C}_3$, we add $\mathbf{R'RC}_2 = \mathbf{R'}$ to both sides of (ii) to give $(\mathbf{R'R}+\mathbf{Z'Z})\mathbf{C}_2 + \mathbf{R'C}_3 = \mathbf{R'}$. Then $\mathbf{R'C}_3 = \mathbf{R'} - (\mathbf{R'R}+\mathbf{Z'Z})\mathbf{C}_2 = \mathbf{R'}\{\mathbf{I} - [\mathbf{R}(\mathbf{R'R}+\mathbf{Z'Z})^{-1}\mathbf{R'}]^{-1}\}$. But, since $\text{Null}(\mathbf{R'}) = 0$, by assumption, this gives

$$\text{(10.38)} \qquad \mathbf{C}_3 = \mathbf{I} - [\mathbf{R}(\mathbf{R'R}+\mathbf{Z'Z})^{-1}\mathbf{R'}]^{-1}.$$

To find an explicit form of $\overset{*}{\boldsymbol{\beta}}$, we may use $\mathbf{RC}_1 = \mathbf{RC}_1' = \mathbf{0}$ from (iii) to write $\overset{*}{\boldsymbol{\beta}} = \mathbf{C}_1\mathbf{Z'g} + \mathbf{C}_2\mathbf{r} = \mathbf{C}_1(\mathbf{Z'g}+\mathbf{R'r}) + \mathbf{C}_2\mathbf{r}$. On substituting for $\mathbf{C}_1$ and $\mathbf{C}_2$ in the last expression, we may obtain, after some manipulation,

$$\text{(10.39)} \qquad \overset{*}{\boldsymbol{\beta}} = \tilde{\boldsymbol{\beta}} - (\mathbf{Z'Z}+\mathbf{R'R})^{-1}\mathbf{R'}[\mathbf{R}(\mathbf{Z'Z}+\mathbf{R'R})^{-1}\mathbf{R'}]^{-1}(\mathbf{R}\tilde{\boldsymbol{\beta}} - \mathbf{r}),$$

$$\tilde{\boldsymbol{\beta}} = (\mathbf{Z'Z}+\mathbf{R'R})^{-1}(\mathbf{Z'g}+\mathbf{R'r}).$$

Using $\mathbf{X'} = [\mathbf{Z'}, \mathbf{R'}]$ and $\mathbf{y'} = [\mathbf{g'}, \mathbf{r'}]$, we may write these more compactly as

$$\text{(10.40)} \qquad \overset{*}{\boldsymbol{\beta}} = \tilde{\boldsymbol{\beta}} - (\mathbf{X'X})^{-1}\mathbf{R'}[\mathbf{R}(\mathbf{X'X})^{-1}\mathbf{R'}]^{-1}(\mathbf{R}\tilde{\boldsymbol{\beta}} - \mathbf{r}),$$

$$\tilde{\boldsymbol{\beta}} = (\mathbf{X'X})^{-1}\mathbf{X'y}.$$

We have now obtained in (10.40) a form of the estimator which is identical to that of the restricted estimator in the case where $\text{Null}(\mathbf{Z}) = 0$, given in (10.18). The difference is that the estimator of (10.18) pertains to the model $(\mathbf{g}, \mathbf{Z}\boldsymbol{\beta} \mid \mathbf{R}\boldsymbol{\beta} = \mathbf{r}, \sigma^2\mathbf{I})$, whereas the present estimator pertains to the model $(\mathbf{y}, \mathbf{X}\boldsymbol{\beta} \mid \mathbf{R}\boldsymbol{\beta} = \mathbf{r}, \sigma^2\mathbf{Q})$ which has a singular dispersion matrix of the form

$$\text{(10.41)} \qquad \sigma^2\mathbf{Q} = D(\boldsymbol{\varepsilon}) = D\begin{bmatrix} \boldsymbol{\eta} \\ \mathbf{0} \end{bmatrix} = \sigma^2\begin{bmatrix} \mathbf{I}_T, & \mathbf{0} \\ \mathbf{0}, & \mathbf{0} \end{bmatrix}.$$

Nevertheless, we are able to exploit the fact that the forms of (10.18) and (10.40) are identical in order to find an unbiased estimator of σ^2 under the general assumption that $\text{Null}(\mathbf{X}) = \text{Null}([\mathbf{Z'}, \mathbf{R'}]') = 0$. First, however, we shall find the dispersion matrix $D(\overset{*}{\boldsymbol{\beta}})$.

To find $D(\overset{*}{\boldsymbol{\beta}})$, we use the fact that $\mathbf{C}_2\mathbf{r}$ is a constant to obtain $D(\overset{*}{\boldsymbol{\beta}})= D(\mathbf{C}_1\mathbf{Z}'\mathbf{g}+\mathbf{C}_2\mathbf{r})=D(\mathbf{C}_1\mathbf{Z}'\mathbf{g})=\mathbf{C}_1\mathbf{Z}'D(\mathbf{g})\mathbf{Z}\mathbf{C}_1'=\sigma^2\mathbf{C}_1\mathbf{Z}'\mathbf{Z}\mathbf{C}_1'$. Next, by premultiplying (i) of (10.34) by $\mathbf{C}_1'=\mathbf{C}_1$ and using $\mathbf{C}_1'\mathbf{R}'=\mathbf{0}$ from (iii) of (10.34), we get $\mathbf{C}_1'\mathbf{Z}'\mathbf{Z}\mathbf{C}_1+\mathbf{C}_1'\mathbf{R}'\mathbf{C}_2'=\mathbf{C}_1'\mathbf{Z}'\mathbf{Z}\mathbf{C}_1=\mathbf{C}_1'$, or

(10.42) $$\mathbf{C}_1'\mathbf{Z}'\mathbf{Z}\mathbf{C}_1=\mathbf{C}_1'=\mathbf{C}_1.$$

From this it follows that

$$\begin{aligned}D(\overset{*}{\boldsymbol{\beta}})&=\sigma^2\mathbf{C}_1\\&=\sigma^2\{(\mathbf{X}'\mathbf{X})^{-1}-(\mathbf{X}'\mathbf{X})^{-1}\mathbf{R}'[\mathbf{R}(\mathbf{X}'\mathbf{X})^{-1}\mathbf{R}']^{-1}\mathbf{R}(\mathbf{X}'\mathbf{X})^{-1}\}.\end{aligned}$$

This compares directly with the expression in (10.24).

Estimating σ^2

In order to find an unbiased estimator of σ^2 from the residual vector $(\mathbf{g}-\mathbf{Z}\overset{*}{\boldsymbol{\beta}})$, we proceed much as we did in the case where $\text{Null}(\mathbf{Z})=0$. Let us therefore note that

(10.43) $\mathbf{P_M}=\mathbf{I}-(\mathbf{X}'\mathbf{X})^{-1}\mathbf{R}'[\mathbf{R}(\mathbf{X}'\mathbf{X})^{-1}\mathbf{R}']^{-1}\mathbf{R}$ is the $\mathbf{X}'\mathbf{X}$-symmetric projector on $\mathcal{N}(\mathbf{R})$ along $\mathcal{N}(\mathbf{R}^*)=\mathcal{M}[(\mathbf{X}'\mathbf{X})^{-1}\mathbf{R}']$ such that $\mathbf{P_M^2}=\mathbf{P_M}$, $\mathbf{X}'\mathbf{X}\mathbf{P_M}=\mathbf{P_M'}\mathbf{X}'\mathbf{X}\mathbf{P_M}=\mathbf{P_M'}\mathbf{X}'\mathbf{X}$, $\mathbf{P_M}(\mathbf{X}'\mathbf{X})^{-1}=\mathbf{P_M}(\mathbf{X}'\mathbf{X})^{-1}\mathbf{P_M'}=(\mathbf{X}'\mathbf{X})^{-1}\mathbf{P_M'}$, and $\mathbf{P_M}(\mathbf{X}'\mathbf{X})^{-1}\mathbf{R}'=\mathbf{0}$.

Since $\mathbf{X}'=[\mathbf{Z}',\mathbf{R}']$ and $\mathbf{X}'\mathbf{Q}=[\mathbf{Z}',\mathbf{0}]$, the last of these conditions implies that

(10.44) $\mathbf{X}\mathbf{P_M}(\mathbf{X}'\mathbf{X})^{-1}\mathbf{X}'=\mathbf{X}\mathbf{P_M}(\mathbf{X}'\mathbf{X})^{-1}[\mathbf{Z}',\mathbf{R}']=\mathbf{X}\mathbf{P_M}(\mathbf{X}'\mathbf{X})^{-1}[\mathbf{Z}',\mathbf{0}]=\mathbf{X}\mathbf{P_M}(\mathbf{X}'\mathbf{X})^{-1}\mathbf{X}'\mathbf{Q}$, whence $\text{Trace}[\mathbf{X}\mathbf{P_M}(\mathbf{X}'\mathbf{X})^{-1}\mathbf{X}'\mathbf{Q}]=\text{Trace}[\mathbf{X}\mathbf{P_M}(\mathbf{X}'\mathbf{X})^{-1}\mathbf{X}']=\text{Trace}(\mathbf{P_M})$.

Now consider the decomposition

(10.45) $$\begin{aligned}&E[(\mathbf{y}-\mathbf{X}\overset{*}{\boldsymbol{\beta}})'(\mathbf{y}-\mathbf{X}\overset{*}{\boldsymbol{\beta}})]\\&=E[(\mathbf{y}-\mathbf{X}\boldsymbol{\beta})'(\mathbf{y}-\mathbf{X}\boldsymbol{\beta})]-E[(\mathbf{X}\overset{*}{\boldsymbol{\beta}}-\mathbf{X}\boldsymbol{\beta})'(\mathbf{X}\overset{*}{\boldsymbol{\beta}}-\mathbf{X}\boldsymbol{\beta})],\end{aligned}$$

which is established in the same manner as (10.25). The first term reduces to $E[(\mathbf{g}-\mathbf{Z}\overset{*}{\boldsymbol{\beta}})'(\mathbf{g}-\mathbf{Z}\overset{*}{\boldsymbol{\beta}})]$. The second term reduces to $E[(\mathbf{g}-\mathbf{Z}\boldsymbol{\beta})'(\mathbf{g}-\mathbf{Z}\boldsymbol{\beta})]=E(\boldsymbol{\eta}'\boldsymbol{\eta})=\sigma^2T$. To find the value of the third term, we use the analogy of (10.19) to write $\mathbf{X}(\overset{*}{\boldsymbol{\beta}}-\boldsymbol{\beta})=\mathbf{X}\mathbf{P_M}(\hat{\boldsymbol{\beta}}-\boldsymbol{\beta})=\mathbf{X}\mathbf{P_M}(\mathbf{X}'\mathbf{X})^{-1}\mathbf{X}'\boldsymbol{\varepsilon}$. Then, from the properties of $\mathbf{P_M}$ given in (10.43), we get $(\mathbf{X}\overset{*}{\boldsymbol{\beta}}-\mathbf{X}\boldsymbol{\beta})'(\mathbf{X}\overset{*}{\boldsymbol{\beta}}-\mathbf{X}\boldsymbol{\beta})=$

$\boldsymbol{\varepsilon}'\mathbf{X}(\mathbf{X}'\mathbf{X})^{-1}\mathbf{P}_{\mathbf{M}}'\mathbf{X}'\mathbf{X}\mathbf{P}_{\mathbf{M}}(\mathbf{X}'\mathbf{X})^{-1}\mathbf{X}'\boldsymbol{\varepsilon} = \boldsymbol{\varepsilon}'\mathbf{X}\mathbf{P}_{\mathbf{M}}(\mathbf{X}'\mathbf{X})^{-1}\mathbf{X}'\boldsymbol{\varepsilon}$. To find the expectation, we use the fact that the trace of a scalar is the value of the scalar itself, and we obtain $E[(\mathbf{X}\overset{*}{\boldsymbol{\beta}} - \mathbf{X}\boldsymbol{\beta})'(\mathbf{X}\overset{*}{\boldsymbol{\beta}} - \mathbf{X}\boldsymbol{\beta})] = E\{\text{Trace}[\boldsymbol{\varepsilon}'\mathbf{X}\mathbf{P}_{\mathbf{M}}(\mathbf{X}'\mathbf{X})^{-1}\mathbf{X}'\boldsymbol{\varepsilon}]\} = \text{Trace}[\mathbf{X}\mathbf{P}_{\mathbf{M}}(\mathbf{X}'\mathbf{X})\mathbf{X}'E(\boldsymbol{\varepsilon}\boldsymbol{\varepsilon}')] = \sigma^2\,\text{Trace}[\mathbf{X}\mathbf{P}_{\mathbf{M}}(\mathbf{X}'\mathbf{X})^{-1}\mathbf{X}'\mathbf{Q}]$. If we now invoke the results of (10.44), we find $E[(\mathbf{X}\overset{*}{\boldsymbol{\beta}} - \mathbf{X}\boldsymbol{\beta})'(\mathbf{X}\overset{*}{\boldsymbol{\beta}} - \mathbf{X}\boldsymbol{\beta})] = \sigma^2\,\text{Trace}(\mathbf{P}_{\mathbf{M}})$. But $\text{Trace}(\mathbf{P}_{\mathbf{M}}) = \text{Trace}(\mathbf{I}_k) - \text{Trace}\{(\mathbf{X}'\mathbf{X})^{-1}\mathbf{R}'[\mathbf{R}(\mathbf{X}'\mathbf{X})^{-1}\mathbf{R}]^{-1}\mathbf{R}\} = \text{Trace}(\mathbf{I}_k) - \text{Trace}\{\mathbf{R}(\mathbf{X}'\mathbf{X})^{-1}\mathbf{R}'[\mathbf{R}(\mathbf{X}'\mathbf{X})^{-1}\mathbf{R}']^{-1}\} = k - j$, so $E[(\mathbf{X}\overset{*}{\boldsymbol{\beta}} - \mathbf{X}\boldsymbol{\beta})'(\mathbf{X}\overset{*}{\boldsymbol{\beta}} - \mathbf{X}\boldsymbol{\beta})] = \sigma^2(k - j)$. Substituting the various results in (10.45) above, we find that $E[(\mathbf{g} - \mathbf{Z}\overset{*}{\boldsymbol{\beta}})'(\mathbf{g} - \mathbf{Z}\overset{*}{\boldsymbol{\beta}})] = \sigma^2(T + j - k)$. Therefore

$$\overset{*}{\sigma}{}^2 = \frac{(\mathbf{g} - \mathbf{Z}\overset{*}{\boldsymbol{\beta}})'(\mathbf{g} - \mathbf{Z}\overset{*}{\boldsymbol{\beta}})}{T + j - k} \tag{10.46}$$

provides an unbiased estimator of σ^2 when $\text{Null}(\mathbf{X}) = \text{Null}([\mathbf{Z}', \mathbf{R}']') = 0$. By comparing (10.46) with (10.26), we can see that we have simply re-established an existing result under more general conditions.

THE MINIMUM VARIANCE PROPERTY OF THE RESTRICTED ESTIMATOR

We wish to prove that

(10.47) The minimum variance linear unbiased estimator of $\mathbf{p}'\boldsymbol{\beta}$ for the model $(\mathbf{g}, \mathbf{Z}\boldsymbol{\beta} \mid \mathbf{R}\boldsymbol{\beta} = \mathbf{r}, \sigma^2\mathbf{I})$ where $\text{Null}(\mathbf{X}) = \text{Null}([\mathbf{Z}', \mathbf{R}']') = 0$ is $\mathbf{p}'\overset{*}{\boldsymbol{\beta}} = \mathbf{q}'\mathbf{X}\overset{*}{\boldsymbol{\beta}} = (\mathbf{k}'\mathbf{Z} + \boldsymbol{\lambda}'\mathbf{R})\overset{*}{\boldsymbol{\beta}}$, where $\overset{*}{\boldsymbol{\beta}}$ is the restricted estimator specified in (10.33) and (10.39).

For this purpose, we may take the model $(\mathbf{g}, \mathbf{Z}\boldsymbol{\beta} \mid \mathbf{R}\boldsymbol{\beta} = \mathbf{r}, \sigma^2\mathbf{I})$ in the form of $(\mathbf{y}, \mathbf{X}\boldsymbol{\beta}, \sigma^2\mathbf{Q})$ and then proceed to demonstrate that the estimator $\mathbf{X}\overset{*}{\boldsymbol{\beta}} = \mathbf{X}(\mathbf{C}_1\mathbf{Z}'\mathbf{g} + \mathbf{C}_2\mathbf{r}) = \mathbf{X}[\mathbf{C}_1\mathbf{Z}', \mathbf{C}_2]\mathbf{y} = \mathbf{P}\mathbf{y}$ satisfies the conditions of the Gauss–Markov Theorem that are stated in (9.7). Thus, given that $\mathcal{M}(\mathbf{P}) \subset \mathcal{M}(\mathbf{X})$, we must show that $\mathbf{P}\mathbf{X} = \mathbf{X}$ and that $\mathbf{P}\mathbf{Q} = \mathbf{P}\mathbf{Q}\mathbf{P}'$.

To show that $\mathbf{P}\mathbf{X} = \mathbf{X}$ we use $\mathbf{C}_1\mathbf{Z}'\mathbf{Z} + \mathbf{C}_2\mathbf{R} = \mathbf{I}$ from (i) of (10.34) to give

$$\mathbf{P}\mathbf{X} = \left(\begin{bmatrix}\mathbf{Z}\\ \mathbf{R}\end{bmatrix}[\mathbf{C}_1\mathbf{Z}', \mathbf{C}_2]\right)\begin{bmatrix}\mathbf{Z}\\ \mathbf{R}\end{bmatrix} = \begin{bmatrix}\mathbf{Z}\\ \mathbf{R}\end{bmatrix}[\mathbf{C}_1\mathbf{Z}'\mathbf{Z} + \mathbf{C}_2\mathbf{R}] = \begin{bmatrix}\mathbf{Z}\\ \mathbf{R}\end{bmatrix} = \mathbf{X}. \tag{10.48}$$

Next, to show that $\mathbf{P}\mathbf{Q}\mathbf{P}' = \mathbf{P}\mathbf{Q}$, we use (iii) and (iv) of (10.34) to write

$$\mathbf{P} = \begin{bmatrix}\mathbf{Z}\mathbf{C}_1\mathbf{Z}', & \mathbf{Z}\mathbf{C}_2\\ \mathbf{R}\mathbf{C}_1\mathbf{Z}', & \mathbf{R}\mathbf{C}_2\end{bmatrix} = \begin{bmatrix}\mathbf{Z}\mathbf{C}_1\mathbf{Z}', & \mathbf{Z}\mathbf{C}_2\\ \mathbf{0}, & \mathbf{I}\end{bmatrix}. \tag{10.49}$$

Then, taking the form of $\mathbf{Q}$ from (10.41) and using the identity $\mathbf{C}_1\mathbf{Z}'\mathbf{Z}\mathbf{C}_1 = \mathbf{C}_1$ given in (10.42), we find that

$$(\mathbf{PQ})\mathbf{P}' = \left(\begin{bmatrix} \mathbf{ZC}_1\mathbf{Z}', & \mathbf{ZC}_2 \\ \mathbf{0}, & \mathbf{I} \end{bmatrix}\begin{bmatrix} \mathbf{I}, & \mathbf{0} \\ \mathbf{0}, & \mathbf{0} \end{bmatrix}\right)\begin{bmatrix} \mathbf{ZC}_2\mathbf{Z}', & \mathbf{0} \\ \mathbf{C}_2'\mathbf{Z}', & \mathbf{I} \end{bmatrix}$$

$$= \begin{bmatrix} \mathbf{ZC}_1\mathbf{Z}'\mathbf{ZC}_1\mathbf{Z}, & \mathbf{0} \\ \mathbf{0}, & \mathbf{0} \end{bmatrix} = \begin{bmatrix} \mathbf{ZC}_1\mathbf{Z}', & \mathbf{0} \\ \mathbf{0}, & \mathbf{0} \end{bmatrix} = \mathbf{PQ},$$

and thus (10.47) is proved.

BIBLIOGRAPHY

The Gauss–Markov Model with Linear Restrictions. Brook and Wallace [**16**], Chipman [**17**], Chipman and Rao [**18**], Rao and Mitra [**98**, Chap. 7, §3], Silvey [**111**, Chap. 3 §10]

CHAPTER 11

Temporal Stochastic Processes

A temporal model is one which postulates a relationship amongst the temporal sequences or time series of a number of variables. The simplest temporal model is one in which, at any instant, the relationship comprises only a single value from each sequence. As an example, we may consider the regression equation

$$y(t)=\beta x(t)+\varepsilon(t) \tag{11.1}$$

which relates the observable output sequence $y(t)$ to an observable input sequence $x(t)$ and an unobservable stochastic sequence $\varepsilon(t)$ consisting of independently and identically distributed random variables. However, to be sufficiently general, we should consider a relationship comprising any number of consecutive values from each of the time series. Thus we might generalize the equation in (11.1) to form

$$\sum_{i=0}^{p} a_i y(t-i)=\sum_{i=0}^{r} \beta_i x(t-i)+\sum_{i=0}^{q} m_i \varepsilon(t-i), \tag{11.2}$$

where any of the sums may be infinite.

Three specializations of the relationship in (11.2) are of particular interest to us. The first of these has the form

$$y(t)=\beta x(t)+\sum_{i=0}^{q} m_i \varepsilon(t-i) \tag{11.3}$$

where the stochastic component $\eta(t)=\sum m_i \varepsilon(t-i)$ is a finite or infinite weighted sum of independent and identically distributed random variables. This is described as a regression model with serially correlated disturbances. The second is the autoregressive regression model of the form

$$\sum_{i=0}^{p} a_i y(t-i)=\beta x(t)+\varepsilon(t). \tag{11.4}$$

This is described alternatively as a regression model with lagged dependent variables. The third is the distributed lag model of the form

$$y(t)=\sum_{i=0}^{r} \beta_i x(t-i)+\varepsilon(t) \tag{11.5}$$

which indicates that the value of the variable x at time t has a determining influence on y not only at that instant but also over a succeeding period.

It is the presence of an observable input sequence $x(t)$ in each of these relationships which accounts for their description as regression models. When $x(t)$ is deleted from (11.3) and (11.4), we obtain the somewhat simpler linear stochastic models described, respectively, as the moving average model and the autoregressive model. We shall treat these linear stochastic models in the present chapter, and in the following chapter we shall deal with the various kinds of temporal regression models.

To help us in unifying our treatment of temporal models, we shall begin by developing the algebra of the lag operator and by examining the properties of linear difference equations.

THE ALGEBRA OF THE LAG OPERATOR

For the sake of rigour, let us define a sequence to be any function $x(t)$ mapping from the set of integers $\mathcal{I}=\{0, \pm 1, \pm 2, \ldots\}$ onto the real line $\mathcal{R}$. Whenever the set of integers represents a sequence of dates separated by a unit time interval, we may describe $x(t)$ as a time series. The value of the function at the point $\tau \in \mathcal{I}$ is denoted by $x_\tau = x(\tau)$. Thus a set of observations of $x(t)$ from the time $t=1$ to the time $t=T$ may be denoted by a vector $\mathbf{x}'=[x_1, \ldots, x_T]$.

We shall make some use of the fact that

(11.6) The set of all time series $\mathcal{X}=\{x(t);\, x \in \mathcal{R},\, t \in \mathcal{I}\}$ constitutes a vector space.

Various linear transformations or operators may be defined on this space $\mathcal{H}$. In particular,

(11.7) The lag operator $L \in \mathcal{L}(\mathcal{X}, \mathcal{X})$ is a linear transformation on $\mathcal{X}$ defined by $Lx(t)=x(t-1)$.

When we apply the lag operator twice in succession, we obtain $L[Lx(t)]= Lx(t-1)=x(t-2)$. Thus it is natural to define L^2 by $L^2x(t)=x(t-2)$ and to define the kth power of the operator by $L^kx(t)=x(t-k)$. Inverse powers of the operator may also be defined such that, in general, $L^{-k}x(t)=x(t+k)$. For the zero-th power, defined by $L^0x(t)=x(t)$, we may use the notation $L^0=I$.

(11.8) The set of lag operators $[I, L, L^2, \ldots, L^{n-1}]$ forms the basis of an n-dimensional vector space $\mathcal{L}^n$.

The generic element of this space is a function $P(L)=\sum_{i=0}^{n-1} p_iL^i$ which is described as a polynomial lag operator of degree $n-1$. Using the notation of the polynomial operator, we can re-express the temporal model in (11.2) as

$$(11.9) \qquad A(L)y(t)=B(L)x(t)+M(L)\varepsilon(t)$$

where, for example,

$$(11.10) \qquad A(L)y(t)=(a_0+a_1L+a_2L^2+\ldots+a_pL^p)y(t) = \sum_{i=0}^{p} a_i y(t-i).$$

The advantage of considering the vector space $\mathcal{L}^n$ lies in the fact that it is isomorphic with the vector space $\mathcal{P}^n$ comprising all real-valued polynomial functions of degree at most $n-1$ in some real scalar variable x. This means that the familiar results concerning the addition and scalar multiplication of polynomials can be invoked to enable us to treat problems concerning the polynomial lag operator. In fact, the n-dimensional space $\mathcal{P}^n$ is of limited interest in comparison with the infinite dimensional space $\mathcal{P}^\infty$ which is closed under the binary operation of polynomial multiplication. An analogous infinite dimensional space $\mathcal{L}^\infty$ can be defined for the polynomial lag operator; and an extended isomorphism may be established between $\mathcal{L}^\infty$ and $\mathcal{P}^\infty$ in respect of the operations of scalar multiplication, polynomial addition and the commutative operation of polynomial multiplication. It is therefore appropriate to recall a number of useful results in the algebra of polynomials.

Polynomial equations

Consider the equation

$$(11.11) \qquad a_0+a_1x+a_2x^2=0$$

with real coefficients a_0, a_1, a_2. On dividing the equation by a_2, we may factorize it to obtain $(x-\lambda_1)(x-\lambda_2)=0$, where λ_1, λ_2 are the roots of the equation. The roots are given by

$$(11.12) \qquad \lambda=\frac{-a_1\pm\sqrt{a_1^2-4a_2a_0}}{2a_2}.$$

If $a_1^2 \geqslant 4a_2a_0$, then the roots λ_1, λ_2 will be real; otherwise they will be conjugate complex numbers $\beta+i\gamma$, $\beta-i\gamma$, where $i=\sqrt{-1}$.

Now consider the general equation of the nth order

$$(11.13) \qquad a_0+a_1x+a_2x^2+\ldots+a_nx^n=0.$$

Dividing through by a_n gives the monic polynomial equation

$$(11.14) \qquad a_0/a_n+a_1x/a_n+\ldots+x^n=0$$

which has unity as the coefficient of the highest power of x. The latter may be factorized as

$$(x-\lambda_1)(x-\lambda_2)\dots(x-\lambda_n)=0 \tag{11.15}$$

where some of the roots $\lambda_1,\dots,\lambda_n$ may be real and others may be complex. The complex roots will occur in conjugate pairs, and the factors containing them may be multiplied together to give real-valued quadratic terms. Thus any polynomial with real coefficients may be expressed as the product of real linear and real quadratic terms.

If the factors in equation (11.15) are multiplied together, we obtain the expression

$$\begin{aligned} x^n-\sum_i \lambda_i x^{n-1}+\sum_i\sum_j \lambda_i\lambda_j x^{n-2} \\ -\dots\pm\lambda_1\lambda_2\dots\lambda_n=0. \end{aligned} \tag{11.16}$$

By comparing the coefficients of this expression with the coefficients in (11.14), we may deduce the result that the sum of the products of all possible combinations of r of the roots is $(-1)^r a_{n-r}/a_n$. In particular, we find that

$$\begin{aligned} \sum_{i=1}^n \lambda_i &= -a_{n-1}/a_n, \\ \prod_{i=1}^n \lambda_i &= (-1)^n a_0/a_n. \end{aligned} \tag{11.17}$$

The second of these gives $a_n = a_0\prod_{i=1}^n(-\lambda_i)^{-1}$, whence we are able to write equation (11.13) variously as

$$\begin{aligned} \sum a_i x^i &= a_n\prod(x-\lambda_i) \\ &= a_0\prod\left(1-\frac{x}{\lambda_i}\right)=0. \end{aligned} \tag{11.18}$$

Rational functions

If $P(x)$ and $Q(x)$ are polynomial expressions of degrees m and n respectively, with $m<n$, then their ratio $P(x)/Q(x)$ is described as a proper rational function. We shall make use, subsequently, of certain rational functions of the lag operator. For an expression such as $[P(L)/Q(L)]y(t)$ to have a meaningful interpretation in the context of a temporal model, it is usually required that it should form a sequence that is bounded in absolute value whenever $y(t)$ is similarly bounded. To ensure such a result, it is

necessary and sufficient that the expansion of $P(x)/Q(x)$ should form a convergent series whenever $|x| \leq 1$. We can investigate whether or not the series is convergent by expressing the ratio $P(x)/Q(x)$ as a sum of partial fractions, each of which has a factor of the polynomial $Q(x)$ in its denominator. The basic result is as follows:

(11.19) If $P(x)/Q(x) = P(x)/[Q_1(x)Q_2(x)]$ is a proper rational function, and if $P(x)$, $Q_1(x)$, $Q_2(x)$ have no common factor, then we may write

$$\frac{P(x)}{Q(x)} = \frac{P_1(x)}{Q_1(x)} + \frac{P_2(x)}{Q_2(x)}$$

where $P_1(x)/Q_1(x)$, $P_2(x)/Q_2(x)$ are uniquely determined proper rational functions.

It follows from repeated applications of this result that, if $Q(x) = q_0\prod_{i=1}^{n}(1 - x\lambda_i^{-1})$, where $\lambda_1, \ldots, \lambda_n$ are distinct roots, then there exists a unique expansion of the form

$$\frac{P(x)}{Q(x)} = \frac{k_1}{(1 - x\lambda_1^{-1})} + \ldots + \frac{k_n}{(1 - x\lambda_n^{-1})}. \tag{11.20}$$

On adding the terms of the right hand side, we obtain a numerator of degree $n-1$. By equating the coefficients of this numerator with the coefficients of $P(x)$, we can determine the constants $k_1, \ldots, k_n$.

As an example, consider $(3+x)/(1-x-6x^2) = (3+x)/[(1-3x)(1+2x)]$. From

$$\frac{3+x}{(1-3x)(1+2x)} = \frac{k_1}{(1-3x)} + \frac{k_2}{(1+2x)},$$

we get the equations $2k_1 - 3k_2 = 1$, $k_1 + k_2 = 3$, whence $k_1 = 2$, $k_2 = 1$ are the values of the constants.

There is also the case where $Q(x)$ has repeated factors. Let $Q(x) = (1 - x\lambda_j^{-1})^r Q_2(x)$. Then

$$\frac{P(x)}{Q(x)} = \frac{P_1(x)}{(1 - x\lambda_j^{-1})^r} + \frac{P_2(x)}{Q_2(x)} \tag{11.21}$$

where $P_1(x)$ is a polynomial of degree less than r which can be expressed as

$$\begin{aligned} P_1(x) = {} & k_{10} + k_{11}(1 - x\lambda_j^{-1}) + k_{12}(1 - x\lambda_j^{-1})^2 + \ldots \\ & + k_{1(r-1)}(1 - x\lambda_j^{-1})^{r-1}. \end{aligned} \tag{11.22}$$

On writing this expression in (11.21), we get

$$(11.23) \qquad \frac{P(x)}{Q(x)} = \frac{k_{10}}{(1-x\lambda_j^{-1})^r} + \frac{k_{11}}{(1-x\lambda_j^{-1})^{r-1}} + \ldots + \frac{k_{1(r-1)}}{(1-x\lambda_j^{-1})} + \frac{P_2(x)}{Q_2(x)}.$$

The matter of convergence is now straightforward. For, when we consider the expressions (11.20) and (11.23) in the light of the fact that

$$(11.24) \qquad \frac{1}{(1-x\lambda_i^{-1})} = 1 + \frac{x}{\lambda_i} + \frac{x^2}{\lambda_i^2} + \frac{x^3}{\lambda_i^3} + \ldots,$$

it becomes clear that $P(x)/Q(x)$ can be expressed as a convergent series for $|x| \leq 1$ if and only if $|\lambda_i| > 1$ for all i.

Linear difference equations

If $x(t)$ is a sequence or a time series, then a relationship of the form

$$(11.25) \qquad a_0x(t) + a_1x(t-1) + \ldots + a_nx(t-n) = u(t)$$

comprising a specified sequence $u(t)$ is called an nth-order linear difference equation in x. Using the lag operator, we may write (11.25) alternatively as

$$(11.26) \qquad (a_0 + a_1L + \ldots + a_nL^n)x(t) = A(L)x(t) = u(t).$$

The equation describes a relationship existing between any $n+1$ consecutive elements of the sequence $x(t)$. Given the n consecutive elements $x_{-1}, x_{-2}, \ldots, x_{-n}$, we can set $t=0$ and use the equation to find the succeeding element x_0. Then, setting $t=1$, we can use $x_0, x_1, \ldots, x_{1-n}$ to find x_1. In this way, we can generate the succeeding sequence. Likewise, we can generate the preceding sequence. Thus we obtain the solution of the difference equation. However, our purpose is not to generate all the values in the range of $x(t)$ but rather to find an analytic form of the function $x(t)$. Such a function will generally comprise a set of n constants $\mathbf{c}' = [c_1, c_2, \ldots, c_n]$ which can be determined once a set of n consecutive elements of the sequence $x(t)$ have been specified. The analytic function $x(t; \mathbf{c})$ is called the general solution of the difference equation.

(11.27) The general solution of the difference equation $A(L)x(t) = u(t)$ may be expressed as the sum $x(t; \mathbf{c}) = y(t) + z(t)$ where $y(t)$ is the general solution of the homogeneous equation $A(L)y(t) = 0$ and $z(t) = A^{-1}(L)u(t)$ is a particular solution to the equation $A(L)z(t) = u(t)$.

This is analogous to the result (2.58) concerning the solution of the inhomogeneous equations $\mathbf{Ax} = \mathbf{y}$.

We solve the difference equation in three steps. First, we find the general solution to the homogeneous equation. Next, we find a particular solution to the difference equation. Finally, we use the specified values of n consecutive elements of the sequence $x(t)$ to enable us to determine the arbitrary constants in the function $x(t;\mathbf{c})$.

We shall concern ourselves in detail only with the general solution of a homogeneous equation.

(11.28) If λ_j is any root of the lag polynomial equation $A(L)=0$ such that $A(\lambda_j)=0$, then $x_j(t)=(1/\lambda_j)^t$ is a solution to the homogeneous difference equation $A(L)x(t)=0$.

To show this, we may use the identity $L^p(1/\lambda_j)^t=(1/\lambda_j)^{t-p}=\lambda_j^p(1/\lambda_j)^t$ to write

(11.29)
$$\begin{aligned}A(L)x_j(t)&=(a_0+a_1L+\ldots+a_nL^n)(1/\lambda_j)^t\\&=(a_0+a_1\lambda_j+\ldots+a_n\lambda_j^n)(1/\lambda_j)^t\\&=A(\lambda_j)x_j(t)=0.\end{aligned}$$

Alternatively, multiplying the factor $(1-\lambda_j^{-1}L)$ of the expansion $A(L)=a_0\prod_{i=1}^n(1-\lambda_i^{-1}L)$ by $x_j(t)=(1/\lambda_j)^t$ gives

(11.30)
$$(1-\lambda_j^{-1}L)(1/\lambda_j)^t=(1/\lambda_j)^t-(1/\lambda_j)^t=0.$$

If $x_j(t)$ is a solution to $A(L)x(t)=0$, then so also is $c_jx_j(t)$ where c_j is an arbitrary constant. In fact,

(11.31) If the roots $\lambda_1, \lambda_2, \ldots, \lambda_n$ of $A(L)=0$ are distinct, then the general solution to the equation $A(L)x(t)=0$ is

$$x(t;\mathbf{c})=c_1(1/\lambda_1)^t+c_2(1/\lambda_2)^t+\ldots+c_n(1/\lambda_n)^t$$

where $\mathbf{c}'=[c_1, c_2, \ldots, c_n]$ is a set of constants.

If $A(L)=0$ has a repeated root so that it contains a factor $(1-\lambda_j^{-1}L)^2$, then both $x_j(t)=(1/\lambda_j)^t$ and $tx_j(t)=t(1/\lambda_j)^t$ are solutions to the equation $A(L)x(t)=0$. To demonstrate this result, we use $x_j(t)=\lambda_j^{-1}x_j(t-1)=\lambda_j^{-2}x_j(t-2)$ to write

(11.32)
$$\begin{aligned}(1-\lambda_j^{-1}L)^2tx_j(t)&=(1-2\lambda_j^{-1}L+\lambda_j^{-2}L^2)tx_j(t)\\&=tx_j(t)-2[t-1]\lambda_j^{-1}x_j(t-1)\\&\quad+[t-2]\lambda_j^{-2}x_j(t-2)\\&=(t-2[t-1]+[t-2])x_j(t)=0.\end{aligned}$$

We can also prove by a simple process of mathematical induction that

(11.33) If $A(L)=0$ has r roots equal to λ_j, then $(1/\lambda_j)^t$, $t(1/\lambda_j)^t, \ldots, t^{r-1}(1/\lambda_j)^t$ are all solutions of the difference equation $A(L)x(t)=0$.

It follows that, if $A(L)=0$ factorizes as

(11.34) $$A(L)=(1-\lambda_1^{-1}L)(1-\lambda_2^{-1}L)\ldots(1-\lambda_p^{-1}L)(1-\lambda_j^{-1}L)^r,$$

then the general solution of $A(L)x(t)=0$ is

(11.35) $$x(t;\mathbf{c})=\sum_{i=1}^{p} c_i(1/\lambda_i)^t+\sum_{k=0}^{r-1} g_k t^k(1/\lambda_j)^t,$$

where $g_k=c_{p+1+k}$.

We should also consider a special case where the roots of $A(L)=0$ are all unity so that $A(L)=(I-L)^d=D^d$, where D is the difference operator defined by $Dx(t)=x(t)-x(t-1)$. The general solution of $A(L)x(t)=D^dx(t)=0$ is then the polynomial time trend $f(t)=\sum_{i=0}^{d-1} c_it^i$. To express this result succinctly, we may state that

(11.36) The dth difference of the polynomial $f(t)=c_0+c_1t+\ldots+c_{d-1}t^{d-1}$ of degree $d-1$ in the integer t is $D^df(t)=0$.

By examining the values of the roots of $A(L)=0$, it is possible to determine whether or not the function $x(t)$ defined by $A(L)x(t)=0$ tends to a limit as t tends to infinity.

(11.37) A necessary and sufficient condition for the convergence of the sequence $x(t)$, where $A(L)x(t)=0$, is that $|\lambda_i|>1$ for every root λ_i of the equation $A(L)=0$.

This follows from the fact that every term of the general solution $x(t;\mathbf{c})$ having the form $c_jx_j(t)=c_j(1/\lambda_j)^t$ or the form $g_kt^kx_j(t)=g_kt^k(1/\lambda_j)^t$ will tend to zero if and only if $|\lambda_i|>1$. We can describe this condition for convergence as the requirement that all the roots of $A(L)=0$ must lie outside the unit circle.

STATIONARY STOCHASTIC PROCESSES

A temporal stochastic process $x(t)$ may be described as a collection of random variables indexed on time. A sequence $\mathbf{x}'_\tau=[x_{\tau+1},\ldots,x_{\tau+T}]$, consisting of T consecutive elements of the stochastic process, is a random vector whose behaviour is described by a T-dimensional probability distribution. Therefore the problems of inference associated with the stochastic process $x(t)$ fall within the ambit of multivariate statistical analysis.

We shall consider only a narrow class of stochastic processes which are distinguished by the fact that every vector $\mathbf{x}_\tau$ of T consecutive elements has the same probability density function regardless of the value of τ. Such processes are described as non-evolutionary or strictly stationary. The property of stationarity implies certain restrictions on the moments of the probability density functions associated with the process. Thus, for example,

(11.38) If $x(t)$ is a stationary process, then $E(x_t)=\mu$ for all t, and $C(x_t, x_s)=\gamma_{|t-s|}<\infty$ for all t, s.

This means that the expected value of the process is independent of time, and that the covariance of any two elements x_t, x_s is a function of their temporal separation or lag $|t-s|=\tau$ regardless of the absolute values of t and s. Therefore we may describe the value γ_τ as an autocovariance of lag τ. The nature of the autocovariances of $x(t)$ implies that the dispersion matrix of the vector $\mathbf{x}'=[x_1, \ldots, x_T]$ has the form

(11.39)
$$D(\mathbf{x})=E\{[(x_t-\mu)(x_s-\mu)]\}$$
$$=\begin{bmatrix} \gamma_0, & \gamma_1, & \gamma_2, \ldots \, \gamma_{T-1} \\ \gamma_1, & \gamma_0 & \gamma_1, \ldots, \gamma_{T-2} \\ \gamma_2, & \gamma_1, & \gamma_0, \ldots, \gamma_{T-3} \\ \cdot & & \\ \cdot & & \\ \cdot & & \\ \gamma_{T-1}, & \gamma_{T-2}, & \gamma_{T-3}, \ldots, \gamma_0 \end{bmatrix}$$

This is described as a Laurent matrix.

In the succeeding development, we shall also use the fourth-order moment matrix

(11.40)
$$F(\mathbf{x}; \tau)=E\{[(x_t-\mu)(x_{t+\tau}-\mu)(x_s-\mu)(x_{s+\tau}-\mu)]\}=[\zeta_{|t-s|}]$$
$$t, s=1, \ldots, T-\tau$$

which specializes to

(11.41)
$$F(\mathbf{x}; 0)=E\{[(x_t-\mu)^2(x_s-\mu)^2]\}=[\delta_{|t-s|}]$$
$$t, s=1, \ldots, T.$$

Both of these are Laurent matrices with forms similar to that of $D(\mathbf{x})=[\gamma_{|t-s|}]$.

Estimating the moments of a stationary process

The vector $\mathbf{x}'=[x_1, \ldots, x_T]$, generated by the stochastic process $x(t)$, represents only a single observation or realization of a T-dimensional probability distribution. There would seem to be little hope of obtaining worthwhile estimates of the parameters of the distribution from this one observation. However, provided that the process $x(t)$ is stationary and provided that the statistical dependencies between widely separated elements of the sequence are weak, it is possible to estimate those parameters of the distribution which express the interdependence of proximate elements of the sequence.

Whenever, by observing a stochastic sequence, we are able to construct consistent estimates of certain parameters of the underlying statistical process, we say that the process is ergodic in respect of those parameters. We shall now establish some conditions which are sufficient to ensure that a process $x(t)$ is ergodic in respect of its mean, its variance and its covariances.

The usual estimator of the population mean is the sample mean $\bar{x} = T^{-1}\sum_{t=1}^{T} x_t$. This is an unbiased estimator since its expectation is

$$E(\bar{x}) = T^{-1}\sum_{t=1}^{T} E(x_t) = T^{-1}T\mu = \mu. \tag{11.42}$$

Its variance is $V(\bar{x}) = T^{-2}V(\mathbf{i}'\mathbf{x}) = T^{-2}\mathbf{i}'D(\mathbf{x})\mathbf{i}$ where $\mathbf{i}' = [1, \ldots, 1]$ is a vector of T units. To express this more explicitly, we may write

$$\begin{aligned} V(\bar{x}) &= E[(\bar{x}-\mu)^2] = T^{-2}E\{[\textstyle\sum (x_t-\mu)]^2\} \\ &= T^{-2}\sum_t\sum_s E[(x_t-\mu)(x_s-\mu)] = T^{-2}\mathbf{i}'D(\mathbf{x})\mathbf{i}. \end{aligned} \tag{11.43}$$

Reference to (11.39) shows that $\mathbf{i}'D(\mathbf{x})\mathbf{i} = T\gamma_0 + 2\sum_{t=1}^{T}(T-t)\gamma_t$, so that

$$V(\bar{x}) = T^{-1}\left[\gamma_0 + 2\sum_{t=1}^{T}\left(1-\frac{t}{T}\right)\gamma_t\right]. \tag{11.44}$$

For $\bar{x}$ to be a consistent estimator, we require that $\lim(T \to \infty)V(\bar{x}) = 0$. For this, it is sufficient that $\lim \sum (1 - t/T)\gamma_t$ should exist, as it does whenever $\lim(t \to \infty)\gamma_t = 0$. Therefore we may conclude that

(11.45) The sample mean $\bar{x}$ is a consistent estimator of the expccted value of the process $x(t)$ if the covariance $\gamma_{|t-s|}$ of the elements x_t, x_s tends to zero as their temporal separation $|t-s|$ increases.

To estimate the covariance γ_τ, we may use

$$\begin{aligned} c_\tau &= (T-\tau)^{-1}\sum_{t=1}^{T-\tau}(x_t-\bar{x}_0)(x_{t+\tau}-\bar{x}_\tau) \\ &= (T-\tau)^{-1}\left[\sum_{t=1}^{T-\tau} x_t x_{t+\tau} - (T-\tau)^{-1}\sum_{t=1}^{T-\tau} x_t \sum_{t=1}^{T-\tau} x_{t+\tau}\right] \end{aligned} \tag{11.46}$$

where $\bar{x}_0$ and $\bar{x}_\tau$ are, respectively, the averages of the first and the last $T-\tau$ elements of the sample. We can also write

$$\begin{aligned} c_\tau = (T-\tau)^{-1}\Bigg[&\sum_{t=1}^{T-\tau}(x_t-\mu)(x_{t+\tau}-\mu) \\ &-(T-\tau)^{-1}\sum_{t=1}^{T-\tau}(x_t-\mu)\sum_{t=1}^{T-\tau}(x_{t+\tau}-\mu)\Bigg]. \end{aligned} \tag{11.47}$$

The expectation is

$$(11.48)\qquad E(c_\tau)=\gamma_\tau-(T-\tau)^{-2}\sum_{t=1}^{T-\tau}\sum_{s=\tau+1}^{T}\gamma_{|t-s|}$$
$$=\gamma_\tau-(T-\tau)^{-2}\mathbf{i}'D_\tau(\mathbf{x})\mathbf{i}$$

where $D_\tau(\mathbf{x})$ is the submatrix of $D(\mathbf{x})$ formed by deleting the elements in the first τ rows and the last τ columns.

Given that $\lim(t\rightarrow\infty)\gamma_t=0$, it follows that $\lim(T\rightarrow\infty)E(c_\tau)=\gamma_\tau$; so the estimate is asymptotically unbiased. To investigate the consistency of c_τ, we must consider the probability limits of the terms

$$(11.49)\qquad c_\tau^*=(T-\tau)^{-1}\sum_{t=1}^{T-\tau}(x_t-\mu)(x_{t+\tau}-\mu)\quad\text{and}$$
$$(\bar{x}_0-\mu)(\bar{x}_\tau-\mu)=(T-\tau)^{-2}\sum_{t=1}^{T-\tau}(x_t-\mu)\sum_{t=1}^{T-\tau}(x_{t+\tau}-\mu)$$

of the formula (11.47). Given that $\text{plim}(\bar{x}_0)=\text{plim}(\bar{x}_\tau)=\mu$ by virtue of the condition that $\lim(t\rightarrow\infty)\gamma_t=0$, it follows that $\text{plim}(\bar{x}_0-\mu)(\bar{x}_\tau-\mu)=0$. Thus, for c_τ to be consistent, it is sufficient that $\text{plim}(c_\tau^*)=\gamma_\tau$. Since $E(c_\tau^*)=\gamma_\tau$, the latter is assured if $\lim(T\rightarrow\infty)V(c_\tau^*)=0$. Therefore we shall examine

$$(11.50)\qquad V(c_\tau^*)=(T-\tau)^{-2}V\{\mathbf{i}'[(x_t-\mu)(x_{t+\tau}-\mu)]\}$$
$$=(T-\tau)^{-2}\mathbf{i}'D\{[(x_t-\mu)(x_{t+\tau}-\mu)]\}\mathbf{i}.$$

The generic element of the $(T-\tau)\times(T-\tau)$ dispersion matrix $D\{[(x_t-\mu)(x_{t+\tau}-\mu)]\}$ is the covariance of $(x_t-\mu)(x_{t+\tau}-\mu)$ and $(x_s-\mu)\times(x_{s+\tau}-\mu)$. This is given by

$$(11.51)\qquad E(\{(x_t-\mu)(x_{t+\tau}-\mu)-E[(x_t-\mu)(x_{t+\tau}-\mu)]\}$$
$$\times\{(x_s-\mu)(x_{s+\tau}-\mu)-E[(x_s-\mu)(x_{s+\tau}-\mu)]\})$$
$$=E[(x_t-\mu)(x_{t+\tau}-\mu)(x_s-\mu)(x_{s+\tau}-\mu)]-\gamma_\tau^2$$
$$=\zeta_{|t-s|}-\gamma_\tau^2.$$

Thus

$$(11.52)\qquad D\{[(x_t-\mu)(x_{t+\tau}-\mu)]\}=[\zeta_{|t-s|}-\gamma_\tau^2]$$
$$=F(\mathbf{x};\tau)-\gamma_\tau^2\mathbf{ii}',$$

and it is apparent that the expression for $V(c_\tau^*)$ has the same structure as the expression for $V(\bar{x})$ in (11.43). Using this analogy, and collecting our various results together, we may conclude that

(11.53) The sample convariance c_τ is a consistent estimator of the autocovariance γ_τ of the process $x(t)$ if the covariance $\gamma_{|t-s|}$ of x_t and x_s and the covariance $\xi_{|t-s|}-\gamma_\tau^2$ of $(x_t-\mu)(x_{t+\tau}-\mu)$ and $(x_s-\mu)(x_{s+\tau}-\mu)$ tend to zero as the temporal separation $|t-s|$ increases.

An alternative estimator of γ_τ is provided by

$$c'_\tau=(T-\tau)^{-1}\sum(x_t-\bar{x})(x_{t+\tau}-\bar{x}), \tag{11.54}$$

which differs from c_τ in having the overall sample mean $\bar{x}=T^{-1}\sum_{t=1}^{T}x_t$ in place of $\bar{x}_0$ and $\bar{x}_\tau$. Since $\bar{x}_0$, $\bar{x}_\tau$ and $\bar{x}$ are all consistent estimates of $E(x_t)=\mu$, it follows that c'_τ and c_τ are asymptotically equivalent.

We should conclude this section by remarking that the conditions under (11.45) and (11.53), that have been shown to be sufficient for the ergodicity of the process $x(t)$ in respect of its mean and its covariances, are sufficiently general to encompass a wide variety of temporal stochastic phenomena. In particular, every stationary linear stochastic process satisfies these conditions.

Tests of serial correlation

Numerous methods are available for testing the hypothesis that the elements of $x(t)$ are distributed independently and identically. The tests fall into two classes. The first contains tests which require no presumption about the exact functional form of the distribution of the elements. These are termed non-parametric tests. The second class contains tests which are based on the presumption that the elements of $x(t)$ are normally distributed. We shall consider only the latter.

A natural way of testing the null hypothesis that $x(t)$ is a purely random non-autocorrelated series is to examine the values of the estimates of the autocorrelation coefficients $\rho_\tau=\gamma_\tau/\gamma_0$ to see whether they are significantly different from zero.

We might estimate ρ_τ by $r_\tau=c_\tau/c_0$. Unfortunately, the problem of deriving the small-sample distribution of r_τ under the assumption that $\mathbf{x}'=[x_1,\ldots,x_T]$ is a purely random normal vector is somewhat intractable on account of the fact that the elements of $\mathbf{x}$ are not equally represented in the formula of c_τ. To overcome this problem, we may use the circular autocorrelation coefficient defined by

$$r_\tau^c=\frac{\sum_{t=1}^{T}x_tx_{t+\tau}-T^{-1}\left(\sum_{t=1}^{T}x_t\right)^2}{\sum_{t=1}^{T}x_t^2-T^{-1}\left(\sum_{t=1}^{T}x_t\right)^2}, \tag{11.55}$$

where the problem of the extra-sample elements is overcome by setting

$$x_{T+1}=x_1,\ldots,x_{T+\tau}=x_\tau.$$

Under the null hypothesis that $\mathbf{x}\sim N(\mu\mathbf{i},\gamma_0\mathbf{I})$, this statistic constitutes the ratio of two quadratic forms of a normal vector, and its exact distribution has been tabulated by Anderson [**6**].

The most commonly used test statistic is the von Neumann ratio defined by

$$(11.56)\qquad v=\frac{\delta^2}{c_0}=\frac{(T-1)^{-1}\sum_{t=1}^{T-1}(x_{t+1}-x_t)^2}{T^{-1}\sum_{t=1}^{T}(x_t-\bar{x})^2}$$

wherein the numerator has an expected value of $2\sigma^2$ and the denominator is the ordinary sample variance. Under the null hypothesis that the series $x(t)$ is purely random, the value of the statistic is expected to be near to 2. If the series is positively autocorrelated, then the value will be smaller. The distribution of v has been extensively tabulated by Hart [**52**].

To understand the nature of the von Neumann ratio, we should recognize that, as the sample size T increases, the value of v tends to that of $2(1-r_1)$. This indicates that the test based on v is asymptotically equivalent to a test based on r_1.

Linear stochastic processes

A linear stochastic process is a sequence of random variables $\eta(t)$ defined by a relationship

$$(11.57)\qquad A(L)\eta(t)=M(L)\varepsilon(t),$$

where $\varepsilon(t)$ is a sequence of independently and identically distributed random variables with zero mean, and where $A(L)=(I+a_1L+\ldots+a_pL^p)=\sum_{i=0}^{p}a_iL^i$ and $M(L)=(I+m_1L+\ldots+m_qL^q)=\sum_{i=0}^{q}m_iL^i$ are polynomial lag operators of finite degree.

The specialized form of the process $\eta(t)$ defined by

$$(11.58)\qquad \eta(t)=M(L)\varepsilon(t)$$

is described as a finite-order moving average process, whereas the opposite specialization defined by

$$(11.59)\qquad A(L)\eta(t)=\varepsilon(t)$$

is described as a finite-order autoregressive process. The general mixed autoregressive moving average process defined in (11.57) may be cast in the alternative rational forms

$$(11.60)\qquad \eta(t)=\frac{M(L)}{A(L)}\varepsilon(t), \qquad \frac{A(L)}{M(L)}\eta(t)=\varepsilon(t).$$

Since the inverse of a finite-degree polynomial is a polynomial of infinite degree these forms may be described respectively as an infinite-order moving average process and an infinite-order autoregressive process. Thus a kind of duality can be seen to exist between autoregressive and moving average processes whereby every autoregressive process, whether of finite or infinite order, is equivalent to some infinite-order moving average process and, conversely, every moving average process is equivalent to some infinite-order autoregressive process.

The autocovariances of a linear process embody the coefficients of the polynomial involved in expressing that process in moving average form. Thus, in particular, the autocovariance of lag τ of the process $\eta(t)$ defined by (11.58) is given by

$$(11.61)\qquad \begin{aligned}\gamma_\tau &= E(\eta_t\eta_{t+\tau})\\ &= E\Big(\sum_i m_i\varepsilon_{t-i}\sum_j m_j\varepsilon_{t+\tau-j}\Big)\\ &= \sum_i\sum_j m_i m_j E(\varepsilon_{t-i}\varepsilon_{t+\tau-j})\\ &= \sigma_\varepsilon^2\sum_i m_i m_{i+\tau},\end{aligned}$$

which follows from the fact that $E(\varepsilon_t\varepsilon_s)=0$ when $t\neq s$ and $E(\varepsilon_t^2)=\sigma_\varepsilon^2$.

Finite-order moving average processes

Although, in econometrics, it is unusual to find a moving average model existing in its own right, it is nevertheless quite common to find one arising in the mathematical manipulation of a temporal regression model. For the moving average model

$$(11.62)\qquad \eta(t)=M(L)\varepsilon(t)=(I+m_1L+m_2L^2+\ldots+m_qL^q)\varepsilon(t)$$

to have any substantive meaning, it is usually required that its expression as an infinite-order autoregressive model should be in terms of past rather than future values of the series $\eta(t)$. When such an expression is available, the moving average process is said to be invertible. Consider, for example, the first-order case

$$(11.63)\qquad \eta(t)=\varepsilon(t)-\theta\varepsilon(t-1)=(I-\theta L)\varepsilon(t).$$

Provided that $|\theta|<1$, we may write

$$(11.64)\qquad \varepsilon(t)=(I-\theta L)^{-1}\eta(t)=(I+\theta L+\theta^2L^2+\ldots)\eta(t)$$
$$=\eta(t)+\theta\eta(t-1)+\theta^2\eta(t-2)+\ldots.$$

However, if $|\theta|\geq 1$, this series fails to converge, and the representation is not viable. Instead we must rewrite the process as

$$(11.65)\qquad \eta(t+1)=\varepsilon(t+1)-\theta\varepsilon(t)=(L^{-1}-\theta)\varepsilon(t)$$
$$=-\theta\left(I-\frac{L^{-1}}{\theta}\right)\varepsilon(t),$$

from which we may obtain an autoregressive representation of the form

$$(11.66)\qquad \varepsilon(t)=-\frac{1}{\theta}\left(I-\frac{L^{-1}}{\theta}\right)^{-1}\eta(t+1)$$
$$=-\left[\frac{\eta(t+1)}{\theta}+\frac{\eta(t+2)}{\theta^2}+\frac{\eta(t+3)}{\theta^3}+\ldots\right].$$

This may have no reasonable substantive meaning.

For the qth-order process $\eta(t)=M(L)\varepsilon(t)$ specified in (11.62) to be invertible, it is necessary and sufficient that the expansion of $M^{-1}(x)$ should converge whenever $|x|\leq 1$. Given the factorization $M(x)=\prod_{i=1}^{q}(1-\lambda_i^{-1}x)$, we can express the inverse of the polynomial in partial fractions as

$$(11.67)\qquad M^{-1}(x)=\sum_{i=1}^{q}\frac{k_i}{(1-\lambda_i^{-1}x)}.$$

For the expansion of every term under the summation to converge, it is necessary and sufficient that $|\lambda_i^{-1}|<1$ for all i; and we may conclude that

(11.68) The moving average process $\eta(t)=M(L)\varepsilon(t)$ is invertible such that $\varepsilon(t)=M^{-1}(L)\eta(t)$ if and only if all the roots of $M(L)=0$ lie outside the unit circle.

We must also consider the property of stationarity. To see that any finite moving average process of the form $\eta(t)=M(L)\varepsilon(t)$ is stationary, we need only consider the fact that $\eta_t=\sum_{i=0}^{q}m_i\varepsilon_{t-i}$ and $\eta_{t+\tau}=\sum_{i=0}^{q}m_i\varepsilon_{t+\tau-i}$ are the same function of the identically distributed random vectors $[\varepsilon_t,\ldots,\varepsilon_{t-q}]$ and $[\varepsilon_{t+\tau},\ldots,\varepsilon_{t+\tau-q}]$. This means that they must have the same distribution for all values of τ.

To find the autocovariances of a finite-order moving average process, we use the formula $\gamma_\tau=\sigma_\varepsilon^2\sum_{i=0}^{q-\tau}m_im_{i+\tau}$ of (11.61). From this we may derive the equations

$$(11.69)\qquad \begin{aligned}\gamma_0&=(m_0^2+m_1^2+\ldots+m_q^2)\sigma_\varepsilon^2\\ \gamma_1&=(m_0m_1+m_1m_2+\ldots+m_{q-1}m_q)\sigma_\varepsilon^2\\ &\;\;\vdots\\ \gamma_q&=m_0m_q\sigma_\varepsilon^2.\end{aligned}$$

For the first-order process $\eta(t)=(I-\theta L)\varepsilon(t)$, we find that

$$(11.70)\qquad \gamma_0=(1+\theta^2)\sigma_\varepsilon^2,\qquad \gamma_1=-\theta\sigma_\varepsilon^2,\qquad \gamma_\tau=0\quad\text{for}\quad |\tau|>1;$$

so that, for a vector $\boldsymbol{\eta}'=[\eta_1,\ldots,\eta_T]$, we have a dispersion matrix of the form

$$(11.71)\qquad D(\boldsymbol{\eta})=\sigma_\varepsilon^2\begin{bmatrix}1+\theta^2, & -\theta, & \ldots\ldots, & 0\\ -\theta, & 1+\theta^2, & \ldots\ldots, & 0\\ \vdots & \vdots & & \vdots\\ 0, & 0, & \ldots\ldots, & 1+\theta^2\end{bmatrix}$$

In general, the dispersion matrix of a vector generated by a qth-order moving average process is a band matrix with $2q+1$ non-zero diagonals.

It is notable that, in the absence of a condition of invertibility, there is more than one set of parameters $m_0,\ldots,m_q$ which will satisfy the equations (11.69) and which will generate the same set of covariances $\gamma_0,\ldots,\gamma_q$. We can illustrate this with the first-order process $\eta(t)=(I-\theta L)\varepsilon(t)$ for which, according to (11.70),

$$(11.72)\qquad -\frac{\gamma_0}{\gamma_1}=\frac{1}{\theta}+\theta.$$

Here we can see that, if θ is a solution for given values of γ_0,γ_1, then so too is θ^{-1}. However, the restriction $|\theta|<1$, which is necessary for invertibility, is sufficient to render the solution unique.

Finite-order autoregressive processes

The pth-order autoregressive process $\eta(t)$ is defined by the equation

$$(11.73)\qquad A(L)\eta(t)=(I+a_1L+a_2L^2+\ldots+a_pL^p)\eta(t)=\varepsilon(t),$$

where $\varepsilon(t)$ is a sequence of independently and identically distributed random variables with a zero mean. Using $A^{-1}(L)$, we can express the process as an infinite-order moving average process $\eta(t)=A^{-1}(L)\varepsilon(t)$.

The polynomial $A(x)$ is factorized as $A(x)=\prod_{i=1}^{p}(1-\lambda_i^{-1}x)$. Its inverse is expressed in partial fractions as

(11.74) $$A^{-1}(x)=\sum_{i=1}^{p}\frac{k_i}{(1-\lambda_i^{-1}x)}.$$

This gives rise to a convergent series when $|x|\leq 1$ if and only if $|\lambda_i^{-1}|<1$ for all i, which is the condition that all the roots of $A(L)=0$ lie outside the unit circle. The convergence of the expansion of $A^{-1}(x)$ is the necessary and sufficient condition for the stationarity of the process. Thus

(11.75) The finite-order autoregressive process $\eta(t)$ defined by $A(L)\eta(t)=\varepsilon(t)$ has a stationary infinite-order moving average representation $\eta(t)=A^{-1}(L)\varepsilon(t)$ if and only if all the roots of $A(L)=0$ lie outside the unit circle.

We should also say that it is true by definition that a finite-order autoregressive process satisfies the condition for invertibility. A comparison of the statement in (11.75) above with the statement in (11.68) bears out the dual nature of the properties of stationarity and invertibility.

For an example of the conditions for stationarity, we may consider the second-order autoregressive process defined by

(11.76) $$(I-\phi_1L-\phi_2L^2)\eta(t)=\varepsilon(t), \quad \text{or}$$
$$\eta(t)=\phi_1\eta(t-1)+\phi_2\eta(t-2)+\varepsilon(t).$$

The roots of the equation $(I-\phi_1L-\phi_2L^2)=0$ are

(11.77) $$\lambda_1=\frac{\phi_1+\sqrt{\phi_1^2+4\phi_2}}{-2\phi_2},$$
$$\lambda_2=\frac{\phi_1-\sqrt{\phi_1^2+4\phi_2}}{-2\phi_2}.$$

Multiplying the roots gives $\lambda_1\lambda_2=-1/\phi_2$, and adding them gives $\lambda_1+\lambda_2=-\phi_1/\phi_2$. Thus

(11.78) $$\frac{1}{\lambda_1\lambda_2}=-\phi_2 \quad \text{and} \quad \frac{\lambda_1+\lambda_2}{\lambda_1\lambda_2}=\frac{1}{\lambda_1}+\frac{1}{\lambda_2}=\phi_1.$$

In view of the stationarity restrictions $|\lambda_1|$, $|\lambda_2|>1$, it follows that the parameters ϕ_1, ϕ_2 must lie in the triangular region defined by

(11.79) $$-1<\phi_2<1$$
$$\phi_2<1-\phi_1$$
$$\phi_2<1+\phi_1.$$

An interesting kind of non-stationary autoregressive model arises whenever one or more of the roots of the autoregressive lag operator $A(L)$ are unity whilst the remainder lie outside the unit circle. When d of the roots are unity, we can factorize the lag operator as $A(L)=A^*(L)(I-L)^d=A^*(L)D^d$ where $D=(I-L)$ is the difference operator such that $Dx(t)=x(t)-x(t-1)$. Thus, on taking $\omega(t)=D^d\eta(t)$ to represent the dth difference of $\eta(t)$, we can write the model

$$(11.80) \qquad A(L)\eta(t)=A^*(L)D^d\eta(t)=\varepsilon(t)$$

in the form of the stationary model

$$(11.81) \qquad A^*(L)\omega(t)=\varepsilon(t).$$

An alternative way of representing this non-stationary model makes use of the fact that the inverse of the difference operator D is the summation operator $S=(I-L)^{-1}=(I+L+L^2+\ldots)$ such that $Sx(t)=\sum_{i=0}^{\infty}x(t-i)$. The infinite sum $Sx(t)$ is described as an integrated sequence. By defining $\zeta(t)=D^{-d}\varepsilon(t)=S^d\varepsilon(t)$, we can write the model in (11.80) in the form of the integrated autoregressive model

$$(11.82) \qquad A^*(L)\eta(t)=\zeta(t).$$

If $d=1$ and $A^*(L)=I$, then we have a process $\eta(t)=S\varepsilon(t)$ which is described as a random walk. This will have the same appearance over a small interval as the process $\varepsilon(t)$ consisting of independently and identically distributed random variables. However, whereas $\varepsilon(t)$ proceeds at the level of its zero expectation, the level of the random walk drifts in a haphazard way. The kind of non-stationarity that results from the presence of one or more latent roots of unit value in the autoregressive lag polynomial is therefore aptly described as stochastic drift.

The autoregressive integrated model has considerable flexibility for representing non-stationary phenomena. For example, let $f(t)=c_0+c_1t+c_2t^2+\ldots+c_{d-1}t^{d-1}$ be a polynomial time trend of degree $d-1$ at most, and let us form the model

$$(11.83) \qquad A^*(L)D^d[\eta(t)+f(t)]=\varepsilon(t).$$

Since, according to (11.36), $D^df(t)=0$, equation (11.83) is indistinguishable from (11.80) and hence the process $\eta(t)+f(t)$ may be assimilated to the autoregressive integrated model.

A somewhat different kind of non-stationary model arises when a stationary autoregressive process $\eta(t)$ combines with a polynomial time trend $f(t)$ of degree $d-1$ to form

$$(11.84) \qquad \phi(t)=f(t)+\eta(t)$$

where

$$(11.85) \qquad A(L)\eta(t)=\varepsilon(t) \quad \text{and} \quad f(t)=\sum_{i=0}^{d-1} c_i t^i.$$

On taking the dth difference of $\phi(t)$, we get the purely stochastic sequence $D^d\phi(t)=D^d[f(t)+\eta(t)]=D^d\eta(t)$ which obeys the relationship

$$(11.86) \qquad A(L)D^d\eta(t)=D^d\varepsilon(t).$$

This differenced sequence provides a basis for investigating the nature of the lag polynomial $A(L)$. The method of reducing a non-stationary series to a stationary series by taking differences is described as the variate difference method; and it has been discussed extensively by Tintner in [**116**].

The autocovariances of a stationary autoregressive process may be found by means of the formula given in (11.61). For the first-order process defined by $(I-\phi L)\eta(t)=\varepsilon(t)$ or, equivalently, by $\eta(t)=(I-\phi L)^{-1}\varepsilon(t)=\sum_{i=0}^{\infty}\phi^i\varepsilon(t-i)$, we have

$$(11.87) \qquad \begin{aligned}\gamma_\tau &= E(\eta_t\eta_{t+\tau})=\sigma_\varepsilon^2\sum_i \phi^i\phi^{i+\tau}\\ &=\sigma_\varepsilon^2\phi^\tau\sum_i \phi^{2i}=\sigma_\varepsilon^2\frac{\phi^\tau}{1-\phi^2}.\end{aligned}$$

The variance of the process is

$$(11.88) \qquad \gamma_0=\frac{\sigma_\varepsilon^2}{1-\phi^2}.$$

Thus the dispersion matrix of the vector $\boldsymbol{\eta}'=[\eta_1,\ldots,\eta_T]$ generated by the first-order process takes the form of

(11.89)

$$D(\boldsymbol{\eta})=\frac{\sigma_\varepsilon^2}{1-\phi^2}\begin{bmatrix} 1, & \phi, & \phi^2 & ,\ldots, & \phi^{T-1}\\ \phi, & 1, & \phi & ,\ldots, & \phi^{T-2}\\ \phi^2, & \phi, & 1 & ,\ldots, & \phi^{T-3}\\ \cdot & \cdot & \cdot & & \cdot\\ \cdot & \cdot & \cdot & & \cdot\\ \cdot & \cdot & \cdot & & \cdot\\ \phi^{T-1}, & \phi^{T-2}, & \phi^{T-3} & ,\ldots, & 1\end{bmatrix}.$$

We may also derive the sequence of the autocovariances of an autoregressive process from the iterative solution of a certain difference equation, or recurrence relationship, in the autocovariance function $\gamma(\tau)$. To derive this relationship, we multiply the terms of $\eta_t + a_1\eta_{t-1} + \ldots + a_p\eta_{t-p} = \varepsilon_t$ by $\eta_{t-\tau}$ and take expectations to obtain

$$E(\eta_t\eta_{t-\tau}) + a_1E(\eta_{t-1}\eta_{t-\tau}) + \ldots + a_pE(\eta_{t-p}\eta_{t-\tau}) = E(\varepsilon_t\eta_{t-\tau}). \tag{11.90}$$

On setting $\tau = 0$ in this relationship, we obtain

$$\gamma_0 + a_1\gamma_1 + \ldots + a_p\gamma_p = \sigma_\varepsilon^2. \tag{11.91}$$

In this result, we have used

$$\begin{aligned} E(\varepsilon_t\eta_t) &= E(\varepsilon_t\{\varepsilon_t - a_1\eta_{t-1} - \ldots - a_p\eta_{t-p}\}) \\ &= E(\varepsilon_t^2) = \sigma_\varepsilon^2, \end{aligned}$$

which follows from the fact that $E(\varepsilon_t\eta_{t-i}) = 0$ for $i > 0$ since ε_t is statistically independent of preceding elements of $\eta(t)$. Next, on dividing the terms of (11.91) by γ_0 and writing $\rho_i = \gamma_i/\gamma_0$ for the ith autocorrelation, we obtain an expression for γ_0 in the form

$$\gamma_0 = \frac{\sigma_\varepsilon^2}{1 + a_1\rho_1 + \ldots + a_p\rho_p}. \tag{11.92}$$

On setting $\tau > 0$ in (11.90), we obtain

$$\gamma_\tau + a_1\gamma_{\tau-1} + \ldots + a_p\gamma_{\tau-p} = 0 \tag{11.93}$$

which indicates that the sequence of autocovariances $\gamma(\tau)$ satisfies a relationship of the form

$$\gamma(\tau) + a_1\gamma(\tau-1) + \ldots + a_p\gamma(\tau-p) = A(L)\gamma(\tau) = 0. \tag{11.94}$$

This is analogous to the relationship $A(L)\eta(t) = \varepsilon(t)$ which describes the stochastic process itself. Moreover, the condition that the roots of $A(L) = 0$ should lie outside the unit circle is necessary and sufficient both for the stationarity of the process $\eta(t)$ and for the convergence to zero of the sequence $\gamma(\tau)$. When we recall that $\lim(\tau \to \infty)\gamma_\tau = 0$ is a sufficient condition for the ergodicity of any stochastic process in respect of its mean, we can recognize in this result an instance of the fact that the conditions for stationarity and ergodicity are equivalent for linear processes.

Given that the parameters of the lag polynomial $A(L)$ are fully specified, the relationship $A(L)\gamma(\tau) = 0$ enables us to generate the sequence of autocovariances once a set of p consecutive values, say $\gamma_0, \ldots, \gamma_{p-1}$, are provided. Alternatively, if the parameters $a_0, a_1, \ldots, a_p$ of the lag polynomial are unknown apart from $a_0 = 1$, they may be inferred from the values of the autocovariances. Thus, on setting $\tau = 1, \ldots, p$ in the equation

$A(L)\gamma(\tau)=0$, we obtain the system of Yule–Walker equations

$$-\begin{bmatrix}\gamma_1\\ \gamma_2\\ \gamma_3\\ \cdot\\ \cdot\\ \cdot\\ \gamma_p\end{bmatrix}=\begin{bmatrix}\gamma_0, & \gamma_1, & \gamma_2 & ,\ldots, & \gamma_{p-1}\\ \gamma_1, & \gamma_0, & \gamma_1 & ,\ldots, & \gamma_{p-2}\\ \gamma_2, & \gamma_1, & \gamma_0 & ,\ldots, & \gamma_{p-3}\\ \cdot & \cdot & \cdot & & \cdot\\ \cdot & \cdot & \cdot & & \cdot\\ \cdot & \cdot & \cdot & & \cdot\\ \gamma_{p-1}, & \gamma_{p-2}, & \gamma_{p-3} & ,\ldots, & \gamma_0\end{bmatrix}\begin{bmatrix}a_1\\ a_2\\ a_3\\ \cdot\\ \cdot\\ \cdot\\ a_p\end{bmatrix} \tag{11.95}$$

which are solved for the unknown parameters.

For an illustration of the use of the Yule–Walker equations, we may consider the second-order process defined by $(I-\phi_1L-\phi_2L^2)\eta(t)=\varepsilon(t)$. By writing the autocorrelation coefficients $\rho_1=\gamma_1/\gamma_0$, $\rho_2=\gamma_2/\gamma_0$ in place of the autocovariances γ_1, γ_2, we may obtain from the Yule–Walker equations the identities

$$\begin{aligned}\rho_1&=\phi_1+\phi_2\rho_1,\\ \rho_2&=\phi_1\rho_1+\phi_2.\end{aligned} \tag{11.96}$$

These are solved for

$$\begin{aligned}\phi_1&=\frac{\rho_1(1-\rho_2)}{1-\rho_1^2},\\ \phi_2&=\frac{\rho_2-\rho_1^2}{1-\rho_1^2}.\end{aligned} \tag{11.97}$$

The equations (11.96) may also be solved to express ρ_1, ρ_2 in terms of ϕ_1, ϕ_2. Thus

$$\begin{aligned}\rho_1&=\frac{\phi_1}{1-\phi_2},\\ \rho_2&=\phi_2+\frac{\phi_1^2}{1-\phi_2}.\end{aligned} \tag{11.98}$$

Using (11.92), we can then find

$$\begin{aligned}\gamma_0&=\frac{\sigma_\varepsilon^2}{1-\rho_1\phi_1-\rho_2\phi_2}\\ &=\left(\frac{1-\phi_2}{1+\phi_2}\right)\frac{\sigma_\varepsilon^2}{[(1-\phi_2)^2-\phi_1^2]}.\end{aligned} \tag{11.99}$$

Mixed autoregressive moving average processes

Our results concerning finite autoregressive processes and finite moving average processes may be brought together to deal with the mixed process $\eta(t)$ defined by

$$A(L)\eta(t)=M(L)\varepsilon(t). \tag{11.100}$$

This may be regarded either as a pth-order autoregressive process defined by $A(L)\eta(t)=\zeta(t)$ wherein $\zeta(t)=M(L)\varepsilon(t)$ follows a qth-order moving average process, or as a qth-order moving average process $\eta(t)=M(L)\omega(t)$ wherein $\omega(t)=A^{-1}(L)\varepsilon(t)$ follows a pth-order autoregressive process. Thus we can see that the process will be stationary if the roots of $A(L)=0$ lie outside the unit circle and that, likewise, it will be invertible if the roots of $M(L)=0$ lie outside the unit circle.

The sequence of the autocovariances of the mixed process is found in the same manner as the autocovariances of an autoregressive process: either by using the formula given in (11.61) or by means of a recurrence relationship in the autocovariance function of the process. To establish the recurrence relationship, we multiply $\eta_t+\sum_{i=1}^{p} a_i\eta_{t-i}=\varepsilon_t+\sum_{i=1}^{q} m_i\varepsilon_{t-i}$ by $\eta_{t-\tau}$ and take expectations to obtain

$$\gamma_\tau+a_1\gamma_{\tau-1}+\ldots+a_p\gamma_{\tau-p}=\lambda_\tau+m_1\lambda_{\tau-1}+\ldots+m_q\lambda_{\tau-q} \tag{11.101}$$

wherein $\gamma_{\tau-i}=E(\eta_{t-i}\eta_{t-\tau})$ and $\lambda_{\tau-i}=E(\varepsilon_{t-i}\eta_{t-\tau})$. Since η_t is not affected by the subsequent disturbances $\varepsilon_{t+1}, \varepsilon_{t+2}, \ldots,$ it follows that $\lambda_\tau=E(\varepsilon_{t+\tau}\eta_t)=0$ whenever $\tau>0$. Thus we have a relationship of the form

$$\begin{aligned} &A(L)\gamma(\tau)=M(L)\gamma(\tau); \qquad |\tau|\leqslant q\\ &A(L)\gamma(\tau)=0; \qquad |\tau|>q. \end{aligned} \tag{11.102}$$

ESTIMATING THE PARAMETERS OF A LINEAR PROCESS

Estimating autoregressive parameters

Let $\eta(t)=x(t)-\mu$ be a stationary autoregressive process satisfying the equation

$$\begin{aligned} x(t)-\mu+a_1[x(t-1)-\mu]+a_2[x(t-2)-\mu]\\ +\ldots+a_p[x(t-p)-\mu]=\varepsilon(t) \end{aligned} \tag{11.103}$$

where $\varepsilon(t)$ is a sequence of independently and identically distributed random variables with zero mean. Then, given observations $x_1, \ldots, x_T$, it is reasonable to estimate the parameters $\mu, a_1, \ldots, a_p$ by finding the values that minimize the sum of squares

$$\sum_{t=p+1}^{T} \varepsilon_t^2 = \sum_{t=p+1}^{T} [(x_t-\mu)+a_1(x_{t+1}-\mu)+\ldots+a_p(x_{t-p}-\mu)]^2. \tag{11.104}$$

This procedure may be justified by showing that it amounts to a maximum-likelihood method on the assumption that $\varepsilon(t)$ is a normal process. On this assumption, the distribution of the elements $\varepsilon_{p+1}, \ldots, \varepsilon_T$ is given by

$$\frac{1}{(2\pi\sigma^2)^{(T-p)/2}} \exp\left\{-\frac{1}{\sigma^2}\sum_{t=p+1}^{T} \varepsilon_t^2\right\}. \tag{11.105}$$

The matrix of the transformation from $[x_{p+1}, \ldots, x_T]'$ to $[\varepsilon_{p+1}, \ldots, \varepsilon_T]'$ is lower triangular with units on its main diagonal. The Jacobian is therefore unity, and it follows that we can write the probability density function of the elements $x_{p+1}, \ldots, x_T$ conditional upon the values $x_1, \ldots, x_p$ as

$$\frac{1}{(2\pi\sigma^2)^{(T-p)/2}} \exp\left\{-\frac{1}{\sigma^2}\sum_{t=p+1}^{T} [(x_t-\mu)+a_1(x_{t-1}-\mu)+\ldots +a_p(x_{t-p}-\mu)]^2\right\}. \tag{11.106}$$

Thus the conditional likelihood function $L(x_{p+1}, \ldots, x_T \mid x_1, \ldots, x_p)$ is maximized by minimizing the sum of squares in (11.104).

An alternative to maximizing the conditional likelihood function is to maximize $L(x_1, \ldots, x_T)$ unconditionally in a way which entails finding estimates of the pre-sample elements $x_0, \ldots, x_{1-p}$. Another alternative is to maximize $L(x_1, \ldots, x_T)$ conditional upon some assigned values of the pre-sample elements. For example, if $E(x_t)=\mu=0$, then we might set $x_0=\ldots=x_{1-p}=0$. However, as the sample size T increases, the results of the various methods will tend to converge.

For the first-order model $x(t)-\mu+a[x(t-1)-\mu]=\varepsilon(t)$, the sum of squares in (11.104) becomes

$$\sum_{t=2}^{T} \varepsilon_t^2 = \sum_{t=2}^{T} [(x_t-\mu)+a(x_{t-1}-\mu)]^2. \tag{11.107}$$

Differentiating with respect to μ and a and setting the results to zero for a minimum gives, after trivial simplification, the normal equations

$$\begin{aligned} &\bar{x}_0-\hat{\mu}+\hat{a}(\bar{x}_1-\hat{\mu})=0, \\ &\sum_{t=2}^{T} (x_{t-1}-\hat{\mu})[(x_t-\hat{\mu})+\hat{a}_1(x_{t-1}-\hat{\mu})]=0, \end{aligned} \tag{11.108}$$

where

$$\bar{x}_0=(x_2+\ldots+x_T)/(T-1),$$
$$\bar{x}_1=(x_1+\ldots+x_{T-1})/(T-1).$$

Solving these equations, we find

(11.109)
$$\hat{\mu} = \frac{\bar{x}_0 + \hat{a}\bar{x}_1}{1+\hat{a}},$$

$$-\hat{a} = \frac{\sum_{t=2}^{T} (x_{t-1} - \hat{\mu})(x_t - \hat{\mu})}{\sum_{t=2}^{T} (x_{t-1} - \hat{\mu})^2}.$$

It is reasonable to approximate $\hat{\mu}$ in these formulae by the overall sample mean $\bar{x} = \sum_{t=1}^{T} x_t/T$.

The estimator $\hat{a}$ is consistent but not unbiased. To understand this, consider the case where $E(x_t) = \mu = 0$ for all t, so that $x(t) + ax(t-1) = \varepsilon(t)$. Then

(11.110)
$$-\hat{a} = \frac{\sum x_{t-1}x_t}{\sum x_{t-1}^2} = -a + \frac{\sum x_{t-1}\varepsilon_t}{\sum x_{t-1}^2},$$

and, since $x(t)$ and $\varepsilon(t)$ are not independent, we have $E(\sum x_{t-1}\varepsilon_t/\sum x_{t-1}^2) \neq \sum E(x_{t-1}/\sum x_{t-1}^2)E(\varepsilon_t) = 0$, and hence, in general, $E(\hat{a}) \neq a$. Nevertheless, since ε_t and x_{t-1} are independent variates, we have

(11.111)
$$\text{plim}\left(\sum x_{t-1}\varepsilon_t/\sum x_{t-1}^2\right)$$
$$= \text{plim}\left(\sum x_{t-1}\varepsilon_t/T\right) \Big/ \text{plim}\left(\sum x_{t-1}^2/T\right) = 0/\sigma_x^2;$$

whence $\text{plim}(\hat{a}) = a$, and the estimator is consistent.

Consideration of the least-squares estimates of the parameters of the second-order autoregressive process $[x(t) - \mu] + a_1[x(t-1) - \mu] + a_2[x(t-2) - \mu] = \varepsilon(t)$ enables us to gain an insight into the general case. By differentiating the appropriate sum of squares, we obtain the normal equations

(11.112)
$$-\begin{bmatrix} \sum (x_t - \hat{\mu})(x_{t-1} - \hat{\mu}) \\ \sum (x_t - \hat{\mu})(x_{t-2} - \hat{\mu}) \end{bmatrix} = \begin{bmatrix} \sum (x_{t-1} - \hat{\mu})^2, & \sum (x_{t-1} - \hat{\mu})(x_{t-2} - \hat{\mu}) \\ \sum (x_{t-1} - \hat{\mu})(x_{t-2} - \hat{\mu}), & \sum (x_{t-2} - \hat{\mu})^2 \end{bmatrix} \begin{bmatrix} \hat{a}_1 \\ \hat{a}_2 \end{bmatrix},$$
$$(\bar{x}_0 - \hat{\mu}) + \hat{a}_1(\bar{x}_1 - \hat{\mu}) + \hat{a}_2(\bar{x}_2 - \hat{\mu}) = 0,$$

where each summation is from $t = 3$ to $t = T$ and where

$$\bar{x}_\tau = (T-2)^{-1} \sum_{t=3}^{T} x_{t-\tau} \quad \text{for} \quad \tau, = 0, 1, 2.$$

On dividing both sides of the first equation (11.112) by $T - 2$, we find that its elements are simply estimates of the variance γ_0 and the autocovariances

γ_1, γ_2 of the process $x(t)$. These estimates are asymptotically equivalent to the estimates c_0, c_1 and c_2 defined in (11.46). Using the latter instead, we obtain the system

$$(11.113) \qquad -\begin{bmatrix} c_1 \\ c_2 \end{bmatrix} = \begin{bmatrix} c_0, c_1 \\ c_1, c_0 \end{bmatrix} \begin{bmatrix} \hat{a}_1 \\ \hat{a}_2 \end{bmatrix}$$

which is the empirical version of the Yule–Walker equations defined in (11.95). The Yule–Walker estimates of the autoregressive parameters a_1 and a_2 are obviously consistent by virtue of the consistency of the estimates c_0, c_1 and c_2. The consistency of the least-squares estimates can easily be established by showing that they are asymptotically equivalent to the Yule–Walker estimates.

Estimating moving average parameters

Let $\eta(t) = x(t) - \mu$ be a stationary moving average process satisfying the equation

$$(11.114) \qquad x(t) - \mu = \varepsilon(t) + m_1\varepsilon(t-1) + \ldots + m_q\varepsilon(t-q).$$

Then, given the observations $x_1, \ldots, x_T$ and a set of pre-sample values $\varepsilon_0, \ldots, \varepsilon_{1-q}$, we can estimate the unknown parameters $\mu, m_1, \ldots, m_q$ by finding the values that minimize

$$(11.115) \qquad \sum_{t=1}^{T} \varepsilon_t^2 = \sum_{t=1}^{T} [(x_t - \mu) - m_1\varepsilon_{t-1} - \ldots - m_q\varepsilon_{t-q}]^2.$$

Under the assumption that $\varepsilon(t)$ is a normal process, these least-squares estimates would also maximize the conditional likelihood function $L(x_1, \ldots, x_T \mid \varepsilon_0, \ldots, \varepsilon_{1-q})$.

We might attempt to find the estimates by differentiating the sum of squares in respect of the unknown parameters and setting the results to zero. This would require writing the sum of squares as a function solely of the data and the parameters; and, since each element ε_t is a non-linear function of the unknown parameters, the approach is hardly viable.

When the moving average process is of low order, it is practical to find a minimum by comparing values of the sum of squares for various choices of the parameters. The elements $\varepsilon_1, \ldots, \varepsilon_T$ that are required in order to evaluate the sum of squares may be generated from the chosen parameter values and the pre-sample elements by a single recursive procedure based on equation (11.114). Since $E(\varepsilon_t) = 0$ for all t, it is natural to specify the pre-sample elements as $\varepsilon_0 = \ldots = \varepsilon_{1-q} = 0$. Alternatively, we can generate "backwards forecasts" of these elements using a method described by Box and Jenkins in [**15**].

There are also a number of direct iterative methods that may be used to estimate the parameters of a moving average process. For example, given a set of initial estimates $\mu_0, m_{1,0}, \ldots, m_{q,0}$ and a set of pre-sample values $\varepsilon_0, \ldots, \varepsilon_{1-q}$, we could begin by generating recursively the values $\varepsilon_{1,0}, \ldots, \varepsilon_{T,0}$. Then, having formed the regression equations

$$x_t = \mu + \sum_{i=1}^{q} m_i \varepsilon_{t-i,0} + \varepsilon_t, \qquad t = 1, \ldots, T, \tag{11.116}$$

we could use ordinary least squares to find revised estimates $\mu_1, m_{1,1}, \ldots, m_{q,1}$. The revised estimates could be used to generate new values $\varepsilon_{1,1}, \ldots, \varepsilon_{T,1}$ and the procedure could be continued in like manner in the hope that the sequence of revised estimates will ultimately converge. If the initial estimates are consistent, then the revised estimates from any stage of the procedure will also be consistent. However, it is not certain that the sequence of estimates will converge nor, if it does converge, is it certain that the resulting estimates will minimize the sum of squares.

We shall outline a more secure iterative method when we come to deal with the estimation of the mixed autoregressive moving average model.

Another approach to estimating the moving average model is to substitute estimates of the covariances of the process into the equations (11.69) which describe a relationship between the true autocovariances and the true parameters of the model. Using the additional constraints arising from the assumption of invertibility, we can then solve the system to obtain unique estimates of the parameters. Thus, for example, in the case of the second-order process $x(t) - \mu = \varepsilon(t) - \theta_1 \varepsilon(t-1) - \theta_2 \varepsilon(t-2)$, we would solve the equations

$$\begin{aligned} c_0 &= (1 + \hat{\theta}_1^2 + \hat{\theta}_2^2)\hat{\sigma}_\varepsilon^2 \\ c_1 &= (-\hat{\theta}_1 + \hat{\theta}_1 \theta_2)\hat{\sigma}_\varepsilon^2 \\ c_2 &= -\hat{\theta}_2 \hat{\sigma}_\varepsilon^2 \end{aligned} \tag{11.117}$$

subject to the invertibility constraints

$$\begin{aligned} -1 &< \hat{\theta}_2 < 1, \\ \hat{\theta}_2 &< 1 - \hat{\theta}_1, \\ \hat{\theta}_2 &< 1 + \hat{\theta}_1. \end{aligned} \tag{11.118}$$

Unlike the analogous Yule–Walker equations for an autoregressive process, these are non-linear in the unknown parameters and their solution presents some problems. Moreover, as Whittle [**121**] has shown, they give rise to inefficient estimates. However, the estimates may be useful as the initial values in an iterative procedure.

Estimating the parameters of a mixed model

The parameters of the mixed autoregressive moving average model

$$x(t)-\mu+a_1[x(t-1)-\mu]+\ldots+a_p[x(t-p)-\mu] = \varepsilon(t)+m_1\varepsilon(t-1)+\ldots+m_q\varepsilon(t-q) \tag{11.119}$$

may be estimated from a sample $x_1, \ldots, x_T$ by finding the values that minimize the sum of squares

$$\sum_{t=1}^{T} \varepsilon_t^2 = \sum_{t=1}^{T} \left[x_t - \mu + \sum_{i=1}^{p} a_i(x_{t-i}-\mu) - \sum_{i=1}^{q} m_i\varepsilon_{t-i} \right]^2 \tag{11.120}$$

subject to a choice of the requisite pre-sample values of $x(t)$ and $\varepsilon(t)$. For this, we may use either a search procedure, as in the case of the moving average model, or an iterative procedure such as the one suggested by Box and Jenkins in [**15**]. To describe the latter, let us write the sample elements of $\varepsilon(t)$ as $\varepsilon_t = f_t(\mathbf{b})$, where $\mathbf{b}' = [a_1, \ldots, a_p, m_1, \ldots, m_q, \mu]$ is a vector containing the $k = p+q+1$ unknown parameters. Then, if $\mathbf{b}_0$ is some initial estimate or starting value, a first-order approximation to $\varepsilon_t = f_t(\mathbf{b})$ would be given by

$$e_t = f_t(\mathbf{b}_0) + \sum_{i=1}^{k} (b_i - b_{i,0}) \left[\frac{\partial f_t(\mathbf{b}_0)}{\partial b_i} \right]. \tag{11.121}$$

Writing $\varepsilon_{t,0} = f_t(\mathbf{b}_0)$ and $z_{it,0} = [\partial f_t(\mathbf{b}_0)/\partial b_i]$ for the value of the derivative of f_t at $\mathbf{b}_0$, we get

$$e_t = \varepsilon_{t,0} + \sum_{i=1}^{k} (b_i - b_{i,0}) z_{it,0}. \tag{11.122}$$

This has the form of a regression equation, and, by applying the method of ordinary least squares, we can obtain estimates of $(b_i - b_{i,0})$ and hence of the unknown parameters b_i. These estimates, which we can denote by $b_{i,1}$, are only the first approximations to the values which minimize the sum of squares in (11.120). To obtain closer approximations, we may repeat the regression procedure using $b_{i,1}$ and the newly evaluated derivatives $z_{it,1} = [\partial f_t(\mathbf{b}_1)/\partial b_i]$ in place of $b_{i,0}$ and $z_{it,0}$. Thus, in the $(r+1)$th iteration of the procedure we would obtain estimates $b_{i,r+1}$, where $i = 1, \ldots, k$, from the regression equation

$$e_t = \varepsilon_{t,r} + \sum_{i=1}^{k} (b_i - b_{i,r}) z_{it,r}. \tag{11.123}$$

The derivatives $z_{it,r}$ that are required by this technique may be obtained either by a simple numerical method or by an analytical method.

In the numerical method, we take a small deviation δ_i around the value $b_{i,r}$ to find

$$(11.124) \qquad z_{it,r} = \frac{f_t(b_{1,r}, \ldots, b_{i,r} + \delta_i, \ldots, b_{k,r}) - f_t(b_{1,r}, \ldots, b_{i,r}, \ldots, b_{k,r})}{\delta_i}.$$

To find the derivatives by the alternative method, we differentiate the sequence $\varepsilon(t) = M^{-1}(L)A(L)\eta(t)$, where $\eta(t) = x(t) - \mu$, to give

$$(11.125) \qquad \begin{aligned} \frac{\partial \varepsilon(t)}{\partial a_i} &= M^{-1}(L)L^i\eta(t) = M^{-1}(L)\eta(t-i) \\ &= A^{-1}(L)\varepsilon(t-i) \end{aligned}$$

and

$$(11.126) \qquad \begin{aligned} \frac{\partial \varepsilon(t)}{\partial m_i} &= -M^{-2}(L)L^iA(L)\eta(t) = -M^{-2}(L)A(L)\eta(t-i) \\ &= -M^{-1}(L)\varepsilon(t-i). \end{aligned}$$

The sequence of derivatives $z_i(t) = \partial\varepsilon(t)/\partial b_i$ therefore satisfies the equivalent relationships

$$(11.127) \qquad \begin{aligned} &A(L)z_i(t) = z_i(t) + a_1 z_i(t-1) + \ldots + a_p z_i(t-p) = \varepsilon(t-i) \\ &M(L)z_i(t) = z_i(t) + m_1 z_i(t-1) + \ldots + m_q z_i(t-q) = \eta(t-i) \\ &\text{for} \quad i = 1, \ldots, p, \end{aligned}$$

and the relationship

$$(11.128) \qquad \begin{aligned} &M(L)z_i(t) = z_i(t) + m_1 z_i(t-1) + \ldots + m_q z_i(t-q) = \varepsilon(t+p-i) \\ &\text{for} \quad i = p+1, \ldots, p+q. \end{aligned}$$

Once we have a set of values for the parameters of $A(L)$ and $M(L)$, we can generate the required values of z_{it}, where $i = 1, \ldots, p+q$ and $t = 1, \ldots, T$, by using a simple recursive procedure based on the relationships in (11.127) and (11.128). For this, we need to specify the pre-sample values $\eta_0, \ldots, \eta_{1-q}$ and $\varepsilon_0, \ldots, \varepsilon_{1-l}$ where $l = \max(p, q)$, and the derivatives $z_{i0}, \ldots, z_{il}$. It is appropriate to set all of these to zero.

We can use the iterative procedure which we have just outlined for estimating the parameters of the simple moving average model. In that case, the algorithm which describes the $(r+1)$th iteration is given by

$$(11.129) \qquad e_t = \varepsilon_{t,r} + \sum_{i=1}^{q} (m_i - m_{i,r}) z_{it,r}.$$

When we approximate the derivatives $z_{it,r} = [\partial f_t(\mathbf{m}_r)/\partial m_i]$ by $-\varepsilon_{t-i}$, the algorithm becomes

$$(11.130) \qquad e_t = \varepsilon_{t,r} - \sum_{i=1}^{q} (m_i - m_{i,r})\varepsilon_{t-i,r}$$

$$= x_t - \mu - \sum_{i=1}^{q} m_i \varepsilon_{t-i,r}.$$

Reference to (11.116) shows that this represents precisely the iterative method that we originally proposed for estimating the parameters of the moving average model.

BIBLIOGRAPHY

Stationary Stochastic Processes. Bartlett [**12**], Jenkins and Watts [**59**], Kendall and Stuart [**62,** Chap. 47]

Estimating the Moments of a Stationary Process. Kendall and Stuart [**62,** Chap. 48], Wilks [**122,** Chap. 17 §4]

Linear Stochastic Processes. Fuller [**39,** Chap. 2], Box and Jenkins [**15,** Chap. 3, 4], Wise [**123**]

Estimating the Parameters of a Linear Process. Box and Jenkins [**15,** Chap. 7], Fuller [**39,** Chap. 8], Jenkins and Watts [**59,** Chap. 5 §4]

CHAPTER 12

Temporal Regression Models

In the previous chapter, we were concerned with the linear stochastic model

$$(12.1)\qquad \sum_{i=0}^{p} a_i y(t-i)=\sum_{i=0}^{q} m_i \varepsilon(t-i)$$

wherein $y(t)$ was an observable stochastic process and $\varepsilon(t)$ was a sequence of independent and identically distributed random variables. The model will now be elaborated by the inclusion of an observable input sequence $x(t)$ to form the relationship

$$(12.2)\qquad \sum_{i=0}^{p} a_i y(t-i)=\sum_{i=0}^{r} \beta_i x(t-i)+\sum_{i=0}^{q} m_i \varepsilon(t-i).$$

This is described as the general form of the temporal regression model. The generalization of the model may be carried even further by having a vector of k input sequences $\mathbf{x}(t)=[x_1(t),\ldots,x_k(t)]$ in place of the single input sequence $x(t)$, and by defining k distinct lag schemes to correspond to each of these sequences.

In practice, we shall be dealing with a number of distinct specializations of the general model; and we shall use the notation of the general model mainly for the purposes of taxonomy.

THE CLASSICAL MODEL WITH STOCHASTIC REGRESSIONS

We shall begin by considering the simple temporal regression model

$$(12.3)\qquad y(t)=\mathbf{x}(t)\boldsymbol{\beta}+\varepsilon(t).$$

Hitherto, in dealing with the regression relationship $y_t=\mathbf{x}_{t.}\boldsymbol{\beta}+\varepsilon_t$, we have assumed that the vector $\mathbf{x}_{t.}=[x_{t1},\ldots,x_{tk}]$ is non-stochastic. We shall now assume that it is generated by a stationary stochastic process $\mathbf{x}(t)$ which is independent of the process $\varepsilon(t)$ generating the disturbances ε_t. Thus, when considering the joint distribution of $\mathbf{x}_{t.}$ and ε_t, we shall specify that

$$(12.4)\qquad \begin{aligned} E(\varepsilon_t\,|\,\mathbf{x}_{t.})&=E(\varepsilon_t)=0,\\ E(\mathbf{x}_{t.}\,|\,\varepsilon_t)&=E(\mathbf{x}_{t.})=\boldsymbol{\mu}', \end{aligned}$$

and that

$$D\begin{bmatrix}\mathbf{x}'_{t.}\\ \varepsilon_t\end{bmatrix}=\begin{bmatrix}D(\mathbf{x}'_{t.}), & C(\mathbf{x}_{t.},\varepsilon_t)\\ C(\varepsilon_t,\mathbf{x}_{t.}), & V(\varepsilon_t)\end{bmatrix}=\begin{bmatrix}\mathbf{M}, & \mathbf{0}\\ \mathbf{0}, & \sigma^2\end{bmatrix}\tag{12.5}$$

where

$$\begin{aligned}\mathbf{M}&=E([\mathbf{x}_{t.}-\boldsymbol{\mu}']'[\mathbf{x}_{t.}-\boldsymbol{\mu}'])\\ &=E(\mathbf{x}'_{t.}\mathbf{x}_{t.})-\boldsymbol{\mu}\boldsymbol{\mu}'\\ &=\mathbf{W}-\boldsymbol{\mu}\boldsymbol{\mu}'.\end{aligned}\tag{12.6}$$

We shall assume that the processes $\mathbf{x}(t)$ and $\varepsilon(t)$ are ergodic in respect of their first and second-order moments so that

$$\begin{aligned}\text{plim}\left(\frac{\mathbf{X}'\mathbf{X}}{T}\right)&=\text{plim}\left(\frac{1}{T}\sum_{t=1}^{T}\mathbf{x}'_{t.}\mathbf{x}_{t.}\right)=\mathbf{W},\\ \text{plim}\left(\frac{\mathbf{X}'\boldsymbol{\varepsilon}}{T}\right)&=\text{plim}\left(\frac{1}{T}\sum_{t=1}^{T}\mathbf{x}'_{t.}\varepsilon_t\right)=\mathbf{0},\\ \text{plim}\left(\frac{\boldsymbol{\varepsilon}'\boldsymbol{\varepsilon}}{T}\right)&=\text{plim}\left(\frac{1}{T}\sum_{t=1}^{T}\varepsilon_t^2\right)=\sigma^2.\end{aligned}\tag{12.7}$$

These results signify that the sample moments are consistent estimators of their corresponding population moments.

The present assumptions extend the scope of the classical linear model without significantly altering the results that we have obtained in Chapter 7. The basic difference is that we must now take care to regard the distributions of $\mathbf{y}$ and of functions of $\mathbf{y}$ as conditional on the set of values realized by $\mathbf{x}(t)$ contained in the data matrix $\mathbf{X}$. Thus, for example, in place of $E(\mathbf{y})=\mathbf{X}\boldsymbol{\beta}$ we must specify

$$E(\mathbf{y}\,|\,\mathbf{X})=E(\mathbf{X}\boldsymbol{\beta}+\boldsymbol{\varepsilon}\,|\,\mathbf{X})=\mathbf{X}\boldsymbol{\beta}+E(\boldsymbol{\varepsilon}\,|\,\mathbf{X})=\mathbf{X}\boldsymbol{\beta}.\tag{12.8}$$

Likewise, for the ordinary least-squares estimator $\hat{\boldsymbol{\beta}}$ we must now specify that

$$\begin{aligned}E(\hat{\boldsymbol{\beta}}\,|\,\mathbf{X})&=\boldsymbol{\beta}+E[(\mathbf{X}'\mathbf{X})^{-1}\mathbf{X}']E(\boldsymbol{\varepsilon}\,|\,\mathbf{X})=\boldsymbol{\beta},\\ D(\hat{\boldsymbol{\beta}}\,|\,\mathbf{X})&=E[(\mathbf{X}'\mathbf{X})^{-1}\mathbf{X}\boldsymbol{\varepsilon}\boldsymbol{\varepsilon}'\mathbf{X}(\mathbf{X}'\mathbf{X})^{-1}\,|\,\mathbf{X}]=\sigma^2(\mathbf{X}'\mathbf{X})^{-1}.\end{aligned}\tag{12.9}$$

The unconditional expectations are simply

$$\begin{aligned}E(\mathbf{y})&=E[E(\mathbf{y}\,|\,\mathbf{X})]=E(\mathbf{X})\boldsymbol{\beta}=\mathbf{i}\boldsymbol{\mu}'\boldsymbol{\beta},\\ E(\hat{\boldsymbol{\beta}})&=E[E(\boldsymbol{\beta}\,|\,\mathbf{X})]=\boldsymbol{\beta},\\ D(\hat{\boldsymbol{\beta}})&=E[D(\hat{\boldsymbol{\beta}}\,|\,\mathbf{X})]=\sigma^2\mathbf{W}^{-1}/T.\end{aligned}\tag{12.10}$$

The asymptotic properties of the ordinary least-squares regression are also conserved. Thus the estimator $\hat{\boldsymbol{\beta}}$ is still consistent, since from $\hat{\boldsymbol{\beta}} = \boldsymbol{\beta} + (\mathbf{X}'\mathbf{X})^{-1}\mathbf{X}'\boldsymbol{\varepsilon}$ we continue to get

$$\text{(12.11)} \qquad \begin{aligned} \text{plim}(\hat{\boldsymbol{\beta}}) &= \boldsymbol{\beta} + \text{plim}\left(\frac{\mathbf{X}'\mathbf{X}}{T}\right)^{-1} \text{plim}\left(\frac{\mathbf{X}'\boldsymbol{\varepsilon}}{T}\right) \\ &= \boldsymbol{\beta} + \mathbf{W}^{-1}\mathbf{0} = \boldsymbol{\beta}. \end{aligned}$$

Equally we find, as in (7.63), that

(12.12) The distribution of $\sqrt{T}(\hat{\boldsymbol{\beta}} - \boldsymbol{\beta}) = (\mathbf{X}'\mathbf{X}/T)^{-1}(\mathbf{X}'\boldsymbol{\varepsilon}/\sqrt{T})$ tends to the distribution $N(\mathbf{0}, \sigma^2\mathbf{W}^{-1})$ as T tends to infinity.

To obtain this result, we use the central limit theorem of (17.68) to deduce that the distribution of $\mathbf{X}'\boldsymbol{\varepsilon}/\sqrt{T} = \sum \mathbf{x}'_{t.}\varepsilon_t/\sqrt{T}$ converges to the normal distribution $N(\mathbf{0}, \sigma^2\mathbf{W})$. Then, given that $\text{plim}(\mathbf{X}'\mathbf{X}/T) = \mathbf{W}$, we can easily deduce the limiting distribution of $(\mathbf{X}'\mathbf{X}/T)^{-1}(\mathbf{X}'\boldsymbol{\varepsilon}/\sqrt{T})$.

REGRESSION MODELS WITH LAGGED DEPENDENT VARIABLES

When the equation $\sum_{i=0}^{p} a_i y(t-i) = \beta x(t) + \varepsilon(t)$ is written as

$$\text{(12.13)} \qquad y(t) = \beta x(t) - \sum_{i=1}^{p} a_i y(t-i) + \varepsilon(t),$$

it assumes the form of a regression relationship explaining the value of the current element of $y(t)$ in terms of previous elements of that sequence and the current value of the input sequence $x(t)$. This relationship is described alternatively as an autoregressive regression or as a regression with lagged dependent variables amongst the explanatory variables.

When the sequence of explanatory variables contains lagged dependent variables, it is clearly not independent of the sequence of disturbances $\varepsilon(t)$. It follows that we cannot sustain the results of the previous section. In particular, the ordinary least-squares estimator is no longer unbiased. However, the fact that the regressors $y_{t-1}, \ldots, y_{t-p}$ are independent of the disturbance ε_t and of all succeeding disturbances is sufficient, in normal circumstances, to ensure the consistency and the asymptotic normality of the ordinary least-squares estimates. Thus it may be proved that

(12.14) The ordinary least-squares estimates $\hat{\beta}, \hat{a}_1, \ldots, \hat{a}_p$ of the parameters of the relationship in (12.13) are consistent whenever $x(t)$ is a stationary stochastic process and the roots of the equation $A(z) = 1 + a_1 z + \cdots + a_p z^p = 0$ lie outside the unit circle.

In addition it can be proved that

(12.15) The joint distribution of the elements $\sqrt{T}(\hat{\beta}-\beta)$, $\sqrt{T}(\hat{a}_1-a_1),\ldots,\sqrt{T}(\hat{a}_p-a_p)$ tends asymptotically with T to a normal distribution with zero mean and a dispersion matrix which is σ^2 times the inverse of the matrix whose elements are the probability limits of the sample moments $\sum x_t y_{t-i}/T$; $i=1,\ldots,p$ and $\sum y_{t-i}y_{t-j}/T$; $i,j=1,\ldots,p$.

These results were first established by Mann and Wald in [**83**]. In essence, their proof is an extension of one which establishes the consistency and asymptotic normality of the ordinary least-squares regression estimates of the parameters of the simple autoregressive model $\sum_{i=0}^{p} a_i y(t-i)=\varepsilon(t)$. A very accessible version of this proof is provided by Grenander and Rosenblatt [**46**].

If $x(t)$ is a linear stochastic process, then the relationship in (12.13) may be placed in the context of the bivariate stochastic process

$$(12.16)\qquad \begin{bmatrix} A(L), & B(L) \\ C(L), & D(L) \end{bmatrix}\begin{bmatrix} y(t) \\ x(t) \end{bmatrix}=\begin{bmatrix} \varepsilon_1(t) \\ \varepsilon_2(t) \end{bmatrix}.$$

To obtain the relationship in (12.13), we require only the specializations $B(L)=-\beta$, $C(L)=0$. The bivariate process is stationary whenever all the roots of the equation

$$(12.17)\qquad \det\begin{bmatrix} A(z), & B(z) \\ C(z), & D(z) \end{bmatrix}=0$$

lie outside the unit circle. With our present specializations, the requirement is simply that the roots of $A(z)=0$ and $D(z)=0$ should lie outside the unit circle.

It should be emphasized that the results of this section, concerning the consistency of the ordinary least-squares estimator in the presence of lagged dependent variables, do not apply when the disturbance terms are serially correlated. Malinvaud [**82**] provides a powerful numerical illustration of this fact by considering a regression model with a lagged dependent variable and a disturbance term generated by a first-order autoregressive process.

REGRESSION MODELS WITH SERIALLY CORRELATED DISTURBANCES

For a temporal regression model, it is reasonable to assume that the disturbances are serially correlated. We commonly imagine that the disturbance term is compounded from a large number of minor factors that are too insignificant individually to be included in the systematic structure of the model. A significant number of these factors might vary quite gradually in time, with the result that the sequence of disturbances will manifest some degree of inertia. This will be reflected in positive correlations among proximate elements of the sequence. To take account of this phenomenon of serial correlation, we must replace the simple temporal regression model $y(t)=\mathbf{x}(t)\boldsymbol{\beta}+\varepsilon(t)$, wherein $\varepsilon(t)$ is a sequence of independent and identically distributed random variables, by a model

$$(12.18) \qquad y(t)=\mathbf{x}(t)\boldsymbol{\beta}+\eta(t),$$

wherein $\eta(t)$ is some stationary linear stochastic process.

We are rarely in the position of knowing the parameters of the process $\eta(t)$. Thus we may not be able to define the estimation procedure which is most appropriate to the relationship underlying the data. Instead, we might make do with the method of ordinary least-squares regression. According to the familiar argument, the ordinary least-squares estimates will be unbiased provided that the processes $\mathbf{x}(t)$ and $\eta(t)$ are uncorrelated. To demonstrate the consistency and asymptotic normality of the estimates is less straightforward. However, Grenander has shown in **[45]** that consistency is assured whenever $\eta(t)$ is a stationary linear process and the vector sequence $\mathbf{x}(t)$ conforms to our assumption in (12.7).

REGRESSION MODELS WITH AUTOREGRESSIVE DISTURBANCES

We are often prepared to make assumptions about the nature of the process $\eta(t)$; and, in econometrics, it is common to assume that it is an autoregressive process of low order. When $\eta(t)$ is a first-order autoregressive process, the equation (12.18) becomes

$$(12.19) \qquad y(t)=\mathbf{x}(t)\boldsymbol{\beta}+(I-\phi L)^{-1}\varepsilon(t).$$

On multiplying both sides by $(I-\phi L)$, we get

$$(12.20) \qquad y(t)-\phi y(t-1)=\mathbf{x}(t)\boldsymbol{\beta}-\phi\mathbf{x}(t-1)\boldsymbol{\beta}+\varepsilon(t).$$

Given a sample of T observations comprised in $\mathbf{y}'=[y_1,\ldots,y_T]$ and $\mathbf{X}'=[\mathbf{x}'_{1.},\ldots,\mathbf{x}'_{T.}]$, it seem appropriate to estimate the parameters $\boldsymbol{\beta}$, ϕ by finding the values that minimize the sum of squares

$$(12.21) \qquad S(\boldsymbol{\beta},\phi)=\sum_{t=2}^{T}[y_t-\phi y_{t-1}-\mathbf{x}_{t.}\boldsymbol{\beta}+\phi\mathbf{x}_{t-1.}\boldsymbol{\beta}]^2.$$

For a given value of ϕ, this is equivalent to applying ordinary least-squares regression to the transformed data **Ty**, **TX**, where

$$\text{(12.22)}\qquad \mathbf{T}=\begin{bmatrix} -\phi, & 1, & 0, & \ldots, & 0, & 0 \\ 0, & -\phi, & 1, & \ldots, & 0, & 0 \\ \cdot & \cdot & \cdot & & \cdot & \cdot \\ \cdot & \cdot & \cdot & & \cdot & \cdot \\ \cdot & \cdot & \cdot & & \cdot & \cdot \\ 0, & 0, & 0, & \ldots, & 1, & 0 \\ 0, & 0, & 0, & \ldots, & -\phi, & 1 \end{bmatrix}$$

is a $(T-1)\times T$ matrix which is the sample analogue of the linear operator $(I-\phi L)$. Thus the minimand can also be written as

$$\text{(12.23)}\qquad S(\boldsymbol{\beta},\phi)=[\mathbf{y}-\mathbf{X}\boldsymbol{\beta}]'\mathbf{T}'(\phi)\mathbf{T}(\phi)[\mathbf{y}-\mathbf{X}\boldsymbol{\beta}].$$

The fact that the transformation **T** is singular with Null(**T**) = 1 suggests that the procedure entails a small loss of information. We are therefore motivated to examine the alternative of applying the method of Gaussian regression in the $\mathbf{Q}^{-1}$-metric to the model $(\mathbf{y}, \mathbf{X}\boldsymbol{\beta}, \sigma_\varepsilon^2\mathbf{Q})$, where $\sigma_\varepsilon^2\mathbf{Q}$ is the dispersion matrix of the vector $\boldsymbol{\eta}'=[\eta_1,\ldots,\eta_T]$ which is specified in (11.89). The inverse of the matrix **Q** is

$$\text{(12.24)}\qquad \mathbf{Q}^{-1}=\begin{bmatrix} 1, & -\phi, & 0, & \ldots, & 0, & 0 \\ -\phi, & 1+\phi^2, & -\phi, & \ldots, & 0, & 0 \\ 0, & -\phi, & 1+\phi^2, & \ldots, & 0, & 0 \\ \cdot & \cdot & \cdot & & \cdot & \cdot \\ \cdot & \cdot & \cdot & & \cdot & \cdot \\ \cdot & \cdot & \cdot & & \cdot & \cdot \\ 0, & 0, & 0, & \ldots, & 1+\phi^2, & -\phi \\ 0, & 0, & 0, & \ldots, & -\phi, & 1 \end{bmatrix}.$$

This may be factorized as $\mathbf{Q}^{-1}=\mathbf{M}'\mathbf{M}$ where

$$\text{(12.25)}\qquad \mathbf{M}=\begin{bmatrix} \sqrt{1-\phi^2}, & 0, & 0, & \ldots, & 0, & 0 \\ -\phi, & 1, & 0, & \ldots, & 0, & 0 \\ 0, & -\phi, & 1, & \ldots, & 0, & 0 \\ \cdot & \cdot & \cdot & & \cdot & \cdot \\ \cdot & \cdot & \cdot & & \cdot & \cdot \\ \cdot & \cdot & \cdot & & \cdot & \cdot \\ 0, & 0, & 0, & \ldots, & 1, & 0 \\ 0, & 0, & 0, & \ldots, & -\phi, & 1 \end{bmatrix}$$

is a $T\times T$ matrix which differs from **T** in (12.22) only by having an extra row. The minimum $\mathbf{Q}^{-1}$-distance estimate of $\boldsymbol{\beta}$ can be found by applying the method of ordinary least squares to the transformed data **My**, **MX** to yield

(12.26)
$$\hat{\boldsymbol{\beta}} = (\mathbf{X}'\mathbf{M}'\mathbf{M}\mathbf{X})^{-1}\mathbf{X}'\mathbf{M}'\mathbf{M}\mathbf{y} = (\mathbf{X}'\mathbf{Q}^{-1}\mathbf{X})^{-1}\mathbf{X}'\mathbf{Q}^{-1}\mathbf{y}.$$

By using the matrix **M** to transform the data instead of the matrix **T**, we manage to include an additional piece of information in the form of the first natural observation $[y_1, \mathbf{x}_{1.}]$ scaled by the factor $\sqrt{1-\phi^2}$. The effect of the scaling is that $V(\sqrt{1-\phi^2}y_1) = V(y_t - \phi y_{t-1}) = \sigma_\varepsilon^2$. Thus the extra element of information acquires the same variance as the other elements; and the scaling can be interpreted as a device which is designed to ensure the efficiency of the method of ordinary least squares.

It is difficult to know how much value to place upon the inclusion of the extra element of information. Kadiyala in [**61**] cites a perverse case where neglecting the information by using the transformation **T** leads to estimates which are less efficient than those which would result from applying ordinary least squares to the untransformed data. However, this result is attributable to an uncommon structure in the matrix **X** comprising the observations on the input variables.

As we have shown in Chapter 6, the minimum $\mathbf{Q}^{-1}$-distance estimator of $\boldsymbol{\beta}$ in the model $(\mathbf{y}, \mathbf{X}\boldsymbol{\beta}, \sigma_\varepsilon^2\mathbf{Q})$ is also the maximum-likelihood estimator on the assumption that the vector of disturbances is normally distributed. However, in the case where ϕ is an unknown parameter, the values of $\boldsymbol{\beta}$ and ϕ which jointly minimize the function

(12.27)
$$S^*(\boldsymbol{\beta}, \phi) = [\mathbf{y} - \mathbf{X}\boldsymbol{\beta}]'\mathbf{Q}^{-1}(\phi)[\mathbf{y} - \mathbf{X}\boldsymbol{\beta}]$$

diverge from the maximum-likelihood estimates.

To demonstrate this, we consider the likelihood function

(12.28)
$$L(\boldsymbol{\beta}, \sigma_\varepsilon^2\mathbf{Q}) = (2\pi)^{-T/2}|\sigma_\varepsilon^2\mathbf{Q}|^{-1/2} \times \exp\left\{-\frac{1}{2\sigma_\varepsilon^2}[\mathbf{y} - \mathbf{X}\boldsymbol{\beta}]'\mathbf{Q}^{-1}(\phi)[\mathbf{y} - \mathbf{X}\boldsymbol{\beta}]\right\}.$$

Using the result that the determinant of $\mathbf{Q}^{-1}$ is $|\mathbf{Q}^{-1}| = 1 - \phi^2$, we write the log of the likelihood function as

(12.29)
$$L^* = -\frac{T}{2}\log(2\pi) - \frac{T}{2}\log\sigma_\varepsilon^2 + \tfrac{1}{2}\log(1-\phi^2) - \frac{1}{2\sigma_\varepsilon^2}[\mathbf{y} - \mathbf{X}\boldsymbol{\beta}]'\mathbf{Q}^{-1}(\phi)[\mathbf{y} - \mathbf{X}\boldsymbol{\beta}].$$

By maximizing L^* partially in respect of $\boldsymbol{\beta}$ and σ_ε^2, we obtain the estimators

(12.30)
$$\hat{\boldsymbol{\beta}}(\phi) = [\mathbf{X}'\mathbf{Q}^{-1}(\phi)\mathbf{X}]^{-1}\mathbf{X}'\mathbf{Q}^{-1}(\phi)\mathbf{y},$$
$$\hat{\sigma}_\varepsilon^2(\phi) = \frac{1}{T}[\mathbf{y} - \mathbf{X}\hat{\boldsymbol{\beta}}(\phi)]'\mathbf{Q}^{-1}(\phi)[\mathbf{y} - \mathbf{X}\hat{\boldsymbol{\beta}}(\phi)].$$

Substituting these in (12.29) gives the concentrated likelihood function

$$L^*(\phi) = -\frac{T}{2}[\log(2\pi)+1] + \tfrac{1}{2}\log(1-\phi^2) - \frac{T}{2}\log\sigma_\varepsilon^2(\phi) \tag{12.31}$$

$$= -\frac{T}{2}[\log(2\pi)+1] - \frac{T}{2}\log\frac{\sigma_\varepsilon^2(\phi)}{(1-\phi^2)^{1/T}}.$$

Thus, maximizing the likelihood function in respect of ϕ and $\boldsymbol{\beta}$ is equivalent to minimizing $\sigma_\varepsilon^2/(1-\phi^2)^{1/T} = T^{-1}S^*(\boldsymbol{\beta}, \phi)/(1-\phi^2)^{1/T}$. However, since $\lim(T\to\infty)(1-\phi^2)^{1/T} = 1$, the difference between the maximum-likelihood criterion and the criterion of minimizing $S^*(\boldsymbol{\beta}, \phi)$ becomes negligible in large samples.

A variety of methods have been proposed for obtaining estimates of $\boldsymbol{\beta}$ and ϕ in fulfilment of either the criterion of minimizing $S(\boldsymbol{\beta}, \phi)$ or the criterion of minimizing $S^*(\boldsymbol{\beta}, \phi)$. To simplify the exposition, we shall describe the methods only in relation to the minimand $S(\boldsymbol{\beta}, \phi)$.

A straightforward way of seeking the global minimum $\min S(\boldsymbol{\beta}, \phi)$ is to compare values of the conditional minima $\min S(\boldsymbol{\beta} \mid \phi)$ arising from the application of ordinary least-squares regression to the transformed data $\mathbf{T}(\phi)\mathbf{y}$, $\mathbf{T}(\phi)\mathbf{X}$ when ϕ is assigned various values in the open interval $(-1, 1)$. The estimates of $\boldsymbol{\beta}$ and ϕ are the values associated with the minimum of the conditional minima.

To conduct the search efficiently, we should begin by comparing values of $\min S(\boldsymbol{\beta} \mid \phi)$ for widely spaced values of ϕ in the interval $(-1, 1)$. Then, in the second round of the search, we should compare values of $\min S(\boldsymbol{\beta} \mid \phi)$ for more closely spaced values of ϕ in the region of the value which gives the relative minimum in the first round. Further rounds of the search can be conducted along the lines of the second round.

By far the most common approach to the problem of estimation is to use an iterative procedure due to Cochrane and Orcutt [**24**]. For an initial value of ϕ, say ϕ_0, the function $S(\boldsymbol{\beta}, \phi)$ is minimized in respect of $\boldsymbol{\beta}$ to give an estimate $\boldsymbol{\beta}_1$. Next, with $\boldsymbol{\beta}_1$ fixed, the function is minimized in respect of ϕ to produce an estimate ϕ_1. The procedure is then repeated with the new value ϕ_1 in place of ϕ_0; and a succession of iterations may be performed until the sequence of revised estimates converges. To illustrate, we shall consider the simple case where $y(t) = \beta x(t) + \eta(t)$ with $\eta(t) = \phi\eta(t-1) + \varepsilon(t)$. The minimand is then

$$S(\beta, \phi) = \sum_{t=2}^{T} [(y_t - \phi y_{t-1}) - \beta(x_t - \phi x_{t-1})]^2 \tag{12.32}$$

$$= \sum_{t=2}^{T} [(y_t - \beta x_t) - \phi(y_{t-1} - \beta x_{t-1})]^2,$$

and the estimates at the $(r+1)$th iteration are

$$\beta_{r+1}=\frac{\sum(x_t-\phi_r x_{t-1})(y_t-\phi_r y_{t-1})}{\sum(x_t-\phi_r x_{t-1})^2}, \tag{12.33}$$

$$\phi_{r+1}=\frac{\sum(y_{t-1}-\beta_{r+1}x_{t-1})(y_t-\beta_{r+1}x_t)}{\sum(y_{t-1}-\beta_{r+1}x_{t-1})^2}.$$

The elements $y_{t-1}-\beta_{r+1}x_{t-1}=h_{t-1,r+1}$ and $y_t-\beta_{r+1}x_t=h_{t,r+1}$ in the second of these regression equations are simply the residuals from the first regression. Given that $\beta_1,\ldots,\beta_{r+1}$ are all consistent estimators of β, it follows that $h_{t,r+1}$ and $h_{t-1,r+1}$ are consistent estimates of the corresponding disturbances η_t and η_{t-1}. The consistency of the estimator ϕ_{r+1} can therefore be established by the arguments of Chapter 11 concerning the application of ordinary least-squares regression to the estimation of the parameters of an autoregressive process.

A more sophisticated approach than the foregoing is one which attempts to estimate the parameters in $\boldsymbol{\theta}'=[\beta,\phi]$ by using a Newton–Raphson procedure to solve the equation $\partial S(\boldsymbol{\theta})/\partial\boldsymbol{\vartheta}=\mathbf{0}$. To elucidate this procedure, let us consider a Taylor series expansion

$$f(b)=f(a)+(b-a)Df(a)+\frac{(b-a)^2}{2!}D^2f(a)+\ldots+\frac{(b-a)^n}{n!}D^nf(a)+\ldots \tag{12.34}$$

wherein $D^if(a)$ represents the ith derivative of $f(x)$ evaluated at the point $x=a$. As a first-order approximation to the equation, we may write

$$f(b)\simeq f(a)+(b-a)Df(a). \tag{12.35}$$

Let b be the value for which $f(b)=0$. Then

$$0\simeq f(a)+(b-a)Df(a) \quad\text{or}\quad b\simeq a-[Df(a)]^{-1}f(a), \tag{12.36}$$

and we have an approximate solution of $f(b)=0$. To seek an accurate solution, we use a sequence of approximations $\{a_0,\ldots,a_r,a_{r+1},\ldots\}$ wherein

$$a_{r+1}=a_r-[Df(a_r)]^{-1}f(a_r), \tag{12.37}$$

and where a_0 is some arbitrary initial value. If a_0 is sufficiently close to b, then we may expect the sequence $\{a_i\}$ to converge to b. The algorithm in (12.37), by which the $(r+1)$th approximation is found from the rth approximation, describes the Newton–Raphson procedure.

On applying a bivariate version of this procedure to the solution of $\partial S(\boldsymbol{\theta})/\partial\boldsymbol{\theta} = \mathbf{0}$, where $\boldsymbol{\theta}' = [\beta, \phi]$, we get

$$\begin{bmatrix}\beta\\ \phi\end{bmatrix}_{r+1} = \begin{bmatrix}\beta\\ \phi\end{bmatrix}_{r} - \begin{bmatrix}\partial^2 S/\partial\beta^2, & \partial^2 S/\partial\beta\,\partial\phi\\ \partial^2 S/\partial\phi\,\partial\beta, & \partial^2 S/\partial\phi^2\end{bmatrix}_r^{-1} \begin{bmatrix}\partial S/\partial\beta\\ \partial S/\partial\phi\end{bmatrix}_r. \tag{12.38}$$

The various derivatives within this expression are evaluated as

$$\begin{aligned}\partial S/\partial\beta &= 2\beta\sum(x_t-\phi x_{t-1})^2 - 2\sum(x_t-\phi x_{t-1})(y_t-\phi y_{t-1}),\\ \partial S/\partial\phi &= 2\phi\sum(y_{t-1}-\beta x_{t-1})^2 - 2\sum(y_{t-1}-\beta x_{t-1})(y_t-\beta x_t),\\ \partial^2 S/\partial\beta^2 &= 2\sum(x_t-\phi x_{t-1})^2,\\ \partial^2 S/\partial\phi^2 &= 2\sum(y_{t-1}-\beta x_{t-1})^2,\\ \partial^2 S/\partial\beta\,\partial\phi &= Q.\end{aligned} \tag{12.39}$$

Thus the algorithm becomes

$$\begin{aligned}\begin{bmatrix}\beta\\ \phi\end{bmatrix}_{r+1} = \begin{bmatrix}\beta\\ \phi\end{bmatrix}_{r} &- \begin{bmatrix}\partial^2 S/\partial\beta^2, & Q\\ Q, & \partial^2 S/\partial\phi^2\end{bmatrix}_r^{-1}\\ &\times\left(\begin{bmatrix}\partial^2 S/\partial\beta^2, & Q\\ Q, & \partial^2 S/\partial\phi^2\end{bmatrix}_r\begin{bmatrix}\beta\\ \phi\end{bmatrix}_r\right.\\ &\left.-\begin{bmatrix}Q\phi + 2\sum(x_t-\phi x_{t-1})(y_t-\phi y_{t-1})\\ Q\beta + 2\sum(y_{t-1}-\beta x_{t-1})(y_t-\beta x_t)\end{bmatrix}_r\right),\end{aligned} \tag{12.40}$$

and, when we multiply both sides by the matrix of second-order derivatives and divide by 2, we get

$$\begin{aligned}&\begin{bmatrix}\sum(x_t-\phi x_{t-1})^2, & Q/2\\ Q/2, & \sum(y_{t-1}-\beta x_{t-1})^2\end{bmatrix}_r\begin{bmatrix}\beta\\ \phi\end{bmatrix}_{r+1}\\ &\qquad= \begin{bmatrix}\sum(x_t-\phi x_{t-1})(y_t-\phi y_{t-1}) + Q\phi/2\\ \sum(y_{t-1}-\beta x_{t-1})(y_t-\beta x_t) + Q\beta/2\end{bmatrix}_r.\end{aligned} \tag{12.41}$$

If we are prepared to accept the approximations $Q_r\phi_{r+1} \simeq Q_r\phi_r$ and $Q_r\beta_{r+1} \simeq Q_r\beta_r$, then we can ignore the cross-derivatives, and the algorithm will yield the estimates

$$\begin{aligned}\beta_{r+1} &= \frac{\sum(x_t-\phi_r x_{t-1})(y_t-\phi_r y_{t-1})}{\sum(x_t-\phi_r x_{t-1})^2},\\ \phi_{r+1} &= \frac{\sum(y_{t-1}-\beta_r x_{t-1})(y_t-\beta_r x_t)}{\sum(y_{t-1}-\beta_r x_{t-1})^2},\end{aligned} \tag{12.42}$$

which are virtually identical to the Cochrane–Orcutt estimates. The sole difference lies in the fact that the present estimator of ϕ incorporates the value β_r as opposed to the value β_{r+1} found in the Cochrane–Orcutt estimator in (12.33).

To complete our account of the available methods, we should mention a suggestion by Durbin in [**30**] that we might find a consistent estimate of ϕ by applying the method of ordinary least-squares regression to observations on the relationship

$$y(t)=\phi y(t-1)+\beta x(t)-\phi\beta x(t-1)+\varepsilon(t). \tag{12.43}$$

With ϕ fixed at its estimated value $\hat{\phi}$, we could then proceed to estimate β by finding the value that minimizes $S(\beta \mid \hat{\phi})$.

In describing the various methods of estimation, we have considered only a first-order autoregressive scheme. Apart from the search procedure, each of these methods may be easily generalized to accommodate autoregressive processes of higher orders. The search procedure becomes impractical when more than two or three parameters are involved.

REGRESSION MODELS WITH MOVING AVERAGE DISTURBANCES

Simple regression models with moving average disturbances are not often postulated in aconometrics. Nevertheless, moving average processes do frequently arise in the mathematical manipulation of temporal regression models involving lag schemes in the observable variables. For the present, we shall ignore the additional complications entailed in such models in order to concentrate solely on the problems of moving average disturbances. We shall therefore consider the model

$$\begin{aligned} y(t)&=\mathbf{x}(t)\boldsymbol{\beta}+\eta(t)\\ &=\mathbf{x}(t)\boldsymbol{\beta}+(I+m_1L+m_2L^2+\ldots+m_qL^q)\varepsilon(t). \end{aligned} \tag{12.44}$$

The simplest case is when the disturbances follow a first-order moving average process to give

$$\begin{aligned} y(t)&=\mathbf{x}(t)\boldsymbol{\beta}+(I-\theta L)\varepsilon(t)\\ &=\mathbf{x}(t)\boldsymbol{\beta}+\varepsilon(t)-\theta\varepsilon(t-1). \end{aligned} \tag{12.45}$$

Let us assume that we have a sample of T observations comprised in $\mathbf{y}$ and $\mathbf{X}$. The corresponding vector of disturbances is $\boldsymbol{\eta}'=[\eta_1,\ldots,\eta_T]$ and, as we have already recorded under (11.71), its dispersion matrix is

$$\begin{aligned} D(\boldsymbol{\eta})&=\sigma_\varepsilon^2\begin{bmatrix} 1+\theta^2, & -\theta, & 0, & \ldots, & 0\\ -\theta, & 1+\theta^2, & -\theta, & \ldots, & 0\\ 0, & -\theta, & 1+\theta^2, & \ldots, & 0\\ \cdot & \cdot & \cdot & & \cdot\\ \cdot & \cdot & \cdot & & \cdot\\ \cdot & \cdot & \cdot & & \cdot\\ 0, & 0, & 0, & \ldots, & 1+\theta^2 \end{bmatrix}\\ &=\sigma_\varepsilon^2\mathbf{Q}. \end{aligned} \tag{12.46}$$

A matrix $\mathbf{MM}'$ which is virtually the same as $\mathbf{Q}$ can be formed from

$$\mathbf{M}=\begin{bmatrix} 1, & 0, & \ldots, & 0, & 0 \\ -\theta, & 1, & \ldots, & 0, & 0 \\ 0, & -\theta, & \ldots, & 0, & 0 \\ \cdot & \cdot & & \cdot & \cdot \\ \cdot & \cdot & & \cdot & \cdot \\ \cdot & \cdot & & \cdot & \cdot \\ 0, & 0, & \ldots, & -\theta, & 1 \end{bmatrix} \tag{12.47}$$

which is the sample analogue of the operator $(I-\theta L)$. The sole difference between the two matrices is in the leading diagonal element which has the value $1+\theta^2$ in $\mathbf{Q}$ and the value of unity in $\mathbf{MM}'$.

If the parameter θ were known, then the efficient estimate of $\boldsymbol{\beta}$ could be found by a minimum $\mathbf{Q}^{-1}$-distance regression. On the assumption that the disturbances follow a normal process, this estimate would also be the value that maximizes the likelihood function. When θ is unknown, we should consider finding estimates by minimizing the function

$$S(\boldsymbol{\beta},\theta)=[\mathbf{y}-\mathbf{X}\boldsymbol{\beta}]'\mathbf{Q}^{-1}(\theta)[\mathbf{y}-\mathbf{X}\boldsymbol{\beta}]. \tag{12.48}$$

As in the case of the model with first-order autoregressive disturbances, these estimates diverge to some extent from the maximum-likelihood estimates. The log of the likelihood function is

$$L^* = -\frac{T}{2}\log(2\pi)-\frac{T}{2}\log\sigma_\varepsilon^2+\tfrac{1}{2}\log|\mathbf{Q}(\theta)|^{-1} \tag{12.49}$$
$$-\frac{1}{2\sigma_\varepsilon^2}[\mathbf{y}-\mathbf{X}\boldsymbol{\beta}]'\mathbf{Q}^{-1}(\theta)[\mathbf{y}-\mathbf{X}\boldsymbol{\beta}].$$

As Durbin records in [**29**], the determinant of $\mathbf{Q}$ is $|\mathbf{Q}|=(1+\theta^{2T+2})/(1-\theta^2)$; and, given that $|\theta|<1$, this tends rapidly to $1/(1-\theta^2)$ as T increases. With $1-\theta^2$ replacing $|\mathbf{Q}|^{-1}$, the log-likelihood function is entirely analogous to the function in (12.29) that relates to the model with first-order autoregressive disturbances. By following the analogy, we can see that maximizing the likelihood is virtually equivalent to minimizing the function $S(\boldsymbol{\beta},\theta)/(1-\theta^2)^{1/T}$; and for samples of reasonable size this is practically the same as minimizing $S(\boldsymbol{\beta},\theta)$. Therefore we need make no practical distinction between the criterion of maximizing the likelihood function and that of minimizing the function in (12.48).

A wide variety of methods are available for obtaining estimates of $\boldsymbol{\beta}$ and θ in fulfilment of our criterion. Perhaps the most secure method of finding the global minimum of $S(\boldsymbol{\beta},\theta)$ and the corresponding estimates of $\boldsymbol{\beta}$ and θ is to compare values of the conditional minima $\min S(\boldsymbol{\beta}\,|\,\theta)$ arising from the minimum $\mathbf{Q}^{-1}(\theta)$-distance regression procedure when a variety of values in the permissible interval $(-1,1)$ are assigned to θ.

However, we might prefer to estimate the matrix $\mathbf{Q}(\theta)$ directly. Thus we can use the residuals of an ordinary least-squares regression to form consistent estimates of the autocovariances of the process $\eta(t)$. By putting the estimated covariances in place of the unknown elements of $\mathbf{Q}$ and using the resulting matrix in a second regression, we can form an asymptotically efficient estimate $\boldsymbol{\beta}$ which possesses the same limiting distribution as the maximum-likelihood estimate. Indeed, a sequence of estimates of $\boldsymbol{\beta}$ can be generated by using the residuals of each regression to form a revised estimate of $\mathbf{Q}$ to be incorporated in a succeeding regression. It is reasonable to expect that such a sequence will converge on the value of $\boldsymbol{\beta}$ which, with the associated value of θ, jointly minimizes the function $S(\boldsymbol{\beta}, \theta)$.

In the present case where the variables comprised in $\mathbf{X}$ are entirely exogenous to the model, every estimate in the sequence of iterations is asymptotically efficient and has the same limiting distribution as an estimate incorporating the true value of $\mathbf{Q}$. However, as Maddala [**81**] has demonstrated, conditions are radically altered when the matrix of regressors contains lagged dependent variables. In that case, not only does the asymptotic distribution of the maximum-likelihood estimate for the case of an unknown dispersion matrix differ from that of the estimate incorporating a known matrix, but also the various estimates in the sequence converging on the maximum-likelihood estimate have different asymptotic distributions. Since the maximum-likelihood estimator is the efficient estimator in these circumstances, the result implies that, when we use an iterative procedure, we should not stop short of full convergence.

There are two ways of implementing the iterative procedure. The first is to form an estimate of the matrix $\mathbf{Q}$ from estimates of the autocovariances of the moving average process and to proceed to find its inverse. The second way is to derive the algebraic expression for the inverse matrix $\mathbf{Q}^{-1}$ and to proceed to estimate its elements from the autocovariances. The second method, although commonly recommended, is hampered, even in the case of the first-order process, by the complexity of the algebraic expression; and approximations are normally used. As Uppuluri and Carpenter [**118**] have demonstrated, the elements of the exact algebraic expression for $\mathbf{Q}^{-1}$ in the first-order case are functions of the parameter θ and of determinants of increasing orders of the matrix $\mathbf{Q}$. An adequate approximation is given by the matrix $\mathbf{M}^{-1\prime}\mathbf{M}^{-1}$, where

$$(12.50) \qquad \mathbf{M}^{-1} = \begin{bmatrix} 1, & 0, & 0, & \dots, & 0 \\ \theta, & 1, & 0, & \dots, & 0 \\ \theta^2, & \theta, & 1, & \dots, & 0 \\ \cdot & \cdot & \cdot & & \cdot \\ \cdot & \cdot & \cdot & & \cdot \\ \cdot & \cdot & \cdot & & \cdot \\ \theta^{T-1}, & \theta^{T-2}, & \theta^{T-3}, & \dots, & 1 \end{bmatrix},$$

which is the inverse of the matrix defined in (12.47), is the sample analogue of the operator $(I-\theta L)^{-1}$. It is readily confirmed that $\mathbf{M}^{-1\prime}\mathbf{M}^{-1}=\mathbf{R}-\mathbf{S}$ where

$$\text{(12.51)} \qquad \mathbf{R}=\frac{1}{1-\theta^2}\begin{bmatrix} 1, & \theta, & \theta^2, & \dots, & \theta^{T-1} \\ \theta, & 1, & \theta, & \dots, & \theta^{T-2} \\ \theta^2, & \theta, & 1, & \dots, & \theta^{T-3} \\ \cdot & \cdot & \cdot & & \cdot \\ \cdot & \cdot & \cdot & & \cdot \\ \cdot & \cdot & \cdot & & \cdot \\ \theta^{T-1}, & \theta^{T-2}, & \theta^{T-3}, & \dots, & 1 \end{bmatrix}$$

and

$$\text{(12.52)} \qquad \mathbf{S}=\frac{1}{1-\theta^2}\begin{bmatrix} \theta^{2T}, & \theta^{2T-1}, & \theta^{2T-2}, & \dots, & \theta^{T+1} \\ \theta^{2T-1}, & \theta^{2T-2}, & \theta^{2T-3}, & \dots, & \theta^{T} \\ \theta^{2T-2}, & \theta^{2T-3}, & \theta^{2T-4}, & \dots, & \theta^{T-1} \\ \cdot & \cdot & \cdot & & \cdot \\ \cdot & \cdot & \cdot & & \cdot \\ \cdot & \cdot & \cdot & & \cdot \\ \theta^{T+1}, & \theta^{T}, & \theta^{T-1}, & \dots, & \theta^2 \end{bmatrix}$$

A coarser approximation is to use the matrix $\mathbf{R}$ in place of $\mathbf{Q}^{-1}$.

To illustrate the nature of our approximation, let us reconsider the equation

$$\text{(12.53)} \qquad y(t)=\beta x(t)+(I-\theta L)\varepsilon(t).$$

On multiplying both sides by the operator $(I-\theta L)^{-1}$, we obtain the equation

$$\text{(12.54)} \qquad (I-\theta L)^{-1}y(t)=\beta(I-\theta L)^{-1}x(t)+\varepsilon(t).$$

The expressions $(I-\theta L)^{-1}y(t)$ and $(I-\theta L)^{-1}x(t)$ represent sequences whose elements at time t are given, respectively, by the infinite sums $\sum_{i=0}^{\infty}\theta^i y_{t-i}$ and $\sum_{i=0}^{\infty}\theta^i x_{t-i}$. On replacing the infinite sums by truncated versions comprising only the sample elements of $y(t)$ and $x(t)$, we can write a set of T regression equations in the form

$$\text{(12.55)} \qquad \sum_{i=0}^{t-1}\theta^i y_{t-i}=\beta\sum_{i=0}^{t-1}\theta^i x_{t-i}+\varepsilon_t.$$

Using the matrix $\mathbf{M}^{-1}$ defined in (12.50), these can be written alternatively as

$$\text{(12.56)} \qquad \mathbf{M}^{-1}\mathbf{y}=\beta\mathbf{M}^{-1}\mathbf{x}+\boldsymbol{\varepsilon}$$

where $\mathbf{y}'=[y_1,\dots,y_T]$, $\mathbf{x}'=[x_1,\dots,x_T]$ and $\boldsymbol{\varepsilon}'=[\varepsilon_1,\dots,\varepsilon_T]$. By applying ordinary least squares, we can obtain an estimator of β in the form of

$\hat{\beta} = (\mathbf{x}'\mathbf{M}^{-1\prime}\mathbf{M}^{-1}\mathbf{x})^{-1}\mathbf{x}'\mathbf{M}^{-1\prime}\mathbf{M}^{-1}\mathbf{y}$. This is the approximation of the minimum $\mathbf{Q}^{-1}$-distance estimator obtained by replacing $\mathbf{Q}^{-1}$ by the matrix $\mathbf{M}^{-1\prime}\mathbf{M}^{-1}$. Thus what we have succeeded in demonstrating is that the approximation of $\mathbf{Q}^{-1}$ by $\mathbf{M}^{-1\prime}\mathbf{M}^{-1}$ is precisely equivalent to the approximation entailed in replacing the infinite sums $\sum_{i=0}^{\infty} \theta^i y_{t-i}$ and $\sum_{i=0}^{\infty} \theta^i x_{t-i}$ by their truncated versions. We shall return to this point when we come to consider the regression model with a geometric lag scheme in the input variable x_t.

Methods that involve finding the inverse of the dispersion matrix of the disturbances tend to become intractable when the number of parameters involved in the moving average process exceed two or three. However, the difficulties may be circumvented if we adopt an alternative formulation of the problem that was proposed by Phillips [**91**] and which has been used by Trivedi [**117**].

To describe their procedure, we shall consider the regression model in (12.44) where the disturbances follow a qth-order moving average process. Let us write T realizations of the relationship as

$$\mathbf{y} = \mathbf{X}\boldsymbol{\beta} + \mathbf{M}_*\boldsymbol{\varepsilon}_* + \mathbf{M}\boldsymbol{\varepsilon}, \tag{12.57}$$

where $\boldsymbol{\varepsilon}_*' = [\varepsilon_{1-q}, \varepsilon_{2-q}, \ldots, \varepsilon_0]$ is a vector of q pre-sample values of $\varepsilon(t)$ and $\boldsymbol{\varepsilon}' = [\varepsilon_1, \ldots, \varepsilon_T]$ is a vector of values from the sample period, and where

(12.58)

$$[\mathbf{M}_*, \mathbf{M}] = \left[\begin{array}{ccc|cccccccc} m_q, & m_{q-1}, & \ldots & 1, & 0, & \ldots, & 0, & 0, & \ldots, & 0 \\ 0, & m_q, & \ldots & m_1, & 1, & \ldots, & 0, & 0, & \ldots, & 0 \\ & & \ddots & & & \ddots & & & & \\ 0, & 0, & \ldots & m_q, & m_{q-1}, & \ldots, & 1, & 0, & \ldots, & 0 \\ 0, & 0, & \ldots & 0, & m_q, & \ldots, & m_1, & 1, & \ldots, & 0 \\ & & & & & \ddots & & & \ddots & \\ 0, & 0, & \ldots & 0, & 0, & \ldots, & m_q, & m_{q-1}, & \ldots, & 1 \end{array}\right]$$

The $T \times 1$ vector $\mathbf{M}_*\boldsymbol{\varepsilon}_*$, which contains non-zero elements in the first q places and zeros elsewhere, can be written as

$$\mathbf{M}_*\boldsymbol{\varepsilon}_* = \mathbf{J}\mathbf{c} \tag{12.59}$$

where $\mathbf{J}' = [\mathbf{I}_q, \mathbf{0}]$ and $\mathbf{c}' = [c_1, \ldots, c_q]$. In this alternative notation, the regression equations are

$$\begin{aligned} \mathbf{y} &= [\mathbf{X}, \mathbf{J}]\begin{bmatrix} \boldsymbol{\beta} \\ \mathbf{c} \end{bmatrix} + \mathbf{M}\boldsymbol{\varepsilon} \\ &= \mathbf{Z}\mathbf{d} + \mathbf{M}\boldsymbol{\varepsilon}. \end{aligned} \tag{12.60}$$

If we regard the pre-sample elements as constants and assume that $\varepsilon(t)$ is a normal process, then, using the fact that $\text{Det}(\mathbf{M})=1$, we can write the likelihood function of the sample as

$$(12.61)\qquad L(\mathbf{d},\mathbf{M})=(2\pi\sigma_\varepsilon^2)^{-T/2}\exp\left\{\frac{-(\mathbf{y}-\mathbf{Z}\mathbf{d})'\mathbf{M}^{-1\prime}\mathbf{M}^{-1}(\mathbf{y}-\mathbf{Z}\mathbf{d})}{2\sigma_\varepsilon^2}\right\}.$$

Therefore, we can obtain maximum-likelihood estimates by minimizing

$$(12.62)\qquad \begin{aligned} S(\mathbf{d},\mathbf{m})&=(\mathbf{y}-\mathbf{Z}\mathbf{d})'\mathbf{M}^{-1\prime}\mathbf{M}^{-1}(\mathbf{y}-\mathbf{Z}\mathbf{d})\\ &=\boldsymbol{\varepsilon}'\boldsymbol{\varepsilon}.\end{aligned}$$

Since this function is still highly non-linear in the parameters, we require an iterative method to achieve the minimization. Trivedi, who has followed the suggestion of Phillips, has used a Gauss–Newton method of the sort that we have already encountered in Chapter 11 in dealing with the estimation of the autoregressive moving average model.

Let us recapitulate on this method. Using $\boldsymbol{\theta}'=[\mathbf{d}',\mathbf{m}']$ to represent the parameters of the model, our objective is to minimize $S(\boldsymbol{\theta})=\boldsymbol{\varepsilon}'\boldsymbol{\varepsilon}$ via the first-order condition $\partial S(\boldsymbol{\theta})/\partial\boldsymbol{\theta}=\mathbf{0}$. Consider the expression

$$(12.63)\qquad \boldsymbol{\varepsilon}(\boldsymbol{\theta})\simeq\boldsymbol{\varepsilon}(\boldsymbol{\theta}_0)+\frac{\partial\boldsymbol{\varepsilon}(\boldsymbol{\theta}_0)}{\partial\boldsymbol{\theta}}(\boldsymbol{\theta}-\boldsymbol{\theta}_0)$$

wherein $\partial\boldsymbol{\varepsilon}(\boldsymbol{\theta}_0)/\partial\boldsymbol{\theta}$ stands for the first derivative of $\boldsymbol{\varepsilon}(\boldsymbol{\theta})$ evaluated at $\boldsymbol{\theta}=\boldsymbol{\theta}_0$. From this approximation, we obtain

$$(12.64)\qquad \begin{aligned} S(\boldsymbol{\theta})&=\boldsymbol{\varepsilon}(\boldsymbol{\theta})'\boldsymbol{\varepsilon}(\boldsymbol{\theta})\\ &\simeq\boldsymbol{\varepsilon}(\boldsymbol{\theta}_0)'\boldsymbol{\varepsilon}(\boldsymbol{\theta}_0)+(\boldsymbol{\theta}-\boldsymbol{\theta}_0)'\frac{\partial\boldsymbol{\varepsilon}(\boldsymbol{\theta}_0)'}{\partial\boldsymbol{\theta}}\frac{\partial\boldsymbol{\varepsilon}(\boldsymbol{\theta}_0)}{\partial\boldsymbol{\theta}}(\boldsymbol{\theta}-\boldsymbol{\theta}_0)\\ &\quad+2\boldsymbol{\varepsilon}(\boldsymbol{\theta}_0)'\frac{\partial\boldsymbol{\varepsilon}(\boldsymbol{\theta}_0)}{\partial\boldsymbol{\theta}}(\boldsymbol{\theta}-\boldsymbol{\theta}_0).\end{aligned}$$

Hence

$$(12.65)\qquad \frac{\partial S(\boldsymbol{\theta})}{\partial\boldsymbol{\theta}}\simeq2(\boldsymbol{\theta}-\boldsymbol{\theta}_0)'\frac{\partial\boldsymbol{\varepsilon}(\boldsymbol{\theta}_0)'}{\partial\boldsymbol{\theta}}\frac{\partial\boldsymbol{\varepsilon}(\boldsymbol{\theta}_0)}{\partial\boldsymbol{\theta}}+2\boldsymbol{\varepsilon}(\boldsymbol{\theta}_0)'\frac{\partial\boldsymbol{\varepsilon}(\boldsymbol{\theta}_0)}{\partial\boldsymbol{\theta}};$$

and an approximate solution to the equation $\partial S(\boldsymbol{\theta})/\partial\boldsymbol{\theta}=\mathbf{0}$ is given by

$$(12.66)\qquad \boldsymbol{\theta}=\boldsymbol{\theta}_0-\left[\frac{\partial\boldsymbol{\varepsilon}(\boldsymbol{\theta}_0)'}{\partial\boldsymbol{\theta}}\frac{\partial\boldsymbol{\varepsilon}(\boldsymbol{\theta}_0)}{\partial\boldsymbol{\theta}}\right]^{-1}\frac{\partial\boldsymbol{\varepsilon}(\boldsymbol{\theta}_0)'}{\partial\boldsymbol{\theta}}\boldsymbol{\varepsilon}(\boldsymbol{\theta}_0).$$

To obtain a sequence of approximate solutions $\{\boldsymbol{\theta}_0,\ldots,\boldsymbol{\theta}_r,\boldsymbol{\theta}_{r+1},\ldots\}$ which can be expected to converge on the exact solution, we use the algorithm

$$(12.67)\qquad \boldsymbol{\theta}_{r+1}=\boldsymbol{\theta}_r-\left[\frac{\partial\boldsymbol{\varepsilon}'}{\partial\boldsymbol{\theta}}\frac{\partial\boldsymbol{\varepsilon}}{\partial\boldsymbol{\theta}}\right]_r^{-1}\left(\frac{\partial\boldsymbol{\varepsilon}}{\partial\boldsymbol{\theta}}\right)_r'\boldsymbol{\varepsilon}_r.$$

This algorithm bears a close comparison with the algorithm of the Newton–Raphson method which, using the same notation, may be expressed as

$$(12.68)\qquad \boldsymbol{\theta}_{r+1}=\boldsymbol{\theta}_r-\left[\frac{\partial(\partial S/\partial\boldsymbol{\theta})'}{\partial\boldsymbol{\theta}}\right]_r^{-1}\left(\frac{\partial S}{\partial\boldsymbol{\theta}}\right)_r'.$$

To find the derivatives which will enable us to apply the Gauss–Newton method to our present problem, it is easiest to argue in terms of differentials. Consider, therefore, the expression

$$(12.69)\qquad \begin{aligned}\mathbf{0}&=\delta\mathbf{y}\\ &=\mathbf{Z}(\delta\mathbf{d})+\mathbf{M}(\delta\boldsymbol{\varepsilon})+(\delta\mathbf{M})\boldsymbol{\varepsilon}\end{aligned}$$

which is obtained from equation (12.60). Now

$$(12.70)\qquad \mathbf{M}\boldsymbol{\varepsilon}=\boldsymbol{\varepsilon}+\mathbf{E}\mathbf{m}$$

where

$$(12.71)\qquad \mathbf{E}=\begin{bmatrix}0, & 0, & \ldots, & 0\\ \varepsilon_1, & 0, & \ldots, & 0\\ \varepsilon_2, & \varepsilon_1, & \ldots, & 0\\ \cdot & \cdot & \cdot & \cdot\\ \cdot & \cdot & \cdot & \cdot\\ \cdot & \cdot & \cdot & \cdot\\ \varepsilon_q, & \varepsilon_{q-1}, & \ldots, & \varepsilon_1\\ \cdot & \cdot & & \cdot\\ \cdot & \cdot & & \cdot\\ \cdot & \cdot & & \cdot\\ \varepsilon_{T-1}, & \varepsilon_{T-2}, & \ldots, & \varepsilon_{T-q}\end{bmatrix},\qquad \mathbf{m}=\begin{bmatrix}m_1\\ m_2\\ \cdot\\ \cdot\\ \cdot\\ m_q\end{bmatrix}$$

Hence

$$(12.72)\qquad (\delta\mathbf{M})\boldsymbol{\varepsilon}=\mathbf{E}(\delta\mathbf{m}).$$

Substituting the latter in (12.69) gives $\mathbf{0}=\mathbf{Z}(\delta\mathbf{d})+\mathbf{M}(\delta\boldsymbol{\varepsilon})+\mathbf{E}(\delta\mathbf{m})$ or

$$(12.73)\qquad \delta\boldsymbol{\varepsilon}=-\mathbf{M}^{-1}\mathbf{Z}(\delta\mathbf{d})-\mathbf{M}^{-1}\mathbf{E}(\delta\mathbf{m}).$$

The required derivatives are therefore given by

$$(12.74)\qquad \begin{aligned}\frac{\partial\boldsymbol{\varepsilon}}{\partial\boldsymbol{\theta}}&=\left[\frac{\partial\boldsymbol{\varepsilon}}{\partial\mathbf{d}},\frac{\partial\boldsymbol{\varepsilon}}{\partial\mathbf{m}}\right]\\ &=-\mathbf{M}^{-1}[\mathbf{Z},\mathbf{E}]=\mathbf{W}.\end{aligned}$$

Hence the algorithm becomes

$$(12.75)\qquad \boldsymbol{\theta}_{r+1}=\boldsymbol{\theta}_r-(\mathbf{W}_r'\mathbf{W}_r)^{-1}\mathbf{W}_r'\boldsymbol{\varepsilon}_r.$$

DISTRIBUTED LAGS

Whenever the current value of the output sequence $y(t)$ is determined by a weighted sum of previous values of the input sequence $x(t)$, we have a relationship of the form

$$\begin{aligned}(12.76)\qquad y(t) &= B(L)x(t)+\varepsilon(t)\\ &= \sum_{i=0}^{r} \beta_i x(t-i)+\varepsilon(t)\end{aligned}$$

which is described in econometrics as a regression equation with distributed lags. In some formulations, the entire sequence of past values of $x(t)$ enters the regression, while, in others, only a limited number of recent values are present. In either case, we are unlikely to obtain precise estimates of the parameters of the model unless we can avail ourselves of some additional *a priori* information regarding the lag polynomial $B(L)$. Thus, as it stands, the model comprising an infinite number of lagged values of $x(t)$ is incapable of complete estimation by any method. On the other hand, the application of ordinary least-squares regression to the model with a finite number of lagged values is likely to yield weak results, since the regressors $x_t, \ldots, x_{t-r}$ are often highly correlated.

The restrictions that we would normally impose upon the parameters of the polynomial $B(L)$ are highly non-linear. Consequently, the methods of Chapter 10 are inappropriate to the problem, and special techniques must be developed. We shall deal first with the problems of estimating the parameters of a restricted finite lag scheme, and we shall then consider some special instances of infinite lag schemes.

Finite lag schemes

A useful way of reducing the number of parameters to be estimated in the model

$$(12.77)\qquad y(t)=\sum_{i=0}^{r} \beta_i x(t-i)+\varepsilon(t)$$

is to assume that the $r+1$ coefficients $\beta_0, \ldots, \beta_r$ can be represented as ordinates of a polynomial $P(\tau)$ of a degree k which is less than r. Thus it may be specified that

$$(12.78)\qquad \beta_i = P(i) = \sum_{j=0}^{k} \lambda_j i^j.$$

On substituting this in (12.77), we get

$$y(t)=\sum_{i=0}^{r}\sum_{j=0}^{k}\lambda_j i^j x(t-i)+\varepsilon(t) \tag{12.79}$$

$$=\sum_{j=0}^{k}\lambda_j z_j(t)+\varepsilon(t)$$

where $z_j(t)=\sum_{i=0}^{r} i^j x(t-i)$. Given a set of T observations $(x_1, y_1), \ldots, (x_T, y_T)$, we can form the variables $z_{0t}, \ldots, z_{kt}$ for $t=r+1, \ldots, T$. Then, by using the method of ordinary least squares to regress y_t on these variables, we can find estimates of the polynomial parameters $\lambda_0, \ldots, \lambda_k$. Finally, by substituting the estimates into the equation (12.78), we obtain a relationship from which we can find estimates of the lag coefficients $\beta_0, \ldots, \beta_r$. If the scheme in (12.78) correctly specifies the coefficients, then we will obtain consistent estimates of the polynomial parameters; and it follows that the derived estimates of the lag coefficients will also be consistent.

A useful elaboration of this method arises when we are able to specify certain co-ordinates of the polynomial $P(\tau)$. For example, we can tie down the polynomial at either end of the set of lag coefficients by specifying that $P(-1)=P(r+1)=0$.

The procedure which is commonly used for incorporating such information was originally suggested by Almon in [**4**]. It employs an alternative form of the kth-degree polynomial $P(\tau)$ which takes account of the fact that, if $\tau_0, \ldots, \tau_k$ are any $k+1$ points in the domain of $P(\tau)$, then $P(\tau)$ is completely specified by knowing the values $p_0=P(\tau_0), \ldots, p_k=P(\tau_k)$. Taking these values as our parameters, we can write the alternative representation as

$$P(\tau)=\sum_{j=0}^{k} p_j\delta_j(\tau) \tag{12.80}$$

wherein

$$\delta_j(\tau)=\frac{\prod_{l\neq j}(\tau-\tau_l)}{\prod_{l\neq j}(\tau_j-\tau_l)} \tag{12.81}$$

is a polynomial of degree k with the property that $\delta_j(\tau_j)=1$ and $\delta_j(\tau_l)=0$ for all $l\neq j$. The functions $\delta_j(\tau)$; $j=0, \ldots, k$ are called Lagrangean interpolation polynomials, and together they form a basis of the vector space $\mathcal{P}^{k-1}$ comprising all polynomials of degrees less than or equal to k.

If, instead of the expression in (12.78), we substitute into (12.77) the expression

$$\beta_i = P(i) = \sum_{j=0}^{k} p_j \delta_j(i), \tag{12.82}$$

we obtain the equation

$$\begin{aligned} y(t) &= \sum_{i=0}^{r} \sum_{j=0}^{k} p_j \delta_j(i) x(t-i) + \varepsilon(t) \\ &= \sum_{j=0}^{k} p_j z_j(t) + \varepsilon(t), \end{aligned} \tag{12.83}$$

where $z_j(t) = \sum_{i=0}^{r} \delta_j(i) x(t-i)$. Given a set of T observations, we can estimate the lag coefficients in the following way. First, we choose the arbitrary values $\tau_0, \ldots, \tau_k$. Then, having formed the associated Lagrangean interpolation polynomials, we can find the $T-r$ values of the transformed variables $z_{0t}, \ldots, z_{kt}$. Next, the estimates of the polynomial parameters $p_0, \ldots, p_k$ are found by using the method of ordinary least squares to regress y_t on the transformed variables. Finally, the estimates of the lag coefficients $\beta_0, \ldots, \beta_r$ can be obtained from equation (12.82) by putting the estimates of the polynomial parameters in place of the unknown values.

Let us now imagine that the points $\tau_0, \ldots, \tau_q$, where $q < k$, are the elements in the domain of the polynomial corresponding to the known values $p_0 = P(\tau_0), \ldots, p_q = P(\tau_q)$. Then we can write the polynomial as

$$P(\tau) = \sum_{j=0}^{q} p_j \delta_j(\tau) + \sum_{j=q+1}^{k} p_j \delta_j(\tau) \tag{12.84}$$

where all the elements of the first term of the RHS are known. On substituting this expression into (12.77) via (12.82), we find that we need only estimate the $k-q$ parameters $p_{q+1}, \ldots, p_k$. In particular, if it is known that $P(-1) = P(r+1) = 0$, then we may choose $\tau_0 = -1$, $\tau_1 = r+1$ to correspond to $p_0 = 0$, $p_1 = 0$. The expression in (12.84) then reduces simply to

$$P(\tau) = \sum_{j=2}^{k} p_j \delta_j(\tau). \tag{12.85}$$

It should be understood that the polynomial $P(\tau)$ can be expressed as a linear combination of any set of polynomials spanning the space $\mathcal{P}^{k-1}$. Thus, although the choice of the Lagrangean interpolation polynomials as a basis renders the problem of incorporating certain types of *a priori* information particularly tractable, it may be less useful for incorporating other types of information.

Infinite lag schemes

We might expect the input variable x_t to have an effect on every succeeding value of the output sequence $y(t)$. It amounts to the same thing when we imagine that every previous value of the input sequence $x(t)$ has contributed to the determination of the current output y_t. In such cases we have a distributed lag model of the form

$$y(t)=B(L)x(t)+\varepsilon(t) \tag{12.86}$$

comprising an infinite-order lag polynomial $B(L)$. If this polynomial were to contain an infinite number of distinct parameters, the estimation of the model would be qutie infeasible. Therefore we must seek to specify the polynomial in a way that limits the number of distinct parameters. This is quite easily accomplished for, as Jorgenson has pointed out in **[60]**, an infinite-degree polynomial can be approximated to any degree of accuracy by a ratio of two polynomials of finite degree. Thus, from a practical point of view, the most general form of the infinite distributed lag model is the rational form

$$y(t)=\frac{B(L)}{A(L)}x(t)+\varepsilon(t) \tag{12.87}$$

wherein $A(L)$ and $B(L)$ are both finite-degree polynomials. In fact, by setting $A(L)=I$, we can accommodate within the rational form the finite-lag models which we have already considered.

On multiplying both sides of (12.87) by $A(L)$, we obtain the relationship

$$A(L)y(t)=B(L)x(t)+A(L)\varepsilon(t). \tag{12.88}$$

From here it is a small step to the relationship

$$A(L)y(t)=B(L)x(t)+M(L)\varepsilon(t) \tag{12.89}$$

associated with the general form of the temporal regression model. Therefore, once we have treated the rational model, we shall pass to the general model. However, to begin with, we shall deal extensively with the specialization of the rational model which arises from setting $B(L)=\alpha I$ and $A(L)=(I-\lambda L)$. This is the geometric lag model.

THE GEOMETRIC LAG

The basic form of our relationship is

$$\begin{aligned} y(t)&=\alpha(I-\lambda L)^{-1}x(t)+\varepsilon(t)\\ &=\alpha(I+\lambda L+\lambda^2L+\ldots)x(t)+\varepsilon(t). \end{aligned} \tag{12.90}$$

On multiplying both sides by the operator $(I-\lambda L)$, we obtain the equation

$$\begin{aligned}(12.91)\qquad y(t) &= \lambda L y(t)+\alpha x(t)+\varepsilon(t)-\lambda L\varepsilon(t)\\ &= \lambda y(t-1)+\alpha x(t)+\varepsilon(t)-\lambda\varepsilon(t-1)\end{aligned}$$

which is described as the autoregressive form. In estimating the parameters of the model either form may be used. A direct approach to estimation via the basic form leads to the problem of having an infinite number of pre-sample values amongst the input variables. On the other hand, an indirect approach via the autoregressive form leads to the problems of a relationship that has both a lagged dependent variable amongst the regressors and a disturbance term that is part of serially correlated sequence. We shall begin by considering a number of indirect approaches.

Indirect estimation of the geometric lag model

To obtain estimates of the parameters in the equation (12.91), we might consider using the method of ordinary least squares to regress y_t on x_t and y_{t-1}. The probability limit of the estimates could be expressed along the lines of (12.11) as

$$(12.92)\qquad \operatorname{plim}\begin{bmatrix}\hat{\lambda}\\ \hat{\alpha}\end{bmatrix}=\begin{bmatrix}\lambda\\ \alpha\end{bmatrix}+\operatorname{plim}\left(T^{-1}\begin{bmatrix}\sum y_{t-1}^2, & \sum y_{t-1}x_t\\ \sum x_t y_{t-1}, & \sum x_t^2\end{bmatrix}\right)^{-1}\times\operatorname{plim}\left(T^{-1}\begin{bmatrix}\sum y_{t-1}\eta_t\\ \sum x_t\eta_t\end{bmatrix}\right)$$

wherein $\eta_t=\varepsilon_t-\lambda\varepsilon_{t-1}$ is the composite disturbance term. However, in contrast to the expression in (12.11), the second term on the RHS has a non-zero value since

$$\operatorname{plim}(\textstyle\sum y_{t-1}\eta_t/T)=\operatorname{plim}(\sum y_{t-1}\varepsilon_t/T)-\lambda\operatorname{plim}(\sum y_{t-1}\varepsilon_{t-1}/T)\neq 0$$

on account of the fact that y_{t-1} is correlated with ε_{t-1}. Thus the estimates would be inconsistent. As Liviatan [**74**] has suggested, the problem may be resolved by replacing the regressor y_{t-1} by the instrumental variable x_{t-1}. For, although x_{t-1} is expected to be highly correlated with y_{t-1}, it is uncorrelated with ε_{t-1}. The resulting estimates are liable to be somewhat inefficient. However, they are easy to compute, and, since they are also consistent, they do provide a useful starting point for a more elaborate iterative procedure.

Some improvement in the efficiency of the instrumental-variables method may be realized by adding a second step employing a revised instrumental variable in the form of $\hat{z}_{t-1}=(x_{t-1}+\hat{\lambda}x_{t-2}+\ldots+\hat{\lambda}^{t-2}x_1)$ wherein $\hat{\lambda}$ is the initial estimate of λ. At the same time, one might also take account of the covariance structure of the compound disturbance η_t by incorporating in the second step a consistent estimate of the dispersion matrix based upon the residuals $h_t = y_t - \hat{\lambda}y_{t-1} - \hat{\alpha}x_t$ from the first step. These suggestions have been made by Amemiya and Fuller [**5**] in the context of their reinterpretation of an estimator proposed by Hannan [**50**]. They have also demonstrated that, when a consistent estimate of the dispersion matrix is incorporated in the second step, the instrumental-variables estimator becomes asymptotically equivalent to a maximum-likelihood estimator.

Another relatively simple consistent estimator is one which was originally devised by Koyk [**69**] and was later expressed in an alternative form by Klein [**63**]. Koyk's approach can be seen as an attempt to obtain a consistent estimator by modifying the normal equations of the ordinary least-squares estimates. Klein's alternative derivation of the estimator is based on the perception that the equation in (12.91) resembles that of an errors-in-variables model. We can see this when we write the equation of the tth observation as

$$(y_t - \varepsilon_t) - \lambda(y_{t-1} - \varepsilon_t) - \alpha x_t = 0; \tag{12.93}$$

for we can regard ε_t and ε_{t-1} as errors besetting the observations y_t and y_{t-1} respectively. On this interpretation, the dispersion matrix associated with the variables in the equation is

$$D\begin{bmatrix} y_t \\ y_{t-1} \\ x_t \end{bmatrix} = \sigma_\varepsilon^2 \begin{bmatrix} 1, & 0, & 0 \\ 0, & 1, & 0 \\ 0, & 0, & 0 \end{bmatrix}. \tag{12.94}$$

Therefore, if we adopt the methods of Chapter 8, we should estimate the parameters by solving the equation

$$\left(\begin{bmatrix} \sum y_t^2, & \sum y_t y_{t-1}, & \sum y_t x_t \\ \sum y_{t-1} y_t, & \sum y_{t-1}^2, & \sum y_{t-1} x_t \\ \sum x_t y_t, & \sum x_t y_{t-1}, & \sum x_t^2 \end{bmatrix} - \mu \begin{bmatrix} 1, & 0, & 0 \\ 0, & 1, & 0 \\ 0, & 0, & 0 \end{bmatrix} \right) \begin{bmatrix} 1 \\ -\lambda \\ -\alpha \end{bmatrix} = \begin{bmatrix} 0 \\ 0 \\ 0 \end{bmatrix} \tag{12.95}$$

subject to the condition that μ assumes the smallest value that renders the system algebraically consistent.

For subsequent reference, it is convenient to solve the first line of this system to give

$$\mu = \sum (y_t - \lambda y_{t-1} - \alpha x_t) y_t \tag{12.96}$$

and to write the remaining lines as

$$\begin{aligned} 0 &= \sum (y_t - \lambda y_{t-1} - \alpha x_t) y_{t-1} + \lambda \mu \\ &= \sum (y_t - \lambda y_{t-1} - \alpha x_t) y_{t-1} + \lambda \sum (y_t - \lambda y_{t-1} - \alpha x_t) y_t \end{aligned} \tag{12.97}$$

and

$$\sum (y_t - \lambda y_{t-1} - \alpha x_t)x_t = 0. \tag{12.98}$$

The Koyk–Klein estimator is not fully efficient since it ignores an intertemporal relationship amongst the errors which arises from the fact that successive vectors of observations $[y_t, y_{t-1}, x_t]$ and $[y_{t+1}, y_t, x_{t+1}]$ have an element in common.

The efficient estimates of the parameters λ, α would be the values that minimize the function

$$S(\alpha, \lambda) = [\mathbf{y} - \lambda\mathbf{y}_{-1} - \alpha\mathbf{x}]'\mathbf{Q}^{-1}(\lambda)[\mathbf{y} - \lambda\mathbf{y}_{-1} - \alpha\mathbf{x}] \tag{12.99}$$

where $\mathbf{y}' = [y_2, y_3, \ldots, y_T]$, $\mathbf{y}'_{-1} = [y_1, y_2, \ldots, y_{T-1}]$, $\mathbf{x}' = [x_2, x_3, \ldots, x_T]$, and where

$$D(\boldsymbol{\eta}) = \sigma_\varepsilon^2 \begin{bmatrix} 1+\lambda^2, & -\lambda, & 0, & \ldots, & 0 \\ -\lambda, & 1+\lambda^2, & -\lambda, & \ldots, & 0 \\ 0, & -\lambda, & 1+\lambda^2, & \ldots, & 0 \\ \cdot & \cdot & \cdot & & \cdot \\ \cdot & \cdot & \cdot & & \cdot \\ \cdot & \cdot & \cdot & & \cdot \\ 0, & 0, & 0, & \ldots, & 1+\lambda^2 \end{bmatrix} = \sigma_\varepsilon^2\mathbf{Q}(\lambda) \tag{12.100}$$

is the dispersion matrix of the vector $\boldsymbol{\eta}' = [\eta_2, \ldots, \eta_T]$ of the composite disturbance terms which follow a first-order moving average process.

A number of procedures that are aimed at fulfilling this criterion have been suggested. Of these, the most straightforward is the search procedure of Dhrymes [**26**] to which we have previously referred in our treatment of the simple regression model with moving average disturbances. An obvious alternative is to use an iterative procedure based on the algorithm

$$\left(\begin{bmatrix} \mathbf{y}'_{-1} \\ \mathbf{x}' \end{bmatrix}\mathbf{Q}_r^{-1}[\mathbf{y}_{-1}, \mathbf{x}]\right)\begin{bmatrix} \lambda \\ \alpha \end{bmatrix}_{r+1} = \begin{bmatrix} \mathbf{y}'_{-1} \\ \mathbf{x}' \end{bmatrix}\mathbf{Q}_r^{-1}\mathbf{y} \tag{12.101}$$

wherein $\mathbf{Q}_r$ is an estimate of the dispersion matrix formed from the residuals of the rth regression. Given consistent estimates for the starting values, the sequence of estimates that are generated by this procedure must also be consistent. However, even when the sequence converges, the limiting values will not constitute the maximum-likelihood estimates. This result may be surprising, but the explanation is straightforward. It arises from the fact that the procedure is based essentially on conditions for minimizing $S(\alpha, \lambda)$ which ignore the fact that the matrix $\mathbf{Q}(\lambda)$ is also a function of λ. To find an estimate which does satisfy the criterion, we may use an iterative procedure that is based on the instrumental variables method of Hannan that has already been mentioned. The algorithm for this is given by

$$(12.102)\qquad \left(\begin{bmatrix} \mathbf{z}'_{-1} \\ \mathbf{x}' \end{bmatrix} \mathbf{Q}^{-1}(\lambda)[\mathbf{y}_{-1}, \mathbf{x}]\right)_r \begin{bmatrix} \lambda \\ \alpha \end{bmatrix}_{r+1} = \left(\begin{bmatrix} \mathbf{z}'_{-1} \\ \mathbf{x}' \end{bmatrix} \mathbf{Q}^{-1}(\lambda)\mathbf{y}\right)_r$$

where $\mathbf{z}'_{-1} = [z_1, \ldots, z_{T-1}]$ is a vector whose generic element is defined by $z_t(\lambda) = (x_t + \lambda x_{t-1} + \ldots + \lambda^{t-1} x_1)$. We shall examine this procedure in greater detail after we have dealt with the direct methods of estimating the geometric model.

Finally, let us consider a method that is aimed at partially fulfilling the maximum-likelihood criterion. This method ignores the off-diagonal elements of the matrix $\mathbf{Q}$ and, in place of minimizing $S(\alpha, \lambda)$, it faces the more modest and tractable problem of finding the values that minimize

$$(12.103)\qquad \frac{1}{1+\lambda^2}(\mathbf{y} - \lambda \mathbf{y}_{-1} - \alpha \mathbf{x})'(\mathbf{y} - \lambda \mathbf{y}_{-1} - \alpha \mathbf{x}) = \frac{1}{1+\lambda^2} \sum (y_t - \lambda y_{t-1} - \alpha x_t)^2.$$

By differentiating this function in respect of λ and α and setting the results to zero for a minimum we get, after eliminating various factors, the equations

$$(12.104)\qquad \begin{aligned} &\sum (y_t - \lambda y_{t-1} - \alpha x_t) y_{t-1} + \frac{\lambda}{1+\lambda^2} \sum (y_t - \lambda y_{t-1} - \alpha x_t)^2 = 0, \\ &\sum (y_t - \lambda y_{t-1} - \alpha x_t) x_t = 0. \end{aligned}$$

The second of these is identical to the equation (12.98) of the Koyk–Klein estimator. The first can be rewritten as

$$(12.105)\qquad \begin{aligned} 0 &= (1+\lambda^2) \sum (y_t - \lambda y_{t-1} - \alpha x_t) y_{t-1} + \lambda \sum (y_t - \lambda y_{t-1} - \alpha x_t)^2 \\ &= (1+\lambda^2) \sum (y_t - \lambda y_{t-1} - \alpha x_t) y_{t-1} \\ &\qquad - \lambda^2 \sum (y_t - \lambda y_{t-1} - \alpha x_t) y_{t-1} \\ &\quad + \lambda \sum (y_t - \lambda y_{t-1} - \alpha x_t) y_t; \end{aligned}$$

and we can see that, with the appropriate cancellations, this is identical to the other equation (12.97) of the Koyk–Klein estimator.

The equations in (12.104) are essentially the quasi-normal equations in Koyk's original formulation of the estimator, and they differ from the normal equations of the ordinary least-squares estimator only by the inclusion of the extra term $\lambda(1+\lambda^2)^{-1} \sum (y_t - \lambda y_{t-1} - \alpha x_t)^2$ in the first equation.

Indirect methods of estimating the geometric model were once favoured on account of the relative simplicity of the autoregressive form. However, there are some distinct advantages to be gained from estimating the model in its basic form. In the autoregressive form, the presence of a lagged dependent variable amongst the regressors makes it certain that methods such as the one by Koyk and Klein will yield inconsistent estimates whenever the stochastic structure is misspecified. Direct methods applied to the basic form are more robust; and a misspecification of the stochastic structure usually results in an estimator which is still consistent albeit somewhat inefficient.

Direct estimation of the geometric lag model

The basic equation (12.90) of the geometric model can be rewritten as

$$(12.106)\qquad \begin{aligned} y(t) &= \alpha[(I-\lambda L)^{-1}x(t)-\lambda^t\gamma]+\alpha\gamma\lambda^t+\varepsilon(t) \\ &= \alpha z(t)+\beta\lambda^t+\varepsilon(t). \end{aligned}$$

The term γ, defined by

$$(12.107)\qquad \gamma=(x_0+\lambda x_{-1}+\lambda^2x_{-2}+\ldots),$$

is a constant called the truncation remainder which is simply a geometrically weighted sum of all the elements of the sequence $x(t)$ prior to the time $t=1$. The sequence $z(t)$ which is a truncated version of the sequence $(I-\lambda L)^{-1}x(t)$ is defined over the positive integers by the recursive system

$$(12.108)\qquad \begin{aligned} z_1 &= x_1 & & \\ z_2 &= x_2+\lambda x_1 & &= x_2+\lambda z_1 \\ &\;\;\vdots & & \;\;\vdots \\ z_t &= x_t+\lambda x_{t-1}+\ldots+\lambda^{t-1}x_1 & &= x_t+\lambda z_{t-1}. \end{aligned}$$

Given the observations (x_t, y_t); $t=1,\ldots,T$, we can form a set of T equations

$$(12.109)\qquad \begin{aligned} y_t &= \alpha\left(\sum_{i=0}^{t-1}\lambda^i x_{t-i}\right)+\beta\lambda^t+\varepsilon_t \\ &= \alpha z_t+\beta\lambda^t+\varepsilon_t. \end{aligned}$$

If the value of λ were known, we could form the variables z_t and λ^t for $t=1,\ldots,T$ and proceed to estimate the parameters α and β by the method of ordinary least squares.

On the assumption that $\varepsilon(t)$ is a normal sequence, such estimates would also maximize the likelihood function. In practice, λ is always unknown, so we must find estimates by minimizing the sum of squares $S(\alpha, \beta, \lambda)$ in respect of all three parameters. A straightforward way of seeking the global minimum is to compare values of the conditional minimum $\min S(\alpha, \beta \mid \lambda)$ arising from the application of ordinary least-squares regression to the equations (12.109) when λ is assigned various values in the interval $[0, 1)$. A search procedure which is analogous to the one proposed for the simple regression model with first-order autoregressive disturbances can be used. From a mathematical point of view, any value of λ in the open interval $(-1, 1)$ is admissible on the grounds that it will ensure the boundedness of the sequence $(I-\lambda L)^{-1}x(t)$ whenever $x(t)$ is bounded. In practice, however, values in the interval $(-1, 0)$ are excluded since these would give rise to a sequence of lag coefficients with alternating signs for which there would be no reasonable substantive interpretation.

Our procedure may be simplified to some extent by ignoring the truncation parameter β. Since β is associated with the variable λ^t which tends to zero as t increases, disregarding it should not unduly affect the estimates of α and λ when the sample size is large. Nevertheless, to estimate β is not unduly burdensome; and it should certainly be estimated when sample is small. Therefore our tendency to ignore the parameter in the account that follows should not be interpreted as a recommendation to do so in practice but rather as a means of facilitating our exposition.

A variety of direct iterative methods are available for computing the parameters. To describe these, let us define the truncated sequence

$$q(t)=(I-\lambda L)^{-1}y(t)-\lambda^t\delta \tag{12.110}$$

wherein $\delta=(y_0+\lambda y_{-1}+\lambda^2 y_{-2}+\ldots)$. This is formed from $y(t)$ in the same way as $z(t)$ is formed from $x(t)$. Multiplying both sides of the equation by $I-\lambda L$ gives $(I-\lambda L)q(t)=y(t)-(I-\lambda L)\lambda^t\delta=y(t)$, whence

$$y(t)=q(t)-\lambda q(t-1). \tag{12.111}$$

On substituting the latter into the relationship (12.106) and rearranging, we have

$$q(t)=\lambda q(t-1)+\alpha z(t)+\beta\lambda^t+\varepsilon(t). \tag{12.112}$$

A simple procedure now suggests itself. From an initial estimate of λ, say λ_0, which might be obtained by the indirect method of instrumental variables, we can form the variables $q_{t,0}$, $q_{t-1,0}$ and $z_{t,0}$ for $t=2,\ldots,T$. By substituting these values in our equation and applying the method of ordinary least squares, we can find the estimates λ_1, α_1, β_1. For the next round, we can use λ_1 to form the revised regressors $q_{t,1}$ and $z_{t,1}$ which will enable us to find revised estimates λ_2, α_2, β_2. By reiterating the procedure, we can generate a sequence of estimates which may converge upon a definitive set of values. We do not necessarily expect the sequence to converge upon the values that give the global minimum of $S(\alpha, \beta, \lambda)$. Nevertheless, given that the initial estimate λ_0 is consistent, it follows that any estimate in the sequence is also consistent.

The estimation might be simplified by ignoring the truncation parameter β. In that case, our algorithm would have the form

$$\text{(12.113)}\qquad \begin{bmatrix} \sum q_{t-1}^2 & \sum q_{t-1}z_t \\ \sum z_t q_{t-1}, & \sum z_t^2 \end{bmatrix}_r \begin{bmatrix} \lambda \\ \alpha \end{bmatrix}_{r+1} = \begin{bmatrix} \sum q_{t-1}q_t \\ \sum z_t q_t \end{bmatrix}_r .$$

Our reasons for doubting that our procedure will yield least-squares or maximum-likelihood estimates is that it is based on equations that are only approximations to the first-order conditions for minimizing

$$\text{(12.114)}\qquad \begin{aligned} S(\alpha, \beta, \lambda) &= \sum_{t=2}^{T} (y_t - \alpha z_t - \beta\lambda^t)^2 \\ &= \sum_{t=2}^{T} (q_t - \lambda q_{t-1} - \alpha z_t - \beta\lambda^t)^2. \end{aligned}$$

In a seminal paper [**112**], Steiglitz and McBride proposed a procedure that is based upon the true first-order conditions which are obtained by differentiating the function $S(\alpha, \beta, \lambda)$ in awareness of the fact that z_t depends upon the value of λ. In order to describe their procedure, we must first consider the derivative

$$\text{(12.115)}\qquad \begin{aligned} \frac{\partial z_t}{\partial\lambda} &= \frac{\partial}{\partial\lambda}\left(\sum_{i=0}^{t-1} \lambda^i x_{t-i}\right) \\ &= \sum_{i=1}^{t-1} i\lambda^{i-1}x_{t-i} \\ &= s_t. \end{aligned}$$

We can recognize s_t as an element of a sequence $s(t)$ which is the truncated version of

$$\text{(12.116)}\qquad \begin{aligned} \frac{\partial}{\partial\lambda}(I-\lambda L)^{-1}x(t) &= (I-\lambda L)^{-2}Lx(t). \\ &= x(t-1)+2\lambda x(t-2)+3\lambda^2 x(t-3) \\ &\quad +\ldots+(t-1)\lambda^{t-2}x(1)+\ldots. \end{aligned}$$

In practice, the elements of the sequence $s(t)$ may be generated by the recursive system

$$\text{(12.117)}\qquad \begin{aligned} s_2 &= z_1 \\ s_3 &= z_2 + \lambda z_1 && = z_2 + \lambda s_2 \\ &\ \ \vdots && \ \ \vdots \\ s_t &= z_{t-1} + \lambda z_{t-2} + \ldots + \lambda^{t-2} z_1 && = z_{t-1} + \lambda s_{t-1} \end{aligned}$$

where z_t; $t = 1, \ldots, T-1$ is generated by the system in (12.108).

Let us now differentiate the function $S(\alpha, \beta, \lambda)$ in respect of α and λ to obtain

$$\text{(12.118)} \qquad \begin{aligned}\frac{\partial S}{\partial \lambda} &= -2\sum (y_t - \alpha z_t - \beta\lambda^t)(\alpha s_t + \beta t\lambda^{t-1}) \\ &= -2\sum (q_t - \lambda q_{t-1} - \alpha z_t - \beta\lambda^t)(\alpha s_t + \beta t\lambda^{t-1})\end{aligned}$$

and

$$\text{(12.119)} \qquad \begin{aligned}\frac{\partial S}{\partial \alpha} &= -2\sum (y_t - \alpha z_t - \beta\lambda^t)z_t \\ &= -2\sum (q_t - \lambda q_{t-1} - \alpha z_t - \beta\lambda^t)z_t.\end{aligned}$$

By setting these derivatives to zero, we obtain two of the first-order conditions for minimizing the function. If we are prepared to ignore the truncation problem by setting $\beta = 0$, then these conditions provide us with the estimating equations

$$\text{(12.120)} \qquad \begin{bmatrix} \sum q_{t-1}s_t, & \sum z_t s_t \\ \sum q_{t-1}z_t, & \sum z_t^2 \end{bmatrix} \begin{bmatrix} \lambda \\ \alpha \end{bmatrix} = \begin{bmatrix} \sum s_t q_t \\ \sum z_t q_t \end{bmatrix}$$

wherein the summation is for $t = 2, \ldots, T$. The equations can be solved by a simple iterative procedure. Given the rth approximation λ_r, we can form the elements $q_{t,r}$, $s_{t,r}$, and $z_{t,r}$. When these are substituted in the equations, they may be solved for the revised estimates λ_{r+1}, α_{r+1}.

One drawback of this method is that it cannot always be relied upon to produce a convergent sequence of estimates. The difficulty is related to the fact that the matrix of cross-products on the LHS of (12.120) is neither positive definite nor symmetric. The suggestion has therefore been made that s_t should be replaced by q_{t-1}. With this amendment, we obtain precisely the estimating system that is depicted in equation (12.113).

Perhaps a more secure way of obtaining the maximum-likelihood estimates is to use a Newton–Raphson or a Gauss–Newton procedure to solve the equations of the first-order conditions. The Gauss–Newton procedure is the more accessible since it involves finding derivatives only of the first order. The requisite derivatives are

$$\text{(12.121)} \qquad \begin{aligned}\frac{\partial \varepsilon_t}{\partial \lambda} &= -\alpha\frac{\partial z_t}{\partial \lambda} - \beta t\lambda^{t-1} \\ &= -\alpha s_t - \beta t\lambda^{t-1}, \\ \frac{\partial \varepsilon_t}{\partial \alpha} &= -z_t.\end{aligned}$$

Let us ignore the truncation parameter by setting $\beta = 0$. Then reference to

(12.67) shows that we can write the algorithm as

$$(12.122)\qquad \begin{bmatrix}\lambda\\ \alpha\end{bmatrix}_{r+1}=\begin{bmatrix}\lambda\\ \alpha\end{bmatrix}_{r}+\begin{bmatrix}\alpha^2\sum s_t^2, & \alpha\sum s_t z_t\\ \alpha\sum z_t s_t, & \sum z_t^2\end{bmatrix}_r^{-1}\begin{bmatrix}\alpha\sum s_t\varepsilon_t\\ \sum z_t\varepsilon_t\end{bmatrix}_r$$

where the summation is for $t=2,\ldots,T$. On substituting for $\varepsilon_t=y_t-\alpha z_t$ and rearranging, we can express the algorithm as

$$(12.123)\qquad \begin{bmatrix}\alpha\sum s_t^2, & \sum s_t z_t\\ \alpha\sum z_t s_t, & \sum z_t^2\end{bmatrix}_r\begin{bmatrix}\lambda\\ \alpha\end{bmatrix}_{r+1}=\begin{bmatrix}\lambda\alpha\sum s_t^2+\sum s_t y_t\\ \lambda\alpha\sum z_t s_t+\sum z_t y_t\end{bmatrix}_r.$$

Perhaps it is worth noting that, by writing $y_t=q_t-\lambda q_{t-1}$ in this equation and by eliminating from either side the terms that tend to equality with the convergence of the sequence of estimates, we can derive the estimating equations (12.120) that are the basis of the method of Steiglitz and McBride. This simply demonstrates that both methods are aimed at satisfying the same criterion.

So far, we have assumed that the disturbances in the basic equation (12.90) of the geometric model are generated by a stochastic process $\varepsilon(t)$ consisting of a sequence of independent and identically distributed random variables. A model which may be more realistic can be obtained by replacing $\varepsilon(t)$ by a first-order autoregressive process $\eta(t)=(I-\phi L)^{-1}\varepsilon(t)$. The basic equation is then

$$(12.124)\qquad y(t)-\alpha(I-\lambda L)^{-1}x(t)+(I-\phi L)^{-1}\varepsilon(t).$$

In these circumstances, we may still obtain consistent estimates of α and λ by using our existing direct methods; but the estimates are liable to be inefficient. To obtain efficient estimates, we can quite simply combine our existing direct methods of estimation with the methods that are commonly applied to simple regression models with autoregressive disturbances. To illustrate, let us consider multiplying both sides of equation (12.124) by the operator $(I-\phi L)$ to obtain

$$(12.125)\qquad \begin{aligned} y(t)-\phi y(t-1)&=\alpha[(I-\lambda L)^{-1}x(t)-\phi(I-\lambda L)^{-1}x(t-1)]+\varepsilon(t)\\ &=\alpha[z(t)-\phi z(t-1)]+\beta(\lambda^t-\phi\lambda^{t-1})+\varepsilon(t).\end{aligned}$$

The function to be minimized is now $\sum\varepsilon_t^2=S(\alpha,\beta,\lambda,\phi)$. As Dhrymes [**27**] has argued, there is no difficulty in extending our existing search procedure to accommodate the extra parameter ϕ. Thus we can seek the global minimum of the function by comparing the values of its conditional minima $\min S(\alpha,\beta\mid\lambda,\phi)$ that arise from the application of ordinary least-squares to the model when various admissible values are assigned to the parameters λ, ϕ. The set of admissible values correspond to the points in the rectangle $(0<\lambda<1, -1<\phi<1)$.

Extensions of our iterative methods are also simple to devise. the Gauss–Newton method for example is readily extended; and Amemiya and Fuller [**5**] have given a full account of the resulting estimator.

Equivalent methods of estimating the geometric model

Often econometric estimators which appear, at first, to be quite distinct are seen, at length, to be nothing but alternative computational procedures aimed at fulfilling, with varying degrees of approximation, a common criterion of estimation. This is certainly true of many of the alternative methods that have been proposed for estimating the parameters of the geometric model. Therefore we may be justified in having provided a less than exhaustive account of these methods.

It is interesting to discover that the equivalences amongst the alternative estimators transcend the distinction that we have made between direct and indirect methods of estimation. We are able to show, for example, that the indirect and the direct maximum-likelihood estimators fulfill the same criterion.

Let us recall that the indirect maximum-likelihood method of estimation consists of seeking the values of λ and α which minimize the function

$$[\mathbf{y}-\lambda\mathbf{y}_{-1}-\alpha\mathbf{x}]'\mathbf{Q}^{-1}(\lambda)[\mathbf{y}-\lambda\mathbf{y}_{-1}-\alpha\mathbf{x}] \tag{12.126}$$

previously specified in (12.99). The matrix $\mathbf{Q}^{-1}$ is the dispersion matrix of a first-order moving average process. It can be closely approximated by $\mathbf{M}^{-1\prime}\mathbf{M}^{-1}$ wherein $\mathbf{M}^{-1}(\lambda)$ is the sample analogue of the operator $(I-\lambda L)^{-1}$, defined exactly as $\mathbf{M}^{-1}(\theta)$ was defined in (12.50). By replacing $\mathbf{Q}^{-1}$ by $\mathbf{M}^{-1\prime}\mathbf{M}^{-1}$, we obtain the expression

$$\begin{aligned}(\mathbf{M}^{-1}\mathbf{y}-\lambda\mathbf{M}^{-1}\mathbf{y}_{-1}-\alpha\mathbf{M}^{-1}\mathbf{x})'(\mathbf{M}^{-1}\mathbf{y}-\lambda\mathbf{M}^{-1}\mathbf{y}_{-1}-\alpha\mathbf{M}^{-1}\mathbf{x})\\ =(\mathbf{q}-\lambda\mathbf{q}_{-1}-\alpha\mathbf{z})'(\mathbf{q}-\lambda\mathbf{q}_{-1}-\alpha\mathbf{z})\end{aligned} \tag{12.127}$$

wherein

$$\begin{aligned}\mathbf{M}^{-1}\mathbf{y}&=\mathbf{q}=[q_2,\ldots,q_T]',\\ \mathbf{M}^{-1}\mathbf{y}_{-1}&=\mathbf{q}_{-1}=[q_1,\ldots,q_{T-1}]',\\ \mathbf{M}^{-1}\mathbf{x}&=\mathbf{z}=[z_2,\ldots,z_T]'\end{aligned} \tag{12.128}$$

are vectors comprising elements of the truncated sequences $q(t)$, $q(t-1)$, and $z(t)$ respectively. On writing the expression in scalar notation, we get

$$\sum_{t=2}^{T}(q_t-\lambda q_{t-1}-\alpha z_t)^2. \tag{12.129}$$

Apart from the omission of the truncation term $\beta\lambda^t$, this is the criterion function $S(\alpha, \beta, \lambda)$ of the direct maximum-likelihood method given in (12.114). What is particularly interesting is that approximation of $\mathbf{Q}^{-1}$ by $\mathbf{M}^{-1\prime}\mathbf{M}^{-1}$ in the indirect method is the exact counterpart of the approximation entailed by setting $\beta = 0$ in the direct method.

The equivalence can also be demonstrated in terms of the estimating equations of the direct and indirect methods. The indirect maximum-likelihood estimates generated by the iterative version of Hannan's procedure satisfy the equation

$$\left(\begin{bmatrix} \mathbf{z}'_{-1} \\ \mathbf{x}' \end{bmatrix} \mathbf{Q}^{-1}(\lambda)[\mathbf{y}_{-1}, \mathbf{x}]\right)\begin{bmatrix} \lambda \\ \alpha \end{bmatrix} = \begin{bmatrix} \mathbf{z}'_{-1} \\ \mathbf{x}' \end{bmatrix} \mathbf{Q}^{-1}(\lambda)\mathbf{y}. \tag{12.130}$$

On replacing $\mathbf{Q}^{-1}$ by $\mathbf{M}^{-1\prime}\mathbf{M}^{-1}$, we obtain the expression

$$\begin{bmatrix} (\mathbf{M}^{-1}\mathbf{z}_{-1})'(\mathbf{M}^{-1}\mathbf{y}_{-1}), & (\mathbf{M}^{-1}\mathbf{z}_{-1})'(\mathbf{M}^{-1}\mathbf{x}) \\ (\mathbf{M}^{-1}\mathbf{x})'(\mathbf{M}^{-1}\mathbf{y}_{-1}), & (\mathbf{M}^{-1}\mathbf{x})'(\mathbf{M}^{-1}\mathbf{x}) \end{bmatrix}\begin{bmatrix} \lambda \\ \alpha \end{bmatrix} = \begin{bmatrix} (\mathbf{M}^{-1}\mathbf{z}_{-1})'(\mathbf{M}^{-1}\mathbf{y}) \\ (\mathbf{M}^{-1}\mathbf{x})'(\mathbf{M}^{-1}\mathbf{y}) \end{bmatrix} \tag{12.131}$$

wherein

$$\mathbf{M}^{-1}\mathbf{z}_{-1} = \mathbf{s} = [s_2, \ldots, s_T]' \tag{12.132}$$

is a vector comprising elements of the truncated sequence $s(t)$. Using the remaining definitions under (12.128), we can write the expression in scalar notation as

$$\begin{bmatrix} \sum s_t q_{t-1}, & \sum s_t z_t \\ \sum z_t q_{t-1}, & \sum z_t^2 \end{bmatrix}\begin{bmatrix} \lambda \\ \alpha \end{bmatrix} = \begin{bmatrix} \sum s_t q_t \\ \sum z_t q_t \end{bmatrix}. \tag{12.133}$$

This is instantly recognizable as the equation (12.120) upon which the direct method of obtaining maximum-likelihood estimates that is due to Steiglitz and McBride is based.

It is possible to demonstrate other equivalences. For example, we have depicted in (12.101) the algorithm of an indirect method that falls short of the maximum-likelihood criterion. We attributed the shortfall to the fact that the conditions on which the method is based are the result of ignoring the dependence of $\mathbf{Q}^{-1}$ on λ. We have also depicted in (12.113) the algorithm of a direct method which likewise falls short of the maximum-likelihood criterion. In this case, we attributed the shortfall to the fact that the method is based on conditions that ignore the dependence of z_t on λ. It is a simple exercise to demonstrate that these two methods are related in precisely the way that the direct and indirect maximum-likelihood methods are related to each other.

THE RATIONAL LAG

The rational lag model may be represented by the equation

$$y(t)=\frac{B(L)}{A(L)}x(t)+\varepsilon(t) \tag{12.134}$$

wherein $B(L)=(\beta_0+\beta_1L+\ldots+\beta_rL^r)$ and $A(L)=(I-\alpha_1L-\ldots-\alpha_pL^p)$ are polynomial lag operators of finite degrees. It is reasonable to impose the restriction that $[B(L)/A(L)]x(t)$ should be a bounded sequence whenever $x(t)$ is bounded. For this, we require the roots of $A(L)=0$ to lie outside the unit circle.

Let us define the sequence $w(t)=A^{-1}(L)x(t)$. Then the equation (12.134) can be written as

$$y(t)=B(L)w(t)+\varepsilon(t), \tag{12.135}$$

and the model reduces to one with a finite lag scheme in the input variable. In order to exploit this simplification in the process of estimating the model, we must be able to provide a reasonable representation of the sequence $w(t)$ based on estimated values of the parameters of $A(L)$. It is therefore appropriate to examine this sequence more closely.

Let us begin by writing $A(L)=I-C(L)$ where $C(L)=(\alpha_1L+\ldots+\alpha_pL^p)$. By applying the operator $I-C(L)$ to both sides of the equation $w(t)=A^{-1}(L)x(t)=[I-C(L)]^{-1}x(t)$ and rearranging the result, we get

$$\begin{aligned} w(t)&=x(t)+C(L)w(t)\\ &=x(t)+\alpha_1w(t-1)+\ldots+\alpha_pw(t-p). \end{aligned} \tag{12.136}$$

This is a pth-order linear difference equation in w. Given p consecutive values $w_0=\gamma_1$, $w_{-1}=\gamma_2,\ldots,w_{1-p}=\gamma_p$ and the values x_t; $t=1,\ldots,T$, we can generate the values w_t; $t=1,\ldots,T$ by the recursive system

$$\begin{aligned}
w_1 &= x_1 + \alpha_1\gamma_1 + \alpha_2\gamma_2 + \ldots + \alpha_p\gamma_p\\
w_2 &= x_2 + \alpha_1 w_1 + \alpha_2\gamma_1 + \ldots + \alpha_p\gamma_{p-1}\\
&\;\;\vdots\\
w_p &= x_p + \alpha_1 w_{p-1} + \alpha_2 w_{p-2} + \ldots + \alpha_p\gamma_1\\
w_{p+1} &= x_{p+1} + \alpha_1 w_p + \alpha_2 w_{p-1} + \ldots + \alpha_p w_1\\
&\;\;\vdots\\
w_t &= x_t + \alpha_1 w_{t-1} + \alpha_2 w_{t-2} + \ldots + \alpha_p w_{t-p}.
\end{aligned} \tag{12.137}$$

In practice, we wish to decompose the sequence $w(t)$ into the sum of a truncated sequence $z(t)$ whose elements for $t=1,\ldots,T$ comprise only the sample values x_t; $t=1,\ldots,T$ and a remainder sequence $r(t)$ whose elements comprise the pre-sample values of w_t in the form of $\gamma_1,\ldots,\gamma_p$. The appropriate method of decomposition is adequately illustrated by considering the case where $A(L)=(I-\alpha_1L-\alpha_2L^2)$ is a quadratic function of the lag operator. Then $w(t)=x(t)+\alpha_1w(t-1)+\alpha_2w(t-2)$ and, given the presample values $w_0=\gamma_1$, $w_{-1}=\gamma_2$, we can generate the elements of $z(t)$ and $r(t)$ for the positive integers by the recursive systems

(12.138)
$$\begin{aligned}
z_1&=x_1 & r_1&=\alpha_1\gamma_1+\alpha_2\gamma_2\\
z_2&=x_2+\alpha_1z_1 & r_2&=\alpha_1r_1+\alpha_2\gamma_1\\
z_3&=x_3+\alpha_1z_2+\alpha_2z_1 & r_3&=\alpha_1r_2+\alpha_2r_1\\
&\;\vdots & &\;\vdots\\
z_t&=x_t+\alpha_1z_{t-1}+\alpha_2z_{t-2} & r_t&=\alpha_1r_{t-1}+\alpha_2r_{t-2}.
\end{aligned}$$

It is readily confirmed that

(12.139)
$$\begin{aligned}
w_1&=z_1+r_1=x_1+\alpha_1\gamma_1 &&+\alpha_2\gamma_2\\
w_2&=z_2+r_2=x_2+\alpha_1(z_1+r_1) &&+\alpha_2\gamma_1\\
w_3&=z_3+r_3=x_3+\alpha_1(z_2+r_2) &&+\alpha_2(z_1+r_1)\\
&\;\vdots && \;\vdots\\
w_t&=z_t+r_t=x_t+\alpha_1(z_{t-1}+r_{t-1})&&+\alpha_2(z_{t-2}+r_{t-2}).
\end{aligned}$$

Thus, with $w(t)=z(t)+r(t)$, our equation becomes

(12.140)
$$y(t)=B(L)z(t)+B(L)r(t)+\varepsilon(t).$$

There are a variety of ways in which we can treat the truncation term $B(L)r(t)$ when we come to estimate the model. The simplest method, albeit the one which is least adequate, is to avoid the truncation problem altogether by setting each of the pre-sample values $\gamma_1,\ldots,\gamma_p$ to zero. We are left with the equation $y(t)=B(L)z(t)+\varepsilon(t)$ so that, in effect, this amounts to approximating the sequence $w(t)$ in our original equation (12.135) by the truncated sequence $z(t)$. The adequacy of the approximation will depend upon the rate at which the remainder sequence $r(t)$ tends to zero as t increases. The remainder sequence satisfies the equation $A(L)r(t)=0$. Thus, if the roots of $A(L)=0$ lie close to the unit circle, $r(t)$ will tend only gradually to zero and the effect of the approximation will endure. Conversely, if the roots are remote from the unit circle, then effect will be transient.

A more adequate way of treating the truncation problem is to provide an explicit representation of the remainder sequence. A number of alternative parametrizations are available. For example, if the roots $\lambda_1, \ldots, \lambda_p$ of $A(L)=0$ are distinct, then it follows from (11.31) that we can represent the general solution of $A(L)r(t)=0$ by

$$r(t)=c_1\lambda_1^{-t}+c_2\lambda_2^{-t}+\ldots+c_p\lambda^{-t} \tag{12.141}$$

where $c_1, \ldots, c_p$ are parameters to be estimated. This representation is inconvenient for, except when $A(L)=0$ is a quadratic equation, it is a tiresome business to find the roots.

A simpler way is to represent the remainder sequence as

$$r(t)=\gamma_1 g_1(t)+\ldots+\gamma_p g_p(t) \tag{12.142}$$

wherein $g_1(t), \ldots, g_p(t)$ are sequences depending only on the values $\alpha_1, \ldots, \alpha_p$. To illustrate, we can consider the case where $A(L)=(I-\alpha_1 L-\alpha_2 L^2)$. Then the remainder sequence is

$$r(t)=\gamma_1 g(t)+\gamma_2 h(t) \tag{12.143}$$

and the elements of $g(t)$ and $h(t)$ can be generated by the systems

$$\begin{aligned} g_1 &= \alpha_1 & h_1 &= \alpha_2 \\ g_2 &= \alpha_1 g_1 & h_2 &= \alpha_1 h_1 \\ g_3 &= \alpha_1 g_2 + \alpha_2 g_1 & h_3 &= \alpha_1 h_2 + \alpha_2 h_1 \\ &\vdots & &\vdots \\ g_t &= \alpha_1 g_{t-1}+\alpha_2 g_{t-2} & h_t &= \alpha_1 h_{t-1}+\alpha_2 h_{t-2}. \end{aligned} \tag{12.144}$$

On substituting the expression for $r(t)$ in (12.142) into the equation (12.140), we get

$$y(t)=B(L)[z(t)+\gamma_1 g_1(t)+\ldots+\gamma_p g_p(t)]+\varepsilon(t). \tag{12.145}$$

Thus the tth element of $y(t)$ can be expressed as

$$y_t=\sum_{i=0}^{r}\beta_i z_{t-i}+\gamma_1\sum_{i=0}^{r}\beta_i g_{1,t-i}+\ldots+\gamma_p\sum_{i=0}^{r}\beta_i g_{p,t-i}+\varepsilon_t; \tag{12.146}$$

and, given the values y_t, z_t, $g_{1t}, \ldots, g_{pt}$ for $t=1, \ldots, T$, we can form the values of ε_t for $t=r+1, \ldots, T$.

The appropriate criterion for estimating the parameters of the rational lag model is to minimize the sum of squares $S(\boldsymbol{\beta}, \boldsymbol{\alpha}, \boldsymbol{\gamma})=\sum_{t=r+1}^{T}\varepsilon_t^2$ in respect to the parameters $\boldsymbol{\beta}=[\beta_0, \ldots, \beta_r]'$, $\boldsymbol{\alpha}=[\alpha_1, \ldots, \alpha_p]'$, and $\gamma=[\gamma_1, \ldots, \gamma_p]'$. The function $S(\boldsymbol{\beta}, \boldsymbol{\alpha}, \boldsymbol{\gamma})$ is non-linear in the parameters and, therefore, we must use an iterative procedure. As in the case of the geometric lag model, the

Gauss–Newton procedure seems both secure and accessible; and it has the advantage of requiring derivatives of only the first order. The requisite derivatives have the forms

$$(12.147)\qquad \frac{\partial \varepsilon_t}{\partial \beta_i} = -z_{t-i} - \gamma_1 g_{1,t-i} - \ldots - \gamma_p g_{p,t-i},$$

$$\frac{\partial \varepsilon_t}{\partial \alpha_j} = -\sum_{i=0}^{r} \beta_i \frac{\partial z_{t-i}}{\partial \alpha_j} - \gamma_1 \sum_{i=0}^{r} \beta_i \frac{\partial g_{1,t-i}}{\partial \alpha_j} - \ldots - \gamma_p \sum_{i=0}^{r} \beta_i \frac{\partial g_{p,t-i}}{\partial \alpha_j},$$

$$\frac{\partial \varepsilon_t}{\partial \gamma_j} = -\sum_{i=0}^{r} \beta_i g_{j,t-i};$$

and the only complication here lies in finding the derivatives $\partial z_t/\partial \alpha_j$ and $\partial g_{k,t}/\partial \alpha_j$. These may be generated by recursive systems. For example, the sequence of the derivatives $s_{1,t} = \partial z_t/\partial \alpha_1$ may be generated by the system

$$(12.148)\qquad \begin{aligned} s_{1,1} &= 0 \\ s_{1,2} &= z_1 \\ s_{1,3} &= z_2 + \alpha_1 s_{1,2} \\ &\vdots \\ s_{1,t} &= z_{t-1} + \alpha_1 s_{1,t-1} + \ldots + \alpha_p s_{1,t-p}. \end{aligned}$$

More generally, we can recognize that for $t = 1, \ldots, j$ the derivative $\partial z_t/\partial \alpha_j$ has a zero value and that for $t = j+1, \ldots, T$ it has the same values as the elements of the truncated version of the sequence

$$(12.149)\qquad \frac{\partial}{\partial \alpha_j} A^{-1}(L)x(t) = A^{-2}(L)L^j x(t).$$

The Gauss–Newton procedure is by no means the only method that is available for estimating the parameters of the rational lag model. Indeed, the method that is commonly described in the literature is an elaboration of the method of Steiglitz and McBride for estimating the geometric model. This method, which was proposed by Dhrymes, Klein, and Steiglitz [**28**], has certain drawbacks. In the first place, it often fails to provide a convergent sequence of estimates and, in the second place, it somewhat overlooks the truncation problem.

Whatever an iterative procedure is used, there is a problem of finding initial estimates for the starting values. It has been argued that these should be obtained by the statistically consistent method of instrumental variables.

However, there should be no disadvantage in using estimates obtained by applying the inconsistent method of ordinary least squares to the equations

$$(12.150) \qquad y_t = \sum_{i=1}^{p} \alpha_i y_{t-i} \sum_{i=0}^{r} \beta_i x_{t-i} + \eta_t$$

which arise from the relationship

$$(12.151) \qquad A(L)y(t) = B(L)x(t) + A(L)\varepsilon(t).$$

Indeed, it was the ordinary least-squares method alone that Jorgenson used in his original empirical applications of the rational lag model.

It is also interesting to recall that Jorgenson [**60**] proposed—but apparently never implemented—an estimation technique based on the relationship

$$(12.152) \qquad A(L)[y(t) - \varepsilon(t)] - B(L)x(t) = 0$$

which was a direct extension of Klein's method for the indirect estimation of the geometric model.

The rational lag model may be elaborated by replacing the stochastic process $\varepsilon(t)$, consisting of a sequence of independent and identically distributed random variables, by an autoregressive process $\eta(t) = P(L)^{-1}\varepsilon(t)$. If $\eta(t)$ is a first-order process, then the equation of the model becomes

$$(12.153) \qquad y(t) = \frac{B(L)}{A(L)} x(t) + \frac{\varepsilon(t)}{(I - \phi L)}$$
$$= B(L)w(t) + (I - \phi L)^{-1}\varepsilon(t).$$

Multiplying both sides by $(I - \phi L)$ gives

$$(12.154) \qquad y(t) - \phi y(t-1) = B(L)[w(t) - \phi w(t-1)] + \varepsilon(t).$$

In this form the model is amenable, with little extra complication, to the Gauss–Newton estimation procedure that we have already described.

The general temporal regression model

The most general temporal regression model that we need to consider can be represented by the equation

$$(12.155) \qquad y(t) = \frac{B(L)}{A(L)} x(t) + \frac{Q(L)}{P(L)} \varepsilon(t).$$

This model comprises a rational lag scheme in the observable input variable and a disturbance term that follows a mixed autoregressive moving average scheme. In the language of Box and Jenkins [**15**], the equation (12.155) provides the most parsimonious general representation of the phenomena that we are studying. That is to say, the equation accommodates the full range of possible relationships amongst $y(t)$, $x(t)$, and $\varepsilon(t)$ with the use of the fewest parameters.

In practice, all the generality that we are likely to require in econometric applications is provided by the equation

$$y(t)=\frac{B(L)}{A(L)}x(t)+\frac{\varepsilon(t)}{P(L)} \tag{12.156}$$

which represents a rational lag model with autoregressive disturbances. It is heartening to realize that we have already dealt with this case.

Even with this simpler model, the problem of estimation may be daunting; and we may wish to alleviate this at the cost of increasing the number of parameters. Let us therefore consider writing the equation (12.156) in the form

$$P(L)A(L)y(t)=P(L)B(L)x(t)+A(L)\varepsilon(t). \tag{12.157}$$

If we are prepared to ignore the fact that some of the parameters occur on both sides of the equation, then we can assimilate it to the form

$$A(L)y(t)=B(L)x(t)+M(L)\varepsilon(t) \tag{12.158}$$

which was our original way of representing the general temporal regression model. Although the number of distinct parameters is increased, the problem of estimation is considerably simplified; for we now face a regression model with a moving average disturbance and finite lag schemes in the observable variables to which the methods that we described in connection with the simple regression model with moving average disturbances are wholly applicable.

The conflict between parsimony and ease of estimation is quite widespread in econometrics. However, experience suggests that, at any level of generality, it is the parsimonious representations that are eventually preferred.

BIBLIOGRAPHY

Temporal Regression Models. Aigner [**2**], Dhrymes [**27**], Fuller [**39**], Griliches [**47**]

Regression Models with Autoregressive Disturbances. Dhrymes [**27**, Chap. 4 §6], Durbin [**30**], Kadiyala [**61**], Sargan [**104**]

Regression Models with Moving Average Disturbances. Nicholls, Pagan and Terrell [**89**], Trivedi [**117**]

Finite Lag Schemes. Almon [**4**], Dhrymes [**27,** Chap. 3, 8]

The Geometric Lag. Amemiya and Fuller [**5**], Dhrymes [**27,** Chap. 4–7], Hannan [**50**], Klein [**63**], Koyk [**69**], Steiglitz and McBride [**112**], Zellner and Geisel [**126**]

The Rational Lag. Dhrymes [**27,** Chap. 9], Dhrymes, Klein and Steiglitz [**28**], Jorgenson [**60**]

The General Temporal Model. Box and Jenkins [**15,** Chap. 10, 11]

Non-linear Computation. Goldfeld and Quandt [**43**], Hartley [**53**], Hartley and Brooker [**54**], Marquardt [**84**]

CHAPTER 13

Sets of Linear Regressions

In previous chapters, we have considered various forms of a linear regression system relating a single observable output y_t to K observable inputs comprised in the vector $\mathbf{x}_{t.} = [x_{t1}, \ldots, x_{tK}]$. We shall now consider a multiple system which relates each of the M outputs comprised in the vector $\mathbf{y}_{t.} = [y_{t1}, \ldots, y_{tM}]$ to the K input variables. An important example of this system is provided by the reduced form of a simultaneous-equation econometric model. We shall use the notation that is commonly associated with the reduced form to represent our system by

$$(13.1) \qquad \mathbf{y}_{t.} = \mathbf{x}_{t.}\mathbf{\Pi} + \mathbf{v}_{t.}.$$

On writing this in finer detail, we get

$$(13.2) \qquad [y_{t1}, \ldots, y_{tM}] = \mathbf{x}_{t.}[\boldsymbol{\pi}_{.1}, \ldots, \boldsymbol{\pi}_{.M}] + [v_{t1}, \ldots, v_{tM}]$$

which is simply an array of M regression equations of the generic form $y_{tm} = \mathbf{x}_{t.}\boldsymbol{\pi}_{.m} + v_{tm}$, each accounting for a different output in terms of a common set of input variables. In some cases, certain inputs are known to be absent from an equation, and we shall be able to take account of this by specifying that the corresponding elements in the parameter vector are zeros.

A set of T realizations of the relationship in (13.1) can be compiled in the usual way to give the matrix equation

$$(13.3) \qquad \mathbf{Y} = \mathbf{X\Pi} + \mathbf{V}$$

which can be rewritten in vector form as

$$(13.4) \qquad \mathbf{Y}^c = (\mathbf{I} \otimes \mathbf{X})\mathbf{\Pi}^c + \mathbf{V}^c.$$

The latter equation conveniently represents the multiple-output system in the format of a single-output system; and it is clear that we can establish an isomorphic relationship between the two types of system. By exploiting this relationship, we are able to apply many of the results from previous chapters to our present problems.

There is a strong presumption that the disturbances of the M equations of the multiple system are statistically inter-related. To justify this, let us recall that a disturbance term is commonly supposed to be compounded out of a large number of individually insignificant and unobservable stochastic inputs. If, on this understanding, we suppose that, as well as having a common set of observable inputs, the constituent equations have a significant number of stochastic inputs in common, then we are bound to envisage a statistical relationship amongst their disturbances.

We shall adopt two sets of detailed assumptions concerning the disturbances. To begin, we shall assume that the vector $\mathbf{v}_{t.}$ is generated by a stochastic process that is independent of time such that, for all values of $t=1,\ldots,T$, we have

$$(13.5)\qquad E(\mathbf{v}_{t.})=\mathbf{0},\qquad D(\mathbf{v}'_{t.})=\mathbf{\Omega},$$

where $\mathbf{\Omega}=[\omega_{ml}]$ is a dispersion matrix containing the variances and covariances of M contemporaneous disturbance terms. The assumption that the stochastic process is independent of time also means that for the vectors $\mathbf{v}'_{.m}=[v_{1m}, v_{2m}, \ldots, v_{Tm}]$ and $\mathbf{v}'_{.l}$, consisting of T consecutive values of the disturbance terms of the mth and the lth equations respectively, we have

$$(13.6)\qquad \begin{aligned} &E(\mathbf{v}_{.m})=E(\mathbf{v}_{.l})=\mathbf{0},\\ &C(\mathbf{v}_{.m},\mathbf{v}_{.l})=\omega_{ml}\mathbf{I}_T \quad \text{if} \quad m\neq l,\\ &C(\mathbf{v}_{.m},\mathbf{v}_{.l})=D(\mathbf{v}_{.m})=\omega_{mm}\mathbf{I}_T \quad \text{if} \quad m=l. \end{aligned}$$

In order to represent the stochastic structure of the entire system of M equations throughout the T periods of observation, we write

$$(13.7)\qquad E(\mathbf{V}^c)=\mathbf{0},\qquad D(\mathbf{V}^c)=\mathbf{\Omega}\otimes\mathbf{I};$$

and this subsumes both (13.5) and (13.6). Using a notation that was introduced in Chapter 6, we can represent our model of the multiple system under the assumptions above by $[\mathbf{Y}^c, (\mathbf{I}\otimes\mathbf{X})\mathbf{\Pi}^c, \mathbf{\Omega}\otimes\mathbf{I}]$.

At a later stage, we shall adopt the assumption that the disturbances are generated by a first-order vector autoregressive process. Denoting the disturbance vector by $\boldsymbol{\eta}_{t.}$, we shall specify that

$$(13.8)\qquad \boldsymbol{\eta}_{t.}=\boldsymbol{\eta}_{t-1.}\mathbf{\Phi}+\mathbf{v}_{t.}$$

where $\mathbf{v}_{t.}$ is a stochastic vector with the properties specified under (13.5).

EFFICIENT ESTIMATION OF THE UNRESTRICTED MODEL

For estimating the parameters of our model, it seems appropriate to adopt a system-wide approach based on the equation (13.4); for such an approach should enable us to incorporate information relating to the contemporaneous covariance structure of the disturbances of the M equations. It is somewhat surprising to find that, in the absence of *a priori* restrictions, the efficient estimator of $\boldsymbol{\Pi}^c$ in the model $[\mathbf{Y}, (\mathbf{I}\otimes\mathbf{X})\boldsymbol{\Pi}^c, \boldsymbol{\Omega}\otimes\mathbf{I}]$ takes no account of the dispersion matrix $\boldsymbol{\Omega}$ and that, in fact, it decomposes into a set of ordinary least-squares estimators of the parameters of the constituent single-equation models. Let us demonstrate this. First we should refer to (6.7) to establish that the efficient estimator of $(\mathbf{I}\otimes\mathbf{X})\boldsymbol{\Pi}^c$ is obtained by the $(\boldsymbol{\Omega}\otimes\mathbf{I})^{-1}$-orthogonal projection of $\mathbf{Y}^c$ on $\mathcal{M}(\mathbf{I}\otimes\mathbf{X})$ such as to minimize the distance function

$$(13.9)\qquad \begin{aligned}&[\mathbf{Y}^c-(\mathbf{I}\otimes\mathbf{X})\boldsymbol{\Pi}^c]'(\boldsymbol{\Omega}^{-1}\otimes\mathbf{I})[\mathbf{Y}^c-(\mathbf{I}\otimes\mathbf{X})\boldsymbol{\Pi}^c]\\ &\quad=\text{Trace}[(\mathbf{Y}-\mathbf{X}\boldsymbol{\Pi})'(\mathbf{Y}-\mathbf{X}\boldsymbol{\Pi})\boldsymbol{\Omega}^{-1}].\end{aligned}$$

Thus, given that $\text{Null}(\mathbf{I}\otimes\mathbf{X})=0$ in consequence of $\text{Null}(\mathbf{X})=0$, we have

$$(13.10)\qquad \hat{\boldsymbol{\Pi}}^c=[(\mathbf{I}\otimes\mathbf{X})'(\boldsymbol{\Omega}\otimes\mathbf{I})^{-1}(\mathbf{I}\otimes\mathbf{X})]^{-1}(\mathbf{I}\otimes\mathbf{X})'(\boldsymbol{\Omega}\otimes\mathbf{I})^{-1}\mathbf{Y}^c.$$

By consolidating terms, we get

$$(13.11)\qquad \begin{aligned}\hat{\boldsymbol{\Pi}}^c&=(\boldsymbol{\Omega}^{-1}\otimes\mathbf{X}'\mathbf{X})^{-1}(\boldsymbol{\Omega}^{-1}\otimes\mathbf{X}')\mathbf{Y}^c\\ &=[\mathbf{I}\otimes(\mathbf{X}'\mathbf{X})^{-1}\mathbf{X}']\mathbf{Y}^c;\end{aligned}$$

whence

$$(13.12)\qquad \hat{\boldsymbol{\Pi}}=(\mathbf{X}'\mathbf{X})^{-1}\mathbf{X}'\mathbf{Y},$$

which can be broken down into M separate ordinary least-squares estimates of the generic from $\hat{\boldsymbol{\pi}}_{.m}=(\mathbf{X}'\mathbf{X})^{-1}\mathbf{X}'\mathbf{y}_{.m}$.

On referring to (6.9), we can see that the dispersion matrix of the estimator is

$$(13.13)\qquad \begin{aligned}D(\hat{\boldsymbol{\Pi}}^c)&=[(\mathbf{I}\otimes\mathbf{X})'(\boldsymbol{\Omega}\otimes\mathbf{I})^{-1}(\mathbf{I}\otimes\mathbf{X})]^{-1}\\ &=\boldsymbol{\Omega}\otimes(\mathbf{X}'\mathbf{X})^{-1}.\end{aligned}$$

It is only for the purpose of determining the statistical properties of the estimates that a knowledge of $\boldsymbol{\Omega}$ is required. In normal circumstances, the elements of $\boldsymbol{\Omega}$ are unknown and we must rely upon estimates formed from the residuals of the ordinary least-squares regression. According to (7.8), an unbiased estimate of ω_{mm} in the model $(\mathbf{y}_{.m}, \mathbf{X}\boldsymbol{\pi}_{.m}, \omega_{mm}\mathbf{I})$ is provided by

$$(13.14)\qquad \hat{\omega}_{mm}=\frac{\mathbf{y}'_{.m}(\mathbf{I}-\mathbf{P})\mathbf{y}_{.m}}{T-K}=\frac{(\mathbf{y}_{.m}-\mathbf{X}\hat{\boldsymbol{\pi}}_{.m})'(\mathbf{y}_{.m}-\mathbf{X}\hat{\boldsymbol{\pi}}_{.m}}{T-K}$$

where $\mathbf{P}=\mathbf{X}(\mathbf{X}'\mathbf{X})^{-1}\mathbf{X}'$. By a very similar argument, it can be shown that an unbiased estimator of the covariance ω_{ml} of the disturbances of the mth and lth equations is provided by

$$(13.15)\qquad \hat{\omega}_{ml}=\frac{\mathbf{y}'_{.m}(\mathbf{I}-\mathbf{P})\mathbf{y}_{.l}}{T-K}=\frac{(\mathbf{y}_{.m}-\mathbf{X}\hat{\boldsymbol{\pi}}_{.m})'(\mathbf{y}_{.l}-\mathbf{X}\hat{\boldsymbol{\pi}}_{.l})}{T-K}$$

Taking these results together, we can see that an unbiased estimator of $\mathbf{\Omega}$ is provided by

$$\hat{\mathbf{\Omega}} = \frac{\mathbf{Y}'(\mathbf{I}-\mathbf{P})\mathbf{Y}}{T-K} = \frac{(\mathbf{Y}-\mathbf{X}\hat{\mathbf{\Pi}})'(\mathbf{Y}-\mathbf{X}\hat{\mathbf{\Pi}})}{T-K}. \tag{13.16}$$

An interesting way of characterizing the fact that the efficient system-wide estimator of $\mathbf{\Pi}^c$ in the model $[\mathbf{Y}^c, (\mathbf{I}\otimes\mathbf{X})\mathbf{\Pi}^c, \mathbf{\Omega}\otimes\mathbf{I}]$ reduces to an ordinary least-squares estimator is to say that the $(\mathbf{\Omega}\otimes\mathbf{I})^{-1}$-metric of the efficient estimator and the $(\mathbf{I}\otimes\mathbf{I})$-metric of the system wide ordinary least-squares estimator are equivalent in the context of the model. According to (5.10), the necessary and sufficient condition for the equivalence of these two metrics is that

$$(\mathbf{\Omega}\otimes\mathbf{I})^{-1}\mathcal{M}(\mathbf{I}\otimes\mathbf{X}) = (\mathbf{I}\otimes\mathbf{I})\mathcal{M}(\mathbf{I}\otimes\mathbf{X}) \tag{13.17}$$

which means that the image of the manifold $\mathcal{M}(\mathbf{I}\otimes\mathbf{X})$ is the same under the two transformations $(\mathbf{\Omega}\otimes\mathbf{I})^{-1}$ and $(\mathbf{I}\otimes\mathbf{I})$. The condition in (13.17) is also equivalent to the condition $\mathcal{M}(\mathbf{\Omega}\otimes\mathbf{X}) = \mathcal{M}(\mathbf{I}\otimes\mathbf{X})$. To show that the latter is satisfied, let us write the jth partition of $\mathbf{\Omega}\otimes\mathbf{X}$ as

$$\begin{bmatrix} \omega_{1j}\mathbf{X} \\ \omega_{2j}\mathbf{X} \\ \cdot \\ \cdot \\ \cdot \\ \omega_{Mj}\mathbf{X} \end{bmatrix} = \omega_{1j}\begin{bmatrix} \mathbf{X} \\ \mathbf{0} \\ \cdot \\ \cdot \\ \cdot \\ \mathbf{0} \end{bmatrix} + \omega_{2j}\begin{bmatrix} \mathbf{0} \\ \mathbf{X} \\ \cdot \\ \cdot \\ \cdot \\ \mathbf{0} \end{bmatrix} + \ldots + \omega_{Mj}\begin{bmatrix} \mathbf{0} \\ \mathbf{0} \\ \cdot \\ \cdot \\ \cdot \\ \mathbf{X} \end{bmatrix} \tag{13.18}$$

This demonstrates that the vectors generating the manifold $\mathcal{M}(\mathbf{\Omega}\otimes\mathbf{X})$ are linear combinations of the vectors generating the manifold $\mathcal{M}(\mathbf{I}\otimes\mathbf{X})$, which can only mean that the two manifolds are identical. The efficiency of the ordinary least-squares estimator for the model $[\mathbf{Y}^c, (\mathbf{I}\otimes\mathbf{X})\mathbf{\Pi}^c, \mathbf{\Omega}\otimes\mathbf{I}]$ depends upon the absence of any *a priori* restrictions on the parameters and upon the fact that the same input variables appear in each of the constituent equations of the system. Whenever there is *a priori* information relating to the parameters, or whenever some of the system's inputs are absent from some of its equations, the efficient estimator has to comprehend the information relating to the covariance structure of the disturbances comprised in $\mathbf{\Omega}$.

Maximum likelihood estimation of the unrestricted model

If we can assume that the vectors of contemporaneous disturbances are independently and identically distributed according to a normal law so that $\mathbf{v}_{t.} \sim N(\mathbf{0}, \mathbf{\Omega})$ for $t=1,\ldots,T$, and if we can regard the vectors $\mathbf{x}_{t.}$ as fixed, then $\mathbf{y}_{t.} \sim N(\mathbf{x}_{t.}\mathbf{\Pi}, \mathbf{\Omega})$, and the likelihood function of the sample becomes

$$(13.19)\qquad L = \prod_{t=1}^{T} N(\mathbf{y}_{t.}; \mathbf{x}_{t.}\mathbf{\Pi}, \mathbf{\Omega})$$

$$= (2\pi)^{-MT/2} |\mathbf{\Omega}|^{-T/2} \exp\left\{-\tfrac{1}{2}\sum_{t=1}^{T} (\mathbf{y}_{t.} - \mathbf{x}_{t.}\mathbf{\Pi})\mathbf{\Omega}^{-1}(\mathbf{y}_{t.} - \mathbf{x}_{t.}\mathbf{\Pi})'\right\}.$$

The logarithm of this function is

$$(13.20)\qquad L^*(\mathbf{\Pi}, \mathbf{\Omega}) = -\frac{MT}{2}\log(2\pi) - \frac{T}{2}\log|\mathbf{\Omega}|$$

$$-\tfrac{1}{2}\,\mathrm{Trace}[(\mathbf{Y} - \mathbf{X\Pi})'(\mathbf{Y} - \mathbf{X\Pi})\mathbf{\Omega}^{-1}],$$

since

$$(13.21)\qquad \sum_{t=1}^{T} (\mathbf{y}_{t.} - \mathbf{x}_{t.}\mathbf{\Pi})\mathbf{\Omega}^{-1}(\mathbf{y}_{t.} - \mathbf{x}_{t.}\mathbf{\Pi})' = \mathrm{Trace}[(\mathbf{Y} - \mathbf{X\Pi})\mathbf{\Omega}^{-1}(\mathbf{Y} - \mathbf{X\Pi})']$$

$$= \mathrm{Trace}[(\mathbf{Y} - \mathbf{X\Pi})'(\mathbf{Y} - \mathbf{X\Pi})\mathbf{\Omega}^{-1}].$$

We can find the maximum-likelihood estimates of $\mathbf{\Pi}$ and $\mathbf{\Omega}$ from the first-order conditions for the maximization of $L^*(\mathbf{\Pi}, \mathbf{\Omega})$ which are

$$(13.22)\qquad \partial\frac{L^*(\mathbf{\Pi}, \mathbf{\Omega})}{\partial\mathbf{\Omega}^{-1}} = \mathbf{0},$$

$$(13.23)\qquad \partial\frac{L^*(\mathbf{\Pi}, \mathbf{\Omega})}{\partial\mathbf{\Pi}} = \mathbf{0}.$$

To evaluate (13.22), we must use (4.80) and (4.74) to find

$$(13.24)\qquad \frac{\partial \log|\mathbf{\Omega}|}{\partial\mathbf{\Omega}^{-1c}} = \frac{\partial \log|\mathbf{\Omega}|}{\partial\mathbf{\Omega}^{c}}\frac{\partial\mathbf{\Omega}^{c}}{\partial\mathbf{\Omega}^{-1c}}$$

$$= -\mathbf{\Omega}^{-1r}(\mathbf{\Omega}\otimes\mathbf{\Omega}),$$

which, on account of the conventions that $\partial y/\partial\mathbf{X}^{c} = (\partial y/\partial\mathbf{X})^{r}$ and that $(\mathbf{AXB}')^{r} = \mathbf{X}^{r}(\mathbf{A}'\otimes\mathbf{B}')$, gives

$$(13.25)\qquad \frac{\partial \log|\mathbf{\Omega}|}{\partial\mathbf{\Omega}^{-1}} = -\mathbf{\Omega}.$$

We must also use (4.83) to find

$$(13.26)\qquad \frac{\partial\,\mathrm{Trace}[(\mathbf{Y} - \mathbf{X\Pi})'(\mathbf{Y} - \mathbf{X\Pi})\mathbf{\Omega}^{-1}]}{\partial\mathbf{\Omega}^{-1}} = (\mathbf{Y} - \mathbf{X\Pi})'(\mathbf{Y} - \mathbf{X\Pi}).$$

Thus (13.22) is evaluated as

$$(13.27)\qquad \frac{\partial L^*}{\partial\mathbf{\Omega}^{-1}} = \frac{T}{2}\mathbf{\Omega} - \tfrac{1}{2}(\mathbf{Y} - \mathbf{X\Pi})'(\mathbf{Y} - \mathbf{X\Pi}) = \mathbf{0}$$

which gives the estimating equation

$$(13.28) \qquad \mathbf{\Omega}(\mathbf{\Pi}) = \frac{(\mathbf{Y}-\mathbf{X\Pi})'(\mathbf{Y}-\mathbf{X\Pi})}{T}.$$

To evaluate (13.23), we must use (4.82) to find

$$(13.29) \qquad \frac{\partial \,\mathrm{Trace}[(\mathbf{Y}-\mathbf{X\Pi})'(\mathbf{Y}-\mathbf{X\Pi})\mathbf{\Omega}^{-1}]}{\partial \mathbf{\Pi}^c}$$

$$= \frac{\partial \,\mathrm{Trace}[(\mathbf{Y}-\mathbf{X\Pi})'(\mathbf{Y}-\mathbf{X\Pi})\mathbf{\Omega}^{-1}]}{\partial(\mathbf{Y}-\mathbf{X\Pi})^c}\frac{\partial(\mathbf{Y}-\mathbf{X\Pi})^c}{\partial \mathbf{\Pi}^c}$$

$$= -2(\mathbf{Y}-\mathbf{X\Pi})^{c\prime}(\mathbf{\Omega}^{-1}\otimes\mathbf{I})(\mathbf{I}\otimes\mathbf{X})$$

$$= -2(\mathbf{Y}-\mathbf{X\Pi})^{\prime r}(\mathbf{\Omega}^{-1}\otimes\mathbf{X})$$

which gives

$$(13.30) \qquad \frac{\partial \,\mathrm{Trace}[(\mathbf{Y}-\mathbf{X\Pi})'(\mathbf{Y}-\mathbf{X\Pi})\mathbf{\Omega}^{-1}]}{\partial \mathbf{\Pi}} = -2\mathbf{\Omega}^{-1}(\mathbf{Y'X}-\mathbf{\Pi'X'X}).$$

Thus the condition (13.23) is evaluated as

$$(13.31) \qquad \frac{\partial L^*}{\partial \mathbf{\Pi}} = \mathbf{\Omega}^{-1}(\mathbf{Y'X}-\mathbf{\Pi'X'X}) = \mathbf{0}$$

from which, by cancelling $\mathbf{\Omega}^{-1}$ and rearranging, we get the estimator

$$(13.32) \qquad \tilde{\mathbf{\Pi}} = (\mathbf{X'X})^{-1}\mathbf{X'Y}.$$

On comparing this with the equation (13.12), we find that the maximum-likelihood estimator of $\mathbf{\Pi}$ coincides with the least-squares estimator. This is hardly surprising since both estimators are effectively derived from the minimand specified in (13.9). By contrast, the maximum-likelihood estimator of $\mathbf{\Omega}$,

$$(13.33) \qquad \tilde{\mathbf{\Omega}} = \frac{(\mathbf{Y}-\mathbf{X}\tilde{\mathbf{\Pi}})'(\mathbf{Y}-\mathbf{X}\tilde{\mathbf{\Pi}})}{T} = \frac{\mathbf{Y'(I-P)Y}}{T},$$

which is obtained by taking $\mathbf{\Pi}=\tilde{\mathbf{\Pi}}$ in equation (13.28), is related to the least-squares estimator $\hat{\mathbf{\Omega}}$ by the formula $\tilde{\mathbf{\Omega}} = \hat{\mathbf{\Omega}}(T-K)/T$.

Second-order derivatives of the log likelihood function

Under very general conditions, the asymptotic dispersion matrix of a maximum-likelihood estimator $\tilde{\mathbf{\theta}}$ is given by $\mathbf{\Sigma} = -[\partial(\partial L^*/\partial\mathbf{\theta})'/\partial\mathbf{\theta}]^{-1}$ when this is evaluated at the true value of $\mathbf{\theta}$, and the asymptotic distribution of $\tilde{\mathbf{\theta}}$ is $N(\mathbf{\theta}, \mathbf{\Sigma})$.

In the present instance, we have little need of the first part of this result, since we already know from (13.13) the form that the dispersion matrix $D(\tilde{\mathbf{\Pi}}^c) = D(\hat{\mathbf{\Pi}}^c)$ takes in samples of all sizes. Nevertheless, it is worth our while to extract the second-order partial derivatives of $L^*(\mathbf{\Pi}, \mathbf{\Omega})$, partly because the exercise provides a useful example of the theory and partly because we shall find use for these derivatives at a later stage. In fact, since we have little interest in finding the asymptotic dispersion matrix of $\tilde{\mathbf{\Omega}}$, we shall work with the concentrated log-likelihood function $L^*(\mathbf{\Pi}) = L^*[\mathbf{\Pi}, \mathbf{\Omega}(\mathbf{\Pi})]$. This may be obtained from (13.20) by replacing $\mathbf{\Omega}$ by the maximum-likelihood expression given in (13.28). Thus we have

$$(13.34) \qquad L^*(\mathbf{\Pi}) = -\frac{MT}{2}\log(2\pi) - \frac{T}{2}\log\left|\frac{(\mathbf{Y}-\mathbf{X\Pi})'(\mathbf{Y}-\mathbf{X\Pi})}{T}\right| - \frac{MT}{2}.$$

Using (4.81), we can find that

$$(13.35) \qquad \begin{aligned}\frac{\partial L^*(\mathbf{\Pi})}{\partial \mathbf{\Pi}} &= T[(\mathbf{Y}-\mathbf{X\Pi})'(\mathbf{Y}-\mathbf{X\Pi})]^{-1}(\mathbf{Y'X}-\mathbf{\Pi'X'X}) \\ &= \mathbf{\Omega}^{-1}(\mathbf{\Pi})(\mathbf{Y'X}-\mathbf{\Pi'X'X})\end{aligned}$$

which, when equated to zero, provides us with the maximum-likelihood estimator $\tilde{\mathbf{\Pi}}$.

It is worth pointing out that the present derivation of $\tilde{\mathbf{\Pi}}$ from the concentrated function $L^*(\mathbf{\Pi})$ indicates that our estimate of $\mathbf{\Pi}$ may also be derived by the criterion of minimizing the generalized residual variance

$$(13.36) \qquad \left|\frac{(\mathbf{Y}-\mathbf{X\Pi})'(\mathbf{Y}-\mathbf{X\Pi})}{T}\right|$$

in respect of $\mathbf{\Pi}$.

To obtain the second-order derivatives, we use the product rule of (4.67) to give

$$(13.37) \qquad \begin{aligned}\frac{\partial(\partial L^*/\partial \mathbf{\Pi}^c)'}{\partial \mathbf{\Pi}^c} &= \frac{\partial[(\mathbf{X'Y}-\mathbf{X'X\Pi})\mathbf{\Omega}^{-1}]^c}{\partial \mathbf{\Pi}^c} \\ &= [\mathbf{I}\otimes(\mathbf{X'Y}-\mathbf{X'X\Pi})]\frac{\partial \mathbf{\Omega}^{-1c}}{\partial \mathbf{\Omega}^c}\frac{\partial \mathbf{\Omega}^c}{\partial \mathbf{\Pi}^c} \\ &\quad + (\mathbf{\Omega}^{-1}\otimes\mathbf{I})\frac{\partial(\mathbf{X'Y}-\mathbf{X'X\Pi})^c}{\partial \mathbf{\Pi}^c}.\end{aligned}$$

Using $\partial(\mathbf{X'X\Pi})^c/\partial\mathbf{\Pi}^c = \mathbf{I}\otimes\mathbf{X'X}$ and $\partial(\mathbf{X'Y})^c/\partial\mathbf{\Pi}^c = \mathbf{0}$, the second term of the latter expression is readily evaluated as

$$(13.38) \qquad (\mathbf{\Omega}^{-1}\otimes\mathbf{I})\frac{\partial(\mathbf{X'Y}-\mathbf{X'X\Pi})^c}{\partial \mathbf{\Pi}^c} = -(\mathbf{\Omega}^{-1}\otimes\mathbf{X'X}).$$

Within the first term we find that

$$\text{(13.39)} \qquad \frac{\partial \mathbf{\Omega}^{-1c}}{\partial \mathbf{\Omega}^{c}} = -(\mathbf{\Omega}^{-1} \otimes \mathbf{\Omega}^{-1}),$$

and that

$$\text{(13.40)} \qquad \frac{\partial \mathbf{\Omega}^{c}}{\partial \mathbf{\Pi}^{c}} = \frac{1}{T} \frac{\partial (\mathbf{Y}'\mathbf{Y} - \mathbf{\Pi}'\mathbf{X}'\mathbf{Y} - \mathbf{Y}'\mathbf{X}\mathbf{\Pi} + \mathbf{\Pi}'\mathbf{X}'\mathbf{X}\mathbf{\Pi})^{c}}{\partial \mathbf{\Pi}^{c}}$$

$$= \frac{1}{T}[-(\mathbf{Y}'\mathbf{X} \otimes \mathbf{I})Ⓣ - (\mathbf{I} \otimes \mathbf{Y}'\mathbf{X}) + (\mathbf{\Pi}'\mathbf{X}'\mathbf{X} \otimes \mathbf{I})Ⓣ + (\mathbf{I} \otimes \mathbf{\Pi}'\mathbf{X}'\mathbf{X})].$$

By assembling the various constituent parts, we find that

$$\text{(13.41)} \qquad \frac{\partial (\partial L^{*}/\partial \mathbf{\Pi}^{c})'}{\partial \mathbf{\Pi}^{c}} = \frac{1}{T}[\mathbf{I} \otimes (\mathbf{X}'\mathbf{Y} - \mathbf{X}'\mathbf{X}\mathbf{\Pi})](\mathbf{\Omega}^{-1} \otimes \mathbf{\Omega}^{-1})$$

$$\times [(\mathbf{Y}'\mathbf{X} \otimes \mathbf{I})Ⓣ + (\mathbf{I} \otimes \mathbf{Y}'\mathbf{X}) - (\mathbf{\Pi}'\mathbf{X}'\mathbf{X} \otimes \mathbf{I})Ⓣ$$

$$- (\mathbf{I} \otimes \mathbf{\Pi}'\mathbf{X}'\mathbf{X})] - (\mathbf{\Omega}^{-1} \otimes \mathbf{X}'\mathbf{X}).$$

Now let us assume that the explanatory variables of the model are generated in such a way that $\text{plim}(\mathbf{V}'\mathbf{X}/T) = \mathbf{0}$ and $\text{plim}(\mathbf{X}'\mathbf{X}/T) = \mathbf{M}$ is a matrix of finite and constant values. It is easy to show that, under these assumptions, the estimators $\tilde{\mathbf{\Pi}}$ and $\tilde{\mathbf{\Omega}}$ are consistent and that

$$\text{(13.42)} \qquad \text{plim}\left(\frac{\mathbf{Y}'\mathbf{X}}{T}\right) = \text{plim}\left(\frac{\mathbf{\Pi}'\mathbf{X}'\mathbf{X}}{T}\right) = \mathbf{\Pi}'\mathbf{M}.$$

On applying this to (13.40), we find that $\text{plim}(\partial \mathbf{\Omega}^{c}/\partial \mathbf{\Pi}^{c}) = \mathbf{0}$. Since the derivative $\partial \mathbf{\Omega}^{c}/\partial \mathbf{\Pi}^{c}$ is a factor in the first term of the expression for $\partial(\partial L^{*}/\partial \mathbf{\Pi}^{c})'\partial \mathbf{\Pi}^{c}$ in (13.41), it follows that, as T tends to infinity, the latter tends in probability to the value of its second term $-(\mathbf{\Omega}^{-1} \otimes \mathbf{X}'\mathbf{X})$. On the strength of this result, we may now deduce that

$$\text{(13.43)} \qquad -\text{plim}\left[\frac{\partial (\partial L^{*}/\partial \mathbf{\Pi}^{c})'}{\partial \mathbf{\Pi}^{c}}\right]^{-1} = T^{-1}\,\text{plim}\left[\mathbf{\Omega}^{-1} \otimes \left(\frac{\mathbf{X}'\mathbf{X}}{T}\right)\right]^{-1}$$

$$= T^{-1}[\mathbf{\Omega} \otimes \mathbf{M}^{-1}].$$

Reference to (13.13) shows that this expression is, without doubt, the asymptotic form of the dispersion matrix $D(\tilde{\mathbf{\Pi}}^{c}) = D(\hat{\mathbf{\Pi}}^{c})$.

RESTRICTED MODELS

We shall now consider the case where our model is subject to *a priori* restrictions on the regression parameters. To facilitate a subsequent comparison with the structural form of a simultaneous-equation system, we shall alter our notation by rewriting the equation in (13.4) as

$$\text{(13.44)} \qquad \mathbf{Y}^c = (\mathbf{I} \otimes \mathbf{X})\mathbf{B}^c + \mathbf{U}^c$$

and by specifying the stochastic structure as

$$\text{(13.45)} \qquad E(\mathbf{U}^c) = \mathbf{0}, \qquad D(\mathbf{U}^c) = \mathbf{\Sigma} \otimes \mathbf{I}.$$

We shall write the *a priori* restrictions on the regression parameters as

$$\text{(13.46)} \qquad \mathbf{R}\mathbf{B}^c = \mathbf{r}.$$

This expression is of sufficient generality to accommodate not only relationships amongst the parameters of single equations but also relationships amongst the parameters of several different equations. With these restrictions, the model may be represented by the summary notation $[\mathbf{Y}^c, (\mathbf{I} \otimes \mathbf{X})\mathbf{B}^c \mid \mathbf{R}\mathbf{B}^c = \mathbf{r}, \mathbf{\Sigma I}]$.

Whenever such *a priori* information is available, we are obliged, if we wish to obtain efficient estimates, to take account of the covariance structure of the disturbances. To illustrate, let us consider the case where the *a priori* restrictions specify that some of the parameters are zeros. It amounts to the same thing to say that some of the inputs are known to be absent from some of the equations. Thus we can take account of the restrictions by writing the constituent equations of the system as

$$\text{(13.47)} \qquad \mathbf{y}_{.m} = \mathbf{X}_m \boldsymbol{\delta}_m + \mathbf{u}_{.m}; \qquad m = 1, \ldots, M$$

where $\boldsymbol{\delta}_m$ is formed from $\boldsymbol{\beta}_{.m}$ by deleting the zero parameters, and $\mathbf{X}_m$ contains a corresponding subset of the vectors of $\mathbf{X}$. The M equations may be compiled to form the system

$$\text{(13.48)} \qquad \begin{bmatrix} \mathbf{y}_{.1} \\ \mathbf{y}_{.2} \\ \vdots \\ \mathbf{y}_{.M} \end{bmatrix} = \begin{bmatrix} \mathbf{X}_1, & \mathbf{0} & , \ldots, & \mathbf{0} \\ \mathbf{0}, & \mathbf{X}_2 & , \ldots, & \mathbf{0} \\ \vdots & \vdots & & \vdots \\ \mathbf{0}, & \mathbf{0} & , \ldots, & \mathbf{X}_M \end{bmatrix} \begin{bmatrix} \boldsymbol{\delta}_1 \\ \boldsymbol{\delta}_2 \\ \vdots \\ \boldsymbol{\delta}_M \end{bmatrix} + \begin{bmatrix} \mathbf{u}_{.1} \\ \mathbf{u}_{.2} \\ \vdots \\ \mathbf{u}_{.M} \end{bmatrix}$$

or

$$\text{(13.49)} \qquad \mathbf{Y}^c = \mathbf{W}\boldsymbol{\delta} + \mathbf{U}^c$$

which is simply a contracted version of the system in (13.44) obtained by eliminating the zero parameters and the corresponding columns of $(\mathbf{I} \otimes \mathbf{X})$.

The efficient estimator of $\boldsymbol{\delta}$ is given by

$$\text{(13.50)} \qquad \hat{\boldsymbol{\delta}} = [\mathbf{W}'(\mathbf{\Sigma} \otimes \mathbf{I})^{-1}\mathbf{W}]^{-1}\mathbf{W}'(\mathbf{\Sigma} \otimes \mathbf{I})^{-1}\mathbf{Y}^c.$$

It is clear that, in general, this will not reduce to a system-wide ordinary least-squares estimator. In the absence of a knowledge of $\mathbf{\Sigma} = [\sigma_{ml}]$, we might estimate its typical element by

$$(13.51) \qquad \hat{\sigma}_{ml} = \frac{(\mathbf{y}_{.m} - \mathbf{X}_m \hat{\boldsymbol{\delta}}_m)'(\mathbf{y}_{.l} - \mathbf{X}_l \hat{\boldsymbol{\delta}}_l)}{T-K}.$$

However, when $\hat{\boldsymbol{\Sigma}} = [\hat{\sigma}_{ml}]$ replaces the unknown $\boldsymbol{\Sigma}$ in (13.50), we are faced with a set of non-linear equations in $\hat{\boldsymbol{\delta}}$ and $\hat{\boldsymbol{\Sigma}}$ which can only be solved by an iterative method. A practical way of avoiding this difficulty is to estimate $\boldsymbol{\Sigma}$ from the residuals of an ordinary least-squares regression applied to the equation (13.49). However, we shall defer the discussion of this and other proposals until we have examined the nature of the maximum-likelihood estimator of a restricted system.

The maximum-likelihood estimator of the restricted system

We shall continue to assume that the vectors of contemporaneous disturbances are independently and identically distributed according to a normal law such that $\mathbf{u}_{t.} \sim N(\mathbf{0}, \boldsymbol{\Sigma})$ for all t. Therefore, apart from the change of notation, we retain the likelihood function specified in (13.19). The estimates of the parameters of our model are now obtained from the maximization of the log-likelihood function subject to the restrictions. Thus the function to be maximized is

$$(13.52) \qquad L^{\mathrm{R}} = L^*(\mathbf{B}, \boldsymbol{\Sigma}) - \boldsymbol{\lambda}'(\mathbf{R}\mathbf{B}^{\mathrm{c}} - \mathbf{r})$$

where $\boldsymbol{\lambda}$ is a vector of Lagrangean multipliers. The first-order conditions for a maximum are

$$(13.53) \qquad \frac{\partial L^{\mathrm{R}}}{\partial \boldsymbol{\Sigma}^{-1}} = \frac{\partial L^*}{\partial \boldsymbol{\Sigma}^{-1}} = \mathbf{0},$$

$$(13.54) \qquad \frac{\partial L^{\mathrm{R}}}{\partial \mathbf{B}^{\mathrm{c}}} = \frac{\partial L^*}{\partial \mathbf{B}^{\mathrm{c}}} - \boldsymbol{\lambda}'\mathbf{R} = \mathbf{0},$$

$$(13.55) \qquad \frac{\partial L^{\mathrm{R}}}{\partial \boldsymbol{\lambda}} = -(\mathbf{R}\mathbf{B}^{\mathrm{c}} - \mathbf{r})' = \mathbf{0},$$

The derivatives that are required in order to evaluate these conditions are

$$(13.56) \qquad \frac{\partial L^{\mathrm{R}}}{\partial \boldsymbol{\Sigma}^{-1}} = \frac{\partial L^*}{\partial \boldsymbol{\Sigma}^{-1}} = \frac{T}{2}\boldsymbol{\Sigma} - \frac{1}{2}(\mathbf{Y} - \mathbf{X}\mathbf{B})'(\mathbf{Y} - \mathbf{X}\mathbf{B})$$

and

$$\frac{\partial L^{\mathrm{R}}}{\partial \mathbf{B}^{\mathrm{c}}}=\frac{\partial L^{*}}{\partial \mathbf{B}^{\mathrm{c}}}-\boldsymbol{\lambda}'\mathbf{R} \tag{13.57}$$
$$=[\boldsymbol{\Sigma}^{-1}(\mathbf{Y}'\mathbf{X}-\mathbf{B}'\mathbf{X}'\mathbf{X})]^{\mathrm{r}}-\boldsymbol{\lambda}'\mathbf{R}.$$

Transposing the latter gives

$$\left(\frac{\partial L^{\mathrm{R}}}{\partial \mathbf{B}^{\mathrm{c}}}\right)'=\left(\frac{\partial L^{*}}{\partial \mathbf{B}^{\mathrm{c}}}\right)'-\mathbf{R}'\boldsymbol{\lambda} \tag{13.58}$$
$$=(\boldsymbol{\Sigma}^{-1}\otimes\mathbf{X}'\mathbf{Y})\mathbf{I}^{\mathrm{c}}-(\boldsymbol{\Sigma}^{-1}\otimes\mathbf{X}'\mathbf{X})\mathbf{B}^{\mathrm{c}}-\mathbf{R}'\boldsymbol{\lambda}.$$

On substituting these derivatives into the conditions, we see that we are faced, once more, with the problem of the simultaneous solution of a set of non-linear equations. A wide variety of iterative methods for dealing with such problems are available; and of these we shall examine the Newton–Raphson procedure. In order to economize our notation, let us first eliminate from our system of equations one of the unknown quantities by solving (13.56) to give

$$\boldsymbol{\Sigma}(\mathbf{B})=\frac{(\mathbf{Y}-\mathbf{XB})'(\mathbf{Y}-\mathbf{XB})}{T}, \tag{13.59}$$

which is substituted in place of $\boldsymbol{\Sigma}$ in (13.54). Our problem is then reduced to one of solving the equations

$$\frac{\partial L^{\mathrm{R}}(\mathbf{B},\boldsymbol{\lambda})}{\partial \mathbf{B}^{\mathrm{c}}}=\frac{\partial L^{*}(\mathbf{B})}{\partial \mathbf{B}^{\mathrm{c}}}-\boldsymbol{\lambda}'\mathbf{R}=\mathbf{0}, \tag{13.60}$$

$$\frac{\partial L^{\mathrm{R}}(\mathbf{B},\boldsymbol{\lambda})}{\partial \boldsymbol{\lambda}}=\mathbf{0}, \tag{13.61}$$

where $L^{*}(\mathbf{B})$ is the logarithm of the concentrated likelihood function. For these concentrated equations, the Newton–Raphson algorithm is

$$\begin{bmatrix}\mathbf{B}^{\mathrm{c}}\\ \boldsymbol{\lambda}\end{bmatrix}_{k+1}=\begin{bmatrix}\mathbf{B}^{\mathrm{c}}\\ \boldsymbol{\lambda}\end{bmatrix}_{k}-\begin{bmatrix}\dfrac{\partial(\partial L^{\mathrm{R}}/\partial\mathbf{B}^{\mathrm{c}})'}{\partial\mathbf{B}^{\mathrm{c}}}, & \dfrac{\partial(\partial L^{\mathrm{R}}/\partial\mathbf{B}^{\mathrm{c}})'}{\partial\boldsymbol{\lambda}}\\ \dfrac{\partial(\partial L^{\mathrm{R}}/\partial\boldsymbol{\lambda})'}{\partial\mathbf{B}^{\mathrm{c}}}, & \dfrac{\partial(\partial L^{\mathrm{R}}/\partial\boldsymbol{\lambda})'}{\partial\boldsymbol{\lambda}}\end{bmatrix}_{k}^{-1}\begin{bmatrix}\left(\dfrac{\partial L^{\mathrm{R}}}{\partial\mathbf{B}^{\mathrm{c}}}\right)'\\ \left(\dfrac{\partial L^{\mathrm{R}}}{\partial\boldsymbol{\lambda}}\right)'\end{bmatrix}_{k} \tag{13.62}$$

where the subscripts on the vector of first derivatives and the matrix of second derivatives indicate that they are evaluated at $\mathbf{B}_k, \boldsymbol{\lambda}_k$.

Some consideration of the derivatives will show that, on the understanding that successive estimates obey the restrictions, we can rewrite the algorithm as

$$(13.63)\qquad \begin{bmatrix}\mathbf{B}^c\\ \boldsymbol{\lambda}\end{bmatrix}_{k+1} = \begin{bmatrix}\mathbf{B}^c\\ \boldsymbol{\lambda}\end{bmatrix}_{k} - \begin{bmatrix}\dfrac{\partial(\partial L^*/\partial \mathbf{B}^c)'}{\partial \mathbf{B}^c}, & -\mathbf{R}'\\ -\mathbf{R}, & \mathbf{0}\end{bmatrix}_k^{-1} \begin{bmatrix}\left(\dfrac{\partial L^*}{\partial \mathbf{B}^c}\right)' - \mathbf{R}'\boldsymbol{\lambda}\\ \mathbf{0}\end{bmatrix}_k$$

where $\partial(\partial L^*/\partial \mathbf{B}^c)'/\partial \mathbf{B}^c$ is obtained from (13.41) through a suitable change of notation.

An interesting modification of the Newton–Raphson algorithm results when we replace the second derivative $[\partial(\partial L^*/\partial \mathbf{B}^c)'/\partial \mathbf{B}^c]_k$ by $-\mathbf{Q}_k$ where

$$(13.64)\qquad \mathbf{Q}_k = \boldsymbol{\Sigma}^{-1}(\mathbf{B}_k)\otimes \mathbf{X}'\mathbf{X}$$

which is, of course, an approximation to the large sample form of the derivative. On defining

$$(13.65)\qquad \mathbf{P}_k = \boldsymbol{\Sigma}^{-1}(\mathbf{B}_k)\otimes \mathbf{X}'\mathbf{Y}$$

and writing

$$\left[\left(\frac{\partial L^*}{\partial \mathbf{B}^c}\right)' - \mathbf{R}'\boldsymbol{\lambda}\right]_k = \mathbf{P}_k\mathbf{I}^c - \mathbf{Q}_k\mathbf{B}_k^c - \mathbf{R}'\boldsymbol{\lambda}_k,$$

we can represent the modified algorithm as

$$(13.66)\qquad \begin{aligned}\begin{bmatrix}\mathbf{B}^c\\ \boldsymbol{\lambda}\end{bmatrix}_{k+1} &= \begin{bmatrix}\mathbf{B}^c\\ \boldsymbol{\lambda}\end{bmatrix}_{k} - \begin{bmatrix}\mathbf{Q}, & \mathbf{R}'\\ \mathbf{R}, & \mathbf{0}\end{bmatrix}_k^{-1} \begin{bmatrix}\mathbf{Q}\mathbf{B}^c + \mathbf{R}'\boldsymbol{\lambda} - \mathbf{P}\mathbf{I}^c\\ \mathbf{0}\end{bmatrix}_k\\ &= \begin{bmatrix}\mathbf{B}^c\\ \boldsymbol{\lambda}\end{bmatrix}_{k} - \begin{bmatrix}\mathbf{Q}, & \mathbf{R}'\\ \mathbf{R}, & \mathbf{0}\end{bmatrix}_k^{-1} \left(\begin{bmatrix}\mathbf{Q}, & \mathbf{R}'\\ \mathbf{R}, & \mathbf{0}\end{bmatrix}_k \begin{bmatrix}\mathbf{B}^c\\ \boldsymbol{\lambda}\end{bmatrix}_{k} - \begin{bmatrix}\mathbf{P}\mathbf{I}^c\\ \mathbf{r}\end{bmatrix}_k\right)\\ &= \begin{bmatrix}\mathbf{Q}, & \mathbf{R}'\\ \mathbf{R}, & \mathbf{0}\end{bmatrix}_k^{-1} \begin{bmatrix}\mathbf{P}\mathbf{I}^c\\ \mathbf{r}\end{bmatrix}_k.\end{aligned}$$

On writing $\mathbf{Q}_k$ and $\mathbf{P}_k$ explicitly, we have

$$(13.67)\qquad \begin{bmatrix}\mathbf{B}\\ \boldsymbol{\lambda}\end{bmatrix}_{k+1} = \begin{bmatrix}\boldsymbol{\Sigma}_k^{-1}\otimes \mathbf{X}'\mathbf{X}, & \mathbf{R}'\\ \mathbf{R}, & \mathbf{0}\end{bmatrix}^{-1} \begin{bmatrix}(\boldsymbol{\Sigma}_k^{-1}\otimes \mathbf{X}'\mathbf{Y})\mathbf{I}^c\\ \mathbf{r}\end{bmatrix}.$$

It will be recognized that this equation has the familiar format of the restricted least-squares estimator. Thus it transpires that the modified Newton–Raphson procedure amounts to nothing more than the repeated application of a conventional regression procedure with successive revisions of the estimate of $\boldsymbol{\Sigma}$.

In practice, we may begin the iterative procedure by setting $\boldsymbol{\Sigma}_0 = \mathbf{I}$. Then the first estimate $\mathbf{B}_1$ is simply the ordinary restricted least-squares estimate. From the residuals of the first regression, we may form $\boldsymbol{\Sigma}_1 = (\mathbf{Y}-\mathbf{X}\mathbf{B}_1)'(\mathbf{Y}-\mathbf{X}\mathbf{B}_1)/T$ for use in the following regression. Although an indefinite number of regressions may be performed in the hope of obtaining a convergent sequence of estimates, it is quite common to stop at the second regression—as, indeed, we have already described in connection with the model containing exclusion restrictions alone.

THE UNRESTRICTED MODEL WITH AUTOREGRESSIVE DISTURBANCES

Let us now consider the system

$$\mathbf{y}(t) = \mathbf{x}(t)\mathbf{B} + \boldsymbol{\eta}(t) \tag{13.68}$$

wherein

$$\boldsymbol{\eta}(t) = \boldsymbol{\eta}(t-1)\boldsymbol{\Phi} + \mathbf{v}(t) \tag{13.69}$$

is a stationary first-order vector autoregressive process. We assume that the process $\mathbf{v}(t)$ is a non-autocorrelated stochastic sequence whose elements $\mathbf{v}_{t.}$ are independently and identically distributed according to the specification in (13.5). Therefore it is necessary and sufficient for the stationarity of the process $\boldsymbol{\eta}(t)$ that every root of the matrix $\boldsymbol{\Phi}$ has an absolute value less than unity. Since no other restrictions are placed on $\boldsymbol{\Phi}$, we must assume that, in general, the value of any element of the current disturbance vector $\boldsymbol{\eta}_{t.}$ is influenced by every element in the preceding disturbance vector $\boldsymbol{\eta}_{t-1.}$. However, when $\boldsymbol{\Phi}$ is a diagonal matrix, the vector process decomposes into M separate and self-contained scalar processes each of which is specific to a single equation.

On substituting the expression for $\boldsymbol{\eta}(t)$ in (13.69) into the equation (13.68), we get

$$\mathbf{y}(t) = \mathbf{x}(t)\mathbf{B} + \boldsymbol{\eta}(t-1)\boldsymbol{\Phi} + \mathbf{v}(t). \tag{13.70}$$

Taking

$$\mathbf{y}(t-1)\boldsymbol{\Phi} = \mathbf{x}(t-1)\mathbf{B}\boldsymbol{\Phi} + \boldsymbol{\eta}(t-1)\boldsymbol{\Phi} \tag{13.71}$$

from this gives

$$\mathbf{y}(t) - \mathbf{y}(t-1)\boldsymbol{\Phi} = \mathbf{x}(t)\mathbf{B} - \mathbf{x}(t-1)\mathbf{B}\boldsymbol{\Phi} + \mathbf{v}(t) \tag{13.72}$$

which compares readily with the analogous equation (12.20) for the simple regression model with autoregressive disturbances.

We shall assume that we have a set of $T+1$ observations on $\mathbf{y}(t)$ and $\mathbf{x}(t)$ running from $t=0$ to $t=T$. We can compile the first and last T observations into the data matrices $\mathbf{Y}'_{-1} = [\mathbf{y}'_{0.}, \ldots, \mathbf{y}'_{T-1.}]$ $\mathbf{Y}' = [\mathbf{y}'_{1.}, \ldots, \mathbf{y}'_{T.}]$, $\mathbf{X}'_{-1}$ and $\mathbf{X}'$. For the stochastic processes $\boldsymbol{\eta}(t)$ and $\mathbf{v}(t)$, we define the analogous matrices $\mathbf{H}_{-1}, \mathbf{H}$ and $\mathbf{V}_{-1}, \mathbf{V}$ respectively. Using this notation, we can compile T realizations of the relationship (13.68) to give

$$\mathbf{Y} = \mathbf{X}\mathbf{B} + \mathbf{H} \tag{13.73}$$

or, in the alternative form corresponding to (13.72),

$$\mathbf{Y}-\mathbf{Y}_{-1}\boldsymbol{\Phi}=\mathbf{XB}-\mathbf{X}_{-1}\mathbf{B}\boldsymbol{\Phi}+\mathbf{V} \tag{13.74}$$

whch may be written in vector form as

$$\mathbf{Y}^c-(\boldsymbol{\Phi}'\otimes\mathbf{I})\mathbf{Y}^c_{-1}=(\mathbf{I}\otimes\mathbf{X})\mathbf{B}^c-(\boldsymbol{\Phi}'\otimes\mathbf{X}_{-1})\mathbf{B}^c+\mathbf{V}^c \tag{13.75}$$

or

$$\mathbf{Q}^c=\mathbf{ZB}^c+\mathbf{V}^c, \tag{13.76}$$

where

$$\begin{aligned}\mathbf{Q}^c&=\mathbf{Y}^c-(\boldsymbol{\Phi}'\otimes\mathbf{I})\mathbf{Y}^c_{-1}\quad\text{and}\\ \mathbf{Z}&=(\mathbf{I}\otimes\mathbf{X})-(\boldsymbol{\Phi}'\otimes\mathbf{X}_{-1}).\end{aligned} \tag{13.77}$$

We shall approach the problem of estimation under the assumption that the vectors $\mathbf{v}_{t.}$ are normally distributed so that $\mathbf{v}_{t.}\sim N(\mathbf{0},\boldsymbol{\Omega})$ for all t. On this basis, the logarithm of the likelihood function of the vectors $\mathbf{Y}$ given $\mathbf{X}, \mathbf{X}_{-1}$ and $\mathbf{y}_0$ is

$$\begin{aligned}L^*(\mathbf{B},\boldsymbol{\Omega},\boldsymbol{\Phi})=&-\frac{MT}{2}\log(2\pi)-\frac{T}{2}\log|\boldsymbol{\Omega}|\\ &-\tfrac{1}{2}\,\mathrm{Trace}(\mathbf{V}'\mathbf{V}\boldsymbol{\Omega}^{-1})\end{aligned} \tag{13.78}$$

where

$$\begin{aligned}\mathbf{V}&=(\mathbf{Y}-\mathbf{Y}_{-1}\boldsymbol{\Phi})-(\mathbf{XB}-\mathbf{X}_{-1}\mathbf{B}\boldsymbol{\Phi})\\ &=(\mathbf{Y}-\mathbf{XB})-(\mathbf{Y}_{-1}-\mathbf{X}_{-1}\mathbf{B})\boldsymbol{\Phi}\\ &=\mathbf{H}-\mathbf{H}_{-1}\boldsymbol{\Phi}.\end{aligned} \tag{13.79}$$

This has the same structure as the likelihood function in (13.20).

The maximum-likelihood estimators of $\mathbf{B}$, $\boldsymbol{\Omega}$ and $\boldsymbol{\Phi}$ are obtained from the conditions

$$\frac{\partial L^*}{\partial\mathbf{B}}=\mathbf{0}, \tag{13.80}$$

$$\frac{\partial L^*}{\partial\boldsymbol{\Omega}^{-1}}=\mathbf{0}, \tag{13.81}$$

$$\frac{\partial L^*}{\partial\boldsymbol{\Phi}}=\mathbf{0}. \tag{13.82}$$

The first condition is equivalent to

$$\begin{aligned}\frac{\partial\,\mathrm{Trace}(\mathbf{V}'\mathbf{V}\boldsymbol{\Omega}^{-1})}{\partial\mathbf{B}^c}&=\frac{\partial(\mathbf{Q}^c-\mathbf{ZB}^c)'(\boldsymbol{\Omega}^{-1}\otimes\mathbf{I})(\mathbf{Q}^c-\mathbf{ZB}^c)}{\partial\mathbf{B}^c}\\ &=\mathbf{0}.\end{aligned} \tag{13.83}$$

It yields the estimating equation

$$\mathbf{B}^c(\mathbf{\Omega}, \mathbf{\Phi}) = [\mathbf{Z}'(\mathbf{\Omega}^{-1} \otimes \mathbf{I})\mathbf{Z}]^{-1}\mathbf{Z}'(\mathbf{\Omega}^{-1} \otimes \mathbf{I})\mathbf{Q}^c. \tag{13.84}$$

The second condition yields the estimating equation

$$\mathbf{\Omega}(\mathbf{B}, \mathbf{\Phi}) = \frac{\mathbf{V}'\mathbf{V}}{T}. \tag{13.85}$$

The third condition is equivalent to

$$\frac{\partial \operatorname{Trace}[(\mathbf{H} - \mathbf{H}_{-1}\mathbf{\Phi})'(\mathbf{H} - \mathbf{H}_{-1}\mathbf{\Phi})\mathbf{\Omega}^{-1}]}{\partial \mathbf{\Phi}} = \mathbf{0} \tag{13.86}$$

which yields the estimating equation

$$\mathbf{\Phi}(\mathbf{B}) = (\mathbf{H}'_{-1}\mathbf{H}_{-1})^{-1}\mathbf{H}'_{-1}\mathbf{H}. \tag{13.87}$$

The maximum-likelihood estimates of $\mathbf{B}$, $\mathbf{\Omega}$ and $\mathbf{\Phi}$ are obtained from the simultaneous solution of the equations (13.84), (13.85) and (13.87). Since they constitute a non-linear system, an iterative procedure is required.

We may recall that, in the absence of serial correlation amongst the disturbances, the unrestricted model is efficiently estimated by ordinary least-squares regression. Clearly, the serial correlation drastically affects the ease with which we can obtain efficient estimates.

BIBLIOGRAPHY

Sets of Linear Regressions. Kmenta and Gilbert [**65**], Malinvaud [**82**, Chap. 6], Zellner [**125**]

Sets of Regressions with Autoregressive Disturbances. Guilkey and Schmidt [**48**], Parks [**90**]

CHAPTER 14

Systems of Simultaneous Equations

THE MODEL

In the previous chapter, we considered a system of equations which produced an observable relationship between K inputs and M outputs. The model will now be elaborated by considering the possibility that there is a feedback process, whereby the output variables of some parts of the system re-enter other parts of the system as inputs. We can represent the structure of the mth equation of such a model by

(14.1)
$$\begin{aligned} y_{tm} &= \mathbf{y}_{t.}\mathbf{c}_{.m} + \mathbf{x}_{t.}\boldsymbol{\beta}_{.m} + u_{tm} \\ &= \mathbf{z}_{t.}\mathbf{a}_{.m} + u_{tm}, \end{aligned}$$

where

y_{tm} is an observation on the output specific to the mth equation,
$\mathbf{y}_{t.}$ is an observation on the M output variables of the whole system,
$\mathbf{x}_{t.}$ is an observation on the K input variables of the whole system,
u_{tm} is the unobserved stochastic input,
$\mathbf{a}'_{.m} = [\mathbf{c}'_{.m}, \boldsymbol{\beta}'_{.m}]$ is the vector of parameters of the mth equation, and
$\mathbf{z}_{t.} = [\mathbf{y}_{t.}, \mathbf{x}_{t.}]$.

We will always be able to specify *a priori* some of the parameter values of the structural equations. In particular,

(14.2) The parameter corresponding to the variable y_{tm} on the RHS of the mth equation is identically zero; that is, $c_{mm} = 0$ for all m.

This restriction prevents the variable in question from appearing on both sides of the equation. The complete system of M equations can be written as

(14.3)
$$\begin{aligned} [y_{t1}, \ldots, y_{tM}] &= \mathbf{y}_{t.}[\mathbf{c}_{.1}, \ldots, \mathbf{c}_{.M}] \\ &\quad + \mathbf{x}_{t.}[\boldsymbol{\beta}_{.1}, \ldots, \boldsymbol{\beta}_{.M}] + [u_{t1}, \ldots, u_{tM}], \end{aligned}$$

or

(14.4) $$\mathbf{y}_{t.} = \mathbf{y}_{t.}\mathbf{C} + \mathbf{x}_{t.}\mathbf{B} + \mathbf{u}_{t.},$$

so that over T periods we have

(14.5) $$\begin{aligned}\mathbf{Y} &= \mathbf{YC} + \mathbf{XB} + \mathbf{U}\\ &= \mathbf{ZA} + \mathbf{U},\end{aligned}$$

or

(14.6) $$\begin{aligned}\mathbf{Y}^c &= (\mathbf{I} \otimes [\mathbf{Y}, \mathbf{X}])\begin{bmatrix}\mathbf{C}\\ \mathbf{B}\end{bmatrix}^c + \mathbf{U}^c\\ &= (\mathbf{I} \otimes \mathbf{Z})\mathbf{A}^c + \mathbf{U}^c.\end{aligned}$$

For some purposes, it is convenient to represent the equations of the system in homogeneous form. Thus we may rewrite (14.4) as

(14.7) $$\begin{aligned}\mathbf{0} &= \mathbf{y}_{t.}(\mathbf{C} - \mathbf{I}) + \mathbf{x}_{t.}\mathbf{B} + \mathbf{u}_{t.}\\ &= \mathbf{y}_{t.}\mathbf{\Gamma} + \mathbf{x}_{t.}\mathbf{B} + \mathbf{u}_{t.}\\ &= \mathbf{z}_{t.}\mathbf{\Theta} + \mathbf{u}_{t.}.\end{aligned}$$

In place of the restrictions (14.2), it now becomes appropriate to specify that

(14.8) The diagonal elements of the parameter matrix $\mathbf{\Gamma}$ are $\gamma_{mm} = -1$ for all m.

These restrictions are conventionally referred to as the normalization rules.

Since the feedback is instantaneous, we are able to write a reduced form of the system which expresses each of the M outputs as functions of the K inputs alone. Thus, in place of (14.4) or (14.7), we can write

(14.9) $$\mathbf{y}_{t.} = \mathbf{x}_{t.}\mathbf{\Pi} + \mathbf{v}_{t.}.$$

By comparing this with (14.4) and using $(\mathbf{C} - \mathbf{I}) = \mathbf{\Gamma}$, we can see that

(14.10) $$\begin{aligned}\mathbf{\Pi} &= -\mathbf{B}(\mathbf{C} - \mathbf{I})^{-1}\\ &= -\mathbf{B}\mathbf{\Gamma}^{-1}\end{aligned}$$

and

(14.11) $$\mathbf{v}_{t.} = -\mathbf{u}_{t.}\mathbf{\Gamma}^{-1}.$$

The stochastic specification that we give to the structural form of the system is identical to that of the system without feedback considered in the previous chapter. We assume that the row vectors $\mathbf{u}_{t.}$ are mutually independent and have identical distributions with

(14.12) $$E(\mathbf{u}_{t.}) = \mathbf{0}, \qquad D(\mathbf{u}_{t.}') = \mathbf{\Sigma} \quad \text{for all } t.$$

For the sample of T observations, we have

$$E(\mathbf{U})=\mathbf{0}, \qquad D(\mathbf{U}^c)=\mathbf{\Sigma}\otimes\mathbf{I}. \tag{14.13}$$

It follows from (14.11) that the row vectors of the reduced-form disturbances $\mathbf{v}_{t.}$ are distributed independently with

$$E(\mathbf{v}_{t.})=\mathbf{0} \quad \text{and} \quad D(\mathbf{v}'_{t.})=\mathbf{\Omega}=\mathbf{\Gamma}'^{-1}\mathbf{\Sigma}\mathbf{\Gamma}^{-1} \quad \text{for all } t. \tag{14.14}$$

from which

$$E(\mathbf{V})=\mathbf{0} \quad \text{and} \quad D(\mathbf{V}^c)=\mathbf{\Omega}\otimes\mathbf{I}. \tag{14.15}$$

Our assumption that the disturbances are independently and identically distributed enables us to write the probability density function of $\mathbf{u}_{t.}$ as $f(\mathbf{u}_{t.};\mathbf{\Sigma})$ for all t. To obtain the probability density function of the random vector $\mathbf{y}_{t.}$ from $f(\mathbf{u}_{t.})$, we use (14.7) to find $\partial\mathbf{u}_{t.}/\partial\mathbf{y}_{t.}=-\mathbf{\Gamma}$. Then, denoting the absolute value of the determinant of $\partial\mathbf{u}_{t.}/\partial\mathbf{y}_{t.}$ by $\|\mathbf{\Gamma}\|$, we find

$$\begin{aligned} f(\mathbf{y}_{t.};\mathbf{\Sigma}) &= \|\partial\mathbf{u}_{t.}/\partial\mathbf{y}_{t.}\|\, f(\mathbf{u}_{t.}:\mathbf{\Sigma}) \\ &= \|\mathbf{\Gamma}\|\, f(\mathbf{y}_{t.}\mathbf{\Gamma}+\mathbf{x}_{t.}\mathbf{B};\mathbf{\Sigma}). \end{aligned} \tag{14.16}$$

Thus the probability density function of the sample of T observations on $\mathbf{y}_{t.}$ is

$$f(\mathbf{y}_{1.},\ldots,\mathbf{y}_{T.}\,|\,\mathbf{x}_{1.},\ldots,\mathbf{x}_{T.};\mathbf{\Gamma},\mathbf{B},\mathbf{\Sigma})=\|\mathbf{\Gamma}\|^T\prod_{t=1}^{T} f(\mathbf{y}_{t.}\mathbf{\Gamma}+\mathbf{x}_{t.}\mathbf{B};\mathbf{\Sigma}). \tag{14.17}$$

We can also characterize the probability laws underlying the observations of $\mathbf{y}_{t.}$ in terms of the reduced-form parameters. Thus, if we denote the probability density function of the vector $\mathbf{v}_{t.}$ by $f(\mathbf{v}_{t.};\mathbf{\Omega})$ and use (14.9) to find $\|\partial\mathbf{v}_{t.}/\partial\mathbf{y}_{t.}\|=|\mathbf{I}|=1$, we obtain

$$\begin{aligned} f(\mathbf{y}_{t.};\mathbf{\Omega}) &= \|\partial\mathbf{v}_{t.}/\partial\mathbf{y}_{t.}\|\, f(\mathbf{v}_{t.};\mathbf{\Omega}) \\ &= f(\mathbf{y}_{t.}-\mathbf{x}_{t.}\mathbf{\Pi};\mathbf{\Omega}), \end{aligned} \tag{14.18}$$

so that the probability density function of the T observations on $\mathbf{y}_{t.}$ may also be written as

$$f(\mathbf{y}_{1.},\ldots,\mathbf{y}_{T.}\,|\,\mathbf{x}_{1.},\ldots,\mathbf{x}_{T.};\mathbf{\Pi},\mathbf{\Omega})=\prod_{t=1}^{T} f(\mathbf{y}_{t.}-\mathbf{x}_{t.}\mathbf{\Pi};\mathbf{\Omega}). \tag{14.19}$$

To demonstrate directly the equivalence of

$$f(\mathbf{y}_{t.};\mathbf{\Sigma})=\|\mathbf{\Gamma}\|\, f(\mathbf{u}_{t.};\mathbf{\Sigma})$$

of (14.16) and

$$f(\mathbf{y}_{t.};\mathbf{\Omega})$$

of (14.18), we use $f(\mathbf{u}_{t.};\mathbf{\Sigma})=\|\partial\mathbf{y}_{t.}/\partial\mathbf{u}_{t.}\|\,f(\mathbf{y}_{t.};\mathbf{\Omega})=\|\mathbf{\Gamma}^{-1}\|\,f(\mathbf{y}_{t.};\mathbf{\Omega})$; for, by substituting the latter in (14.16) and cancelling $\|\mathbf{\Gamma}\|$ with $\|\mathbf{\Gamma}^{-1}\|=\|\mathbf{\Gamma}\|^{-1}$, we obtain (14.18).

THE PROBLEM OF IDENTIFICATION

The probability law underlying the observation of $\mathbf{y}_{t.}$ is characterized by a unique mean vector $\boldsymbol{\mu}_{t.}=\mathbf{x}_{t.}\mathbf{\Pi}$ and a unique dispersion matrix $D(\mathbf{v}'_{t.})=\mathbf{\Omega}$. That is to say, there are no other values of these parameters for which the probability density function $f(\mathbf{y}_{t.})$ assumes the same values over the entire range of $\mathbf{y}_{t.}$. It follows that, if $\mathbf{x}_{t.}$ is fixed in repeated samplings of $\mathbf{y}_{t.}$, we can obtain unique consistent estimates of $\boldsymbol{\mu}$ and $\mathbf{\Omega}$. If, instead, $\mathbf{x}_{t.}$ varies freely from sample to sample, we can obtain consistent estimates of $\mathbf{\Pi}$ and $\mathbf{\Omega}$.

The probability law associated with the observations of $\mathbf{y}_{t.}$ does not, however, imply a unique set of values for the structural-form parameters. To demonstrate this, let us consider $\mathbf{\Gamma}$, $\mathbf{B}$, and $\mathbf{\Sigma}$ to be the true values of the structural parameters, so that

$$(14.20)\qquad \mathbf{\Pi}=-\mathbf{B}\mathbf{\Gamma}^{-1},\quad\text{and}\quad \mathbf{\Omega}=\mathbf{\Gamma}'^{-1}\mathbf{\Sigma}\mathbf{\Gamma}^{-1}$$

are the unique values of the reduced-form parameters. Let us also define $\mathbf{\Gamma}_*=\mathbf{\Gamma}\mathbf{M}$, $\mathbf{B}_*=\mathbf{B}\mathbf{M}$, and $\mathbf{\Sigma}_*=\mathbf{M}'\mathbf{\Sigma}\mathbf{M}$, where $\mathbf{M}$ is an arbitrary non-singular matrix of order M. Then,

$$\begin{aligned}-\mathbf{B}_*\mathbf{\Gamma}_*^{-1}&=-\mathbf{B}\mathbf{M}\mathbf{M}^{-1}\mathbf{\Gamma}^{-1}\\&=\mathbf{\Pi}\end{aligned}$$

and

$$\begin{aligned}\mathbf{\Gamma}_*'^{-1}\mathbf{\Sigma}_*\mathbf{\Gamma}_*^{-1}&=\mathbf{\Gamma}'^{-1}\mathbf{M}'^{-1}\mathbf{M}'\mathbf{\Sigma}\mathbf{M}\mathbf{M}^{-1}\mathbf{\Gamma}^{-1}\\&=\mathbf{\Omega}.\end{aligned}$$

Thus $\mathbf{\Gamma}$, $\mathbf{B}$, $\mathbf{\Sigma}$, and $\mathbf{\Gamma}_*$, $\mathbf{B}_*$, $\mathbf{\Sigma}_*$ are clearly equivalent values from the point of view of the probability distribution of $\mathbf{y}_{t.}$; and it follows that the sample information provides no basis for distinguishing between these two sets of values. Thus the structural parameters are determined by the probability laws only up to an arbitrary non-singular transformation of order M; and unless we are able to place sufficient restrictions upon the set of possible values of $\mathbf{\Gamma}$, $\mathbf{B}$, $\mathbf{\Sigma}$, we shall not be able to obtain unique estimates of the true values. The problem of establishing conditions which are sufficient for obtaining unique estimates of the structural parameters is called the problem of identification.

We may discuss the problem of identification most effectively by considering the parameter spaces of the reduced form and the structural form. The total parameter space of the structural form is the vector space of dimension

M^2+MK containing $\boldsymbol{\Theta}^c$ where $\boldsymbol{\Theta}'=[\boldsymbol{\Gamma}', \mathbf{B}']$. The admissible parameter set of the structural form is a set $\{\boldsymbol{\Theta}^c; \mathbf{R}\boldsymbol{\Theta}^c=\mathbf{r}\}$ containing all values of $\boldsymbol{\Theta}^c$ obeying the restrictions

$$(14.21) \qquad \mathbf{R}\boldsymbol{\Theta}^c=\mathbf{r} \quad \text{or} \quad \mathbf{R}\begin{bmatrix}\boldsymbol{\Gamma}\\ \mathbf{B}\end{bmatrix}^c=\mathbf{r}$$

that are postulated for the model. These are independent linear equations. Therefore the admissible parameter set is an affine linear subspace of the total parameter space; so we shall refer to it as the admissible parameter space.

The total parameter space of the reduced form is the vector space of dimension MK containing $\boldsymbol{\Pi}^c$. There are no direct restrictions on the reduced form. However, the restrictions on the structural form are conveyed to the reduced form by the identity $\boldsymbol{\Pi}=-\mathbf{B}\boldsymbol{\Gamma}^{-1}$. Thus the structural restrictions give rise to a set of non-linear restrictions on $\boldsymbol{\Pi}^c$ which serve to define an admissible parameter set $\{[\boldsymbol{\Pi}(\boldsymbol{\Theta})]^c; \mathbf{R}\boldsymbol{\Theta}^c=\mathbf{r}\}$ within the parameter space. However, under certain conditions it is possible for the admissible parameter set virtually to coincide with the total parameter space, and thus, in practice, $\boldsymbol{\Pi}^c$ may be unrestricted.

As it is commonly conceived, the problem of identification is one of determining the conditions that must be satisfied by the restrictions $\mathbf{R}\boldsymbol{\Theta}^c=\mathbf{r}$ in order to ensure that there is a one-to-one correspondence between a compact set of admissible values surrounding the true value of $\boldsymbol{\Pi}^c$ and a similar set of admissible values surrounding the true value of $\boldsymbol{\Theta}^c$. This interpretation of the problem is appropriate whenever the available satistical information enables us to locate a unique estimate of $\boldsymbol{\Pi}^c$ in the admissible parameter set close to the true value. However, if the condition $\text{Null}(\mathbf{X})=0$ is not satisfied, then the statistical information will not afford a unique estimate. In that case, since $\mathbf{X}\boldsymbol{\Pi}$ is always estimable, it becomes appropriate to consider the problem of constructing a one-to-one correspondence between a compact set of admissible values of the mean vector $(\mathbf{X}\boldsymbol{\Pi})^c$ and a similar set of admissible values of $\boldsymbol{\Theta}^c$.

Whenever there is a unique value of $\boldsymbol{\Theta}^c$ corresponding to some specified value of $\boldsymbol{\Pi}^c$ or $(\mathbf{X}\boldsymbol{\Pi})^c$, we say that $\boldsymbol{\Theta}^c$ is identified for that value. It transpires that, whenever $\boldsymbol{\Theta}^c$ is identified for some such value, it is identified for virtually every admissible value. Thus, in practice, $\boldsymbol{\Theta}^c$ is often characterized as identified or unidentified in an unqualified way.

Of course, it is quite possible that some elements of $\boldsymbol{\Theta}^c$ will be identified whilst others will not. This possibility of partial identification complicates the problem considerably, and so we shall begin our account by making a simplifying assumption. Our assumption is that the matrix $\mathbf{R}$ of the restrictions (14.21) consists entirely of non-zero elements. This implies that each restriction binds the entire vector of parameters so that, in effect, the possibility of the identification of only part of the vector is excluded. The assumption is unrealistic; for, in practice, the restrictions are often confined to single equations or to small groups of equations. We shall also confine our attention to the case where the statistical information is sufficient to locate a unique estimate of $\mathbf{\Pi}$. Thus we shall deal in terms of the relationship

$$(14.22) \qquad [\mathbf{\Pi}, \mathbf{I}]\begin{bmatrix}\mathbf{\Gamma}\\ \mathbf{B}\end{bmatrix} = \mathbf{0} \quad \text{or} \quad [\mathbf{\Pi}, \mathbf{I}]\mathbf{\Theta} = \mathbf{0}$$

comprising the reduced-form and structural-form parameters. In vector form, this becomes

$$(14.23) \qquad (\mathbf{I} \otimes [\mathbf{\Pi}, \mathbf{I}])\begin{bmatrix}\mathbf{\Gamma}\\ \mathbf{B}\end{bmatrix}^c = \mathbf{0}$$

which is a full-rank system of MK independent equations in $MK+M^2$ unknowns. When we compound these equations with the J independent linear restrictions of (14.21), we obtain the system

$$(14.24) \qquad \begin{bmatrix}\mathbf{I} \otimes [\mathbf{\Pi}, \mathbf{I}]\\ \mathbf{R}\end{bmatrix}\begin{bmatrix}\mathbf{\Gamma}\\ \mathbf{B}\end{bmatrix}^c = \begin{bmatrix}\mathbf{0}\\ \mathbf{r}\end{bmatrix}$$

comprising $MK+J$ equations in $MK+M^2$ unknowns.

To determine the necessary and sufficient conditions for the identification of the structural parameters, we need only determine the conditions for a unique solution of the equation (14.24). There are three aspects of the conditions. First there is the requirement that there be a sufficient number of equations in relation to the number of unknowns. This is known as the order condition for identifiability. Next is the requirement that the matrix of the system should have full column rank; that is, a rank of $MK+M^2$. This is known as the rank condition for identifiability and it subsumes the order condition. The third requirement is that the system should be algebraically consistent. As we shall see, this condition relates only to the admissibility of the value of $\mathbf{\Pi}$. Given that we have characterized the problem of identification as one of finding a unique admissible structural-form parameter value from an admissible reduced-form value, it follows that the rank condition is the necessary and sufficient condition for identification.

To illustrate these conditions, let us consider some cases. First, let us imagine that the number of restrictions J is less than M^2. Then neither the order condition nor the rank condition are satisfied, and therefore the structural parameters are unidentified. However, given our assumptions concerning the matrix $\mathbf{R}$, it is virtually certain that the matrix

$$(14.25) \qquad \begin{bmatrix}\mathbf{I} \otimes [\mathbf{\Pi}, \mathbf{I}]\\ \mathbf{R}\end{bmatrix}$$

will have full row rank. This is so because the set of all values of $\mathbf{\Pi}$ which would render the rows of $\mathbf{I} \otimes [\mathbf{\Pi}, \mathbf{I}]$ linearly dependent on the rows of $\mathbf{R}$ is of negligible extent in the context of the total reduced-form parameter space. When the matrix has full row rank, the system (14.24) is certain to be algebraically consistent, since the vector on the RHS falls within the manifold of the matrix. Since virtually any value of $\mathbf{\Pi}$ will assure consistency, the upshot is that the admissible parameter set of the reduced form is practically unrestricted and almost coincides with the total parameter space.

Now consider the case where the number of restrictions J is equal to M^2. Then the matrix in (14.25) is square and, given our assumptions regarding $\mathbf{R}$, it is virtually certain to be non-singular. According to the result in (2.56), the non-singularity of the matrix guarantees the consistency of the system and the uniqueness of its solution. Thus the structural-form parameters will almost certainly be identified. Moreover, as in the previous case, the admissible parameter set of the reduced form remains virtually unrestricted. Since the present circumstances border on the previous case where the parameters were unidentified, we say that they are now just identified.

Lastly, consider the situation where $J > M^2$. There are now more equations than unknowns. Therefore the order condition is satisfied. Our assumptions make it virtually certain that the rank condition will also be satisfied. However, the algebraic consistency of the system is no longer guaranteed; for, if $\mathbf{\Pi}$ assumes an arbitrary value, it is unlikely that the vector on the RHS will fall in the manifold of the matrix. In fact, the set of values of $\mathbf{\Pi}$ that render the system consistent is of negligible extent in the context of the total reduced-form parameter space. In other words, the admissible parameter set of the reduced form is a set of measure zero. The upshot is that we now face a difficult statistical problem in locating an estimate of $\mathbf{\Pi}^c$ within the admissible parameter set. We describe these circumstances by saying that the structural parameters are over-identified.

The relatively uncomplicated nature of our treatment so far of the problem of identification in the system as a whole stems from the fact that we have considered a rather limited class of restrictions. The nature of these restrictions is such that a linear dependence between the rows of the matrix $\mathbf{I} \otimes [\mathbf{\Pi}, \mathbf{I}]$ and any set of at most M^2 rows taken from $\mathbf{R}$ is unlikely to arise. Unfortunately, this specification of $\mathbf{R}$ excludes the kind of restrictions that are most likely to arise in practice. These are the so-called exclusion restrictions which set individual parameters to zero, thereby eliminating certain variables from certain equations. When such restrictions are spread unevenly through the system, we are likely to find that some parts of the structure are identified whilst others are not. Thus, even when the necessary order condition for identifiability is satisfied, there is no certainty that the necessary and sufficient rank condition will be fulfilled. In fact, it is one of the bugbears of simultaneous equation estimation that, when we wish to ascertain whether or not the structural parameters are identified, we have to examine small subsystems and even single equations in detail.

Example. Consider the system

$$[y_{t1}, y_{t2}]\begin{bmatrix}\gamma_{11}, & \gamma_{12}\\ \gamma_{21}, & \gamma_{22}\end{bmatrix}+[x_{t1}, x_{t2}]\begin{bmatrix}\beta_{11}, & \beta_{12}\\ \beta_{21}, & \beta_{22}\end{bmatrix}+[u_{t1}, u_{t2}]=[0,0]$$

of $M=2$ structural equations, and imagine that, in addition to the normalization rules $\gamma_{11}=-1$, $\gamma_{22}=-1$, we have the exclusion restrictions $\beta_{12}=\beta_{22}=0$. Then the total number of restrictions is $M^2=4$, and thus the order condition is satisfied. However, the rank condition is not satisfied. To show this, we write the equation of (14.24) *in detail:*

$$\left[\begin{array}{cccc|cccc}
\pi_{11}, & \pi_{12}, & 1. & 0 & 0, & \cdot & \cdot, & 0\\
\pi_{21}, & \pi_{22}, & 0, & 1 & 0, & \cdot & \cdot, & 0\\
\hline
0, & \cdot & \cdot, & 0 & \pi_{11}, & \pi_{12}, & 1, & 0\\
0, & \cdot & \cdot, & 0 & \pi_{21}, & \pi_{22}, & 0, & 1\\
\hline
1, & 0, & \cdot & \cdot & \cdot & \cdot & \cdot, & 0\\
\hline
0, & \cdot & \cdot & \cdot & 0, & 1, & 0, & 0\\
0, & \cdot & \cdot & \cdot & \cdot, & 0, & 1, & 0\\
0, & \cdot & \cdot & \cdot & \cdot & \cdot, & 0, & 1
\end{array}\right]
\begin{bmatrix}\gamma_{11}\\ \gamma_{21}\\ \beta_{11}\\ \beta_{21}\\ \gamma_{12}\\ \gamma_{22}\\ \beta_{12}\\ \beta_{22}\end{bmatrix}
=
\left[\begin{array}{c}0\\ 0\\ \hline 0\\ 0\\ \hline -1\\ \hline -1\\ 0\\ 0\end{array}\right]$$

Multiplying the third row of the matrix by π_{21}/π_{11} and subtracting the fourth row gives a vector wherein all but the last three elements are zeros. This vector is linearly dependent on the last three rows of the matrix. Thus the matrix is singular and the vector of structural parameters as a whole is unidentified. However, the lack of identification affects only three elements of the vector. Consider substituting the known values of γ_{11}, γ_{22}, β_{12}, and β_{22} into the first four equations to obtain

$$\text{(i)}\ -\pi_{11}+\pi_{12}\gamma_{21}+\beta_{11}=0, \quad \text{(ii)}\ -\pi_{21}+\pi_{22}\gamma_{21}+\beta_{21}=0,$$
$$\text{(iii)}\ \pi_{11}\gamma_{12}-\pi_{12}=0, \quad \text{(iv)}\ \pi_{21}\gamma_{12}-\pi_{22}=0.$$

Then we can see that γ_{12} is determined both by (iii) *and by* (iv)*; which also implies that the elements of the admissible reduced-form parameter matrix* **Π** *are constrained to obey the relationship $\pi_{12}/\pi_{11}=\pi_{22}/\pi_{21}$. This is actually equivalent to the condition that the matrix be of rank $M-1=1$. On the other hand,* (i) *and* (ii) *together contain three undetermined values γ_{21}, β_{11}, and β_{21}; and these are the unidentified elements of the vector. Thus, apart from*

$\gamma_{11}=-1$, *the parameters of the first structural equation are unidentified, whereas the parameters of the second equation are wholly identified.*

Identification of single equations

The problems of estimating systems of simultaneous equations are considerably simplified by treating each of the M equations separately. When we adopt a single-equation approach, we are forced to dispense with any *a priori* information that relates the parameters of different equations. It is therefore worthwhile to consider the specialized problem of identifying the parameters of a single equation by using information that is entirely specific to that equation.

In dealing with the mth equation, we must consider the relationship

$$(14.26) \qquad [\mathbf{\Pi}, \mathbf{I}]\begin{bmatrix}\boldsymbol{\gamma}_{.m}\\ \boldsymbol{\beta}_{.m}\end{bmatrix}=\mathbf{0},$$

which is contained within (14.22). We can write the linear restrictions on the parameters $\boldsymbol{\gamma}_{.m}$, $\boldsymbol{\beta}_{.m}$ as

$$(14.27) \qquad \mathbf{R}_m\begin{bmatrix}\boldsymbol{\gamma}_{.m}\\ \boldsymbol{\beta}_{.m}\end{bmatrix}=\mathbf{r}_m;$$

and these are understood to contain the normalization rule $\boldsymbol{\gamma}_{mm}=-1$. The problem of the identification of the ith equation is now a matter of the necessary and sufficient conditions for the solution of the system

$$(14.28) \qquad \begin{bmatrix}\mathbf{\Pi}, & \mathbf{I}\\ & \mathbf{R}_m\end{bmatrix}\begin{bmatrix}\boldsymbol{\gamma}_{.m}\\ \boldsymbol{\beta}_{.m}\end{bmatrix}=\begin{bmatrix}\mathbf{0}\\ \mathbf{r}_m\end{bmatrix}.$$

There are $M+K$ unknowns in (14.28). The relationship (14.26) provides K independent equations. Thus the necessary order condition for a unique solution is the requirement that there must be at least M restrictions in (14.27); or $M-1$ restrictions if we do not count the normalization rule. The rank condition is straightforward.

The treatment of the identification problem of a single equation often proceeds on the assumption that, apart from the normalization rule, the *a priori* restrictions all take the form of exclusion rules which indicate that certain variables appearing in the system as a whole are absent from the equation. To discuss this, we shall rewrite the mth equation as

$$(14.29) \qquad [\mathbf{y}_{t\Delta}, \mathbf{y}_{t\Delta\Delta}]\begin{bmatrix}\boldsymbol{\gamma}_{\Delta m}\\ \mathbf{0}\end{bmatrix}+[\mathbf{x}_{t*}, \mathbf{x}_{t**}]\begin{bmatrix}\boldsymbol{\beta}_{*m}\\ \mathbf{0}\end{bmatrix}+u_{tm}=0$$

where

> $\mathbf{y}_{t\Delta}$ is an observation on the $M_\Delta = M - M_{\Delta\Delta}$ output variables included in the relationship,
> $\mathbf{x}_{t_*}$ is an observation on the $K_* = K - K_{**}$ input variables included in the relationship,
> $\boldsymbol{\gamma}_{\Delta m}$, $\boldsymbol{\beta}_{*m}$ are the parameters associated with the variables included in the relationship, and
> $\mathbf{y}_{t\Delta\Delta}$, $\mathbf{x}_{t_{**}}$ are observations on the variables not included in the relationship.

In this notation, the reduced-form relationship is written as

$$(14.30)\qquad [\mathbf{y}_{t\Delta}, \mathbf{y}_{t\Delta\Delta}] = [\mathbf{x}_{t_*}, \mathbf{x}_{t_{**}}]\begin{bmatrix}\boldsymbol{\Pi}_{*\Delta}, & \boldsymbol{\Pi}_{*\Delta\Delta}\\ \boldsymbol{\Pi}_{**\Delta}, & \boldsymbol{\Pi}_{**\Delta\Delta}\end{bmatrix} + [\mathbf{v}_{t\Delta}, \mathbf{v}_{t\Delta\Delta}].$$

Thus the identity (14.26) becomes

$$(14.31)\qquad \begin{bmatrix}\boldsymbol{\Pi}_{*\Delta}, & \boldsymbol{\Pi}_{*\Delta\Delta}\\ \boldsymbol{\Pi}_{**\Delta}, & \boldsymbol{\Pi}_{**\Delta\Delta}\end{bmatrix}\begin{bmatrix}\boldsymbol{\gamma}_{\Delta m}\\ \mathbf{0}\end{bmatrix} + \begin{bmatrix}\mathbf{I}, & \mathbf{0}\\ \mathbf{0}, & \mathbf{I}\end{bmatrix}\begin{bmatrix}\boldsymbol{\beta}_{*m}\\ \mathbf{0}\end{bmatrix} = \begin{bmatrix}\mathbf{0}\\ \mathbf{0}\end{bmatrix},$$

or

$$(14.32)\qquad \begin{bmatrix}\boldsymbol{\Pi}_{*\Delta}, & \mathbf{I}\\ \boldsymbol{\Pi}_{**\Delta}, & \mathbf{0}\end{bmatrix}\begin{bmatrix}\boldsymbol{\gamma}_{\Delta m}\\ \boldsymbol{\beta}_{*m}\end{bmatrix} = \begin{bmatrix}\mathbf{0}\\ \mathbf{0}\end{bmatrix}.$$

To determine the parameters uniquely, we need to be able to solve (14.32) up to a factor of proportionality; for then we can scale the solution by the normalization rule to obtain the unique result. The necessary and sufficient condition for such a solution is

$$(14.33)\qquad \text{Null}\begin{bmatrix}\boldsymbol{\Pi}_{*\Delta}, & \mathbf{I}\\ \boldsymbol{\Pi}_{**\Delta}, & \mathbf{0}\end{bmatrix} = 1.$$

The matrix in question has an order of $K \times (M_\Delta + K_*)$, so that (14.33) is equivalent to the condition that the matrix has a Rank of $M_\Delta + K_* - 1$. The submatrix $[\boldsymbol{\Pi}_{*\Delta}, \mathbf{I}]$ certainly has a rank of K_* and is also linearly independent of the submatrix $[\boldsymbol{\Pi}_{**\Delta}, \mathbf{0}]$. Thus it follows that

(14.34) The necessary and sufficient rank condition for the identification of the equation (14.29) is that $\text{Rank}(\boldsymbol{\Pi}_{**\Delta}) = M_\Delta - 1$.

The condition (14.33) also implies that the number of columns of the matrix cannot exceed the number of the rows by more than 1. Thus

(14.35) The necessary order condition for the identification of the equation (14.29) is that $K_* + M_\Delta - 1 \leqslant K$, which states that the total number of variables included in the relationship cannot exceed the number of input variables in the whole system by more than 1.

THE ESTIMATION OF THE STRUCTURAL FORM

The structural form of the simultaneous equation system generating T observations is written as

$$(14.36) \qquad \mathbf{Y\Gamma} + \mathbf{XB} + \mathbf{U} = \mathbf{0},$$

and the corresponding reduced-form relationship is written as

$$(14.37) \qquad \mathbf{Y} = \mathbf{X\Pi} + \mathbf{V}.$$

Combining the two gives

$$(14.38) \qquad \begin{aligned} \mathbf{0} &= (\mathbf{X\Pi} + \mathbf{V})\mathbf{\Gamma} + \mathbf{XB} + \mathbf{U} \\ &= [\mathbf{X\Pi}, \mathbf{X}]\begin{bmatrix}\mathbf{\Gamma}\\ \mathbf{B}\end{bmatrix} + \mathbf{U} + \mathbf{V\Gamma} \\ &= [\mathbf{X\Pi}, \mathbf{X}]\begin{bmatrix}\mathbf{\Gamma}\\ \mathbf{B}\end{bmatrix}; \end{aligned}$$

the last of which follows since, by (14.11), we have $-\mathbf{U} = \mathbf{V\Gamma}$. In vector form, (14.38) becomes

$$(14.39) \qquad (\mathbf{I} \otimes [\mathbf{X\Pi}, \mathbf{X}])\begin{bmatrix}\mathbf{\Gamma}\\ \mathbf{B}\end{bmatrix}^c = \mathbf{0}.$$

In addition to these equations, we have the *a priori* information which is expressed as

$$(14.40) \qquad \mathbf{R}\begin{bmatrix}\mathbf{\Gamma}\\ \mathbf{B}\end{bmatrix}^c = \mathbf{r} \quad \text{or} \quad \mathbf{R\Theta}^c = \mathbf{r}.$$

The set of all values of $\mathbf{\Theta}^c$ that obey the restrictions (14.40) is said to constitute the admissible structural-form parameter space, and the set of all values of $(\mathbf{X\Pi})^c$ such that $\mathbf{X\Pi}$ obeys the restriction

$$(14.41) \qquad (\mathbf{I} \otimes [\mathbf{X\Pi}, \mathbf{X}])\mathbf{\Theta}^c = \mathbf{0}$$

for at least one admissible value of $\mathbf{\Theta}^c$ is said to constitute the admissible parameter set of the reduced form.

Familiar considerations suggest that, in order to estimate the structural parameters, we should adopt a procedure of two steps. The first step is to find an estimate of $\mathbf{X\Pi}$ within the admissible parameter set according to the criterion

$$\text{(14.42)} \qquad \text{Minimize} \quad (\mathbf{Y}-\mathbf{X\Pi})^{c\prime}(\mathbf{\Omega}^{-1}\otimes\mathbf{I})(\mathbf{Y}-\mathbf{X\Pi})^{c}.$$

Having found the estimate $\mathbf{X}\overset{*}{\mathbf{\Pi}}$, then, subject to the conditions for uniqueness, the second step is to obtain the estimates of $\mathbf{\Gamma}$ and $\mathbf{B}$ as solutions of the consistent system

$$\text{(14.43)} \qquad \begin{bmatrix} \mathbf{I}\otimes[\mathbf{X}\overset{*}{\mathbf{\Pi}}, \mathbf{X}] \\ \mathbf{R} \end{bmatrix}\begin{bmatrix} \mathbf{\Gamma} \\ \mathbf{B} \end{bmatrix}^{c} = \begin{bmatrix} \mathbf{0} \\ \mathbf{r} \end{bmatrix}.$$

If the condition $\text{Null}(\mathbf{X})=0$ is fulfilled, we can obtain unique estimates of $\mathbf{\Pi}$ itself. It then becomes possible to define the parameter set of the reduced form as the set of all $\mathbf{\Pi}^c$ such that $\mathbf{\Pi}$ obeys the restriction

$$\text{(14.44)} \qquad (\mathbf{I}\otimes[\mathbf{\Pi}, \mathbf{I}])\mathbf{\Theta}^{c}=\mathbf{0}$$

for at least one admissible value of $\mathbf{\Theta}^c$, and we may replace the system (14.43) by

$$\text{(14.45)} \qquad \begin{bmatrix} \mathbf{I}\otimes[\overset{*}{\mathbf{\Pi}}, \mathbf{I}] \\ \mathbf{R} \end{bmatrix}\begin{bmatrix} \mathbf{\Gamma} \\ \mathbf{B} \end{bmatrix}^{c} = \begin{bmatrix} \mathbf{0} \\ \mathbf{r} \end{bmatrix}.$$

The practicability of the two-step method depends largely upon the status of the model.

If the model is just identified, so that the admissible reduced-form parameter set virtually coincides with the total parameter space, then the method is relatively straightforward. For, in the absence of restrictions on the parameter space, the criterion (14.42) yields the ordinary least-squares estimator $\mathbf{X}\hat{\mathbf{\Pi}}=\mathbf{X}(\mathbf{X}'\mathbf{X})^{-}\mathbf{X}'\mathbf{Y}$. Thus any problems of implementing the criterion that might have arisen from our ignorance of the true value of $\mathbf{\Omega}$ are circumvented. The next step of solving (14.43) or (14.45) for $\mathbf{\Gamma}$ and $\mathbf{B}$ represents no problem; for, under the conditions that we have assumed, these are virtually certain to be algebraically consistent systems of full column rank. The statistical consistency of the estimates of $\mathbf{\Gamma}$ and $\mathbf{B}$ is also assured under any circumstances which allow for consistent estimates of $\mathbf{X\Pi}$ or $\mathbf{\Pi}$; for, when $\mathbf{X}\hat{\mathbf{\Pi}}$ or $\hat{\mathbf{\Pi}}$ assume their limiting values which, by the assumption of the consistency of the estimators, are the true values of $\mathbf{X\Pi}$ and $\mathbf{\Pi}$, we are bound to get the true values of $\mathbf{\Gamma}$ and $\mathbf{B}$ as solutions to (14.43) or (14.45). The two-step method outlined here is usually described, whenever it is practicable, as indirect least squares.

If the model is over-identified, then the admissible reduced-form parameter set has a measure of zero in the context of the reduced-form parameter space. This means that it is virtually certain that, in finite samples, the unrestricted regression estimate of $\mathbf{\Pi}$ or $\mathbf{X\Pi}$ will fall outside the admissible parameter set and so fail to satisfy the restrictions. Furthermore, with an inadmissible value in place of $\overset{*}{\mathbf{\Pi}}$ or $\mathbf{X}\overset{*}{\mathbf{\Pi}}$ the systems (14.43) and (14.45) will become algebraically inconsistent so that no solution in $\mathbf{\Gamma}$ and $\mathbf{B}$ will be available. Therefore the method of indirect least squares becomes inoperative unless we are prepared to reduce our model to one which is just identified by ignoring a sufficient number of *a priori* restrictions.

One recourse in the case of an over-identified model is to take explicit account of the restrictions affecting the reduced-form parameters. To do this, we may adopt a restricted version of the criterion (14.42) of the form:

(14.46) Minimize

$$L=[\mathbf{Y}-\mathbf{X\Pi}(\mathbf{\Theta})]^{c\prime}(\mathbf{\Omega}^{-1}\otimes\mathbf{I})[\mathbf{Y}-\mathbf{X\Pi}(\mathbf{\Theta})]^{c}-\boldsymbol{\lambda}'(\mathbf{R\Theta}^{c}-\mathbf{r}).$$

To evaluate this, we use the conditions of stationariness which are

$$\frac{\partial L}{\partial\mathbf{\Pi}^{c}}\frac{\partial\mathbf{\Pi}^{c}}{\partial\mathbf{\Theta}^{c}}-\boldsymbol{\lambda}'\mathbf{R}=\mathbf{0} \quad \text{and} \tag{14.47}$$

$$\mathbf{R\Theta}^{c}-\mathbf{r}=\mathbf{0}, \tag{14.48}$$

where, by definition,

$$[\mathbf{\Pi},\mathbf{I}]\mathbf{\Theta}=\mathbf{0}. \tag{14.49}$$

These three equations constitute a non-linear system that can only be solved $\mathbf{\Gamma}$ and $\mathbf{B}$ by an iterative process. To solve the system, we must attribute some value to the matrix $\mathbf{\Omega}$ which enters the expression of (14.47). In the absence of a knowledge of its true value, we might set $\mathbf{\Omega}$ to some arbitrary value such as $\mathbf{I}$. Alternatively, we can replace it in (14.47) by its estimate

$$\mathbf{\Omega}(\mathbf{\Theta})=\frac{[\mathbf{Y}-\mathbf{X\Pi}(\mathbf{\Theta})]'[\mathbf{Y}-\mathbf{X\Pi}(\mathbf{\Theta})]}{T}. \tag{14.50}$$

It is interesting to know that we can derive the equation which results from this substitution directly from the minimum generalized variance criterion:

(14.51) Minimize

$$\left|\frac{[\mathbf{Y}-\mathbf{X\Pi}(\mathbf{\Theta})]'[\mathbf{Y}-\mathbf{X\Pi}(\mathbf{\Theta})]}{T}\right|.$$

This is equivalent to the maximum-likelihood criterion under the assumption that the disturbances of the model have a normal distribution.

An alternative approach to the problem of obtaining estimates of the structural parameters of over-identified models, which is less sophisticated than the one mentioned above, has been investigated in various forms by

Basmann [**13**], Theil [**114**], and Zellner and Theil [**128**]. To portray the method, let us write (14.39) in normalized form as

$$(14.52)\qquad (\mathbf{I}\otimes[\mathbf{X\Pi},\mathbf{X}])\begin{bmatrix}\mathbf{C}\\ \mathbf{B}\end{bmatrix}^{c}=(\mathbf{X\Pi})^{c}.$$

The restrictions (14.40) must then be written conformably as

$$(14.53)\qquad \mathbf{R}\begin{bmatrix}\mathbf{C}\\ \mathbf{B}\end{bmatrix}^{c}=\mathbf{r}+\mathbf{R}\begin{bmatrix}\mathbf{I}\\ \mathbf{0}\end{bmatrix}^{c}=\mathbf{p}\quad\text{or}\quad \mathbf{RA}^{c}=\mathbf{p}.$$

Now consider estimating $\mathbf{X\Pi}$ by ordinary least squares to get $\mathbf{X\hat{\Pi}}=\mathbf{X}(\mathbf{X'X})^{-}\mathbf{X'Y}$. Substituting this in (14.52) and combining the latter with (14.53) gives

$$(14.54)\qquad \begin{bmatrix}\mathbf{I}\otimes[\mathbf{X\hat{\Pi}},\mathbf{X}]\\ \mathbf{R}\end{bmatrix}\begin{bmatrix}\mathbf{C}\\ \mathbf{B}\end{bmatrix}^{c}=\begin{bmatrix}(\mathbf{X\hat{\Pi}})^{c}\\ \mathbf{p}\end{bmatrix}.$$

In cases where the model is over-identified, the system (14.54) is bound to be inconsistent. It is therefore proposed that, in order to obtain the estimates, we should resolve this inconsistency by the usual method of projecting the vector on the right of the equation into the manifold of the matrix, and that we should then solve the resulting consistent system for $\mathbf{C}=\mathbf{\Gamma}+\mathbf{I}$, and $\mathbf{B}$. We require that these operations should be performed in a way which ensures that the estimates obey the restriction $\mathbf{RA}^{c}=\mathbf{p}$. The appropriate method consists of applying a form of restricted least-squares regression to (14.54). In order to specify the method completely, we must indicate our choice of a regression metric to be defined on the space containing the vector $(\mathbf{X\hat{\Pi}})^{c}$ and the manifold $\mathcal{M}(\mathbf{I}\otimes[\mathbf{X\hat{\Pi}},\mathbf{X}])$. The choice of the unitary metric $(\mathbf{I}\otimes\mathbf{I})$ leads to the estimator known as two-stage least squares. The three-stage least-squares estimator uses as its metric the matrix $(\overset{*}{\mathbf{\Sigma}}{}^{-1}\otimes\mathbf{I})$, wherein $\overset{*}{\mathbf{\Sigma}}=(\mathbf{Y}-\mathbf{Z}\overset{*}{\mathbf{A}})'(\mathbf{Y}-\mathbf{Z}\overset{*}{\mathbf{A}})/T$ is an estimate of the structural-form dispersion matrix based on the two-stage least-squares estimates of the structural parameters which we write as $\overset{*}{\mathbf{A}}$ where $\overset{*}{\mathbf{A}}{}'=[\overset{*}{\mathbf{C}}{}',\overset{*}{\mathbf{B}}{}']$.

The statistical consistency of estimates generated by these methods is readily established by the argument which was applied to indirect least squares. This argument asserts that, if $\mathbf{X\hat{\Pi}}$ assumes the true value of $\mathbf{X\Pi}$ in the limit, then the system (14.54), which will become algebraically consistent, will generate the true values of $\mathbf{C}=\mathbf{\Gamma}+\mathbf{I}$ and $\mathbf{B}$.

We shall give two-stage and three-stage least squares the generic name of quasi-Gaussian estimators. This is to allude to the fact that they are essentially applications of single-equation Gaussian regression methods to the equation (14.54).

A peculiar characteristic of the quasi-Gaussian methods is that the algebraically consistent equations, which are solved to obtain estimates of the structural parameters, contain two different representations of $\mathbf{X\Pi}$. These equations are obtained from (14.54) by replacing $(\mathbf{X\hat{\Pi}})^c$ on the right by a value $(\mathbf{X\overset{*}{\Pi}})^c$ which is found in $\mathcal{M}(\mathbf{I}\otimes[\mathbf{X\Pi},\mathbf{X}])$. Using a new notation $\mathbf{X\hat{\Pi}}=\mathbf{X\Pi}_1$, $\mathbf{X\overset{*}{\Pi}}=\mathbf{X\Pi}_2$, we can write the equations in the form of

$$(14.55)\qquad \begin{bmatrix}\mathbf{I}\otimes[\mathbf{X\Pi}_1,\mathbf{X}]\\ \mathbf{R}\end{bmatrix}\begin{bmatrix}\mathbf{C}\\ \mathbf{B}\end{bmatrix}^c=\begin{bmatrix}(\mathbf{X\Pi}_2)^c\\ \mathbf{p}\end{bmatrix},$$

where it is to be understood that, in general, $\mathbf{X\Pi}_1\neq\mathbf{X\Pi}_2$.

An interesting proposal which is aimed at amending this situation has been made by H. Wold in [**124**]. In essence, his suggestion is that we should attempt to bring the two representations of $\mathbf{X\Pi}$ into equality by repeated applications of the regression procedure. To extend our present procedure, we should reform (14.55) by replacing the equation

$$(14.56)\qquad (\mathbf{I}\otimes[\mathbf{X\Pi}_1,\mathbf{X}])\mathbf{A}^c=(\mathbf{X\Pi}_2)^c$$

by

$$(14.57)\qquad (\mathbf{I}\otimes[\mathbf{X\Pi}_2,\mathbf{X}])\mathbf{A}^c=(\mathbf{X\Pi}_2)^c.$$

Since the change is bound to make the system inconsistent, it necessitates a further resolution by applying the regression procedure to find $(\mathbf{X\Pi}_3)^c$ in $\mathcal{M}(\mathbf{I}\otimes[\mathbf{X\Pi}_2,\mathbf{X}])$ to replace $(\mathbf{X\Pi}_2)^c$ on the right of (14.57). At this stage, new estimates of the structural parameters might be obtained. It is to be expected that $\mathbf{X\Pi}_2$ will be somewhat nearer to $\mathbf{X\Pi}_3$ than to $\mathbf{X\Pi}_1$. Thus we can hope that, if the procedure is repeated an indefinite number of times, the two representations of $\mathbf{X\Pi}$ in the consistent system will virtually coincide at a limiting value $\mathbf{X\Pi}^0$. The latter will be some value in the admissible parameter set of the reduced form. When $\mathbf{X\Pi}^0$ is reached, the definitive estimates of the structural parameters are obtained.

It is not obvious which choice of the regression metric is the appropriate one for the procedure that we have outlined. Consequently, it is not apparent that the limiting value $\mathbf{X\Pi}^0$, however it is obtained, will satisfy any suitable criterion such as (14.42) or (14.51).

In our exposition of the method, we have considered finding $(\mathbf{X\Pi}_{k+1})^c$ in the manifold $\mathcal{M}(\mathbf{I}\otimes[\mathbf{X\Pi}_k,\mathbf{X}])$ at a minimum distance from $(\mathbf{X\Pi}_k)^c$. In his original proposal of the so-called fix-point method, Wold considered finding $(\mathbf{X\Pi}_{k+1})^c$ at a minimum distance from $\mathbf{Y}^c$ according to the simple criterion

$$\text{Minimize}$$

$$(\mathbf{Y}-\mathbf{X\Pi}_{k+1})^{c\prime}(\mathbf{Y}-\mathbf{X\Pi}_{k+1}).$$

It is interesting to discover that there is one greatly modified version of the fix-point procedure which satisfies the criterion (14.51) in the limit. This is an iterative instrumental variables procedure which can be regarded as an extension of three-stage least squares, involving successive revisions of the regression metric. We shall consider this, in a subsequent chapter, not as a fix-point procedure but as a computational procedure that is designed to fulfill the maximum-likelihood criterion. In that context, the method must be attributed to Durbin [**31**].

BIBLIOGRAPHY

The Problem of Identification. Fisher [**35**], Koopmans, Rubin and Leipnik [**68**], Malinvaud [**82,** Chap. 18], Rothenberg [**99**], [**100**], Wegge [**120**]

Fix-point Methods of Estimation. Lyttkens [**76**], Mosbaek and Wold [**87**]

Quasi-Gaussian Methods of Estimation. Basmann [**13**], Theil [**114**], Zellner and Theil [**128**]

CHAPTER 15

Quasi-Gaussian Methods

In the previous chapter, we gave a summary description of the quasi-Gaussian methods for estimating the structural parameters of a simultaneous equation system. The common feature of these methods is that they are based upon the unrestricted ordinary least-squares estimates of the reduced-form parameters. We shall now examine in detail the three-stage least-squares and two-stage least-squares estimators. The former is a full-information method which must be applied to the system of structural equations as a whole. The latter is a limited-information method which, in the absence of *a priori* parametric restrictions running across the structural equations, can be applied to any of the equations in isolation provided only that the requisite conditions for identifiability are satisfied.

For didactic purposes, it is best to begin by developing the limited-information estimator in the context of a single structural equation and to proceed by generalization to the full-information system-wide estimator.

SINGLE EQUATION ESTIMATION

A set of T realizations of the full system of structural equations may be represented, as in (14.5), by

$$\text{(15.1)} \qquad \mathbf{Y}=\mathbf{YC}+\mathbf{XB}+\mathbf{U}$$

where $\mathbf{Y}$ is a $T\times M$ matrix of the output variables, $\mathbf{X}$ is a $T\times K$ matrix of the input variables and $\mathbf{U}$ is a $T\times M$ matrix of stochastic disturbances. Let us extract from this system a single structural equation; and let us presume that some of the coefficients of the equation are zeros so that certain of the system's variables are effectively excluded. In that case, T realizations of the single structural equation may be represented by

$$\text{(15.2)} \qquad \begin{aligned} \mathbf{y} &= \mathbf{Y}_1\mathbf{c}+\mathbf{X}_1\boldsymbol{\beta}+\mathbf{u} \\ &= \mathbf{Z}_1\mathbf{a}+\mathbf{u} \end{aligned}$$

where $\mathbf{y}$ is the $T\times 1$ vector of output, $\mathbf{Y}_1$ is a $T\times(M_\Delta-1)$ matrix of output variables generated by other equations of the system, $\mathbf{X}_1$ is a $T\times K_1$ matrix of input variables and $\mathbf{u}$ is the $T\times 1$ vector of the stochastic disturbance.

Excluded from the present equation, but appearing elsewhere in the system, are the M_2 output variables of the matrix $\mathbf{Y}_2$ and the K_2 input variables of the matrix $\mathbf{X}_2$. A comparison of the present notation with the notation used in (14.29) shows that $[\mathbf{y}, \mathbf{Y}_1] = \mathbf{Y}_\Delta$, $\mathbf{Y}_2 = \mathbf{Y}_{\Delta\Delta}$, $\mathbf{X}_1 = \mathbf{X}_*$ and $\mathbf{X}_2 = \mathbf{X}_{**}$.

To reflect the distinction between the included and excluded variables, we may write the reduced form of the system as a whole as

$$(15.3) \qquad [\mathbf{y}, \mathbf{Y}_1, \mathbf{Y}_2] = [\mathbf{X}_1, \mathbf{X}_2]\begin{bmatrix} \boldsymbol{\pi}_{10}, & \boldsymbol{\Pi}_{11}, & \boldsymbol{\Pi}_{12} \\ \boldsymbol{\pi}_{20}, & \boldsymbol{\Pi}_{21}, & \boldsymbol{\Pi}_{22} \end{bmatrix} + [\mathbf{v}, \mathbf{V}_1, \mathbf{V}_2]$$
$$= \mathbf{X}[\boldsymbol{\pi}_{\mathbf{X}0}, \boldsymbol{\Pi}_{\mathbf{X}1}, \boldsymbol{\Pi}_{\mathbf{X}2}] + [\mathbf{v}, \mathbf{V}_1, \mathbf{V}_2].$$

The structural-form and the reduced-form parameters are related to each other by the identity $\boldsymbol{\Pi\Gamma} + \mathbf{B} = \mathbf{0}$ previously given under (14.10). With $\boldsymbol{\Gamma} = \mathbf{C} - \mathbf{I}$, this becomes $\boldsymbol{\Pi} = \boldsymbol{\Pi}\mathbf{C} + \mathbf{B}$, and from the latter we can extract the identity

$$(15.4) \qquad \begin{bmatrix} \boldsymbol{\pi}_{10} \\ \boldsymbol{\pi}_{20} \end{bmatrix} = \begin{bmatrix} \boldsymbol{\Pi}_{11}, & \mathbf{I} \\ \boldsymbol{\Pi}_{21}, & \mathbf{0} \end{bmatrix} \begin{bmatrix} \mathbf{c} \\ \boldsymbol{\beta} \end{bmatrix}$$

which relates the parameters of our single equation to the parameters of the reduced form. Equally, on substituting the reduced-form expressions for $\mathbf{y}$ and $\mathbf{Y}_1$ from (15.3) into the structural equation in (15.2) and cancelling the various stochastic terms that are related by the identity

$$(15.5) \qquad \mathbf{u} = \mathbf{V}_1\mathbf{c} - \mathbf{v},$$

we get the relationship

$$(15.6) \qquad \mathbf{X}\boldsymbol{\pi}_{\mathbf{X}0} = [\mathbf{X}\boldsymbol{\Pi}_{\mathbf{X}1}, \mathbf{X}_1]\begin{bmatrix} \mathbf{c} \\ \boldsymbol{\beta} \end{bmatrix},$$

which is simply the equation in (15.4) premultiplied by $\mathbf{X} = [\mathbf{X}_1, \mathbf{X}_2]$.

To estimate the structural parameters $\mathbf{c}$, $\boldsymbol{\beta}$, we use an empirical version of equation (15.6) which is derived by replacing the unknown values $\mathbf{X}\boldsymbol{\pi}_{\mathbf{X}0}$, $\mathbf{X}\boldsymbol{\Pi}_{\mathbf{X}1}$ by appropriate estimates. According to the arguments of Chapter 13, the efficient estimate of $\mathbf{X}\boldsymbol{\Pi}$ in the unrestricted reduced-form model $(\mathbf{Y}, \mathbf{X}\boldsymbol{\Pi}, \boldsymbol{\Omega} \otimes \mathbf{I})$ is the ordinary least-squares estimate which, allowing for the possibility that $\text{Null}(\mathbf{X}) \neq 0$, is given by

$$(15.7) \qquad \mathbf{X}\hat{\boldsymbol{\Pi}} = \mathbf{X}(\mathbf{X}'\mathbf{X})^{-}\mathbf{X}'\mathbf{Y} = \mathbf{P}\mathbf{Y}.$$

By substituting the ordinary least-squares estimates for the unknown elements of $\mathbf{X}\boldsymbol{\Pi}$ in equation (15.6), we derive the equation

$$(15.8) \qquad \mathbf{X}\hat{\boldsymbol{\pi}}_{\mathbf{X}0} = [\mathbf{X}\hat{\boldsymbol{\Pi}}_{\mathbf{X}1}, \mathbf{X}_1]\begin{bmatrix} \mathbf{c} \\ \boldsymbol{\beta} \end{bmatrix}$$

or, equivalently,

(15.9) $$\mathbf{Py} = [\mathbf{PY}_1, \mathbf{X}_1]\begin{bmatrix}\mathbf{c}\\ \boldsymbol{\beta}\end{bmatrix} = \mathbf{PZ}_1\mathbf{a}.$$

Except in limiting cases, the equation (15.8) is almost certain to be algebraically inconsistent. This inconsistency is analogous to that of the empirical equations $\mathbf{y}=\mathbf{X}\boldsymbol{\beta}$ obtained from the realizations of the regression relationship $y_t = \mathbf{x}_{t.}\boldsymbol{\beta} + \varepsilon_t$. The quasi-Gaussian estimates of the structural parameters $\mathbf{c}$, $\boldsymbol{\beta}$ are obtained by applying a method of Gaussian regression to the equation (15.8). As in Chapter 5, we may distinguish two steps in the application of the method. The first step is to resolve the inconsistency by replacing the vector $\mathbf{X}\hat{\boldsymbol{\pi}}_{X0}$ by its image in the manifold $\mathcal{M}[\mathbf{X}\hat{\boldsymbol{\Pi}}_{X1}, \mathbf{X}_1]$ obtained by the use of an appropriate projector. The second step is to find estimates of $\mathbf{c}$ and $\boldsymbol{\beta}$ as ordinary algebraic solutions of the reformed system. If we wish to envisage the method in one step, then we may consider using a left inverse to find an approximate solution of the equation (15.8) of the form

(15.10) $$\begin{bmatrix}\overset{*}{\mathbf{c}}\\ \overset{*}{\boldsymbol{\beta}}\end{bmatrix} = [\mathbf{X}\hat{\boldsymbol{\Pi}}_{X1}, \mathbf{X}_1]^{L}\mathbf{X}\hat{\boldsymbol{\pi}}_{X0}$$

or, in the equivalent terms of (15.9),

(15.11) $$\overset{*}{\mathbf{a}} = (\mathbf{PZ}_1)^{L}\mathbf{Py}.$$

Clearly, the existence of unique quasi-Gaussian estimates depends upon the existence of the left inverse $[\mathbf{X}\hat{\boldsymbol{\Pi}}_{X1}, \mathbf{X}_1]^{L} = (\mathbf{PZ}_1)^{L}$. For this, it is necessary and sufficient, according to (2.36), that $\text{Null}(\mathbf{PZ}_1)=0$. Equivalently,

(15.12) The parameters $\mathbf{c}$, $\boldsymbol{\beta}$ in the structural equation (15.2) are estimable if and only if both $\text{Null}(\mathbf{Z}_1)=0$ and $\text{Rank}(\mathbf{PZ}_1) = \text{Rank}(\mathbf{Z}_1)$.

In examining the implications of these conditions, it is safe to assume that the matrices $\mathbf{X}$ and $\mathbf{Z}_1 = [\mathbf{Y}_1, \mathbf{X}_1]$ have maximum rank. Adding the fact that $\text{Rank}(\mathbf{P}) = \text{Rank}(\mathbf{X})$, we can express this assumption by stating the conditions

(15.13) (*a*) $\text{Rank}(\mathbf{P}) = \text{Rank}(\mathbf{X}) = \min(T, K)$,

(*b*) $\text{Rank}(\mathbf{Z}_1) = \min\{T, (M_\Delta - 1) + K_1\}$.

If (15.13) *b* is granted, then the condition $\text{Null}(\mathbf{Z}_1)=0$ is equivalent to the condition $T \geqslant (M_\Delta - 1) + K_1$. The condition that $\text{Rank}(\mathbf{PZ}_1) = \text{Rank}(\mathbf{Z}_1)$ implies, by the theorem in (2.23), that $\text{Rank}(\mathbf{Z}_1) = \text{Rank}(\mathbf{PZ}_1) \leqslant \min\{\text{Rank}(\mathbf{P}), \text{Rank}(\mathbf{Z}_1)\}$ or simply that $\text{Rank}(\mathbf{Z}_1) \geqslant \text{Rank}(\mathbf{P})$; and, if (15.13) *a* is granted, the latter is equivalent to the condition that $\min(T, K) \geqslant \min\{T, (M_\Delta - 1) + K_1\}$. Thus, by combining the implications of the two conditions in (15.12), we can deduce that a necessary condition for the existence of a left inverse $(\mathbf{PZ}_1)^{\mathrm{L}}$ is that $\min(T, K) \geqslant (M_\Delta - 1) + K_1$.

Given the assumptions in (15.13), the condition $\min(T, K) \geqslant (M_\Delta - 1) + K_1$ is also virtually sufficient for the existence of the left inverse. In the first place, the condition $T \geqslant (M_\Delta - 1) + K_1$ ensures that $\text{Null}(\mathbf{Z}_1) = 0$. In the second place, the condition $\min(T, K) \geqslant (M_\Delta - 1) + K_1$ ensures that the dimension of $\mathcal{R}^T$ equals or exceeds the sum of the dimensions of its subspaces $\mathcal{N}(\mathbf{P})$ and $\mathcal{R}(\mathbf{Z}_1)$. In such circumstances, it is almost certain that $\mathcal{N}(\mathbf{P})$ and $\mathcal{R}(\mathbf{Z}_1)$ will constitute virtually disjoint subspaces of $\mathcal{R}^T$ with $\mathcal{R}(\mathbf{Z}_1) \cap \mathcal{N}(\mathbf{P}) = \mathbf{0}$; in which case $\text{Rank}(\mathbf{PZ}_1) = \text{Rank}(\mathbf{Z}_1)$. Thus, whenever $\min(T, K) \geqslant (M_\Delta - 1) + K_1$, we are almost certain to get $\text{Rank}(\mathbf{PZ}_1) = \text{Rank}(\mathbf{Z}_1)$.

Our examination of the implications of the conditions in (15.12) enables us to conclude that

(15.14) The parameters $\mathbf{c}$, $\boldsymbol{\beta}$ in the structural equation are only estimable if $\min(T, K) \geqslant (M_\Delta - 1) + K_1$, in which case they are virtually certain to be estimable.

Reference to (14.35) shows that these conditions for estimability entail the conditions for identifiability. It is important to understand the distinction between the two sets of conditions. The conditions for identifiability concern the possibility of deducing the values of the structural parameters from presumed values of the reduced-form parameters. The conditions for estimability concern the possibility of inferring the values of the structural parameters from a set of T sample observations. There is no requirement in the latter conditions that the reduced-form parameter matrix should be uniquely estimable. Herein lies a cause for confusion; for the conventional exposition of the identification problem which we provided in Chapter 14 has a tendency to suggest that the estimability of the reduced-form parameters is a prerequisite for the estimability of the structural parameters. In fact, the necessary and sufficient condition for the estimability of the reduced-form parameters is that $\text{Null}(\mathbf{X}) = 0$. Given that $\mathbf{X}$ has maximum rank, this is equivalent to the condition that $T \geqslant K$; and we can see that the latter has no place in the estimability conditions of (15.14).

Before we consider specific estimators, we may briefly examine the question of the statistical consistency of the whole class of quasi-Gaussian estimators. All that need be said on this matter is that the consistency of the estimates of the structural parameters is guaranteed by any conditions that ensure the consistency of the estimates of the reduced-form parameters. For, if the probability limits of the reduced-form estimates are the true parameter values, then the estimates of $\mathbf{c}$, $\boldsymbol{\beta}$ that are derived from equation (15.10) must also tend in probability to the true values of the structural parameters. The consistency of the reduced-form estimates is certainly assured whenever the elements of $\mathbf{X}$ and of the disturbance matrix $\mathbf{V}$ are generated by mutually uncorrelated stochastic processes such that

$$\text{(15.15)} \qquad \operatorname{plim}\left(\frac{\mathbf{X}'\mathbf{X}}{T}\right)=\mathbf{M} \quad \text{is finite and}$$

$$\operatorname{plim}\left(\frac{\mathbf{X}'\mathbf{V}}{T}\right)=\mathbf{0}.$$

TWO-STAGE LEAST-SQUARES ESTIMATES

The two-stage least-squares estimator was derived independently by Theil in [**114**] and by Basmann in [**13**]. The estimates are obtained by applying the ordinary least-squares regression procedure to the equations in (15.8) or (15.9), and they may be expressed as

$$\text{(15.16)} \qquad \begin{bmatrix} \overset{*}{\mathbf{c}} \\ \overset{*}{\boldsymbol{\beta}} \end{bmatrix} = \begin{bmatrix} \hat{\boldsymbol{\Pi}}'_{X1}\mathbf{X}'\mathbf{X}\hat{\boldsymbol{\Pi}}_{X1}, & \hat{\boldsymbol{\Pi}}'_{X1}\mathbf{X}'\mathbf{X}_1 \\ \mathbf{X}'_1\mathbf{X}\hat{\boldsymbol{\Pi}}_{X1}, & \mathbf{X}'_1\mathbf{X}_1 \end{bmatrix}^{-1} \begin{bmatrix} \hat{\boldsymbol{\Pi}}'_{X1}\mathbf{X}'\mathbf{X}\hat{\boldsymbol{\pi}}_{X0} \\ \mathbf{X}'_1\mathbf{X}\hat{\boldsymbol{\pi}}_{X0} \end{bmatrix}$$

or, equivalently, as

$$\text{(15.17)} \qquad \begin{bmatrix} \overset{*}{\mathbf{c}} \\ \overset{*}{\boldsymbol{\beta}} \end{bmatrix} = \begin{bmatrix} \mathbf{Y}'_1\mathbf{P}\mathbf{Y}_1, & \mathbf{Y}'_1\mathbf{X}_1 \\ \mathbf{X}'_1\mathbf{Y}_1, & \mathbf{X}'_1\mathbf{X}_1 \end{bmatrix}^{-1} \begin{bmatrix} \mathbf{Y}'_1\mathbf{P}\mathbf{y} \\ \mathbf{X}'_1\mathbf{y} \end{bmatrix},$$

which can be written more compactly as

$$\text{(15.18)} \qquad \overset{*}{\mathbf{a}} = (\mathbf{Z}'_1\mathbf{P}\mathbf{Z}_1)^{-1}\mathbf{Z}'_1\mathbf{P}\mathbf{y}.$$

To derive the latter expressions from (15.9), we use the symmetry and idempotency of $\mathbf{P}$ and the fact that $\mathbf{P}\mathbf{X}_1=\mathbf{X}_1$.

For the estimates to exist, the condition $\min(T, K) \geqslant (M_\Delta - 1) + K_1$ given in (15.14) must be satisfied. Granted this condition, the estimating equations may be specialized in one of two ways according to whether $T \geqslant K$ or $K \geqslant T$. If $T \geqslant K$ there is a further specialization when $K=(M_\Delta-1)+K_1$, whereas if $K \geqslant T$ there is a further specialization when $T=(M_\Delta-1)+K_1$.

Let us consider first the case where $T \geqslant K$. Then, by the assumptions in (15.13), we have $\operatorname{Rank}(\mathbf{X})=K$ or, equivalently, $\operatorname{Null}(\mathbf{X})=0$, so that $(\mathbf{X}'\mathbf{X})^{-1}$ exists. In consequence, each of the reduced-form parameters is uniquely estimable and we can factorize the expression in (15.16) to give

$$\text{(15.19)} \qquad \begin{bmatrix} \overset{*}{\mathbf{c}} \\ \overset{*}{\boldsymbol{\beta}} \end{bmatrix} = \left(\begin{bmatrix} \hat{\boldsymbol{\Pi}}'_{11}, & \hat{\boldsymbol{\Pi}}'_{21} \\ \mathbf{I}, & \mathbf{0} \end{bmatrix} \mathbf{X}'\mathbf{X} \begin{bmatrix} \hat{\boldsymbol{\Pi}}_{11}, & \mathbf{I} \\ \hat{\boldsymbol{\Pi}}_{21}, & \mathbf{0} \end{bmatrix} \right)^{-1}$$

$$\times \begin{bmatrix} \hat{\boldsymbol{\Pi}}'_{11}, & \hat{\boldsymbol{\Pi}}'_{21} \\ \mathbf{I}, & \mathbf{0} \end{bmatrix} \mathbf{X}'\mathbf{X} \begin{bmatrix} \hat{\boldsymbol{\pi}}_{10} \\ \hat{\boldsymbol{\pi}}_{20} \end{bmatrix}.$$

This has the form

$$(15.20)\qquad \begin{bmatrix} \overset{*}{\mathbf{c}} \\ \overset{*}{\boldsymbol{\beta}} \end{bmatrix} = \begin{bmatrix} \hat{\boldsymbol{\Pi}}_{11}, & \mathbf{I} \\ \hat{\boldsymbol{\Pi}}_{21}, & \mathbf{0} \end{bmatrix}^{L} \begin{bmatrix} \hat{\boldsymbol{\pi}}_{10} \\ \hat{\boldsymbol{\pi}}_{20} \end{bmatrix}.$$

In the special case where $K=(M_\Delta-1)+K_1$, the matrix in (15.20) is square and, given the assumptions in (15.13), it is also non-singular. Thus, according to the result in (2.50), the left inverse becomes a uniquely specified regular inverse and we obtain the so-called indirect least-squares estimates. In fact, we can also obtain the indirect least-squares estimating equations directly from (15.19), in this special case, by cancelling various non-singular factors to give, once more,

$$(15.21)\qquad \begin{bmatrix} \overset{*}{\mathbf{c}} \\ \overset{*}{\boldsymbol{\beta}} \end{bmatrix} = \begin{bmatrix} \hat{\boldsymbol{\Pi}}_{11}, & \mathbf{I} \\ \hat{\boldsymbol{\Pi}}_{21}, & \mathbf{0} \end{bmatrix}^{-1} \begin{bmatrix} \hat{\boldsymbol{\pi}}_{10} \\ \hat{\boldsymbol{\pi}}_{20} \end{bmatrix}.$$

The peculiar simplicity of the indirect least-squares estimator is due to the fact that, under our special assumptions, the equation (15.8) becomes algebraically consistent.

Now let us consider the case where $K \geqslant T$. Then, by the assumptions in (15.13), $\text{Rank}(\mathbf{X})=T$ or, equivalently, $\text{Null}(\mathbf{X}')=0$; and it follows that $\mathbf{P}=\mathbf{X}(\mathbf{X}'\mathbf{X})^{-}\mathbf{X}'$, which is formally the projector of $\mathcal{R}^T$ on $\mathcal{M}(\mathbf{X})=\mathcal{R}^T$, is now just the identity transformation $\mathbf{I}_T$. Substituting $\mathbf{P}=\mathbf{I}$ in (15.17), we find that

$$(15.22)\qquad \begin{bmatrix} \overset{*}{\mathbf{c}} \\ \overset{*}{\boldsymbol{\beta}} \end{bmatrix} = \begin{bmatrix} \mathbf{Y}_1'\mathbf{Y}_1, & \mathbf{Y}_1'\mathbf{X}_1 \\ \mathbf{X}_1'\mathbf{Y}_1, & \mathbf{X}_1'\mathbf{X}_1 \end{bmatrix}^{1} \begin{bmatrix} \mathbf{Y}_1'\mathbf{y} \\ \mathbf{X}_1'\mathbf{y} \end{bmatrix},$$

from which we can see that the two-stage least-squares estimator has collapsed into an ordinary least-squares estimator. The limiting specialization of the estimator arises when $T=(M_\Delta-1)+K_1$. In that case, the matrix $[\mathbf{Y}_1, \mathbf{X}_1]=\mathbf{Z}_1$ is square and, by the assumption of (15.13), it is also non-singular. It follows that the estimating equations reduce to

$$(15.23)\qquad \begin{bmatrix} \overset{*}{\mathbf{c}} \\ \overset{*}{\boldsymbol{\beta}} \end{bmatrix} = [\mathbf{Y}_1, \mathbf{X}_1]^{-1}\mathbf{y}.$$

Asymptotic properties of the two-stage least-squares estimator

We have already argued that the quasi-Gaussian estimators are statistically consistent whenever the least-squares estimator $\hat{\boldsymbol{\Pi}}$ of the reduced-form parameter matrix is consistent. We shall now establish the consistency and asymptotic normality of the two-stage least-squares estimator under the particular assumptions that the row vectors $\mathbf{x}_{t.}$ and $\mathbf{u}_{t.}$ comprised within $\mathbf{X}$ and $\mathbf{U}$ of equation (15.1) are generated by mutually uncorrelated stochastic processes such that, when T goes to infinity, we get

$$\text{(15.24)} \qquad \operatorname{plim}\left(\frac{\mathbf{X}'\mathbf{X}}{T}\right)=\operatorname{plim}\left(\sum_{t=1}^{T}\frac{\mathbf{x}_{t.}'\mathbf{x}_{t.}}{T}\right)=\mathbf{M},$$

$$\operatorname{plim}\left(\frac{\mathbf{X}'\mathbf{U}}{T}\right)=\operatorname{plim}\left(\sum_{t=1}^{T}\frac{\mathbf{x}_{t}'\mathbf{u}_{t}}{T}\right)=\mathbf{0},$$

$$\operatorname{plim}\left(\frac{\mathbf{U}'\mathbf{U}}{T}\right)=\operatorname{plim}\left(\sum_{t=1}^{T}\frac{\mathbf{u}_{t.}'\mathbf{u}_{t.}}{T}\right)=\mathbf{\Sigma},$$

where $\mathbf{\Sigma}=[\sigma_{ml}]$ is the dispersion matrix $D(\mathbf{u}_{t.}')$ of the structural-form disturbances. Using the identities $\mathbf{V}=-\mathbf{U}\mathbf{\Gamma}^{-1}$ and $\mathbf{Y}=\mathbf{X}\mathbf{\Pi}-\mathbf{U}\mathbf{\Gamma}^{-1}$, we can deduce from these assumptions that

$$\text{(15.25)} \qquad \operatorname{plim}\left(\frac{\mathbf{V}'\mathbf{X}}{T}\right)=\mathbf{0},$$

$$\operatorname{plim}\left(\frac{\mathbf{Y}'\mathbf{X}}{T}\right)=\mathbf{\Pi}'\mathbf{M},$$

$$\operatorname{plim}\left(\frac{\mathbf{Z}'\mathbf{X}}{T}\right)=\operatorname{plim}\begin{bmatrix}\dfrac{\mathbf{Y}'\mathbf{X}}{T}\\[2ex]\dfrac{\mathbf{X}'\mathbf{X}}{T}\end{bmatrix}=\begin{bmatrix}\mathbf{\Pi}'\mathbf{M}\\ \mathbf{M}\end{bmatrix}.$$

We should begin by establishing the consistency of the reduced-form estimate. This is straightforward, for, on taking the probability limit of $\hat{\mathbf{\Pi}}=(\mathbf{X}'\mathbf{X})^{-1}\mathbf{X}'\mathbf{Y}=\mathbf{\Pi}+(\mathbf{X}'\mathbf{X}/T)^{-1}\mathbf{X}'\mathbf{V}/T$, we get

$$\text{(15.26)} \qquad \begin{aligned}\operatorname{plim}(\hat{\mathbf{\Pi}})&=\mathbf{\Pi}+\operatorname{plim}\left(\frac{\mathbf{X}'\mathbf{X}}{T}\right)^{-1}\operatorname{plim}\left(\frac{\mathbf{X}'\mathbf{V}}{T}\right)\\ &=\mathbf{\Pi}\end{aligned}$$

since $\operatorname{plim}(\mathbf{X}'\mathbf{X}/T)^{-1}=\mathbf{M}^{-1}$ and $\operatorname{plim}(\mathbf{X}'\mathbf{V}/T)=\mathbf{0}$.

Now consider using the notation of (15.18) to write the two-stage least-squares estimator as

$$\text{(15.27)} \qquad \overset{*}{\mathbf{a}}=\mathbf{a}+\left(\frac{\mathbf{Z}_1'\mathbf{P}\mathbf{Z}_1}{T}\right)^{-1}\frac{\mathbf{Z}_1'\mathbf{P}\mathbf{u}}{T}.$$

The probability limits of the stochastic factors are

$$(15.28)\qquad \operatorname{plim}\left(\frac{\mathbf{Z}_1'\mathbf{P}\mathbf{Z}_1}{T}\right)=\operatorname{plim}\begin{bmatrix}\hat{\mathbf{\Pi}}_{\mathbf{X}1}'\left(\frac{\mathbf{X}'\mathbf{X}}{T}\right)\hat{\mathbf{\Pi}}_{\mathbf{X}1}, & \hat{\mathbf{\Pi}}_{\mathbf{X}1}'\left(\frac{\mathbf{X}'\mathbf{X}_1}{T}\right)\\ \left(\frac{\mathbf{X}_1'\mathbf{X}}{T}\right)\hat{\mathbf{\Pi}}_{\mathbf{X}1}, & \left(\frac{\mathbf{X}_1'\mathbf{X}_1}{T}\right)\end{bmatrix}$$

$$=\begin{bmatrix}\mathbf{\Pi}_{\mathbf{X}1}'\mathbf{M}_{\mathbf{XX}}\mathbf{\Pi}_{\mathbf{X}1}, & \mathbf{\Pi}_{\mathbf{X}1}'\mathbf{M}_{\mathbf{XX}_1}\\ \mathbf{M}_{\mathbf{X}_1\mathbf{X}}\mathbf{\Pi}_{\mathbf{X}1}, & \mathbf{M}_{\mathbf{X}_1\mathbf{X}_1}\end{bmatrix},$$

where $\mathbf{M}_{\mathbf{XX}_1}$, $\mathbf{M}_{\mathbf{X}_1\mathbf{X}}$, and $\mathbf{M}_{\mathbf{X}_1\mathbf{X}_1}$ are submatrices of $\mathbf{M}_{\mathbf{XX}}=\operatorname{plim}(\mathbf{X}'\mathbf{X}/T)$, and

$$(15.29)\qquad \operatorname{plim}\left(\frac{\mathbf{Z}_1'\mathbf{P}\mathbf{u}}{T}\right)=\operatorname{plim}\left(\begin{bmatrix}\left(\frac{\mathbf{Y}_1'\mathbf{X}}{T}\right)\\ \left(\frac{\mathbf{X}_1'\mathbf{X}}{T}\right)\end{bmatrix}\left(\frac{\mathbf{X}'\mathbf{X}}{T}\right)^{-1}\left(\frac{\mathbf{X}'\mathbf{u}}{T}\right)\right)$$

$$=\mathbf{0},$$

which results from $\operatorname{plim}(\mathbf{X}'\mathbf{u}/T)=\mathbf{0}$. It follows immediately that

$$(15.30)\qquad \operatorname{plim}(\overset{*}{\mathbf{a}})=\mathbf{a}+\operatorname{plim}\left(\frac{\mathbf{Z}_1'\mathbf{P}\mathbf{Z}_1}{T}\right)^{-1}\operatorname{plim}\left(\frac{\mathbf{Z}_1\mathbf{P}\mathbf{u}}{T}\right)$$

$$=\mathbf{a},$$

and the consistency of the estimator is demonstrated.

Now, consider the expression

$$(15.31)\qquad \sqrt{T}(\overset{*}{\mathbf{a}}-\mathbf{a})=\left(\frac{\mathbf{Z}_1'\mathbf{P}\mathbf{Z}_1}{T}\right)^{-1}\frac{\mathbf{Z}_1'\mathbf{X}}{T}\left(\frac{\mathbf{X}'\mathbf{X}}{T}\right)^{-1}\frac{\mathbf{X}'\mathbf{u}}{\sqrt{T}}.$$

On the assumption that the elements of $\mathbf{u}$ are independently and identically distributed such that $E(\mathbf{u})=\mathbf{0}$ and $D(\mathbf{u})=\sigma^2\mathbf{I}_T$, it follows from the central limit theorem of (17.68) that the distribution of $\mathbf{X}'\mathbf{u}/\sqrt{T}=\sum_{t=1}^{T}\mathbf{x}_{t.}'u_t/\sqrt{T}$ converges to the normal distribution $N(\mathbf{0},\sigma^2\mathbf{M})$ as T tends to infinity. The remaining factors in the expression have known finite probability limits that are comprised in (15.24), (15.25), and (15.28). It is therefore straightforward to deduce that the random variable $\sqrt{T}(\overset{*}{\mathbf{a}}-\mathbf{a})$ has a limiting normal distribution with zero mean and a dispersion matrix of

$$(15.32)\qquad \sigma^2\begin{bmatrix}\mathbf{\Pi}_{\mathbf{X}1}'\mathbf{M}_{\mathbf{XX}}\mathbf{\Pi}_{\mathbf{X}1}, & \mathbf{\Pi}_{\mathbf{X}1}'\mathbf{M}_{\mathbf{XX}_1}\\ \mathbf{M}_{\mathbf{X}_1\mathbf{X}}\mathbf{\Pi}_{\mathbf{X}1}, & \mathbf{M}_{\mathbf{X}_1\mathbf{X}_1}\end{bmatrix}^{-1}.$$

The classical analogy

Basmann's original derivation of the two-stage least-squares estimator, which he described as a generalized classical linear estimator, was predicated upon an analogy between the structural equation in (15.2) and the equation $\mathbf{y}=\mathbf{Za}+\mathbf{u}$ of the classical linear regression model $(\mathbf{y}, \mathbf{Za}, \sigma^2\mathbf{I})$. The classical model embodies two crucial assumptions which are necessary for the statistical efficiency and consistency of the ordinary least-squares estimates of $\mathbf{a}$. The first is that the elements of $\mathbf{u}$ are distributed independently and identically so that $E(\mathbf{u})=\mathbf{0}$ and $D(\mathbf{u})=\sigma^2\mathbf{I}$. The second is that the elements of $\mathbf{u}$ and the elements of $\mathbf{Z}$ are distributed independently of each other such that $\text{plim}(\mathbf{Z}'\mathbf{u}/T)=\mathbf{0}$ and $\text{plim}(\mathbf{Z}'\mathbf{Z}/T)$ is finite. When the latter conditions are satisfied, the probability limit of the ordinary least-squares estimates is

$$(15.33) \qquad \begin{aligned}\text{plim}(\hat{\mathbf{a}}) &= \mathbf{a}+\text{plim}(\mathbf{Z}'\mathbf{Z}/T)^{-1}\text{plim}(\mathbf{Z}'\mathbf{u}/T)\\ &= \mathbf{a},\end{aligned}$$

and this demonstrates their statistical consistency.

The structural equation $\mathbf{y}=\mathbf{Z}_1\mathbf{a}+\mathbf{u}$ of the simultaneous system conforms to the first assumption of the classical linear model. However, since the structural disturbances within the vector $\mathbf{u}$ are correlated with the elements of $\mathbf{Y}_1$ within the matrix $\mathbf{Z}_1=[\mathbf{Y}_1, \mathbf{X}_1]$, the second assumption is violated; and we have $\text{plim}(\mathbf{Z}_1'\mathbf{u}/T)\neq\mathbf{0}$. As a consequence the ordinary least-squares estimates of the structural parameters are statistically inconsistent.

In order to apply the method of ordinary least-squares successfully to the structural equation, we must first transform it to eliminate the causes of the statistical inconsistency. We should seek to do so in a way which preserves the statistical properties of the disturbance term; for then we can expect the method to retain some of the efficiency that it possesses in its application to the classical model. One way is to premultiply the structural equation by the transpose of an orthonormal matrix $\mathbf{S}$ whose vectors constitute a basis of $\mathcal{M}(\mathbf{X})$. From the example following (3.79) we see that $\mathbf{S}'\mathbf{S}=\mathbf{I}_K$ and that, when $\text{Null}(\mathbf{X})=0$, $\mathbf{SS}'=\mathbf{P}=\mathbf{X}(\mathbf{X}'\mathbf{X})^{-1}\mathbf{X}'$. Thus, given $D(\mathbf{u})=\sigma^2\mathbf{I}$, it follows that the disturbance vector $\mathbf{S}'\mathbf{u}$ of the transformed model

$$(15.34) \qquad \mathbf{S}'\mathbf{y}=\mathbf{S}'\mathbf{Z}_1\mathbf{a}+\mathbf{S}'\mathbf{u}$$

has a dispersion matrix of $D(\mathbf{S}'\mathbf{u})=\mathbf{S}'D(\mathbf{u})\mathbf{S}=\sigma^2\mathbf{I}_K$ which is analogous to that of the classical model. Moreover, on applying ordinary least squares to the transformed model we obtain the estimates

$$(15.35) \qquad \begin{aligned}\overset{*}{\mathbf{a}} &= (\mathbf{Z}_1'\mathbf{SS}'\mathbf{Z}_1)^{-1}\mathbf{Z}_1'\mathbf{SS}'\mathbf{y}\\ &= (\mathbf{Z}_1'\mathbf{PZ}_1)^{-1}\mathbf{Z}_1'\mathbf{Py};\end{aligned}$$

and these are precisely the two-stage least-squares estimates of which the statistical consistency is already established under broad assumptions.

An alternative way of pursuing the classical analogy is to consider premultiplying the structural equation by the projector $\mathbf{P}=\mathbf{X}(\mathbf{X}'\mathbf{X})^{-}\mathbf{X}'$, as we have done in (15.9), to obtain the model

$$\mathbf{P}\mathbf{y}=\mathbf{P}\mathbf{Z}_1\mathbf{a}+\mathbf{P}\mathbf{u}, \tag{15.36}$$

which has a singular dispersion matrix $D(\mathbf{P}\mathbf{u})=\sigma^2\mathbf{P}$. This model falls within the scope of the methods of Chapter 9. Since the manifold $\mathcal{M}(\mathbf{P}\mathbf{Z}_1)\subset\mathcal{M}(\mathbf{X})$ of the regressors is contained within the manifold of the dispersion matrix, it follows from (9.12) that the appropriate estimator is one which embodies an arbitrary generalized inverse of the dispersion matrix. Thus the estimator is

$$\begin{aligned}\overset{*}{\mathbf{a}}&=(\mathbf{Z}_1'\mathbf{P}'\mathbf{P}^{-}\mathbf{P}\mathbf{Z}_1)^{-1}\mathbf{Z}_1'\mathbf{P}'\mathbf{P}^{-}\mathbf{P}\mathbf{y}\\&=(\mathbf{Z}_1'\mathbf{P}\mathbf{Z}_1)^{-1}\mathbf{Z}_1\mathbf{P}\mathbf{y},\end{aligned}$$

which, again, is precisely the two-stage least-squares estimator. Amongst the generalized inverses of $\mathbf{P}=\mathbf{P}'$ is the identity matrix $\mathbf{I}_T$. When we substitute this in place of $\mathbf{P}^{-}$ in the equation above we see immediately that the method that we are applying to equation (15.36) amounts to ordinary least squares.

The errors-in-variables analogy

A structural equation of a simultaneous system has some of the essential characteristics of the equation of an errors-in-variables model. To see this, let us write the equation (15.6) in homogeneous form as

$$[\mathbf{X}\boldsymbol{\pi}_{X0},\mathbf{X}\boldsymbol{\Pi}_{X1}]\begin{bmatrix}-1\\\mathbf{c}\end{bmatrix}+\mathbf{X}_1\boldsymbol{\beta}=\mathbf{0} \tag{15.37}$$

On substituting $\mathbf{y}-\mathbf{v}=\mathbf{X}\boldsymbol{\pi}_{X0}$ and $\mathbf{Y}_1-\mathbf{V}_1=\mathbf{X}\boldsymbol{\Pi}_{X1}$ from the reduced-form relationship in (15.3), this becomes

$$[\mathbf{y}-\mathbf{v},\mathbf{Y}_1-\mathbf{V}_1]\begin{bmatrix}-1\\\mathbf{c}\end{bmatrix}+\mathbf{X}_1\boldsymbol{\beta}=\mathbf{0}; \tag{15.38}$$

and we may regard $\mathbf{v}$ and $\mathbf{V}_1$ as the errors comprised in the observations $\mathbf{y}$ and $\mathbf{Y}_1$ respectively. The contemporaneous covariance structure of these errors is given by the dispersion matrix

$$\boldsymbol{\Omega}_{\Delta\Delta}=\begin{bmatrix}\boldsymbol{\omega}_{00}, & \boldsymbol{\omega}_{01}\\\boldsymbol{\omega}_{10}, & \boldsymbol{\Omega}_{11}\end{bmatrix}. \tag{15.39}$$

If this matrix were known, we might use the methods of Chapter 8 to find estimates of $\mathbf{c}$, $\boldsymbol{\beta}$ by solving the equation

$$(15.40)\qquad \left(\begin{bmatrix} \mathbf{y}'\mathbf{y}, & \mathbf{y}'\mathbf{Y}_1, & \mathbf{y}'\mathbf{X}_1 \\ \mathbf{Y}_1'\mathbf{y}, & \mathbf{Y}_1'\mathbf{Y}_1, & \mathbf{Y}_1'\mathbf{X}_1 \\ \mathbf{X}_1'\mathbf{y}, & \mathbf{X}_1'\mathbf{Y}_1, & \mathbf{X}_1'\mathbf{X}_1 \end{bmatrix} - \lambda \begin{bmatrix} \omega_{00}, & \boldsymbol{\omega}_{01}, & \mathbf{0} \\ \boldsymbol{\omega}_{10}, & \boldsymbol{\Omega}_{11}, & \mathbf{0} \\ \mathbf{0}, & \mathbf{0}, & \mathbf{0} \end{bmatrix}\right) \begin{bmatrix} -1 \\ \mathbf{c} \\ \boldsymbol{\beta} \end{bmatrix} = \begin{bmatrix} 0 \\ \mathbf{0} \\ \mathbf{0} \end{bmatrix}$$

subject to the condition that λ assumes the smallest value that renders the system algebraically consistent. It is interesting to interpret the method of two-stage least squares in the light of this procedure.

To begin, let us take the equations

$$(15.41)\qquad \begin{aligned} \overset{*}{\mathbf{a}} &= (\mathbf{Z}_1'\mathbf{P}\mathbf{Z}_1)^{-1}\mathbf{Z}_1'\mathbf{P}\mathbf{y}, \\ T\mu &= \mathbf{y}'\mathbf{P}\mathbf{y} - \mathbf{y}'\mathbf{P}\mathbf{Z}_1(\mathbf{Z}_1'\mathbf{P}\mathbf{Z}_1)^{-1}\mathbf{Z}_1'\mathbf{P}\mathbf{y}. \end{aligned}$$

The first of these gives the two-stage least-squares estimates and the second is an expression for the residual sum of squares of the second-stage regression. Reference to (5.58) shows that, on expanding $\mathbf{P}\mathbf{Z}_1 = [\mathbf{P}\mathbf{Y}_1, \mathbf{X}_1]$, we may write these equations together in the system

$$(15.42)\qquad \left(\begin{bmatrix} \mathbf{y}'\mathbf{P}\mathbf{y}, & \mathbf{y}'\mathbf{P}\mathbf{y}_1, & \mathbf{y}'\mathbf{X}_1 \\ \mathbf{Y}_1'\mathbf{P}\mathbf{y}, & \mathbf{Y}_1'\mathbf{P}\mathbf{Y}_1, & \mathbf{Y}_1'\mathbf{X}_1 \\ \mathbf{X}_1'\mathbf{y}, & \mathbf{X}_1'\mathbf{Y}_1, & \mathbf{X}_1'\mathbf{X}_1 \end{bmatrix} - T \begin{bmatrix} \mu, \mathbf{0}, \mathbf{0} \\ \mathbf{0}, \mathbf{0}, \mathbf{0} \\ \mathbf{0}, \mathbf{0}, \mathbf{0} \end{bmatrix}\right) \begin{bmatrix} -1 \\ \mathbf{c} \\ \boldsymbol{\beta} \end{bmatrix} = \begin{bmatrix} 0 \\ \mathbf{0} \\ \mathbf{0} \end{bmatrix}.$$

Let us now recall that, according to (13.33), we can write the expression $\mathbf{Y}'\mathbf{P}\mathbf{Y}$ as

$$(15.43)\qquad \begin{aligned} \mathbf{Y}'\mathbf{P}\mathbf{Y} &= \mathbf{Y}'\mathbf{Y} - \mathbf{Y}'(\mathbf{I} - \mathbf{P})\mathbf{Y} \\ &= \mathbf{Y}'\mathbf{Y} - T\hat{\boldsymbol{\Omega}}, \end{aligned}$$

where $\hat{\boldsymbol{\Omega}}$ is an estimate of the dispersion matrix of contemporaneous reduced-form disturbances. If we extract the appropriate equations from (15.43) and substitute them into (15.42) above we obtain

$$(15.44)\qquad \left(\begin{bmatrix} \mathbf{y}'\mathbf{y}, & \mathbf{y}'\mathbf{Y}_1, & \mathbf{y}'\mathbf{X}_1 \\ \mathbf{Y}_1'\mathbf{y}, & \mathbf{Y}_1'\mathbf{Y}_1, & \mathbf{Y}_1'\mathbf{X}_1 \\ \mathbf{X}_1'\mathbf{y}, & \mathbf{X}_1'\mathbf{Y}_1, & \mathbf{X}_1'\mathbf{X}_1 \end{bmatrix} - T \begin{bmatrix} \mu + \hat{\omega}_{00}, & \hat{\boldsymbol{\omega}}_{01}, & \mathbf{0} \\ \hat{\boldsymbol{\omega}}_{10}, & \hat{\boldsymbol{\Omega}}_{11}, & \mathbf{0} \\ \mathbf{0}, & \mathbf{0}, & \mathbf{0} \end{bmatrix}\right) \begin{bmatrix} -1 \\ \mathbf{c} \\ \boldsymbol{\beta} \end{bmatrix} = \begin{bmatrix} 0 \\ \mathbf{0} \\ \mathbf{0} \end{bmatrix}$$

wherein $\hat{\omega}_{00}$, $\hat{\boldsymbol{\omega}}_{01}$, and $\hat{\boldsymbol{\Omega}}_{11}$ are estimates of the corresponding elements of $\boldsymbol{\Omega}_{\Delta\Delta}$ of (15.39). The comparison between the estimating equations of two-stage least squares as represented above and the equations (15.40) of the errors-in-variables method is now straightforward. For, apart from the fact that the elements of $\boldsymbol{\Omega}_{\Delta\Delta}$ are represented in (15.44) by their estimates, the sole difference lies in the replacement of the latent root λ by the constant T and the assumption of the role of λ by the new variable μ. In summary, we might say that the two-stage least-squares estimating equations represent a linearized version of errors-in-variables equations. In the following chapter we shall be treating the errors-in-variables estimator in its own right, and we shall have occasion to make further comparisons with the two-stage least-squares estimator.

SYSTEM-WIDE ESTIMATION

The limited-information quasi-Gaussian method of estimating single structural relationships takes little account of the fact that the structural equation is embedded in a system of simultaneous stochastic equations. There are at least two ways in which we can profit from taking a system-wide approach to estimation. In the first place, to adopt such an approach enables us to use the sort of *a priori* information that establishes relationships amongst the parameters of several equations. In the second place, by taking into account the system-wide information on the contemporaneous covariance structure of the structural disturbances that is provided by the sample, we are able to improve the statistical efficiency of the estimates. We have already shown in Chapter 13 how both kinds of information can be used in estimating the parameters of a set of non-simultaneous or seemingly-unrelated regression equations. Thus we should be able to visualize the developments of the following section as the results of the application of established methods to a more complex problem.

Let us begin our account by recalling some of the details of the notation that was established in Chapter 14. The set of T realizations of the entire system of simultaneous relationships was written in (14.5) as the matrix equation

$$(15.45)\qquad \begin{aligned}\mathbf{Y}&=\mathbf{YC}+\mathbf{XB}+\mathbf{U}\\&=\mathbf{ZA}+\mathbf{U}\end{aligned}$$

which, in vector form, becomes

$$(15.46)\qquad \begin{aligned}\mathbf{Y}^c&=(\mathbf{I}\otimes[\mathbf{Y},\mathbf{X}])\begin{bmatrix}\mathbf{C}\\\mathbf{B}\end{bmatrix}^c+\mathbf{U}^c\\&=(\mathbf{I}\otimes\mathbf{Z})\mathbf{A}^c+\mathbf{U}^c.\end{aligned}$$

By eliminating the stochastic components from both sides of (15.45), we obtain the equation

$$(15.47)\qquad \mathbf{X\Pi}=\mathbf{X\Pi C}+\mathbf{XB}$$

which, in vector form, becomes

$$(15.48)\qquad (\mathbf{X\Pi})^c = (\mathbf{I}\otimes[\mathbf{X\Pi}, \mathbf{X}])\begin{bmatrix}\mathbf{C}\\ \mathbf{B}\end{bmatrix}^c.$$

We shall presume that sufficient *a priori* information is available to enable us to estimate the entire set of structural parameters. This information is represented in general by the linear equation

$$(15.49)\qquad \mathbf{R}\begin{bmatrix}\mathbf{C}\\ \mathbf{B}\end{bmatrix}^c = \mathbf{R}\mathbf{A}^c = \mathbf{p}.$$

When this equation contains only exclusion restrictions specifying that certain elements of $\mathbf{C}$ and $\mathbf{B}$ are zeros, we may apply the restrictions to (15.46) to obtain the contracted system

(15.50)

$$\begin{bmatrix}\mathbf{y}_{.1}\\ \mathbf{y}_{.2}\\ \cdot\\ \cdot\\ \cdot\\ \mathbf{y}_{.M}\end{bmatrix} = \begin{bmatrix}[\mathbf{Y}_1, \mathbf{X}_1], & \mathbf{0}, & \dots, & \mathbf{0}\\ \mathbf{0}, & [\mathbf{Y}_2, \mathbf{X}_2], & \dots, & \mathbf{0}\\ \cdot & \cdot & & \cdot\\ \cdot & \cdot & & \cdot\\ \cdot & \cdot & & \cdot\\ \mathbf{0}, & \mathbf{0}, & \dots, & [\mathbf{Y}_M, \mathbf{X}_M]\end{bmatrix}\begin{bmatrix}\begin{bmatrix}\mathbf{c}_1\\ \boldsymbol{\beta}_1\end{bmatrix}\\ \begin{bmatrix}\mathbf{c}_2\\ \boldsymbol{\beta}_2\end{bmatrix}\\ \cdot\\ \cdot\\ \cdot\\ \begin{bmatrix}\mathbf{c}_M\\ \boldsymbol{\beta}_M\end{bmatrix}\end{bmatrix} + \begin{bmatrix}\mathbf{u}_{.1}\\ \mathbf{u}_{.2}\\ \cdot\\ \cdot\\ \cdot\\ \mathbf{u}_{.M}\end{bmatrix}$$

which we shall write in summary notation as

$$(15.51)\qquad \mathbf{Y}^c = \mathbf{W}\boldsymbol{\delta} + \mathbf{U}^c.$$

System-wide two-stage least squares

We can now formulate a system-wide version of the two-stage least-squares estimator. Our first object is to replace the unknown elements of $\mathbf{X\Pi}$ in the equation (15.48) by the corresponding elements of the least-squares estimate $\mathbf{X}\hat{\mathbf{\Pi}} = \mathbf{PY}$. On consolidating the resulting equation with the restrictions of (15.49), we obtain the system

$$(15.52)\qquad \begin{bmatrix}(\mathbf{X}\hat{\mathbf{\Pi}})^c\\ \mathbf{p}\end{bmatrix} = \begin{bmatrix}\mathbf{I}\otimes[\mathbf{X}\hat{\mathbf{\Pi}}, \mathbf{X}]\\ \mathbf{R}\end{bmatrix}\begin{bmatrix}\mathbf{C}\\ \mathbf{B}\end{bmatrix}^c.$$

The next object is to resolve the algebraic inconsistency of this system whilst constraining the solution of the reformed system to satisfy the *a priori* restrictions. To achieve this, we place the burden of adjustment upon the vector $(\mathbf{X}\hat{\mathbf{\Pi}})^c$. This is replaced by a vector $\mathbf{Q}^c = (\mathbf{I}\otimes[\mathbf{X}\hat{\mathbf{\Pi}}, \mathbf{X}])\overset{*}{\mathbf{A}}{}^c$ which lies in the manifold $\mathcal{M}(\mathbf{I}\otimes[\mathbf{X}\hat{\mathbf{\Pi}},\mathbf{X}])$ and which is subject to the restriction that $\mathbf{R}\overset{*}{\mathbf{A}}{}^{c}=\mathbf{p}$. The method of two-stage least squares is to locate $\mathbf{Q}^{c}$ at a minimum distance from $(\mathbf{X}\hat{\mathbf{\Pi}})^{c}$; and in practice this involves applying the method of restricted least squares to the equation (15.52).

The application of ordinary restricted least squares to the model $(\mathbf{g},\mathbf{Z}\boldsymbol{\beta}\,|\,\mathbf{R}\boldsymbol{\beta}=\mathbf{r},\sigma^2\mathbf{I})$ yields the estimating equations

$$\begin{bmatrix}\mathbf{Z}'\mathbf{Z}, & \mathbf{R}'\\ \mathbf{R}, & \mathbf{0}\end{bmatrix}\begin{bmatrix}\overset{*}{\boldsymbol{\beta}}\\ \boldsymbol{\lambda}\end{bmatrix}=\begin{bmatrix}\mathbf{Z}'\mathbf{g}\\ \mathbf{r}\end{bmatrix}$$

previously given under (10.16). By using these for our guidance, and by noting the fact that

$$(15.53)\qquad (\mathbf{I}\otimes[\mathbf{X}\hat{\mathbf{\Pi}},\mathbf{X}])'(\mathbf{X}\hat{\mathbf{\Pi}})^{c}=\left(\mathbf{I}\otimes\begin{bmatrix}\hat{\mathbf{\Pi}}'\mathbf{X}'\mathbf{X}\hat{\mathbf{\Pi}}\\ \mathbf{X}'\mathbf{X}\hat{\mathbf{\Pi}}\end{bmatrix}\right)\mathbf{I}^{c},$$

we can readily establish that the system-wide two-stage least-squares estimates are given by the solution of the equations

$$(15.54)\qquad \begin{bmatrix}\mathbf{I}\otimes\begin{bmatrix}\hat{\mathbf{\Pi}}'\mathbf{X}'\mathbf{X}\hat{\mathbf{\Pi}}, & \hat{\mathbf{\Pi}}'\mathbf{X}'\mathbf{X}\\ \mathbf{X}'\mathbf{X}\hat{\mathbf{\Pi}}, & \mathbf{X}'\mathbf{X}\end{bmatrix}, & \mathbf{R}'\\ \mathbf{R}, & \mathbf{0}\end{bmatrix}\begin{bmatrix}\begin{bmatrix}\mathbf{C}\\ \mathbf{B}\end{bmatrix}^{c}\\ \boldsymbol{\lambda}\end{bmatrix}=\begin{bmatrix}\left(\mathbf{I}\otimes\begin{bmatrix}\hat{\mathbf{\Pi}}'\mathbf{X}'\mathbf{X}\hat{\mathbf{\Pi}}\\ \mathbf{X}'\mathbf{X}\hat{\mathbf{\Pi}}\end{bmatrix}\right)\mathbf{I}^{c}\\ \mathbf{p}\end{bmatrix}$$

As in the case of the single equation estimator, there are a variety of ways in which we can write the system-wide two-stage least-squares estimator. Thus any of the alternative forms in the identity

$$(15.55)\qquad \begin{bmatrix}\hat{\mathbf{\Pi}}'\mathbf{X}'\mathbf{X}\hat{\mathbf{\Pi}}, & \hat{\mathbf{\Pi}}\mathbf{X}'\mathbf{X}\\ \mathbf{X}'\mathbf{X}\hat{\mathbf{\Pi}}, & \mathbf{X}'\mathbf{X}\end{bmatrix}=\begin{bmatrix}\mathbf{Y}'\mathbf{P}\mathbf{Y}, & \mathbf{Y}'\mathbf{X}\\ \mathbf{X}'\mathbf{Y}, & \mathbf{X}'\mathbf{X}\end{bmatrix}=\begin{bmatrix}\mathbf{Y}'\mathbf{Y}-T\hat{\mathbf{\Omega}}, & \mathbf{Y}'\mathbf{X}\\ \mathbf{X}'\mathbf{Y}, & \mathbf{X}'\mathbf{X}\end{bmatrix}$$

may be employed for the cross-product matrix.

THREE-STAGE LEAST SQUARES

The two-stage least-squares estimator fails to take full account of the contemporaneous covariance structure of the structural-form disturbances. To demonstrate how information on this aspect of the system can be incorporated, let us pursue the classical analogy that we have previously used in connection with the single-equation two-stage least-squares estimator. We can begin by recognizing that the application of restricted least-squares to the untransformed system (15.46) would result in statistically inconsistent estimates. To eliminate the causes of the inconsistency, we must premultiply the equation by a matrix $\mathbf{I}\otimes\mathbf{S}'$ wherein $\mathbf{S}$ is a matrix whose vectors constitute an orthonormal basis of the manifold $\mathcal{M}(\mathbf{X})$. Our transformed system is

$$(15.56)\qquad (\mathbf{I}\otimes\mathbf{S}')\mathbf{Y}^c=(\mathbf{I}\otimes\mathbf{S}'[\mathbf{Y},\mathbf{X}])\begin{bmatrix}\mathbf{C}\\\mathbf{B}\end{bmatrix}^c+(\mathbf{I}\otimes\mathbf{S}')\mathbf{U}^c,$$

and the dispersion matrix of the transformed disturbances is

$$(15.57)\qquad \begin{aligned} D[(\mathbf{I}\otimes\mathbf{S}')\mathbf{U}^c]&=(\mathbf{I}\otimes\mathbf{S}')D(\mathbf{U}^c)(\mathbf{I}\otimes\mathbf{S})\\ &=(\mathbf{I}\otimes\mathbf{S}')(\boldsymbol{\Sigma}\otimes\mathbf{I})(\mathbf{I}\otimes\mathbf{S})\\ &=\boldsymbol{\Sigma}\otimes\mathbf{I}_K. \end{aligned}$$

Given a knowledge of the matrix $\boldsymbol{\Sigma}$, we could find efficient estimates of the structural-form parameters by a restricted least-squares regression in the $(\boldsymbol{\Sigma}\otimes\mathbf{I})^{-1}$-metric. The estimating equations would be

$$(15.58)\qquad \begin{aligned} &(\mathbf{I}\otimes\mathbf{S}'[\mathbf{Y},\mathbf{X}])'(\boldsymbol{\Sigma}\otimes\mathbf{I})^{-1}(\mathbf{I}\otimes\mathbf{S}'[\mathbf{Y},\mathbf{X}])\begin{bmatrix}\mathbf{C}\\\mathbf{B}\end{bmatrix}^c+\mathbf{R}'\boldsymbol{\lambda}\\ &\qquad\qquad=(\mathbf{I}\otimes\mathbf{S}'[\mathbf{Y},\mathbf{X}])'(\boldsymbol{\Sigma}\otimes\mathbf{I})^{-1}(\mathbf{I}\otimes\mathbf{S}')\mathbf{Y}^c,\\ &\mathbf{R}\begin{bmatrix}\mathbf{C}\\\mathbf{B}\end{bmatrix}^c=\mathbf{p}. \end{aligned}$$

By collecting various terms of the expression and using $\mathbf{SS}'=\mathbf{P}$ and $\mathbf{P}^2=\mathbf{P}$, we can rewrite the first of these as

$$(15.59)\qquad \left(\boldsymbol{\Sigma}^{-1}\otimes\begin{bmatrix}\mathbf{Y}'\mathbf{PY}, & \mathbf{Y}'\mathbf{X}\\ \mathbf{X}'\mathbf{Y}, & \mathbf{X}'\mathbf{X}\end{bmatrix}\right)\begin{bmatrix}\mathbf{C}\\\mathbf{B}\end{bmatrix}^c+\mathbf{R}'\boldsymbol{\lambda}=\left(\boldsymbol{\Sigma}^{-1}\otimes\begin{bmatrix}\mathbf{Y}'\mathbf{PY}\\\mathbf{X}'\mathbf{Y}\end{bmatrix}\right)\mathbf{I}^c.$$

However, the dispersion matrix $\boldsymbol{\Sigma}$ is unknown so that, in a viable procedure, it must be replaced by an estimate. The suggestion of Zellner and Theil in [**128**] is that we should use

$$(15.60)\qquad \begin{aligned} \overset{*}{\boldsymbol{\Sigma}}&=\frac{(\mathbf{Y}-\mathbf{Y}\overset{*}{\mathbf{C}}-\mathbf{X}\overset{*}{\mathbf{B}})'(\mathbf{Y}-\mathbf{Y}\overset{*}{\mathbf{C}}-\mathbf{X}\overset{*}{\mathbf{B}})}{T}\\ &=\frac{\overset{*}{\mathbf{U}}{}'\overset{*}{\mathbf{U}}}{T} \end{aligned}$$

where $\overset{*}{\mathbf{C}}$, $\overset{*}{\mathbf{B}}$ are the matrices of the two-stage least-squares estimates of the structural parameters. Since $\overset{*}{\mathbf{C}}$, $\overset{*}{\mathbf{B}}$ are consistent estimates, it follows that $\overset{*}{\mathbf{U}}$ is a consistent estimate of the matrix of structural disturbances. Thus it follows from the assumption in (15.24) that $\overset{*}{\boldsymbol{\Sigma}}$ is a consistent estimate of $\boldsymbol{\Sigma}$.

On substituting $\overset{*}{\boldsymbol{\Sigma}}$ for $\boldsymbol{\Sigma}$ in (15.59) and using an alternative expression for the matrix of cross-products provided by the identity (15.55), we can write the estimating equations as

$$(15.61)\qquad \begin{bmatrix} \overset{*}{\boldsymbol{\Sigma}}^{-1}\otimes\begin{bmatrix}\mathbf{Y}'\mathbf{Y}-T\hat{\boldsymbol{\Omega}}, & \mathbf{Y}'\mathbf{X}\\ \mathbf{X}'\mathbf{Y}, & \mathbf{X}'\mathbf{X}\end{bmatrix}, & \mathbf{R}'\\ \mathbf{R}, & \mathbf{0}\end{bmatrix}\begin{bmatrix}\begin{bmatrix}\mathbf{C}\\ \mathbf{B}\end{bmatrix}^{c}\\ \boldsymbol{\lambda}\end{bmatrix}=\begin{bmatrix}\left(\overset{*}{\boldsymbol{\Sigma}}^{-1}\otimes\begin{bmatrix}\mathbf{Y}'\mathbf{Y}-T\hat{\boldsymbol{\Omega}}\\ \mathbf{X}'\mathbf{Y}\end{bmatrix}\right)\mathbf{I}^{c}\\ \mathbf{p}\end{bmatrix}$$

The solutions of the equations are the three-stage least-squares estimates.

The method of three-stage least squares was originally proposed by Zellner and Theil in the context of the system (15.50) which arises when the *a priori* information is entirely in the form of exclusion restrictions. Let us derive the estimates for this special case. The first step is to apply the transformation $(\mathbf{I}\otimes\mathbf{S}')$ to the summary representation of the condensed equations to give

$$(15.62)\qquad (\mathbf{I}\otimes\mathbf{S}')\mathbf{Y}^{c}=(\mathbf{I}\otimes\mathbf{S}')\mathbf{W}\boldsymbol{\delta}+(\mathbf{I}\otimes\mathbf{S}')\mathbf{U}^{c}.$$

Next, we apply ordinary least-squares to the transformed equations to obtain a set of two-stage least-squares estimates in the form of

$$(15.63)\qquad \begin{aligned}\overset{*}{\boldsymbol{\delta}}&=[\mathbf{W}'(\mathbf{I}\otimes\mathbf{S})(\mathbf{I}\otimes\mathbf{S}')\mathbf{W}]^{-1}\mathbf{W}'(\mathbf{I}\otimes\mathbf{S})(\mathbf{I}\otimes\mathbf{S}')\mathbf{Y}^{c}\\ &=[\mathbf{W}'(\mathbf{I}\otimes\mathbf{P})\mathbf{W}]^{-1}\mathbf{W}'(\mathbf{I}\otimes\mathbf{P})\mathbf{Y}^{c}.\end{aligned}$$

This expression stands for an array of single-equation estimates. The elements of the estimated dispersion matrix $\overset{*}{\boldsymbol{\Sigma}}=[\overset{*}{\sigma}_{ml}]$ are now given by

$$(15.64)\qquad \overset{*}{\boldsymbol{\sigma}}_{ml}=\frac{(\mathbf{y}_{.m}-\mathbf{Y}_m\overset{*}{\mathbf{c}}_m-\mathbf{X}_m\overset{*}{\boldsymbol{\beta}}_m)'(\mathbf{y}_{.l}-\mathbf{Y}_l\overset{*}{\mathbf{c}}_l-\mathbf{X}_l\overset{*}{\boldsymbol{\beta}}_l)}{T}.$$

Having composed the matrix $\overset{*}{\boldsymbol{\Sigma}}$ from these elements, we can proceed to find the revised three-stage least-squares estimates from the equation

$$(15.65)\qquad \tilde{\boldsymbol{\delta}}=[\mathbf{W}'(\overset{*}{\boldsymbol{\Sigma}}^{-1}\otimes\mathbf{P})\mathbf{W}]^{-1}\mathbf{W}'(\overset{*}{\boldsymbol{\Sigma}}^{-1}\otimes\mathbf{P})\mathbf{Y}^{c}.$$

Asymptotic properties of the three-stage least-squares estimator

We shall now deduce the asymptotic properties of the three-stage least-squares estimator under the assumptions in (15.24). It might be argued that this exercise is superfluous. In the first place, we already know that a quasi-Gaussian estimator of the structural parameters is consistent whenever the estimator of the reduced-form parameters is consistent. In the second place, our experience of the two-stage least-squares estimator strongly suggests that the asymptotic properties of the three-stage estimator can be inferred from a straightforward analogy with the properties of the restricted least-squares estimator of $\boldsymbol{\beta}$ in the model $(\mathbf{g}, \mathbf{Z}\boldsymbol{\beta} \mid \mathbf{R}\boldsymbol{\beta}=\mathbf{r}, \sigma^2\mathbf{I})$ of Chapter 10. Nevertheless, we shall derive our results directly, using the material of Chapter 10 only to lend familiarity to our algebraic manipulations.

We may begin by writing the three-stage least-squares estimating equations in the form

$$\begin{bmatrix} \overset{*}{\boldsymbol{\Sigma}}{}^{-1} \otimes \mathbf{Z'PZ}, & \mathbf{R'} \\ \mathbf{R}, & \mathbf{0} \end{bmatrix} \begin{bmatrix} \mathbf{A}^c \\ \boldsymbol{\lambda} \end{bmatrix} = \begin{bmatrix} (\overset{*}{\boldsymbol{\Sigma}}{}^{-1} \otimes \mathbf{Z'PY})\mathbf{I}^c \\ \mathbf{p} \end{bmatrix}. \tag{15.66}$$

To avoid a problem of singularity with the matrix of this equation as T tends to infinity, we shall give the submatrix $\mathbf{R}$ and the vector $\mathbf{p}$ the same order as T which will make $\mathbf{R}/T$ and $\mathbf{p}/T$ constant. This is permissible since $\mathbf{R}$ and $\mathbf{p}$ are only determined up to a common scalar factor. By solving the equation (15.66), we obtain the three-stage least-squares estimator

$$\tilde{\mathbf{A}}^c = \mathbf{C}_1(\overset{*}{\boldsymbol{\Sigma}}{}^{-1} \otimes \mathbf{Z'PY})\mathbf{I}^c + \mathbf{C}_2\mathbf{p} \tag{15.67}$$

wherein $\mathbf{C}_1$ and $\mathbf{C}_2$ are submatrices of the partitioned inverse

$$\begin{bmatrix} \overset{*}{\boldsymbol{\Sigma}}{}^{-1} \otimes \mathbf{Z'PZ}, & \mathbf{R'} \\ \mathbf{R}, & \mathbf{0} \end{bmatrix}^{-1} = \begin{bmatrix} \mathbf{C}_1, & \mathbf{C}_2 \\ \mathbf{C}_2', & \mathbf{C}_3 \end{bmatrix}. \tag{15.68}$$

These submatrices obey the identities

$$\mathbf{C}_1(\overset{*}{\boldsymbol{\Sigma}}{}^{-1} \otimes \mathbf{Z'PZ}) + \mathbf{C}_2\mathbf{R} = \mathbf{I} \tag{15.69}$$

and

$$\mathbf{C}_1'(\overset{*}{\boldsymbol{\Sigma}}{}^{-1} \otimes \mathbf{Z'PZ})\mathbf{C}_1 = \mathbf{C}_1 \tag{15.70}$$

which are analogous, respectively, to those under (10.34) and (10.42).

Let us now substitute $\mathbf{ZA} + \mathbf{U} = \mathbf{Y}$ and $\mathbf{RA}^c = \mathbf{p}$ in (15.67) to obtain

$$\begin{aligned} \tilde{\mathbf{A}}^c &= \mathbf{C}_1[\overset{*}{\boldsymbol{\Sigma}}{}^{-1} \otimes \mathbf{Z'P(ZA+U)}]\mathbf{I}^c + \mathbf{C}_2\mathbf{RA}^c \\ &= \mathbf{C}_1(\overset{*}{\boldsymbol{\Sigma}}{}^{-1} \otimes \mathbf{Z'PZ})\mathbf{A}^c + \mathbf{C}_2\mathbf{RA}^c + \mathbf{C}_1(\overset{*}{\boldsymbol{\Sigma}}{}^{-1} \otimes \mathbf{Z'PU})\mathbf{I}^c \\ &= \mathbf{A}^c + \mathbf{C}_1(\overset{*}{\boldsymbol{\Sigma}}{}^{-1} \otimes \mathbf{Z'PU})\mathbf{I}^c. \end{aligned} \tag{15.71}$$

To show that $\tilde{\mathbf{A}}^c$ is a consistent estimator, we need only demonstrate that the second term of the final expression has a zero probability limit. For this purpose, we need the results that

$$\text{plim}(\overset{*}{\boldsymbol{\Sigma}}) = \boldsymbol{\Sigma}, \tag{15.72}$$

$$\text{plim}\left(\overset{*}{\boldsymbol{\Sigma}}{}^{-1} \otimes \frac{\mathbf{Z'PZ}}{T}\right) = \boldsymbol{\Sigma}^{-1} \otimes \begin{bmatrix} \boldsymbol{\Pi}'\mathbf{M}\boldsymbol{\Pi}, & \boldsymbol{\Pi}'\mathbf{M} \\ \mathbf{M}\boldsymbol{\Pi}, & \mathbf{M} \end{bmatrix}, \tag{15.73}$$

$$\text{plim}\left(\frac{\mathbf{Z'PU}}{T}\right) = \mathbf{0} \tag{15.74}$$

which can be deduced from the assumptions in (15.24) and the results in (15.25). Combining (15.73) with the fact that $\mathbf{R}/T$ is constant enables us to deduce that the matrix which is T times the inverse matrix in (15.68) has a finite probability limit. Hence $\text{plim}(T\mathbf{C}_1)$ is a finite matrix. It follows that

$$(15.75)\qquad \begin{aligned}\text{plim}(\tilde{\mathbf{A}}^c) &= \mathbf{A}^c + \text{plim}(T\mathbf{C}_1)\left[\text{plim}(\overset{*}{\boldsymbol{\Sigma}}{}^{-1})\otimes\text{plim}\left(\frac{\mathbf{Z}'\mathbf{P}\mathbf{U}}{T}\right)\right]\mathbf{I}^c\\ &= \mathbf{A}^c\end{aligned}$$

which demonstrates the consistency of $\tilde{\mathbf{A}}^c$.

Now let us consider the expression

$$(15.76)\qquad \begin{aligned}\sqrt{T}(\tilde{\mathbf{A}}^c - \mathbf{A}^c) &= T\mathbf{C}_1\left[\overset{*}{\boldsymbol{\Sigma}}{}^{-1}\otimes\frac{\mathbf{Z}'\mathbf{X}}{T}\left(\frac{\mathbf{X}'\mathbf{X}}{T}\right)^{-1}\frac{\mathbf{X}'\mathbf{U}}{\sqrt{T}}\right]\mathbf{I}^c\\ &= T\mathbf{C}_1\left[\overset{*}{\boldsymbol{\Sigma}}{}^{-1}\otimes\frac{\mathbf{Z}'\mathbf{X}}{T}\left(\frac{\mathbf{X}'\mathbf{X}}{T}\right)^{-1}\right]\left(\frac{\mathbf{I}\otimes\mathbf{X}'}{\sqrt{T}}\right)\mathbf{U}^c.\end{aligned}$$

Within this expression, we have

$$(15.77)\qquad \left(\frac{\mathbf{I}\otimes\mathbf{X}'}{\sqrt{T}}\right)\mathbf{U}^c = \frac{1}{\sqrt{T}}\begin{bmatrix}\mathbf{X}'\mathbf{u}_{.1}\\ \mathbf{X}'\mathbf{u}_{.2}\\ \cdot\\ \cdot\\ \cdot\\ \mathbf{X}'\mathbf{u}_{.M}\end{bmatrix}$$

where $\mathbf{u}_{.1}, \mathbf{u}_{.2}, \ldots, \mathbf{u}_{.M}$ are successive columns of the disturbance matrix $\mathbf{U}$. On the assumption that the elements of the generic vector $\mathbf{u}_{.m}$ are independently and identically distributed such that $E(\mathbf{u}_{.m}) = \mathbf{0}$ and $D(\mathbf{u}_{.m}) = \sigma_m^2\boldsymbol{I}_T$, it follows from the central limit theorem in (17.68) that the distribution of $\mathbf{X}'\mathbf{u}_{.m}/\sqrt{T}$ converges to the normal distribution $N(\mathbf{0}, \sigma_m^2\mathbf{M})$ as T tends to infinity. It also follows from an extension of that theorem that the distribution of the complete vector in (15.77) tends to the normal distribution $N(\mathbf{0}, \boldsymbol{\Sigma}\otimes\mathbf{M})$. The remaining factors in expression in (15.76) have known finite probability limits—those of $\mathbf{Z}'\mathbf{X}/T$ and $\mathbf{X}'\mathbf{X}/T$ being given under (15.25) and (15.24) respectively. Thus we may deduce that the vector $\sqrt{T}(\tilde{\mathbf{A}}^c - \mathbf{A}^c)$ has a limiting normal distribution with zero mean and a dispersion matrix of

$$(15.78)\qquad \begin{aligned}&\text{plim}(T\mathbf{C}_1)\left(\boldsymbol{\Sigma}^{-1}\otimes\begin{bmatrix}\boldsymbol{\Pi}'\\ \mathbf{I}\end{bmatrix}\right)(\boldsymbol{\Sigma}\otimes\mathbf{M})\left(\boldsymbol{\Sigma}^{-1}\otimes[\boldsymbol{\Pi}, \mathbf{I})\right)\text{plim}(T\mathbf{C}_1)\\ &= \text{plim}(T\mathbf{C}_1)\left(\boldsymbol{\Sigma}^{-1}\otimes\begin{bmatrix}\boldsymbol{\Pi}'\mathbf{M}\boldsymbol{\Pi}, & \boldsymbol{\Pi}'\mathbf{M}\\ \mathbf{M}\boldsymbol{\Pi}, & \mathbf{M}\end{bmatrix}\right)\text{plim}(T\mathbf{C}_1).\end{aligned}$$

This is the probability limit of T times the expression in (15.70); so the dispersion matrix of the limiting distribution is simply $\text{plim}(T\mathbf{C}_1)$.

We should conclude matters by considering the special case of the three-stage least-squares estimator where the *a priori* information is entirely in the form of exclusion restrictions. In that case, the limiting distribution of the vector $\sqrt{T}(\tilde{\boldsymbol{\delta}}-\boldsymbol{\delta})$ is a normal distribution with a zero mean and a dispersion matrix which is the inverse of a matrix that is found by deleting the appropriate rows and columns from

$$\boldsymbol{\Sigma}^{-1}\otimes\begin{bmatrix}\boldsymbol{\Pi}'\mathbf{M}\boldsymbol{\Pi}, & \boldsymbol{\Pi}'\mathbf{M}\\ \mathbf{M}\boldsymbol{\Pi}, & \mathbf{M}\end{bmatrix}. \tag{15.79}$$

Interpretations of the three-stage least-squares estimator

We have described how the system-wide quasi-Gaussian estimates are obtained by a process that resolves the algebraic inconsistency of the system in (15.52). The peculiar characteristic of the reformed system from which the estimates are derived as ordinary algebraic solutions is that it contains two separate representations of the elements of the matrix $\mathbf{X}\boldsymbol{\Pi}$. This arises from the fact that the estimate $(\mathbf{X}\hat{\boldsymbol{\Pi}})^c$ on the LHS of (15.52) is replaced in the reformed system by an estimate $\mathbf{Q}^c$ located in the manifold $\mathcal{M}(\mathbf{I}\otimes[\mathbf{X}\hat{\boldsymbol{\Pi}},\mathbf{X}])$. This peculiarity emerges in the context of the three-stage least-squares estimating equation (15.61) in a somewhat disguised fashion as a disparity between the estimates $\hat{\boldsymbol{\Omega}}$ and $\overset{*}{\boldsymbol{\Sigma}}$ of the reduced-form and structural-form dispersion matrices. Ideally, these estimates should conform to the relationship

$$\boldsymbol{\Omega}=\boldsymbol{\Gamma}'^{-1}\boldsymbol{\Sigma}\boldsymbol{\Gamma}^{-1}$$

postulated to exist amongst the true parameters. However,

$$\hat{\boldsymbol{\Omega}}=\frac{(\mathbf{Y}-\mathbf{X}\hat{\boldsymbol{\Pi}})'(\mathbf{Y}-\mathbf{X}\hat{\boldsymbol{\Pi}})}{T}$$

is an estimate based upon the unrestricted least-squares estimate of the reduced-form parameters, whereas

$$\overset{*}{\boldsymbol{\Sigma}}=\frac{(\mathbf{Y}\overset{*}{\boldsymbol{\Gamma}}+\mathbf{X}\overset{*}{\mathbf{B}})'(\mathbf{Y}\overset{*}{\boldsymbol{\Gamma}}+\mathbf{X}\overset{*}{\mathbf{B}})}{T}$$

is based upon the two-stage least-squares estimates $\overset{*}{\boldsymbol{\Gamma}}=\overset{*}{\mathbf{C}}-\mathbf{I}$ and $\overset{*}{\mathbf{B}}$ which embody the structural-form restrictions. It follows that we cannot expect $\hat{\boldsymbol{\Omega}}$ to equal $\overset{*}{\boldsymbol{\Omega}}=\overset{*}{\boldsymbol{\Gamma}}'^{-1}\overset{*}{\boldsymbol{\Sigma}}\overset{*}{\boldsymbol{\Gamma}}^{-1}$ as, ideally, it should since

$$\overset{*}{\boldsymbol{\Omega}}=\frac{(\mathbf{Y}+\mathbf{X}\overset{*}{\mathbf{B}}\overset{*}{\boldsymbol{\Gamma}}^{-1})'(\mathbf{Y}+\mathbf{X}\overset{*}{\mathbf{B}}\overset{*}{\boldsymbol{\Gamma}}^{-1})}{T}$$

is based on a restricted estimate $\overset{*}{\boldsymbol{\Pi}}=-\overset{*}{\mathbf{B}}\overset{*}{\boldsymbol{\Gamma}}^{-1}$.

It would be satisfying to have a fully conformable set of estimates of $\mathbf{\Omega}$, $\mathbf{\Sigma}$, $\mathbf{\Gamma}$, $\mathbf{B}$, and $\mathbf{\Pi}$ obeying all the relationships postulated to exist amongst these parameters. To obtain such estimates, we would have to use the method of full-information maximum likelihood. In fact, in the next chapter we shall show that the three-stage least-squares estimator is essentially a modified version of the full-information maximum-likelihood estimator which achieves a measure of computational simplicity at the cost of violating certain of the relationships existing amongst the parameters.

BIBLIOGRAPHY

Two-stage and Three-stage Least-squares Estimators. Basman [**13**], Fisher [**36**], Theil [**114**], Zellner and Theil [**128**]

Estimation with Undersized Samples. Fisher and Wadycki [**37**], Swamy and Holmes [**113**]

Asymptotic Properties of Three-stage Least-squares. Madansky [**79**], Sargan [**105**]

CHAPTER 16

Maximum-Likelihood Methods

The problem of estimating the parameters of a simultaneous-equation econometric system was first examined in detail by members of the Cowles Commission for Research in Economics. Their principal findings were collected in two volumes of articles edited by Koopmans [**66**] and by Hood and Koopmans [**57**] and published, respectively, in 1950 and 1953. Their method of obtaining estimates was to attribute to the parameters the values that maximized the likelihood of the sample data. In many ways, the resulting limited-information and full-information maximum-likelihood estimators represented the definitive solutions to the problems that had been broached. However, the Commission's estimators were not readily adopted. They had two outstanding drawbacks. In the first place, the derivations of the estimators were lengthy and difficult. In the second place, the computational problems, particularly those associated with the full-information estimator, taxed the resources of the available computers and placed the estimators beyond the reach of the practical research worker. It is probably true to say that the practice of estimating simultaneous systems only became widespread with the advent of the more tractable two-stage and three-stage least-squares estimators.

The two-stage and three-stage least-squares estimators, or the quasi-Gaussian estimators as we have called them, were derived along quite different lines from those followed by the Cowles Commission; and, at first, it was not widely appreciated how closely related to the Cowles Commission estimators they were. The truth of the matter is that the quasi-Gaussian estimators can be derived by making very minor modifications to the Cowles Commission estimators; and, indeed, we might have adopted such an approach were it not for the fact that the original derivations presented in the previous chapter provide interesting perspectives in which to view the problems of simultaneous-equation estimation.

In presenting the Cowles Commission estimators, we still have to contend with the peculiar complexity of their derivations. This complexity is largely due to the fact that the maximum-likelihood estimating systems involve the simultaneous determination of the parameters of the systematic structure of the model and the parameters of the dispersion matrices. The problem is greatly simplified if the dispersion matrices are assumed to be known *a priori* or if their determination can be assigned to a separate estimating system. As we shall see, it is precisely by using separate estimating systems for the dispersion parameters that the quasi-Gaussian methods achieve their relative simplicity.

FULL-INFORMATION ESTIMATION

Let us recall the notation of the simultaneous-equation econometric model. We represent a single realization of the M structural relationships by

$$\mathbf{y}_{t.}\boldsymbol{\Gamma}+\mathbf{x}_{t.}\mathbf{B}+\mathbf{u}_{t.}=\mathbf{0} \tag{16.1}$$

or, more compactly, by

$$\mathbf{z}_{t.}\boldsymbol{\Theta}+\mathbf{u}_{t.}=\mathbf{0} \tag{16.2}$$

where $\mathbf{z}_{t.}=[\mathbf{y}_{t.},\mathbf{x}_{t.}]$ and $\boldsymbol{\Theta}'=[\boldsymbol{\Gamma}',\mathbf{B}']$. The restrictions on the structural parameters are written as

$$\mathbf{R}\begin{bmatrix}\boldsymbol{\Gamma}\\ \mathbf{B}\end{bmatrix}^{c}=\mathbf{R}\boldsymbol{\Theta}^{c}=\mathbf{r}. \tag{16.3}$$

The reduced form of the equation (16.1) is

$$\begin{aligned}\mathbf{y}_{t.}&=-\mathbf{x}_{t.}\mathbf{B}\boldsymbol{\Gamma}^{-1}-\mathbf{u}_{t.}\boldsymbol{\Gamma}^{-1}\\ &=\mathbf{x}_{t.}\boldsymbol{\Pi}+\mathbf{v}_{t.}\,.\end{aligned} \tag{16.4}$$

In order to specify the probability density function of a sample $\mathbf{y}_{1.},\ldots,\mathbf{y}_{T.}$ for the given set of values $\mathbf{x}_{1.},\ldots,\mathbf{x}_{T.}$, we must specify the density functions of the stochastic inputs $\mathbf{u}_{t.}$ of the structural relationship. It is both reasonable and convenient to assume that these are independently and normally distributed. If we assume that

$$\mathbf{u}_{t.}\sim N(\mathbf{0},\boldsymbol{\Sigma}) \quad \text{for all } t, \tag{16.5}$$

then it follows that

$$\mathbf{v}_{t.}\sim N(\mathbf{0},\boldsymbol{\Omega}), \qquad \boldsymbol{\Omega}=\boldsymbol{\Gamma}^{-1\prime}\boldsymbol{\Sigma}\boldsymbol{\Gamma}^{-1}, \quad \text{for all } t. \tag{16.6}$$

Thus, on referring to (16.4), we find that

$$\mathbf{y}_{t.}\sim N(\mathbf{x}_{t.}\boldsymbol{\Pi},\boldsymbol{\Omega}) \quad \text{for all } t. \tag{16.7}$$

It follows that the probability density function of the sample $\mathbf{y}_{1.},\ldots,\mathbf{y}_{T.}$ and, equally, the likelihood function of parameters is given by

$$\begin{aligned}L&=\prod_{t=1}^{T}N(\mathbf{y}_{t.};\mathbf{x}_{t.}\boldsymbol{\Pi},\boldsymbol{\Omega})\\ &=(2\pi)^{-MT/2}\,|\boldsymbol{\Omega}|^{-T/2}\exp\left\{-\tfrac{1}{2}\sum_{t=1}^{T}(\mathbf{y}_{t.}-\mathbf{x}_{t.}\boldsymbol{\Pi})\boldsymbol{\Omega}^{-1}(\mathbf{y}_{t.}-\mathbf{x}_{t.}\boldsymbol{\Pi})'\right\}.\end{aligned} \tag{16.8}$$

The logarithm of the likelihood function is therefore

$$L^*(\mathbf{\Pi}, \mathbf{\Omega}) = -\frac{MT}{2}\log(2\pi) - \frac{T}{2}\log|\mathbf{\Omega}| - \tfrac{1}{2}\operatorname{Trace}[(\mathbf{Y}-\mathbf{X\Pi})'(\mathbf{Y}-\mathbf{X\Pi})\mathbf{\Omega}^{-1}]. \tag{16.9}$$

By using the identities $\mathbf{\Pi} = -\mathbf{B\Gamma}^{-1}$, $\mathbf{\Omega}^{-1} = \mathbf{\Gamma\Sigma}^{-1}\mathbf{\Gamma}'$ and $|\mathbf{\Omega}| = |\mathbf{\Gamma}|^{-2}|\mathbf{\Sigma}|$, we can rewrite this function in terms of the structural parameters as

$$L^*(\mathbf{\Gamma}, \mathbf{B}, \mathbf{\Sigma}) = -\frac{MT}{2}\log(2\pi) + T\log|\mathbf{\Gamma}| - \frac{T}{2}\log|\mathbf{\Sigma}| - \tfrac{1}{2}\operatorname{Trace}[(\mathbf{Y\Gamma}+\mathbf{XB})'(\mathbf{Y\Gamma}+\mathbf{XB})\mathbf{\Sigma}^{-1}]. \tag{16.10}$$

The maximum-likelihood estimates of the structural parameters are obtained from the first-order conditions for the maximization of the log-likelihood function subject to the structural constraints in (16.3). Thus the function to be maximized is

$$L^R = L^* - \boldsymbol{\lambda}'(\mathbf{R\Theta}^c - \mathbf{r}) \tag{16.11}$$

where $\boldsymbol{\lambda}$ is a vector of Lagrangean multipliers. The first-order conditions can be given in the form

$$\left(\frac{\partial L^R}{\partial \mathbf{\Sigma}^{-1c}}\right)' = \left(\frac{\partial L^*}{\partial \mathbf{\Sigma}^{-1c}}\right)' = \mathbf{0}, \tag{16.12}$$

$$\left(\frac{\partial L^R}{\partial \mathbf{\Theta}^c}\right)' = \left(\frac{\partial L^*}{\partial \mathbf{\Theta}^c}\right)' - \mathbf{R}'\boldsymbol{\lambda} = \mathbf{0}, \tag{16.13}$$

$$\left(\frac{\partial L^R}{\partial \boldsymbol{\lambda}}\right)' = -(\mathbf{R\Theta}^c - \mathbf{r}) = \mathbf{0}. \tag{16.14}$$

We might attempt to evaluate these conditions by obtaining the derivatives $\partial L^*/\partial \mathbf{\Sigma}^{-1c}$, $\partial L^*/\partial \mathbf{\Theta}^c$ from the likelihood function $L^*(\mathbf{\Theta}, \mathbf{\Sigma})$ given in (16.10). However, we shall adopt the alternative procedure of obtaining the derivatives from the function $L^*(\mathbf{\Pi}, \mathbf{\Omega})$ of (16.9) in the forms $(\partial L^*/\partial \mathbf{\Omega}^{-1c}) \times (\partial \mathbf{\Omega}^{-1c}/\partial \mathbf{\Sigma}^{-1c})$ and $(\partial L^*/\partial \mathbf{\Pi}^c)(\partial \mathbf{\Pi}^c/\partial \mathbf{\Theta}^c)$. Our reasons are twofold. In the first place, we have already accomplished the arduous task of finding the derivatives $\partial L^*/\partial \mathbf{\Omega}^{-1c}$ and $\partial L^*/\partial \mathbf{\Pi}^c$ in Chapter 13; and we can make good use of these results. In the second place, our method of evaluating the derivatives enables us to envisage the problem of estimation as essentially one of minimizing the distance function

$$\begin{aligned} &\sum_{t=1}^{T} (\mathbf{y}_{t.} - \mathbf{x}_{t.}\mathbf{\Pi})\mathbf{\Omega}^{-1}(\mathbf{y}_{t.} - \mathbf{x}_{t.}\mathbf{\Pi})' \\ &= [\mathbf{Y}^c - (\mathbf{I}\otimes\mathbf{X})\mathbf{\Pi}^c]'(\mathbf{\Omega}^{-1}\otimes\mathbf{I})[\mathbf{Y}^c - (\mathbf{I}\otimes\mathbf{X})\mathbf{\Pi}^c] \\ &= \operatorname{Trace}(\mathbf{Y}-\mathbf{X\Pi})'(\mathbf{Y}-\mathbf{X\Pi})\mathbf{\Omega}^{-1} \end{aligned} \tag{16.15}$$

in respect of the set of admissible values of $\mathbf{\Pi}=-\mathbf{B}\mathbf{\Gamma}^{-1}$ that are compounded from values of $\mathbf{\Theta}'=[\mathbf{\Gamma}',\mathbf{B}']$ obeying the structural restrictions. This engenders a familiar interpretation of the problem of econometric estimation.

The derivative $\partial L^*/\partial\mathbf{\Sigma}^{-1c}$

We may begin by evaluating the condition under (16.12) which we shall write as

$$(16.16)\qquad \left(\frac{\partial L^*}{\partial\mathbf{\Sigma}^{-1c}}\right)'=\left(\frac{\partial\mathbf{\Omega}^{-1c}}{\partial\mathbf{\Sigma}^{-1c}}\right)'\left(\frac{\partial L^*}{\partial\mathbf{\Omega}^{-1c}}\right)'=\mathbf{0}.$$

To evaluate the first of the factors, we write $\mathbf{\Omega}^{-1}=\mathbf{\Gamma}\mathbf{\Sigma}^{-1}\mathbf{\Gamma}'$ as $\mathbf{\Omega}^{-1c}=(\mathbf{\Gamma}\otimes\mathbf{\Gamma})\mathbf{\Sigma}^{-1c}$. It follows that

$$(16.17)\qquad \left(\frac{\partial\mathbf{\Omega}^{-1c}}{\partial\mathbf{\Sigma}^{-1c}}\right)'=(\mathbf{\Gamma}'\otimes\mathbf{\Gamma}').$$

To evaluate the second factor, we obtain $\partial L^*/\partial\mathbf{\Omega}^{-1}$ from (13.27) and we use the relationship $(\partial L^*/\partial\mathbf{\Omega}^{-1c})'=(\partial L^*/\partial\mathbf{\Omega}^{-1})'^{c}$ to give

$$(16.18)\qquad \left(\frac{\partial L^*}{\partial\mathbf{\Omega}^{-1c}}\right)'=\left[\frac{T}{2}\mathbf{\Omega}-\tfrac{1}{2}(\mathbf{Y}-\mathbf{X}\mathbf{\Pi})'(\mathbf{Y}-\mathbf{X}\mathbf{\Pi})\right]^{c}.$$

On substituting both results in (16.16), we find that

$$(16.19)\qquad \left(\frac{\partial L^*}{\partial\mathbf{\Sigma}^{-1c}}\right)'=(\mathbf{\Gamma}'\otimes\mathbf{\Gamma}')\left[\frac{T}{2}\mathbf{\Omega}-\tfrac{1}{2}(\mathbf{Y}-\mathbf{X}\mathbf{\Pi})'(\mathbf{Y}-\mathbf{X}\mathbf{\Pi})\right]^{c}$$

$$=\left[\frac{T}{2}\mathbf{\Gamma}'\mathbf{\Omega}\mathbf{\Gamma}-\tfrac{1}{2}\mathbf{\Gamma}'(\mathbf{Y}-\mathbf{X}\mathbf{\Pi})'(\mathbf{Y}-\mathbf{X}\mathbf{\Pi})\mathbf{\Gamma}\right]^{c}=\mathbf{0}.$$

Since $\mathbf{\Gamma}'\mathbf{\Omega}\mathbf{\Gamma}=\mathbf{\Sigma}$ and $-\mathbf{\Pi}\mathbf{\Gamma}=\mathbf{B}$, this condition gives us the estimating equation

$$(16.20)\qquad \mathbf{\Sigma}(\mathbf{\Theta})=\frac{(\mathbf{Y}\mathbf{\Gamma}+\mathbf{X}\mathbf{B})'(\mathbf{Y}\mathbf{\Gamma}+\mathbf{X}\mathbf{B})}{T}.$$

The estimating equation

$$(16.21)\qquad \mathbf{\Omega}(\mathbf{\Pi})=\frac{(\mathbf{Y}-\mathbf{X}\mathbf{\Pi})'(\mathbf{Y}-\mathbf{X}\mathbf{\Pi})}{T}$$

of the reduced-form dispersion matrix may be obtained either through the relationship $\mathbf{\Omega}(\mathbf{\Pi})=\mathbf{\Gamma}^{-1\prime}\mathbf{\Sigma}(\mathbf{\Theta})\mathbf{\Gamma}^{-1}$ or directly from the condition $\partial L^*/\partial\mathbf{\Omega}^{-1}=\mathbf{0}$.

The derivative $\partial L^*/\partial \boldsymbol{\Theta}^c$

The condition under (16.13) can be written as

$$\left(\frac{\partial L^*}{\partial \boldsymbol{\Gamma}}, \frac{\partial L^*}{\partial \mathbf{B}}\right)'^{c} - \mathbf{R}'\boldsymbol{\lambda} = \mathbf{0}. \tag{16.22}$$

We shall begin by evaluating

$$\left(\frac{\partial L^*}{\partial \mathbf{B}^c}\right)' = \left(\frac{\partial \boldsymbol{\Pi}^c}{\partial \mathbf{B}^c}\right)'\left(\frac{\partial L^*}{\partial \boldsymbol{\Pi}^c}\right)'. \tag{16.23}$$

To find the first factor of this expression, we write the relationship $\boldsymbol{\Pi} = -\mathbf{B}\boldsymbol{\Gamma}^{-1}$ in the form $\boldsymbol{\Pi}^c = -(\boldsymbol{\Gamma}^{-1\prime} \otimes \mathbf{I})\mathbf{B}^c$. It follows that

$$\left(\frac{\partial \boldsymbol{\Pi}^c}{\partial \mathbf{B}^c}\right)' = -(\boldsymbol{\Gamma}^{-1} \otimes \mathbf{I}). \tag{16.24}$$

To find the second factor, we take the derivative $\partial L^*/\partial \boldsymbol{\Pi}$ from (13.31) and we use the relationship $(\partial L^*/\partial \boldsymbol{\Pi}^c)' = (\partial L^*/\partial \boldsymbol{\Pi})'^c$ to give

$$\left(\frac{\partial L^*}{\partial \boldsymbol{\Pi}^c}\right)' = [(\mathbf{X}'\mathbf{Y} - \mathbf{X}'\mathbf{X}\boldsymbol{\Pi})\boldsymbol{\Omega}^{-1}]^c. \tag{16.25}$$

By combining the two factors, we find that

$$\begin{aligned}(\partial L^*/\partial \mathbf{B}^c)' &= -(\boldsymbol{\Gamma}^{-1} \otimes \mathbf{I})[(\mathbf{X}'\mathbf{Y} - \mathbf{X}'\mathbf{X}\boldsymbol{\Pi})\boldsymbol{\Omega}^{-1}]^c \\ &= -[(\mathbf{X}'\mathbf{Y} - \mathbf{X}'\mathbf{X}\boldsymbol{\Pi})\boldsymbol{\Omega}^{-1}\boldsymbol{\Gamma}^{-1\prime}]^c \\ &= -[(\mathbf{X}'\mathbf{Y}\boldsymbol{\Gamma} + \mathbf{X}'\mathbf{X}\mathbf{B})\boldsymbol{\Sigma}^{-1}]^c \\ &= (\partial L^*/\partial \mathbf{B})'^c.\end{aligned} \tag{16.26}$$

Next we evaluate

$$\left(\frac{\partial L^*}{\partial \boldsymbol{\Gamma}^c}\right)' = \left(\frac{\partial \boldsymbol{\Pi}^c}{\partial \boldsymbol{\Gamma}^c}\right)'\left(\frac{\partial L^*}{\partial \boldsymbol{\Pi}^c}\right)'. \tag{16.27}$$

To find the first factor, we write the relationship $\boldsymbol{\Pi} = -\mathbf{B}\boldsymbol{\Gamma}^{-1}$ in the form $\boldsymbol{\Pi}^c = -(\mathbf{I} \otimes \mathbf{B})\boldsymbol{\Gamma}^{-1c}$ from which it follows that

$$\begin{aligned}\left(\frac{\partial \boldsymbol{\Pi}^c}{\partial \boldsymbol{\Gamma}^c}\right)' &= \left(\frac{\partial \boldsymbol{\Gamma}^{-1c}}{\partial \boldsymbol{\Gamma}^c}\right)'\left(\frac{\partial \boldsymbol{\Pi}^c}{\partial \boldsymbol{\Gamma}^{-1c}}\right)' \\ &= (\boldsymbol{\Gamma}^{-1} \otimes \boldsymbol{\Gamma}^{-1\prime})(\mathbf{I} \otimes \mathbf{B}') \\ &= -(\boldsymbol{\Gamma}^{-1} \otimes \boldsymbol{\Pi}').\end{aligned} \tag{16.28}$$

By substituting this and the expression for $(\partial L^*/\partial \mathbf{\Pi}^c)'$ under (16.25) into (16.27), we get

$$\begin{aligned}(16.29)\qquad \left(\frac{\partial L^*}{\partial \mathbf{\Gamma}^c}\right)' &= -(\mathbf{\Gamma}^{-1}\otimes\mathbf{\Pi}')[(\mathbf{X}'\mathbf{Y}-\mathbf{X}'\mathbf{X}\mathbf{\Pi})\mathbf{\Omega}^{-1}]^c\\ &= -[\mathbf{\Pi}'(\mathbf{X}'\mathbf{Y}-\mathbf{X}'\mathbf{X}\mathbf{\Pi})\mathbf{\Omega}^{-1}\mathbf{\Gamma}^{-1\prime}]^c\\ &= -[(\mathbf{\Pi}'\mathbf{X}'\mathbf{Y}\mathbf{\Gamma}+\mathbf{\Pi}'\mathbf{X}'\mathbf{X}\mathbf{B})\mathbf{\Sigma}^{-1}]^c\\ &= (\partial L^*/\partial\mathbf{\Gamma})'^c.\end{aligned}$$

The derivative $(\partial L^*/\partial \mathbf{\Gamma})'$ may be expressed in any of the forms comprised in the identity

$$\begin{aligned}(16.30)\qquad (\partial L^*/\partial\mathbf{\Gamma})' &= -(\mathbf{\Pi}'\mathbf{X}'\mathbf{Y}+\mathbf{\Pi}'\mathbf{X}'\mathbf{X}\mathbf{B})\mathbf{\Sigma}^{-1}\\ &= -\{[\mathbf{Y}'\mathbf{Y}-T\mathbf{\Omega}(\mathbf{\Pi})]\mathbf{\Gamma}+\mathbf{Y}'\mathbf{X}\mathbf{B}\}\mathbf{\Sigma}^{-1}\\ &= [T\mathbf{\Gamma}^{-1\prime}-(\mathbf{Y}'\mathbf{Y}+\mathbf{Y}'\mathbf{X}\mathbf{B})\mathbf{\Sigma}^{-1}].\end{aligned}$$

Consider

$$\begin{aligned}(16.31)\qquad T\mathbf{\Omega}(\mathbf{\Pi})\mathbf{\Gamma} &= (\mathbf{Y}-\mathbf{X}\mathbf{\Pi})'(\mathbf{Y}-\mathbf{X}\mathbf{\Pi})\mathbf{\Gamma}\\ &= (\mathbf{Y}'\mathbf{Y}-\mathbf{Y}'\mathbf{X}\mathbf{\Pi}-\mathbf{\Pi}'\mathbf{X}'\mathbf{Y}+\mathbf{\Pi}'\mathbf{X}'\mathbf{X}\mathbf{\Pi})\mathbf{\Gamma}\\ &= \mathbf{Y}'\mathbf{Y}\mathbf{\Gamma}+\mathbf{Y}'\mathbf{X}\mathbf{B}-\mathbf{\Pi}'\mathbf{X}'\mathbf{Y}\mathbf{\Gamma}-\mathbf{\Pi}'\mathbf{X}'\mathbf{X}\mathbf{B}.\end{aligned}$$

On rearranging the final equation, we get

$$(16.32)\qquad (\mathbf{Y}'\mathbf{Y}-T\mathbf{\Omega})\mathbf{\Gamma}+\mathbf{Y}'\mathbf{X}\mathbf{B}=\mathbf{\Pi}'\mathbf{X}'\mathbf{Y}\mathbf{\Gamma}+\mathbf{\Pi}'\mathbf{X}'\mathbf{X}\mathbf{B}$$

which is sufficient to establish the first identity in (16.30). To establish the second identity, we consider

$$\begin{aligned}(16.33)\qquad ([\mathbf{Y}'\mathbf{Y}-T\mathbf{\Omega}]\mathbf{\Gamma}+\mathbf{Y}'\mathbf{X}\mathbf{B})\mathbf{\Sigma}^{-1} &= -T\mathbf{\Omega}\mathbf{\Gamma}\mathbf{\Sigma}^{-1}+(\mathbf{Y}'\mathbf{Y}\mathbf{\Gamma}+\mathbf{Y}'\mathbf{X}\mathbf{B})\mathbf{\Sigma}^{-1}\\ &= -T\mathbf{\Gamma}^{-1\prime}+(\mathbf{Y}'\mathbf{Y}\mathbf{\Gamma}+\mathbf{Y}'\mathbf{X}\mathbf{B})\mathbf{\Sigma}^{-1}.\end{aligned}$$

Let us finally assemble the various results under (16.26) and (16.30) to obtain

$$\begin{aligned}(16.34)\qquad \left(\frac{\partial L^*}{\partial \mathbf{\Theta}^c}\right)' &= \begin{bmatrix}(\partial L^*/\partial\mathbf{\Gamma})'\\ (\partial L^*/\partial\mathbf{B})'\end{bmatrix}^c\\ &= -\left(\begin{bmatrix}\mathbf{\Pi}'\mathbf{X}'\mathbf{Y}, & \mathbf{\Pi}'\mathbf{X}'\mathbf{X}\\ \mathbf{X}'\mathbf{Y}, & \mathbf{X}'\mathbf{X}\end{bmatrix}\begin{bmatrix}\mathbf{\Gamma}\\ \mathbf{B}\end{bmatrix}\mathbf{\Sigma}^{-1}\right)^c\\ &= -\left(\begin{bmatrix}\mathbf{Y}'\mathbf{Y}-T\mathbf{\Omega}, & \mathbf{Y}'\mathbf{X}\\ \mathbf{X}'\mathbf{Y}, & \mathbf{X}'\mathbf{X}\end{bmatrix}\begin{bmatrix}\mathbf{\Gamma}\\ \mathbf{B}\end{bmatrix}\mathbf{\Sigma}^{-1}\right)^c\\ &= \left(T\begin{bmatrix}\mathbf{\Gamma}^{-1\prime}\\ \mathbf{0}\end{bmatrix}-\begin{bmatrix}\mathbf{Y}'\mathbf{Y}, & \mathbf{Y}'\mathbf{X}\\ \mathbf{X}'\mathbf{Y}, & \mathbf{X}'\mathbf{X}\end{bmatrix}\begin{bmatrix}\mathbf{\Gamma}\\ \mathbf{B}\end{bmatrix}\mathbf{\Sigma}^{-1}\right)^c.\end{aligned}$$

The full-information maximum-likelihood estimating equations

The equations that directly determine the estimates of the structural parameters comprised in $\mathbf{\Theta}' = [\mathbf{\Gamma}', \mathbf{B}']$ are obtained by substituting any of the expressions of $(\partial L^*/\partial \mathbf{\Theta}^c)'$ given in (16.34) into the first-order condition (16.13) and by compounding the result with the equations of the restrictions given under (16.14). Thus, allowing for a change of sign, we obtain the system

$$(16.35)\qquad \begin{bmatrix} \mathbf{\Sigma}^{-1} \otimes \begin{bmatrix} \mathbf{\Pi}'\mathbf{X}'\mathbf{Y}, & \mathbf{\Pi}'\mathbf{X}'\mathbf{X} \\ \mathbf{X}'\mathbf{Y}, & \mathbf{X}'\mathbf{X} \end{bmatrix}, & \mathbf{R}' \\ \mathbf{R}, & \mathbf{0} \end{bmatrix} \begin{bmatrix} \begin{bmatrix} \mathbf{\Gamma} \\ \mathbf{B} \end{bmatrix}^c \\ \boldsymbol{\lambda} \end{bmatrix} = \begin{bmatrix} \mathbf{0} \\ \mathbf{0} \\ \mathbf{r} \end{bmatrix},$$

or, equally, the equivalent system

$$(16.36)\qquad \begin{bmatrix} \mathbf{\Sigma}^{-1} \otimes \begin{bmatrix} \mathbf{Y}'\mathbf{Y} - T\mathbf{\Omega}, & \mathbf{Y}'\mathbf{X} \\ \mathbf{X}'\mathbf{Y}, & \mathbf{X}'\mathbf{X} \end{bmatrix}, & \mathbf{R} \\ \mathbf{R}, & \mathbf{0} \end{bmatrix} \begin{bmatrix} \begin{bmatrix} \mathbf{\Gamma} \\ \mathbf{B} \end{bmatrix}^c \\ \boldsymbol{\lambda} \end{bmatrix} = \begin{bmatrix} \mathbf{0} \\ \mathbf{0} \\ \mathbf{r} \end{bmatrix}.$$

To these we must add the subsidiary equations

$$(16.37)\qquad \mathbf{\Sigma}(\mathbf{\Theta}) = \frac{(\mathbf{Y\Gamma} + \mathbf{XB})'(\mathbf{Y\Gamma} + \mathbf{XB})}{T},$$

$$(16.38)\qquad \mathbf{\Omega}(\mathbf{\Pi}) = \frac{(\mathbf{Y} - \mathbf{X\Pi})'(\mathbf{Y} - \mathbf{X\Pi})}{T} = \mathbf{\Gamma}^{-1\prime}\mathbf{\Sigma}(\mathbf{\Theta})\mathbf{\Gamma}^{-1},$$

$$(16.39)\qquad \mathbf{\Pi} = -\mathbf{B\Gamma}^{-1}.$$

The full-information maximum-likelihood estimates of $\mathbf{\Gamma}$, $\mathbf{B}$, $\mathbf{\Sigma}$, $\mathbf{\Omega}$, and $\mathbf{\Pi}$ are obtained by the simultaneous solution of one or other of (16.35) and (16.36) together with (16.37), (16.38), and (16.39). We shall shortly be describing a procedure for finding a solution.

Second-order derivatives of the log-likelihood function

The theory of maximum-likelihood estimation indicates that the limiting distribution of the vector $\sqrt{T}(\hat{\mathbf{\Theta}}^c - \mathbf{\Theta}^c)$ comprising the full-information maximum-likelihood estimate $\hat{\mathbf{\Theta}}$ will be the normal distribution $N(\mathbf{0}, \mathbf{C}_1)$ where $\mathbf{C}_1$ is defined by

$$(16.40)\qquad \begin{bmatrix} \mathbf{C}_1, & \mathbf{C}_2 \\ \mathbf{C}_2', & \mathbf{C}_3 \end{bmatrix} = \begin{bmatrix} -\operatorname{plim}\left[T^{-1}\dfrac{\partial(\partial L^*/\partial \mathbf{\Theta}^c)'}{\partial \mathbf{\Theta}^c}\right], & \mathbf{R}' \\ \mathbf{R}, & \mathbf{0} \end{bmatrix}^{-1}.$$

In this equation, the expression $\partial(\partial L^*/\partial \mathbf{\Theta}^c)'/\partial \mathbf{\Theta}^c$ stands for the second-order derivatives of the concentrated log-likelihood function $L^*(\boldsymbol{\Theta}) = L^*[\boldsymbol{\Theta}, \boldsymbol{\Sigma}(\boldsymbol{\Theta})]$ which is obtained from $L^*(\boldsymbol{\Theta}, \boldsymbol{\Sigma})$ of (16.10) by replacing the unknown $\boldsymbol{\Sigma}$ by its maximum-likelihood estimate $\boldsymbol{\Sigma}(\boldsymbol{\Theta})$ given in (16.20). The result was established by Aitchison and Silvey [**3**] and is recorded by Silvey [**111**].

Let us evaluate the matrix of second-order derivatives. We begin by noting that the derivative $\partial L^*(\boldsymbol{\Theta})/\partial\boldsymbol{\Theta}^c$ of the concentrated function is precisely the derivative $\partial L^*(\boldsymbol{\Theta}, \boldsymbol{\Sigma})/\partial\boldsymbol{\Theta}^c$ evaluated at $\boldsymbol{\Sigma} = \boldsymbol{\Sigma}(\boldsymbol{\Theta})$. Thus, using the final expression under (16.34), we can write the derivatives in the form

$$(16.41)\qquad \left(\frac{\partial L^*}{\partial\boldsymbol{\Theta}^c}\right)' = \left(T\begin{bmatrix}\boldsymbol{\Gamma}^{-1\prime}\\ \mathbf{0}\end{bmatrix} - \begin{bmatrix}\mathbf{Y}'\mathbf{Y}, & \mathbf{Y}'\mathbf{X}\\ \mathbf{X}'\mathbf{Y}, & \mathbf{X}'\mathbf{X}\end{bmatrix}\begin{bmatrix}\boldsymbol{\Gamma}\\ \mathbf{B}\end{bmatrix}\boldsymbol{\Sigma}^{-1}(\boldsymbol{\Theta})\right)^c$$

$$= T\left\{\begin{bmatrix}\boldsymbol{\Gamma}^{-1\prime}\\ \mathbf{0}\end{bmatrix} - \begin{bmatrix}\mathbf{Y}'\mathbf{Y}, & \mathbf{Y}'\mathbf{X}\\ \mathbf{X}'\mathbf{Y}, & \mathbf{X}'\mathbf{X}\end{bmatrix}\begin{bmatrix}\boldsymbol{\Gamma}\\ \mathbf{B}\end{bmatrix} \times\left((\boldsymbol{\Gamma}', \mathbf{B}')\begin{bmatrix}\mathbf{Y}'\mathbf{Y}, & \mathbf{Y}'\mathbf{X}\\ \mathbf{X}'\mathbf{Y}, & \mathbf{X}'\mathbf{X}\end{bmatrix}\begin{bmatrix}\boldsymbol{\Gamma}\\ \mathbf{B}\end{bmatrix}\right)^{-1}\right\}^c$$

$$= T\left\{\begin{bmatrix}\boldsymbol{\Gamma}^{-1\prime}\\ \mathbf{0}\end{bmatrix} - \mathbf{W}\boldsymbol{\Theta}(\boldsymbol{\Theta}'\mathbf{W}\boldsymbol{\Theta})^{-1}\right\}^c,$$

where

$$\mathbf{W} = T^{-1}\begin{bmatrix}\mathbf{Y}'\mathbf{Y}, & \mathbf{Y}'\mathbf{X}\\ \mathbf{X}'\mathbf{Y}, & \mathbf{X}'\mathbf{X}\end{bmatrix}.$$

Now consider

$$(16.42)\qquad T^{-1}\frac{\partial(\partial L^*/\partial\boldsymbol{\Theta}^c)'}{\partial\boldsymbol{\Theta}^c} = \frac{\partial[\boldsymbol{\Gamma}^{-1}, \mathbf{0}]'^c}{\partial\boldsymbol{\Theta}^c} - \frac{\partial[\mathbf{W}\boldsymbol{\Theta}(\boldsymbol{\Theta}'\mathbf{W}\boldsymbol{\Theta})^{-1}]^c}{\partial\boldsymbol{\Theta}^c}.$$

Within this expression,

$$(16.43)\qquad \frac{\partial[\mathbf{W}\boldsymbol{\Theta}(\boldsymbol{\Theta}'\mathbf{W}\boldsymbol{\Theta})^{-1}]^c}{\partial\boldsymbol{\Theta}^c} = (\mathbf{I}\otimes\mathbf{W}\boldsymbol{\Theta})\frac{\partial(\boldsymbol{\Theta}'\mathbf{W}\boldsymbol{\Theta})^{-1c}}{\partial\boldsymbol{\Theta}^c} + [(\boldsymbol{\Theta}'\mathbf{W}\boldsymbol{\Theta})^{-1}\otimes\mathbf{I}]\frac{\partial(\mathbf{W}\boldsymbol{\Theta})^c}{\partial\boldsymbol{\Theta}^c}$$

where, according to (4.74) and (4.75),

$$(16.44)\qquad \frac{\partial(\boldsymbol{\Theta}'\mathbf{W}\boldsymbol{\Theta})^{-1c}}{\partial\boldsymbol{\Theta}^c} = \frac{\partial(\boldsymbol{\Theta}'\mathbf{W}\boldsymbol{\Theta})^{-1c}}{\partial(\boldsymbol{\Theta}'\mathbf{W}\boldsymbol{\Theta})^c}\frac{\partial(\boldsymbol{\Theta}'\mathbf{W}\boldsymbol{\Theta})^c}{\partial\boldsymbol{\Theta}^c}$$

$$= -[(\boldsymbol{\Theta}'\mathbf{W}\boldsymbol{\Theta})^{-1}\otimes(\boldsymbol{\Theta}'\mathbf{W}\boldsymbol{\Theta})^{-1}] \times[(\boldsymbol{\Theta}'\mathbf{W}\otimes\mathbf{I})\textcircled{T} + (\mathbf{I}\otimes\boldsymbol{\Theta}'\mathbf{W})]$$

$$= -[(\boldsymbol{\Theta}'\mathbf{W}\boldsymbol{\Theta})^{-1}\boldsymbol{\Theta}'\mathbf{W}\otimes(\boldsymbol{\Theta}'\mathbf{W}\boldsymbol{\Theta})^{-1}]\textcircled{T} - [(\boldsymbol{\Theta}'\mathbf{W}\boldsymbol{\Theta})^{-1}\otimes(\boldsymbol{\Theta}'\mathbf{W}\boldsymbol{\Theta})^{-1}\boldsymbol{\Theta}'\mathbf{W}]$$

and

$$\frac{\partial(\mathbf{W\Theta})^c}{\partial\mathbf{\Theta}^c}=(\mathbf{I}\otimes\mathbf{W})\frac{\partial\mathbf{\Theta}^c}{\partial\mathbf{\Theta}^c}=\mathbf{I}\otimes\mathbf{W}. \tag{16.45}$$

By placing (16.44) and (16.45) in (16.43), we get

$$\begin{aligned}\frac{\partial[\mathbf{W\Theta}(\mathbf{\Theta'M\Theta})^{-1}]^c}{\partial\mathbf{\Theta}^c}=&-[(\mathbf{\Theta'W\Theta})^{-1}\mathbf{\Theta'W}\otimes\mathbf{W\Theta}(\mathbf{\Theta'W\Theta})^{-1}]\textcircled{T}\\&-[(\mathbf{\Theta'W\Theta})^{-1}\otimes\mathbf{W\Theta}(\mathbf{\Theta'W\Theta})^{-1}\mathbf{\Theta'W}]\\&+[(\mathbf{\Theta'W\Theta})^{-1}\otimes\mathbf{W}].\end{aligned} \tag{16.46}$$

Also within the expression in (16.42) is the term

$$\frac{\partial[\mathbf{\Gamma}^{-1},\mathbf{0}]'^c}{\partial\mathbf{\Theta}^c}=\partial\begin{bmatrix}\mathbf{\Gamma}^{-1'}\\\mathbf{0}\end{bmatrix}^c\Big/\partial\begin{bmatrix}\mathbf{\Gamma}\\\mathbf{B}\end{bmatrix}^c. \tag{16.47}$$

The easiest way of evaluating this is to find first the derivative

$$\begin{aligned}\partial\begin{bmatrix}\mathbf{\Gamma}^{-1'c}\\\mathbf{0}^c\end{bmatrix}\Big/\partial\begin{bmatrix}\mathbf{\Gamma}^c\\\mathbf{B}^c\end{bmatrix}&=\begin{bmatrix}\partial\mathbf{\Gamma}^{-1'c}/\partial\mathbf{\Gamma}^c, & \partial\mathbf{\Gamma}^{-1'c}/\partial\mathbf{B}^c\\\mathbf{0}\otimes\mathbf{0}, & \mathbf{0}\otimes\mathbf{0}\end{bmatrix}\\&=-\begin{bmatrix}(\mathbf{\Gamma}^{-1}\otimes\mathbf{\Gamma}^{-1'})\textcircled{T}, & \mathbf{0}\otimes\mathbf{0}\\\mathbf{0}\otimes\mathbf{0}, & \mathbf{0}\otimes\mathbf{0}\end{bmatrix}.\end{aligned} \tag{16.48}$$

By rearranging this, we get

$$\frac{\partial[\mathbf{\Gamma}^{-1},\mathbf{0}]'^c}{\partial\mathbf{\Theta}^c}=-\left([\mathbf{\Gamma}^{-1},\mathbf{0}]\otimes\begin{bmatrix}\mathbf{\Gamma}^{-1'}\\\mathbf{0}\end{bmatrix}\right)\textcircled{T} \tag{16.49}$$

By substituting the expressions under (16.46) and (16.49) into the expression under (16.42), we finally arrive at

$$\begin{aligned}T^{-1}\frac{\partial(\partial L^*/\partial\mathbf{\Theta}^c)'}{\partial\mathbf{\Theta}^c}=&-\left([\mathbf{\Gamma}^{-1},\mathbf{0}]\otimes\begin{bmatrix}\mathbf{\Gamma}^{-1'}\\\mathbf{0}\end{bmatrix}\right)\textcircled{T}\\&+[(\mathbf{\Theta'W\Theta})^{-1}\mathbf{\Theta'W}\otimes\mathbf{W\Theta}(\mathbf{\Theta'W\Theta})^{-1}]\textcircled{T}\\&+[(\mathbf{\Theta'W\Theta})^{-1}\otimes\mathbf{W\Theta}(\mathbf{\Theta'W\Theta})^{-1}\mathbf{\Theta'W}]\\&-[(\mathbf{\Theta'W\Theta})\otimes\mathbf{W}].\end{aligned} \tag{16.50}$$

We shall now find the probability limit of this expression. We shall invoke the usual assumption that the explanatory variables comprised in the matrix $\mathbf{X}$ are generated in such a way that $\text{plim}(\mathbf{X'X}/T)=\mathbf{M_{XX}}$ is a matrix of finite values and $\text{plim}(\mathbf{X'U}/T)=\mathbf{0}$. The latter assumption implies that $\text{plim}(\mathbf{X'V}/T)=-\text{plim}(\mathbf{X'U}/T)\mathbf{\Gamma}^{-1}=\mathbf{0}$. From our assumptions concerning the distributions of the vectors $\mathbf{u}_{t.}$ and $\mathbf{v}_{t.}$ come the further results that

$\text{plim}(\mathbf{U}'\mathbf{U}/T) = \boldsymbol{\Sigma}$ and $\text{plim}(\mathbf{V}'\mathbf{V}/T) = \boldsymbol{\Omega}$. We may deduce that

$$\text{(16.51)} \qquad \text{plim}\left(\frac{\mathbf{X}'\mathbf{Y}}{T}\right) = \mathbf{M}_{\mathbf{XX}}\boldsymbol{\Pi},$$

$$\text{(16.52)} \qquad \text{plim}\left(\frac{\mathbf{Y}'\mathbf{Y}}{T}\right) = \mathbf{M}_{\mathbf{YY}} = \boldsymbol{\Pi}'\mathbf{M}_{\mathbf{XX}}\boldsymbol{\Pi} + \boldsymbol{\Omega}.$$

All that we require now in order to find probability limit of $T^{-1}\,\partial(\partial L^*/\partial\boldsymbol{\Theta}^c)'/\partial\boldsymbol{\Theta}^c$ are the probability limits of $\mathbf{W}\boldsymbol{\Theta}$ and $\boldsymbol{\Theta}'\mathbf{W}\boldsymbol{\Theta}$. These are

$$\text{(16.53)} \qquad \begin{aligned} \text{plim}(\mathbf{W}\boldsymbol{\Theta}) &= \text{plim}\left(T^{-1}\begin{bmatrix}\mathbf{Y}'\mathbf{Y}\boldsymbol{\Gamma} + \mathbf{Y}'\mathbf{X}\mathbf{B} \\ \mathbf{X}'\mathbf{Y}\boldsymbol{\Gamma} + \mathbf{X}'\mathbf{X}\mathbf{B}\end{bmatrix}\right) \\ &= \text{plim}\left(T^{-1}\begin{bmatrix}(\mathbf{Y}'\mathbf{Y} - \mathbf{Y}'\mathbf{X}\boldsymbol{\Pi})\boldsymbol{\Gamma} \\ \mathbf{X}'\mathbf{U}\end{bmatrix}\right) = \begin{bmatrix}\boldsymbol{\Omega} \\ \mathbf{0}\end{bmatrix}\boldsymbol{\Gamma} \end{aligned}$$

and

$$\text{(16.54)} \qquad \begin{aligned} \text{plim}(\boldsymbol{\Theta}'\mathbf{W}\boldsymbol{\Theta}) &= \text{plim}\,\frac{(\mathbf{Y}\boldsymbol{\Gamma} + \mathbf{X}\mathbf{B})'(\mathbf{Y}\boldsymbol{\Gamma} + \mathbf{X}\mathbf{B})}{T} \\ &= \text{plim}\left(\frac{\mathbf{U}'\mathbf{U}}{T}\right) = \boldsymbol{\Sigma}. \end{aligned}$$

Thus, by taking the probability limits of the factors of the expression in (16.50), we get

$$\text{(16.55)} \qquad \begin{aligned} \text{plim}\left(T^{-1}\frac{\partial(\partial L^*/\partial\boldsymbol{\Theta}^c)'}{\partial\boldsymbol{\Theta}^c}\right) = &-\left([\boldsymbol{\Gamma}^{-1}, \mathbf{0}] \otimes \begin{bmatrix}\boldsymbol{\Gamma}^{-1\prime} \\ \mathbf{0}\end{bmatrix}\right)\textcircled{T} \\ &+\left(\boldsymbol{\Sigma}^{-1}\boldsymbol{\Gamma}'[\boldsymbol{\Omega}, \mathbf{0}] \otimes \begin{bmatrix}\boldsymbol{\Omega} \\ \mathbf{0}\end{bmatrix}\boldsymbol{\Gamma}\boldsymbol{\Sigma}^{-1}\right)\textcircled{T} \\ &+\left(\boldsymbol{\Sigma}^{-1} \otimes \begin{bmatrix}\boldsymbol{\Omega} \\ \mathbf{0}\end{bmatrix}\boldsymbol{\Gamma}\boldsymbol{\Sigma}^{-1}\boldsymbol{\Gamma}'[\boldsymbol{\Omega}, \mathbf{0}]\right) \\ &-(\boldsymbol{\Sigma} \otimes \mathbf{M}) \end{aligned}$$

where $\mathbf{M} = \text{plim}(\mathbf{W})$. The first two terms of this expression cancel each other and the last two terms combine to give

$$\text{(16.56)} \qquad \begin{aligned} \text{plim}\left(T^{-1}\frac{\partial(\partial L^*/\partial\boldsymbol{\Theta}^c)'}{\partial\boldsymbol{\Theta}^c}\right) &= -\left(\boldsymbol{\Sigma}^{-1} \otimes \begin{bmatrix}\mathbf{M}_{\mathbf{YY}} - \boldsymbol{\Omega}, & \mathbf{M}_{\mathbf{YX}} \\ \mathbf{M}_{\mathbf{XY}}, & \mathbf{M}_{\mathbf{XX}}\end{bmatrix}\right) \\ &= -\left(\boldsymbol{\Sigma}^{-1} \otimes \begin{bmatrix}\boldsymbol{\Pi}'\mathbf{M}_{\mathbf{XX}}\boldsymbol{\Pi}, & \boldsymbol{\Pi}'\mathbf{M}_{\mathbf{XX}} \\ \mathbf{M}_{\mathbf{XX}}\boldsymbol{\Pi}, & \mathbf{M}_{\mathbf{XX}}\end{bmatrix}\right). \end{aligned}$$

To find the dispersion matrix $\mathbf{C}_1$ of the limiting distribution of the vector $\sqrt{T}(\hat{\boldsymbol{\Theta}} - \boldsymbol{\Theta})$, we carry the expression above to the equation in (16.40).

We may conclude our business by considering the case of the full-information estimates where the *a priori* information is in the form of exclusion restrictions specifying that certain variables are absent from certain equations and normalization rules identifying the dependent variables in each of the M structural equations. In that case, the dispersion matrix of the estimates of the coefficients of the explanatory variables is the inverse of a matrix obtained from

$$(16.57) \qquad \boldsymbol{\Sigma}^{-1} \otimes \begin{bmatrix} \boldsymbol{\Pi}'\mathbf{M}_{\mathbf{XX}}\boldsymbol{\Pi}, & \boldsymbol{\Pi}'\mathbf{M}_{\mathbf{XX}} \\ \mathbf{M}_{\mathbf{XX}}\boldsymbol{\Pi}, & \mathbf{M}_{\mathbf{XX}} \end{bmatrix}$$

by deleting the rows and columns corresponding to the restrictions.

The limiting distribution of the full-information maximum-likelihood estimates is the same as the limiting distribution of the three-stage least-squares estimates. There is no difficulty in understanding this result once a comparison is made of the two sets of estimating equations under (15.61) and (16.36).

The computation of the full-information maximum-likelihood estimates

If the values of $\boldsymbol{\Sigma}$ and $\boldsymbol{\Omega}$ were known, then we would be able to obtain full-information maximum-likelihood or FIML estimates of the structural parameters $\boldsymbol{\Gamma}$, $\mathbf{B}$ by the simple process of solving a set of linear equations in the form of (16.36). However, when $\boldsymbol{\Sigma}$ and $\boldsymbol{\Omega}$ are unknown, we must use the values specified by the estimating equations (16.37) and (16.38). The latter equations comprise the unknown values $\boldsymbol{\Gamma}$, $\mathbf{B}$, and $\boldsymbol{\Pi}=-\mathbf{B}\boldsymbol{\Gamma}^{-1}$, and so we find ourselves confronted by a complicated system of non-linear equations in $\boldsymbol{\Gamma}$, $\mathbf{B}$, $\boldsymbol{\Omega}$, and $\boldsymbol{\Sigma}$ which is incapable of being solved by any direct algebraic method.

One way of avoiding this difficulty is to assign the determination of the values of $\boldsymbol{\Sigma}$ and $\boldsymbol{\Omega}$ to a separate estimating system not depending on the FIML values of $\boldsymbol{\Gamma}$, $\mathbf{B}$; and, in fact, this is the approach adopted in the method of three-stage least-squares. To obtain true FIML estimates, we must devise an iterative procedure that will give rise to a sequence of estimates converging on a set of values that satisfy all of the estimating equations simultaneously.

To describe one such procedure, let us imagine that the kth iteration has provided us with the estimates $\boldsymbol{\Gamma}_k$, $\mathbf{B}_k$, $\boldsymbol{\Sigma}_k$ and $\boldsymbol{\Omega}_k$. We can proceed to set $\boldsymbol{\Sigma}=\boldsymbol{\Sigma}_k$ and $\boldsymbol{\Omega}=\boldsymbol{\Omega}_k$ in the equation (16.36). Solving the resulting system provides us with the revised estimates $\boldsymbol{\Gamma}_{k+1}$, $\mathbf{B}_{k+1}$. Next we can set $\boldsymbol{\Gamma}=\boldsymbol{\Gamma}_{k+1}$, $\mathbf{B}=\mathbf{B}_{k+1}$, and $\boldsymbol{\Pi}=\boldsymbol{\Pi}_{k+1}=-\mathbf{B}_{k+1}\boldsymbol{\Gamma}_{k+1}^{-1}$ in equations (16.37) and (16.38) to obtain from each respectively the revised estimates $\boldsymbol{\Sigma}_{k+1}$ and $\boldsymbol{\Omega}_{k+1}$. The algorithm can be represented by the equations

$$(16.58)\qquad \begin{bmatrix} \boldsymbol{\Sigma}_k^{-1}\otimes\begin{bmatrix}\mathbf{Y}'\mathbf{Y}-T\boldsymbol{\Omega}_k, & \mathbf{Y}'\mathbf{X}\\ \mathbf{X}'\mathbf{Y}, & \mathbf{X}'\mathbf{X}\end{bmatrix}, & \mathbf{R}'\\ \mathbf{R}, & \mathbf{0}\end{bmatrix}\begin{bmatrix}\begin{bmatrix}\boldsymbol{\Gamma}\\ \mathbf{B}\end{bmatrix}^c_{k+1}\\ \boldsymbol{\lambda}_{k+1}\end{bmatrix}=\begin{bmatrix}\mathbf{0}\\ \mathbf{0}\\ \mathbf{r}\end{bmatrix},$$

$$\boldsymbol{\Sigma}_{k+1}=\frac{(\mathbf{Y}\boldsymbol{\Gamma}_{k+1}+\mathbf{X}\mathbf{B}_{k+1})'(\mathbf{Y}\boldsymbol{\Gamma}_{k+1}+\mathbf{X}\mathbf{B}_{k+1})}{T},$$

$$\boldsymbol{\Omega}_{k+1}=\frac{(\mathbf{Y}-\mathbf{X}\boldsymbol{\Pi}_{k+1})'(\mathbf{Y}-\mathbf{X}\boldsymbol{\Pi}_{k+1})}{T}=\boldsymbol{\Gamma}'^{-1}_{k+1}\boldsymbol{\Omega}_{k+1}\boldsymbol{\Gamma}^{-1}_{k+1}.$$

To specify this procedure completely, we must choose the initial conditions. It seems reasonable to set $\boldsymbol{\Sigma}_0=\mathbf{I}$ and $\boldsymbol{\Omega}_0=\mathbf{Y}'[\mathbf{I}-\mathbf{X}(\mathbf{X}'\mathbf{X})^{-1}\mathbf{X}']\mathbf{Y}/T$. The latter is the unrestricted maximum-likelihood estimator of the reduced-form dispersion matrix that was previously given in (13.33).

Reference to (15.54) and (15.55) shows that, with the present choice of initial conditions, the estimates $\boldsymbol{\Gamma}_1$, $\mathbf{B}_1$ of the first iteration are simply the two-stage least-squares estimates. The revised estimates $\boldsymbol{\Gamma}_2$, $\mathbf{B}_2$ of the second iteration, which are obtained by replacing $\boldsymbol{\Sigma}_0$ and $\boldsymbol{\Omega}_0$ in the estimating equations by $\boldsymbol{\Sigma}_1$ and $\boldsymbol{\Omega}_1$ respectively, are not the same as the three-stage least-squares estimates. The three-stage least-squares estimating equations incorporate the revised estimate $\boldsymbol{\Sigma}_1$ but retain the original estimate $\boldsymbol{\Omega}_0$. There can be little justification for this failure to revise the estimate of $\boldsymbol{\Omega}$.

Our method of obtaining FIML estimates is simply an extension of the method proposed in Chapter 13 for finding the maximum-likelihood estimates of $\mathbf{B}$ and $\boldsymbol{\Sigma}$ in the restricted model $[\mathbf{Y}^c, (\mathbf{I}\otimes\mathbf{X})\mathbf{B}^c \mid \mathbf{R}\mathbf{B}^c=\mathbf{r}, \boldsymbol{\Sigma}\otimes\mathbf{I}]$. We demonstrated that the latter method amounted to a modified version of the Newton–Raphson procedure wherein the derivative $\partial(\partial L^*/\partial\mathbf{B}^c)'/\partial\mathbf{B}^c$ required by the algorithm had been replaced by an approximation of its large sample value in the form of the matrix $-\boldsymbol{\Sigma}_k^{-1}\otimes\mathbf{X}'\mathbf{X}$. It is easy to demonstrate along similar lines that our present method also amounts to a modified Newton–Raphson procedure. In this case, the derivative $\partial(\partial L^*/\partial\boldsymbol{\Theta}^c)'/\partial\boldsymbol{\Theta}^c$ has been replaced by the approximation

$$(16.59)\qquad -\boldsymbol{\Sigma}_k^{-1}\otimes\begin{bmatrix}\mathbf{Y}'\mathbf{Y}-T\boldsymbol{\Omega}_k, & \mathbf{Y}'\mathbf{X}\\ \mathbf{X}'\mathbf{Y}, & \mathbf{X}'\mathbf{X}\end{bmatrix}.$$

Amongst the various procedures for finding the FIML estimates is one that has been proposed by Durbin [**31**] and which is based on the alternative form of the estimating equations given in (16.35). This procedure is similar to the one we have described except that it involves successive revisions of $\boldsymbol{\Sigma}$ and $\boldsymbol{\Pi}$ within the estimating equations instead of $\boldsymbol{\Sigma}$ and $\boldsymbol{\Omega}$. The same procedure has been presented by Lyttkens in [**76**] under the guise of an iterative instrumental variables method.

LIMITED-INFORMATION ESTIMATION

A limited-information method is one which concentrates upon a subset of the equations of a simultaneous system, which is usually a single equation, while disregarding the structural relationships and parametric restrictions which bind the system as a whole.

There are various reasons that prompt the study of limited-information methods. In the first place, while it is true that the fullest use of the available information results in the most efficient estimator, the system-wide full-information methods impose a considerable computational burden. Therefore it is quite common to accept the loss of efficiency entailed in estimating each equation separately in order to save time and expense in computation. In the second place, a lack of identification of some of the equations may prevent the use of a system-wide full-information procedure. Equally, doubts about the appropriate specifications in parts of the system may encourage the investigator to adopt methods whose success depends only upon a correct specification within the subsystem currently being estimated. Finally, there are cases where interest lies only in estimating a single relationship within the system and where the trouble involved in estimating the entire system would vastly outweigh the benefit of improving the efficiency of the desired estimates.

The classical limited-information maximum-likelihood or LIML estimator of single equations which was originally derived by Anderson and Rubin [**9**] applies to the conventional case where the *a priori* information relating to the structural parameters takes the form of a set of exclusion restrictions and a normalization rule. The original derivation has the peculiarity that the normalization rule, which serves to identify the dependent variable in the structural equation, is largely ignored and is only imposed after the estimate of the vector of structural parameters has been determined up to a scalar factor. If the normalization rule is imposed throughout the derivation, then an alternative estimator arises which is closer in some respects to the two-stage least-squares or 2SLS estimator than is the classical estimator of Anderson and Rubin.

We shall follow the original derivation of Anderson and Rubin in most respects, but we shall begin by representing the restrictions in a rather general form which allows us to incorporate the normalization rule and which avoids the complications that arise from partitioning the data matrices into sets of included and excluded variables. We shall then specialize the restrictions to the conventional form. Finally, by suppressing the normalization rule, we shall derive the classical estimator as a special case.

If we ignore the subscripts which indicate the location of the single structural equation within the system as a whole, then we can write this equation as

$$(16.60) \qquad \mathbf{y}_{t.}\boldsymbol{\gamma}+\mathbf{x}_{t.}\boldsymbol{\beta}+u_t=0.$$

The identity relating the structural parameters to the reduced-form parameters can be written as

$$(16.61) \qquad \boldsymbol{\Pi\gamma}+\boldsymbol{\beta}=\mathbf{0},$$

and the restrictions on the structural parameters can be represented in the general manner by writing

$$(16.62) \qquad \mathbf{R}_1\boldsymbol{\gamma}+\mathbf{R}_2\boldsymbol{\beta}=\mathbf{r}.$$

We retain our existing assumptions concerning the distribution of the stochastic elements of the model. Therefore, if we take L^* to represent the log-likelihood function in (16.9), we can write the function that is to be maximized as

$$(16.63) \qquad L^{\mathrm{R}}=L^*-\boldsymbol{\delta}'(\boldsymbol{\Pi\gamma}+\boldsymbol{\beta})-\boldsymbol{\phi}'(\mathbf{R}_1\boldsymbol{\gamma}+\mathbf{R}_2\boldsymbol{\beta}-\mathbf{r}).$$

The estimating equations of the reduced-form parameters

On differentiating L^{R} with respect to $\boldsymbol{\Pi}$ and setting the result to zero, we obtain the condition

$$(16.64) \qquad (\mathbf{X}'\mathbf{Y}-\mathbf{X}'\mathbf{X}\boldsymbol{\Pi})\boldsymbol{\Omega}^{-1}-\boldsymbol{\delta\gamma}'=\mathbf{0}$$

which gives us

$$(16.65) \qquad \boldsymbol{\Pi}=(\mathbf{X}'\mathbf{X})^{-1}\mathbf{X}'\mathbf{Y}-(\mathbf{X}'\mathbf{X})^{-1}\boldsymbol{\delta\gamma}'\boldsymbol{\Omega}.$$

The first term in this expression is simply the ordinary least-squares estimate of $\boldsymbol{\Pi}$, and the second term owes its presence to the restrictions. Postmultiplying both sides of the equation by $\boldsymbol{\gamma}$ and using the condition $\boldsymbol{\Pi\gamma}=-\boldsymbol{\beta}$ enables us to find

$$(16.66) \qquad \boldsymbol{\delta}=(\boldsymbol{\gamma}'\boldsymbol{\Omega\gamma})^{-1}\mathbf{X}'(\mathbf{Y}\boldsymbol{\gamma}+\mathbf{X}\boldsymbol{\beta}).$$

Inserting this back in (16.65) gives us an equation which enables us to express the estimator of $\boldsymbol{\Pi}$ as

$$(16.67) \qquad \tilde{\boldsymbol{\Pi}}=(\mathbf{X}'\mathbf{X})^{-1}\mathbf{X}'\mathbf{Y}-(\tilde{\boldsymbol{\gamma}}'\tilde{\boldsymbol{\Omega}}\tilde{\boldsymbol{\gamma}})^{-1}(\mathbf{X}'\mathbf{X})^{-1}\mathbf{X}'(\mathbf{Y}\tilde{\boldsymbol{\gamma}}+\mathbf{X}\tilde{\boldsymbol{\beta}})\tilde{\boldsymbol{\gamma}}'\tilde{\boldsymbol{\Omega}}$$

where $\tilde{\boldsymbol{\gamma}}$, $\tilde{\boldsymbol{\beta}}$ and $\tilde{\boldsymbol{\Omega}}$ are the estimates that have yet to be determined.

The estimating equation of the dispersion matrix

Our restricted estimate $\tilde{\mathbf{\Omega}}$ of the reduced-form dispersion matrix is derived from the maximum-likelihood estimating equation

$$\mathbf{\Omega}(\mathbf{\Pi}) = \frac{(\mathbf{Y}-\mathbf{X\Pi})'(\mathbf{Y}-\mathbf{X\Pi})}{T} \tag{16.68}$$

previously given in (16.21).

From (16.67), we obtain the expression

$$(\mathbf{Y}-\mathbf{X}\tilde{\mathbf{\Pi}}) = (\mathbf{I}-\mathbf{P})\mathbf{Y} + (\tilde{\boldsymbol{\gamma}}'\tilde{\mathbf{\Omega}}\tilde{\boldsymbol{\gamma}})^{-1}\mathbf{P}(\mathbf{Y}\tilde{\boldsymbol{\gamma}}+\mathbf{X}\tilde{\boldsymbol{\beta}})\tilde{\boldsymbol{\gamma}}'\tilde{\mathbf{\Omega}} \tag{16.69}$$

where $\mathbf{P}=\mathbf{X}(\mathbf{X}'\mathbf{X})^{-1}\mathbf{X}$ is the orthogonal projector on $\mathcal{M}(\mathbf{X})$. By substituting this into (16.68), and using the symmetry and idempotency of $\mathbf{P}$ and $\mathbf{I}-\mathbf{P}$ and the condition $\mathbf{P}'(\mathbf{I}-\mathbf{P})=\mathbf{0}$, we find that

$$\tilde{\mathbf{\Omega}} = \frac{\mathbf{Y}'(\mathbf{I}-\mathbf{P})\mathbf{Y}}{T} + \left\{\frac{(\mathbf{Y}\tilde{\boldsymbol{\gamma}}+\mathbf{X}\tilde{\boldsymbol{\beta}})'\mathbf{P}(\mathbf{Y}\tilde{\boldsymbol{\gamma}}+\mathbf{X}\tilde{\boldsymbol{\beta}})}{T(\tilde{\boldsymbol{\gamma}}'\tilde{\mathbf{\Omega}}\tilde{\boldsymbol{\gamma}})^2}\right\}\tilde{\mathbf{\Omega}}\tilde{\boldsymbol{\gamma}}\tilde{\boldsymbol{\gamma}}'\tilde{\mathbf{\Omega}}. \tag{16.70}$$

We can recognize the first term on the RHS of this equation as the unrestricted estimate

$$\hat{\mathbf{\Omega}} = \frac{\mathbf{Y}'(\mathbf{I}-\mathbf{P})\mathbf{Y}}{T} = \mathbf{W} \tag{16.71}$$

of the reduced-form dispersion matrix. To distinguish this estimate from $\tilde{\mathbf{\Omega}}$, we shall denote it by $\mathbf{W}$ throughout the present section, but thereafter we shall revert to the notation $\hat{\mathbf{\Omega}}$. Postmultiplying both sides of (16.70) by $\tilde{\boldsymbol{\gamma}}$ gives

$$\tilde{\mathbf{\Omega}}\tilde{\boldsymbol{\gamma}} = \frac{\mathbf{Y}'(\mathbf{I}-\mathbf{P})\mathbf{Y}\tilde{\boldsymbol{\gamma}}}{T} + \left\{\frac{(\mathbf{Y}\tilde{\boldsymbol{\gamma}}+\mathbf{X}\tilde{\boldsymbol{\beta}})'\mathbf{P}(\mathbf{Y}\tilde{\boldsymbol{\gamma}}+\mathbf{X}\tilde{\boldsymbol{\beta}})}{T\tilde{\boldsymbol{\gamma}}'\tilde{\mathbf{\Omega}}\tilde{\boldsymbol{\gamma}}}\right\}\tilde{\mathbf{\Omega}}\tilde{\boldsymbol{\gamma}}. \tag{16.72}$$

Then, on premultiplying by $\tilde{\boldsymbol{\gamma}}'$ and using $\mathbf{PX}=\mathbf{X}$, we find that

$$\begin{aligned}\tilde{\boldsymbol{\gamma}}'\tilde{\mathbf{\Omega}}\tilde{\boldsymbol{\gamma}} &= \frac{\tilde{\boldsymbol{\gamma}}'\mathbf{Y}'(\mathbf{I}-\mathbf{P})\mathbf{Y}\tilde{\boldsymbol{\gamma}} + (\mathbf{Y}\tilde{\boldsymbol{\gamma}}+\mathbf{X}\tilde{\boldsymbol{\beta}})'\mathbf{P}(\mathbf{Y}\tilde{\boldsymbol{\gamma}}+\mathbf{X}\tilde{\boldsymbol{\beta}})}{T} \\ &= \frac{(\mathbf{Y}\tilde{\boldsymbol{\gamma}}+\mathbf{X}\tilde{\boldsymbol{\beta}})'(\mathbf{Y}\tilde{\boldsymbol{\gamma}}+\mathbf{X}\tilde{\boldsymbol{\beta}})}{T}.\end{aligned} \tag{16.73}$$

Putting this back in (16.72) gives

$$\begin{aligned}\frac{\mathbf{Y}'(\mathbf{I}-\mathbf{P})\mathbf{Y}\tilde{\boldsymbol{\gamma}}}{T} &= \left\{1 - \frac{(\mathbf{Y}\tilde{\boldsymbol{\gamma}}+\mathbf{X}\tilde{\boldsymbol{\beta}})'\mathbf{P}(\mathbf{Y}\tilde{\boldsymbol{\gamma}}+\mathbf{X}\tilde{\boldsymbol{\beta}})}{(\mathbf{Y}\tilde{\boldsymbol{\gamma}}+\mathbf{X}\tilde{\boldsymbol{\beta}})'(\mathbf{Y}\tilde{\boldsymbol{\gamma}}+\mathbf{X}\tilde{\boldsymbol{\beta}})}\right\}\tilde{\mathbf{\Omega}}\tilde{\boldsymbol{\gamma}} \\ &= \left\{\frac{\tilde{\boldsymbol{\gamma}}'\mathbf{Y}'(\mathbf{I}-\mathbf{P})\mathbf{Y}\tilde{\boldsymbol{\gamma}}}{(\mathbf{Y}\tilde{\boldsymbol{\gamma}}+\mathbf{X}\tilde{\boldsymbol{\beta}})'(\mathbf{Y}\tilde{\boldsymbol{\gamma}}+\mathbf{X}\tilde{\boldsymbol{\beta}})}\right\}\tilde{\mathbf{\Omega}}\tilde{\boldsymbol{\gamma}};\end{aligned} \tag{16.74}$$

and, since $\mathbf{Y}'(\mathbf{I}-\mathbf{P})\mathbf{Y}/T=\mathbf{W}$, the latter provides

$$(16.75)\qquad T\tilde{\mathbf{\Omega}}\tilde{\boldsymbol{\gamma}}=\left\{\frac{(\mathbf{Y}\tilde{\boldsymbol{\gamma}}+\mathbf{X}\tilde{\boldsymbol{\beta}})'(\mathbf{Y}\tilde{\boldsymbol{\gamma}}+\mathbf{X}\tilde{\boldsymbol{\beta}})}{\tilde{\boldsymbol{\gamma}}'\mathbf{W}\tilde{\boldsymbol{\gamma}}}\right\}\mathbf{W}\tilde{\boldsymbol{\gamma}}.$$

By using the expression for $\tilde{\mathbf{\Omega}}\tilde{\boldsymbol{\gamma}}$ resulting from this equation, we can derive from (16.70) a restricted estimator of $\mathbf{\Omega}$ of the form

$$(16.76)\qquad \tilde{\mathbf{\Omega}}=\mathbf{W}+\left\{\frac{(\mathbf{Y}\tilde{\boldsymbol{\gamma}}+\mathbf{X}\tilde{\boldsymbol{\beta}})'\mathbf{P}(\mathbf{Y}\tilde{\boldsymbol{\gamma}}+\mathbf{X}\tilde{\boldsymbol{\beta}})}{T(\tilde{\boldsymbol{\gamma}}'\mathbf{W}\tilde{\boldsymbol{\gamma}})^2}\right\}\mathbf{W}\tilde{\boldsymbol{\gamma}}\tilde{\boldsymbol{\gamma}}'\mathbf{W}.$$

Estimating the structural parameters

Now let us differentiate the function L^R in respect of the structural parameters. Setting the derivatives to zero gives the conditions

$$(16.77)\qquad \tilde{\mathbf{\Pi}}'\boldsymbol{\delta}+\mathbf{R}_1'\boldsymbol{\phi}=\mathbf{0}$$

and

$$(16.78)\qquad \boldsymbol{\delta}+\mathbf{R}_2'\boldsymbol{\phi}=\mathbf{0}.$$

By substituting the expressions for $\tilde{\mathbf{\Pi}}$ and $\boldsymbol{\delta}$ from (16.67) and (16.66) respectively into the first of these conditions, we obtain the equation

$$(16.79)\qquad (\tilde{\boldsymbol{\gamma}}'\tilde{\mathbf{\Omega}}\tilde{\boldsymbol{\gamma}})^{-1}\left\{\mathbf{Y}'\mathbf{P}(\mathbf{Y}\tilde{\boldsymbol{\gamma}}+\mathbf{X}\tilde{\boldsymbol{\beta}})-\frac{(\mathbf{Y}\tilde{\boldsymbol{\gamma}}+\mathbf{X}\tilde{\boldsymbol{\beta}})'\mathbf{P}(\mathbf{Y}\tilde{\boldsymbol{\gamma}}+\mathbf{X}\tilde{\boldsymbol{\beta}})\tilde{\mathbf{\Omega}}\tilde{\boldsymbol{\gamma}}}{\tilde{\boldsymbol{\gamma}}'\tilde{\mathbf{\Omega}}\boldsymbol{\gamma}}\right\} +\mathbf{R}_1'\boldsymbol{\phi}=\mathbf{0}.$$

But, as equations (16.73) and (16.74) together indicate, we have

$$(16.80)\qquad \begin{aligned}\left\{\frac{(\mathbf{Y}\tilde{\boldsymbol{\gamma}}+\mathbf{X}\tilde{\boldsymbol{\beta}})'\mathbf{P}(\mathbf{Y}\tilde{\boldsymbol{\gamma}}+\mathbf{X}\tilde{\boldsymbol{\beta}})}{\tilde{\boldsymbol{\gamma}}'\tilde{\mathbf{\Omega}}\tilde{\boldsymbol{\gamma}}}\right\}\tilde{\mathbf{\Omega}}\tilde{\boldsymbol{\gamma}}&=T\left\{\frac{(\mathbf{Y}\tilde{\boldsymbol{\gamma}}+\mathbf{X}\tilde{\boldsymbol{\beta}})'\mathbf{P}(\mathbf{Y}\tilde{\boldsymbol{\gamma}}+\mathbf{X}\tilde{\boldsymbol{\beta}})}{(\mathbf{Y}\tilde{\boldsymbol{\gamma}}+\mathbf{X}\tilde{\boldsymbol{\beta}})'(\mathbf{Y}\tilde{\boldsymbol{\gamma}}+\mathbf{X}\tilde{\boldsymbol{\beta}})}\right\}\tilde{\mathbf{\Omega}}\tilde{\boldsymbol{\gamma}}\\&=T\tilde{\mathbf{\Omega}}\tilde{\boldsymbol{\gamma}}-\mathbf{Y}'(\mathbf{I}-\mathbf{P})\mathbf{Y}\tilde{\boldsymbol{\gamma}};\end{aligned}$$

so it follows that (16.79) can be rewritten as

$$(16.81)\qquad (\tilde{\boldsymbol{\gamma}}'\tilde{\mathbf{\Omega}}\tilde{\boldsymbol{\gamma}})^{-1}\{(\mathbf{Y}'\mathbf{Y}-T\tilde{\mathbf{\Omega}})\tilde{\boldsymbol{\gamma}}+\mathbf{Y}'\mathbf{X}\tilde{\boldsymbol{\beta}}\}+\mathbf{R}_1'\boldsymbol{\phi}=\mathbf{0}.$$

Next, by substituting the expression in (16.66) in place of $\boldsymbol{\delta}$ in the second condition (16.78), we find that

$$(16.82)\qquad (\tilde{\boldsymbol{\gamma}}'\tilde{\mathbf{\Omega}}\tilde{\boldsymbol{\gamma}})^{-1}\{\mathbf{X}'\mathbf{Y}\tilde{\boldsymbol{\gamma}}+\mathbf{X}'\mathbf{X}\tilde{\boldsymbol{\beta}}\}+\mathbf{R}_2'\boldsymbol{\phi}=\mathbf{0}.$$

On defining $\boldsymbol{\mu}=(\tilde{\boldsymbol{\gamma}}'\tilde{\mathbf{\Omega}}\tilde{\boldsymbol{\gamma}})\boldsymbol{\phi}$ and compounding the equations (16.81) and (16.82) with the equations of the restrictions from (16.62), we obtain the system

$$(16.83)\qquad \begin{bmatrix}\mathbf{Y}'\mathbf{Y}-T\tilde{\mathbf{\Omega}}, & \mathbf{Y}'\mathbf{X}, & \mathbf{R}_1'\\ \mathbf{X}'\mathbf{Y}, & \mathbf{X}'\mathbf{X}, & \mathbf{R}_2'\\ \mathbf{R}_1, & \mathbf{R}_2, & \mathbf{0}\end{bmatrix}\begin{bmatrix}\tilde{\boldsymbol{\gamma}}\\ \tilde{\boldsymbol{\beta}}\\ \boldsymbol{\mu}\end{bmatrix}=\begin{bmatrix}\mathbf{0}\\ \mathbf{0}\\ \mathbf{r}\end{bmatrix}$$

wherein $\tilde{\boldsymbol{\Omega}}$ is the restricted maximum-likelihood estimate of the dispersion matrix provided by the equation (16.76). However, reference to (16.75) shows that the restricted maximum-likelihood estimate of the dispersion matrix is related to the unrestricted estimate $\hat{\boldsymbol{\Omega}}=\mathbf{W}$ by the identity

$$T\tilde{\boldsymbol{\Omega}}\tilde{\boldsymbol{\gamma}}=\lambda\hat{\boldsymbol{\Omega}}\tilde{\boldsymbol{\gamma}} \tag{16.84}$$

where

$$\lambda=\frac{(\mathbf{Y}\tilde{\boldsymbol{\gamma}}+\mathbf{X}\tilde{\boldsymbol{\beta}})'(\mathbf{Y}\tilde{\boldsymbol{\gamma}}+\mathbf{X}\tilde{\boldsymbol{\beta}})}{\tilde{\boldsymbol{\gamma}}'\hat{\boldsymbol{\Omega}}\tilde{\boldsymbol{\gamma}}}. \tag{16.85}$$

Therefore the system (16.83) is equivalent to the system

$$\begin{bmatrix}\mathbf{Y}'\mathbf{Y}-\lambda\hat{\boldsymbol{\Omega}}, & \mathbf{Y}'\mathbf{X}, & \mathbf{R}_1' \\ \mathbf{X}'\mathbf{Y}, & \mathbf{X}'\mathbf{X}, & \mathbf{R}_2' \\ \mathbf{R}_1, & \mathbf{R}_2, & \mathbf{0}\end{bmatrix}\begin{bmatrix}\tilde{\boldsymbol{\gamma}} \\ \tilde{\boldsymbol{\beta}} \\ \boldsymbol{\mu}\end{bmatrix}=\begin{bmatrix}\mathbf{0} \\ \mathbf{0} \\ \mathbf{r}\end{bmatrix} \tag{16.86}$$

The computation of the limited-information maximum-likelihood estimates

It is now apparent that, given $\mathbf{r}\neq\mathbf{0}$, there are two distinct procedures that may be used in finding the limited-information maximum-likelihood estimates. The first procedure involves the iterative solution of the equations (16.83) and (16.76). We begin by replacing $\tilde{\boldsymbol{\Omega}}$ by an initial value which can only be the unrestricted estimate $\mathbf{W}=\hat{\boldsymbol{\Omega}}$. By solving the resulting system, we obtain first-round estimates of $\boldsymbol{\gamma}$ and $\boldsymbol{\beta}$ which are, in fact, the two-stage least-squares estimates. These estimates can be put in place of $\tilde{\boldsymbol{\gamma}}$ and $\tilde{\boldsymbol{\beta}}$ in equation (16.76) to obtain a revised estimate of $\boldsymbol{\Omega}$ to be used in the second round of estimation. By repeating the procedure indefinitely, we can generate sequences of estimates of $\boldsymbol{\gamma}$, $\boldsymbol{\beta}$ and $\boldsymbol{\Omega}$ which should converge on values that satisfy both equations at once.

The alternative procedure involves the iterative solution of equations (16.85) and (16.86). We may begin by setting $\lambda=T$ in equation (16.86). By solving the resulting system, we obtain the same first-round estimates of $\boldsymbol{\gamma}$ and $\boldsymbol{\beta}$ as in the previous procedure. These estimates are put in place of $\tilde{\boldsymbol{\gamma}}$ and $\tilde{\boldsymbol{\beta}}$ in equation (16.85) to provide a revised value of λ for use in the second round. Once more, if the procedure is continued, we should generate convergent sequences of estimates.

A more elaborate procedure, combining aspects of both procedures described above, is also available. Thus, basing ourselves on equations (16.76), (16.85) and (16.86), and using the same initial values as before, we can generate sequences of estimates of λ, $\boldsymbol{\Omega}$, $\boldsymbol{\gamma}$ and $\boldsymbol{\beta}$ which should converge on T, $\tilde{\boldsymbol{\Omega}}$, $\tilde{\boldsymbol{\gamma}}$ and $\tilde{\boldsymbol{\beta}}$ respectively.

Conventional specializations of the limited-information maximum-likelihood estimator

According to the usual assumptions, the *a priori* information in (16.62) consists solely of exclusion restrictions specifying that certain elements of $\boldsymbol{\gamma}$ and $\boldsymbol{\beta}$ are zeros and a normalization rule setting one of the elements of $\boldsymbol{\gamma}$ to -1. By imposing these restrictions on $\boldsymbol{\gamma}'$ and $\boldsymbol{\beta}'$ and re-ordering their elements as required, we obtain the vectors $[\gamma_0, \boldsymbol{\gamma}_1', \boldsymbol{\gamma}_2'] = [-1, \boldsymbol{\gamma}_1', \mathbf{0}]$ and $[\boldsymbol{\beta}_1', \boldsymbol{\beta}_2'] = [\boldsymbol{\beta}_1', \mathbf{0}]$. On ordering and partitioning $\mathbf{Y}$ and $\mathbf{X}$ correspondingly, we obtain $[\mathbf{y}_0, \mathbf{Y}_1, \mathbf{Y}_2]$ and $[\mathbf{X}_1, \mathbf{X}_2]$. It also helps to define $\boldsymbol{\gamma}_\Delta' = [\gamma_0, \boldsymbol{\gamma}_1']$ and $\mathbf{Y}_\Delta = [\mathbf{y}_0, \mathbf{Y}_1]$.

When we apply the exclusion restrictions to (16.85) and (16.86), we obtain the estimating equations

$$(16.87)\qquad \lambda = \frac{(\mathbf{Y}_\Delta\tilde{\boldsymbol{\gamma}}_\Delta + \mathbf{X}_1\tilde{\boldsymbol{\beta}}_1)'(\mathbf{Y}_\Delta\tilde{\boldsymbol{\gamma}}_\Delta + \mathbf{X}_1\tilde{\boldsymbol{\beta}}_1)}{\tilde{\boldsymbol{\gamma}}_\Delta'\hat{\boldsymbol{\Omega}}_{\Delta\Delta}\tilde{\boldsymbol{\gamma}}_\Delta}$$

and

$$(16.88)\qquad \begin{bmatrix} \mathbf{y}_0'\mathbf{y}_0 - \lambda\hat{\omega}_{00}, & \mathbf{y}_0'\mathbf{Y}_1 - \lambda\hat{\boldsymbol{\omega}}_{01}, & \mathbf{y}_0'\mathbf{X}_1, & 1 \\ \mathbf{Y}_1'\mathbf{y}_0 - \lambda\hat{\boldsymbol{\omega}}_{10}, & \mathbf{Y}_1'\mathbf{Y}_1 - \lambda\hat{\boldsymbol{\Omega}}_{11}, & \mathbf{Y}_1'\mathbf{X}_1, & \mathbf{0} \\ \mathbf{X}_1'\mathbf{y}_0, & \mathbf{X}_1'\mathbf{Y}_1, & \mathbf{X}_1'\mathbf{X}_1, & \mathbf{0} \\ 1, & \mathbf{0}, & \mathbf{0}, & 0 \end{bmatrix} \begin{bmatrix} \tilde{\gamma}_0 \\ \tilde{\boldsymbol{\gamma}}_1 \\ \tilde{\boldsymbol{\beta}}_1 \\ \mu \end{bmatrix} \begin{bmatrix} 0 \\ \mathbf{0} \\ \mathbf{0} \\ -1 \end{bmatrix}$$

where

$$(16.89)\qquad \hat{\boldsymbol{\Omega}}_{\Delta\Delta} = \begin{bmatrix} \hat{\omega}_{00}, & \hat{\boldsymbol{\omega}}_{01} \\ \hat{\boldsymbol{\omega}}_{10}, & \hat{\boldsymbol{\Omega}}_{11} \end{bmatrix} = \frac{\mathbf{Y}_\Delta'(\mathbf{I} - \mathbf{P})\mathbf{Y}_\Delta}{T}$$

is the unrestricted estimate of the dispersion matrix of the vector $\mathbf{y}_{t\Delta} = [y_{t0}, \mathbf{y}_{t1}]$ comprising those of the system's output variables that are present in our single structural equation.

The equation (16.88) may be condensed to give

$$(16.90)\qquad \begin{bmatrix} \mathbf{y}_0'\mathbf{y}_0 - (\lambda\hat{\omega}_{00} + \mu), & \mathbf{y}_0'\mathbf{Y}_1 - \lambda\hat{\boldsymbol{\omega}}_{01}, & \mathbf{y}_0'\mathbf{X}_1 \\ \mathbf{Y}_1'\mathbf{y}_0 - \lambda\hat{\boldsymbol{\omega}}_{10}, & \mathbf{Y}_1'\mathbf{Y}_1 - \lambda\hat{\boldsymbol{\Omega}}_{11}, & \mathbf{Y}_1'\mathbf{X}_1 \\ \mathbf{X}_1'\mathbf{y}_0, & \mathbf{X}_1'\mathbf{Y}_1, & \mathbf{X}_1'\mathbf{X}_1 \end{bmatrix} \begin{bmatrix} -1 \\ \tilde{\boldsymbol{\gamma}}_1 \\ \tilde{\boldsymbol{\beta}}_1 \end{bmatrix} = \begin{bmatrix} 0 \\ \mathbf{0} \\ \mathbf{0} \end{bmatrix}$$

Then, if we eliminate the first row and rearrange the remainder, we get

$$(16.91)\qquad \begin{bmatrix} \mathbf{Y}_1'\mathbf{Y}_1 - \lambda\hat{\boldsymbol{\Omega}}_{11}, & \mathbf{Y}_1'\mathbf{X}_1 \\ \mathbf{X}_1'\mathbf{Y}_1, & \mathbf{X}_1'\mathbf{X}_1 \end{bmatrix} \begin{bmatrix} \tilde{\boldsymbol{\gamma}}_1 \\ \tilde{\boldsymbol{\beta}}_1 \end{bmatrix} = \begin{bmatrix} \mathbf{Y}_1'\mathbf{y}_0 - \lambda\hat{\boldsymbol{\omega}}_{10} \\ \mathbf{X}_1'\mathbf{y}_0 \end{bmatrix}.$$

An expression for $\tilde{\boldsymbol{\beta}}_1$ in terms of $\tilde{\boldsymbol{\gamma}}_\Delta$ of the form

$$(16.92)\qquad \tilde{\boldsymbol{\beta}}_1 = -(\mathbf{X}_1'\mathbf{X}_1)^{-1}\mathbf{X}_1'\mathbf{Y}_\Delta\tilde{\boldsymbol{\gamma}}_\Delta$$

may be obtained from any of these alternative representations of the basic estimating equation. Defining $\mathbf{P}_1=\mathbf{X}_1(\mathbf{X}_1'\mathbf{X}_1)^{-1}\mathbf{X}_1'$ and substituting $-\mathbf{P}_1\mathbf{Y}_\Delta\tilde{\boldsymbol{\gamma}}_\Delta=\mathbf{X}_1\tilde{\boldsymbol{\beta}}_1$ into equation (16.87), we find that

$$
\begin{aligned}
\lambda &= \frac{(\mathbf{Y}_\Delta\tilde{\boldsymbol{\gamma}}_\Delta-\mathbf{P}_1\mathbf{Y}_\Delta\tilde{\boldsymbol{\gamma}}_\Delta)'(\mathbf{Y}_\Delta\tilde{\boldsymbol{\gamma}}_\Delta-\mathbf{P}_1\mathbf{Y}_\Delta\tilde{\boldsymbol{\gamma}}_\Delta)}{\tilde{\boldsymbol{\gamma}}_\Delta'\hat{\boldsymbol{\Omega}}_{\Delta\Delta}\tilde{\boldsymbol{\gamma}}_\Delta} \\
&= T\frac{\tilde{\boldsymbol{\gamma}}_\Delta'\mathbf{Y}_\Delta'(\mathbf{I}-\mathbf{P}_1)\mathbf{Y}_\Delta\tilde{\boldsymbol{\gamma}}_\Delta}{\tilde{\boldsymbol{\gamma}}_\Delta'\mathbf{Y}_\Delta'(\mathbf{I}-\mathbf{P})\mathbf{Y}_\Delta\tilde{\boldsymbol{\gamma}}_\Delta}.
\end{aligned}
\tag{16.93}
$$

Since $\mathbf{P}-\mathbf{P}_1=(\mathbf{I}-\mathbf{P}_1)\mathbf{X}_2[\mathbf{X}_2'(\mathbf{I}-\mathbf{P}_1)\mathbf{X}_2]^{-1}\mathbf{X}_2'(\mathbf{I}-\mathbf{P}_1)$ is a symmetric positive-semidefinite matrix, it follows that the value of the quadratic form in the numerator of the above expression cannot be less than the value of the quadratic form in the denominator. Hence we have the inequality $\lambda \geq T$.

The alternative estimating equation in (16.83) has the expression $T\tilde{\boldsymbol{\Omega}}$ in place of $\lambda\hat{\boldsymbol{\Omega}}$ in (16.86). The submatrix of the restricted estimate $\tilde{\boldsymbol{\Omega}}$ corresponding to the vector $\mathbf{y}_{t\Delta}=[y_{t0},\mathbf{y}_{t1}]$ can be expressed as

$$
\begin{aligned}
\tilde{\boldsymbol{\Omega}}_{\Delta\Delta} &= \hat{\boldsymbol{\Omega}}_{\Delta\Delta}+\left\{\frac{(\mathbf{Y}_\Delta\tilde{\boldsymbol{\gamma}}_\Delta+\mathbf{X}_1\tilde{\boldsymbol{\beta}}_1)'\mathbf{P}(\mathbf{Y}\tilde{\boldsymbol{\gamma}}_\Delta+\mathbf{X}\tilde{\boldsymbol{\beta}}_1)}{T\tilde{\boldsymbol{\gamma}}_\Delta'\hat{\boldsymbol{\Omega}}_{\Delta\Delta}\tilde{\boldsymbol{\gamma}}_\Delta}\right\}\hat{\boldsymbol{\Omega}}_{\Delta\Delta}\tilde{\boldsymbol{\gamma}}_\Delta\tilde{\boldsymbol{\gamma}}_\Delta'\hat{\boldsymbol{\Omega}}_{\Delta\Delta} \\
&= \hat{\boldsymbol{\Omega}}_{\Delta\Delta}+\left\{\frac{\tilde{\boldsymbol{\gamma}}_\Delta'\mathbf{Y}_\Delta'(\mathbf{P}-\mathbf{P}_1)\mathbf{Y}_\Delta\tilde{\boldsymbol{\gamma}}_\Delta}{\tilde{\boldsymbol{\gamma}}_\Delta'\mathbf{Y}_\Delta'(\mathbf{I}-\mathbf{P})\mathbf{Y}_\Delta\tilde{\boldsymbol{\gamma}}_\Delta}\right\}\hat{\boldsymbol{\Omega}}_{\Delta\Delta}\tilde{\boldsymbol{\gamma}}_\Delta\tilde{\boldsymbol{\gamma}}_\Delta'\hat{\boldsymbol{\Omega}}_{\Delta\Delta},
\end{aligned}
\tag{16.94}
$$

and the condensed version of the equation (16.83) may be written as

$$
\begin{bmatrix}
\mathbf{y}_0'\mathbf{y}_0-(T\tilde{\omega}_{00}+\mu), & \mathbf{y}_0'\mathbf{Y}_1-T\tilde{\boldsymbol{\omega}}_{01}, & \mathbf{y}_0'\mathbf{X}_1 \\
\mathbf{Y}_1'\mathbf{y}_0-T\tilde{\boldsymbol{\omega}}_{10}, & \mathbf{Y}_1'\mathbf{Y}_1-T\tilde{\boldsymbol{\Omega}}_{11}, & \mathbf{Y}_1'\mathbf{X}_1 \\
\mathbf{X}_1'\mathbf{y}_0, & \mathbf{X}_1'\mathbf{Y}_1, & \mathbf{X}_1'\mathbf{X}_1
\end{bmatrix}
\begin{bmatrix} -1 \\ \tilde{\boldsymbol{\gamma}}_1 \\ \tilde{\boldsymbol{\beta}}_1 \end{bmatrix}
=
\begin{bmatrix} 0 \\ \mathbf{0} \\ \mathbf{0} \end{bmatrix}
\tag{16.95}
$$

which becomes

$$
\begin{bmatrix}
\mathbf{Y}_1'\mathbf{Y}_1-T\tilde{\boldsymbol{\Omega}}_{11}, & \mathbf{Y}_1'\mathbf{X}_1 \\
\mathbf{X}_1'\mathbf{Y}_1, & \mathbf{X}_1'\mathbf{X}_1
\end{bmatrix}
\begin{bmatrix} \tilde{\boldsymbol{\gamma}}_1 \\ \tilde{\boldsymbol{\beta}}_1 \end{bmatrix}
=
\begin{bmatrix} \mathbf{Y}_1'\mathbf{y}_0-T\tilde{\boldsymbol{\omega}}_{10} \\ \mathbf{X}_1'\mathbf{y}_0 \end{bmatrix}
\tag{16.96}
$$

when we eliminate the first row and rearrange the remainder.

Equation (16.95) enables us to recognize the remarkable affinity between our LIML estimator and the 2SLS estimator. For, as reference to (15.44) shows, the only difference is that 2SLS uses the unrestricted estimator $\hat{\boldsymbol{\Omega}}$ in place of the restricted estimator $\tilde{\boldsymbol{\Omega}}$.

The classical LIML estimator of Anderson and Rubin may be obtained from equation (16.90) by suppressing the normalization rule which sets $\gamma_0=-1$ and which is also responsible for the presence of the Lagrangean multiplier μ. By setting $\mu=0$ and by consolidating $[\gamma_0,\boldsymbol{\gamma}_1']=\boldsymbol{\gamma}_\Delta'$ and $[\mathbf{y}_0,\mathbf{Y}_1]=\mathbf{Y}_\Delta$, we obtain the equation

$$
\begin{bmatrix}
\mathbf{Y}_\Delta'\mathbf{Y}_\Delta-\lambda\hat{\boldsymbol{\Omega}}_{\Delta\Delta}, & \mathbf{Y}_\Delta'\mathbf{X}_1 \\
\mathbf{X}_1'\mathbf{Y}_\Delta, & \mathbf{X}_1'\mathbf{X}_1
\end{bmatrix}
\begin{bmatrix} \tilde{\boldsymbol{\gamma}}_\Delta \\ \tilde{\boldsymbol{\beta}}_1 \end{bmatrix}
=
\begin{bmatrix} \mathbf{0} \\ \mathbf{0} \end{bmatrix}.
\tag{16.97}
$$

This is a homogeneous system which is amenable to a non-trivial solution only if λ is adjusted so as to induce a degree of linear dependence amongst the columns of the matrix. By writing the solution $\mathbf{X}_1\tilde{\boldsymbol{\beta}}_1 = -\mathbf{P}_1\mathbf{Y}_\Delta\tilde{\boldsymbol{\gamma}}_\Delta$ in the first line of the system, we obtain the equation

$$[\mathbf{Y}_\Delta'(\mathbf{I}-\mathbf{P}_1)\mathbf{Y}_\Delta - \lambda\hat{\boldsymbol{\Omega}}_{\Delta\Delta}]\tilde{\boldsymbol{\gamma}}_\Delta = \mathbf{0}. \tag{16.98}$$

Thus we see that the scalar λ is a characteristic root of the matrix $\mathbf{Y}_\Delta'(\mathbf{I}-\mathbf{P}_1)\mathbf{Y}_\Delta$ in the metric defined by $\hat{\boldsymbol{\Omega}}_{\Delta\Delta} = \mathbf{Y}_\Delta'(\mathbf{I}-\mathbf{P})\mathbf{Y}_\Delta/T$. To obtain estimates, we use the characteristic root of least absolute value. The estimate of $\boldsymbol{\gamma}_\Delta$, which is only determined up to a scalar factor by equation (16.98), is rendered unique by the normalization rule. By using this estimate in equation (16.92), we may obtain the solution for $\tilde{\boldsymbol{\beta}}_1$.

The peculiar feature of this procedure is that the normalization rule is used in such a way that it has no bearing on the relative values of the elements in the vector $[\tilde{\boldsymbol{\gamma}}_\Delta', \tilde{\boldsymbol{\beta}}_1']$. Any other normalization will determine a vector with the same relative values. Since none of them is truly singled out as the dependent variable, we can describe the variables in $\mathbf{y}_{t\Delta}$ as jointly dependent.

We ought to demonstrate now that, by setting λ to the smallest possible value, we are indeed satisfying the criterion of maximizing the log-likelihood function. However, this will become evident in the next section where we shall provide an alternative derivation of the estimating equation (16.86) by minimizing λ subject to restrictions.

An alternative derivation of the limited-information maximum-likelihood estimator

Let us reconsider the structural equation in (16.60). We can see from (16.4) that the structural disturbance u_t is related to the disturbance vector $\mathbf{v}_{t.}$ of the reduced-form equation by the identity $u_t = -\mathbf{v}_{t.}\boldsymbol{\gamma}$. Therefore we can re-express the structural equation as

$$(\mathbf{y}_{t.} - \mathbf{v}_{t.})\boldsymbol{\gamma} + \mathbf{x}_{t.}\boldsymbol{\beta} = 0 \tag{16.99}$$

where $\mathbf{y}_{t.} - \mathbf{v}_{t.} = \mathbf{x}_{t.}\boldsymbol{\Pi} = \boldsymbol{\mu}_{t.}$ is the systematic component of the reduced-form equation.

Given observations on $\mathbf{x}_{t.}$ and $\mathbf{y}_{t.}$ for $t = 1, \ldots, T$, our task is to find corresponding estimates $\hat{\boldsymbol{\mu}}_{t.}$ of the systematic component which will render the equations

$$\hat{\boldsymbol{\mu}}_{t.}\boldsymbol{\gamma} + \mathbf{x}_{t.}\boldsymbol{\beta} = 0; \qquad t = 1, \ldots, T \tag{16.100}$$

both mutually consistent and consistent with the equations of the *a priori* restrictions in (16.62). Provided that there are sufficient restrictions, such estimates should enable us to determine uniquely the estimates of $\boldsymbol{\gamma}$ and $\boldsymbol{\beta}$.

Having regard to the log-likelihood function in (16.9), it should be apparent that the maximum-likelihood estimates are obtained by minimizing

$$\text{Trace}[(\mathbf{Y}-\mathbf{X\Pi})'(\mathbf{Y}-\mathbf{X\Pi})\mathbf{\Omega}^{-1}]=\sum(\mathbf{y}_{t.}-\boldsymbol{\mu}_{t.})\mathbf{\Omega}^{-1}(\mathbf{y}_{t.}-\boldsymbol{\mu}_{t.})' \tag{16.101}$$

subject to the restrictions and the conditions in (16.100). This minimand is the sum of squares of the distances measured in the $\mathbf{\Omega}^{-1}$-metric from the data points $\mathbf{y}_{t.}$ to the corresponding points $\boldsymbol{\mu}_{t.}$ in the hyperplane defined by the relationship $\boldsymbol{\mu}_{t.}\boldsymbol{\gamma}+\mathbf{x}_{t.}\boldsymbol{\beta}=0$. To find an expression in terms of the sought-after parameters for the distance between $\mathbf{y}_{t.}$ and the nearest point in the hyperplane, we must differentiate the Lagrangean

$$L=(\mathbf{y}_{t.}-\boldsymbol{\mu}_{t.})\mathbf{\Omega}^{-1}(\mathbf{y}_{t.}-\boldsymbol{\mu}_{t.})'+2\lambda(\boldsymbol{\mu}_{t.}\boldsymbol{\gamma}+\mathbf{x}_{t.}\boldsymbol{\beta}) \tag{16.102}$$

in respect of $\boldsymbol{\mu}_{t.}$. By setting the result to zero, we obtain the condition

$$(\mathbf{y}_{t.}-\boldsymbol{\mu}_{t.})\mathbf{\Omega}^{-1}=\lambda\boldsymbol{\gamma}'. \tag{16.103}$$

This gives

$$(\mathbf{y}_{t.}-\boldsymbol{\mu}_{t.})\mathbf{\Omega}^{-1}(\mathbf{y}_{t.}-\boldsymbol{\mu}_{t.})'=\lambda^2\boldsymbol{\gamma}'\mathbf{\Omega}\boldsymbol{\gamma} \tag{16.104}$$

and

$$\lambda=(\boldsymbol{\gamma}'\mathbf{\Omega}\boldsymbol{\gamma})^{-1}(\mathbf{y}_{t.}-\boldsymbol{\mu}_{t.})\boldsymbol{\gamma}. \tag{16.105}$$

Using the condition $-\boldsymbol{\mu}_{t.}\boldsymbol{\gamma}=\mathbf{x}_{t.}\boldsymbol{\beta}$, we find that

$$\lambda=(\boldsymbol{\gamma}'\mathbf{\Omega}\boldsymbol{\gamma})^{-1}(\mathbf{y}_{t.}\boldsymbol{\gamma}+\mathbf{x}_{t.}\boldsymbol{\beta}); \tag{16.106}$$

so equation (16.104) gives

$$(\mathbf{y}_{t.}-\boldsymbol{\mu}_{t.})\mathbf{\Omega}^{-1}(\mathbf{y}_{t.}-\boldsymbol{\mu}_{t.})'=(\boldsymbol{\gamma}'\mathbf{\Omega}\boldsymbol{\gamma})^{-1}(\mathbf{y}_{t.}\boldsymbol{\gamma}+\mathbf{x}_{t.}\boldsymbol{\beta})^2. \tag{16.107}$$

The latter enables us to represent our problem in terms of minimizing the Lagrangean expression

$$L=(\boldsymbol{\gamma}'\mathbf{\Omega}\boldsymbol{\gamma})^{-1}(\mathbf{Y}\boldsymbol{\gamma}+\mathbf{X}\boldsymbol{\beta})'(\mathbf{Y}\boldsymbol{\gamma}+\mathbf{X}\boldsymbol{\beta})+2\boldsymbol{\phi}'(\mathbf{R}_1\boldsymbol{\gamma}+\mathbf{R}_2\boldsymbol{\beta}-\mathbf{r}). \tag{16.108}$$

The derivatives with respect to $\boldsymbol{\gamma}$ and $\boldsymbol{\beta}$ are

$$\begin{aligned}\left(\frac{\partial L}{\partial \boldsymbol{\gamma}}\right)'&=2(\boldsymbol{\gamma}'\mathbf{\Omega}\boldsymbol{\gamma})^{-1}\mathbf{Y}'(\mathbf{Y}\boldsymbol{\gamma}+\mathbf{X}\boldsymbol{\beta})\\&\quad-2(\boldsymbol{\gamma}'\mathbf{\Omega}\boldsymbol{\gamma})^{-2}(\mathbf{Y}\boldsymbol{\gamma}+\mathbf{X}\boldsymbol{\beta})'(\mathbf{Y}\boldsymbol{\gamma}+\mathbf{X}\boldsymbol{\beta})\mathbf{\Omega}\boldsymbol{\gamma}+2\mathbf{R}_1'\boldsymbol{\phi},\\\left(\frac{\partial L}{\partial \boldsymbol{\beta}}\right)'&=2(\boldsymbol{\gamma}'\mathbf{\Omega}\boldsymbol{\gamma})^{-1}\mathbf{X}'(\mathbf{Y}\boldsymbol{\gamma}+\mathbf{X}\boldsymbol{\beta})+2\mathbf{R}_2'\boldsymbol{\phi}.\end{aligned} \tag{16.09}$$

On setting these to zero, defining

$$\lambda=\frac{(\mathbf{Y}\boldsymbol{\gamma}+\mathbf{X}\boldsymbol{\beta})'(\mathbf{Y}\boldsymbol{\gamma}+\mathbf{X}\boldsymbol{\beta})}{\boldsymbol{\gamma}'\mathbf{\Omega}\boldsymbol{\gamma}}, \tag{16.110}$$

and compounding the resulting equations with the restrictions in (16.62), we obtain the system

$$(16.111)\qquad \begin{bmatrix} \mathbf{Y'Y}-\lambda\mathbf{\Omega}, & \mathbf{Y'X}, & \mathbf{R}_1' \\ \mathbf{X'Y}, & \mathbf{X'X}, & \mathbf{R}_2' \\ \mathbf{R}_1, & \mathbf{R}_2, & \mathbf{0} \end{bmatrix} \begin{bmatrix} \boldsymbol{\gamma} \\ \boldsymbol{\beta} \\ \boldsymbol{\mu} \end{bmatrix} = \begin{bmatrix} \mathbf{0} \\ \mathbf{0} \\ \mathbf{r} \end{bmatrix}$$

wherein $\boldsymbol{\mu}=(\boldsymbol{\gamma}'\mathbf{\Omega}\boldsymbol{\gamma})\boldsymbol{\phi}$ is a freely determined Lagrangean multiplier.

We may now recognize that (16.111) simply repeats the form of the estimating equation in (16.86). Moreover, reference to (16.108) shows that it has been derived by minimizing λ subject to the restrictions.

It makes no difference to the ultimate solution of this estimating equation whether $\mathbf{\Omega}$ has the value of the unrestricted estimate $\hat{\mathbf{\Omega}}$ or the value of the restricted estimate $\tilde{\mathbf{\Omega}}$. For $\mathbf{\Omega}$ affects the system via the expression $\lambda\mathbf{\Omega}\boldsymbol{\gamma}=\{(\mathbf{Y}\boldsymbol{\gamma}+\mathbf{X}\boldsymbol{\beta})'(\mathbf{Y}\boldsymbol{\gamma}+\mathbf{X}\boldsymbol{\beta})/(\boldsymbol{\gamma}'\mathbf{\Omega}\boldsymbol{\gamma})\}\mathbf{\Omega}\boldsymbol{\gamma}$ and, as we can see by referring to equation (16.73) and equation (16.75), wherein $\hat{\mathbf{\Omega}}=\mathbf{W}$, we have

$$(16.112)\qquad \begin{aligned} \frac{(\mathbf{Y}\tilde{\boldsymbol{\gamma}}+\mathbf{X}\tilde{\boldsymbol{\beta}})'(\mathbf{Y}\tilde{\boldsymbol{\gamma}}+\mathbf{X}\tilde{\boldsymbol{\beta}})}{\tilde{\boldsymbol{\gamma}}'\tilde{\mathbf{\Omega}}\tilde{\boldsymbol{\gamma}}}\tilde{\mathbf{\Omega}}\tilde{\boldsymbol{\gamma}} &= T\tilde{\mathbf{\Omega}}\tilde{\boldsymbol{\gamma}} \\ &= \frac{(\mathbf{Y}\tilde{\boldsymbol{\gamma}}+\mathbf{X}\tilde{\boldsymbol{\beta}})'(\mathbf{Y}\tilde{\boldsymbol{\gamma}}+\mathbf{X}\tilde{\boldsymbol{\beta}})}{\tilde{\boldsymbol{\gamma}}\hat{\mathbf{\Omega}}\tilde{\boldsymbol{\gamma}}}\hat{\mathbf{\Omega}}\tilde{\boldsymbol{\gamma}}. \end{aligned}$$

The asymptotic properties of the limited-information maximum-likelihood estimator

Let $\tilde{\boldsymbol{\theta}}'=[\tilde{\boldsymbol{\gamma}}',\tilde{\boldsymbol{\beta}}']$ represent the vector of maximum-likelihood estimates and let $\boldsymbol{\theta}'$ be the vector of the true parameter values. Then, as the theory of maximum-likelihood estimation indicates, the limiting distribution of $\sqrt{T}(\tilde{\boldsymbol{\theta}}-\boldsymbol{\theta})$ will be the normal distribution $N(\mathbf{0},\mathbf{C}_1)$ where $\mathbf{C}_1$ is a matrix defined by the identity

$$(16.113)\qquad \begin{bmatrix} \mathbf{C}_1, & \mathbf{C}_2 \\ \mathbf{C}_1', & \mathbf{C}_3 \end{bmatrix} = \begin{bmatrix} -\operatorname{plim}\left[T^{-1}\dfrac{\partial(\partial L^*/\partial\boldsymbol{\theta})'}{\partial\boldsymbol{\theta}}\right], & \mathbf{R}' \\ \mathbf{R}, & \mathbf{0} \end{bmatrix}^{-1}$$

wherein $\mathbf{R}=[\mathbf{R}_1,\mathbf{R}_2]$. In this context L^* stands for the concentrated log-likelihood function

$$(16.114)\qquad L^*(\boldsymbol{\theta})=-\frac{MT}{2}\log(2\pi)-\frac{T}{2}\log|\mathbf{\Omega}(\boldsymbol{\theta})|-\frac{MT}{2}$$

which incorporates an expression for $\mathbf{\Omega}$ in terms of $\boldsymbol{\gamma}$ and $\boldsymbol{\beta}$ in the form of (16.76). It can be shown that

$$(16.115)\qquad -\operatorname{plim}\left[T^{-1}\frac{\partial(\partial L^*/\partial\boldsymbol{\theta})'}{\partial\boldsymbol{\theta}}\right]=\sigma^{-2}\begin{bmatrix} \mathbf{\Pi}'\mathbf{M}_{\mathbf{XX}}\mathbf{\Pi}, & \mathbf{\Pi}'\mathbf{M}_{\mathbf{XX}} \\ \mathbf{M}_{\mathbf{XX}}\mathbf{\Pi}, & \mathbf{M}_{\mathbf{XX}}, \end{bmatrix}$$

where $\mathbf{M_{XX}} = \text{plim}\,(\mathbf{X'X}/T)$ and $\sigma^2 = \boldsymbol{\gamma}'\boldsymbol{\Omega}\boldsymbol{\gamma} = V(u_t)$ is the variance of the structural disturbance.

On specializing these results to the conventional case where our *a priori* information consists of exclusion restrictions and a normalization rule, we find that the dispersion matrix of the limiting distribution of the vector $\sqrt{T}([\tilde{\boldsymbol{\gamma}}_1', \tilde{\boldsymbol{\beta}}_1'] - [\boldsymbol{\gamma}_1', \boldsymbol{\beta}_1'])'$ is

$$\sigma^2 \begin{bmatrix} \boldsymbol{\Pi}_{\mathbf{X}1}'\mathbf{M_{XX}}\boldsymbol{\Pi}_{\mathbf{X}1}, & \boldsymbol{\Pi}_{\mathbf{X}1}'\mathbf{M}_{\mathbf{X}1} \\ \mathbf{M}_{1\mathbf{X}}\boldsymbol{\Pi}_{\mathbf{X}1}, & \mathbf{M}_{11} \end{bmatrix}^{-1} \tag{16.116}$$

wherein $\mathbf{M}_{\mathbf{X}1} = \mathbf{M}_{1\mathbf{X}}' = \text{plim}\,(\mathbf{X}'\mathbf{X}_1/T)$ and $\boldsymbol{\Pi}_{\mathbf{X}1}$ is the corresponding submatrix of $\boldsymbol{\Pi}$. In fact, these asymptotic properties are identical to those of the 2SLS estimator as reference to Chapter 15 will show.

The estimating equations of 2SLS in (15.44) differ from those of LIML in (16.95) only by having the unrestricted estimate $\hat{\boldsymbol{\Omega}}$ of the reduced-form dispersion matrix in place of the restricted estimate $\tilde{\boldsymbol{\Omega}}$. The asymptotic equivalence of 2SLS and LIML is a direct consequence of the convergence of $\hat{\boldsymbol{\Omega}}$ and $\tilde{\boldsymbol{\Omega}}$.

BIBLIOGRAPHY

Derivations of the FIML Estimating Equations. Fisk [**38**], Koopmans, Rubin and Leipnik [**68**], Rothenberg and Leenders [**101**]

Computation of the FIML Estimates. Chow [**21**], Fisk [**38**, Chap. 4], Malinvaud [**82,** Chap. 19 §7]

3SLS and FIML Hendry [**56**], Rothenberg and Leenders [**101**], Sargan [**105**]

The Classical LIML Estimator. Anderson [**7**], Anderson and Rubin [**9**], [**10**], Goldberger and Olkin [**42**], Koopmans and Hood [**67**]

LIML Estimation of Multi-equation Subsystems. Chow and Ray-Chaudhuri [**22**], Ghosh [**40**], Hannan [**51**]

LIML and 2SLS. Chow [**20**], Theil [**114,** pp. 231–237]

Relationships amongst Estimators. Chow [**20**], Hendry [**56**]

Maximum Likelihood Estimation of Simultaneous Systems with Autoregressive Disturbances. Hendry [**55**], Sargan [**103**], Zellner and Palm [**127**]

CHAPTER 17

Appendix of Statistical Theory

The purpose of this appendix is to provide a brief summary of certain salient results in statistical theory which are referred to in the body of the text. A more thorough treatment can be found in very many textbooks. Two texts which together are all but definitive for our purposes are T. W. Anderson's *Introduction to Multivariate Statistical Analysis* [**8**] and C. R. Rao's *Linear Statistical Inference and its Applications* [**93**]. An excellent survey of much of the statistical theory which is requisite to econometrics can be found in A. S. Goldberger's *Econometric Theory* [**41**].

DISTRIBUTIONS

We shall be concerned exclusively with random vectors and scalars of the continuous type which—roughly speaking—can assume a non-denumerable infinity of values in any interval within their range. We shall restrict our attention to variates that have either the normal distribution or some associated distribution. The justification for this comes not from any supposition that economic data are distributed in such ways, but rather from the central limit theorem which indicates that, for large samples at least, the distributions of our statistical estimates will be approximately normal. We begin with the basic definitions.

Multivariate density functions

An n-dimensional random vector $\mathbf{x} \in \mathcal{R}^n$ is an ordered set of real numbers $[x_1, x_2, \ldots, x_n]'$ each of which represents some aspect of a statistical event. A scalar-valued function $F(\mathbf{x})$, whose value at $\boldsymbol{\phi} = [\phi_1, \phi_2, \ldots, \phi_n]'$ is the probability of the event $(x_1 \leqslant \phi_1, x_2 \leqslant \phi_2, \ldots, x_n \leqslant \phi_n)$, is called a cumulative distribution function.

(17.1) If $F(\mathbf{x})$ has the representation

$$F(\mathbf{x}) = \int_{-\infty}^{x_n} \cdots \int_{-\infty}^{x_1} f(x_1, \ldots, x_n)\, dx_1 \ldots dx_n,$$

which can also be written as

$$F(\mathbf{x})=\int_{-\infty}^{\mathbf{x}} f(\mathbf{x})\,dx,$$

then we say that it is absolutely continuous; in which case $f(\mathbf{x})=f(x_1,\ldots,x_n)$ is called a continuous probability density function.

When $\mathbf{x}$ has the probability density function $f(\mathbf{x})$, we say that it is distributed as $f(\mathbf{x})$, and we denote this by writing $\mathbf{x}\sim f(\mathbf{x})$.

The function $f(\mathbf{x})$ has the following properties:

(17.2) (i) $f(\mathbf{x})\geqslant 0$ for all $\mathbf{x}\in\mathcal{R}^n$.

(ii) If $\mathcal{A}\subset\mathcal{R}^n$ is a set of values for $\mathbf{x}$, then the probability that $\mathbf{x}$ is in $\mathcal{A}$ is

$$P(\mathcal{A})=\int_{\mathcal{A}} f(\mathbf{x})\,d\mathbf{x}.$$

(iii) $P(\mathbf{x}\in\mathcal{R}^n)=\int_{\mathbf{x}} f(\mathbf{x})\,d\mathbf{x}=1.$

Strictly speaking, the set $\mathcal{A}\subset\mathcal{R}^n$ must be a Borel set of a sort that can be formed by a finite or a denumerably infinite number of unions, intersections and complements of a set of half-open intervals of the type $(\mathbf{a}<\mathbf{x}\leqslant\mathbf{b})$. The probability $P(\mathcal{A})$ can then be expressed as a sum of ordinary multiple integrals. However, the requirement imposes no practical restrictions, since any set in $\mathcal{R}^n$ can be represented as a limit of a sequence of Borel sets.

We may wish to characterize the statistical event in terms of only a subset of the elements in $\mathbf{x}$. This leads us to define the marginal distribution of these elements.

(17.3) Let the $n\times 1$ random vector $\mathbf{x}\sim f(\mathbf{x})$ be partitioned such that $\mathbf{x}'=[\mathbf{x}_1',\mathbf{x}_2']$ where $\mathbf{x}_1'=[x_1,\ldots,x_m]$ and $\mathbf{x}_2'=[x_{m+1},\ldots,x_n]$. Then, on writing $f(\mathbf{x})=f(\mathbf{x}_1,\mathbf{x}_2)$, we may define the marginal probability density function of $\mathbf{x}_1$ as

$$f(\mathbf{x}_1)=\int_{\mathbf{x}_2} f(\mathbf{x}_1,\mathbf{x}_2)\,d\mathbf{x}_2,$$

which can also be written as

$$f(x_1,\ldots,x_m)$$

$$=\int_{x_n}\cdots\int_{x_{m+1}} f(x_1,\ldots,x_m,x_{m+1},\ldots,x_n)\,dx_{m+1}\ldots dx_n.$$

Using the marginal probability density function, we can express the probability that $\mathbf{x}_1$ will assume a value in the set $\mathscr{B}$, without reference to the value of $\mathbf{x}_2$, as

$$P(\mathscr{B}) = \int_{\mathscr{B}} f(\mathbf{x}_1)\, d\mathbf{x}_1.$$

Next we consider conditional probabilities.

(17.4) The probability of the event $\mathbf{x}_1 \in \mathscr{A}$ given the event $\mathbf{x}_2 \in \mathscr{B}$ is

$$P(\mathscr{A} \mid \mathscr{B}) = \frac{P(\mathscr{A} \cap \mathscr{B})}{P(\mathscr{B})} = \frac{\int_{\mathscr{A}} \int_{\mathscr{B}} f(\mathbf{x}_1, \mathbf{x}_2)\, d\mathbf{x}_1\, d\mathbf{x}_2}{\int_{\mathscr{B}} f(\mathbf{x}_2)\, d\mathbf{x}_2}.$$

We also wish to define the probability $P(\mathscr{A} \mid \mathbf{x}_2 = \boldsymbol{\phi})$ of the event $\mathbf{x}_1 \in \mathscr{A}$ given that $\mathbf{x}_2$ has the specific value $\boldsymbol{\phi}$. We may approach this problem by finding the limiting value of $P(\mathscr{A} \mid \boldsymbol{\phi} < \mathbf{x}_2 \leq \boldsymbol{\phi} + \Delta\mathbf{x}_2)$ as $\Delta\mathbf{x}_2$ tends to zero. Defining the event $\mathscr{B} = \{\mathbf{x}_2; \phi < \mathbf{x}_2 \leq \boldsymbol{\phi} + \Delta\mathbf{x}_2\}$, we have, according to the mean value theorem,

$$P(\mathscr{B}) = \int_{\boldsymbol{\phi}}^{\boldsymbol{\phi}+\Delta\mathbf{x}_2} f(\mathbf{x}_2)\, d\mathbf{x}_2 = f(\boldsymbol{\phi}^0)\, \Delta\mathbf{x}_2$$

where $\boldsymbol{\phi} \leq \boldsymbol{\phi}^0 \leq \boldsymbol{\phi} + \Delta\mathbf{x}_2$. Likewise we have

$$P(\mathscr{A} \cap \mathscr{B}) = \int_{\mathscr{A}} f(\mathbf{x}_1, \boldsymbol{\phi}^*)\, \Delta\mathbf{x}_2\, d\mathbf{x}_1$$

where $\boldsymbol{\phi} \leq \boldsymbol{\phi}^* \leq \boldsymbol{\phi} + \Delta\mathbf{x}_2$. Thus, provided that $f(\boldsymbol{\phi}^0) > 0$,

$$P(\mathscr{A} \mid \mathscr{B}) = \frac{\int_{\mathscr{A}} f(\mathbf{x}_1, \boldsymbol{\phi}^*)\, d\mathbf{x}_1}{f(\boldsymbol{\phi}^0)};$$

and we can define the probability $P(\mathscr{A} \mid \mathbf{x}_2 = \boldsymbol{\phi})$ as the limit this integral as $\Delta\mathbf{x}_2$ tends to zero and both $\boldsymbol{\phi}^0$ and $\boldsymbol{\phi}^*$ tend to $\boldsymbol{\phi}$. Thus, in general,

(17.5) If $\mathbf{x}' = [\mathbf{x}_1', \mathbf{x}_2']$, then the conditional probability density function of $\mathbf{x}_1$ given $\mathbf{x}_2$ is defined as

$$f(\mathbf{x}_1 \mid \mathbf{x}_2) = \frac{f(\mathbf{x})}{f(\mathbf{x}_2)} = \frac{f(\mathbf{x}_1, \mathbf{x}_2)}{f(\mathbf{x}_2)}.$$

Notice that the probability density function of $\mathbf{x}$ can now be written as $f(\mathbf{x}) = f(\mathbf{x}_1 \mid \mathbf{x}_2) f(\mathbf{x}_2) = f(\mathbf{x}_2 \mid \mathbf{x}_1) f(\mathbf{x}_1)$.

We can proceed to give a definition of statistical independence.

(17.6) The vectors $\mathbf{x}_1$, $\mathbf{x}_2$ are statistically independent if their joint distribution is $f(\mathbf{x}_1, \mathbf{x}_2) = f(\mathbf{x}_1)f(\mathbf{x}_2)$ or, equivalently, if $f(\mathbf{x}_1 \mid \mathbf{x}_2) = f(\mathbf{x}_1)$ and $f(\mathbf{x}_2 \mid \mathbf{x}_1) = f(\mathbf{x}_2)$.

Functions of random vectors

Consider a random vector $\mathbf{y} \sim g(\mathbf{y})$ that is a continuous function $\mathbf{y} = \mathbf{y}(\mathbf{x})$ of another random vector $\mathbf{x} \sim f(\mathbf{x})$, and imagine that the inverse function $\mathbf{x} = \mathbf{x}(\mathbf{y})$ is uniquely defined. Then, if $\mathscr{A}$ is a statistical event defined as a set of values of $\mathbf{x}$, and if $\mathscr{B} = \{\mathbf{y}; \mathbf{y} = \mathbf{y}(\mathbf{x}), \mathbf{x} \in \mathscr{A}\}$ is the same event defined in terms of $\mathbf{y}$, it follows that

(17.7)
$$\int_{\mathscr{A}} f(\mathbf{x})\, d\mathbf{x} = P(\mathscr{A})$$
$$= P(\mathscr{B}) = \int_{\mathscr{B}} g(\mathbf{y})\, d\mathbf{y}.$$

When the probability density function $f(\mathbf{x})$ is known, it is quite easy to find $g(\mathbf{y})$.

For the existence of a uniquely defined inverse transformation $\mathbf{x} = \mathbf{x}(\mathbf{y})$, it is necessary and sufficient that the determinant $|\partial \mathbf{x}/\partial \mathbf{y}|$, known as the Jacobian, should be non-zero for all values of $\mathbf{y}$; which means that it must either be strictly positive or strictly negative. We can make use of the Jacobian to change the variable under the first integral in (17.7) from $\mathbf{x}$ to $\mathbf{y}$ to give the identity

$$\int_{\mathscr{B}} f\{\mathbf{x}(\mathbf{y})\}\, |\partial \mathbf{x}/\partial \mathbf{y}|\, d\mathbf{y} = \int_{\mathscr{B}} g(\mathbf{y})\, d\mathbf{y}.$$

Within this expression, we have $f\{\mathbf{x}(\mathbf{y})\} \geqslant 0$ and $g(\mathbf{y}) \geqslant 0$. Thus, if $|\partial \mathbf{x}/\partial \mathbf{y}| > 0$, we can identify the probability density function of $\mathbf{y}$ as $g(\mathbf{y}) = f\{\mathbf{x}(\mathbf{y})\}\, |\partial \mathbf{x}/\partial \mathbf{y}|$. However, if $|\partial \mathbf{x}/\partial \mathbf{y}| < 0$, then $g(\mathbf{y})$ defined in this way is no longer positive. Our recourse is to change the signs of the axes of $\mathbf{y}$. Thus, in general, the probability density function of $\mathbf{y}$ is defined as $g(\mathbf{y}) = f\{\mathbf{x}(\mathbf{y})\}\, \|\partial \mathbf{x}/\partial \mathbf{y}\|$ where $\|\partial \mathbf{x}/\partial \mathbf{y}\|$ is the absolute value of the determinant. Let us summarize by stating that

(17.8) If $\mathbf{x} \sim f(\mathbf{x})$ and $\mathbf{y} = \mathbf{y}(\mathbf{x})$ is a transformation with a uniquely defined inverse $\mathbf{x} = \mathbf{x}(\mathbf{y})$, then $\mathbf{y} \sim g(\mathbf{y}) = f\{\mathbf{x}(\mathbf{y})\}\, \|\partial \mathbf{x}/\partial \mathbf{y}\|$ where $\|\partial \mathbf{x}/\partial \mathbf{y}\|$ is the absolute value of the determinant of the matrix $\partial \mathbf{x}/\partial \mathbf{y}$.

Even when $\mathbf{y} = \mathbf{y}(\mathbf{x})$ has no uniquely defined inverse, it is still possible to find a probability density function $g(\mathbf{y})$ by the above method provided that the transformation is surjective; that is to say, provided that the range of the transformation is coextensive with the vector space within which the random vector $\mathbf{y}$ resides. Imagine that $\mathbf{x}$ is a vector in $\mathcal{R}^n$ and that $\mathbf{y}$ is a vector in $\mathcal{R}^m$ where $m<n$. Then the technique is to devise an invertible transformation $\mathbf{q}=\mathbf{q}(\mathbf{x})$ where $\mathbf{q}'=[\mathbf{y}',\mathbf{z}']$ comprises, in addition to the vector $\mathbf{y}$, a vector $\mathbf{z}$ of $n-m$ dummy variables. Having found the probability density function of $\mathbf{q}$, we can proceed to find the marginal probability density function $g(\mathbf{y})$ by a process of integration.

Expectations

(17.9) If $x \sim f(x)$ is a random variable, its expected value is defined by

$$E(x)=\int_x f(x)\,dx.$$

The expected value of a function of x may be found without first determining its own probability density function. Thus

(17.10) If $y=y(x)$ is a function of $x\sim f(x)$, and if $y\sim g(y)$, then

$$E(y)=\int_y yg(y)\,dy=\int_x y(x)f(x)\,dx.$$

We can talk of an expectations operator E and we can list some of its properties as follows:

(17.11)
(i) If $x\geqslant 0$, then $E(x)\geqslant 0$.
(ii) If c is a constant, then $E(c)=c$.
(iii) If c is a constant and x a random variable, then $E(cx)=cE(x)$.
(iv) $E(x_1+x_2)=E(x_1)+E(x_2)$.
(v) If x_1, x_2 are independent random variables, then $E(x_1x_2)=E(x_1)E(x_2)$.

These are readily established from the definitions (17.9) and (17.10). By combining the properties (iii) and (iv), we have

$$E(c_1x_1+c_2x_2)=c_1E(x_1)+c_2E(x_2)$$

when c_1, c_2 are constants. Thus the expectations operator is seen to be a linear operator.

Moments of a multivariate distribution

We shall now define some of the more important moments of a multivariate distribution and record their properties. Elsewhere in the text we define more complicated moments of higher orders which it would not be particularly instructive to consider here.

(17.12) The expected value of the element x_i of the random vector $\mathbf{x} \sim f(\mathbf{x})$ is defined by

$$E(x_i) = \int_{\mathbf{x}} x_i f(\mathbf{x})\, d\mathbf{x} = \int_{x_i} x_i f(x_i)\, dx_i$$

where $f(x_i)$ is the marginal distribution of x_i.

The variance of x_i is defined by

$$\begin{aligned} V(x_i) &= E\{[x_i - E(x_i)]^2\} \\ &= \int_{\mathbf{x}} [x_i - E(x_i)]^2 f(\mathbf{x})\, d\mathbf{x} = \int_{x_i} [x_i - E(x_i)]^2 f(x_i)\, dx_i. \end{aligned}$$

The covariance of x_i and x_j is defined as

$$\begin{aligned} C(x_i, x_j) &= E\{[x_i - E(x_i)][x_j - E(x_j)]\} \\ &= \int_{\mathbf{x}} [x_i - E(x_i)][x_j - E(x_j)] f(\mathbf{x})\, d\mathbf{x} \\ &= \int_{x_j}\int_{x_i} [x_i - E(x_i)][x_j - E(x_j)] f(x_i, x_j)\, dx_i\, dx_j \end{aligned}$$

where $f(x_i, x_j)$ is the marginal distribution of x_i and x_j.

On expanding the expression for the covariance, we get $C(x_i, x_j) = E[x_i x_j - E(x_i)x_j - E(x_j)x_i + E(x_i)E(x_j)] = E(x_i x_j) - E(x_i)E(x_j)$. We can set $x_j = x_i$ to obtain a similar expression for the variance $V(x_i) = C(x_i, x_i)$. Thus

(17.13)
$$\begin{aligned} C(x_i, x_j) &= E(x_i x_j) - E(x_i)E(x_j), \\ V(x_i) &= E(x_i^2) - [E(x_i)]^2. \end{aligned}$$

We may observe that the property of the expectations operator given under (17.11)(i) implies $V(x_i) \geq 0$. Also, let us use the property under (17.11)(v) to deduce from the expression for $C(x_i, x_j)$ above that

(17.14) If x_i, x_j are independently distributed, then $C(x_i, x_j) = 0$.

Another important result is that

(17.15) $$V(x_i + x_j) = V(x_i) + V(x_j) + 2C(x_i, x_j).$$

This comes from expanding the final expression in

$$\begin{aligned} V(x_i + x_j) &= E\{[(x_i + x_j) - E(x_i + x_j)]^2\} \\ &= E(\{[x_i - E(x_i)] + [x_j - E(x_j)]\}^2). \end{aligned}$$

It is convenient to assemble the expectations, variances, and covariances of a multivariate distribution in matrices.

(17.16) If $\mathbf{x} \sim f(\mathbf{x})$ is an $n \times 1$ random vector, then its expected value

$$E(\mathbf{x}) = [E(x_i), \ldots, E(x_n)]'$$

is a vector comprising the expected values of the n elements. Its dispersion matrix

$$\begin{aligned} D(\mathbf{x}) &= E\{[\mathbf{x} - E(\mathbf{x})][\mathbf{x} - E(\mathbf{x})]'\} \\ &= E(\mathbf{x}\mathbf{x}') - E(\mathbf{x})E(\mathbf{x}') \end{aligned}$$

is a symmetric $n \times n$ matrix comprising the variances and covariances of its elements. If $\mathbf{x}$ is partitioned such that $\mathbf{x}' = [\mathbf{x}_1', \mathbf{x}_2']$, then the covariance matrix

$$\begin{aligned} C(\mathbf{x}_1, \mathbf{x}_2) &= E\{[\mathbf{x}_1 - E(\mathbf{x}_1)][\mathbf{x}_2 - E(\mathbf{x}_2)]'\} \\ &= E(\mathbf{x}_1\mathbf{x}_2') - E(\mathbf{x}_1)E(\mathbf{x}_2') \end{aligned}$$

is a matrix comprising the covaraince of the two sets of elements.

The dispersion matrix is non-negative definite. We see this by writing $\mathbf{a}'D(\mathbf{x})\mathbf{a} = \mathbf{a}'\{E[\mathbf{x} - E(\mathbf{x})][\mathbf{x} - E(\mathbf{x})]'\}\mathbf{a} = E\{[\mathbf{a}'\mathbf{x} - \mathbf{a}'E(\mathbf{x})][\mathbf{a}'\mathbf{x} - \mathbf{a}'E(\mathbf{x})]'\} = E\{[\mathbf{a}'\mathbf{x} - E(\mathbf{a}'\mathbf{x})]^2\} = V(\mathbf{a}'\mathbf{x}) \geqslant 0$, which uses the fact that variance of any scalar is non-negative.

Some properties of the operators which it is useful to record are as follows:

(17.17) If $\mathbf{x}$, $\mathbf{y}$, $\mathbf{z}$ are random vectors of appropriate orders, then

(i) $E(\mathbf{x} + \mathbf{y}) = E(\mathbf{x}) + E(\mathbf{y})$,
(ii) $D(\mathbf{x} + \mathbf{y}) = D(\mathbf{x}) + D(\mathbf{y}) + C(\mathbf{x}, \mathbf{y}) + C(\mathbf{y}, \mathbf{x})$,
(iii) $C(\mathbf{x} + \mathbf{y}, \mathbf{z}) = C(\mathbf{x}, \mathbf{z}) + C(\mathbf{y}, \mathbf{z})$.

Also

(17.18) If $\mathbf{x}$, $\mathbf{y}$ are random vectors and $\mathbf{A}$, $\mathbf{B}$ are matrices of appropriate orders, then

(i) $E(\mathbf{A}\mathbf{x}) = \mathbf{A}E(\mathbf{x})$,
(ii) $D(\mathbf{A}\mathbf{x}) = \mathbf{A}D(\mathbf{x})\mathbf{A}'$,
(iii) $C(\mathbf{A}\mathbf{x}, \mathbf{B}\mathbf{y}) = \mathbf{A}C(\mathbf{x}, \mathbf{y})\mathbf{B}'$.

Degenerate random vectors

An n-element random vector $\mathbf{x}$ is said to be degenerate if its values are contained within a subset of $\mathcal{R}^n$ of Lebesgue measure zero. In particular, $\mathbf{x}$

is degenerate if it is confined to a vector subspace or an affine subspace of $\mathscr{R}^n$. Let $\mathscr{A} \subset \mathscr{R}^n$ be the affine subspace containing the values of $\mathbf{x}$, and let $\mathbf{a} \in \mathscr{A}$ be any fixed value. Then $\mathscr{A} - \mathbf{a}$ is a vector subspace, and there exists a non-zero linear transformation $\mathbf{R}$ on $\mathscr{R}^n$ such that $\mathbf{R}(\mathbf{x}-\mathbf{a}) = \mathbf{0}$ for all $\mathbf{x} \in \mathscr{A}$. Clearly, if $\mathbf{x} \in \mathscr{A}$, then $E(\mathbf{x}) \in \mathscr{A}$ and we can set $\mathbf{a} = E(\mathbf{x})$. Thus we can state that

(17.19) The random vector $\mathbf{x} \in \mathscr{R}^n$ is degenerate if there exists a non-zero matrix $\mathbf{R}$ such that $\mathbf{R}[\mathbf{x} - E(\mathbf{x})] = \mathbf{0}$ for all values of $\mathbf{x}$.

To provide an alternative characterization of this sort of degenerate random vector, we may prove that

(17.20) The condition $\mathbf{R}[\mathbf{x} - E(\mathbf{x})] = \mathbf{0}$ is equivalent to the condition $\mathbf{R}D(\mathbf{x}) = \mathbf{0}$.

Proof. The condition $\mathbf{R}[\mathbf{x} - E(\mathbf{x})] = \mathbf{0}$ implies $E\{\mathbf{R}[\mathbf{x} - E(\mathbf{x})][\mathbf{x} - E(\mathbf{x})]'\mathbf{R}'\} = \mathbf{R}D(\mathbf{x})\mathbf{R}' = \mathbf{0}$ or, equivalently, that $\mathbf{R}D(\mathbf{x}) = \mathbf{0}$. Conversely, if $\mathbf{R}D(\mathbf{x}) = \mathbf{0}$, then $\mathbf{R}D(\mathbf{x})\mathbf{R}' = D\{\mathbf{R}[\mathbf{x} - E(\mathbf{x})]\} = \mathbf{0}$. But, by definition, $E\{\mathbf{R}[\mathbf{x} - E(\mathbf{x})]\} = \mathbf{0}$, so this implies $\mathbf{R}[\mathbf{x} - E(\mathbf{x})] = \mathbf{0}$ with a probability of 1.

The minimal vector subspace $\mathscr{A} - E(\mathbf{x}) = \mathscr{S} \subset \mathscr{R}^n$ containing $\boldsymbol{\varepsilon} = \mathbf{x} - E(\mathbf{x})$ is called the support of $\boldsymbol{\varepsilon}$. If $\text{Dim}(\mathscr{S}) = q$, we can find a matrix $\mathbf{R}$ with $\text{Null}(\mathbf{R}) = q$ whose null space $\mathscr{N}(\mathbf{R}) = \mathscr{S}$ is identical to the support of $\boldsymbol{\varepsilon}$. It follows from (17.20) that this null space will also be identical to the manifold $\mathscr{M}[D(\mathbf{x})]$ of the dispersion matrix of $\mathbf{x}$. Thus

(17.21) If $\mathscr{S}$ is the minimal vector subspace containing $\boldsymbol{\varepsilon} = \mathbf{x} - E(\mathbf{x})$, and if $D(\mathbf{x}) = \mathbf{Q}$, then $\mathscr{S} = \mathscr{M}(\mathbf{Q})$ and, for every $\boldsymbol{\varepsilon}$, there is some vector $\boldsymbol{\lambda}$ such that $\boldsymbol{\varepsilon} = \mathbf{Q}\boldsymbol{\lambda}$.

A useful way of visualizing the degenerate random vector $\mathbf{x}$ with $E(\mathbf{x}) = \boldsymbol{\mu}$ and $D(\mathbf{x}) = \mathbf{Q}$ is to imagine that it is formed as $\mathbf{x} = \mathbf{L}\boldsymbol{\eta} + \boldsymbol{\mu}$, where $\boldsymbol{\eta}$ has $E(\boldsymbol{\eta}) = \mathbf{0}$ and $D(\boldsymbol{\eta}) = \mathbf{I}$, and $\mathbf{L}$ is an $n \times q$ matrix such that $\mathbf{L}\mathbf{L}' = \mathbf{Q}$. To demonstrate that we can always express $\mathbf{x} = \boldsymbol{\mu} + \boldsymbol{\varepsilon}$ in this form, let $\mathbf{T}$ be a non-singular matrix such that

$$\mathbf{T}\mathbf{Q}\mathbf{T}' = \begin{bmatrix} \mathbf{I}_q, & \mathbf{0} \\ \mathbf{0}, & \mathbf{0} \end{bmatrix}.$$

On partitioning $\mathbf{T}\mathbf{x}$ to conform with this matrix, we get

$$\begin{bmatrix} \mathbf{T}_1\mathbf{x} \\ \mathbf{T}_2\mathbf{x} \end{bmatrix} = \begin{bmatrix} \mathbf{T}_1\boldsymbol{\mu} \\ \mathbf{T}_2\boldsymbol{\mu} \end{bmatrix} + \begin{bmatrix} \boldsymbol{\eta} \\ \mathbf{0} \end{bmatrix}$$

where $\boldsymbol{\eta} \sim (\mathbf{0}, \mathbf{I}_q)$. Now define $[\mathbf{L}, \mathbf{M}] = \mathbf{T}^{-1}$. Then $\mathbf{x} = [\mathbf{L}, \mathbf{M}]\mathbf{T}\mathbf{x} = \mathbf{L}\mathbf{T}_1\boldsymbol{\mu} + \mathbf{M}\mathbf{T}_2\boldsymbol{\mu} + \mathbf{L}\boldsymbol{\eta} = \mathbf{L}\boldsymbol{\eta} + \boldsymbol{\mu}$, or simply $\mathbf{x} = \mathbf{L}\boldsymbol{\eta} + \boldsymbol{\mu}$ as we require.

Finally, we should understand that a degenerate random vector has no density function in the ordinary meaning of this term. This is because the probability density is zero everywhere in $\mathcal{R}^n$ except over a set $\mathcal{A}$ which, having a measure of zero, is of negligible extent.

The multivariate normal distribution

We say that the $n \times 1$ random vector $\mathbf{x}$ is normally distributed with a mean $E(\mathbf{x}) = \boldsymbol{\mu}$ and a dispersion matrix $D(\mathbf{x}) = \boldsymbol{\Sigma}$ if its probability density function is

$$(17.22) \qquad N(\mathbf{x}; \boldsymbol{\mu}, \boldsymbol{\Sigma}) = (2\pi)^{-n/2} |\boldsymbol{\Sigma}|^{-1/2} \exp\{-\tfrac{1}{2}(\mathbf{x}-\boldsymbol{\mu})'\boldsymbol{\Sigma}^{-1}(\mathbf{x}-\boldsymbol{\mu})\}.$$

It is understood that $\mathbf{x}$ is non-degenerate with $\text{Rank}(\boldsymbol{\Sigma}) = n$ and $|\boldsymbol{\Sigma}| \neq 0$. To denote that $\mathbf{x}$ has this distribution, we can write $\mathbf{x} \sim N(\boldsymbol{\mu}, \boldsymbol{\Sigma})$.

We shall demonstrate two notable features of the normal distribution. The first feature is that the conditional and marginal distributions associated with a normally distributed vector are also normal. The second is that any linear function of a normally distributed vector is itself normally distributed.

We shall base our arguments on two fundamental facts. The first is that

(17.23) If $\mathbf{x} \sim N(\boldsymbol{\mu}, \boldsymbol{\Sigma})$ and if $\mathbf{y} = \mathbf{A}(\mathbf{x}-\mathbf{b})$ where $\mathbf{A}$ is non-singular, then $\mathbf{y} \sim N(\mathbf{A}(\boldsymbol{\mu}-\mathbf{b}), \mathbf{A}\boldsymbol{\Sigma}\mathbf{A}')$.

This may be illustrated by considering the case where $\mathbf{b} = \mathbf{0}$. Then, according to the result in (17.8), $\mathbf{y}$ has the distribution

$$(17.24) \qquad \begin{aligned} &N(\mathbf{A}^{-1}\mathbf{y}; \boldsymbol{\mu}, \boldsymbol{\Sigma}) \, \|\partial\mathbf{x}/\partial\mathbf{y}\| \\ &\quad = (2\pi)^{-n/2} |\boldsymbol{\Sigma}|^{-1/2} \exp\{-\tfrac{1}{2}(\mathbf{A}^{-1}\mathbf{y} - \boldsymbol{\mu})'\boldsymbol{\Sigma}^{-1}(\mathbf{A}^{-1}\mathbf{y} - \boldsymbol{\mu})\} \, \|\mathbf{A}^{-1}\| \\ &\quad = (2\pi)^{-n/2} |\mathbf{A}\boldsymbol{\Sigma}\mathbf{A}'|^{-1/2} \exp\{-\tfrac{1}{2}(\mathbf{y} - \mathbf{A}\boldsymbol{\mu})'(\mathbf{A}\boldsymbol{\Sigma}\mathbf{A}')^{-1}(\mathbf{y} - \mathbf{A}\boldsymbol{\mu})\}; \end{aligned}$$

so, clearly, $\mathbf{y} \sim N(\mathbf{A}\boldsymbol{\mu}, \mathbf{A}\boldsymbol{\Sigma}\mathbf{A}')$.

The second of the fundamental facts is that

(17.25) If $\mathbf{x} \sim N(\boldsymbol{\mu}, \boldsymbol{\Sigma})$ can be written in partitioned form as

$$\begin{bmatrix} \mathbf{x}_1 \\ \mathbf{x}_2 \end{bmatrix} \sim N\left(\begin{bmatrix} \boldsymbol{\mu}_1 \\ \boldsymbol{\mu}_2 \end{bmatrix}, \begin{bmatrix} \boldsymbol{\Sigma}_{11}, & \mathbf{0} \\ \mathbf{0}, & \boldsymbol{\Sigma}_{22} \end{bmatrix} \right),$$

then $\mathbf{x}_1 \sim N(\boldsymbol{\mu}_1, \boldsymbol{\Sigma}_{11})$ and $\mathbf{x}_2 \sim N(\boldsymbol{\mu}_2, \boldsymbol{\Sigma}_{22})$ are independently distributed normal variates.

To see this, we need only consider the quadratic form

$$\begin{aligned} &(\mathbf{x}-\boldsymbol{\mu})'\boldsymbol{\Sigma}^{-1}(\mathbf{x}-\boldsymbol{\mu}) \\ &\qquad = (\mathbf{x}_1 - \boldsymbol{\mu}_1)'\boldsymbol{\Sigma}_{11}^{-1}(\mathbf{x}_1 - \boldsymbol{\mu}_1) + (\mathbf{x}_2 - \boldsymbol{\mu}_2)'\boldsymbol{\Sigma}_{22}^{-1}(\mathbf{x}_2 - \boldsymbol{\mu}_2), \end{aligned}$$

that arises in this particular case. On substituting it into the expression for $N(\mathbf{x}; \boldsymbol{\mu}, \boldsymbol{\Sigma})$ in (17.22) and using $|\boldsymbol{\Sigma}| = |\boldsymbol{\Sigma}_{11}|\,|\boldsymbol{\Sigma}_{22}|$, we get

$$\begin{aligned}N(\mathbf{x}; \boldsymbol{\mu}, \boldsymbol{\Sigma}) &= (2\pi)^{-m/2}\,|\boldsymbol{\Sigma}_{11}|^{-1/2} \exp\{-\tfrac{1}{2}(\mathbf{x}_1 - \boldsymbol{\mu}_1)'\boldsymbol{\Sigma}_{11}^{-1}(\mathbf{x}_1 - \boldsymbol{\mu}_1)\}\\ &\quad\times (2\pi)^{(m-n)/2}\,|\boldsymbol{\Sigma}_{22}|^{-1/2} \exp\{-\tfrac{1}{2}(\mathbf{x}_2 - \boldsymbol{\mu}_2)'\boldsymbol{\Sigma}_{22}^{-1}(\mathbf{x}_2 - \boldsymbol{\mu}_2)\}\\ &= N(\mathbf{x}_1; \boldsymbol{\mu}_1, \boldsymbol{\Sigma}_{11})N(\mathbf{x}_2; \boldsymbol{\mu}_2, \boldsymbol{\Sigma}_{22}).\end{aligned}$$

The latter can only be the product of the marginal distributions of $\mathbf{x}_1$ and $\mathbf{x}_2$, which proves that these vectors are independently distributed.

The essential feature of the result is that

(17.26) If $\mathbf{x}_1$ and $\mathbf{x}_2$ are normally distributed with $C(\mathbf{x}_1, \mathbf{x}_2) = \mathbf{0}$, then they are mutually independent.

A zero covariance does not generally imply statistical independence.

Even when $\mathbf{x}_1$, $\mathbf{x}_2$ are not independently distributed, their marginal distributions are still formed in the same way from the appropriate components of $\boldsymbol{\mu}$ and $\boldsymbol{\Sigma}$. This is entailed in the first of our two main results which is that

(17.27) If $\mathbf{x} \sim N(\boldsymbol{\mu}, \boldsymbol{\Sigma})$ is partitioned as

$$\begin{bmatrix}\mathbf{x}_1\\ \mathbf{x}_2\end{bmatrix} \sim N\left(\begin{bmatrix}\boldsymbol{\mu}_1\\ \boldsymbol{\mu}_2\end{bmatrix}, \begin{bmatrix}\boldsymbol{\Sigma}_{11}, & \boldsymbol{\Sigma}_{12}\\ \boldsymbol{\Sigma}_{21}, & \boldsymbol{\Sigma}_{22}\end{bmatrix}\right),$$

then the marginal distribution of $\mathbf{x}_1$ is $N(\boldsymbol{\mu}_1, \boldsymbol{\Sigma}_{11})$ and the conditional distribution of $\mathbf{x}_2$ given $\mathbf{x}_1$ is

$$N(\mathbf{x}_2 \,|\, \mathbf{x}_1; \boldsymbol{\mu}_2 + \boldsymbol{\Sigma}_{21}\boldsymbol{\Sigma}_{11}^{-1}(\mathbf{x}_1 - \boldsymbol{\mu}_1), \boldsymbol{\Sigma}_{22} - \boldsymbol{\Sigma}_{21}\boldsymbol{\Sigma}_{11}^{-1}\boldsymbol{\Sigma}_{12}).$$

Proof. Consider a non-singular transformation

$$\begin{bmatrix}\mathbf{y}_1\\ \mathbf{y}_2\end{bmatrix} = \begin{bmatrix}\mathbf{I}, & \mathbf{0}\\ \mathbf{F}, & \mathbf{I}\end{bmatrix}\begin{bmatrix}\mathbf{x}_1\\ \mathbf{x}_2\end{bmatrix}$$

such that $C(\mathbf{y}_2, \mathbf{y}_1) = C(\mathbf{F}\mathbf{x}_1 + \mathbf{x}_2, \mathbf{x}_1) = \mathbf{F}D(\mathbf{x}_1) + C(\mathbf{x}_2, \mathbf{x}_1) = \mathbf{0}$. Writing this condition as $\mathbf{F}\boldsymbol{\Sigma}_{11} + \boldsymbol{\Sigma}_{21} = \mathbf{0}$ gives $\mathbf{F} = -\boldsymbol{\Sigma}_{21}\boldsymbol{\Sigma}_{11}^{-1}$. It follows that

$$E\begin{bmatrix}\mathbf{y}_1\\ \mathbf{y}_2\end{bmatrix} = \begin{bmatrix}\boldsymbol{\mu}_1\\ \boldsymbol{\mu}_2 - \boldsymbol{\Sigma}_{21}\boldsymbol{\Sigma}_{11}^{-1}\boldsymbol{\mu}_1\end{bmatrix};$$

and, since $D(\mathbf{y}_1) = \boldsymbol{\Sigma}_{11}$, $C(\mathbf{y}_1, \mathbf{y}_2) = \mathbf{0}$ and

$$\begin{aligned}D(\mathbf{y}_2) &= D(\mathbf{F}\mathbf{x}_1 + \mathbf{x}_2)\\ &= \mathbf{F}D(\mathbf{x}_1)\mathbf{F}' + D(\mathbf{x}_2) + \mathbf{F}C(\mathbf{x}_1, \mathbf{x}_2) + C(\mathbf{x}_2, \mathbf{x}_1)\mathbf{F}'\\ &= \boldsymbol{\Sigma}_{21}\boldsymbol{\Sigma}_{11}^{-1}\boldsymbol{\Sigma}_{11}\boldsymbol{\Sigma}_{11}^{-1}\boldsymbol{\Sigma}_{12} + \boldsymbol{\Sigma}_{22} - \boldsymbol{\Sigma}_{21}\boldsymbol{\Sigma}_{11}^{-1}\boldsymbol{\Sigma}_{12} - \boldsymbol{\Sigma}_{21}\boldsymbol{\Sigma}_{11}^{-1}\boldsymbol{\Sigma}_{12}\\ &= \boldsymbol{\Sigma}_{22} - \boldsymbol{\Sigma}_{21}\boldsymbol{\Sigma}_{11}^{-1}\boldsymbol{\Sigma}_{12},\end{aligned}$$

it also follows that

$$D\begin{bmatrix}\mathbf{y}_1\\ \mathbf{y}_2\end{bmatrix}=\begin{bmatrix}\boldsymbol{\Sigma}_{11}, & \mathbf{0}\\ \mathbf{0}, & \boldsymbol{\Sigma}_{22}-\boldsymbol{\Sigma}_{21}\boldsymbol{\Sigma}_{11}^{-1}\boldsymbol{\Sigma}_{12}\end{bmatrix}.$$

Therefore, according to (17.25), we can write the joint density function of $\mathbf{y}_1$, $\mathbf{y}_2$ as

$$N(\mathbf{y}_1;\boldsymbol{\mu}_1,\boldsymbol{\Sigma}_{11})N(\mathbf{y}_2;\boldsymbol{\mu}_2-\boldsymbol{\Sigma}_{21}\boldsymbol{\Sigma}_{11}^{-1}\boldsymbol{\mu}_1,\boldsymbol{\Sigma}_{22}-\boldsymbol{\Sigma}_{21}\boldsymbol{\Sigma}_{11}^{-1}\boldsymbol{\Sigma}_{12}).$$

Integrating with respect to $\mathbf{y}_2$ gives the marginal distribution of $\mathbf{x}_1=\mathbf{y}_1$ as $N(\mathbf{x}_1;\boldsymbol{\mu}_1,\boldsymbol{\Sigma}_{11})$.

Now consider the inverse transformation $\mathbf{x}=\mathbf{x}(\mathbf{y})$. The Jacobian of this transformation is unity. Thus, to obtain an expression for $N(\mathbf{x};\boldsymbol{\mu},\boldsymbol{\Sigma})$, we need only write $\mathbf{y}_2=\mathbf{x}_2-\boldsymbol{\Sigma}_{21}\boldsymbol{\Sigma}_{11}^{-1}\mathbf{x}_1$ and $\mathbf{y}_1=\mathbf{x}_1$ in the expression for the joint distribution of $\mathbf{y}_1$, $\mathbf{y}_2$. This gives us

$$\begin{aligned}N(\mathbf{x};\boldsymbol{\mu},\boldsymbol{\Sigma})&=N(\mathbf{x}_1;\boldsymbol{\mu}_1,\boldsymbol{\Sigma}_{11})\\&\quad\times N(\mathbf{x}_2-\boldsymbol{\Sigma}_{21}\boldsymbol{\Sigma}_{11}^{-1}\mathbf{x}_1;\boldsymbol{\mu}_2-\boldsymbol{\Sigma}_{21}\boldsymbol{\Sigma}_{11}^{-1}\boldsymbol{\mu}_1,\boldsymbol{\Sigma}_{22}-\boldsymbol{\Sigma}_{21}\boldsymbol{\Sigma}_{11}^{-1}\boldsymbol{\Sigma}_{12})\end{aligned}$$

which is the product of the marginal distribution of $\mathbf{x}_1$ and the conditional distribution $N(\mathbf{x}_2\,|\,\mathbf{x}_1;\boldsymbol{\mu}_2+\boldsymbol{\Sigma}_{21}\boldsymbol{\Sigma}_{11}^{-1}(\mathbf{x}_1-\boldsymbol{\mu}_1),\boldsymbol{\Sigma}_{22}-\boldsymbol{\Sigma}_{21}\boldsymbol{\Sigma}_{11}^{-1}\boldsymbol{\Sigma}_{12})$ of $\mathbf{x}_2$ given $\mathbf{x}_1$.

The linear function $E(\mathbf{x}_2\,|\,\mathbf{x}_1)=\boldsymbol{\mu}_2+\boldsymbol{\Sigma}_{21}\boldsymbol{\Sigma}_{11}^{-1}(\mathbf{x}_1-\boldsymbol{\mu}_1)$ that defines the expected value of $\mathbf{x}_2$ for given values of $\mathbf{x}_1$ is described as the regression of $\mathbf{x}_2$ on $\mathbf{x}_1$. The matrix $\boldsymbol{\Sigma}_{21}\boldsymbol{\Sigma}_{11}^{-1}$ is the matrix of the regression coefficients.

Now that we have established in general the form of the marginal distribution, we can prove that any non-degenerate random vector that represents a linear function of a normal vector is itself normally distributed. To this end we prove that

(17.28) If $\mathbf{x}\sim N(\boldsymbol{\mu},\boldsymbol{\Sigma})$ and $\mathbf{y}=\mathbf{B}(\mathbf{x}-\mathbf{b})$ where $\text{Null}(\mathbf{B}')=0$ or, equivalently, $\mathbf{B}$ has full row rank, then $\mathbf{y}\sim N(\mathbf{B}(\boldsymbol{\mu}-\mathbf{b}),\mathbf{B}\boldsymbol{\Sigma}\mathbf{B}')$.

Proof. If $\mathbf{B}$ has full row rank, then there exists a non-singular matrix $\mathbf{A}'=[\mathbf{B}',\mathbf{C}']$ such that

$$\mathbf{q}=\begin{bmatrix}\mathbf{y}\\ \mathbf{z}\end{bmatrix}=\begin{bmatrix}\mathbf{B}\\ \mathbf{C}\end{bmatrix}(\mathbf{x}-\mathbf{b}).$$

Then $\mathbf{q}$ has the distribution $N(\mathbf{q};\mathbf{A}(\boldsymbol{\mu}-\mathbf{b}),\mathbf{A}\boldsymbol{\Sigma}\mathbf{A}')$ where

$$\mathbf{A}(\boldsymbol{\mu}-\mathbf{b})=\begin{bmatrix}\mathbf{B}(\boldsymbol{\mu}-\mathbf{b})\\ \mathbf{C}(\boldsymbol{\mu}-\mathbf{b})\end{bmatrix},\qquad \mathbf{A}\boldsymbol{\Sigma}\mathbf{A}'=\begin{bmatrix}\mathbf{B}\boldsymbol{\Sigma}\mathbf{B}', & \mathbf{B}\boldsymbol{\Sigma}\mathbf{C}'\\ \mathbf{C}\boldsymbol{\Sigma}\mathbf{B}', & \mathbf{C}\boldsymbol{\Sigma}\mathbf{C}'\end{bmatrix}.$$

It follows from (17.27) that $\mathbf{y}$ has the marginal distribution

$$N(\mathbf{B}(\boldsymbol{\mu}-\mathbf{b}),\mathbf{B}\boldsymbol{\Sigma}\mathbf{B}').$$

It is desirable to have a theory that applies to all linear transformations of a normal vector without restriction. In order to generalize our theory to that extent, we require a definition of a normal vector which includes the degenerate case. Therefore we shall say that

(17.29) A vector $\mathbf{x}$ with $E(\mathbf{x})=\boldsymbol{\mu}$ and $D(\mathbf{x})=\mathbf{Q}=\mathbf{LL}'$, where $\mathbf{Q}$ may be singular, has a normal distribution if it can be expressed as $\mathbf{x}=\mathbf{L}\boldsymbol{\eta}+\boldsymbol{\mu}$ where $\boldsymbol{\eta}\sim N(\mathbf{0},\mathbf{I})$.

Then, regardless of the rank of $\mathbf{Q}$, we may express the normality of $\mathbf{x}$ by writing $\mathbf{x}\sim N(\boldsymbol{\mu},\mathbf{Q})$. We can now assert, quite generally, that

(17.30) If $\mathbf{x}\sim N(\boldsymbol{\mu},\boldsymbol{\Sigma})$ is an $n\times 1$ random vector and if $\mathbf{y}=\mathbf{B}(\mathbf{x}-\mathbf{b})$ where $\mathbf{B}$ is any $q\times n$ matrix, then $\mathbf{y}\sim N(\mathbf{B}(\boldsymbol{\mu}-\mathbf{b}),\mathbf{B\Sigma B}')$.

All that we need to demonstrate, in order to justify this statement, is that $\mathbf{y}$ can be written in the form $\mathbf{y}=\mathbf{N}\boldsymbol{\eta}+\mathbf{p}$ where $\boldsymbol{\eta}\sim N(\mathbf{0},\mathbf{I})$ and $\mathbf{p}=E(\mathbf{y})$. This is clearly so, for $\mathbf{x}$ can be written as $\mathbf{x}=\mathbf{L}\boldsymbol{\eta}+\boldsymbol{\mu}$ where $\mathbf{LL}'=\boldsymbol{\Sigma}$, whether or not it is degenerate, whence $\mathbf{y}=\mathbf{BL}\boldsymbol{\eta}+\mathbf{B}(\boldsymbol{\mu}-\mathbf{b})=\mathbf{N}\boldsymbol{\eta}+\mathbf{p}$ with $\mathbf{N}=\mathbf{BL}$ and $\mathbf{p}=\mathbf{B}(\boldsymbol{\mu}-\mathbf{b})=E(\mathbf{y})$.

Distributions associated with the normal distribution

(17.31) Let $\boldsymbol{\eta}\sim N(\mathbf{0},\mathbf{I})$ be an $n\times 1$ vector of independently and identically distributed normal variates $\eta_i\sim N(0,1)$; $i=1,\ldots,n$. Then $\boldsymbol{\eta}'\boldsymbol{\eta}=\sum \eta_i^2$ has a chi-square distribution of n degrees of freedom denoted by $\chi^2(n)$.

The cumulative chi-square distribution is tabulated in most statistics text-books; typically for degrees of freedom from $n=1$ to $n=30$. We shall not bother with the formula for the density function; but we may note that if $w\sim\chi^2(n)$, then $E(w)=n$ and $V(w)=2n$.

(17.32) Let $x\sim N(0,1)$ be a standard normal variate, and let $w\sim\chi^2(n)$ be a chi-square variate of n degrees of freedom. Then the ratio $t=x/\sqrt{w/n}$ has a t distribution of n degrees of freedom denoted $t(n)$.

The t distribution, which is perhaps the most important of the sampling distributions, is also extensively tabulated. Again, we shall not give the formula for the density function; but we may note that the distribution is symmetrical and that $E(t)=0$ and $V(t)=n/(n-2)$. The distribution $t(n)$ approaches the standard normal $N(0,1)$ as n tends to infinity. This results from the fact that, as n tends to infinity, the distribution of the denominator in the ratio defining the t variate becomes increasingly concentrated around the value of unity, thus allowing the variate to be dominated by the numerator.

Finally,

(17.33) Let $w_1 \sim \chi^2(n)$ and $w_2 \sim \chi^2(m)$ be independently distributed chi-square variates of n and m degrees of freedom respectively. Then $F = \{(w_1/n)/(w_2/m)\}$ has an F distribution of n and m degrees of freedom denoted $F(n, m)$.

We may record that $E(F) = m/(m-2)$ and $V(F) = 2m^2[1+(m-2)/n]/(m-2)^2(m-4)$.

We should recognize that

(17.34) If $t \sim t(n)$, then $t^2 \sim F(1, n)$.

This follows from the definition in (17.33); for we have $t^2 = \{(x^2/1)/(w/n)\}$ where $w \sim \chi^2(n)$, and $x^2 \sim \chi^2(1)$ since $x \sim N(0, 1)$.

Quadratic functions of normal vectors

We shall now establish a number of specialized results concerning quadratic functions of normally distributed vectors. We shall change our usual notation for the dispersion matrix of a random vector $\boldsymbol{\varepsilon}$ from $D(\boldsymbol{\varepsilon}) = \boldsymbol{\Sigma}$ to $D(\boldsymbol{\varepsilon}) = \mathbf{Q}$. This is in order to facilitate the application of some of the following results to certain problems that arise in the text. When it becomes important to know that the random vector $\boldsymbol{\varepsilon} \sim N(\mathbf{0}, \mathbf{Q})$ has the order $p \times 1$, we shall write $\boldsymbol{\varepsilon} \sim N_p(\mathbf{0}, \mathbf{Q})$.

We begin with some specialized results concerning the standard normal distribution $N(\boldsymbol{\eta}; \mathbf{0}, \mathbf{I})$.

(17.35) If $\boldsymbol{\eta} \sim N(\mathbf{0}, \mathbf{I})$ and $\mathbf{C}$ is an orthonormal matrix such that $\mathbf{C}'\mathbf{C} = \mathbf{C}\mathbf{C}' = \mathbf{I}$, then $\mathbf{C}'\boldsymbol{\eta} \sim N(\mathbf{0}, \mathbf{I})$.

This is a straightforward specialization of the basic result in (17.23). More generally,

(17.36) If $\boldsymbol{\eta} \sim N_n(\mathbf{0}, \mathbf{I})$ is an $n \times 1$ vector and $\mathbf{C}$ is an $n \times r$ matrix of orthonormal vectors, where $r \leq n$, such that $\mathbf{C}'\mathbf{C} = \mathbf{I}_r$, then $\mathbf{C}'\boldsymbol{\eta} \sim N_r(\mathbf{0}, \mathbf{I})$.

This is a specialization of the more general result under (17.28).

Occasionally we shall wish to transform the non-degenerate vector $\boldsymbol{\varepsilon} \sim N(\mathbf{0}, \mathbf{Q})$ to a standard normal vector.

(17.37) Let $\boldsymbol{\varepsilon} \sim N(\mathbf{0}, \mathbf{Q})$ where $\text{Null}(\mathbf{Q}) = 0$. Then there exists a non-singular matrix $\mathbf{T}$ such that $\mathbf{T}'\mathbf{T} = \mathbf{Q}^{-1}$, $\mathbf{T}\mathbf{Q}\mathbf{T}' = \mathbf{I}$, and it follows that $\mathbf{T}\boldsymbol{\varepsilon} \sim N(\mathbf{0}, \mathbf{I})$.

We can use this result immediately to prove our first result concerning quadratic forms:

(17.38) If $\boldsymbol{\varepsilon} \sim N_n(\mathbf{0}, \mathbf{Q})$ and $\mathbf{Q}^{-1}$ exists, then $\boldsymbol{\varepsilon}'\mathbf{Q}^{-1}\boldsymbol{\varepsilon} \sim \chi^2(n)$.

This follows since, if $\mathbf{T}$ is a matrix such that $\mathbf{T}'\mathbf{T} = \mathbf{Q}^{-1}$, $\mathbf{TQT}' = \mathbf{I}$, we have $\boldsymbol{\eta} = \mathbf{T}\boldsymbol{\varepsilon} \sim N_n(\mathbf{0}, \mathbf{I})$; whence, from (17.31), we have $\boldsymbol{\eta}'\boldsymbol{\eta} = \boldsymbol{\varepsilon}'\mathbf{T}'\mathbf{T}\boldsymbol{\varepsilon} = \boldsymbol{\varepsilon}'\mathbf{Q}^{-1}\boldsymbol{\varepsilon} \sim \chi^2(n)$.

This result shows how we may form a chi-square variate from a normally distributed vector by standardizing it and then forming the inner product. The next result shows that, given a standard normal vector, there are a limited variety of ways in which we can form a chi-square variate.

(17.39) If $\boldsymbol{\eta} \sim N_n(\mathbf{0}, \mathbf{I})$, then $\boldsymbol{\eta}'\mathbf{P}\boldsymbol{\eta} \sim \chi^2(p)$ when $\mathbf{P}$ is symmetric if and only if $\mathbf{P} = \mathbf{P}^2$ and $\text{Rank}(\mathbf{P}) = p$

Proof. If $\mathbf{P}$ is symmetric and idempotent such that $\mathbf{P} = \mathbf{P}' = \mathbf{P}^2$, and if $\text{Rank}(\mathbf{P}) = p$, then there exists a matrix $\mathbf{C}$, comprising p orthonormal vectors, such that $\mathbf{CC}' = \mathbf{P}$ and $\mathbf{C}'\mathbf{C} = \mathbf{I}_p$. Thus, $\boldsymbol{\eta}'\mathbf{P}\boldsymbol{\eta} = \boldsymbol{\eta}'\mathbf{CC}'\boldsymbol{\eta} = \mathbf{z}'\mathbf{z}$ where $\mathbf{z} = \mathbf{C}'\boldsymbol{\eta} \sim N_p(\mathbf{0}, \mathbf{I})$, according to (17.35), which implies $\boldsymbol{\eta}'\mathbf{P}\boldsymbol{\eta} = \mathbf{z}'\mathbf{z} \sim \chi^2(p)$.

Conversely, if $\mathbf{P}$ is a symmetric matrix, there exists an orthonormal matrix $\mathbf{C}$, comprising n vectors, such that $\mathbf{C}'\mathbf{PC} = \boldsymbol{\Lambda}$ is a diagonal matrix of the characteristic roots of $\mathbf{P}$. Now, since $\mathbf{C}'\mathbf{C} = \mathbf{CC}' = \mathbf{I}$, we have $\boldsymbol{\eta}'\mathbf{P}\boldsymbol{\eta} = \boldsymbol{\eta}'\mathbf{CC}'\mathbf{PCC}'\boldsymbol{\eta} = \boldsymbol{\eta}'\mathbf{C}\boldsymbol{\Lambda}\mathbf{C}'\boldsymbol{\eta} = \mathbf{z}'\boldsymbol{\Lambda}\mathbf{z}$ where $\mathbf{z} = \mathbf{C}'\boldsymbol{\eta} \sim N_n(\mathbf{0}, \mathbf{I})$. Hence $\boldsymbol{\eta}'\mathbf{P}\boldsymbol{\eta} = \mathbf{z}'\boldsymbol{\Lambda}\mathbf{z} \sim \chi^2(p)$ only if the diagonal matrix $\boldsymbol{\Lambda}$ comprises p units and $T - p$ zeros on the diagonal and zeros elsewhere. This means that we must have $\text{Rank}(\mathbf{P}) = p$ and $\boldsymbol{\Lambda} = \boldsymbol{\Lambda}^2$. Furthermore, $\mathbf{C}'\mathbf{PC} = \boldsymbol{\Lambda}$ implies $\mathbf{P} = \mathbf{C}\boldsymbol{\Lambda}\mathbf{C}'$. Hence $\mathbf{P}^2 = \mathbf{C}\boldsymbol{\Lambda}\mathbf{C}'\mathbf{C}\boldsymbol{\Lambda}\mathbf{C}' = \mathbf{C}\boldsymbol{\Lambda}^2\mathbf{C}' = \mathbf{C}\boldsymbol{\Lambda}\mathbf{C} = \mathbf{P}$, so $\mathbf{P}$ must also be idempotent.

The only $n \times n$ idempotent matrix of rank n is the identity matrix. Thus we see, as a corollary of (17.39), that, if $\boldsymbol{\eta} \sim N_n(\mathbf{0}, \mathbf{I})$, then $\boldsymbol{\eta}'\mathbf{P}\boldsymbol{\eta} \sim \chi^2(n)$ if and only if $\mathbf{P} = \mathbf{I}$.

The result (17.39) may be used to prove a more general result concerning the formation of chi-square variates from normal vectors.

(17.40) Let $\boldsymbol{\varepsilon} \sim N_n(\mathbf{0}, \mathbf{Q})$ where $\mathbf{Q}$ may be singular. Then, when $\mathbf{A}$ is symmetric, $\boldsymbol{\varepsilon}'\mathbf{A}\boldsymbol{\varepsilon} \sim \chi^2(p)$ if and only if $\mathbf{QAQAQ} = \mathbf{QAQ}$ and $\text{Rank}(\mathbf{QAQ}) = p$.

Proof. Let $\mathbf{Q} = \mathbf{LL}'$ with $\text{Null}(\mathbf{L}) = 0$, so that $\boldsymbol{\varepsilon} = \mathbf{L}\boldsymbol{\eta}$ where $\boldsymbol{\eta} \sim N(\mathbf{0}, \mathbf{I})$. Then, by the previous theorem, $\boldsymbol{\eta}'\mathbf{L}'\mathbf{AL}\boldsymbol{\eta} \sim \chi^2(p)$ if and only if $(\mathbf{L}'\mathbf{AL})^2 = \mathbf{L}'\mathbf{AL}$ and $\text{Rank}(\mathbf{L}'\mathbf{AL}) = p$. We must establish that these two conditions are equivalent to $\mathbf{QAQAQ} = \mathbf{QAQ}$ and $\text{Rank}(\mathbf{QAQ}) = p$ respectively. Premultiplying the equation $(\mathbf{L}'\mathbf{AL})^2 = \mathbf{L}'\mathbf{AL}$ by $\mathbf{L}$ and postmultiplying it by $\mathbf{L}'$ gives $\mathbf{LL}'\mathbf{ALL}'\mathbf{ALL}' = \mathbf{QAQAQ} = \mathbf{LL}'\mathbf{ALL}' = \mathbf{QAQ}$. Conversely, since $\text{Null}(\mathbf{L}) = 0$ implies that $\mathbf{L}^{L}$ and $\mathbf{L}'^{R}$ exist, we may premultiply and postmultiply the equation $\mathbf{QAQAQ}=\mathbf{QAQ}$ to obtain $\mathbf{L}^L\mathbf{QAQAQL}'^R=\mathbf{L}'\mathbf{ALL}'\mathbf{AL}=(\mathbf{L}'\mathbf{AL})^2=\mathbf{L}^L\mathbf{QAQL}'^R=\mathbf{L}'\mathbf{AL}$. Thus the first equivalence is established. To establish the second equivalence, we invoke the results under (2.24) and (2.25) to show that $\text{Null}(\mathbf{L})=0$ implies $\text{Rank}(\mathbf{QAQ})=\text{Rank}(\mathbf{LL}'\mathbf{ALL}')=\text{Rank}(\mathbf{L}'\mathbf{AL})$.

A straightforward corollary of the result (17.40) which is also an immediate generalization of (17.38) is that

(17.41) If $\boldsymbol{\varepsilon}\sim N_n(\mathbf{0},\mathbf{Q})$, then $\boldsymbol{\varepsilon}'\mathbf{Q}^-\boldsymbol{\varepsilon}\sim\chi^2(q)$ where $q=\text{Rank}(\mathbf{Q})$.

This follows because, when $\mathbf{A}=\mathbf{Q}^-$, the condition $\mathbf{QQ}^-\mathbf{Q}=\mathbf{Q}$ implies that $\mathbf{QAQAQ}=\mathbf{QAQ}$ and $\text{Rank}(\mathbf{QAQ})=\text{Rank}(\mathbf{Q})$.

The decomposition of a chi-square variate

We have shown that, given any kind of normally distributed vector in $\mathcal{R}^n$, we can construct a quadratic form that is distributed as a chi-square variate. We shall now show that this chi-square variate can be decomposed, in turn, into a sum of statistically independent chi-square variates of lesser orders.

Associated with the decomposition of the chi-square variate is a parallel decomposition of the normal vector into a sum of independently distributed component vectors residing in virtually disjoint subspaces of $\mathcal{R}^n$. Each component of the decomposed chi-square variate can be expressed as a quadratic form in one of these components of the normal vector.

The algebraic details of these decompositions depend upon the specification of the distribution of the normal vector. We shall deal successively with the standard normal vector $\boldsymbol{\eta}\sim N(\mathbf{0},\mathbf{I})$, a non-degenerate normal vector $\boldsymbol{\varepsilon}\sim N(\mathbf{0},\mathbf{Q})$ and a degenerate normal vector. Thus we shall present a sequence of results of increasing generality that has the same progression as the sequence of results in the previous section.

Let us begin by considering the transformation of the standard normal vector into k mutually orthogonal vectors. Our purpose is to show that the ordinary inner products of these vectors constitute a set of mutually independent chi-square variates. The transformation of $\boldsymbol{\eta}$ into the k vectors $\mathbf{P}_1\boldsymbol{\eta},\ldots,\mathbf{P}_k\boldsymbol{\eta}$ is effected by using a set of symmetric idempotent matrices $\mathbf{P}_1,\ldots,\mathbf{P}_k$ with the properties that $\mathbf{P}_i=\mathbf{P}_i^2$ and $\mathbf{P}_i\mathbf{P}_j=\mathbf{0}$. The condition $\mathbf{P}_i=\mathbf{P}_i^2$ implies, according to (2.28), that the matrices are projectors, and the condition $\mathbf{P}_i\mathbf{P}_j=\mathbf{0}$ implies that $\mathcal{R}(\mathbf{P}_i)\perp\mathcal{R}(\mathbf{P}_j)$ which means that every vector in the range space of $\mathbf{P}_i$ is orthogonal to every vector in the range space of $\mathbf{P}_j$. To understand the latter, consider any two vectors $\mathbf{x},\mathbf{y}\in\mathcal{R}^n$. Then $\mathbf{x}'\mathbf{P}_i\mathbf{P}_j\mathbf{y}=\mathbf{x}'\mathbf{P}_i'\mathbf{P}_j\mathbf{y}=\mathbf{0}$, so that $\mathbf{P}_i\mathbf{x}\perp\mathbf{P}_j\mathbf{y}$. The condition $\mathbf{P}_i\mathbf{P}_j=\mathbf{0}$ also implies, of course, that $\mathcal{R}(\mathbf{P}_i)\cap\mathcal{R}(\mathbf{P}_j)=\mathbf{0}$, so that $\mathcal{R}(\mathbf{P}_1)\oplus\ldots\oplus\mathcal{R}(\mathbf{P}_k)$ is a direct sum of virtually disjoint subspaces.

In proving our theorem we shall make use of the following result.

(17.42) Let $\mathbf{P}_1, \ldots, \mathbf{P}_k$ be a set of symmetric idempotent matrices such that $\mathbf{P}_i = \mathbf{P}_i^2$ and $\mathbf{P}_i\mathbf{P}_j = \mathbf{0}$ when $i \neq j$. Then there exists a partitioned matrix of orthonormal vectors $\mathbf{C} = [\mathbf{C}_1, \ldots, \mathbf{C}_k]$ such that $\mathbf{C}_i\mathbf{C}_i' = \mathbf{P}_i$ and $\mathbf{C}_i'\mathbf{C}_j = \mathbf{0}$.

Proof. Let $\mathbf{C}_i$ be an orthonormal matrix whose vectors constitute a basis of $\mathcal{R}(\mathbf{P}_i)$. Then $\mathbf{C}_i\mathbf{C}_i' = \mathbf{P}_i$ satisfies the conditions $\mathbf{P}_i' = \mathbf{P}_i = \mathbf{P}_i^2$. Also, since $\mathbf{P}_i\mathbf{P}_j = \mathbf{0}$, we have $\mathbf{C}_i'\mathbf{C}_j = \mathbf{0}$. For, with $\text{Null}(\mathbf{C}_i) = 0$ and $\text{Null}(\mathbf{C}_j) = 0$, we have $\text{Rank}(\mathbf{C}_i'\mathbf{C}_j) = \text{Rank}(\mathbf{C}_i\mathbf{C}_i'\mathbf{C}_j\mathbf{C}_j') = \text{Rank}(\mathbf{P}_i\mathbf{P}_j) = 0$ or, equivalently, $\mathbf{C}_i'\mathbf{C}_j = \mathbf{0}$.

There are, in fact, a number of alternative ways in which we may characterize the set of projectors $\mathbf{P}_1, \ldots, \mathbf{P}_k$. To begin with,

(17.43) Let $\mathbf{C} = [\mathbf{C}_1, \ldots, \mathbf{C}_k]$ be a matrix of orthonormal vectors such that $\mathbf{C}_i'\mathbf{C}_j = \mathbf{0}$ when $i \neq j$. Then $\mathbf{C}'\mathbf{C} = \mathbf{I}$, and $\mathbf{CC}' = \mathbf{C}_1\mathbf{C}_1' + \ldots + \mathbf{C}_k\mathbf{C}_k'$ is a sum of symmetric idempotent matrices. Denoting $\mathbf{CC}' = \mathbf{P}$ and $\mathbf{C}_i\mathbf{C}_i' = \mathbf{P}_i$, we have

(a) $\mathbf{P}_i^2 = \mathbf{P}_i$,
(b) $\mathbf{P}_i\mathbf{P}_j = \mathbf{0}$,
(c) $\mathbf{P}^2 = \mathbf{P}$,

(d) $\text{Rank}(\mathbf{P}) = \sum_{i=1}^{k} \text{Rank}(\mathbf{P}_i)$.

All of this is easily confirmed. What actually enables us to provide the alternative characterizations is the following result:

(17.44) Given condition (c), conditions (a), (b), and (d) of (17.43) are equivalent. Also conditions (a), (b) together imply condition (c).

Proof. (i) The conditions (c), (d) imply the conditions (a), (b): with $\mathbf{P} = \mathbf{P}_1 + \ldots + \mathbf{P}_k$ (d) implies that $\mathcal{R}(\mathbf{P}) = \mathcal{R}(\mathbf{P}_1) \oplus \ldots \oplus \mathcal{R}(\mathbf{P}_k)$ is a direct sum of virtually disjoint subspaces. (c) implies that $\mathbf{y} = \mathbf{Py}$ if $\mathbf{y} \in \mathcal{R}(\mathbf{P})$. Consider $\mathbf{y} = \mathbf{P}_j\mathbf{x} \in \mathcal{R}(\mathbf{P})$. Then $\mathbf{P}_j\mathbf{x} = \mathbf{PP}_j\mathbf{x} = (\sum \mathbf{P}_i)\mathbf{P}_j\mathbf{x}$. But the range spaces of $\mathbf{P}_1, \ldots, \mathbf{P}_k$ are virtually disjoint, so this implies that $\mathbf{P}_i\mathbf{P}_j\mathbf{x} = \mathbf{0}$ and $\mathbf{P}_j^2\mathbf{x} = \mathbf{P}_j\mathbf{x}$ for all $\mathbf{x}$ or $\mathbf{P}_i\mathbf{P}_j = \mathbf{0}$, $\mathbf{P}_i^2 = \mathbf{P}_i$.

(ii) The conditions (c), (b) imply the condition (a): (b) implies $\mathbf{PP}_i = (\sum \mathbf{P}_j)\mathbf{P}_i = \mathbf{P}_i^2$. Let λ and $\mathbf{x}$ be any latent root and vector of $\mathbf{P}_i$ such that $\lambda\mathbf{x} = \mathbf{P}_i\mathbf{x}$. Then $\lambda\mathbf{Px} = \mathbf{PP}_i\mathbf{x} = \mathbf{P}_i^2\mathbf{x} = \lambda\mathbf{P}_i\mathbf{x}$. Cancelling λ from $\lambda\mathbf{Px} = \lambda\mathbf{P}_i\mathbf{x}$ gives $\mathbf{Px} = \mathbf{P}_i\mathbf{x} = \lambda\mathbf{x}$, so λ and $\mathbf{x}$ are also a characteristic root and vector of $\mathbf{P}$. Now $\mathbf{P}_i = \mathbf{P}_i^2$ if and only if $\mathbf{P}_i\mathbf{x} = \lambda\mathbf{x}$ implies $\lambda = 0$ or 1. But, by (c), $\mathbf{P} = \mathbf{P}^2$, so $\mathbf{Px} = \lambda\mathbf{x}$ implies $\lambda = 0$ or 1; hence $\mathbf{P}_i\mathbf{x} = \lambda\mathbf{x}$ implies $\mathbf{P}_i^2 = \mathbf{P}_i$.

(iii) The conditions (c), (a) imply the condition (d): (a) implies $\text{Rank}(\mathbf{P}_i)=\text{Trace}(\mathbf{P}_i)$ and (c) implies $\text{Rank}(\mathbf{P})=\text{Trace}(\mathbf{P})$; hence $\text{Trace}(\mathbf{P})=\text{Trace}(\sum\mathbf{P}_i)=\sum[\text{Trace}(\mathbf{P}_i)]$ implies $\text{Rank}(\mathbf{P})=\sum\text{Rank}(\mathbf{P}_i)$.

We have shown that (c), (d) $\Rightarrow$ (b), that (c), (b) $\Rightarrow$ (a) and that (c), (a) $\Rightarrow$ (d). Thus, given (c), we have (d) $\Rightarrow$ (b) $\Rightarrow$ (a) $\Rightarrow$ (d); so the conditions (a), (b), (d) are equivalent.

(iv) Conditions (a), (b) imply (c): with $\mathbf{P}=\sum\mathbf{P}_i$ (a) implies $\mathbf{P}^2=\sum\mathbf{P}_i^2+\sum_{i\neq j}\sum\mathbf{P}_i\mathbf{P}_j=\sum\mathbf{P}_i+\sum\sum_{i\neq j}\mathbf{P}_i\mathbf{P}_j$, whence (b) implies $\mathbf{P}^2=\sum\mathbf{P}_i^2=\sum\mathbf{P}_i=\mathbf{P}$.

An alternative and logically equivalent way of stating the theorem in (17.44) is to say that any two of the conditions (a), (b), (c) in (17.43) imply all four conditions (a), (b), (c), (d), and the conditions (c), (b) together imply the conditions (a), (b).

These equivalences amongst sets of conditions provide us with a number of alternative ways of stating our basic theorem concerning the formation of a set of mutually independent chi-square variates from the standard normal vector $\boldsymbol{\eta}\sim N(\mathbf{0},\mathbf{I})$. Our preferred way of stating the theorem is as follows:

(17.45) Let $\boldsymbol{\eta}\sim N(\mathbf{0},\mathbf{I})$, and let $\mathbf{P}=\sum\mathbf{P}_i$ be a sum of k symmetric matrices with $\text{Rank}(\mathbf{P})=r$ and $\text{Rank}(\mathbf{P}_i)=r_i$ such that $\mathbf{P}_i=\mathbf{P}_i^2$ and $\mathbf{P}_i\mathbf{P}_j=\mathbf{0}$ when $i\neq j$. Then $\boldsymbol{\eta}'\mathbf{P}_i\boldsymbol{\eta}\sim\chi^2(r_i)$; $i=1,\ldots,k$ are independent chi-square variates such that $\sum\boldsymbol{\eta}'\mathbf{P}_i\boldsymbol{\eta}=\boldsymbol{\eta}'\mathbf{P}\boldsymbol{\eta}\sim\chi^2(r)$ with $r=\sum r_i$.

Proof. If the conditions of the theorem are satisfied, then there exists a partitioned $n\times r$ matrix of orthonormal vectors $\mathbf{C}=[\mathbf{C}_1,\ldots,\mathbf{C}_k]$ such that $\mathbf{C}'\mathbf{C}=\mathbf{I}_r$, $\mathbf{C}_i'\mathbf{C}_j=\mathbf{0}$ and $\mathbf{C}_i\mathbf{C}_i'=\mathbf{P}_i$. If $\boldsymbol{\eta}\sim N_n(\mathbf{0},\mathbf{I})$, then $\mathbf{C}'\boldsymbol{\eta}\sim N_r(\mathbf{0},\mathbf{I})$; and this can be written as

$$\mathbf{C}'\boldsymbol{\eta}=\begin{bmatrix}\mathbf{C}_1'\boldsymbol{\eta}\\ \mathbf{C}_2'\boldsymbol{\eta}\\ \cdot\\ \cdot\\ \cdot\\ \mathbf{C}_k'\boldsymbol{\eta}\end{bmatrix}\sim N_r\left(\begin{bmatrix}\mathbf{0}\\ \mathbf{0}\\ \cdot\\ \cdot\\ \cdot\\ \mathbf{0}\end{bmatrix},\begin{bmatrix}\mathbf{I}_{r_1}, & \mathbf{0}, & \ldots, & \mathbf{0}\\ \mathbf{0}, & \mathbf{I}_{r_2}, & \ldots, & \mathbf{0}\\ \cdot & \cdot & & \cdot\\ \cdot & \cdot & & \cdot\\ \cdot & \cdot & & \cdot\\ \mathbf{0}, & \mathbf{0}, & \ldots, & \mathbf{I}_{r_k}\end{bmatrix}\right)$$

wherein $\mathbf{C}_i\boldsymbol{\eta}\sim N_{r_i}(\mathbf{0},\mathbf{I})$ for $i=1,\ldots,k$ are mutually independent standard normal variates. Thus $\boldsymbol{\eta}'\mathbf{C}\mathbf{C}'\boldsymbol{\eta}\sim\chi^2(r)$ is a chi-square variate and also $\boldsymbol{\eta}'\mathbf{C}_i\mathbf{C}_i'\boldsymbol{\eta}\sim\chi^2(r_i)$ for $i=1,\ldots,k$ constitute a set of mutually independent chi-square variates. Now observe that $\boldsymbol{\eta}'\mathbf{C}\mathbf{C}'\boldsymbol{\eta}=\boldsymbol{\eta}'[\mathbf{C}_1\mathbf{C}_1'+\ldots+\mathbf{C}_k\mathbf{C}_k']\boldsymbol{\eta}=\sum\boldsymbol{\eta}'\mathbf{C}_i\mathbf{C}_i'\boldsymbol{\eta}$. Thus, using $\mathbf{P}_i=\mathbf{C}_i\mathbf{C}_i'$ and the notation $\mathbf{P}=\mathbf{C}\mathbf{C}'$, we have $\sum\boldsymbol{\eta}'\mathbf{P}_i\boldsymbol{\eta}=\boldsymbol{\eta}'\mathbf{P}\boldsymbol{\eta}\sim\chi^2(r)$. Finally, it is clear from the construction that $r=\sum r_i$.

Actually, the conditions $\mathbf{P}_i=\mathbf{P}_i^2$ and $\mathbf{P}_i\mathbf{P}_j=\mathbf{0}$ are both necessary and sufficient for the result. For, according to (17.39), $\boldsymbol{\eta}'\mathbf{P}_i\boldsymbol{\eta}$ is a chi-square if and only if $\mathbf{P}_i = \mathbf{P}_i^2$ and, according to a theorem that we have not proved, $\boldsymbol{\eta}'\mathbf{P}_i\boldsymbol{\eta}$ and $\boldsymbol{\eta}'\mathbf{P}_j\boldsymbol{\eta}$ are independent if and only if $\mathbf{P}_i\mathbf{P}_j = \mathbf{0}$.

The theorem in (17.45) was originally proved by Cochran [**23**] for the case where $\mathbf{P} = \mathbf{I}_n$ with the implicit condition $\mathbf{P} = \mathbf{P}^2$ and the condition $\sum \text{Rank}(\mathbf{P}_i) = n$ replacing $\mathbf{P}_i = \mathbf{P}_i^2$ and $\mathbf{P}_i\mathbf{P}_j = \mathbf{0}$.

We can readily generalize the theorem to apply to the case of a non-degenerate random vector $\boldsymbol{\varepsilon} \sim N(\mathbf{0}, \mathbf{Q})$.

(17.46) Let $\boldsymbol{\varepsilon} \sim N(\mathbf{0}, \mathbf{Q})$, and let $\mathbf{P} = \sum \mathbf{P}_i$ be a sum of k $\mathbf{Q}^{-1}$-symmetric matrices with $\text{Rank}(\mathbf{P}) = r$ and $\text{Rank}(\mathbf{P}_i) = r_i$ such that $\mathbf{P}_i = \mathbf{P}_i^2$ and $\mathbf{P}_i\mathbf{P}_j = \mathbf{0}$. Then $\boldsymbol{\varepsilon}'\mathbf{P}_i\mathbf{Q}^{-1}\mathbf{P}_i\boldsymbol{\varepsilon} = \boldsymbol{\varepsilon}'\mathbf{Q}^{-1}\mathbf{P}_i\boldsymbol{\varepsilon} \sim \chi^2(r_i)$; $i = 1, \ldots, k$ are independent chi-square variates such that $\sum \boldsymbol{\varepsilon}'\mathbf{P}_i'\mathbf{Q}^{-1}\mathbf{P}_i\boldsymbol{\varepsilon} = \boldsymbol{\varepsilon}'\mathbf{P}'\mathbf{Q}^{-1}\mathbf{P}\boldsymbol{\varepsilon} = \boldsymbol{\varepsilon}'\mathbf{Q}^{-1}\mathbf{P}\boldsymbol{\varepsilon} \sim \chi^2(r)$ with $r = \sum r_i$.

Proof. Since $\mathbf{P}_i$ is $\mathbf{Q}^{-1}$-symmetric, we have $\mathbf{Q}^{-1}\mathbf{P}_i = \mathbf{P}_i'\mathbf{Q}^{-1}$. With $\mathbf{P}_i = \mathbf{P}_i^2$ it follows that $\mathbf{P}_i'\mathbf{Q}^{-1}\mathbf{P}_i = \mathbf{Q}^{-1}\mathbf{P}_i\mathbf{P}_i = \mathbf{Q}^{-1}\mathbf{P}_i$, which explains the alternative ways of writing the variates.

Now let $\mathbf{T}$ be a non-singular matrix such that $\mathbf{TQT}' = \mathbf{I}$, $\mathbf{T}'\mathbf{T} = \mathbf{Q}^{-1}$. Then $\mathbf{TP}_i\mathbf{T}^{-1}$, $\mathbf{TP}_j\mathbf{T}^{-1}$ are symmetric matrices such that $(\mathbf{TP}_i\mathbf{T}^{-1})^2 = \mathbf{TP}_i\mathbf{T}^{-1}$ and $(\mathbf{TP}_i\mathbf{T}^{-1})(\mathbf{TP}_j\mathbf{T}^{-1}) = \mathbf{0}$. It follows that $\sum \mathbf{TP}_i\mathbf{T}^{-1} = \mathbf{T}(\sum \mathbf{P}_i)\mathbf{T}^{-1} = \mathbf{TPT}^{-1}$ is a sum of symmetric matrices obeying the conditions of the theorem (17.45). Next consider that $\boldsymbol{\varepsilon} \sim N(\mathbf{0}, \mathbf{Q})$ implies $\boldsymbol{\varepsilon} = \mathbf{T}^{-1}\boldsymbol{\eta}$ where $\boldsymbol{\eta} \sim N(\mathbf{0}, \boldsymbol{I})$. Therefore it follows from the theorem that $\boldsymbol{\varepsilon}'\mathbf{P}_i'\mathbf{Q}^{-1}\mathbf{P}_i\boldsymbol{\varepsilon} = \boldsymbol{\eta}'\mathbf{T}^{-1\prime}\mathbf{P}_i'\mathbf{T}'\mathbf{TP}_i\mathbf{T}^{-1}\boldsymbol{\eta} = \boldsymbol{\eta}'(\mathbf{TP}_i\mathbf{T}^{-1})^2\boldsymbol{\eta} \sim \chi^2(r_i)$; $i = 1, \ldots, k$ are independent chi-square variates.

Finally, $\mathbf{P}_i\mathbf{P}_j = \mathbf{0}$ gives $\sum \mathbf{P}_i'\mathbf{Q}^{-1}\mathbf{P}_i = (\sum \mathbf{P}_i)'\mathbf{Q}^{-1}(\sum \mathbf{P}_i) = \mathbf{P}'\mathbf{Q}^{-1}\mathbf{P}$. Also $\sum \mathbf{P}_i'\mathbf{Q}^{-1}\mathbf{P}_i = \sum \mathbf{Q}^{-1}\mathbf{P}_i = \mathbf{Q}^{-1}\mathbf{P}$. Thus the two expressions for the sum of the variates are justified.

The following result is more general.

(17.47) Let $\boldsymbol{\varepsilon} \sim N(\mathbf{0}, \mathbf{Q})$, where $\mathbf{Q}$ may be singular, and let $\mathbf{A}_1, \ldots, \mathbf{A}_k$ be a set of matrices such that $\sum \mathbf{QA}_i\mathbf{Q} = \mathbf{QAQ}$ with $\text{Rank}(\mathbf{QA}_i\mathbf{Q}) = r_i$ and $\text{Rank}(\mathbf{QAQ}) = r$. Then, if $\mathbf{QA}_i\mathbf{QA}_i\mathbf{Q} = \mathbf{QA}_i\mathbf{Q}$ for all i and $\mathbf{QA}_i\mathbf{QA}_j\mathbf{Q} = \mathbf{0}$ when $i \neq j$, it follows that $\boldsymbol{\varepsilon}'\mathbf{A}_i\boldsymbol{\varepsilon} \sim \chi^2(r_i)$; $i = 1, \ldots, k$ are independent chi-square variates such that $\sum \boldsymbol{\varepsilon}'\mathbf{A}_i\boldsymbol{\varepsilon} = \boldsymbol{\varepsilon}'\mathbf{A}\boldsymbol{\varepsilon} \sim \chi^2(r)$ with $r = \sum_{r_i}$.

Proof. Let $\mathbf{L}$ with $\text{Null}(\mathbf{L}) = 0$ be such that $\mathbf{LL}' = \mathbf{Q}$. Then $\sum \mathbf{QA}_i\mathbf{Q} = \mathbf{QAQ}$ is equivalent to $\sum \mathbf{L}'\mathbf{A}_i\mathbf{L} = \mathbf{L}'\mathbf{AL}$. Likewise, the condition $\mathbf{QA}_i\mathbf{QA}_i\mathbf{Q} = \mathbf{QA}_i\mathbf{Q}$ is equivalent to $(\mathbf{L}'\mathbf{A}_i\mathbf{L})^2 = \mathbf{L}'\mathbf{A}_i\mathbf{L}$, and $\mathbf{QA}_i\mathbf{QA}_j\mathbf{Q} = \mathbf{0}$ is equivalent to $(\mathbf{L}'\mathbf{A}_i\mathbf{L})(\mathbf{L}'\mathbf{A}_j\mathbf{L}) = \mathbf{0}$. Now consider the fact that $\boldsymbol{\varepsilon} \sim N(\mathbf{0}, \mathbf{Q})$ implies that $\boldsymbol{\varepsilon} = \mathbf{L}\boldsymbol{\eta}$ for some $\boldsymbol{\eta} \sim N(\mathbf{0}, \mathbf{I})$. It follows that $\boldsymbol{\varepsilon}'\mathbf{A}_i\boldsymbol{\varepsilon} = \boldsymbol{\eta}'\mathbf{L}'\mathbf{A}_i\mathbf{L}\boldsymbol{\eta} = \boldsymbol{\eta}'\mathbf{P}_i\boldsymbol{\eta}$, where $\mathbf{P}_i = \mathbf{L}'\mathbf{A}_i\mathbf{L}$; $i = 1, \ldots, k$, obey all the conditions of theorem (17.45). Therefore the propositions above follow immediately.

We shall conclude this section by proving a result that is used in Chapter 9 in dealing with the regression model $(\mathbf{y}, \mathbf{X}\boldsymbol{\beta}, \sigma^2\mathbf{Q})$ where $\mathbf{Q}$ is a singular matrix.

(17.48) Let $\boldsymbol{\varepsilon} \sim N(\mathbf{0}, \mathbf{Q})$ where $\mathbf{Q}$ may be singular, and let $\mathbf{PQ} = \sum \mathbf{P}_i\mathbf{Q}$ be a sum of matrices such that $\mathbf{P}_i\mathbf{Q} = \mathbf{P}_i\mathbf{QP}_i' = \mathbf{QP}_i'$ for all i and $\mathbf{P}_i\mathbf{QP}_j' = \mathbf{0}$ if $i \neq j$, and let $\text{Rank}(\mathbf{P}_i\mathbf{Q}) = r_i$ and $\text{Rank}(\mathbf{PQ}) = r$. Then $\boldsymbol{\varepsilon}'\mathbf{P}_i'\mathbf{Q}^-\mathbf{P}_i\boldsymbol{\varepsilon} \sim \chi^2(r_i)$; $i = 1, \ldots, k$ are mutually independent chi-square variates such that $\sum \boldsymbol{\varepsilon}'\mathbf{P}_i'\mathbf{Q}^-\mathbf{P}_i\boldsymbol{\varepsilon} = \boldsymbol{\varepsilon}'\mathbf{P}'\mathbf{Q}^-\mathbf{P}\boldsymbol{\varepsilon} \sim \chi^2(r)$ where $r = \sum r_i$.

Proof. We need only demonstrate that $\mathbf{A}_i = \mathbf{P}_i'\mathbf{Q}^-\mathbf{P}_i$; $i = 1, \ldots, k$ satisfy the conditions of the previous theorem (17.47).

First, we use $\mathbf{P}_i\mathbf{Q} = \mathbf{P}_i\mathbf{QP}_i' = \mathbf{QP}_i'$ and its implication $\mathbf{QP}_i' = \mathbf{QP}_i'\mathbf{P}_i'$ to show that $(\mathbf{QP}_i')\mathbf{Q}^-(\mathbf{P}_i\mathbf{Q})\mathbf{P}_i'\mathbf{Q}^-\mathbf{P}_i\mathbf{Q} = \mathbf{P}_i(\mathbf{QQ}^-\mathbf{Q})\mathbf{P}_i'\mathbf{P}_i'\mathbf{Q}^-\mathbf{P}_i\mathbf{Q} = \mathbf{P}_i(\mathbf{QP}_i'\mathbf{P}_i')\mathbf{Q}^-\mathbf{P}_i\mathbf{Q} = (\mathbf{P}_i\mathbf{QP}_i')\mathbf{Q}^-\mathbf{P}_i\mathbf{Q} = \mathbf{QP}_i'\mathbf{Q}^-\mathbf{P}_i\mathbf{Q}$ or simply $\mathbf{Q}(\mathbf{P}_i'\mathbf{Q}^-\mathbf{P}_i)\mathbf{Q}(\mathbf{P}_i'\mathbf{Q}^-\mathbf{P}_i)\mathbf{Q} = \mathbf{Q}(\mathbf{P}_i'\mathbf{Q}^-\mathbf{P}_i)\mathbf{Q}$.

Next, $\mathbf{Q}(\mathbf{P}_i'\mathbf{Q}^-\mathbf{P}_i)\mathbf{Q}(\mathbf{P}_j'\mathbf{Q}^-\mathbf{P}_j)\mathbf{Q} = \mathbf{0}$ follows immediately from the condition $\mathbf{P}_i\mathbf{QP}_j' = \mathbf{0}$.

Finally, $\mathbf{QP}_i'\mathbf{Q}^-\mathbf{P}_i\mathbf{Q} = \mathbf{P}_i\mathbf{QQ}^-\mathbf{QP}_i' = \mathbf{P}_i\mathbf{QP}_i' = \mathbf{P}_i\mathbf{Q}$ and $\mathbf{QP}'\mathbf{Q}^-\mathbf{PQ} = (\sum \mathbf{QP}_i')\mathbf{Q}^-(\sum \mathbf{P}_i\mathbf{Q}) = (\sum \mathbf{P}_i\mathbf{Q})\mathbf{Q}^-(\sum \mathbf{QP}_i') = \sum\sum_{ij} \mathbf{P}_i\mathbf{QP}_j' = \sum \mathbf{P}_i\mathbf{QP}_i' = \sum \mathbf{P}_i\mathbf{Q}$ serve to show that $\sum \mathbf{Q}(\mathbf{P}_i'\mathbf{Q}^-\mathbf{P}_i)\mathbf{Q} = \mathbf{Q}(\mathbf{P}'\mathbf{Q}^-\mathbf{P})\mathbf{Q}$.

LIMIT THEOREMS

Consider making repeated measurements of some quantity where each measurement is beset by an unknown error. To estimate the quantity, we can form the average of the measurements. Under a wide variety of conditions concerning the propagation of the errors, we are liable to find that the average converges upon the true value of the quantity.

To illustrate this convergence, let us imagine that each error is propagated independently with a zero expected value and a finite variance. Then there is an upper bound on the probability that an error will exceed a certain size. In the process of averaging the measurements, these bounds are transmuted into an upper bound on the probability of finite deviations of the average from the true value of the unknown quantity; and, as the number of measurements comprised in the average increases indefinitely, this bound tends to zero.

We shall demonstrate this result mathematically. Let $\{x_t; t = 1, \ldots, T, \ldots\}$ be the sequence of measurements, and let μ be the unknown quantity. Then the errors are $x_t - \mu$, and, by our assumptions $E(x_t - \mu) = 0$ and $E[(x_t - \mu)^2] = \sigma_t^2$. Equivalently, $E(x_t) = \mu$ and $V(x_t) = \sigma_t^2$.

We begin by establishing an upper bound for the probability $P(|x_t - \mu| > \varepsilon)$. Let $g(x)$ be a non-negative function of $x \sim f(x)$, and let $\mathcal{S} = \{x; g(x) > k\}$ be the set of all values of x for which $g(x)$ exceeds a certain constant. Then

$$E[g(x)] = \int_x g(x)f(x)\,dx$$

$$\geq \int_{\mathcal{S}} kf(x)\,dx = kP[g(x) > k];$$

and it follows that

(17.49) If $g(x)$ is a non-negative function of a random variable x, then for every $k > 0$ we have $P[g(x) > k] \leq E[g(x)]/k$.

This result is known as Chebyshev's inequality. Now let $g(x_t) = |x_t - \mu|^2$. Then $E[g(x_t)] = V(x_t) = \sigma_t^2$ and, setting $k = \varepsilon^2$, we have $P(|x_t - \mu|^2 > \varepsilon^2) \leq \sigma^2/\varepsilon^2$. Thus

(17.50) If $x_t \sim f(x_t)$ has $E(x_t) = \mu$ and $V(x_t) = \sigma_t^2$, then $P(|x_t - \mu| > \varepsilon) \leq \sigma_t^2/\varepsilon^2$;

and this gives the upper bound on the probability that an error will exceed a certain magnitude.

Now consider the average $\bar{x} = \sum x_t/T$. Since the errors are independently distributed, we have $V(\bar{x}) = \sum V(x_t)/T^2 = \sum \sigma_t^2/T^2$. Also $E(\bar{x}) = \mu$. On replacing x_t, $E(x_t)$ and $V(x_t)$ in the inequality in (17.50) by $\bar{x}_T$, $E(\bar{x}_T)$, and $V(\bar{x}_T)$, we get

$$P(|\bar{x}_T - \mu| > \varepsilon) \leq \sum \sigma_t^2/(\varepsilon T)^2;$$

and, on taking limits as $T \to \infty$, we find that $\lim P(|\bar{x}_T - \mu| > \varepsilon) = 0$. Thus, in the limit, the probability that $\bar{x}$ diverges from μ by any finite quantity is zero. We have proved a version of a fundamental limit theorem known as the law of large numbers.

Although the limiting distribution of $\bar{x}$ is degenerate, we still wish to know how $\bar{x}$ is distributed in large samples. If we are prepared to make specific assumptions about the distributions of the elements x_t, then we may be able to derive the distribution of $\bar{x}$. Unfortunately, the problem is liable to prove intractable unless we can assume that the elements are normally distributed. However, what is remarkable is that, given that the elements are independent, and provided that their sizes are constrained by the condition that

$$\lim(T \to \infty) P\left(\left| (x_t - \mu) \middle/ \sum_{t=1}^{T} \sigma_t^2 \right| > \varepsilon \right) = 0,$$

the distribution of $\bar{x}$ tends to normal distribution $N(\mu, \sum \sigma_t^2/T^2)$. This result, which we shall prove in a restricted form, is known as the central limit theorem.

The law of large numbers and the central limit theorem provide the basis for determining the asymptotic properties of econometric estimators. In demonstrating these asymptotic properties, we are usually faced with a number of subsidiary complications. To prove the central limit theorem and to dispose properly of the subsidiary complications, we require a number of additional results. Ideally these results should be stated in terms of vectors, since it is mainly to vectors that they will be applied. However, to do so would be tiresome, and so our treatment is largely confined to scalar random variables.

A more extensive treatment of the issues raised in the following section can be found in Rao [**93**]; and an exhaustive treatment is provided by Loève [**75**].

Stochastic convergence

It is a simple matter to define what is meant by the convergence of a sequence of constants $\{a_n\}$. We say that the sequence is convergent or, equivalently, that it tends to a constant a if, for any positive number ε, there exists a number $N=N(\varepsilon)$ such that $|a_n-a|<\varepsilon$ for all $n>N$. This is indicated by writing $\lim(n\to\infty)a_n=a$ or, alternatively, by stating that $a_n\to a$ as $n\to\infty$.

The question of the convergence of a sequence of random variables is less straightforward, and there are a variety of modes of convergence.

(17.51) Let $\{x_t\}$ be a sequence of random variables and let c be a constant. Then

(a) x_t converges to c weakly in probability, written $x_t \xrightarrow{P} c$ or $\text{plim}(x_t)=c$, if for every $\varepsilon>0$

$$\lim(t\to\infty)P(|x_t-c|>\varepsilon)=0,$$

(b) x_t converges to c strongly in probability or almost certainly written $x_t \xrightarrow{a.s.} c$, if for every $\varepsilon>0$

$$\lim(\tau\to\infty)P\left(\bigcup_{t>\tau}|x_t-c|>\varepsilon\right)=0,$$

(c) x_t converges in mean square to c, written $x_t \xrightarrow{m.s.} c$, if

$$\lim(t\to\infty)E(|x_t-c|^2)=0.$$

In the same way, we may define the convergence of a sequence of random variables to a random variable.

(17.52) A sequence of random variables $\{x_t\}$ is said to converge to a random variable x in the sense of (a), (b), or (c) of (17.51) if the sequence $\{x_t-x\}$ converges to zero in that sense.

Of these three criteria of convergence, weak convergence in probability is the most commonly used in econometrics. The other criteria are too stringent. Consider the criterion of almost certain convergence which can also be written as $\lim(\tau\to\infty)P(\bigcap_{t>\tau}|x_t-c|\leq\varepsilon)=1$. This requires that, in the limit, all the elements of $\{x_t\}$ with $t>\tau$ should lie simultaneously in the interval $[c-\varepsilon, c+\varepsilon]$ with a probability of one. The condition of weak convergence in probability requires much less: it requires only that single elements, taken separately, should have a probability of one of lying in this interval. Clearly,

(17.53) If x_t converges almost certainly to c, then it also converges to c weakly in probability. Thus $x_t \xrightarrow{a.s.} c$ implies $x_t \xrightarrow{P} c$.

The disadvantage of the criterion of mean-square convergence is that it requires the existence of second-order moments; and in many econometric applications it cannot be guaranteed that an estimator will possess such moments. In fact

(17.54) If x_t converges in mean square, then it also converges weakly in probability, so that $x_t \xrightarrow{m.s.} c$ implies $x_t \xrightarrow{P} c$.

This follows directly from Chebychev's inequality whereby

$$P(|x_t-c|>\varepsilon)\leq\frac{E[(x_t-c)^2]}{\varepsilon^2}.$$

A result which we shall use to a considerable extent is the following:

(17.55) If g is a continuous function and if x_t converges in probability to x, then $g(x_t)$ converges in probability to $g(x)$. Thus $x_t \xrightarrow{P} x$ implies $g(x_t)\xrightarrow{P} g(x)$.

Proof. If x is a constant, then the proof is straightforward. Let $\delta>0$ be an arbitrary value. Then, since g is a continuous function, there exists a value ε such that $|x_t-x|\leq\varepsilon$ implies $|g(x_t)-g(x)|\leq\delta$. Hence $P(|g(x_t)-g(x)|\leq\delta)\geq P(|x_t-x|\leq\varepsilon)$; and so $x_t\xrightarrow{P}x$, which may be expressed as $\lim P(|x_t-x|\leq\varepsilon)=1$, implies $\lim P(|g(x_t)-g(x)|\leq\delta)=1$ or, equivalently, $g(x_t)\xrightarrow{P}g(x)$.

When x is random, we let δ be an arbitrary value in the interval $(0, 1)$, and we choose an interval $\mathscr{A}$ such that $P(x\in\mathscr{A})=1-\delta/2$. Then, for $x\in\mathscr{A}$, there exists some value ε such that $|x_t-x|\leq\varepsilon$ implies $|g(x_t)-g(x)|\leq\delta$. Hence

$$\begin{aligned}P(|g(x_t)-g(x)|\leq\delta)&\geq P(\{|x_t-x|\leq\varepsilon\}\cap\{x\in\mathscr{A}\})\\&\geq P(|x_t-x|\leq\varepsilon)+P(x\in\mathscr{A})-1.\end{aligned}$$

But there is some value τ such that for $t \geqslant \tau$ we have $P(|x_t - x| \leqslant \varepsilon) > 1 - \delta/2$. Therefore for $t > \tau$ we have $P(|g(x_t) - g(x)| \leqslant \delta) > 1 - \delta$, and letting $\delta \to 0$ shows that $g(x_t) \xrightarrow{P} g(x)$.

The proofs of such propositions are often considerably more complicated than the intuitive notions to which they are intended to lend rigour. The special case of the proposition above where x_t converges in probability to a constant c is frequently invoked in the text. We may state this case as follows:

(17.56) If $g(x_t)$ is a continuous function and if $\text{plim}(x_t) = c$ is a constant, then $\text{plim}[g(x_t)] = g[\text{plim}(x_t)]$.

This is known as Slutsky's theorem. In common with every theorem so far stated, Slutsky's theorem applies equally to vectors and matrices. For example, if $\mathbf{X}$ is a $T \times k$ matrix of stochastic elements and if $\text{plim}(T \to \infty)(\mathbf{X}'\mathbf{X}/T) = \mathbf{M}$, then the theorem indicates that $\text{plim}(\mathbf{X}'\mathbf{X}/T)^{-1} = \mathbf{M}^{-1}$.

The concept of convergence in distribution has equal importance in econometrics with the concept of convergence in probability. It is fundamental in the proof of the central limit theorem.

(17.57) Let $\{x_t\}$ be a sequence of random variables and let $\{F_t\}$ be the corresponding sequence of distribution functions. Then x_t is said to converge in distribution to a random variable x with distribution function F, written $x_t \xrightarrow{D} x$, if F_t converges to F at all points of continuity of the latter.

This means simply that, if x^* is any point in the domain of F such that $F(x^*)$ is a continuity point, then $F_t(x^*)$ converges to $F(x^*)$ in the ordinary mathematical sense. We call F the limiting distribution or asymptotic distribution of x_t.

Weak convergence in probability is sufficient to ensure a convergence in distribution. Thus

(17.58) If x_t converges to the random variable x weakly in probability, it also converges to x in distribution. That is, $x_t \xrightarrow{P} x$ implies $x_t \xrightarrow{D} x$.

Proof. Let F and F_t denote the distribution functions of x and x_t respectively, and define $z_t = x - x_t$. Then $x_t \xrightarrow{P} x$ implies $\lim P(|z_t| > \varepsilon) = 0$ for any

$\varepsilon>0$. Let y be any continuity point of F. Then

$$\begin{aligned}P(x_t<y)&=P(x<y+z_t)\\&=P([x<y+z_t]\cap[z_t\leqslant\varepsilon])+P([x<y+z_t]\cap[z_t>\varepsilon])\\&\leqslant P(x<y+\varepsilon)+P(z_t>\varepsilon),\end{aligned}$$

where the inequality follows from the fact that the events in the final expression subsume the events of the preceeding expression. Taking limits as $t\to\infty$ gives $\lim P(x_t<y)\leqslant P(x<y+\varepsilon)$. By a similar argument, we may show that $\lim P(x_t<y)\geqslant P(x<y-\varepsilon)$. By letting $\varepsilon\to 0$, we see that $\lim P(x_t<y)=P(x<y)$ or simply that $\lim F_t(y)=F(y)$, which proves the theorem.

A theorem of considerable importance, which lies on our way towards the central limit theorem, is the Helly–Bray theorem as follows:

(17.59) Let $\{F_t\}$ be a sequence of distribution functions converging to the distribution function F, and let g be any bounded continuous function in the same argument. Then $\int g\,dF_t\to\int g\,dF$ as $t\to\infty$.

A proof of this is to be found in Rao [**93,** p. 97]. The theorem indicates, in particular, that, if $g(x_t)=\mu_t^r$ is the rth moment of x_t and if $g(x)=\mu^r$ is the rth moment of x, then $x_t\xrightarrow{D}x$ implies $\mu_t^r\to\mu^r$. However, this result must be strongly qualified, for it presumes that the rth moment exists for all elements of the sequence $\{x_t\}$; and this cannot always be guaranteed.

It is one of the bugbears of econometric estimation that whereas, for any reasonable estimator, there is usually a limiting distribution possessing finite moments up to the order r, the small-sample distributions often have no such moments. We must therefore preserve a clear distinction between the moments of the limiting distribution and the limits of the moments of the sampling distributions. Since the small-sample moments often do not exist, the latter concept has little operational validity.

We can establish that a sequence of distributions converges to a limiting distribution by demonstrating the convergence of their characteristic functions.

(17.60) The characteristic function of a random variable x is defined by $\phi(h)=E(\exp\{ihx\})$ where $i=\sqrt{-1}$.

The essential property of a characteristic function is that it uniquely determines the distribution function. In particular, if x has the probability density function $f(x)$ so that

$$\phi(h)=\int_{-\infty}^{+\infty}e^{ihx}f(x)\,dx,$$

then an inversion relation holds whereby

$$f(x) = \frac{1}{2\pi}\int_{-\infty}^{+\infty} e^{-ihx}\phi(h)\,dh.$$

Thus the characteristic function and the probability density function are just Fourier transforms of each other.

Example. The standard normal variate $x \sim N(0, 1)$ *has the probability density function*

$$f(x) = \frac{1}{\sqrt{2\pi}} e^{-x^2/2}.$$

The corresponding characteristic function is

$$\begin{aligned}\phi(h) &= \frac{1}{\sqrt{2\pi}}\int_{-\infty}^{+\infty} e^{ihx - x^2/2}\,dx \\ &= e^{-h^2/2}\frac{1}{\sqrt{2\pi}}\int e^{-(x-ih)^2/2}\,dx \\ &= e^{-h^2/2}\frac{1}{\sqrt{2\pi}}\int e^{-z^2/2}\,dz,\end{aligned}$$

where $z = x - ih$ *is a complex variable. The integral of the complex function* $e^{-z^2/2}$ *can be shown to be equal to the integral of the corresponding function defined on the real line. The latter has the value of* $\sqrt{2\pi}$, *so*

$$\phi(h) = e^{-h^2/2}.$$

Thus the probability density function and the characteristic function of the standard normal variate have the same form. Also, it is trivial to confirm, in this instance, that $f(x)$ *and* $\phi(h)$ *satisfy the inversion relation.*

The theorem which is used to establish the convergence of a sequence of distributions states that

(17.61) If $\phi_t(h)$ is the characteristic function of x_t and $\phi(h)$ is that of x, then x_t converges in distribution to x if and only if $\phi_t(h)$ converges to $\phi(h)$. That is, $x_t \xrightarrow{D} x$ if and only if $\phi_t(h) \to \phi(h)$.

Proof. The Helly–Bray theorem establishes that $\phi_t \to \phi$ if $x_t \xrightarrow{D} x$. To establish the converse, let F be the distribution function corresponding to ϕ and let $\{F_t\}$ be a sequence of distribution functions corresponding to the sequence $\{\phi_t\}$. Choose a subsequence $\{F_m\}$ tending to a non-decreasing bounded function G. Now G must be a distribution function; for, by taking limits in the expression $\phi_m(h)=\int e^{ihx}\,dF_m$, we get $\phi(h)=\int e^{ihx}\,dG$, and setting $h=0$ gives $\phi(0)=\int dG=1$ since, by definition, $\phi(0)=e^0\int dF=1$. But the distribution function corresponding to $\phi(h)$ is unique, so $G=F$. All subsequences must necessarily converge to the same distribution function, so $\phi_t\rightarrow\phi$ implies $F_t\rightarrow F$ or, equivalently, $x_t\xrightarrow{D}x$.

We shall invoke this theorem in proving the central limit theorem.

Finally let us consider an econometric estimator $\hat{\boldsymbol{\theta}}_T$ of a parameter vector $\boldsymbol{\theta}$. Quite commonly, $\hat{\boldsymbol{\theta}}_T$ satisfies an equation of the form $\sqrt{T}(\hat{\boldsymbol{\theta}}_T-\boldsymbol{\theta})=\mathbf{M}_T^{-1}\boldsymbol{\eta}_T$ where $\mathbf{M}_T$ is a stochastic matrix tending in probability to a constant matrix $\mathbf{M}$ as $T\rightarrow\infty$ and where $\boldsymbol{\eta}_T$ is a random vector tending in distribution to a normal vector $\boldsymbol{\eta}\sim N(\mathbf{0},\mathbf{Q})$. We can determine the limiting distribution of $\sqrt{T}(\hat{\boldsymbol{\theta}}_T-\boldsymbol{\theta})$ in view of the following theorem which is due to Cramér [**25**].

(17.62) Let $\{x_t, y_t\}$ be a sequence of random variables such that x_t converges in distribution to x and y_t converges in probability to c; that is $x_t\xrightarrow{D}x$ and $y_t\xrightarrow{P}c$. Then

(a) $x_t+y_t\xrightarrow{D}x+c$,

(b) $x_ty_t\xrightarrow{D}cx$,

(c) $x_t/y_t\xrightarrow{D}x/c$,

(d) if $y_t\xrightarrow{P}c=0$, then $x_ty_t\xrightarrow{P}0$.

These results are proven in a straightforward way by Rao [**93,** p. 102]. Together with the theorem under (17.56), they enable us to deduce that the limiting distribution of the vector $\sqrt{T}(\hat{\boldsymbol{\theta}}_T-\boldsymbol{\theta})$ is the normal distribution $N(\mathbf{0},\mathbf{M}^{-1}\mathbf{Q}\mathbf{M}^{-1\prime})$.

The law of large numbers and the central limit theorem

The theorems of the previous section contribute to the proofs of the two limit theorems that are fundamental to the theory of estimation. The first if the law of large numbers. We have already proved that

(17.63) If $\{x_t\}$ is a sequence of independent random variables with $E(x_t)=\mu$ and $V(x_t)=\sigma_t^2$, and if $\bar{x}=\sum_{t=1}^T x_t/T$, then $\lim(T\rightarrow\infty)P(|\bar{x}-\mu|>\varepsilon)=0$.

This theorem states that $\bar{x}$ converges to μ weakly in probability and it is called, for that reason, the weak law of large numbers. In fact, if we assume that the elements of $\{x_t\}$ are independent and identically distributed, we no longer need the assumption that their second moments exist in order to prove the convergence of $\bar{x}$. Thus Khinchine's theorem states that

(17.64) If $\{x_t\}$ is a sequence of independent and identically distributed random variables with $E(x_t)=\mu$, then $\bar{x}$ tends weakly in probability to μ.

Proof. Let $\phi(h)=E(\exp(ihx_t))$ be the characteristic function of x_t. Expanding in a neighbourhood of $h=0$ we get

$$\phi(h)=E\left[1+ihx_t+\frac{(ihx_t)^2}{2!}+\ldots\right],$$

and, since the mean $E(x_t)=\mu$ exists, we can write this as

$$\phi(h)=1+i\mu h+o(h),$$

where $o(h)$ is a remainder term of a smaller order than h, so that $\lim(h\to 0)[o(h)/h]=0$. Since $\bar{x}=\sum x_t/T$ is a sum of independent and identically distributed random variables x_t/T, its characteristic function can be written as

$$\begin{aligned}\phi_T^*&=E\left[\exp\left\{ih\left(\frac{x_1}{T}+\ldots+\frac{x_T}{T}\right)\right\}\right]\\&=\prod_{t=1}^{T}E\left(\exp\left\{\frac{ihx_t}{T}\right\}\right)=\left[\phi\left(\frac{h}{T}\right)\right]^T.\end{aligned}$$

On taking limits, we get

$$\begin{aligned}\lim(T\to\infty)\phi_T^*&=\lim\left[1+i\frac{h}{T}\mu+o\left(\frac{h}{T}\right)\right]^T\\&=\exp\{ih\mu\}\end{aligned}$$

which is the characteristic function of a degenerate random variable with the probability mass concentrated on μ. This proves the convergence of $\bar{x}$.

It is possible to prove Khinchine's theorem without using the characteristic function as is shown, for example, by Rao [**93**]. However, the proof that we have just given has an interesting affinity with the proof of the central limit theorem. The Lindeberg–Levy version of the theorem is as follows:

(17.65) Let $\{x_t\}$ be a sequence of independent and identically distributed random variables with $E(x_t)=\mu$ and $V(x_t)=\sigma^2$. Then $z_T=(1/\sqrt{T})\sum_{t=1}^{T}(x_t-\mu)/\sigma$ converges in distribution to $z\sim N(0, 1)$. Equivalently, the limiting distribution of $\sqrt{T}\bar{x}$ is the normal distribution $N(\mu, \sigma^2)$.

Proof. First we recall that the characteristic function of the standard normal variate $z \sim N(0, 1)$ is $\phi(h) = \exp\{-h^2/2\}$. We must show that the characteristic function ϕ_T of z_T converges to ϕ as $T \to \infty$. Let us write $z_T = T^{-1/2} \sum z_t$ where $z_t = (x_t - \mu)/\sigma$ has $E(z_t) = 0$ and $E(z_t^2) = 1$. The characteristic function of z_t can be written as

$$\begin{aligned}\phi^0(h) &= 1 + ihE(z_t) - \frac{h^2 E(z_t^2)}{2} + o(h^2)\\ &= 1 - \frac{h^2}{2} + o(h^2).\end{aligned}$$

Since $z_T = T^{-1/2} \sum z_t$ is a sum of independent and identically distributed random variables, it follows that its characteristic function can be written, in turn, as

$$\begin{aligned}\phi_T\left(\frac{h}{\sqrt{T}}\right) &= \left[\phi^0\left(\frac{h}{\sqrt{T}}\right)\right]^T\\ &= \left[1 - \frac{h^2}{2T} + o\left(\frac{h^2}{T}\right)\right]^T.\end{aligned}$$

Letting $T \to \infty$ we find that $\lim \phi_T = \exp\{-h^2/2\} = \phi$, which proves the theorem.

A useful extension of the theorem is the following:

(17.66) Let $\{x_t\}$ be a sequence of independent and identically distributed random variables with $E(x_t) = \mu$ and $V(x_t) = \sigma^2$, and let $g = g(x)$ be a function with a continuous first derivative in the neighbourhood of $x = \mu$ such that $\partial g(\mu)/\partial x \neq 0$. Then $z_T = \sqrt{T}[g(\bar{x}) - g(\mu)]$ converges in distribution to $z \sim N(0, \sigma^2[\partial g(\mu)/\partial x]^2)$.

Proof. By Taylor's theorem, $g(\bar{x}) = g(\mu) + [\partial g(x^*)/\partial x](\bar{x} - \mu)$ where x^* lies between $\bar{x}$ and μ. Therefore z_T can be written as

$$\begin{aligned}z_T &= \sqrt{T}[g(\bar{x}) - g(\mu)]\\ &= [\partial g(x^*)/\partial x]\sqrt{T}(\bar{x} - \mu).\end{aligned}$$

By the law of large numbers, $\bar{x} \xrightarrow{P} \mu$ and so $x^* \xrightarrow{P} \mu$. Since $\partial g(x)/\partial x$ is a continuous function, we also have $\partial g(x^*)/\partial x \xrightarrow{P} \partial g(\mu)/\partial x$. By the central limit theorem, $\sqrt{T}(\bar{x} - \mu)$ converges in distribution to $N(0, \sigma^2)$. Therefore, on invoking Cramer's theorem (17.62), we find that z_T tends in distribution to $z \sim N(0, \sigma^2[\partial g(\mu)/\partial x]^2)$.

Example. Let the elements x_t of the sequence be continuously distributed with a probability density function $f(x_t)$ that has a positive value at $x=0$, and consider the function $g(\bar{x})=1/\bar{x}$. According to the theorem, $\sqrt{T}/\bar{x}$ has a normal limiting distribution with mean $1/\mu$ and variance σ^2/μ^4. However, $\sqrt{T}/\bar{x}$ has no finite moments for any value of T. To understand this, consider the fact that $f(0)\neq 0$. This implies a finite probability that $\bar{x}$ will fall in the interval $[-\varepsilon, \varepsilon]$ about zero. It follows that $1/\bar{x}$ will have the same probability of falling in a corresponding set of unbounded values. Therefore the integral defining the expected value of $g(\bar{x})=1/\bar{x}$ cannot converge.

This example of a sequence of random variables without finite moments, converging in distribution to a random variable with well defined moments, illustrates the nature of many econometric estimators.

The multivariate extension of the Lindeberg–Levy central limit theorem is straightforward.

(17.67) Let $\{\mathbf{x}_t\}$ be a sequence of independent and identically distributed random vectors with $E(\mathbf{x}_t)=\boldsymbol{\mu}$ and $D(\mathbf{x}_t)=\boldsymbol{\Sigma}$. Then $\mathbf{z}_T=(1/\sqrt{T})\sum_{t=1}^{T}(\mathbf{x}_t-\boldsymbol{\mu})$, which has $E(\mathbf{z}_T)=\mathbf{0}$ and $D(\mathbf{z}_T)=\boldsymbol{\Sigma}$, converges in distribution to the normal vector $\mathbf{z}\sim N(\mathbf{0},\boldsymbol{\Sigma})$.

To prove this, we consider any scalar function $y_t=\boldsymbol{\alpha}'(\mathbf{x}_t-\boldsymbol{\mu})$. This has $E(y_t)=0$ and $V(y_t)=\boldsymbol{\alpha}'\boldsymbol{\Sigma}\boldsymbol{\alpha}$. It follows, by the central limit theorem (17.65), that $\boldsymbol{\alpha}'\mathbf{z}_T=\sum y_t/\sqrt{T}$ converges in distribution to $y=\boldsymbol{\alpha}'\mathbf{z}\sim N(0,\boldsymbol{\alpha}'\boldsymbol{\Sigma}\boldsymbol{\alpha})$. Since $\boldsymbol{\alpha}$ is arbitrary, this shows that every linear combination of the vector $\mathbf{z}_T$ has a normal limiting distribution; and it follows that $\mathbf{z}_T$ must have the limiting normal distribution $N(\mathbf{0},\boldsymbol{\Sigma})$.

In a number of econometric applications, we find ourselves considering the limiting distribution of a random vector $\boldsymbol{\eta}_T=\mathbf{X}'\boldsymbol{\varepsilon}/\sqrt{T}=\sum_{t=1}^{T}\mathbf{x}_{t.}'\varepsilon_t/\sqrt{T}$ where $\boldsymbol{\varepsilon}'=[\varepsilon_1,\ldots,\varepsilon_T]$ is a vector of independent and identically distributed random variables with $E(\varepsilon_t)=0$, and $\mathbf{X}'=[\mathbf{x}_{1.}',\ldots,\mathbf{x}_{T.}']$ is either a matrix formed from the non-stochastic row vectors $\mathbf{x}_{t.}$ such that $\lim(\mathbf{X}'\mathbf{X}/T)=\lim(\sum_{t=1}^{T}\mathbf{x}_{t.}'\mathbf{x}_{t.}/T)=\mathbf{M}$, or else a matrix of stochastic vectors such that $\text{plim}(\mathbf{X}'\mathbf{X}/T)=\mathbf{M}$ where $\mathbf{M}=E(\mathbf{x}_{t.}'\mathbf{x}_{t.})$.

The case where $\mathbf{X}$ is non-stochastic is relatively tractable. Let us consider the scalar quantity $\boldsymbol{\alpha}'\mathbf{X}'\boldsymbol{\varepsilon}/\sqrt{T}=\sum\boldsymbol{\alpha}'\mathbf{x}_{t.}'\varepsilon_t/\sqrt{T}$, where $\boldsymbol{\alpha}$ is an arbitrary vector. This has the characteristic function

$$\phi_T\left(\frac{h}{\sqrt{T}}\right)=\prod_{t=1}^{T}\left[1-\frac{h^2\sigma^2(\boldsymbol{\alpha}'\mathbf{x}_{t.}')^2}{2T}+o\left(\frac{h^2}{T}\right)\right].$$

Taking natural logarithms, and using the expansion of $\log(1+z)=$

$\log 1+z[\partial \log(1)/\partial z]+r=0+z+r$ given by Cramér [**25**, p. 217], we get

$$\log \phi_T = \sum \log\left[1-\frac{h^2\sigma^2(\boldsymbol{\alpha}'\mathbf{x}'_{t.})^2}{2T}+o\left(\frac{h^2}{T}\right)\right]$$

$$= -\tfrac{1}{2}h^2\sigma^2\boldsymbol{\alpha}'\left(\frac{\sum \mathbf{x}'_{t.}\mathbf{x}_{t.}}{T}\right)\boldsymbol{\alpha}+To'\left(\frac{h^2}{T}\right).$$

Given that $\lim(T\to\infty)\sum \mathbf{x}'_{t.}\mathbf{x}_{t.}/T=\mathbf{M}$ we find that $\log \phi_T \to \log\phi$ where

$$\phi=\exp\{-\tfrac{1}{2}h^2\sigma^2\boldsymbol{\alpha}'\mathbf{M}\boldsymbol{\alpha}\}.$$

This is the characteristic function of the normal variate $y\sim N(0,\sigma^2\boldsymbol{\alpha}'\mathbf{M}\boldsymbol{\alpha})$, and we can infer that $\boldsymbol{\alpha}'\boldsymbol{\eta}_T$ tends in distribution to this variable. Since this is true for all $\boldsymbol{\alpha}$, it follows that $\boldsymbol{\eta}_T$ tends in distribution to the normal vector $\boldsymbol{\eta}\sim N(\mathbf{0},\sigma^2\mathbf{M})$.

The cases where $\mathbf{X}$ is a stochastic matrix are more complicated. However, given that the elements $\mathbf{x}_{t.}$ are independently and identically distributed, we can still apply the theorem in (17.67) to vector $\boldsymbol{\eta}_T=\sum \mathbf{x}'_{t.}\varepsilon_t/\sqrt{T}$. Greater problems arise when the elements $\mathbf{x}_{t.}$ are serially correlated. Nevertheless, we can make the following statement:

(17.68) Let $\{\varepsilon_t\}$ be a sequence of independent and identically distributed random variables with $E(\varepsilon_t)=0$ and $V(\varepsilon_t)=\sigma^2$, and let $\mathbf{x}_{t.}=[x_{t1},\ldots,x_{tk}]$ be a vector such that either

$$\lim\left(\sum_{t=1}^{T}\mathbf{x}'_{t.}\mathbf{x}_{t.}/T\right)=\mathbf{M} \quad \text{or else}$$

$$\text{plim}\left(\sum_{t=1}^{T}\mathbf{x}'_{t.}\mathbf{x}_{t.}/T\right)=E(\mathbf{x}'_{t.}\mathbf{x}_{t.})=\mathbf{M}.$$

Then $\boldsymbol{\eta}_T=\sum \mathbf{x}'_{t.}\varepsilon_t/\sqrt{T}$ tends in distribution to the random vector $\boldsymbol{\eta}\sim N(\mathbf{0},\sigma^2\mathbf{M})$.

THE THEORY OF ESTIMATION

Let $\mathbf{X}'=[\mathbf{x}'_{1.},\ldots,\mathbf{x}'_{T.}]$ be a data matrix comprising T realizations of a random vector $\mathbf{x}$ whose probability density function $f(\mathbf{x};\boldsymbol{\theta})$ is characterized by the parameter vector $\boldsymbol{\theta}'=[\theta_1,\ldots,\theta_k]$. Then any function $\hat{\boldsymbol{\theta}}=\hat{\boldsymbol{\theta}}(\mathbf{X})$ of the data which purports to provide a useful approximation to the parameter vector is called a point estimator. The set $\mathcal{S}$ comprising all possible values of the data matrix is called a sample space, and the set $\mathcal{A}$ of all values of $\boldsymbol{\theta}$ which conform to whatever restrictions have been postulated is called the admissible parameter set. A point estimator is therefore a function which associates with every value in $\mathcal{S}$ a unique value in $\mathcal{A}$.

We must begin by defining the conditions under which it is possible to make valid inferences about $\boldsymbol{\theta}$. Clearly, we can estimate this parameter only if its particular value is in some way reflected in the realized values of $\mathbf{x}$. The basic requirement, therefore, is that distinct values of $\boldsymbol{\theta}$ should lead to distinct probability density functions. Thus

(17.69) The parameter $\boldsymbol{\theta}$ is said to be identifiable if and only if $\boldsymbol{\theta}_1 \neq \boldsymbol{\theta}_2$ implies, for some value of $\mathbf{x}$, that $f(\mathbf{x};\boldsymbol{\theta}_1) \neq f(\mathbf{x};\boldsymbol{\theta}_2)$.

This concept of identifiability makes no reference to the actual data that is to be used in estimating $\boldsymbol{\theta}$. A parameter that is identifiable in this sense might not be estimable from the data at hand or from any other data arising from the specified sample space. Such is the case when, for example, the admissible parameter set is a vector space of a dimension k exceeding the dimension T of the sample space. To settle the question of estimability we must consider the family of probability density functions $L(\mathbf{X};\boldsymbol{\theta})$ defined over the set $\mathscr{A} \times \mathscr{S}$ of all pairs of values of the parameter vector and the sample data. Clearly, it makes sense to say that

(17.70) The parameter $\boldsymbol{\theta}$ is estimable if $\boldsymbol{\theta}_1 \neq \boldsymbol{\theta}_2$ implies $L(\mathbf{X};\boldsymbol{\theta}_1) \neq L(\mathbf{X};\boldsymbol{\theta}_2)$ for almost all $\mathbf{X} \in \mathscr{S}$.

An alternative definition which is frequently used states that

(17.71) The parameter $\boldsymbol{\theta}$ is (unbiasedly) estimable if there exists a function $\hat{\boldsymbol{\theta}} = \hat{\boldsymbol{\theta}}(\mathbf{X})$ such that $E(\hat{\boldsymbol{\theta}}) = \boldsymbol{\theta}$.

Unfortunately, this definition is not wholly adequate in econometrics since it may be difficult, if not impossible, to prove that an unbiased estimator actually exists. It may even be the case that none of the estimators that are worth considering have any finite moments.

To be of any worth, an estimator must possess a probability distribution that is closely concentrated around the true value of the unknown parameter. A natural measure of the closeness of a scalar estimate $\hat{\theta}$ to the parameter value θ is provided by the mean-square error.

(17.72) The mean-square error of the estimator $\hat{\theta}$ is defined by $E(\hat{\theta} - \theta)^2$.

This is the expected value of a squared distance. We see at once that

$$\begin{aligned} E(\hat{\theta} - \theta)^2 &= E[\{\hat{\theta} - E(\hat{\theta})\} + \{E(\hat{\theta}) - \theta\}]^2 \\ &= V(\hat{\theta}) + [E(\hat{\theta}) - \theta]^2, \end{aligned}$$

since the cross-product term in the expansion is equal to zero. The quantity $E(\hat{\theta}) - \theta$ defines the bias of the estimator. The corresponding multivariate measure of closeness is not uniquely defined since it depends upon a choice of metric for the parameter set.

(17.73) The mean-square error of the estimator $\hat{\boldsymbol{\theta}}$ measured in the $\mathbf{Q}$-metric is

$$E[(\hat{\boldsymbol{\theta}} - \boldsymbol{\theta})'\mathbf{Q}(\hat{\boldsymbol{\theta}} - \boldsymbol{\theta})] = \text{Trace}\{E[(\boldsymbol{\theta} - \hat{\boldsymbol{\theta}})(\boldsymbol{\theta} - \hat{\boldsymbol{\theta}})']\mathbf{Q}\}.$$

The equality in this definition follows from the fact that if x is a scalar then $E(x)=E[\text{Trace}(x)]=\text{Trace}[E(x)]$ and from the fact that the trace of a matrix product is invariant with respect to the cyclical permutation of its factors.

Estimators having a minimum mean-square error for all $\boldsymbol{\theta}\in\mathscr{A}$ do not exist. For the fact that the mean-square error of an estimator $\hat{\boldsymbol{\theta}}$ is zero at the point in $\mathscr{A}$ where $\boldsymbol{\theta}=\hat{\boldsymbol{\theta}}$ means that, to meet the requirement, an estimator must have a zero mean-square error for every $\boldsymbol{\theta}$; and this is impossible. To overcome this problem, we commonly impose the condition that our optimal estimator should also be unbiased. The criterion of unbiasedness is somewhat arbitrary, and it may have the effect of excluding from our consideration estimators with uniformly smaller mean-square errors. For an unbiased estimator, the mean-square error is the same thing as the variance; so we may talk of a minimum variance unbiased estimator. We say that

(17.74) The scalar function $\hat{\theta}$ is a minimum variance unbiased estimator or best estimator of θ if $E(\hat{\theta})=\theta$ and $V(\hat{\theta})\leqslant V(\tilde{\theta})$, where $\tilde{\theta}$ is any other unbiased estimator with $E(\tilde{\theta})=\theta$.

Applying the condition $E(\hat{\boldsymbol{\theta}})=\boldsymbol{\theta}$ of unbiasedness to the multivariate measure in (17.73) gives us the quantity $\text{Trace}[D(\hat{\boldsymbol{\theta}})\mathbf{Q}]$. Thus, for a particular choice of $\mathbf{Q}$ defining a metric on the parameter space, we might define $\hat{\boldsymbol{\theta}}$ to be the best estimator if $\text{Trace}[D(\hat{\boldsymbol{\theta}})\mathbf{Q}]\leqslant\text{Trace}[D(\tilde{\boldsymbol{\theta}})\mathbf{Q}]$ for all $\boldsymbol{\theta}$, where $\tilde{\boldsymbol{\theta}}$ is any other unbiased estimator. However, if $D(\tilde{\boldsymbol{\theta}})-D(\hat{\boldsymbol{\theta}})$ is positive semidefinite for all $\mathbf{X}\in\mathscr{S}$, then the inequality is satisfied for any choice of $\mathbf{Q}$. Also, the condition that $D(\tilde{\boldsymbol{\theta}})-D(\hat{\boldsymbol{\theta}})$ is positive semidefinite is equivalent to the condition that $V(\mathbf{q}'\hat{\boldsymbol{\theta}})=\mathbf{q}'D(\hat{\boldsymbol{\theta}})\mathbf{q}\leqslant\mathbf{q}'D(\tilde{\boldsymbol{\theta}})\mathbf{q}=V(\mathbf{q}'\tilde{\boldsymbol{\theta}})$ for all $\mathbf{q}$. Therefore

(17.75) We say that $\hat{\boldsymbol{\theta}}=\hat{\boldsymbol{\theta}}(\mathbf{X})$ is the minimum variance unbiased estimator of $\boldsymbol{\theta}$ if $E(\hat{\boldsymbol{\theta}})=\boldsymbol{\theta}$ and if $D(\tilde{\boldsymbol{\theta}})-D(\hat{\boldsymbol{\theta}})$ is positive semidefinite or, equivalently, if $V(\mathbf{q}'\hat{\boldsymbol{\theta}})\leqslant V(\mathbf{q}'\tilde{\boldsymbol{\theta}})$ for all $\mathbf{q}$, where $\tilde{\boldsymbol{\theta}}$ is any other unbiased estimator with $E(\tilde{\boldsymbol{\theta}})=\boldsymbol{\theta}$.

A unbiased estimator that meets this criterion is said to be efficient.

We can prove that

(17.76) If the minimum variance unbiased estimator exists, it is unique.

Proof. Let $\boldsymbol{\theta}^1$ and $\boldsymbol{\theta}^2$ be minimum variance unbiased estimators of $\boldsymbol{\theta}$ with $D(\boldsymbol{\theta}^1)=D(\boldsymbol{\theta}^2)=\mathbf{Q}$. Then $V(\mathbf{q}'\boldsymbol{\theta}^1-\mathbf{q}'\boldsymbol{\theta}^2)=V(\mathbf{q}'\boldsymbol{\theta}^1)+V(\mathbf{q}'\boldsymbol{\theta}^2)-2C(\mathbf{q}'\boldsymbol{\theta}^1,\mathbf{q}'\boldsymbol{\theta}^2)$ for any $\mathbf{q}$, and, since this is a non-negative quantity, we have the inequality

$$\begin{aligned}2\mathbf{q}'\mathbf{Q}\mathbf{q}&=V(\mathbf{q}'\boldsymbol{\theta}^1)+V(\mathbf{q}'\boldsymbol{\theta}^2)\\&\geqslant 2C(\mathbf{q}'\boldsymbol{\theta}^1,\mathbf{q}'\boldsymbol{\theta}^2).\end{aligned}$$

Now consider the unbiased estimator $\boldsymbol{\theta}^3 = \frac{1}{2}(\boldsymbol{\theta}^1 + \boldsymbol{\theta}^2)$. Using the inequality we find that

$$\begin{aligned} V(\mathbf{q}'\boldsymbol{\theta}^3) &= \tfrac{1}{4}V(\mathbf{q}'\boldsymbol{\theta}^1) + \tfrac{1}{4}V(\mathbf{q}'\boldsymbol{\theta}^2) + \tfrac{1}{2}C(\mathbf{q}'\boldsymbol{\theta}^1, \mathbf{q}'\boldsymbol{\theta}^2) \\ &\leqslant \mathbf{q}'\mathbf{Q}\mathbf{q}. \end{aligned}$$

But, unless an equality holds, this contradicts the assumption that $\boldsymbol{\theta}^1$ and $\boldsymbol{\theta}^2$ are minimum variance unbiased estimators. An equality holds when $V(\mathbf{q}'\boldsymbol{\theta}^1) + V(\mathbf{q}'\boldsymbol{\theta}^2) = 2C(\mathbf{q}'\boldsymbol{\theta}^1, \mathbf{q}'\boldsymbol{\theta}^2)$ or, equivalently, when $V(\mathbf{q}'\boldsymbol{\theta}^1 - \mathbf{q}'\boldsymbol{\theta}^2) = 0$ which implies that $c = \mathbf{q}'\boldsymbol{\theta}^1 - \mathbf{q}'\boldsymbol{\theta}^2$ is a constant. But, since $E(\boldsymbol{\theta}^1) = E(\boldsymbol{\theta}^2)$ by assumption, we must have $c = 0$ and hence $\boldsymbol{\theta}_1 = \boldsymbol{\theta}_2$, since $\mathbf{q}$ is any vector.

Given that the probability density function is normal—which is the conventional assumption in econometrics—we can usually find an unbiased estimator that has minimum variance uniformly for all $\boldsymbol{\theta} \in \mathscr{A}$ provided we can find one that is unbiased. However, the criterion presumes the existence of the first-order and second-order moments of the estimator for all sample sizes T; and it is clearly inappropriate to many econometric estimators for which there is no guarantee of the existence of these moments. In such cases we must select our estimators according to a criterion of efficiency which relates to the limiting distribution of the estimator. We usually begin by restricting our attention to consistent estimators.

(17.77) A consistent estimator $\hat{\boldsymbol{\theta}}_T$ of $\boldsymbol{\theta}$ is one that converges to $\boldsymbol{\theta}$ in probability as $T \to \infty$. Thus $\hat{\boldsymbol{\theta}}_T$ is consistent if $\hat{\boldsymbol{\theta}}_T \xrightarrow{P} \boldsymbol{\theta}$ or, equivalently, if $\operatorname{plim}(\hat{\boldsymbol{\theta}}_T) = \boldsymbol{\theta}$.

We can often presume that such an estimator will have a normal limiting distribution with an expected value equal to the value of the unknown parameter $\boldsymbol{\theta}$. In this context we can define an estimator to be asymptotically efficient if its limiting distribution satisfies the conditions in (17.75). Therefore

(17.78) Let $\boldsymbol{\theta}_T^1$ and $\boldsymbol{\theta}_T^2$ be consistent estimators of $\boldsymbol{\theta}$ such that $\sqrt{T}(\boldsymbol{\theta}_T^1 - \boldsymbol{\theta})$ and $\sqrt{T}(\boldsymbol{\theta}_T^2 - \boldsymbol{\theta})$ have respectively the normal limiting distributions $N(\mathbf{0}, \boldsymbol{\Sigma}_1)$ and $N(\mathbf{0}, \boldsymbol{\Sigma}_2)$. Then $\boldsymbol{\theta}_T^1$ is said to be asymptotically efficient relative to $\boldsymbol{\theta}_T^2$ if $\boldsymbol{\Sigma}_2 - \boldsymbol{\Sigma}_1$ is positive semidefinite or, equivalently, if $\mathbf{q}'\boldsymbol{\Sigma}_1\mathbf{q} \leqslant \mathbf{q}'\boldsymbol{\Sigma}_2\mathbf{q}$ for all $\mathbf{q}$.

The most efficient estimator on this criterion is called the best asymptotic normal estimator.

Our enquiries into the efficiency of econometric estimators are usually conducted on the basis of certain regularity assumptions concerning the probability density function $L(\mathbf{X}; \boldsymbol{\theta})$ of the sample data $\mathbf{X}$.

(17.79) The probability density function $L(\mathbf{X}; \boldsymbol{\theta})$ is said to be regular if

(a) The set $\mathscr{S}$ of all values of $\mathbf{X}$ for which $L(\mathbf{X}; \boldsymbol{\theta})$ is strictly positive does not depend on $\boldsymbol{\theta}$,

(b) The density is a smooth function of $\boldsymbol{\theta}$ such that, for all $\boldsymbol{\theta} \in \mathcal{A}$ and $\mathbf{X} \in \mathcal{S}$, $L(\mathbf{X}; \boldsymbol{\theta})$ and $L^* = \log L(\mathbf{X}; \boldsymbol{\theta})$ have finite-valued partial derivatives up to the third order,

(c) The dispersion matrix of $\partial L^*/\partial \boldsymbol{\theta} = \partial \log L(\mathbf{X}; \boldsymbol{\theta})/\partial \boldsymbol{\theta}$ is positive definite everywhere in $\mathcal{A}$.

(d) The expression $\int L(\mathbf{X}; \boldsymbol{\theta})\, d\mathbf{X}^c$ is twice differentiable under the integral.

In addition, it is commonly assumed that

(17.80) The density arises from independent sampling so that

$$L(\mathbf{X}; \boldsymbol{\theta}) = \prod_{t=1}^{T} f(\mathbf{x}_{t.}; \boldsymbol{\theta}).$$

Subject to these conditions, we can establish a lower bound for the variance of an unbiased estimator.

(17.81) Let $L(\mathbf{X}; \boldsymbol{\theta})$ be the density function of the sample $\mathbf{X}$, and let $L^* = \log L$. Then, if $\hat{\boldsymbol{\theta}} = \hat{\boldsymbol{\theta}}(\mathbf{X})$ is an unbiased estimator of $\boldsymbol{\theta}$, we have

$$V(\mathbf{q}'\hat{\boldsymbol{\theta}}) \geqslant -\mathbf{q}'\left\{E\left[\frac{\partial(\partial L^*/\partial \boldsymbol{\theta})'}{\partial \boldsymbol{\theta}}\right]\right\}^{-1}\mathbf{q}.$$

This is known as the Cramer–Rao inequality.

Let us proceed to demonstrate this inequality. To begin, consider

$$\int_{\mathcal{S}} L(\mathbf{X}; \boldsymbol{\theta})\, d\mathbf{X}^c = 1.$$

Differentiating once with respect to $\boldsymbol{\theta}$ gives

$$\int \frac{\partial L(\mathbf{X}; \boldsymbol{\theta})}{\partial \boldsymbol{\theta}}\, d\mathbf{X}^c = \int \frac{\partial L^*(\mathbf{X}; \boldsymbol{\theta})}{\partial \boldsymbol{\theta}} L(\mathbf{X}; \boldsymbol{\theta})\, d\mathbf{X}^c = \mathbf{0}$$

where the first equality follows from $\partial \log L/\partial \boldsymbol{\theta} = (1/L)(\partial L/\partial \boldsymbol{\theta})$. We can write this result as

(17.82) $$E\left(\frac{\partial L^*}{\partial \boldsymbol{\theta}}\right) = \mathbf{0}.$$

Differentiating a second time with respect to $\boldsymbol{\theta}$ gives

$$\begin{aligned}
&\int \left[\frac{\partial(\partial L^*/\partial \boldsymbol{\theta})'}{\partial \boldsymbol{\theta}} L(\mathbf{X}; \boldsymbol{\theta}) + \left(\frac{\partial L^*}{\partial \boldsymbol{\theta}}\right)'\left(\frac{\partial L}{\partial \boldsymbol{\theta}}\right)\right] d\mathbf{X}^c \\
&= \int \left[\frac{\partial(\partial L^*/\partial \boldsymbol{\theta})'}{\partial \boldsymbol{\theta}} + \left(\frac{\partial L^*}{\partial \boldsymbol{\theta}}\right)'\left(\frac{\partial L^*}{\partial \boldsymbol{\theta}}\right)\right] L(\mathbf{X}; \boldsymbol{\theta})\, d\mathbf{X}^c \\
&= E\left[\frac{\partial(\partial L^*/\partial \boldsymbol{\theta})'}{\partial \boldsymbol{\theta}}\right] + E\left[\left(\frac{\partial L^*}{\partial \boldsymbol{\theta}}\right)'\left(\frac{\partial L^*}{\partial \boldsymbol{\theta}}\right)\right] = \mathbf{0}.
\end{aligned}$$

Since $E(\partial L^*/\partial\boldsymbol{\theta}) = \mathbf{0}$, the last equality shows that

$$D\left(\frac{\partial L^*}{\partial\boldsymbol{\theta}}\right) = -E\left[\frac{\partial(\partial L^*/\partial\boldsymbol{\theta})'}{\partial\boldsymbol{\theta}}\right]. \tag{17.83}$$

Next consider

$$E[\hat{\boldsymbol{\theta}}(\mathbf{X})] = \int \hat{\boldsymbol{\theta}}(\mathbf{X})L(\mathbf{X};\boldsymbol{\theta})\, d\mathbf{X}^c.$$

Differentiation gives

$$\begin{aligned}\frac{\partial E[\hat{\boldsymbol{\theta}}(\mathbf{X})]}{\partial\boldsymbol{\theta}} &= \int \hat{\boldsymbol{\theta}}(\mathbf{X})\frac{\partial L(\mathbf{X};\boldsymbol{\theta})}{\partial\boldsymbol{\theta}}\, d\mathbf{X}^c \\ &= \int \hat{\boldsymbol{\theta}}(\mathbf{X})\frac{\partial L^*(\mathbf{X};\boldsymbol{\theta})}{\partial\boldsymbol{\theta}} L(\mathbf{X};\boldsymbol{\theta})\, d\mathbf{X}^c \\ &= E\left(\hat{\boldsymbol{\theta}}\frac{\partial L^*}{\partial\boldsymbol{\theta}}\right).\end{aligned}$$

Now $E(\hat{\boldsymbol{\theta}}) = \boldsymbol{\theta}$ implies that $\partial E(\hat{\boldsymbol{\theta}})/\partial\boldsymbol{\theta} = \mathbf{I}$. Also we have from (17.82) that $E(\partial L^*/\partial\boldsymbol{\theta}) = \mathbf{0}$. Therefore the equality $\partial E(\hat{\boldsymbol{\theta}})/\partial\boldsymbol{\theta} = E(\hat{\boldsymbol{\theta}}\partial L^*/\partial\boldsymbol{\theta})$ can be written as

$$C(\hat{\boldsymbol{\theta}}, \partial L^*/\partial\boldsymbol{\theta}) = \mathbf{I}. \tag{17.84}$$

By compiling the results under (17.83) and (17.84), we find that

$$\begin{aligned}D\begin{bmatrix}\hat{\boldsymbol{\theta}} \\ \left(\dfrac{\partial L^*}{\partial\boldsymbol{\theta}}\right)'\end{bmatrix} &= \begin{bmatrix} D(\hat{\boldsymbol{\theta}}), & C(\hat{\boldsymbol{\theta}}, \partial L^*/\partial\boldsymbol{\theta}) \\ C(\partial L^*/\partial\boldsymbol{\theta}, \hat{\boldsymbol{\theta}}), & D(\partial L^*/\partial\boldsymbol{\theta})\end{bmatrix} \\ &= \begin{bmatrix} D(\hat{\boldsymbol{\theta}}), & \mathbf{I} \\ \mathbf{I}, & -E\left[\dfrac{\partial(\partial L^*/\partial\boldsymbol{\theta})'}{\partial\boldsymbol{\theta}}\right]\end{bmatrix}.\end{aligned}$$

This is a positive-semidefinite matrix. Hence, defining $\mathbf{Q}^{-1} = -E[\partial(\partial L^*/\partial\boldsymbol{\theta})'/\partial\boldsymbol{\theta}]$, we have

$$[\mathbf{q}', -\mathbf{q}'\mathbf{Q}]\begin{bmatrix} D(\hat{\boldsymbol{\theta}}), & \mathbf{I} \\ \mathbf{I}, & \mathbf{Q}^{-1}\end{bmatrix}\begin{bmatrix}\mathbf{q} \\ -\mathbf{Q}\mathbf{q}\end{bmatrix} = \mathbf{q}'D(\hat{\boldsymbol{\theta}})\mathbf{q} - \mathbf{q}'\mathbf{Q}\mathbf{q} \geq 0.$$

Using $\mathbf{q}'D(\hat{\boldsymbol{\theta}})\mathbf{q} = V(\mathbf{q}'\hat{\boldsymbol{\theta}})$, we find, on substituting for $\mathbf{Q}$, that

$$V(\mathbf{q}'\hat{\boldsymbol{\theta}}) \geq -\mathbf{q}'\left\{E\left[\frac{\partial(\partial L^*/\partial\boldsymbol{\theta})'}{\partial\boldsymbol{\theta}}\right]\right\}^{-1}\mathbf{q}$$

which is the desired result.

Let us now consider the case where $\hat{\boldsymbol{\theta}}$ attains the minimum variance bound. Then $V(\mathbf{q}'\hat{\boldsymbol{\theta}}) - \mathbf{q}'\mathbf{Q}\mathbf{q} = \mathbf{q}'D(\hat{\boldsymbol{\theta}})\mathbf{q} - \mathbf{q}'\mathbf{Q}\mathbf{q} = 0$ or, equivalently,

$$[\mathbf{q}', -\mathbf{q}'\mathbf{Q}]D\begin{bmatrix} \hat{\boldsymbol{\theta}} \\ \left(\dfrac{\partial L^*}{\partial \boldsymbol{\theta}}\right)' \end{bmatrix}\begin{bmatrix} \mathbf{q} \\ -\mathbf{Q}\mathbf{q} \end{bmatrix} = 0.$$

But, according to (17.20), the latter is equivalent to the condition

$$[\mathbf{q}', -\mathbf{q}'\mathbf{Q}]\begin{bmatrix} \hat{\boldsymbol{\theta}} - E(\hat{\boldsymbol{\theta}}) \\ \left(\dfrac{\partial L^*}{\partial \boldsymbol{\theta}}\right)' - E\left(\dfrac{\partial L^*}{\partial \boldsymbol{\theta}}\right)' \end{bmatrix} = 0,$$

whence, using $E(\hat{\boldsymbol{\theta}}) = \boldsymbol{\theta}$ and $E(\partial L^*/\partial \boldsymbol{\theta}) = \mathbf{0}$ from (17.82), we get

$$\mathbf{q}'(\hat{\boldsymbol{\theta}} - \boldsymbol{\theta}) - \mathbf{q}'\mathbf{Q}\left(\frac{\partial L^*}{\partial \boldsymbol{\theta}}\right)' = 0.$$

Since this holds for all $\mathbf{q}$, we must have $\hat{\boldsymbol{\theta}} - \boldsymbol{\theta} = \mathbf{Q}(\partial L^*/\partial \boldsymbol{\theta})'$. What we have shown is that

(17.85) Subject to the regularity conditions in (17.79), there exists an unbiased estimator $\hat{\boldsymbol{\theta}}(\mathbf{X})$ whose variance attains the Cramer–Rao minimum variance bound if and only if $\partial L^*(\mathbf{X}; \boldsymbol{\theta})/\partial \boldsymbol{\theta}$ can be expressed in the form

$$\left(\frac{\partial L^*}{\partial \boldsymbol{\theta}}\right)' = -E\left[\frac{\partial(\partial L^*/\partial \boldsymbol{\theta})'}{\partial \boldsymbol{\theta}}\right](\hat{\boldsymbol{\theta}} - \boldsymbol{\theta}).$$

This is, of course, an exceedingly strong requirement; and therefore it is only in somewhat exceptional circumstances that the minimum variance bound can be attained. However, as we shall see shortly, whenever the regularity conditions are satisfied the bound is invariably approached asymptotically by the maximum-likelihood estimator if it is not actually attained for finite samples.

Maximum-likelihood estimation

When the value of $\boldsymbol{\theta}$ is given, $L(\mathbf{X}; \boldsymbol{\theta})$ defines a probability density function over the sample space $\mathcal{S}$. When $\boldsymbol{\theta}$ is unknown and $\mathbf{X}$ is a given or realized value of the data matrix, $L(\mathbf{X}; \boldsymbol{\theta})$ is regarded as a likelihood function defined over the parameter set $\mathcal{A}$.

The principle of maximum-likelihood estimation indicates that we should estimate $\boldsymbol{\theta}$ by choosing the value that renders L as large as possible. Formally

(17.86) A maximum-likelihood estimate $\hat{\boldsymbol{\theta}} = \hat{\boldsymbol{\theta}}(\mathbf{X})$ is an element of the admissible parameter set $\mathcal{A}$ such that $L(\mathbf{X}; \hat{\boldsymbol{\theta}}) \geqslant L(\mathbf{X}; \boldsymbol{\theta})$ for every $\boldsymbol{\theta} \in \mathcal{A}$.

The underlying intuitive idea is that we should select for our estimate the value of $\boldsymbol{\theta}$ which implies the greatest probability of obtaining such values of $\mathbf{X}$ as the one that we have at hand.

Provided that the regularity conditions under (17.79) are satisfied, and provided that L does not attain a maximum at a boundary point of $\mathscr{A}$, then the maximum-likelihood estimate will be among the solutions of the equation $\partial L(\mathbf{X};\boldsymbol{\theta})/\partial\boldsymbol{\theta}=\mathbf{0}$. We usually make the assumption that the data arise from independent sampling so that $L(\mathbf{X};\boldsymbol{\theta})=\prod_{t=1}^{T} f(\mathbf{x}_{t.};\boldsymbol{\theta})$. It is then more convenient to seek the maximum-likelihood estimate by evaluating the equivalent equation

$$\begin{aligned}\frac{\partial L^*(\mathbf{X};\boldsymbol{\theta})}{\partial\boldsymbol{\theta}}&=\frac{\partial \log L(\mathbf{X};\boldsymbol{\theta})}{\partial\boldsymbol{\theta}}\\&=\sum_{t=1}^{T}\frac{\partial \log f(\mathbf{x}_t;\boldsymbol{\theta})}{\partial\boldsymbol{\theta}}=\mathbf{0}.\end{aligned}$$

In some cases, it is apparent that the equation has a unique solution which corresponds to the global maximum of the likelihood function. In other cases there may be reasonable doubts as to whether or not the function has a single stationary point, and then it may be desirable to seek the maximum-likelihood estimate by evaluating $L(\mathbf{X};\boldsymbol{\theta})$ or $L^*(\mathbf{X};\boldsymbol{\theta})$ over a large set of values of $\boldsymbol{\theta}$.

The consistency of the maximum-likelihood estimator

The consistency of the maximum-likelihood estimator is a direct consequence of the fact that the expectation of $L^*(\mathbf{X};\boldsymbol{\theta})$ is maximized by the true parameter value $\boldsymbol{\theta}_0$. To establish the fact that $E[L^*(\mathbf{X};\boldsymbol{\theta}_0)]\geqslant E[L^*(\mathbf{X};\boldsymbol{\theta})]$ for all $\boldsymbol{\theta}\in\mathscr{A}$ we employ Jensen's inequality which shows that, if $x\sim f(x)$ is a random variable and $g(x)$ is a strictly convex function, then $E[g(x)]>g[E(x)]$. This result, which is little more than a statement that $\lambda g(x_1)+(1-\lambda)g(x_2)>g[\lambda x_1+(1-\lambda)x_2]$ when $0<\lambda<1$, is proved by Rao **[93]**. Noting that $-\log(z)$ is a strictly convex function, we begin by finding that

$$E\left[-\log\frac{L(\mathbf{X};\boldsymbol{\theta})}{L(\mathbf{X};\boldsymbol{\theta}_0)}\right]\geqslant -\log E\left[\frac{L(\mathbf{X};\boldsymbol{\theta})}{L(\mathbf{X};\boldsymbol{\theta}_0)}\right],$$

where the equality arises when $\boldsymbol{\theta}=\boldsymbol{\theta}_0$. Next we find that, on the RHS, we have

$$\begin{aligned}E\left[\frac{L(\mathbf{X};\boldsymbol{\theta})}{L(\mathbf{X};\boldsymbol{\theta}_0)}\right]&=\int\frac{L(\mathbf{X};\boldsymbol{\theta})}{L(\mathbf{X};\boldsymbol{\theta}_0)}L(\mathbf{X};\boldsymbol{\theta}_0)\,d\mathbf{X}^{c}\\&=1.\end{aligned}$$

Substituting this in the inequality gives $E[-\log\{L(\mathbf{X};\boldsymbol{\theta})/L(\mathbf{X};\boldsymbol{\theta}_0)\}]=E[L^*(\mathbf{X};\boldsymbol{\theta}_0)]-E[L^*(\mathbf{X};\boldsymbol{\theta})]\geqslant 0$ which is the desired result. We shall actually employ the inequality in the form

$$(17.87)\qquad E\left[\frac{L^*(\mathbf{X};\boldsymbol{\theta}_0)}{T}\right]\geqslant E\left[\frac{L^*(\mathbf{X};\boldsymbol{\theta})}{T}\right].$$

We are now in a position to prove that

(17.88) If $\hat{\boldsymbol{\theta}}_T$ is the maximum-likelihood estimator satisfying $L^*(\mathbf{X};\hat{\boldsymbol{\theta}}_T)\geqslant L^*(\mathbf{X};\boldsymbol{\theta})$ for all T and for every $\boldsymbol{\theta}\in\mathscr{A}$, then $\hat{\boldsymbol{\theta}}_T\xrightarrow{P}\boldsymbol{\theta}_0$ where $\boldsymbol{\theta}_0$ is the true parameter value. That is to say, the maximum-likelihood estimator is consistent.

Proof. For any value of $\boldsymbol{\theta}$, the function $L^*(\mathbf{X};\boldsymbol{\theta})/T=\sum\log f(\mathbf{x}_{t.};\boldsymbol{\theta})/T$ is the mean of independent and identically distributed random variables with expected values of $E[\log f(\mathbf{x}_{t.};\boldsymbol{\theta})]=E[L^*(\mathbf{X};\boldsymbol{\theta})/T]$ for all t. Hence, by the law of large numbers, $L^*(\mathbf{X};\boldsymbol{\theta})/T\xrightarrow{P}E[L^*(\mathbf{X};\boldsymbol{\theta})/T]$. Therefore, using the inequality in (17.87), we get

$$\begin{aligned}\text{plim}[L^*(\mathbf{X};\boldsymbol{\theta}_0)/T]&=E[L^*(\mathbf{X};\boldsymbol{\theta}_0)/T]\\&\geqslant E[L^*(\mathbf{X};\boldsymbol{\theta})/T]=\text{plim}[L^*(\mathbf{X};\boldsymbol{\theta})/T],\end{aligned}$$

or simply $\text{plim}[L^*(\mathbf{X};\boldsymbol{\theta}_0)/T]\geqslant\text{plim}[L^*(\mathbf{X};\boldsymbol{\theta})/T]$. But, if $\hat{\boldsymbol{\theta}}$ is the maximum-likelihood estimate, then, by definition, $L^*(\mathbf{X};\hat{\boldsymbol{\theta}})/T\geqslant L(\mathbf{X};\boldsymbol{\theta})/T$ for all T and, in particular, $L^*(\mathbf{X};\hat{\boldsymbol{\theta}})/T\geqslant L^*(\mathbf{X};\boldsymbol{\theta}_0)/T$. This cannot be reconciled with the previous inequality unless $\text{plim}[L^*(\mathbf{X};\hat{\boldsymbol{\theta}})/T]=\text{plim}[L^*(\mathbf{X};\boldsymbol{\theta}_0)/T]$. Under very general conditions, this can be taken to imply that $\text{plim}(\hat{\boldsymbol{\theta}})=\boldsymbol{\theta}_0$.

We have given a simplified version of a proof by Wald [**119**]. An exhaustive account of the conditions under which $\text{plim}[L^*(\mathbf{X};\hat{\boldsymbol{\theta}})/T]=\text{plim}[L^*(\mathbf{X};\boldsymbol{\theta}_0)/T]$ implies $\text{plim}(\hat{\boldsymbol{\theta}})=\boldsymbol{\theta}_0$ can be found in Rao [**93**]. We should note that the conditions of the theorem are sufficient to enable us to establish, by invoking the strong law of large numbers, that $L^*(\mathbf{X};\boldsymbol{\theta})/T$ converges strongly in probability, or almost certainly, to $E[L^*(\mathbf{X};\boldsymbol{\theta})/T]$. Therefore we can make an even stronger statement about the certainty of the inequality $L^*(\mathbf{X};\boldsymbol{\theta}_0)/T\geqslant L^*(\mathbf{X};\boldsymbol{\theta})/T$ for large T.

There remains the question of whether more than one solution of the equation $\partial L^*(\mathbf{X};\boldsymbol{\theta})/\partial\boldsymbol{\theta}=\mathbf{0}$ can constitute a consistent estimator. Huzurbazar [**58**] has shown that, under the regularity conditions, as T increases there emerges a unique consistent estimator. That is to say, if $\boldsymbol{\theta}^1$ and $\boldsymbol{\theta}^2$ are two solutions to the equation they are asymptotically equivalent in the sense that $\sqrt{T}(\boldsymbol{\theta}^1-\boldsymbol{\theta}^2)$ converges to zero strongly in probability. The problem of multiple solutions is therefore essentially a small-sample problem.

The efficiency and asymptotic normality of the maximum-likelihood estimator

Maximum-likelihood estimators have certain optimal properties.

To begin with, a rather weak justification of the estimator is provided by the fact that

(17.89) If there exists an unbiased estimator that attains the minimum variance bound, then this coincides with the maximum-likelihood estimator.

For we have already shown in (17.85) that a minimum variance bound estimator $\hat{\boldsymbol{\theta}}$ exists if and only if $(\partial L^*/\partial\boldsymbol{\theta})' = -E[\partial(\partial L^*/\partial\boldsymbol{\theta})'/\partial\boldsymbol{\theta}](\hat{\boldsymbol{\theta}}-\boldsymbol{\theta})$ and, in that case, the only solution to the maximum-likelihood equation $\partial L^*/\partial\boldsymbol{\theta}=\mathbf{0}$ is $\boldsymbol{\theta}=\hat{\boldsymbol{\theta}}$. We may notice that, since the minimum variance unbiased estimator is unique, this also settles the question of the uniqueness of the maximum-likelihood estimator. However, it is doubtful whether we can gain any more information about the uniqueness of the solution to $\partial L^*/\partial\boldsymbol{\theta}=\mathbf{0}$ in this way than can be gained from a simple inspection of the likelihood function.

A much stronger justification of the maximum-likelihood estimator arises from the fact that, if it is not already the minimum variance unbiased estimator, then, under the regularity conditions, it invariably approaches the minimum variance bound asymptotically as $T\to\infty$. We prove this in demonstrating the asymptotic normality of the estimator. Specifically, we shall prove that

(17.90) If $\hat{\boldsymbol{\theta}}$ is the maximum-likelihood estimator obtained from $\partial L^*/\partial\boldsymbol{\theta}=\mathbf{0}$, then $\sqrt{T}(\hat{\boldsymbol{\theta}}-\boldsymbol{\theta}_0)$ has the normal limiting distribution $N(\mathbf{0},\mathbf{M})$ where

$$\mathbf{M}=-\left(E\left\{\frac{1}{T}\frac{\partial[\partial L^*(\mathbf{X};\boldsymbol{\theta}_0)/\partial\boldsymbol{\theta}]'}{\partial\boldsymbol{\theta}}\right\}\right)^{-1}.$$

Proof. If $\hat{\boldsymbol{\theta}}$ is the solution to $\partial L^*/\partial\boldsymbol{\theta}=\mathbf{0}$ and if $\boldsymbol{\theta}_0$ is the true parameter value, then, by Taylor's theorem,

$$\mathbf{0}=\left[\frac{\partial L^*(\mathbf{X};\boldsymbol{\theta}_0)}{\partial\boldsymbol{\theta}}\right]'+\frac{\partial[\partial L^*(\mathbf{X};\boldsymbol{\theta}_0)/\partial\boldsymbol{\theta}]'}{\partial\boldsymbol{\theta}}(\hat{\boldsymbol{\theta}}-\boldsymbol{\theta}_0)+\frac{\mathbf{R}}{2}(\hat{\boldsymbol{\theta}}-\boldsymbol{\theta}_0)$$

where $\mathbf{R}$ is a matrix whose typical element $\sum_j(\partial^3L^*/\partial\theta_i\partial\theta_j\partial\theta_r)(\hat{\theta}_j-\theta_{0,j})$ incorporates a third-order derivative evaluated at some point between $\hat{\boldsymbol{\theta}}$ and $\boldsymbol{\theta}_0$. By rearranging the expression and incorporating the factor $\sqrt{T}$, we get

$$\sqrt{T}(\hat{\boldsymbol{\theta}}-\boldsymbol{\theta}_0)=-\left\{\frac{1}{T}\frac{\partial[\partial L^*(\mathbf{X};\boldsymbol{\theta}_0)/\partial\boldsymbol{\theta}]'}{\partial\boldsymbol{\theta}}+\frac{\mathbf{R}}{2T}\right\}^{-1}\left\{\frac{1}{\sqrt{T}}\frac{\partial L^*(\mathbf{X};\boldsymbol{\theta}_0)'}{\partial\boldsymbol{\theta}}\right\}.$$

We must now find the probability limits of the expressions on the RHS.

First consider the fact that $\partial L^*(\mathbf{X};\boldsymbol{\theta}_0)/\partial\boldsymbol{\theta}=\sum\partial\log f(\mathbf{x}_{t.};\boldsymbol{\theta}_0)/\partial\boldsymbol{\theta}$ is a sum of independent and identically distributed random vectors. Since, according to (17.82) and (17.83), we have $E[\partial L^*(\mathbf{X}; \boldsymbol{\theta}_0)/\partial\boldsymbol{\theta}] = \mathbf{0}$ and $D[\partial L^*(\mathbf{X}; \boldsymbol{\theta}_0)/\partial\boldsymbol{\theta}] = -E\{\partial[\partial L^*(\mathbf{X}; \boldsymbol{\theta}_0)/\partial\boldsymbol{\theta}]'/\partial\boldsymbol{\theta}\} = T\mathbf{M}^{-1}$, it follows from the central limit theorem in (17.67) that $(1/\sqrt{T})[\partial L^*(\mathbf{X}; \boldsymbol{\theta}_0)/\partial\boldsymbol{\theta}]'$ has the limiting normal distribution $N(\mathbf{0}, \mathbf{M}^{-1})$.

Next consider the fact that $\partial[\partial L^*(\mathbf{X}; \boldsymbol{\theta}_0)/\partial\boldsymbol{\theta}]'/\partial\boldsymbol{\theta} = \sum \partial[\partial \log f(\mathbf{x}_{t.}; \boldsymbol{\theta}_0)/\partial\boldsymbol{\theta}]'/\partial\boldsymbol{\theta}$ is a sum of independent and identically distributed random matrices. It follows, therefore, from the law of large numbers in (17.64) that $(1/T)\partial[\partial L^*(\mathbf{X}; \boldsymbol{\theta}_0)/\partial\boldsymbol{\theta}]'/\partial\boldsymbol{\theta}$ converges in probability to its expected value $-\mathbf{M}^{-1}$.

Finally, we can invoke the regularity condition (17.79)(b) concerning the boundedness of partial derivatives of the third order to show that $\mathbf{R}/T$ tends to zero as $T \to \infty$.

On compiling these three results, we see that $\sqrt{T}(\hat{\boldsymbol{\theta}} - \boldsymbol{\theta}_0)$ tends in distribution to a random vector $\mathbf{M}\boldsymbol{\eta}$ where $\boldsymbol{\eta} \sim N(\mathbf{0}, \mathbf{M}^{-1})$; and we conclude that $\sqrt{T}(\hat{\boldsymbol{\theta}} - \boldsymbol{\theta}_0)$ has the normal limiting distribution $N(\mathbf{0}, \mathbf{M})$.

To establish that the maximum-likelihood estimator approaches the minimum variance bound as $T \to \infty$, we need only to confirm that the asymptotic dispersion matrix $\mathbf{M}$ defined in (17.90) is simply T times the matrix $\mathbf{Q}$ entailed in thc Cramer–Rao inequality $V(\mathbf{q}'\hat{\boldsymbol{\theta}}) \geqslant \mathbf{q}'\mathbf{Q}\mathbf{q}$ in (17.81). We should remind ourselves that this result concerns the moments of a limiting distribution rather than the limits of the moments of the sampling distributions; although, of course, there are some cases where there is no distinction between the two.

An alternative way of representing the dispersion matrix of the limiting distribution of the estimator is to write it as

$$\mathbf{M} = -\text{plim}\left\{\frac{1}{T}\frac{\partial[\partial L^*(\mathbf{X}; \hat{\boldsymbol{\theta}})/\partial\boldsymbol{\theta}]'}{\partial\boldsymbol{\theta}}\right\}^{-1}.$$

This is justified by the fact that $\text{plim}(\hat{\boldsymbol{\theta}}) = \boldsymbol{\theta}_0$ and by the fact that, on account of the law of large numbers, the expression within the first bracket tends to its expected value as $T \to \infty$.

We have demonstrated the asymptotic efficiency and normality of the maximum-likelihood estimator only for the case where the data arises from independent sampling. The case of non-independent sampling is also of interest to us since it affects the temporal regression models that we consider in Chapter 12. The necessary extensions were made in 1943 by Mann and Wald [**83**] who demonstrated the consistency and asymptotic normality of the maximum-likelihood estimators of such models under very general assumptions. However, they did not demonstrate rigorously that the estimates retain the property of efficiency. The reader who wishes to confirm that optimal properties of the estimators are retained in cases of dependent observations may consult an article by Bhat [**14**].

Bibliography

An extensive bibliography of econometric literature may be found in Theil's *Principles of Econometrics* [**115**]. Klein's *A Textbook of Econometrics* [**64**] and Madansky's *Foundations of Econometrics* [**80**] both contain selective annotated bibliographies at the ends of chapters. A bibliography that is specific to the problems of simultaneous-equation estimation may be found in Fisk's *Stochastically Dependent Equations* [**38**]. The following references have been cited in this book either in the text or at the ends of chapters.

[**1**] Afriat, S. N. (1957), 'Orthogonal and Oblique Projectors and the Characteristics of Pairs of Vector Spaces', *Proceedings of the Cambridge Phil. Soc.*, **53,** 800–816.

[**2**] Aigner, D. J. (1971), 'A Compendium on Estimation of the Autoregressive Moving Average Model for Time Series Data', *International Econometric Review*, **12,** 348–371.

[**3**] Aitchison, J. and S. D. Silvey (1958), 'Maximum Likelihood Estimation of Parameters Subject to Restraints', *Annals of Mathematical Statistics*, **29,** 813–828.

[**4**] Almon, S. (1965), 'The Distributed Lag between Capital Appropriations and Expenditures', *Econometrica*, **33,** 178–196.

[**5**] Amemiya, T. and W. A. Fuller (1967), 'A Comparative Study of Alternative Estimators in a Distributed Lag Model', *Econometrica*, **35,** 509–529.

[**6**] Anderson, R. L. (1942), 'Distribution of the Serial Correlation Coefficient', *Annals of Mathematical Statistics*, **13,** 1–13.

[**7**] Anderson, T. W. (1950), 'Estimation of the Parameters of a Single Equation by the Limited-Information Maximum-Likelihood Method', Chapter 9 in *Statistical Inference in Dynamic Economic Models*, T. C. Koopmans (editor), Cowles Foundation for Research in Economics, Monograph No. 10, New York: John Wiley and Sons.

[**8**] Anderson, T. W. (1958), *An Introduction to Multivariate Statistical Analysis*, New York: John Wiley and Sons.

[**9**] Anderson, T. W. and H. Rubin (1949), 'Estimation of the Parameters of a Single Equation in a Complete System of Stochastic Equations', *Annals of Mathematical Statistics*, **20,** 46–63.

[**10**] Anderson T. W. and H. Rubin (1950), 'The Asymptotic Properties of Estimates of the Parameters of a Single Equation in a Complete System of Stochastic Equations', *Annals of Mathematical Statistics*, **21,** 570–582.

[**11**] Barnard, G. A. (1975), 'On the Geometry of Estimation', in *Perspectives in Probability and Statistics: Papers in Honour of M. S. Bartlett*, J. Gani (editor), London: Academic Press.

[**12**] Bartlett, M. S. (1955), *An Introduction to Stochastic Processes with Special Reference to Methods and Applications*, Cambridge: Cambridge University Press.

[**13**] Basmann, R. L. (1957), 'A Generalized Classical Method of Linear Estimation of Coefficients in a Structural Equation', *Econometrica*, **25,** 77–84.

[**14**] Bhat, B. R. (1974), 'On the Method of Maximum Likelihood for Dependent Observations', *Journal of the Royal Statistical Society*, Series B, **36,** 48–53.

[**15**] Box, G. E. P. and G. M. Jenkins (1970), *Time Series Analysis: Forecasting and Control*, San Francisco: Holden-Day.

[**16**] Brook, R. and T. D. Wallace (1973), 'A Note on Extraneous Information in Regression', *Journal of Econometrics*, **1,** 315–316.

[**17**] Chipman, J. S. (1964), 'On Least Squares with Insufficient Observations', *Journal of the American Statistical Association*, **59,** 1078–1111.

[**18**] Chipman, J. S. and M. M. Rao (1964), 'The Treatment of Linear Restrictions in Regression Analysis', *Econometrica*, **32,** 198–209.

[**19**] Chipman, J. S. and M. M. Rao (1964), 'Projections, Generalized Inverses, and Quadratic Forms', *Journal of Mathematical Analysis and Applications*, **9,** 1–11.

[**20**] Chow, G. C. (1964), 'A Comparison of Alternative Estimators for Simultaneous Equations', *Econometrica*, **32,** 532–553.

[**21**] Chow, G. C. (1968), 'Two Methods of Computing Full-Information Maximum Likelihood Estimates in Simultaneous Stochastic Equations', *International Economic Review*, **9,** 100–112.

[**22**] Chow, G. C. and D. K. Ray-Chaudhuri (1967), 'An Alternative Proof of Hannan's Theorem on Canonical Correlation and Multiple Equation Systems', *Econometrica*, **35,** 139–142.

[**23**] Cochran, W. G. (1934), 'The Distribution of Quadratic Forms in a Normal System, with Applications to the Analysis of Variance', *Proceedings of the Cambridge Phil. Soc.*, **30,** 178–191.

[**24**] Cochrane, D. and G. H. Orcutt (1949), 'Application of Least-Squares Regression to Relationships Containing Autocorrelated Error Terms', *Journal of the American Statistical Association*, **44,** 32–61.

[**25**] Cramér, H. (1946), *Mathematical Methods of Statistics*, Princeton University Press.

[**26**] Dhrymes, P. J. (1966), 'On the Treatment of Certain Recurrent Non-Linearities in Regression Analysis', *Southern Economic Journal*, **33,** 187–196.

[**27**] Dhrymes, P. J. (1971), *Distributed Lags: Problems of Estimation and Formulation*, Edinburgh: Oliver and Boyd, San Francisco: Holden–Day.

[**28**] Dhrymes, P. J., L. R. Klein, and K. Steiglitz (1970), 'Estimation of Distributed Lags', *International Economic Review*, **11,** 235–250.

[**29**] Durbin, J. (1959), 'Efficient Estimation of Parameters in Moving Average Models', *Biometrika*, **46,** 306–316.

[**30**] Durbin, J. (1960), 'Estimation of Parameters in Time Series Regression Models', *Journal of the Royal Statistical Society*, Series B, **22,** 139–153.

[**31**] Durbin, J. (1963), 'Maximum Likelihood Estimation of the Parameters of a System of Simultaneous Regression Equations', paper presented at the Copenhagen meeting of the Econometric Society.

[**32**] Durbin, J. and M. G. Kendall (1951), 'The Geometry of Estimation', *Biometrika*, **38,** 150–158.

[**33**] Dwyer, P. S. (1967), 'Some Applications of Matrix Derivatives in Multivariate Analysis', *Journal of the American Statistical Association*, **62,** 607–625.

[**34**] Dwyer, P. S. and M. S. MacPhail (1948), 'Symbolic Matrix Derivatives', *Annals of Mathematical Statistics*, **19,** 517–534.

[**35**] Fisher, F. M. (1966), *The Identification Problem in Econometrics*, New York: McGraw-Hill.

[**36**] Fisher, G. R. (1972), 'The Algebra of Estimation in Linear Econometric Systems', *International Journal of Mathematical Education in Science and Technology*, **3,** 385–403.

[**37**] Fisher, W. D. and W. J. Wadycki (1971) 'Estimating a Structural Equation in a Large System', *Econometrica*, **39,** 461–465.

[**38**] Fisk, P. R. (1967), *Stochastically Dependent Equations: An Introductory Text for Econometricians*, London: Charles Griffin and Co.

[**39**] Fuller, W. A. (1976), *Introduction to Statistical Time Series*, New York: John Wiley and Sons.

[**40**] Ghosh, S. K. (1972), 'Canonical Correlation and Extended Limited-Information Methods Under General Linear Restrictions on Parameters', *International Economic Review*, **13,** 728–736.

[**41**] Goldberger, A. S. (1964), *Econometric Theory*, New York: John Wiley and Sons.

[**42**] Goldberger, A. S. and I. Olkin (1971), 'A Minimum-Distance Interpretation of Limited-Information Estimation', *Econometrica*, **39,** 635–639.

[**43**] Goldfeld, S. M. and R. E. Quandt (1972), *Non-Linear Methods in Econometrics*, Amsterdam: North-Holland Publishing Co.

[**44**] Goldman, A. J. and M. Zelen (1964), 'Weak Generalized Inverses and Minimum Variance Linear Unbiased Estimation', *Journal of Research of the National Bureau of Standards*, Series B, **68,** 151–172.

[**45**] Grenander, U. (1954), 'On the Estimation of Regression Coefficients in the Case of an Autocorrelated Disturbance', *Annals of Mathematical Statistics*, **25,** 252–272.

[**46**] Grenander, U. and M. Rosenblatt (1957), *Statistical Analysis of Stationary Time Series*, New York: John Wiley and Sons.

[**47**] Griliches, Z. (1967), 'Distributed Lags: A Survey', *Econometrica*, **35,** 16–49.

[**48**] Guilkey, D. K. and P. Schmidt (1973), 'Estimation of Seemingly Unrelated Regressions with Vector Autoregressive Errors', *Journal of the American Statistical Association*, **68,** 642–648.

[**49**] Halmos, P. R. (1958), *Finite Dimensional Vector Spaces*, New York: Van Nostrand–Reinhold Co.

[**50**] Hannan, E. J. (1965), 'The Estimation of Relationships Involving Distributed Lags', *Econometrica*, **33,** 206–224.

[**51**] Hannan, E. J. (1967), 'Canonical Correlation and Multiple Equation Systems in Economics', *Econometrica*, **35,** 123–138.

[**52**] Hart, B. I. (1942), 'Tabulation of the Probabilities of the Ratio of the Mean Square Successive Difference to the Variance', *Annals of Mathematical Statistics*, **13,** 207–214.

[**53**] Hartley, H. O. (1961), 'The Modified Gauss–Newton Method for the Fitting of Non-Linear Regression Functions by Least Squares', *Technometrics*, **3,** 269–280.

[**54**] Hartley, H. O. and A. Brooker (1965), 'Non-Linear Least-Squares Estimation', *Annals of Mathematical Statistics*, **36,** 638–650.

[**55**] Hendry, D. F. (1971), 'Maximum Likelihood Estimation of Systems of Simultaneous Regression Equations with Errors Generated by a Vector Autoregressive Process', *International Economic Review*, **12,** 257–271.

[**56**] Hendry, D. F. (1976), 'The Structure of Simultaneous Equations Estimators', *Journal of Econometrics*, **4,** 51–88.

[**57**] Hood, W. C. and T. C. Koopmans (editors) (1953), *Studies in Econometric Method*, Cowles Foundation for Research in Economics, Monograph No. 14, New York: John Wiley and Sons.

[**58**] Huzurbazar, V. S. (1948), 'The Likelihood Equation, Consistency and the Maxima of the Likelihood Function', *Annals of Eugenics*, **14,** 185–200.

[**59**] Jenkins, G. M. and D. G. Watts (1968), *Spectral Analysis and its Applications*, San Francisco: Holden–Day.

[**60**] Jorgenson, D. W. (1966), 'Rational Distributed Lag Functions', *Econometrica*, **34,** 135–149.

[**61**] Kadiyala, K. R. (1968), 'A Transformation Used to Circumvent the Problem of Autocorrelation', *Econometrica*, **36,** 93–96.

[**62**] Kendall, M. G. and A. Stuart (1958, 1961, 1966), *The Advanced Theory of Statistics*, Three Volume Edition, London: Charles Griffin and Co.

[**63**] Klein, L. R. (1958), 'The Estimation of Distributed Lags', *Econometrica*, **26,** 553–565.

[**64**] Klein, L. R. (1974), *A Textbook of Econometrics—2nd Edition*, Englewood Cliffs, New Jersey: Prentice–Hall.

[**65**] Kmenta, J. and R. F. Gilbert (1968), 'Small Sample Properties of Alternative Estimators of Seemingly Unrelated Regressions', *Journal of the American Statistical Association*, **63,** 1180–1200.

[**66**] Koopmans, T. C. (editor) (1950), *Statistical Inference in Dynamic Economic Models*, Cowles Foundation for Research in Economics, Monograph No. 10, New York: John Wiley and Sons.

[**67**] Koopmans, T. C. and W. M. Hood (1953), 'The Estimation of Simultaneous Linear Economic Relationships', Chapter 6 in *Studies in Econometric Method*, W. C. Hood and T. C. Koopmans (editors), Cowles Foundation for Research in Economics, Monograph No. 14, New York: John Wiley and Sons.

[**68**] Koopmans, T. C., H. Rubin, and R. B. Leipnik (1950), 'Measuring the Equation Systems of Dynamic Economics', Chapter 2 in *Statistical Inference in Dynamic Economic Models*, T. C. Koopmans (editor), Cowles Foundation for Research in Economics, Monograph No. 10, New York: John Wiley and Sons.

[**69**] Koyck, L. M. (1954), *Distributed Lags and Investment Analysis*, Amsterdam: North-Holland Publishing Co.

[**70**] Kreider, D. L., R. G. Kuller, D. R. Ostberg, and F. W. Perkins (1966), *An Introduction to Linear Analysis*, Reading, Mass.: Addison–Wesley Publishing Co.

[**71**] Kruskal, W. (1968), 'When are Gauss–Markov and Least Squares Estimators Identical? A Coordinate-Free Approach', *Annals of Mathematical Statistics*, **39,** 70-75.

[**72**] Kruskal, W. (1975), 'The Geometry of Generalized Inverses', *Journal of the Royal Statistical Society*, Series B, **37,** 272–283.

[**73**] Lang, S. (1966), *Linear Algebra*, Reading, Mass.: Addison–Wesley Publishing Co.

[**74**] Liviatan, N. (1963), 'Consistent Estimation of Distributed Lags', *International Economic Review*, **4,** 44–52.

[**75**] Loève, M. (1960), *Probability Theory*, New York: Van Nostrand Co.

[**76**] Lyttkens, E. (1973), 'The Fix-Point Method for Estimating Interdependent Systems with Underlying Model Specification', *Journal of the Royal Statistical Society*, Series A, **135,** 353–375.

[**77**] MacRae, E. C. (1974), 'Matrix Derivatives with an Application to an Adaptive Linear Decision Problem', *Annals of Statistics*, **2,** 337–346.

[**78**] Madansky, A. (1959), 'The Fitting of Straight Lines when Both Variables are Subject to Error', *Journal of the American Statistical Association*, **54,** 173–205.

[**79**] Madansky, A. (1964), 'On the Efficiency of Three-Stage Least-Squares Estimation', *Econometrica*, **32,** 51–56.

[**80**] Madansky, A. (1976), *Foundations of Econometrics*, Amsterdam: North-Holland Publishing Co.

[**81**] Maddala, G. S. (1971), 'Generalized Least Squares with an Estimated Variance–Covariance Matrix', *Econometrica*, **39,** 23–33.

[**82**] Malinvaud, E. (1966), *Statistical Methods of Econometrics*, Amsterdam: North-Holland Publishing Co.

[**83**] Mann, H. B. and A. Wald (1943), 'On the Statistical Treatment of Linear Stochastic Difference Equations', *Econometrica*, **11,** 173–220.

[**84**] Marquardt, D. W. (1963), 'An Algorithm for Least-Squares Estimation of Non-Linear Parameters', *SIAM Journal on Applied Mathematics*, **11,** 431–441.

[**85**] Mitra, S. K. (1973), 'Unified Least-Squares Approach to Linear Estimation in a General Gauss–Markov Model', *SIAM Journal on Applied Mathematics*, **25,** 671–680.

[**86**] Morrison, D. F. (1967), *Multivariate Statistical Methods*, New York: McGraw-Hill Book Co.

[**87**] Mosbaek, E. J. and H. Wold (1970), *Interdependent Systems: Structure and Estimation*, Amsterdam: North-Holland Publishing Co.

[**88**] Neudecker, H. (1969), 'Some Theorems on Matrix Differentiation with Special Reference to Kronecker Matrix Products', *Journal of the American Statistical Association*, **64,** 953–963.

[**89**] Nicholls, D. F., A. R. Pagan, and R. D. Terell (1975), 'The Estimation and Use of Models with Moving Average Disturbance Terms: A Survey', *International Economic Review*, **16,** 113–134.

[**90**] Parks, R. W. (1967), 'Efficient Estimation of a System of Regression Equations when Disturbances are both Serially and Contemporaneously Correlated', *Journal of the American Statistical Association*, **62,** 500–509.

[**91**] Phillips, A. W. (1966), 'Estimation of Stochastic Difference Equations with Moving Average Disturbances', paper presented at the San Francisco meeting of the Econometric Society.

[**92**] Pringle, R. M. and A. A. Rayner (1971), *Generalized Inverse Matrices with Applications to Statistics*, London: Charles Griffin and Co.

[**93**] Rao, C. R. (1965), *Linear Statistical Inference and its Applications*, New York: John Wiley and Sons.

[**94**] Rao, C. R. (1966), 'Generalized Inverse for Matrices and its Application in Mathematical Statistics', *Research Papers in Statistics*, Festschrift for J. Neyman, New York: John Wiley and Sons.

[**95**] Rao, C. R. (1971), 'Unified Theory of Linear Estimation', *Sankhya*, Series A, **33,** 371–394.

[**96**] Rao, C. R. (1973), 'Representations of Best Linear Unbiased Estimators in the Gauss–Markov Model with a Singular Dispersion Matrix', *Journal of Multivariate Analysis*, **3,** 276–292.

[**97**] Rao, C. R. (1974), 'Projectors, Generalized Inverses and BLUE's', *Journal of the Royal Statistical Society*, Series B, **36,** 442–448.

[**98**] Rao, C. R. and S. K. Mitra (1971), *Generalized Inverse of Matrices and its Applications*, New York: John Wiley and Sons.

[**99**] Rothenberg, T. J. (1971), 'Identification in Parametric Models', *Econometrica*, **39,** 577–591.

[**100**] Rothenberg, T. J. (1973), *Efficient Estimation with A Priori Information*, Cowles Foundation for Research in Economics, Monograph No. 23, New Haven and London: Yale University Press.

[**101**] Rothenberg, T. J. and C. T. Leenders (1964), 'Efficient Estimation of Simultaneous Equation Systems', *Econometrica*, **32,** 57–76.

[**102**] Sargan, J. D. (1958), 'The Estimation of Economic Relationships Using Instrumental Variables', *Econometrica*, **26,** 393–415.

[**103**] Sargan, J. D. (1961), 'The Maximum Likelihood Estimation of Economic Relationships with Autoregressive Residuals', *Econometrica*, **29,** 414–426.

[**104**] Sargan, J. D. (1964), 'Wages and Prices in the United Kingdom: A Study in Econometric Methodology', in *Econometric Analysis for National Economic Planning*, P. E. Hart, G. Mills and J. K. Whitaker (editors), pp. 25–54, London: Butterworth and Co.

[**105**] Sargan, J. D. (1964), 'Three-Stage Least-Squares and Full Maximum Likelihood Estimates', *Econometrica*, **32,** 77–81.

[**106**] Scheffé, H. (1959), *The Analysis of Variance*, New York: John Wiley and Sons.

[**107**] Schönfeld, P. (1975), 'A Note on Least-Squares Estimation and the BLUE in a Generalized Linear Regression Model', *Journal of Econometrics*, **3,** 189–197.

[**108**] Seber, G. A. F. (1966), *The Linear Hypothesis: A General Theory*, London: Charles Griffin and Co.

[**109**] Shephard, G. C. (1966), *Vector Spaces of Finite Dimension*, Edinburgh and London: Oliver and Boyd.

[**110**] Shilov, G. E. (1961), *Theory of Linear Spaces*, Englewood Cliffs, New Jersey: Prentice–Hall.

[**111**] Silvey, S. D. (1970), *Statistical Inference*, Harmondsworth: Penguin Books, Reprinted (1975), London: Chapman and Hall.

[**112**] Steiglitz, K. and L. E. McBride (1965), 'A Technique for the Identification of Linear Systems', *IEEE Transactions on Automatic Control*, **AC-10,** 461–464.

[**113**] Swamy, P. A. V. B. and J. Holmes (1971), 'The Use of Undersized Samples in the Estimation of Simultaneous Equation Systems', *Econometrica*, **39,** 455–459.

[**114**] Theil, H. (1961), *Econometric Forecasts and Policy—2nd Edition*, Amsterdam: North-Holland Publishing Co.

[**115**] Theil, H. (1971), *Principles of Econometrics*, New York: John Wiley and Sons.

[**116**] Tintner, G. (1940), *The Variate Difference Method*, Bloomington, Ind.: Principia Press.

[**117**] Trivedi, P. K. (1970), 'Inventory Behaviour in U.K. Manufacturing, 1956–67', *Review of Economic Studies*, **37,** 517–536.

[**118**] Uppuluri, V. R. R. and J. A. Carpenter (1969), 'The Inverse of a Matrix Occurring in First-Order Moving Average Models', *Sankhya*, Series A, **31,** 79–82.

[**119**] Wald, A. (1949), 'Note on the Consistency of the Maximum Likelihood Estimates', *Annals of Mathematical Statistics*, **20,** 595–601.

[**120**] Wegge, L. L. (1965), 'Identifiability Criteria for a System of Equations as a Whole', *Australian Journal of Statistics*, **7,** 67–77.

[**121**] Whittle, P. (1953), 'Estimation and Information in Stationary Time Series', *Arkiv für Matematik*, **2,** 423–434.

[**122**] Wilks, S. S. (1962), *Mathematical Statistics*, New York: John Wiley and Sons.

[**123**] Wise, J. (1956), 'Stationarity Conditions for Stochastic Processes of the Autoregressive and Moving Average Type', *Biometrika*, **43,** 215–219.

[**124**] Wold, H. (1965), 'A Fix-Point Theorem with Econometric Background', *Arkiv für Matematik*, **6,** 209–240.

[**125**] Zellner, A. (1962), 'An Efficient Method of Estimating Seemingly Unrelated Regressions and Tests for Aggregration Bias', *Journal of the American Statistical Association*, **57,** 348–368.

[**126**] Zellner, A. and M. S. Geisel (1970), 'Analysis of Distributed Lag Models with Applications to Consumption Function Estimation', *Econometrica*, **38,** 865–888.

[**127**] Zellner, A. and F. Palm (1974), 'Time Series Analysis and Simultaneous Equation Econometric Models', *Journal of Econometrics*, **2,** 17–54.

[**128**] Zellner, A. and H. Theil (1962), 'Three-Stage Least Squares: Simultaneous Estimation of Simultaneous Equations', *Econometrica*, **30,** 54–78.

[**129**] Zyskind, G. and F. B. Martin (1969), 'On Best Linear Estimation and a General Gauss–Markov Theorem in Linear Models with Arbitrary Non-Negative Covariance Structure', *SIAM Journal on Applied Mathematics*, **17,** 1190–1202.

Index